P9-DOG-197

PROJECTIONS

✠

Shaping an American Theology for the Future

PROJECTIONS:

Shaping an American Theology for the Future

✠

Edited by Thomas F. O'Meara
and Donald M. Weisser

1970
DOUBLEDAY & COMPANY, INC.
Garden City, New York

LIBRARY OF CONGRESS CATALOG CARD NUMBER 71–89086
COPYRIGHT © 1970 BY DOUBLEDAY & COMPANY, INC.
ALL RIGHTS RESERVED
PRINTED IN THE UNITED STATES OF AMERICA

CONTENTS

Contents

vi

Shaping an American Theology for the Future

✠

THOMAS F. O'MEARA AND
DONALD M. WEISSER

To hope about the future is as old as man. To pictorialize the future—whether with Thomas More's *Utopia* or science fiction's realism of the almost—surfaces with modern man.[1] To predict the future in detail is an illusion; the idolatry of taboos and stars undercuts man's hopes. To shape the future is something new.[2]

[1] "One can hazard the theory that the main energies of the imagination in classical and medieval culture bore backward. . . . To the inner eye of classical and medieval man (I speak only of Western culture), strong light, vivid tints, precise shapes lay in the East. Thus Eden, the Gardens of Adonis, the deep-seated conviction that the beginnings of time and man were to be located in the Orient. . . . The East goes with remembrance, with the past tense of language and imagination. The West goes with the future. And it is when European history starts shifting westward, to the precise imagining and acquisition of new Western worlds, that myths and dreams begin to focus more and more on tomorrow." George Steiner, "It Happened Tomorrow," *The New Yorker* (November 16, 1968), 237.

[2] "Earlier time scales, related more or less to the duration of a few generations, have been superseded. We think habitually of the future of the human race on earth a hundred years from now, or five hundred years, or two thousand years. In the control of natural resources—the soil and its products, food crops, forests, fisheries, water power—we already effectively plan in ways that will determine conditions of life in the next few centuries, and it is in part our ability to do this which gives our life the future pitch it has. But the principal reason for the thrust into the future which makes our state of mind today different from that of earlier man is our knowledge of cosmic and organic evolution. We are aware that we live in an evolving universe, pitched into the future. The world is structured in patterned

Mao Tze-tung, Stanley Kubrick, Carl Rogers, Tom Hayden, Hans Küng are all working at the future. Shaping the future does not mean outlining the next decade or century in novels or by computers. It means tracking the alternatives ahead in our immediate tomorrow. Shaping the future is a flexible consideration of potentialities in and beyond the present. It is a consideration of the future not as Heavenly Jerusalem or as Orwellian Hell but as the mutative evolution of what is already active today. Projecting the future begins with a vision of the present as pluralistic and ambiguous, as multiple and deficient; the future is not envisioned but, rather, coolly contemplated before various possible frameworks. To shape the future means to arrange with charism and science the options for whatever is coming toward us. It means discerning and fashioning "alternative futures."

Critics of Herman Kahn's Hudson Institute or of the *Futuribles* of Paris miss the point when they identify them with nineteenth-century scientific romanticism or with the technological-political naïveté of the post-World War II period. Kahn's *The Year 2000*[3]

---

change. Not only can man change things; he can change the very pattern of change as well." W. Ong, "Knowledge in Time," *Knowledge and the Future of Man* (New York, 1968), 24–25.

[3] New York, 1967. A selected bibliography on these areas might include: *Towards the Year 2000. Work in Progress, Daedalus,* 96 (New York, 1967). William R. Ewald, Jr., ed., *Environment for Man, Environment and Change, Environment and Policy* (Bloomington: Indiana University Press, 1969); H. Kahn, *The Year 2000* (New York: Macmillan, 1967); G. R. Taylor, *Biological Time-Bomb* (New York: Harcourt Brace & World, 1968); Carl Rogers, "Interpersonal Relationships: U.S.A. 2000," *The Journal of Applied Behavioral Science,* 4 (1968), 265ff.; J. Moltmann, *Theology of Hope* (New York: Harper & Row, 1967); H. Richardson, *Towards an American Theology* (New York: Harper & Row, 1967); M. Novak, ed., *American Philosophy and the Future* (New York: Scribners, 1969); M. Novak, *A Theology for Radical Politics* (New York: Herder & Herder, 1969); W. Ong, ed., *Knowledge and the Future of Man* (New York: Holt, Rinehart and Winston, 1968); J. B. Metz, "Creative Hope," *Cross Currents,* 17 (1967), 171ff.; C. Oglesby, R. Shaull, *Containment and Change* (New York: Macmillan, 1967); E. Schillebeeckx, *God the Future of Man* (New York: Sheed and Ward, 1968); R. Fells, C. Walteon, eds., *Man in the City of the Future* (New York: Macmillan, 1968); F. Sontag, *The Future of Theology* (Philadelphia: Westminster, 1969); W. A. Beardslee, ed., *America and the Future of Theology* (Philadelphia: Westminster, 1967); T. F. Green, "Schools and Communities: A Look Forward," *Harvard Educational Review,* 39 (1969), 221ff.

is *not* a cold, self-assured description of what the future will be. Something new in "futurology," it draws out different lines of probability and projects them into the future. The future is shaped not by attempts to predict it but by pondering how the complexity of the present extends into the horizon of coming times. The future tense of verbs, hope, and insight are the mental correlates of human tools—distinguishing man from other species. Yet, something new in history has appeared. Man now has power to form his future—to end it or to transform it. Daniel Bell writes:

> How does one explain this resurgence of interest in "the future"? Some of this is due, undoubtedly, to the lure of the millennial number of the year 2000 . . . ; two-thirds of all Americans now alive will probably witness the turn of that chiliastic year. Some is due to the romance of space—the awareness that within this generation men will have stood upon the moon, and before the end of the century they may even reach out for Venus and Mars. Important as these factors are to the imaginative context of men's efforts—the recurrence of an impulse toward omnipotence—there are more prosaic, yet, paradoxically, more important reasons for this upsurge. It arises from the simple fact that every society today is consciously committed to economic growth, to raising the standard of living of its people, and therefore to the planning, direction, and control of social change. What makes the present studies, therefore, so completely different from those of the past is that they are oriented to specific social-policy purposes; and along with this new dimension, they are fashioned, self-consciously, by a new methodology that gives the promise of providing a more reliable foundation for realistic alternatives and choices, if not for exact prediction.[4]

PROJECTING THE FUTURE

Projections: Shaping an American Theology for the Future is one future projection. It is a projection of Christian faith. How will different currents—politics, language, mass media, education—projected into the future affect the language and mission of the

[4] Daniel Bell, "Introduction," *The Year 2000, ed. cit.,* xxv.

Christian communities? What must the Christian churches do, what must they be as the influence of the behavioral sciences grows? What does it mean to have an inspired scripture for a society which is picture-oriented? Americans, as technology, advertisement, politics, and theology now agree, are remarkably future-oriented. Can a faith survive whose center supposedly lies two millennia in the past? We are concerned not so much with a future theology, but whether in the light of the areas we have selected, theology (like liberal politics and traditional education) has any future. Since theology is not the Word of God itself but man thinking about that Word, the question of its future can be answered only in terms of projections into that future. For future is no longer the fabulous or the otherworldly, but the approach of ourselves and our world out of the future. The future is my present and my world . . . tomorrow.

Secondly, we are concerned with an American theology. If we take seriously pursuing lines with theological implication into the future, we involve ourselves not only as Christians but as Americans. American society is exploding and explosive. American cities search for revolutionary environments; new social systems must be developed to correspond to increased transportation systems; new ethical and psychological norms are needed. The problem is no longer to console men with the otherworldly presence of the City of God, but so to build the City of Man that transcendence and love can flourish there. Society's language has always determined the preaching and living of the Christian Word, from the Semitic Sermon on the Mount through the Parisian Aquinas and the Germanic Luther. Our future as Christians will in some way be American. Although talking about an American theology is exciting and popular, American theology is almost nonexistent. For the Christian theologian, it is embarrassing to walk through Manhattan at noon or to drive along the North Shore in Chicago at dusk, to see churches crowded with doctors, scientists, engineers, and plant managers on Sunday mornings, and to know that, to date, there has been little creative reflection or planning about what has happened and is happening in America.

Many people view the future with hope, a hope based upon the real possibility of improvement. Perhaps a new politics can place human thrust and the radical imperative of peace above military growth fed by espionage and myth; perhaps wheat and protein can be increased a thousandfold; perhaps computers and television can solve the problems of transportation; perhaps we can qualitatively intensify education . . . and perhaps not. Like American society, the Christian churches see the future with two quite different evaluations, and American Christians are becoming increasingly polarized. Some see the changing world and the changing Christian mission as disintegration, a personal threat and a betrayal of orthodoxy. Are our cities simply the epiphanies of original sin—we cannot live together? Are campus disturbances the result of a Communist plot? Others see changing world and church as a liberation of the true spirit of the gospel, the breaking through of ossified offices, forms, and people by the Holy Spirit so that Christ might emerge dynamically in our world. There is an infinite distance between hope and despair, between fear and shaping creativity. Similarly, there is increasing conflict within the churches—not over the Trinity or justification (as in past dogmatic conflicts) but about the present and its future. Ultimately, the deepest conflict is over change itself. Man's greatest (it can almost be said, his *only*) problem is intelligently to assimilate change.[5]

The crisis of the church involves change, authority, polarization between generations, conflict between idea-oriented and person-oriented thought-forms and a shifting of emphasis from personal confession to public apostolic action. This is obviously related to the broader crises in American society (and in the West), so that it can be said to be stimulated by a broad undercurrent. This need not imply that Christianity's form is no more than the cultural product of a particular time. Not infrequently it has been taking the gospel of Christ seriously that has allowed the times to change. On the other hand, once Christianity leaves its ghettos and anathemas and sees its role as prophetic, clarifying, and magnetic for all men of good will, it, like Jesus Christ, is incarnated in a particular time; its community and communication cannot escape the profound impact of a society in turmoil. Herbert Richardson describes this situation, where the underlying presuppositions of our society evolve

---

[5] Carl Rogers, "Interpersonal Relationships: U.S.A. 2000," *The Journal of Applied Behavioral Science,* 4 (1968), 266.

and new ways appear on the horizon either as lights of hope or flames of threat. "In a cultural crisis, the matrix of meaning that undergirds and unifies the various dimensions of man's life breaks down and, with it, all inherited institutions and habitual modes of thought and action. That we are in the midst of such a cultural crisis today is evidenced by the fact that we face not a single problem, but a problem syndrome."[6] Finally, change poses special problems for the Christian, for "Jesus Christ is always the same yesterday, today and forever" (Heb. 13:8).

This book is about Christ, about being a Christian, about love and life. But it is not about Christology, ecclesiology, or biblical theology. It moves on a deeper level than that. It is becoming less humorous and more anxiously incomprehensible to realize that the number of existences in Christ, the relationship of a Catholic judge to Protestant divorce legality, the repeated "destructions" of the history of Jesus, were actually seen as crucial theological questions. That is the "theology" which has been considered as another word for irrelevent dogmatism or unswerving abstract ideology. The revolution in theology is not to be as radical as possible in denial: to go "so far" as to preach the "death of God." The radical revolution in Christianity—a revolution we have by no means espoused—is to allow the Incarnation with its love, to allow the intervention of God in history with its openness for history and culture, to be radically present. But radical presence must involve the issues of questioning Americans: What should I do (not in church, but in the ghetto downtown)? Who am I (not my degrees or memories, but me)? What do I find in Jesus Christ? What do I give to the mystery we call God?

The following probes explore the way men and their Christian faith express themselves. They ask, How do people think and how must the Christian good news employ these thought-forms—some changing, some lasting—to be even heard, much less understood? They presuppose that we must ask, How do Americans today see being-a-man, being-in-a-community? before we can explain our confession that Jesus Christ is the Word made man and that a parish church is a community of Christians. Why are more and

[6] H. Richardson, *Towards an American Theology* (New York, 1967), ix.

6

more people lonely? Does jet transportation cause this and does TV alleviate it? The following essays, drawing on their different perspectives, reflect upon the very encounter of God's Word with human words, on Jesus Christ meeting me in Boston or Omaha.

The present and future we entertain here are assumedly ecumenical and contemporary American. By the former we mean an attitude toward Jesus Christ's gospel which is less dogmatic and more developmental and pastoral; and by the latter we mean Christians who, without diluting faith, live each day in a secular, pluralistic, technological (in terms of automation and media) society. "Secular theologies" and the ecumenical movement have attracted a great deal of attention and notoriety. They are both more and less significant than we may think. The secular horizon is the horizon within which most Americans live (excepting some rural areas for Protestants and some urban areas for Catholics). Recently we have become more aware of this secular horizon. The rise of the city, of urban civilization, is related to the collapse of traditional sacral Christianity. Urbanization constitutes a massive change in the way men live together, and became possible in its contemporary form only with scientific and technological advances. Secularization marks a change in the way men grasp and understand their life. It occurred only when men admitted the relativity of myths and traditions once thought unquestionable. Secular is the dominance of city and country by the skyscraper rather than by the cathedral; it is the predominance of the nonreligious (which does not exclude the dimension of the holy). Faith exists within the individual, working out from his personal confession into the external sphere rather than including automatically each individual in a religious state or a historical-sacral milieu. The secular invites and protects pluralism, hinders technology less and is strengthened by it; it nourishes an authentic personal faith but makes the religious-political encounter more difficult. The secular leads to the continuum of religious and worldly, of human and divine. It has gone beyond theocracy, but is at home with the sacramental and the incarnational. Theology, then, rediscovers that Jesus Christ spoke out of a particular social situation, was crucified for political as well as ecclesiastical reasons. It recognizes again the unity of

7

man, the profound but partial nature of sin, and believes in and listens to one spirit at work in men.

Paradoxically, the ecumenical opening of Christians and their churches highlighted the secular. The secular stood over against the hesitant churches with a fierce pressure. Ideas such as "secular ecumenism" and "the post-ecumenical age" may sound shocking, but it is clear that the ecumenical movement as it was developed in Europe over five decades is ending; it lasted in the United States about ten years. (This view does not overlook the relatively meager yet greatly needed grass-roots ecumenical efforts in local communities.) As the churches left their inter-Christian narrowness, they opened themselves to demands by the world. Through the pressures of effective education and social scandals, of revolutions in the seminary, and the union of long-suffering laity into underground churches, the ecumenical dialogue is moving from being between traditions separated by sixteenth-century theological issues to traditions faced with the same crucial ecclesial and secular problems. For increasing numbers of younger ministers, priests, and informed Christians, ecumenism is not dead but taken for granted. Growing outside pressures direct our attention away from ourselves. Perhaps societal uncertainty, with its threat to the churches, is, unexpectedly, slowly resolving the inter-Christian problems.

THE PRESENT TASK

The trends described above suggested to the editors the idea of inviting Christian theologians to project theology into America's future. These theologians are not known as particularly Protestant or Catholic; they are associated with the general contemporary American scene. Some are intimately involved in the Christian-social encounter—both in the classrooms and in the streets. We asked our contributors to take a particular area—e.g., revolution or the mass media—and to ask how this neutral, secular stimulus now present in our society will in the future make increasing demands upon Christianity. How will theology be written and done? What must a Christian witness to and reject? What should

a church affected by this catalyst be and do in the coming years?
These projections rather parallel Marshall McLuhan's explorations.
He writes:

> I'm making explorations. I don't know where they're going to
> take me. My work is designed for the pragmatic purpose of trying
> to understand our technological environment and its psychic and
> social consequences. But my books constitute the *process* rather
> than the completed product of discovery. My purpose is to employ
> facts as tentative probes, as means of insight, of pattern recognition,
> rather than to use them in the tradition and sterile sense of
> classified data, categories, containers. I want to map new terrain
> rather than chart old landmarks.[7]

We chose ten forces, and ten theologians known for their interest
in these areas. Our choice of the ten was not a random one, yet
it was limited by certain practical considerations. We asked: Of
the many influences in our culture, which are decisive for Christ
being present in our culture? Our final choices were: future,
politics, revolution, culture, history, technology, behavioral sciences,
language, mass media, and education.

THEOLOGY WITHOUT IDEOLOGY

There may be no theology in the future. Without becoming
alarmist, it is thought-provoking to consider that the communication
methods of the first, thirteenth, and sixteenth centuries will soon
be so foreign as perhaps to pass unnoticed in the media revolutions
of the future. Theology is involved in communicating the gospel
to people. It may become—through enmity to change—too ossified
in a *changing* world to accomplish this. Simultaneously, younger
generations have grown irascibly critical of credibility gaps. It has
been said that Christianity is the only religion to which one can
belong and consistently neglect its basic tenets. If the growing-up
of society—a maturing away from accepting as normal, war,
discrimination, and large-scale poverty and exploitation—is really

[7] "Interview: Marshall McLuhan," *Playboy* (March, 1969).

happening (and we see signs that "a world come of age" is a possibility), then a Christian community which compromises the transcendent God and the great command of human love is doomed. Theology, vital theology, is always a possibility as a grace; it is not an inevitability. It is possible for theology—as the living encounter of a culture with revelation in Christ—to be absent. Carl Rogers predicts in his essay on the year 2000:

> By the year 2000, institutionalized religion, already on the wane as a significant factor in everyday life, will have faded to a point where it is of only slight importance in the community. Theology may exist as a scholastic exercise, but in reality the God of authoritative answers will be not only dead but buried. This does not mean at all that the concerns which have been the basis of religion will have vanished. The mysterious process of life, the mystery of the universe and how it came to be, the tragedy of man's alienation from himself and from others, the puzzle of the meaning of individual life—these mysteries will all be very much present. There may, indeed, be a greater appreciation of mystery as our knowledge increases.[8]

Rogers is not writing the epitaph for the kind of gospel and theology the following pages sketch; in fact, he is describing how they may begin to come into existence. But this theology—of mystery, of life, of human unity and love, and their point of intensity in Jesus Christ—will (without being a pure humanism or a demythologized positiveness towards life) have to rediscover the gospel anew in a hundred different ways as each increasingly educated generation struggles with new dangers and new frontiers.

Clearly, by theology we do not mean the Scriptures nor the dogmatic sentences of church authority. Theology is not the enumeration of what must be believed, but rather thinking about and living out what is believed. Theology is not only words and ideas about God and Christ, but the personal reflection of each Christian and each community upon what God, Christ, love, and worship mean. There is an academic theology, but there is also a personal theology. There is an individual theology, but there is also a communal and ecclesial theology. There are lastingly important theologies, but there is also the emerging theology of every Christian

[8] Rogers, *art. cit.*, 277.

10

today. Theology is the creative relationship of Christ to me and my family, to my neighborhood and my country, to my city and my world. The task of theology has always been to shape an access for man—in his particular epoch, in his particular way of understanding the world and himself—to the lived reality of Christian faith. Still, this does not mean that faith's reality is a consequence derived from the understanding of self and society.

Theology does not escape the ecumenical-historical dimension. It is not divorced from the theologians of the past and the history of the church, yet it is not a repetition of their works. Personal theology is present where grace meets the emotions and the subconscious; it is thinking *with:* thinking with the larger community, young and old; thinking with the help of its charisms and authority, its brilliant insights and its pusillanimous hesitations. So we see the importance of asking, How will people think theologically in the future?

It may appear that the following explorations are sociological or psychological rather than theological. Their fundamental purpose is to let Christ be present in our world—not by turning off the world or shutting out our day-to-day life, but by seeing precisely how Christ with his grace and gospel is present in it. Theology can use many thought-forms to explain its belief. These "filters" range from ontology to cybernetics. Sociology, for instance, plans the city, the community, the nation. It also influences the Christian's life, because Christianity is a radically communal religion. Christ in me and others is stifled when neither secular nor Christian community is a real possibility. Theology learns from sociology about today's world, and then fashions its own social theology, which asks, How can Christ and the Christian community exist in this particular society?

THE AMERICAN CHURCHES AND
AMERICAN THEOLOGY

Until the past decade, American Catholicism appeared as the child of Italy and Ireland. Piety, moral theology, and parochial fellowship were Irish; Anglo-Saxon respect for law made the interpretation of European canon law and Vatican utterances compulsively rigorous; a not always theological respect for Rome precluded at times visible and tangible American aspects of the Church. Naturally, there was another side to this story. Independence from European models in adapting to a new pluralistic democracy, initiative in a vast school system, embracing American society and politics (seen from afar as clearly Protestant), brought down the condemnation of mythical "Americanism." The achievements of the American Catholic Church—for instance, the devotion to the parish among American Catholics of every income and age bracket—are enormous.

The late 1950s began to indicate other possibilities in theology, religious education, and liturgy. Some were only titillating; a few were ridiculous; none were radical. Only in the liturgical movement did the American church play any real endemic role. When Vatican II consistently showed the superiority of the thought of men such as Congar and Rahner (previously widely considered as almost demented), and when the pastoral openness of the Council became felt in the United States, a new theological atmosphere burst upon the scene. European theology, preparing since 1945 for such a council, had dominated for two decades, and its impact for both Protestants and Catholics should and does remain. Yet, within a few years, there was a call for an American theology. Why struggle to understand theologies born out of Immanuel Kant? Was not American pragmatism more realistic and fruitful than existentialism? Why lay theological claims demonstrable only via Hegel and Schleiermacher? Why be distracted from pop art and folk rock by a Germanic academe? Such questions have rightly intensified in the half decade since the close of the Council.

The influence of European theologians, especially German and Dutch, on Catholicism has remained; and yet, at the same time, it has diminished. This has happened because in the United States Catholicism has undergone such intensive and rapid change, such turmoil, since Vatican II. But this renewal of Catholic Christianity is still remarkably a-theological, if by "theology" we mean "theoretical (yet relevant) reflection." Extensive renewal by tens of thousands of sisters; the establishment of presbyteries and priests' associations; theologians' and seminarians' critiques of ecclesiastics through public opinion; the emergence of five hundred "floating" or "underground" parishes; a versatility in liturgical experimentation; the charismatic involvement of priests and sisters in movements for justice and peace; the improvement, along with the recognition of multiple crises, in religious education—these are striking signs of the "different" post-conciliar epoch in the United States.

Protestant theology in America was similarly the stepchild of Europeans. Not until the last decade—apart from the social gospel and some less distinguished ventures—did the surge of American life (aided by the bridge building of Paul Tillich) call attention to American theologies. Protestantism has been dominated by a word-centered *dogmatic conflict* between liberalism, orthodoxy, and fundamentalism. For fifty years, parishes and seminaries have taken sides within what appears, increasingly, as a European framework. Theology struggled with the truth-existence dichotomy. Those who argued for existential import had come to that conclusion over a painful road fleeing away from fundamentalism; the neo-orthodox were not able to retain in forms and movements the Protestant commitment to *ecclesia semper reformanda*. This longtime conflict has ended. It has ended with both sides embarrassed before the social crises of contemporary America and before the unexpected renewal in Catholicism. "Liberal" no longer means denying the divinity of Christ, no longer implies lengthy notes on existentialism and Bonhoeffer, but means the openness and willingness of the entire church to renew its ministry and community, to come to grips with people as they are and to re-establish the prophetic voice of the church to what could be an increasingly alien church membership. In short, the depth of God's intervention in Christ and in our lives is all too much needed, but this can take hold—relevantly and meaningfully—only if we change, live, and worship in the midst of our lives. Nothing has become more obvious than that academic abbreviations of the gospel are exceedingly easier than the pastoral renewal of the local church. And so we return again to the social and the political, the pastoral and the American.

How would there be an American theology? Paradoxically, the genius of change in the church is theological in that it is pastoral. The early advocates of American theology were mistaken and doomed to minimal success when they envisaged American theology as a union of Scripture and the American Pragmatists. Pragmatism as a description of the American style of life is not the same as the philosophical view of Pierce or Royce. This false start was excusable, since theology is viewed by many as including the employment of some philosophy—Plato, Aristotle, Hegel, Heidegger. But the present American situation resembles more this attitude: Theology uses all of human reflection, including sociology and psychology, to explain the Word. No doubt it is worthwhile to study the American pragmatists from a religious concern, but American theology will *not* be the synthesis of an ontology with the New Testament, for America is not likely to produce a metaphysics of that sort. America's metaphysics is the social and behavioral sciences; it is the appreciation of the mass media and the plunge into urban planning. That is why *The Secular City* is important. Cox drew upon a general "ontology" of the American urban scene and used this as his nonreligious thought-form for a contemporary theology.[9] It was his valuable insight which was able to draw out the "social ontology," the middle principles between charts and abstractions which could serve as the stimulus, linguistic matrix, and thought-form for Christian theological reflection. And so, the following essays, searching for an American theology, do not turn often to metaphysics (although the benevolent spirits of Aristotle and John Dewey are not unwelcome) but spend time and effort on different aspects of society, behavior, and communications.

There must be an American theology. Otherwise, the United States will lack the prophetic voice of the emerging Christ needful in our time. Not only campus activists but United States Senators recognize that, confronted with enormous decisions, there can no longer be a total exclusion of moral and religious dimensions from policy-making. The present American crises are, above all, moral crises with civil conflict, racial hatred, political persecution, alienation, and addiction as root problems. From another perspective, America dominates the world in technological development. While many excoriate it during its crises, some are wise enough to perceive

[9] New York, 1966. What Merleau-Ponty writes of philosophy is equally true of theology: "We need neither tear down the behavioral sciences to lay the foundations of philosophy, nor tear down philosophy to lay the foundations of the behavioral sciences. Every science secretes an ontology; every ontology anticipates a body of knowledge." *Signs* (Evanston, 1964), 98.

that these are preludes, tests, or preventatives for the rest of the world. J.-J. Servan-Schreiber says that America, as the leading industrial power, is the crucial battlefield. "The crises you are living through we will have to face in the future." There must be a corresponding, critical, and appreciative Christian word to the race forward in automation and transportation, to media and medicine. Otherwise, the church will be reduced to the center of individualistic devotion, catering only to social dropouts or schizophrenics.

Recently Europe, too, has called for a more social and political theology—but the very pages suggesting such a project illustrate how difficult it is for a French or German theologian to depart from the framework of Kant or Descartes. The fact is that only a few North Americans (McLuhan must be included here, although he is not a theologian explicitly) have been able to "do theology"—to rethink the Christ event—from within contemporary patterns such as the urban or media explosions.

Shaping an American theology means laying the groundwork so that out of the American experience we can begin to meditate on Christ or to project a parish in these terms. The experience of living in the United States tends to emphasize the social and the personal—not in terms of subject but of the individual. Our horizon for life, as we noted, is neither the primitive sacral nor the European Christian but the secular. A secular horizon includes democratic participation, pluralism, the preservation of both freedom and social responsibility. Somehow change through technology, loneliness through emptiness and immensity (the largeness of both our cities and our country), intertwine there. And, finally, there is "American pragmatism"—the union of theory and effectiveness, the urge to develop, the unwillingness not to improve what is deficient, a confidence in the future in terms of trust in planned ideas and effective machines.

An American theology need not tend toward exclusivism or chauvinism. As Servan-Schreiber points out, America pioneers the world in the social, technological, and behavioral spheres. It is no longer telling to place American capitalism over against Communism—the new theology must criticize these old and ideological (hence un-American) dichotomies—and yet America is important because it will influence basic options for the rest of the world.

As socialism and capitalism merge, it is not so much the economic system, but the experience of Americans living in this very period of stress and crisis before new goals, which makes imperative American thinking about being-Christ-in-the-world and letting-Christ-be-in-our-world. Herbert Richardson describes some principles of a new theology:

> The three generalizations (of the emerging cultural epoch vis-à-vis theology) I propose are the following: (1) The modern period of history is coming to an end and a new period of history is beginning. The life of this period will be dominated by social techniques developed by the sociological, psychological, economic, and political sciences. (2) The thought of this new "sociotechnic age" will be "metacritical" rather than critical, concerned to organize experience into its simplest part in order to master it. (3) The creative, formative theology of the future will be American.[10]

An American theology cannot completely avoid commitment through articulated faith and through church tradition to certain basic aspects of the Christ event. But initially—in the present volume, for example—the framework does not exist for raising dogmatic questions or disagreements. This does not mean they are unimportant but that the primary concern is pastoral. We are concerned with the deeper questions of how to speak of Christ in the contemporary world.

It is now clear why the God-Is-Dead theology was not an American theology, and why a political theology is. The former was a mistaken attempt to join surface readings of German theology to the American penchant for the sensational. Like most advertising, it became obsolete, and like all repeated past theologies, it did not speak to the heart. Theology, like history, never runs backward. Europe is more fascinated than America by different kinds of "deaths" of religion and God. Why? Because Europe is not yet secular, or, at least, not fully aware of being secular. Karl Rahner speaks of "a diaspora church" but from within a country where baroque Catholicism is all too prominent and where evangelical and Roman Catholic churches gratefully accept benefits bestowed by the state. The greatest problem for the grass-roots renewal of

---

[10] Richardson, *op. cit.*, x.

French Christianity is precisely that France *is* Catholic. The Church is always in the background—in formalities such as First Communion, in cultural and class differences, in the structures of antiquity which can seem as threatening as they did two hundred years ago. The constant tension about introducing God into schools, TV, and space trips is really a reminder for American believers that God is not automatically present. At times, the United States Government spares us this idolatry, although it too clearly prefers priests who advocate order to those who test equality and freedom in marches.

The following essays can attain some measure of success only if they are allowed to act as stimuli. They must be thought-along-with, listened to, criticized, and imagined. They must be allowed to open new vistas for the presence of Christ in the life of man. The essays will never be important for their content. They reflect the strength and the weakness of emerging American and future theologies; they give a clear and courageous beginning, and yet they show how far away is the completion of these insights and suggestions. Can the theologian be aware of what could be and thus have a voice in building the future? Only when he allows the present to rouse him with a passion for what is possible can he celebrate rather than excoriate change. We must, further, learn to think out of new worlds—e.g., men interacting in sociology, revolutions of justice and honesty. The Christian must, paradoxically, enter into these worlds of man, learn to live newly and humanly, before he can articulate his faith meaningfully. Reflection as a keynote of Christian theology means not only to think inwardly— to reflect upon—but to reflect faith outwardly in life and contact. Finally, these essays must be regarded as stimuli to doing. Their purpose is not simply knowledge or theological academics. They are destined primarily for action; they exist to change. Their future is something new in the world. The proof of their being understood is when their insights have driven Christians to being in new structures, to be constantly stimulated to improvement and critical building at every level of Christian life.

In short, as these probes into the future of thinking about Christ are read, they should lead through one idea to many more. They will be successful only if they end in creative reformation.

Man and His Future

✠

CHRISTOPHER F. MOONEY

*What is the future of Christ in America? It is possible that America
has carried pioneering and forging and building so far that—with
the medium as the message—the future is the present. Teilhard de
Chardin writes: "It is a pleasant and dramatic spectacle, that of
Mankind divided to its very depths into two irrevocably opposed
camps—one looking towards the horizon and proclaiming with all
its new-found faith, 'We are moving,' and the other, without
shifting its position, obstinately maintaining, 'Nothing changes.
We are not moving at all.'" Christopher Mooney, S.J., President
of Woodstock Theological College, has written one of the lasting
and significant studies on Teilhard,* Teilhard de Chardin and the
Mystery of Christ *(1966). In the following essay he describes the
new significance of the future in America, the different emerging
theologians of the future, and their relationship to further theological
choices awaiting us in the next decade.*

America is unique, it has been said, because it is the first society
to actually experience the future. Concretely, this experience is one
of accelerating change oriented toward what has been called a
"technetronic" or "cybernetic" society. At a much faster pace than
the rest of the world, cultural, social, and economic life in America
is being altered today by the power of technology and autonomous
control systems. The extraordinary sense of awe which everywhere

18

accompanied viewings of the recent moon flight underscores this sudden awareness that we shall be living in a new type of world sooner than we think. Sober scientists accept as certainties man's power within the next century to eliminate famine and disease, to accumulate knowledge in electronic banks and transmit it directly to the human brain through the nervous system, to stabilize population, even to "engineer" man's genetic development. These predictions are based, it should be noted, not on flights of imagination but upon techniques already known and in operation by which man commits himself to the future in and through decisions made in the present.

This experience of a future rapidly moving into the present has resulted in America in an especially strong desire for both accurate forecast and responsible control. This double desire has in turn given rise to a series of problems that touch contemporary man as man, and, as a consequence, contemporary Christian theology. What is being called "the theology of the future" owes much of its appeal to the fact that it attacks these problems directly. Yet, it does not provide answers so much as a context from Christian revelation for their fuller comprehension. In the pages that follow we shall first outline some of the concrete manifestations of this desire for forecast and control as well as some of the reasons for theology's sudden interest in rethinking the Christian message in function of this contemporary orientation of man and his world. We shall then sketch in broad outline the theology of the future now developing, with its emphasis upon hope as the organizing principle of revelation. Finally, we shall indicate some of the practical consequences for American Christian life stimulated by this change in theological perspective.

TOWARDS THE YEAR 2000

A few years ago, an entire issue of *Daedalus* was devoted to the deliberations of the American Academy of Arts and Sciences' Commission on the Year 2000. Among its riches was a preliminary report by Herman Kahn and his associates at the Hudson Institute, subsequently published in greatly expanded form as a book, *The Year 2000*.[1] Kahn attempts first to identify those long-range trends in America likely to continue into the next century: the world-wide spread of secular humanism, institutionalization of scientific innovation, and continuous economic growth. He then explores a number of "alternative worlds," as he calls them: "scenarios" of future possibilities worked out from extrapolations based on different sets of assumptions. What is important for us here is to observe how his efforts (and those of many others) to forecast the future inevitably focus at the start upon scientific and technological progress already begun and which can reasonably be expected to continue more or less at the same rate. The structure of society within which such developments will take place, however, and the uses to which they will be put, are much more problematic, and depend upon what man decides to do *with* and *in* the world he is creating. Precisely because his areas of choice are widening rapidly, man begins to feel uneasy. The more the consequences of his self-made world become incalculable, the greater is his desire for forecast and the more confused he becomes about ultimate meanings and goals. For, of itself, secular culture can provide him only with short-range, pragmatic means, while the ends to which they are directed, the "alternative worlds," will depend upon value judgments which he has perhaps carelessly made in the past and feels at a loss to make now.

Many thoughtful observers have noted this anomaly in the present outlook on the future. Jacques Ellul has asked how man is to remain master in a world of means, and answers that as yet there is no answer. An individual can inquire after the values to impose on technology, and can also search out the way to remain a man in the fullest sense within a "technetronic" society. But these efforts of the individual are in themselves pointless to resolve in any way the problem in its totality, since to accomplish this would require that *all* men in a given society adopt the same values and the same behavior.[2] In a pluralistic culture, however, such concern

---

[1] *Towards the Year 2000. Work and Progress, Daedalus*, 96 (1967); *The Year 2000* (New York, 1967).

[2] *Technological Society* (New York, 1964).

for ultimate meanings, which alone makes hope of humanization possible, is not a unitive but a divisive force. Hence the insistence of Fred Charles Iklé that predictions for the year 2000 not attempt to *describe* our world but rather to evaluate the *consequences* of alternative courses of action.[3] For any aspect of the future whose consequences do not depend upon our choice here and now is really irrelevant. What man needs, then, is to see the full extent of his burden of freedom and somehow gain the necessary strength to support it.

Nor are there lacking those who deny that such support is likely to be obtained. C. P. Snow has said that "the signs are all pointing the wrong way—objective grounds for hope have gotten less and less and the objective grounds for nonhope have gotten stronger. I have been nearer to despair this year, 1968, than ever in my life."[4] *Homo sapiens*, writes Arthur Koestler in *The Ghost in the Machine*, must have some error or deficiency built into the wiring circuits of his brain. Otherwise, how explain his urge to self-destruction and proneness to delusion, or his extraordinary impulse to make war upon his own species in the name of self-made idols? He must be some kind of biological freak, the result of some remarkable mistake in the evolutionary process. On the level of society this same conviction underlies Herbert Marcuse's *One-Dimensional Man*.[5] He sees the United States fast becoming the most irrational of societies in respect to the values of truth and human living. So hedonistic is its culture, so object-oriented and repressive of the individual, that the only cure seems to be some total regenerative effort destroying the whole system. While technology provides man with material well-being, it has also produced in America a "state of anesthesia," which either absorbs or streamlines all "existence-transcending" forces which oppose it. Today the discrepancy between the emancipation of man's freedom which is possible and the repression which is practiced is greater than it ever was before.

What these writers have done, each in his own way, is to touch

[3] "Can Social Predictions Be Evaluated?" *Daedalus, ed. cit.,* 733–58.
[4] As reported in the New York *Times,* November 12 and 13, 1968.
[5] Boston, 1964.

the nerve center of modern man's anxiety before a future which, in spite of the accuracy of technological prediction, remains unstructured precisely in areas that concern him most personally. "Tomorrow?" asks Teilhard de Chardin. "But who can guarantee us a tomorrow anyway? And without the assurance that this tomorrow exists, can we really go on living, we to whom has been given—perhaps for the first time in the whole history of the universe—the terrible gift of foresight?"[6] What man wants is not greater power to *invent* the future, of which he may already have too much, but greater power to *plan* it, to plan those fulfillments of himself and his society which he has not yet found either in his present or his past. This means looking to the future as a way out from a one-dimensional, utopianless world, an arena where new possibilities can finally be realized, not for technology so much as for human community, where the unfinished character of existence can be redeemed at last. What contemporary man wants most is to actualize "the hope principle" in the depths of his being, that mystique of transcendence rooted in a world of restive change. And what contemporary American man wants is to dream once more the American dream.

What have all these developments, both in America and the world at large, to do with the Christian faith? For our answer we must take briefly into account two large areas of current religious concern. The first is the fundamental question of the relation between Christian theology and the world view of a given culture. There are those like sociologist Peter Berger who have warned that efforts to accommodate religious affirmations to psychological reality structures can become an abdication of theological responsibility in favor of "market research." For in a pluralist society, says Berger, religion resembles a commodity obliged to compete on the open market. But such an endeavor to "sell" the Christian faith can result, as it has in the case of the radical theologians, in a complete secularist reduction.[7] The tactical problem of getting

---

[6] Pierre Teilhard de Chardin, *The Phenomenon of Man* (New York, 1959), 229.

[7] Peter L. Berger, "A Sociological View of the Secularization of Theology," *Journal for the Scientific Study of Religion*, 6 (1967), 3–16. See also *The Sacred Canopy* (New York, 1967).

one's message across to a recalcitrant clientele has a built-in escalation factor: The clientele is likely to become more, not less, recalcitrant in the pluralizing situation. If reality structures of the man in the street are allowed to become the unquestioned standard of cognitive validity, they will necessarily tend to bring with them all the uncertainty that comes from long confrontation with various reality-defining agencies, none of which has compelled allegiance. The question is, therefore, given the problem of translation, Which are the grammars to be used and how? The newly refined tools of biblical and historical scholarship have already become a prominent part of translation procedures, as well as ideas from psychoanalysis, existentialism, sociology, and linguistic analysis. But many theologians who use these tools seem to be unaware that modern man's outlook, which the tools themselves represent, is the result not of some intrinsically superior access to truth but of his existence in a pluralist environment which in fact tends to undermine religious certitude. The enthusiasm of the theologians for adaptation should consequently be tempered with extreme caution, since from the sociological and historical point of view the attitudes of our present age are, cognitively speaking, as relative as those of any other.

Now, this skepticism toward adaptation, whether on the part of sociologists like Berger or on the part of those who, unlike him, feel that defense is the only proper theological attitude, arises from a misunderstanding which can perhaps be clarified by considering a second large area of current religious concern, namely, the problem of God. Everyone is aware that this problem arises today from the fact that in the past the experience of God was to a large extent that of a substitute for powers which man himself lacked. No longer, however, does man need such a God. No longer must he appeal to him for solace or assistance in his helplessness before a world he cannot control. His grasp of the secular sphere is now firm and bold, and demands no recourse to religion to support it. Nevertheless, while *this* role of God is rapidly disappearing in modern culture, it does not follow that this same culture will not be the occasion for a new experience of God coming to birth in harmony with the forces of social and psychological change. Christianity's apparent inability as yet clearly to formulate such an experience in conceptual terms is simply testimony that it has not yet dissociated itself from one cultural pattern or completely made the transition into the one now developing. "In the past," writes Edward Schillebeeckx, "God was an accepted idea—he was the world mover, the last cause, he upheld the moral and political order of the world, and even maintained social stability. In the modern world God has ceased to be an idea and has become a question which both believers and non-believers are never tired of discussing in ordinary conversation, in the newspapers, in books and articles, and on the radio and television. Now that we can no longer feel secure with ideas of God, God himself is the subject of our conversations."[8]

It is not a question, therefore, as Berger suggests, of adaptation by grudging concessions to a recalcitrant clientele in order once again to "sell" Christianity and make it "marketable." Rather, there is the emergence of a new understanding of Christian revelation in and through the experience of a new culture. For God can be known only in relation to the particular world in which men live. Any self-revelation on his part which lay outside a given sphere of human experience simply could not be heard.[9] What makes our knowledge of God what it is are the specific cultural factors which make our world what it is. These cultural factors, however, are in turn becoming more and more characterized by a thrust toward the future. Science and technology have given man the possibility of changing the earth and planning the well-being of mankind as a whole. Such goals are in fact totally new in human history and rivet attention not on the world as it has been and is, but on the world that is to come into being. Such changes in man's experience must necessarily also affect his experience of God, for he cannot be oriented toward the future by his whole culture and pulled toward the past by his religion; his concept of God cannot be relevant to his life if it is at odds with his society.

[8] Edward Schillebeeckx, O.P., "Theology of Renewal Talks About God," *Theology of Renewal*, L. K. Shook, C.S.B., ed. (New York, 1968), I, 98.

[9] Schillebeeckx (*op. cit.*, 100) notes that this is the explicit teaching of Thomas Aquinas in *Summa Theologica*, I, q. 1, a. 7, ad 2. It is, moreover, commonly admitted today that all revelation is functional, that God reveals himself only in what he is for us and does for us in history.

Now, the contemporary theology of the future is precisely an attempt to come to grips with and to articulate the relationship between God and man as these are now being experienced in a new society and culture slowly coming to birth. Adaptation of this type is a questioning of the biblical witness to Christ and arises from our peculiar difficulty in speaking *about* and *to* God in our contemporary world. The same inquiry was not possible for Christians of a former generation simply because they were living in *their* world, not ours. Nor can the Scriptures satisfy our questioning immediately, since their message was directed to men whose inquiry was very different. "The Gospel does not answer questions that are not asked. . . . Every generation asks the Gospel its own questions from the context of its own life. . . . The answer the Gospel gives us will therefore be new, but at the same time, also *evangelical*. This presupposes that we should be ready . . . to change, extend or correct our questioning in the light of Scripture and biblical interpretation given during the Church's whole history."[10] *What the theology of the future is ultimately asking, then, is not so much how the Christian today should speak about God* (although this is obviously a problem), *but how God through Christ now speaks to us.* How is Christian faith to function and be expressed in our new culture without becoming identified with it? Jesus himself as proclaimed by the faith of the apostles is the guiding principle of this readaptation. But while the Gospel inspires our questioning, this questioning itself necessarily interprets the Gospel in confrontation with our future-oriented culture.

HOPE AND ESCHATOLOGY

The theology of the future may be discussed from two points of view. The first centers upon an effort to rethink, in terms of hope, the totality of Christian revelation, with eschatology as the organizing principle. The second concerns itself with the practical consequences, in the Christian life, that follow such a change in theological perspective. The names most frequently associated with

[10] *Ibid.,* 95–96.

the first point of view are Jürgen Moltmann,[11] and Wolfhart Pannenberg[12]; and with the second, Edward Schillebeeckx,[13] Karl Rahner,[14] Johannes Metz,[15] and Harvey Cox.[16] Two others, the German Marxist Ernst Bloch[17] and the French Jesuit Pierre Teilhard de Chardin,[18] elaborated their own systems of thought long before present concern for the future, but their writings continue today to be a source of inspiration both for theory and practical application.

The speculative approach of Moltmann and Pannenberg has to be seen historically as a reaction to the thought of Rudolf Bultmann and others with the same perspective who see New Testament concern for the future in terms of the existential decision of an individual to the "now" of revelation. Such a theology tends indeed to individualize and spiritualize eschatology; it interprets revelation

[11] Jürgen Moltmann, *Theology of Hope* (New York, 1967); "Hope Without Faith," *Concilium*, vol. 16, *Is God Dead?* (New York, 1966), 25–40; "Hoping and Planning," *Cross Currents*, 18 (1968), 307–18; "Hope and Confidence," *Dialog*, 7 (1968), 42–55; "The Category of the New in Christian Theology," *The Future as the Presence of Shared Hope*, Maryellen Muckenhirn, ed., (New York, 1968), 9–33; "Resurrection as Hope," *Harvard Theological Review*, 61 (1968), 129–48.

[12] Wolfhart Pannenberg, *Jesus—God and Man* (Philadelphia, 1968); "Hope as the Arrival of the Future," *Journal of the American Academy of Religion*, 35 (1967), 107–18; "Theology and the Kingdom of God," *Una Sancta*, 24 (1967), 283–94; "Response to the Discussion," in *Theology as History*, James M. Robinson and John B. Cobb, Jr., eds. (New York, 1967), 221–76.

[13] Edward Schillebeeckx, O.P., *God the Future of Man* (New York, 1968), esp. Chapter 6, "Secularization and Man's Future on Earth."

[14] Karl Rahner, S.J., "Building the New Earth," *Dialogue*, 1 (1968), 58–63; "Christentum als Religion der absoluten Zukunft," *Christentum und Marxismus Heute*, Erich Kellner, ed. (Vienna, 1966), 202–13; "Experiment: Man," *Theology Digest*, Sesquicentennial Issue (February, 1968), 57–69.

[15] Johannes Metz, *Theology of the World* (New York, 1969); "The Responsibility of Hope," *Philosophy Today*, 10 (1966), 280–88; "Creative Hope," *Cross Currents*, 17 (1967), 171–80; "Religion and Society in the Light of a Political Theology," *Harvard Theological Review*, 61 (1968), 507–23.

[16] Harvey Cox, *The Secular City* (New York, 1965); *On Not Leaving It to the Snake* (New York, 1967).

[17] Ernst Bloch, *Das Prinzip Hoffnung* (Frankfurt, 1959).

[18] Pierre Teilhard de Chardin, *The Future of Man* (New York, 1964).

primarily as the disclosure of the eternal transcendence breaking into time, and understands the parousia of Christ as his presence rather than his return. This approach, according to its critics, serves only to imprison man in his own finitude and to falsify the central biblical view of revelation as both promise and future fulfillment. Hence the dialogue which they carry on with the Marxist Ernst Bloch, and the use they make of his philosophical categories of "not-yet-being," "frontier," and "the new," for these they see as antidotes to what they believe to be the deleterious influence of Martin Heidegger. In Bloch's system hope is the key to an understanding of man, "the hoping animal" with an "infatuation for the possible," whose innate power is to project himself into the future. Bloch acknowledges, moreover, that it was through the Hebrew-Christian Scriptures that man first realized his innate power of courageously living for a new and better world. "Christian theology," writes Pannenberg, "will be indebted to Ernst Bloch's philosophy of hope if it again finds the courage to deal with its central category: the general concept of eschatology. . . . Bloch has taught us to understand anew the overwhelming significance of a future which is still open, and of the hope which anticipates this future, for the life and thought of mankind and for the ontological peculiarity of all reality. He has regained the eschatological method of thinking of the biblical traditions as a theme for philosophical reflection and also for Christian theology."[19]

The theology of the future, then, wishes to construct an ontology and an anthropology (Pannenberg emphasizing the former, Moltmann the latter) which will understand the future as a divine mode of being, and hope as the "thermal current" in all articles of the Christian faith. The revelation to Israel which culminated in Jesus is where the promise of this future is to be found. Israel lived as a people in the light of God's promises, first to Abraham, then to his descendants, to Moses and the prophets. In contrast to the Hellenic view of life, where "future" was meaningless, the Hebrews lived in continual expectation. This is confirmed by reading the divine name in Exodus 3:14 as "I will be who I will be," so that God is seen to be the "God before us," whose transcendence is revealed

---

[19] Pannenberg, "The God of Hope," 286–87.

precisely as the force of our future. We know this "God before us" in the unfolding history of his promises. Again, in the resurrection of Jesus, God is seen as the one who has raised and will raise the dead. In this event we see something totally new, which in turn is itself a pledge of Christ's lordship over the whole cosmos, a lordship "not yet" actualized but promised. While the accent of Jesus' message differed from the Jewish eschatological hope insofar as he underscored the present impact of the future, this difference cannot be so exaggerated that the futurity of the Kingdom in his message is minimized. "Jesus indeed spoke of the presence of the Kingdom of God, but always in terms of the presence of God's *coming* Kingdom. Futurity is fundamental for Jesus' message."[20]

Both Moltmann and Pannenberg insist upon the centrality of the resurrection for any Christian experience of the presence of the future. "In remembering this one, unique event, we remember the hope for the future of all world history. . . . The expectation of what is to come on the ground of the resurrection of Christ, must then turn all reality that can be experienced and all real experience into an experience that is provisional and a reality that does not yet contain within it what is held in prospect for it."[21] Though the two men understand the historicity of the resurrection differently (Pannenberg stressing the possibility and necessity of knowing it by modern standards of historical research),[22] the event itself, for both, is clearly the guarantee that in the fullness of Jesus the fullness of the whole world is to be realized. It thus provides a hermeneutical principle for judging the Christian proclamation of a future promised but not yet realized. "This event which is revealed in the cross and the Easter experiences points back to the promises of God and forward to an *eschaton* in which his divinity is revealed in all. It must then be understood as the eschatological coming to pass of the faithfulness of God, and at the same time as the eschatological authentication of his promise and as the dawning of its fulfillment. . . . Jesus identifies himself in the Easter appearances as the coming one, and his identity in cross and resurrection points the direction for coming events and makes a path for them. . . . What

20 Pannenberg, "Theology and the Kingdom of God," 5.
21 Moltmann, *Theology of Hope*, 180.
22 Pannenberg, *Jesus—God and Man*, 24–28.

happened to him is understood as the dawn and assured promise of the coming glory of God over all, as the victory of life from God over death."[23]

Yet the centrality of the resurrection must not in any way obscure the reality of the cross in the Christian orientation toward the future. For the real problem of all thinking in terms of hope is the fact of death. Hope in the future can be taken seriously by the Christian only if death is taken seriously. Such hope can thus never be equated with security. It is not an attempt to rob the future of mystery, or to develop a glorified optimism about progress that somehow shuts its eyes to the hard realities of life, especially that suffering which must eventually be the lot of every human being. The final outcome of Jesus' earthly life is in this sense a confirmation that by all human standards the life of man is more tragic than triumphant. Only Jesus' resurrection, made accessible to the Christian through faith, brings the conviction that our immediate experience of life is not an ultimate experience. This hoped-for-future of man, both individual and collective, has in its favor neither facts nor auspicious tendencies on the part of nature, but only the faithfulness of God who stands by his word and his promise. Christian hope is thus a hope contrary to what is seen, as Paul says in Romans 8:24. Because of the resurrection of Christ who was crucified, the Christian can, in the face of death, set his hope on the impossible. The person who trusts in the crucified Christ can in fact surrender to life completely, since death and the pain of a continual self-giving in love ultimately have life as both their source and their achievement.[24]

From what has been said thus far, it will readily be seen why the centrality of the resurrection in the theology of the future inevitably leads it to focus upon the doctrine of God. For the only future to which Christian eschatology can be oriented is what Karl Rahner has called "the absolute future," and Pannenberg, "the ultimate future." All intermediate futures are more or less in the hands of men and must inevitably become pasts, since their achievements will always be partial, and flawed by the ambiguities of suffering and death. But to think in these terms is to raise the

[23] Moltmann, *Theology of Hope,* 201.
[24] Moltmann, "Hope and Confidence," 52–54.

question of the future as a divine mode of being. "The future as a mode of being of God has still not been considered in theology, in spite of the close correlation of God and of the coming reign of God in the eschatological message of Jesus. . . . As the power of the future, the God of the Bible has always been and is still beyond any statements made about him and he has already surpassed every conception of God. . . . The power of the future—and only it—can be an object of hope and trust; for the future has power over that which is temporally present and releases the forces that overcome it."[25]

By thus conceiving God primarily as the power of the future, Pannenberg can speak of the present as an *effect* of the future in contrast to conventional assumption that past and present *cause* the future. This priority of the ultimate future demands, he says, a reversal in our ontological conceptions. "In every event the infinite future separates itself from the finite events which until then had been hidden in this future but are now released into existence. The future lets go of itself to bring into being our present. . . . In every present we confront the infinite future, and in welcoming the particular finite events which spring from that future, we anticipate the coming of God."[26] This concept of the futurity of God, however, does not mean that God is only in the future and not in the past and present as well. For as power of the future he dominates the remotest past. Nor does such a concept exclude that of eternity: "The God of the coming Kingdom must be called eternal because he is not only the future of our present but has been also the future of every past age. . . . He was the future even of that 'nothing' which preceded creation." Such futurity does not therefore imply any development in God, for "what turns out to be true in the future will then be evident as having been true all along." This applies especially to truth about God. "God was present in every past moment as the one who is in his futurity. He was in the past the same one whom he will manifest himself to be in the future."[27]

[25] Pannenberg, "The God of Hope," 289–90.
[26] Pannenberg, "Theology and the Kingdom of God," 9.
[27] *Ibid.*, 11–12.

What Pannenberg is insisting upon, then, is the ontological priority of the future as this becomes evident in the idea of God as the one who is coming. Such rethinking of the doctrine of God in the context of the eschatological message of Jesus constitutes an essential first step in making hope the "thermal current" in all articles of the Christian faith. For to associate the transcendence of God with the absolute future of man is, in a culture oriented toward the future, to enable divine transcendence to have a new significance for the believer. God the wholly Other now becomes God the wholly New. In Jesus Christ this God gives to the world the possibility and responsibility of transcending its past and creating what has never been before. This "New" is not a mere renewal: It can even be, as Paul says (I Corinthians 2:7), the entrance of the totally unexpected, a future determined by the absolute freedom of God. Although faith still has priority in the Christian life, hope would now have the primacy, to use Moltmann's phrasing. Without faith's knowledge of Christ, human hope would become a mere utopia hanging in the air; but without hope, faith becomes fragmented and ultimately dies. It is hope that enables faith to move toward the future and to draw the believer into love; therefore, it will also be hope which mobilizes faith's thinking and reflection upon human nature, history, and society. "Faith hopes in order to know what it believes," says Moltmann, and this is why he can call for Christian theology to follow a new basic principle: *spes quaerens intellectum—spero ut intellegam.*[28] "If one succeeds in conceiving God and the future together," he writes, "then one can see the future in the past, the *eschaton* as initial purpose, transformation in expiation, the Kingdom of God in the resurrection of Christ, and the Promised Land in the Gospel. An eschatological ontology and anthropology will then be able to consider transient matter together with its future, reconciling them with human existence seen together with its glorification. This will be possible because in both (and here we have the most important consideration) the power of the divine future can be made manifest in nothingness itself."[29]

[28] Moltmann, *Theology of Hope,* 20, 33.
[29] Moltmann, "Hope Without Faith," 39.

A TIME FOR DECISION

The changes in theological perspective we have just outlined have opened up a number of problem areas in concrete Christian living, and to these the nascent theology of the future has also been addressing itself. First, however, it has had to defend its right to do so. For it can be readily seen how constant orientation toward the future, in reaction to existentialist theology, could be understood only as an emphasis elaborated at the expense of the present. By concentrating on those past events in salvation history in which God's promises for the future are most clearly manifest, such an emphasis, it is argued, tends to absorb the present either into its past foundation or its future development. Both Moltmann and Pannenberg are sensitive to this kind of criticism and have accordingly taken pains to indicate the importance they attach to the present. Moltmann writes that "the new is never totally new," and "the place where the future of man and of the world is decided is the present, [which is] the front line of the future."[30] His statements that hope's promises always stand in "contradiction to present reality" must not therefore be understood literally.[31] Pannenberg, on the other hand, points to his conviction that God as ultimate future gives a transcendent worth to every present moment. "The future comes to be relevant through the fact that it 'comes into' the present. . . . The confession of the incarnation of God in Jesus Christ affirms, in this sense, that in him the future of God has become present among us, and not only a transitory present . . . but an enduring present—through the spirit of Jesus—because it is a present that has an unbounded future."[32]

---

[30] Moltmann, "The Category of the New in Christian Theology," 14, 24.

[31] Moltmann, *Theology of Hope*, 18. With his usual perception, Philip Hefner concludes a discussion of this question by noting that "contradiction can only refer to the fact that our predictions and visions of those open possibilities are never adequate to the way in which the future actually unfolds." "Questions for Moltmann and Pannenberg," *Una Sancta*, 25 (1968), 37.

[32] Pannenberg, *Theology as History*, 267, note 77.

Nevertheless, it is not Moltmann and Pannenberg who have developed the full practical implications of these statements, but rather theologians like Johannes Metz, Edward Schillebeeckx, and Harvey Cox. Metz speaks of a "political theology"; Harvey Cox theologizes in terms of today's American social scene: urban, secular, mobile, anonymous—yet Christian in a new way. Schillebeeckx recalls the Church's function of "critical negativity." They emphasize that the Christian's eschatological hope, far from disengaging him from the present, forces him to view it as the time for decision; not passive dreams for the future but practical initiatives in the present are called for. For the miseries of the world around us become intolerable in the light of the new creation promised by Christ. To hope, then, is not simply to trust in God but to commit oneself to changing a society always open in its possibilities. It is this joining of hope to realizable possibility which makes it practical, and gives rise to that relationship which exists between that critical character of Christian hope and the contemporary instinct for planning. To plan the future is consciously to execute the transition from the possible to the real. The finite futures which man thereby realizes, however, must always be recognized as finite; they can never be seen as exhausting the possibilities of human development. Human planning can foster man's growth in freedom, but only in the absolute future can this freedom be fully actualized through the powerful intervention of God. Consequently, there must remain a dialectical tension between what is planned by man and what is unforeseen by him, what is anticipated and what comes through the unexpected intervention of God. For the dynamics of "grace" touch the actions of all men, Christian and non-Christian alike, and it is this conviction which gives to Christian hope its desire to cooperate with God in bringing to pass in the present not simply the possible but the new.[33]

For Johannes Metz's incipient political theology, there is an intrinsic relationship between the changing of the world under the free hand of man, and the eschatological horizon of promise. On this horizon the world appears not as a finished reality but as one in process toward a greater future through man's free decision. The

[33] Metz, "The Responsibility of Hope," 284–87; Rahner, "Building the New Earth," 61–63.

Christian doctrine of creation, moreover, as well as the clear acceptance of the transcendence of God, are what historically deprived the world of its divine character in the eyes of men and provided thereby a basis for its new evaluation and use. Once man saw the world as finite, he realized that he had the power, as coworker with God, to control nature and set it to his own purposes. In Christ God accepts this world of man, and through the Incarnation asserts the full reality of himself and the world, at the same time making manifest their eventual convergence. Christian hope for the future cannot be fulfilled if the world and its future are passed over; such hope clings to a single promised future which includes the future of the world. Hence, the responsibility of hope can best be expressed in the concept of "creative eschatology," by which Metz means that the contents of the promise founded on Jesus—freedom, peace, justice, reconciliation—require the assumption of social responsibility. Nor does this mean to identify the Christian promise with any historical condition of society; on the contrary, such identification would involve a surrender of that "eschatological reservation" by reason of which every historically attained status of society appears provisional. Rather, what is important is to see that the Christian approaches the world's future not by contemplating it but by bringing it about through historical demands that are "political" in a truly theological sense.[34]

"I understand political theology," writes Metz, "to be the critical correction of present-day theology inasmuch as this theology shows an extreme privatizing tendency (a tendency, that is, to center upon the private person rather than 'public,' 'political' society). At the same time, I understand this political theology to be a positive attempt to formulate the eschatological message under the conditions of our present society."[35] In this European form, therefore, such a theology is less a question of social involvement than one of theological epistemology: The Christian message does not attribute to the sociopolitical reality some shadowy existence but regards it as an area with which Christian salvation is intrinsically concerned. Here Metz is reacting against what he calls a theology of transcen-

[34] Metz, "Creative Hope," 175–80.
[35] Metz, "Religion and Society in the Light of a Political Theology," 507.

dental, existential, personalist orientation, whose most prominent categories are of the intimate, the private, the apolitical sphere. Charity has been regarded as the virtue of the I-thou relation extending to the field of interpersonal encounter, or at best to charity on the scale of the neighborhood. But Christian love must also mobilize itself socially as an unconditional determination toward justice and freedom, and this must be accomplished through the church as an institution of criticism in society, radically oriented to the future rather than to the maintenance of the status quo.[36]

Edward Schillebeeckx develops a crucial point in Metz's approach with his concept of "critical negativity." This positive power exercises constant pressure to bring about what is most desirable for man in the future, not by explicit formulation but by negative knowledge. "In the long run, situations which are unworthy of man give rise to explicit protest, not in the name of a concept of what . . . is already positively defined, but in the name of human values still being sought and revealed in a negative manner in the contrast-experience of situations unworthy of man. The Christian has as little positive idea as the non-Christian of what is worthy of man, either ultimately or here and now. He too has to seek fumblingly and consider various alternatives, keeping in the back of his mind, as he searches, human values already realized in history."[37] The difference for the Christian, however, is that his eschatological faith in the God of the promise tells him that even though he cannot form the content of the promise in a positive way, God has nonetheless bound himself to the realization of this promise in Christ. What is humanly possible becomes really possible in Jesus.

The Christian's hope thus makes him critical of every attempt to realize a perfect future for the whole of mankind purely on the basis of technological planning. For this would be to attribute solely to the power of man the future he is in process of achieving, whereas in fact the future promised by God must be received from him as a gift. Nor is such reception a purely passive act, since the future so received must thereafter be "made" by man himself. Pre-

---

[36] *Ibid.*, 512–15.
[37] Schillebeeckx, *God the Future of Man*, 191.

cisely because those who make history are sinful men, the realization of a better future cannot come simply from planning but must also come from redemption. Eschatological hope says that everything really worthy of man is possible through the resources of man himself, but this means the resources of *redeemed* man. For it is the sinfulness of man which is continually forcing the question whether what is worthy of man is, ultimately, at all possible. The Christian answer is that it *is* possible, but only if man is open to a transcendence of himself and all his limitations. The critical function of the church is thus directed at everything which would diminish man's being, against every skepticism of man's potential, against every attempt to consider him exclusively as either matter or means for building a completely rationalized technological future. "The distinctively Christian contribution is to be found," concludes Schillebeeckx, "on the one hand, in a commitment to the building up of the world by a concern for man which is radical for the sake of eschatological faith and implemented by all available scientific and technical means, and on the other hand, in a criticism which is based on and inwardly flows from this same Christian hope, a criticism that is directed toward every positive design of man which is presented as the last word or which in any way diminishes man's being."[38]

To end this discussion of the practical consequences of eschatology in today's Christian life, let us consider the theory fashioned by Pierre Teilhard de Chardin in order to explain man's relationship with God in the creation of the future. Teilhard saw the world which man achieves as a "preliminary sketch" or "rough draft" of the final outcome of the evolutionary process. Man plans and works for the new earth in accordance with his own aspirations and desires, but his achievement must be refinished and brought to completion by God just as the work of art begun by the apprentice is completed by the master artist. Thus in the incipient interiority of plants Teilhard saw a "rough sketch" of consciousness, and in the primates he saw a "first draft" of the human person. The structure of human personality at present is therefore only a "faint sketch" of that collectivity of consciousness to emerge at the final state of

[38] *Ibid.*, 196.

the universe. Scientific cooperation, racial integration, international harmony, these likewise represent an "outline" only of that total sense of humanity to become manifest in the future. Transformation, then, is in Teilhard's thought an analogous concept used to describe the part which God plays at every state of man's making of man; the divine hand refinishing the preliminary sketch made by the human hand, and at the Parousia transforming the whole of history. Christian hope thus becomes the creative dynamism enabling man to advance into a future that often terrifies him by its newness and disheartens him by its uncertainty. Because the promised goal of history is the *pleroma* of Christ, the Christian should have an immense and totally human hope, one which constitutes an invitation for Christ to return.[39] Harvey Cox has noted that Teilhard's approach here transcends ordinary teleological approaches by placing in human hands the key to the next stage of the cosmic process. What next happens really *is* up to man. In such a perspective teleology ripens indeed into prophecy, which is the characteristically Hebrew mode of perceiving the future as the open field of human hope and responsibility.[40]

CONCLUSION

The broad outlines of the theology of the future which we have sketched here would seem to justify two concluding remarks. The first is that there is danger in the type of optic we have been discussing only through exclusivity. If one can say in a perfectly correct sense that hope is an unfolding of faith, then one must also say that such unfolding is at the same time an orientation of faith toward the future. What one cannot say is that this dimension of the future is the whole of faith. For faith is oriented also toward the past, whence it takes its origin, and toward the present,

---

[39] Teilhard de Chardin, *The Future of Man*, 223–24, 267–68; on his use of "preliminary sketch" (*ébauche*) see *L'Energie humaine, Oeuvres*, 6 (Paris, 1962) 141–200.

[40] Cox, *On Not Leaving It to the Snake*, 8–9, 40.

where it actually exists. This is why faith has to be the comprehensive principle in theology. While hope obviously comes from faith, faith cannot be explained exclusively in terms of hope. The creed and its contents are more than their future dimension. The author of Hebrews 11:1 says that faith is hope's foundation, its origin and the measure of its truth. Faith must, therefore, have not only the priority but also the primacy. Contrary to Moltmann's view, *credo ut intelligam* remains more fundamental than *spero ut intelligam*. It is faith which enables us to catch the inner unity of God's promises given through the Old and New Testaments. But the life of Jesus is more than an event of promise; it means that grace, justification, and salvation are given to man in the present. Only insofar as man *actually* possesses these, can he have hope in God's future promise. In both Moltmann and Pannenberg we find a tendency to limit this existential aspect of soteriology, whereas in fact there is no reason at all for them to do so. The theology of the future they elaborate provides us with a key for reordering all the various elements in revelation, but in doing so it need not exclude or minimize any of the data. The "not yet" cannot do without the "already."[41]

A second conclusion concerns the relationship between this new theological perspective and human freedom. We noted earlier in this essay man's power today to change himself to a degree previously undreamed of, indeed, to make an experiment of himself. He has in a true sense entered the era of self-creation. As Teilhard saw so clearly, biological evolution has gradually developed into a cultural evolution in which man makes all the decisive choices and does all the systematic planning. This development is in no way inimical to Christianity but is in radical harmony with it, for man is now becoming what the Gospel teaches he should be: a free being under his own responsible control. Christianity insists, however, that this human planning, this active self-fulfillment through the manipulation of reality, is embraced by an event not subject to our purposes

[41] See Moltmann, *Theology of Hope*, 156ff; Pannenberg, *Jesus—God and Man*, 48ff. Heinrich Fries has underscored this criticism in "Spero ut Intelligam: Bemerkungen zu einer Theologie der Hoffnung," *Wahrheit und Verkündigung* (Paderborn, 1967), 368–72.

and beyond all planning. When man pushes forward into the future, he not only sees his own practical achievements, but also experiences what is not his achievement, what is purely given. This mystery of absolute giving the Christian calls God, the mystery of love endlessly giving itself. The Christian finds this mystery in Christ and he confesses it in hope.[42] And it is precisely this eschatological hope which can bring to modern man a sense of security in the God who is to come; trust and confidence therefore rather than fear and anxiety before the awful consequences of freedom.

The source of this confidence, it should be noted, is God's living *presence* to man as he creates his own future. There is no question here of appealing to God as a solver of problems or as a refuge from the harshness of life. For what man is afraid of is not his inability to control his world as he moves into the future, but his inability to control himself. What he needs, then, is a reaffirmation, within the context of the future, of the personal relationship between God and himself. "The future of humanity," said the Second Vatican Council, "lies in the hands of those who are strong enough to provide coming generations with reasons for living and hoping."[43] These reasons somehow must assuage man's sense of loneliness in the cosmos, for ultimately it is loneliness which will make his freedom a burden too heavy to bear. "Man, overburdened in his freedom and left alone even by his fellow men to make free decisions, need not ultimately feel lonely—as St. John observes in a masterly statement in his Gospel, given as a pure interpretation of Jesus' life—'I am not alone; the Father is always with me'" (John 8:16).[44] Within this sphere of trust, then, and of the constant dialogue between God and man, the impossible can actually be undertaken. Indeed, it is only by encouraging the undertaking of the impossible that Christianity can continue to exercise its mission in the modern world. In this way "a new impulse becomes possible and is now beginning to take shape in human consciousness. Born of the psychic combination of two kinds of faith—in the transcendent

[42] See Karl Rahner, "Experiment: Man," 62–66.
[43] *Pastoral Constitution on the Church in the Modern World,* article 31.
[44] Schillebeeckx, *God the Future of Man,* 200.

39

action of a personal God and the innate perfectibility of a world in progress—it is an impulse (or better, a spirit of love) that is truly evolutionary. We can indeed say of it that it is the only kind of spiritual energy capable of causing the formidable human machine, in which, from what we can see, all the future and all the hopes of evolution must henceforth be concentrated, to function at full power, without danger from egotism or from mechanization, and to the full extent of its potentialities."[45]

[45] Teilhard de Chardin, *The Future of Man*, 224–25.

Political Theology for the United States

✠

HARVEY COX

*Recently theologians have been calling for a "political theology."
This means experiencing through the growing social crises the
union between politics and love, and the ambiguous character of
the eschatological Kingdom of God. Political theology may well
demand that "politics" as we know it today die. Harvey Cox is
professor at the Divinity School of Harvard University. His* The
Secular City *(1966) began u new era in theology. From sociologies
and societal observation he found the prism for asking about the
Christian amid the mobility and autonomy of America today. Political theology is the action correlative of his analysis of Christianity
through social dimensions.*

Fashions in theology change so quickly today that the very recent
discussion about the need for a "political theology" has already
elicited a backlash based on its alleged narrowness. Political theology, some critics claim, overlooks the personal aspect of the reality
upon which theologians are called to reflect. It focuses so heavily
on the social dimension that subjectivity often almost disappears.
This structural orientation is especially unfortunate, the critics
continue, when such Marxists as Roger Garaudy are conceding that

Marxism has been weak on the question of human subjectivity and could learn a good deal about it from Christians.[1]

What is the significance of these accusations? Is it true that Christian theologians, by emphasizing the need for a political theology, have left the store untended just as the customers have begun to return? Have the "political theologians" abandoned the citadel in a mistaken sortie out to the periphery of theology?

I do not think so. It is my conviction that only a conceptually deficient version of political theology would overlook the place of the person in the polis. I believe further that theologies which fasten too obsessively on "the person," as have some contemporary Catholic personalists and Protestant existentialists, often succeed in losing the very thing they say they want to preserve. My insistence that, despite all, we must continue to press for a viable "political theology" is premised on the belief that the wholeness of salvation must reach the entire human enterprise and ultimately even the cosmos if individuals are to find fulfillment.

The dichotomy between "personal" and "political" is a questionable one. It is itself a symptom of our age's derangement. But we are learning better. We are now giving up, for example, the venerable distinction between "public health" and some other kind of health. Similarly, we can no longer perpetuate the false dichotomy between the so-called "social gospel" and some other gospel. If man is saved or damned, if he is sound or sick, he is so in inextricable solidarity with the whole human family. Pascal once said, "One Christian is no Christian." Likewise, it is doubtful if we can speak today about the "healthy individual" unless we talk about the healthy family, the good city, even the soundly functioning world and cosmos.

René Dubos once defined health as the capacity to cope with the future. The person, family, city, or nation which cannot innovate and change in response to the future is sick. Political theology is so oriented toward the future. I want to deal here with two issues

[1] See R. Garaudy, *From Anathema to Dialogue* (New York, 1966); R. Garaudy and Q. Lauer, *Christian Communist Dialogue* (New York, 1968); P. Oestereicher, ed., *The Christian-Marxist Dialogue* (New York, 1969).

in particular upon which a viable American political theology must be centered if it is to be both politically sound and theologically substantive in the decades that lie ahead. Not surprisingly, one of these issues seems to display a more conventionally "political" mien, the other a more "personal" one. But my contention is that a successful *political* theology will have to come to terms with both. The two major issues to which I am referring are the search for social justice and the search for self-knowledge, the "outer quest" and the "inner quest." Together they provide the unspoken ambiance within which any political theology will eventually be measured. To succeed, a political theology will not only have to see them both, but see them together, as part of a single quest. Let us look, then, at each.

THE DEATH OF POLITICS?

What about social revolution, the search for justice? We have recently heard from Daniel Bell that the last third of the twentieth century is no longer a time of revolution.[2] The death of politics and the "end of ideology" have been announced and we have been told that large-scale social upheaval is passé. Do we live at the end of ideology? Have all revolutions today become vehicles for cruel power-grabbing by cynical elites and for the colossal deception of the masses?

This judgment has been widely circulated, but I think it is wrong. Even when first circulated it had a provincially Western and even "Northern" bias. It seemed true that in the advanced industrial nations today the terms in which the struggle for power goes on have changed and that earlier revolutionary rhetoric did seem somewhat stale. But Paris, Prague, and the uprisings in the American black ghettos should make us wonder whether even the most "advanced" industrial society is really wholly beyond all aspects of

[2] Daniel Bell, "Introduction," *The Year 2000*, H. Kahn and A. J. Wiener, eds. (New York, 1967), xxi-xxviii; "Notes on the Post-Industrial Society," *The Public Interest*, 7 (1967).

revolutionary change. The sociologist Norman Birnbaum has recently reminded us that, after all, industrial nations are very fragile indeed.[3] Most importantly, however, we have noticed recently how much the international confrontation between the rich nations of the Northern hemisphere and the poor nations of the Southern still breeds revolutionary passions. The "exported proletariat" that picks the coffee, cuts the sugar, and packs the bananas for the American breakfast table will no longer remain deferentially silent. Ours *is* still an age of revolution, now on an international rather than on a merely domestic scale. The poor, the black, the outsiders—those who have been excluded from the world's decision-making councils—now want in. They are insisting on the uprooting and rebuilding of whole national and international political structures so they can share the giddy privileges and awesome responsibilities of power.

Despite the fact that many of us would like it to go away, revolution and the quest for radical social change remain major components of our late-twentieth-century life style. Its constant presence sets the stage on which a political theology must be worked out.

THE JOURNEY INWARD

What about the second component of our emerging future mentality, what I have called the search for self-knowledge and inner wholeness? This is also a vital component of our age. It is shown by our indefatigable interest in the exploration of the inner recesses of the psyche. This inward journey also gives our time its characteristic tone. Our artists and young people revel with endless fascination in the vast reaches of man's dream and fantasy life. Writers plunge into previously tabooed areas. Painters and poets pinch and prod the human psyche in search of expanded modes of experience. We accept with appreciation plays and novels on blood lust, deviancy, criminality, and self-destruction that previous gener-

[3] "Staggering Colossus," *The Nation*, 206 (1968), 167.

ations stashed under the counter. No manic nightmare, no ecstatic vision, no unheard-of permutation of human experience lies outside the range of our insatiable quest for self-knowledge and expanded experience. We want to know ourselves fully.

Thus social revolution and self-revelation form the polar axis of our late-twentieth-century mentality. Neither is wholly new in our century. Revolution has a long history in the West, though its theoreticians wrote mainly in the eighteenth and nineteenth centuries. Some scholars believe the revolutionary impulse has its origin in the Hebrew hope for a messianic era; consequently, it is no accident that the tradition of revolution arose in the Christian West. The quest for self-realization goes even further back, though its peculiarly modern form probably started in the nineteenth century with Kierkegaard and Nietzsche. This impulse may also go back to the Christian idea of the incalculable worth of every person and the hope of the believer to fulfill the destiny for which God has created him. Social revolution and self-revelation both have long histories. *What is important for our time is the convergence of these two streams and the tensions which this convergence produces.* What is particularly significant for us today is the effect this late modern mentality has on the way we think theologically and how theology can deal in the future with this convergence.

We will miss the point in our theologizing today if we do not recognize that the main impact of these two movements bears not on the *content* of ideas but on *how* we look at theological ideas, or at any ideas. We must see that because of our avid interest in structural change and psychic exploration today, we tend to look at any idea in a radically new way, and this is the real challenge. We do not any longer view theological ideas as secure landmarks but as aspects of lived experience. We concern ourselves with their human significance, their validity within the process of social change and self-revelation. Our highest tribute to anything today is that it is "exciting" or "moving." We ask of someone's idea for the staging of a play or the staging of a coup: "Will it work?"

This does not mean that our age has settled for a cheap, utilitarian view of the good. Rather, it is a recognition that any idea which lacks social or personal immediacy is a delusion. We perceive

45

a theological formulation not as a timeless essence but as a historical construct. This may be a recognition of the insistence by modern philosophy of science that all so-called "facts" function within a particular paradigm, a specific human project.[4] It may also be a secularized modern tribute to the biblical notion that truth is not mere accuracy but power and dependability.

This characteristically late modern concern with the capacity of ideas and values to push society toward change or to stir human beings into new modes of perception refers also to religious values. Today religious doctrines and images must face a harrowing new kind of litmus test. The revolutionary asks Buddhism, Christianity, and Islam about the political weight of their messages. He has no interest in the allegedly eternal truth of religious values; he looks to see what *effect they have in the world*. Does this church's Christ sanctify crippling patterns of privilege and exploitation? Or does he summon the dispossessed to participate in casting down the mighty? The revolutionary will not be drawn into debates and dialogues that imply some abstract or duplicative view of whether this or that idea is "true." Truth for him is potency, the power of an idea to awaken those anesthetized by the incantations of the powerful and to expose the myths by which injustice holds its sway.

But what about those artists whose trek carries them into the inner universe? How do they measure ideas? If the revolutionary tests ideas and doctrines for their political valency, the artist feels out their capacity to stretch and nourish the human consciousness. True, he often says of an idea in a play or poem, or of the play or poem itself, that it is "true." But he means true in the sense that a Godard film or a Calder mobile is "true"—because it works. It comes over. It enriches the experience and perspective of the audience; it grants its viewer the glimpse of a new dimension of space. As Susan Sontag rightly says of the role of ideas, including moral and religious ideas, in the contemporary film and drama: They "function as decor, props, sensuous material."[5]

[4] Cf. Thomas Kuhn, *The Structure of Scientific Revolutions* (Chicago, 1962).

[5] *Against Interpretation and Other Essays* (New York, 1966), 171.

THE POWER TO CHANGE

Theologies grip us today only if they have the power to change our inner or outer worlds, to make them more worthy of human habitation. Theological ideas are not something we contemplate or cherish. We chalk them on placards, choreograph them, try them on for size. Then we listen raptly to see if they take. Is the earth enriched, made more just, more interesting, more varied because these ideas have been there? If not, away with them. We banish the ideas that do not make real contact with the human world to the airy oblivion they deserve. In other words, our age demands the incarnation of truth.

Christianity once fought a long and costly but finally successful struggle against Gnosticism. For the Gnostics, values and doctrines must have seemed like discarnate wraiths floating in a filmy world far above the hurly-burly of earthly life. In fact, for the Gnostics, salvation itself was gained by soaring up to this mystical gnosis and leaving the everyday world behind. In our times, it sometimes has seemed that Christianity slides back into the very gnostic heresies it had formally condemned, that it contents itself with "eternal values" severed from the shifting uncertainties of history.

But while the church has often fallen into gnostic errors, the paradox is that our modern world has moved, however unknowingly, toward a biblical instinct for the meaning of truth. Those who think today's political and artistic approach to religious truth demeans it by reducing it to slogans or gimmicks often fail to see the significance of our era's developing view of what it means for something to be "true." Of course, there are demagogues who deliberately pervert ideas to mislead the gullible, and there will always be charlatans who will daub ideas with deceptive rouge to titillate the emotionally retarded. But the basic insight of the genuine revolutionary and the real artist cannot be brushed aside. For them, ideas find their value and truth in the lived world. The hoary old question, "Is Christianity true?" is still being asked today, and the question deserves an answer. But "true" no longer means a Verifax copy of

47

something somewhere else. "Is it true?" means, "Can it survive the test of human experience in all its dimensions?"

This contemporary and very "political" way of looking at truth explains why flurried attempts by theologians to make Christianity more intellectually digestible today are usually greeted with yawns of indifference. Intellectual acceptability is not the problem. Today's religious dropouts leave not because they find Christianity intellectually implausible, but because they find it soporific or spineless. People complain that they find religious services boring, the theological disputes tedious. But they seldom write criticisms of the church for this reason; they just disaffiliate. The most devastating frontal assaults on the church today flay it not for obscurantism but for cowardice, for not living up to its own definition of itself. Thus, Rolf Hochhuth's attack on Pope Pius XII, and in one sense on Christianity as a whole, hit the mark so forcibly because it implied that the world *expected* a word from the Pope, as the vicar of Christ, on the Nazi murder of seven million Jews. Hochhuth blasted the church not because he cannot believe the Nicene Creed, but because it flunked the most critical moral test of the century.

The men of faith today who inspire us are those who enact the Gospel. Martin Luther King and Camilo Torres not only called the church to practice what it preaches. They took real risks to bring justice to black people and peons. And both these very political Christians paid the highest price for the potency of their vision.

Pope John XXIII in his short pontificate managed to persuade millions of people that there might be something to Christianity after all. He did not do so, however, by composing a dazzling defense of Christian doctrine. The peasant pope was not capable of that sort of feat, and no one would have been interested anyway. Rather, he reached the modern world for the gospel by the style and manner of his life. He blessed the animals in a traveling circus menagerie. He visited condemned murderers in Rome's prisons. He poked fun at the pretense of the papal court and at his own infallibility. He summoned a council to discuss questions many people thought were closed forever.

Theology requires continuous reinterpretation of the faith. But theologians frequently fail in the reinterpretative process because they wildly misjudge the mood of the culture to which they so desperately wish to speak. In today's world theological disquisitions often flop because they try to make Christianity credible to a world committed to the incredible. They try to accommodate the faith to the world as it now is, just as the citizens of that world have decided to change it into something else. They have sought to explicate religion within the bounds of reason, in this or that view of the perimeters of reason, just as our secular seers have moved beyond our forefathers' reverence for reason in a soaring quest for prophecy and ecstatic insight. Who can walk away from a "black is beautiful" rally in Mississippi, a De Kooning canvas, or a play by Samuel Beckett and still believe that the secret to evangelism today is to trim off religion's irrational edges?

Religion will survive in the modern world only if it contributes to man's commitment to fashion a more just social order, and if it aids his determination to delve into the hidden depths of his self.

The British psychiatrist R. D. Laing recently drew these two strands of late-twentieth-century life together in a remarkable book entitled *The Politics of Experience*.[6] The very title of the book symbolizes the basic unity of the contemporary drives for justice and peace in society and for more profound self-knowledge. I have argued here that the two should never be separated. Personal conversion and social action should not be sundered from each other. The inner and outer quests, one of which sometimes pushes people to counterproductive violence and the other to the self-destructive misuse of drugs, must both be nourished in productive ways and held together as a common search. All this is the task of an American political theology. But such a theology will not succeed if its ideas and insights merely explain and organize. Theology must now actively contribute to civilizational and individual fulfillment. For too long theologians have simply interpreted the world. The time has come to change it.

[6] New York, 1967.

The Christian in the Vortex of Revolution

✠

RICHARD SHAULL

Faced with the political and the social agonies of establishing real equality for all, many are less and less shocked by the word rev-olution. We are slowly coming to perceive that the preservation of the best in America is not served by suppressing every revolt against the status quo. It was through his years in Colombia and Brazil, where he was intimately involved in the elaboration of the Christian community's role in societies needing social and economic change, that Richard Shaull saw the need for a new encounter of Chris-tianity with revolution. Encounter with Revolution (1952) *was fol-lowed by his collaboration with Carl Oglesby in* Containment and Change (1967). *Richard Shaull is professor of Ecumenics at Prince-ton Theological Seminary. The following essay develops insights of the Old Testament and the Calvinist tradition asking how Christian groups can be active and revolutionary.*

The attempt in this essay to project certain trends in the future of theology's interaction with revolution is based on two major assumptions. The first is that the revolutionary ferment in which we are caught at the present time is no passing phenomenon. Revolu-tion is, rather, one of the central facts with which we will have to deal in the coming decades, and the United States is destined to be in the very center of it. The modernizing revolutions which first broke out in England and France in the seventeenth and eighteenth centuries (which have continued under socialist auspices in our time) have not yet run their course. In fact, the failure of our present structures to meet the rising expectations and awakening self-consciousness of minority groups in the West as well as the peoples of the developing world, suggests that these revolutions of modernization may now be reaching their most intense and global phase. And to our own surprise and chagrin, we in America are discovering that, thanks to the black man, we are confronted by the demands of that revolution in our own society. At the same time, we are the major power striving desperately to stop its spread in Asia, Africa, and Latin America.

As if this were not enough, the success of modernization brings the possibility of a new stage of revolution in the advanced nations of the West as well as in the Communist countries. Modernization was achieved at the cost of personal repression and social domination, now firmly structured into our technological-bureaucratic society. At the same time, the process of secularization has destroyed the power of old authorities and given birth to a new form of human self-consciousness that yearns for freedom. And the success of industrialization in overcoming scarcity now makes such surplus repression unnecessary. To move beyond this impasse will require the development of qualitatively new types of social organization, which is the one thing our advanced technological society seems incapable of producing. Here, too, the United States is in the forefront of the revolutionary struggle.

Our second assumption is that the inner logic of Christian faith pushes us toward involvement in the struggle for revolutionary change. The biblical story focuses on man's life *in the world,* a created world which has lost its divine character. His existence is historical, and history is seen as the realm of divine action, moving toward the establishment of the messianic kingdom, a new order of individual fulfillment and social justice. Man's life is oriented not only toward the future, but toward the expectation of a *new* and *promising* future full of unexpected possibilities. This new reality does not arise naturally and gradually out of the old, but breaks into the present from the future; the old order must often be destroyed in order for the new to take shape. Israel moves through the exodus to the Promised Land; Jesus Christ, through death to resurrection.

I would contend that anyone who comes to understand his faith in these terms and sees his vocation as that of participating in shaping this new future will find himself moving toward the cutting edge of social change, which in our time, may well mean revolution.[1] This may be the logic of faith; it is not the logic of much of our theology and of the established church. And those few Christians who have been captivated by this vision have felt very ill at ease in the church; some of them have left it in disgust. At the same time, there have been a few occasions in modern Christian history when this revolutionary dynamic has broken through, the most significant example of this being provided by the English Calvinists and their participation in the Revolution of 1648. Here, according to Michael Walzer's study of this movement, we have the shaping of the first ideology, organization, and discipline of revolution within the framework of Calvin's theology.[2]

To be sure, Calvin's theology did not produce revolutionaries everywhere it went; the French Huguenot gentlemen, for example, were content to struggle for constitutional government by other means. But among the "unsettled men" of England, uprooted and deeply dissatisfied with the society to which they belonged, Calvinism had a tremendous appeal, and those who adopted it found a perspective on life and the world which gave direction to their efforts; they participated in community which pushed them toward revolutionary struggle and sustained them in it. In a time of social disruption and personal anxiety, Calvinism affirmed the sovereignty of a gracious God, and did this in such a way that it offered a new perspective on the world and the social order as well as on personal existence. This God was seen as doing great things in the world; he called men to participation in this transformation of the world and demanded their total loyalty and obedience. As the old loyalties lost their hold over men, trust in such a God not only freed men from other jurisdictions and authorities but also led to the release of tremendous energy in the direction of revolutionary politics. How this movement occurred can be seen more clearly at several specific points.

[1] For a fuller development of this thesis, see my paper, "Does Religion Demand Social Change?" *Theology Today*, 26 (1969), 5–13.
[2] M. Walzer, *The Revolution of the Saints* (New York, 1968).

TOWARD REVOLUTIONARY POLITICS

During the Middle Ages—and beyond—reality was understood as a vast Chain of Being. The cosmos was an integral part of a hierarchy of being that started with God and moved downward to the smallest stone. It was this conception that provided the foundation for the established order for centuries, as it gave a certain natural inevitability to things, and excluded the possibility of planned reconstruction of the social order.

Calvinism tended to destroy this whole view of cosmic and social reality. For the Calvinist, the central reality was the dynamic action, in the world, of a God who was making all things new. This God reigned over a single, unified domain, and men of all social positions were called to be his instruments. As he was wont to overthrow kingdoms and send churches into precipitous decline, obedience to him broke the old spell, made it possible for men to perceive sovereign power active in those who rebelled against the established order as well as those who maintained it, and opened the way for eventual action to overthrow unjust governments.

In the world in which Calvinism emerged and developed, the Chain of Being was complemented by an organic view of institutions. The political order was the *body* politic, following the analogy of the Church as the Body of Christ. According to Walzer, this meant that society was a harmonious order, and each member of it had a fixed function with no capacity for independent activity.[3] Not only the state but also the world of work and the family were part of this organism, to whose health innovation constituted the greatest possible danger.

Within the Calvinist perspective, institutions gradually came to be seen as *functional*, for their major concern was not that of healing an old body but of constructing a new building. The Puritan preachers spoke not of the body politic but of the ship of state, steered toward specific goals set by God through the action of responsible citizens. The economic order was something to be built by

<hr />

[3] *Ibid.*, 174.

the hard and unremitting work of trained and disciplined men. Even the family was changed. It was no longer the large patriarchal structure, a natural and sacramental community, but a voluntary association, constituted by the free choice of two individuals. Thus, the conjugal relationship was central, and the responsibility of the couple became the dominant thing. Given the Calvinists' passion to remake society, such a functional view of institutions led to the radical devaluation of all the institutions of the status quo and the transformation of politics into a purposive discipline.

Calvinism developed a life style and a form of disciplined community that appealed to the "masterless men" of that time. It overcame their anxiety, strengthened their radicalism, and gave discipline and direction to their politics.

In this way, the religious community did not attempt to tame reckless men, but rather to discipline and support them in a persistent, radical struggle in church and society. Their political exile was further complicated by their religious loyalties. Their contempt for the established order in England was deepened by their experience of the new order in Geneva. And the primary Christian community became an exciting experiment in radical politics. It provided new forms of association for those cut off from the old structures, on the basis of ideological commitment; and those who took part in such groups learned how to evade discipline, how to live outside the system of benefices and survive, and how to be outside the jurisdiction of the bishops. Thus the Christian community provided constant experience in the development of revolutionary politics.

What significance, if any, does this Puritan experience have for us today? Could it possibly provide us with a paradigm for the development of a new theology within a new church which might perform, in our time, the function which the early English Calvinist communities did in theirs? Or is it destined to remain one of those interesting but isolated examples of marginal developments in the life of the church which now have only historical significance?

In recent decades we have had a tremendous revival of this early Calvinistic theology. But it has not pushed neo-orthodoxy toward the front lines of revolutionary struggle today, nor has it provided any significant resources for understanding or action on the part of those who are involved in that struggle. This fact should hardly surprise us. A work of restoration of a theological system which developed in interaction with the world view of the sixteenth century could hardly be expected to operate as a creative force in relation to contemporary human experience. The same conceptual framework which shattered the old order and constituted a force of trangression in thought and society at that time can only function as a conservative force when it is reaffirmed and reconstructed four hundred years later. Especially when this theological development takes place within an acculturated church, now serving as one of the main supports of the myths and structures of the old order, the end result is almost inevitable. And it may well be that the church today is so acculturated and so sclerotic that no amount of confrontation with the transgressive forces in its past will produce creative new developments in theology or give men the courage to overcome the old ecclesiastical order in the expectation of a resurrection of the church.

Our efforts in this area, however, are based on the wager that a different outcome is possible. We are convinced that the inner logic of Christian faith provides resources for unpredictable and uncontrollable explosions—in theory and in praxis—which may occur when they are least expected. Admittedly, there is little ground for hope that the institutional church will encourage or give expression to these new developments; yet, an increasing number of Christians are being pushed, by conviction and circumstance, to take a stance and form communities similar to those of the English Puritans of the late sixteenth and early seventeenth centuries. Whether such communities will have vitality and staying power and become a significant factor in the wider revolutionary struggle may well depend upon the ability of a new generation of theologians to meet the challenge before them.

I admit that there are not many signs, thus far, of this happening. For this to happen would require something of a revolution in the life and work of the theologian himself. By this I mean several things: the willingness to do theology in the midst of revolutionary praxis; the experience on the part of the theologian of a real *exodus* and *exile* in relation to the prevailing culture and dominant social system; a rich knowledge of our theological heritage combined with a full awareness of the bankruptcy of its traditional terms and systems and of the need for the creation of new paradigms; most important of all, perhaps, a willingness to dare to allow dead theological systems to be buried, to stand before the world empty-handed, and to expect a theological resurrection.

In the last few years, there has been a great deal of discussion in Catholic and Protestant circles of a "theology of revolution." Unfortunately, most of it has not arisen out of such a revolution among the theologians. This is not the place for a critical discussion of the various attempts made thus far. But I would like to mention several factors which, to my mind, have stood in the way of more significant progress.

OBSTACLES TO A THEOLOGY OF REVOLUTION

In the United States the extraordinary work of Reinhold Niebuhr should have provided the foundation for this. As a matter of fact, it has not. This has been partly due to the fact that Niebuhr's own thought developed in a context determined by the success of a revitalized liberalism in the era of the New Deal in America and the horrors of the Stalinist era in the Communist world. The result was a gradual movement toward a more conservative position, which was hardly prepared for the revolutionary upheavals in the 1960s. But a number of other negative facts have been operative in the thought of Niebuhr and his associates: (1) Niebuhr's brilliant analysis of the phenomenology of revolution in *Moral Man and Immoral Society*[4] is a description of the shape of the struggle for social justice in the process of modernization. We have now moved to a new stage in the Western process of revolution, which calls for a fundamental restructuring of human relationships and the overcoming of repression under the conditions imposed by advanced technological society. (2) It was possible for Niebuhr to deal with the crises in society through the use of a theological tradition which was still largely intact and had been invigorated by neo-orthodoxy, and as a member of a church which offered a basis for Christian community and social action. Today, all this has changed. The

[4] New York, 1932.

radical Christian finds himself fully involved in a secular revolutionary struggle in which he is all too aware of the almost total crisis in theology and in the life of the church. This can only have far-reaching consequences in the way he goes about his task and structures his thought. (3) Niebuhr discovered the political significance of certain central elements of Christian faith, and developed them in a powerful way, especially in his *Nature and Destiny of Man*.[5] But this strength has turned out to be his weakness, for it tended to obscure certain limitations in his theological system. His recovery of transcendence was expressed essentially in Kierkegaardian terms, as the Absolute, the Vertical which intercepts the horizontal at every moment. At this advanced stage of secularization, that conceptual framework makes very little sense; what is perhaps more serious is the fact that it provides no way of dealing concretely with the ongoing process of redemption in history. Together with this, his lack of interest in the eschatological dimensions of faith has left us without resources for the radical negation of the given order or for the expectation of a qualitatively new future on the other side of change.

Oddly enough, theologians in Europe, especially in Germany, have shown a much more lively interest in the "theology of revolution" than has been evident thus far in the United States. It is likely that, in the course of the next decade or two, the most interesting developments in this area could come from a new generation of Continental theologians. At the moment, however, two serious obstacles seem to me to stand in the way of this. The first of these is the traditional separation, in the academic world, of theory and praxis, which is especially disastrous when attempting to deal with the question of revolution. Any significant advance at this point would require a fundamental break with the academic tradition and a new relationship between the university and the world, the scholar and the political activist. Perhaps because of this isolation, a second element is at work. Much theological discussion of revolution is carried on within the framework provided by the classical Western theological and philosophical systems. And yet one of the most important characteristics of the Western revolutionary today

---

[5] New York, 1949.

is his rejection of the structures of thought and world views that have developed along the philosophical road from Aristotle to Hegel, and his complete lack of interest in theological formulations which are the product of interaction with these thought-forms. This crisis could mean the liberation of theology to explore new ways, but there is not much evidence as yet that this is beginning to happen.

BEYOND THE IMPASSE

Is there any way out of this impasse? Here theological discussion of revolution must become something of a leap into the future, in an attempt to describe a road theology might take in dealing with this problem. The clue for it is to be found, I believe, in the primal Old Testament experience, which represents a revolution in religious consciousness when it occurred and has been all but ignored in most of our theological methodology.[6]

In the midst of the ontocratic, sacral world of olden times, with its static idea of God, something happened which represented a fundamental break in religious thought. The people of Israel found themselves called to embark upon an exodus from a situation of oppression in Egypt. By an act of rebellion they moved out into the desert in the hope of eventually arriving at a land of promise, "flowing with milk and honey." They did this in response to a God who revealed himself as "I will be who I will be"; i.e., a God making himself known to his people on the road to the future.[7] And this exodus was understood as being of ultimate significance for the whole world; its purpose was the redemption of all nations.

Consequently, theological reflection occurs *on the road*, in the

---

[6] I am indebted here to Cornelis Miskotte for his insights into the nature of the Old Testament presented in his book *When the Gods Are Silent* (New York, 1968).

[7] In using this particular translation of God's name, I am not taking sides in the philological discussion, nor am I basing my argument on the correctness of this translation. Rather, I am assuming that the orientation toward the future which it suggests is thoroughly consistent with the nature of the God of the Exodus and with his way of dealing with Israel later on.

midst of a struggle to break out of bondage and move toward the Promised Land. In this context, the Word becomes event, takes on form and makes history. As this happens, the historical experience of the people of Israel is filled with events and stories, words and symbols, which in the framework of their experience as a whole are interpreted in a specific way. Thus, in the midst of their struggle, they discover the possibilities of reflecting on what is happening to them day by day in the light of what has happened in their past. The story of the Exodus and later developments in their history provide a point of reference for the interpretation of each new experience.

Today, confronted as we are with the silence of God and the crisis of all our theological concepts, this may suggest a new point of departure for us as well. We can no longer expect to move ahead by shutting ourselves up in academic isolation, analyzing old theological systems, developing them further and attempting to translate them into contemporary idiom. Our starting point must be in praxis, but praxis of a very special sort: *our own experience of exodus and exile* as we break out of the order of social oppression and personal repression of which we are victims, and move expectantly toward a new land of promise, toward the creation of a new order of social and personal existence.

If the Old Testament experience is revelatory, if it is a disclosure of ultimate reality, we can expect new events to occur which will confront us with new realities and unexpected new possibilities for ourselves as individuals and for our society. We will find that in the midst of our struggle these new events will be illumined by the past experience of the people of God: in the Old Testament, in the New Testament, and in Christian history. Beyond our theological bankruptcy, we will discover new resources for reflection: resources for a new and deeper self-understanding; new perspectives on our history and on the future; new ways of dealing critically and creatively with the problems arising in our revolutionary struggle.

As this happens, the overwhelming problem we face because of the tremendous difference between the world view of the biblical story and old theological systems on the one hand, and contemporary human experience on the other, will not be easily overcome. But we may be provided with signs of a theological resurrection as new words and symbols emerge which break our situation open and gradually take on formative power. To the degree that this miracle occurs, it is possible that theology will be able to play a role similar to that which it played in the days when Calvinistic theology and the Puritan communities were in the center of the revolution.

If we can expect theology to be operative once again in the midst of revolution, the way it will go about its task will, of necessity, be very different. For what the Old Testament model suggests is that the new theology will not undertake to develop a total world view or system, but will rather be a description of a *new reality taking shape in community*, as that community engages in a running dialogue with the historical experience of a community of faith. Contemporary experience being what it is at this stage in the process of secularization, this theology will not be primarily a systematic affirmation of the sovereignty of God but rather an affirmation of life for man, of the possibilities open to him, individually and collectively, in his struggle for liberation from present forms of oppression.

In other words, it will represent in conceptual terms the experience, on the part of a community, of a new politics of transformation, of the discovery of freedom to create a new tomorrow through the transformation of social structures. In a community in which the Christian heritage is operative, this will be fundamentally an experience of freedom. This will include trust in the possibility of eventually overcoming the old order and in the appearance of qualitatively new institutions and structures beyond the crisis and collapse of the old; freedom to transgress the limits set by secular thought in order to negate the presuppositions on which the old order is built, to call into question our own perspectives and thus to work toward the creation of new models for a new society; freedom to engage in this struggle without falling into nihilism or absolutizing revolutionary ideology and strategy.

At the same time, and in the context of this political struggle, theology will be concerned with the description of a new reality of personal existence. In the community of faith we will discover that we are free to call into question and negate the middle-class values we have taken for granted and are free to explore the possibility of developing a new style of life. We will be surprised to find that the community of faith is not an instrument of repression but rather a process by which repression is overcome, and we are made participants in a new experience of personal liberation. And the central Old Testament affirmation of life will break through to us once again, life that is, in some unimaginably deep way, good and full of joy, as pain and suffering are transfigured and the fullness of existence on earth is affirmed under the dominance of grace.

Whenever such an approach to theology has been suggested, the fear has been expressed that it will inevitably lead to a new humanism. While this risk is certainly present, it is by no means inevitable. What does seem to me to be inevitable is the continuance of the rising tide of atheism produced by our insistence on preserving our traditional theological structures. The wager we are called upon to make today is that the proper business of *theo*-logy is to describe the possibilities open before man in the world. And when we do this, rather than ignoring or refusing to face the God question, we will be brought up against it in a new and perhaps inescapable way. The Judaeo-Christian story is the story of the freedom of man —in the political order as well as in personal life—occurring within a particular context. It is freedom which is both a human achievement and something that happens to man. It is a growing awareness of self which is, however, not bondage to self; which is possible because we do not have to establish our own worth, but can start from the assumption that our worth has been already established in spite of our limitations. It is freedom to be fully in the world, without absolutizing any aspect of it. This impossible possibility is, in biblical terms, open to man because he ultimately confronts and responds to a reality *in* the world which is nevertheless *distinguished* from the world. And the words and symbols which provide the foundation for our language about God are the means by which we point to and attempt to describe such a reality.

MAPPING A THEOLOGY OF REVOLUTION

What all this might mean for theological reflection on revolution can perhaps be made clear by a number of examples. We suggested earlier certain specific points at which Calvin's theology brought about a fundamental change in perspective that moved Christians toward revolution and supported their involvement in it. We would here like to suggest how the theological approach outlined above could be operative in today's world in dealing with similar problems.

(1) The religious world of the Middle Ages was immobilized in the face of new events by its conception of reality in terms of a Chain of Being. Calvinism was able to break out of this bind and open the way to the future because of the centrality it gave to the sovereignty of God. Today our secular world is the victim of a myth which has become a new absolute and is just as immobilizing, that of a *Chain of Progression*. And once again, the Christian community and the theological reflection of which it is capable offer the possibility of destroying this myth and opening the way to a new future.

Charles West, in a recent study, has described the basic assumption of liberalism as "the belief that progress toward a future of indeterminate possibilities for mankind is an immanent tendency of human history and that it is institutionalized in the provisions which our political and economic structures make for individual freedom and initiative, and for adjustment of old powers to new vitalities."[8] It is this assumption combined with the working out of the inner logic of technology and bureaucracy which leads to the conclusion that we must take for granted the structures of our present system and work for change according to the rules it has set up. Anything else, it is assumed, will result in anarchy and chaos. The dominance of this perspective is so complete that some of the most outstanding political and intellectual leaders of our country can perceive no other possibility. Consequently, they affirm, time and again, the need for new solutions to new problems, and then proceed to denounce those who are trying to bring about such change because they threaten to disrupt the established order. They can present brilliant analyses of the reasons why the dispossessed in the Third World and in our own ghettos resort to violence in despair, and in the next breath, condemn all violence and disruption without discrimination and insist that law and order must be preserved at all costs. Failing to understand why they are repudiated by those of a younger generation who are committed to social trans-

[8] C. West, "Ethics, Violence and Revolution" (unpublished paper).

formation, they lash out in bitterness against them. And when their efforts at reform fail to solve urgent problems at home and abroad, they become our Security Managers.

The tragedy of all this is that, in acting this way, they are victims of a myth that has been exposed time and again in our Western history. What they fail to see is that the very ideals they most cherish have emerged in the West through the violent destruction of the established order. As Barrington Moore has amply demonstrated in his study of the *Social Origins of Dictatorship and Democracy*,[9] the new principles of social organization which have made our economic development and political democracy possible are products of a series of major social revolutions.

When this fact is ignored, we become victims of a system, increasingly unable to meet new problems. Confronted by demands for the creation of the qualitatively new, we are unable to develop new models or support political strategies by which they could become reality. Thus, to a generation longing for a new social order, the best we can offer is "more and more of the same." As long as we remain victimized by this liberal ideology, we can only become ever more frustrated by the crisis in which we are caught, and our failure to create a new order will lead to greater violence and destruction.

In this wasteland the experience of the community of faith can break the power of old myths by pointing to new dimensions of personal and social existence which these myths have excluded. For the basic experience of faith is the discovery that the end of the road is, in reality, the occasion for a new beginning. We are free to face the death of what we are and what we most cherish because the future offers a new possibility of life on the other side of that destruction. We can allow institutions and structures to die or participate in their destruction, because we can thus open the way for the creation of a new order—yet not for the chaos which Peter Berger most fears, that "political situation in which orderly government disintegrates and Hobbesian forms of brute violence take the place of what we commonly call civilization."[10]

[9] Boston, 1966.
[10] P. Berger, "Between Tyranny and Chaos," *The Christian Century*, 85 (1968), 1365–70.

This does not mean that the Christian is obsessed with destruction or engages in indiscriminate use of violence. What it does mean is that his participation in society is shaped by an ongoing experience of affirmation of life which breaks all the boundaries we commonly set. He finds himself impelled by the desire to overcome every present, and to give creative form to new possibilities. In the words of Miskotte, this primal Old Testament experience is permeated with "tidings of a breakthrough, an end, a fulfillment, which are beyond the grasp of all human action, which, in the full sense of the word, 'overcome' man."[11]

As this reality is experienced in community, it is illuminated by a variety of biblical symbols. The Exodus story is the story of the beginning of a new history, through a break with the established order in an act of rebellion. The history of Israel, as it moves from bondage to the creation of a new nation, which is eventually scattered and gathered again, is seen as a description of the road that the nations of the world follow in their march through history. The symbols of death and resurrection provide us with a clue to the nature and process of human fulfillment in history, and the eschatological imagery of Old and New Testament prepares us for the perception of the qualitatively new future that time and again breaks into our present.

To the degree that this reality is lived and understood in a community of faith, we are prepared for a massive assault on the liberal myths and free to work at the formulation of new social thought and engage in a new politics. Out of this experience can emerge a new style of life especially appropriate for the contemporary situation, a style of personal existence in which we are free to accept the death of our old self and begin again, to leave the old behind and to risk new ventures in all areas of life and thought. And in the midst of the social struggle we will discover that order has to be recreated again and again, and that the new order will be quite irreconcilable with old ways of life. We will be concerned not only with order but also with revolution, with law as well as the overthrow of law, and we will recognize that at certain times and places the introduction of incoherence and violence is essential. Admittedly,

11 Miskotte, *op. cit.*, 66.

this is a risky business, something to be undertaken with fear and trembling. But over against the end of history, which is all the Security Managers can offer us, we can perceive that upheavals which all but wreck the societies in which they occur are often the occasion for major advances of civilization; the values and achievements of the past are preserved as they are subjected to criticism and transformed.

(2) Early Calvinism shattered the authority of old institutions, based as it was on an organic view of reality, and so opened the way for revolutionary change. Today man is once again victimized by institutions because of a new type of *secular* authority: impersonal, objective, and rational. And it is just possible that radical Christian communities may break through this and once again open the way for change.

Whether it be in the economic or in the political order, in social organizations or in bureaucracy, in patterns of work or in family life, the logic of our given institutional structures is simply taken for granted. To call into question the "democratic process," American capitalism, or the bourgeois family is something we have no resources for doing. And yet, it is the logic of these institutions that creates a situation of social oppression and personal repression; a way of life in which we are expected to play a role and conform even though it denies our selfhood; and an acute state of institutional sclerosis, in which we are unable to meet the most pressing demands for basic changes in the nature and functioning of institutions.

Our wager is that small Christian communities will gradually develop in which people will experience liberation from such forms of domination. They will be able to desanctify the secular order, take an honest look at the institutions in which they find themselves, and see more clearly what these structures do to them. Out of this may develop a healthy attitude of disrespect if not contempt for these institutions and their myths. Through participation in this process, they will find that they are free to break with the status quo and experiment in the creation of new patterns of institutional life. What these new forms will be, it is still too early to predict. But certainly they will move in the direction of transforming work into creative play, developing communities in which people can

65

participate in deciding and creating their own future, and moving beyond the dead end of our present bourgeois family life to new types of man-woman and parent-child relationships.

A few centuries ago the resources for this freedom were provided by a theology of sovereignty; today they will be found in a new *experience* of freedom, and reflection on it through the use and interpretation of basic Christian symbols. Our language about God will be taken seriously because of the resources it offers for radical social iconoclasm and for giving new names to new realities. We will have a new understanding of the revolution Jesus provoked in institutions when he defined them in terms of their functional character, and thus freed us to judge each of them according to the contribution it makes to the well-being of man. And the centrality of the eschatological perspective in Christian thought will not only permit us to look at each institution from the perspective of what it can become in the future, but also make it possible for us to live in hope that this future will overcome the present order of things.

(3) Early Calvinism offered unusual resources for the first revolutions of modernization, by breaking the hold of the old structures of domination and creating new forms of discipline and repression, which were then essential in order to get on with the work of economic development and industrialization. Today we are at a new stage of revolution in which the essence of revolution is the overcoming of repression and the creation of a new order of freedom in which psychic energy is released for social reconstuction.

It will not be easy for the Christian community to make any significant contribution in this situation. Protestantism has been so identified with the old order that, as Miskotte observes, the Christian man is a narrow-minded moralist who follows the straight and narrow path under the leadership of a robot-God barking out commands.[12] And yet, we should not be surprised if in the coming years radical Christian communities experience the reality of faith as liberation from repression and take a new look at the Judaeo-Christian heritage with surprising results.

The secular radical may have discovered that, as Marcuse puts it, repression can be overcome only through the eroticization of all of

---

[12] *Ibid.*, 244.

life.[13] But this is not an easy task, nor will it lead inevitably to the creation of a new social order. As Freud clearly understood, the idea of the free, autonomous individual is a myth. Not only is man a victim of oppressive social structures but also of the archaic heritage of history, "frozen manifestation of the general repression of mankind." And he is impelled by the desire to return to the nirvana of the womb from birth on, so that the experience of pleasure can easily become an end in itself, lead to withdrawal from the world, and produce quiescence rather than dynamic social activity.

In this context, we may be surprised to discover certain hidden elements in our tradition which will prove relevant. The Christian doctrine of sin provides a framework for new explorations into the depth of the human. Jesus Christ, as God in the flesh, offers a possibility for the liberation of the *flesh* and the resurrection of the *body*. In Him, agape overcomes law. And the primal Old Testament experience reveals what it means to be human as we are *known* and *loved*, and respond as the heart (understanding, will, feeling, imagination) is kindled. Here is an affirmation of life—of bodily and earthly life—not in terms of self-centered pleasure, but as an encompassing aspiration for joy and happiness in the context of interpersonal relationships and the struggle for justice. And through this experience, eros is directed toward the creation of a new future, and love breaks through the bonds of possessiveness set by our Western bourgeois culture.

In the latter stages of our industrial society, Marx attempted to make love operative through socialist revolution. It may not be entirely absurd to hope that radical Christian communities will be able to contribute something to making love operative at this new stage of social revolution, as they struggle to develop new structures in which surplus repression is overcome, opening up new possibilities for human fulfillment.

(4) The Puritans gave great attention to the development of patterns of congregational life, which appealed to the "masterless men" of that time. They completed their alienation from the established order and offered them the possibility of a new life style

13 See Herbert Marcuse, *Eros and Civilization* (Boston, 1955).

and sustained their revolutionary struggle in church and society. Today, among those who have broken with the old order, few things are more urgently needed than a contemporary equivalent of this: models of radical community in which men and women can experience a real death and rebirth in relation to bourgeois society and its ethos, be able to work gradually at the creation of new life styles, and know the reality of community that is both liberating and supportive.

As the church has been about this task for a long time—with varying degrees of success and failure—it possesses an unusual background of experience with which to face this demand. The only problem is that for the church to make its contribution in this area it will have to negate most of its present forms. Since the average local congregation, in suburbia and elsewhere, provides religious security and protects people from the real conflicts of our world, at the same time that it offers superficial forms of fellowship which deny community, it can make no contribution at this point. Only those who dare break with this, who will engage in the struggle to overcome the present structures of domination and at the same time work out for themselves the dimensions of personal liberation, can hope to give form to community on the new frontiers. Community today means sharing in a process, in a type of personal relationship, in which each is challenged to relate more fully to his world and develop critical awareness of it; to allow self to be called into question again and again, trusting that out of this the new will emerge. It means the freedom to move along this road toward new discoveries of self, of the richness of life and of the meaning of responsibility in the midst of social struggle. And as this happens, such groups will discover that their self-identity is defined over against the established order as well as the established church.

For those who dare to move in this direction, the ecclesiological question will be taken out of the sterile limits now set by the ecumenical movement and become once again a vital issue. For we will be forced to discover what it means for the *ekklesia* to be the community of those who are "called out." We will be compelled, once again, to see ourselves as a people moving from the land of bondage to the Promised Land, as a community that experiences the reality of the "new creation" as it moves through death to resurrection. And our description of our communal existence as being *in* but not *of* the world will be the description of an existential reality, not empty ecclesiastical rhetoric.

We may also rediscover a part of our history that, in recent times, we have tended to ignore: the sectarian heritage. As Troeltsch pointed out in his study of this question, the sect has been the way by which the radical character of the Christian ideal has broken forth again and again with extraordinary power; it has been the means by which a church which is "overwhelmingly conservative" and an "integral part of the existing social order" responds to new challenges. More than this, the sect expresses the fact that, when the church structure becomes rigid and loses its ability to respond to new realities, it is not enough for a few prophetic voices to be raised within the church. The task of reform becomes so overwhelming that it requires individuals and groups with a new self-identity who are able to confront the sclerotic structures, to introduce incoherence and conflict, and to create a new dynamic situation.

Even within the framework of this experience, the task of giving form to community today will not be an easy one. For a new human situation calls for communities that are open rather than closed, liberating not repressive, and oriented toward the creation of a new future. So even the sectarian model must be radically reworked if it is to be of any service to us today.

We have attempted to indicate some of the lines along which we expect a new theology to emerge in the context of revolution. We have been able to do little more than point to certain areas in which we believe creative work can and will be done. Only the future will show whether this wager about the relevance and vitality of theology is justified. But one thing is beyond doubt: such theological developments will focus on new questions in new ways, and so shatter all our old alignments. And they will require the reworking of our whole theological heritage, the development of new paradigms, and the exploration of elements of the tradition which have been largely ignored or forced underground. If theology is the Logos of God, it should demonstrate its freedom to do precisely that.

Social Concreteness in American Theology

✠

MICHAEL NOVAK

*"In one sense, no man speaks for God. In another sense, every man does." These words illustrate the shift in the American religious horizon away from the two-sphere theory of "nature" and "grace." No event is without grace; grace is found by persons in events. The Christian dimension is discovered within the secular as the worlds of university and Congress face the quest for a new moral awareness. Michael Novak is professor of philosophy and theology at the innovative State University of New York College at Old Westbury. His recent books—*A Theology of Radical Politics *(1969),* American Philosophy and the Future *(1969), and* The Experience of Nothingness *(1970)—indicate the tone and direction of his work.*

The prospect offered to theology today is so vast that no one has been able to glimpse the entire range of possibilities.[1] An amazing, an astonishing breakthrough has been achieved. The question is whether, and how, such vast possibilities can be absorbed. If the present generation of theologians does its work well, the bounds of theology tomorrow, by comparison with recent theology, will be

[1] The first part of this article includes material revised from "The New Relativism in American Theology," *The Religious Situation—1968* (Boston: Beacon Press, 1968).

immeasurably expanded. The need pressing upon us is the need for a comprehensive, open, concrete set of methods, enabling us to deal with the variety of materials before us in a way which is not merely chaotic or fortuitous.

The humble catalyst responsible for opening the horizons of theologians has been the enthusiasm of the producers, editors, and correspondents of the mass media: first fruits of technology. Temporarily, theological books and journals follow rather than lead the events of public consciousness. Whereas Paul Tillich and Reinhold Neibuhr spoke a special theological language whose sense eluded many ordinary Christians and non-Christian intellectuals, today theologians find both popular and academic audiences hungry to participate in theological discussion—discussion of alternative politics, myths, and values. Moreover, theologians are beneficiaries of a language newly fashioned for carrying on that discussion.

The mass media and theologians, however, could not raise real issues unless real events were happening. The problem of God is profound and serious in our culture, and was so long before the media forced theologians to confront it publicly. No major institution in our culture—not government or the universities or labor unions or business corporations—has shown itself in recent years as willing as the churches to undertake radical reform. When the media began to look to the churches to see what was happening, they found nuns on picket lines, ministers supporting migrant-worker protests and inner-city projects; they found trenchant critics of repressive social institutions, and scholars able and willing to criticize ideas heretofore held sacred. The scholars of the *last* generation, working and teaching in relative obscurity, inspired many of their students with the vision of a new relationship between theology and culture. These students knew themselves to be a minority and usually were made to feel "too advanced" in their respective churches. But now the mass media have given them a hearing before millions of people, and before their academic colleagues. The media have made the theologian—a little shaken by the knowledge—aware that people are listening.

The scientific frontier for theology, moreover, is no longer physics. The social sciences have opened American theology to a new understanding of the theological task.[2] It has become apparent to theologians that language is a social institution; that the context of language is the life forms, the symbols, and the expectations embodied in social institutions; that reality itself is a social construct.[3] When theologians in the past talked about "what Christians believe," they usually articulated what Christians *should* believe (or what theologians thought they should believe). But sociologists are beginning to learn how to inquire into the attitudes which huge populations actually share. Thus theologians are becoming sensitive to the difference between a theoretical analysis and an empirical study of creeds and attitudes. How do "religious" people pray? Theology is no longer the same when the question is taken to be empirical as well as normative. To what extent can Christianity be said to be unique? To what extent does the relativity introduced by the methods of the social sciences remove the intellectual scandal from Christianity and from Judaism by treating them exactly like other world religions? A functional analysis of religion seems, in particular, to understand Christianity and Judaism as culture religions and to interpret them as filling social and psychological needs.[4]

Modern communications have deeply affected the social consciousness of men and communities heretofore isolated from one another. Confidence in the rightness and the adequacy of limited traditions has been shaken by discovery of the power of other traditions. So accustomed have theologians became to relativity that some have recognized, in John Donne's phrase, "the relativity of relativity." To see that there is no absolute standpoint does not mean that one must absolutize relativism. It is true that men differ and that each man must define his own horizon; it does not follow that one horizon is as adequate as another, but only that there is no way of appealing to an umpire outside the playing field.

[2] H. Richardson, "The Nature of Unbelief," *Continuum*, 5 (1967), 106–17.

[3] P. Berger, "A Sociological View of the Secularization of Theology," *Journal for the Scientific Study of Religion*, 6 (1967), 3–16. See also P. Berger and T. Luckmann, *The Social Construction of Reality: A Treatise in the Sociology of Knowledge* (New York, 1966).

[4] See T. O'Dea, *The Sociology of Religion* (New York, 1966); M. J. Yinger, *Religion, Society and the Individual* (New York, 1957).

Possibly the greatest factor in the opening of theology, however, is the dissolution of the modern form of Western culture. Modern consciousness is losing its coherence, and a new consciousness is dimly taking shape. Some persons still find sustenance in the forms of the receding age; others are intolerably restless. There appear to be four sources of disintegration—or at least of widespread malaise—experienced by religious persons in the United States. First, there is the collapse of the shared meanings which for a long time characterized "the American way of life." Secondly, folk religion—the traditional modality of the world religions—is becoming increasingly difficult to support. Thirdly, the impossibility of simply affirming ("celebrating") the contemporary secular world is painfully obvious.[5] Fourth, the dominating theological tension between the liberalism of Rudolf Bultmann and the neo-orthodoxy of Karl Barth has come to the end of its fruitfulness. This theological effort was, on the one hand, too Germanic in its presuppositions and, on the other, too easily and simply Christian to be of much use to American culture. It is on this last point that I wish to dwell before making my own proposals.

THE USE OF AMERICAN CATEGORIES

In the last few years American theologians have come to appreciate their mutual religious, educational, regional, and other differences in an unprecedented way. Ecumenical conversation has generated friendships and sympathies where none existed before; but it has also sharpened each participant's awareness of the limitations and inadequacies of his own point of view. In contemporary Anglo-American philosophy, the question of justification is becoming central: How does one justify one's point of view, one's presuppositions, one's way of life?[6] Theologians and philosophers are arriving in the same area at the same time. The task is to find a way

[5] For a treatment of these first three points see Novak, *art. cit.*, 203–15.
[6] See M. White, *Toward Reunion in Philosophy* (Cambridge, 1956).

of speaking intelligently and intersubjectively ("objectively" would be both impossible and, if possible, undesirable) of one's own intellectual commitments. I have spoken elsewhere about the concept of "intelligent subjectivity."[7]

The fundamental relativity of each personal starting place has been obscured, however, by the central debate in German theology. German-speaking writers have dominated theological discourse in this century; in particular, the tension between Bultmann and Barth.[8] To put the issue between Bultmann and Barth in a far too simple way, Bultmann wishes to begin from man and "build a bridge" to God, whereas Barth wishes to "begin from God."[9] Both thinkers try to deal with the problem of historical relativity. Both recognize that the sociocultural context of the twentieth century is not that of the sixteenth or the first centuries and that, in consequence, the essential meaning of Christianity must be interpreted afresh.

The difficulty with the problem of relativity as it travels from the German setting to the American is that it becomes a different problem. The German theological tradition appears to be fond of the chasm between Barth and Bultmann; God is set over against man, and the authentic Christian gospel is contrasted with all mere "religion." In the United States, by contrast, the situation is much more fluid, and there appears to be a closer rapport between theologians and members of other faculties of the universities. The American theologian is constantly struck by the wisdom, insight, and courage of many colleagues who, far from being Christians, are atheists of possibly three or four generations' standing. All that he considers to be signs of the presence of grace often seem to be as manifest in such colleagues as they are in Christians. Moreover, even these signs themselves seem, upon reflection, to be forms of human conduct, manner, or style: compassion, patience, joy, kind-

[7] See M. Novak, *Belief and Unbelief* (New York, 1965).

[8] See J. D. Smart, *The Divided Mind of Modern Theology: Karl Barth and Rudolf Bultmann, 1908–1933* (Philadelphia, 1967).

[9] J. D. Smart, *Revolutionary Theology in the Making* (Richmond, 1964), 217; see also M. McLuhan, *Understanding Media: The Extensions of Man* (New York, 1964), 6of., 70; S. Ogden, *Existence and Faith: Shorter Writings of Rudolf Bultmann* (New York, 1960), 31.

ness, long-suffering, and the rest. Why, then, does one remain a Christian? What does it mean to be a Christian?

The context for an American theologian, in short, is less and less the context of theological schools of thought; the context is that of the whole academic community: philosophy and the humanities, the social sciences and psychology, law and business and medicine, the physical and engineering sciences. But in the United States, the wider public also becomes involved in theological discussion; theologians soon become aware of the different interpretation given the same words by whites and blacks, by the upper middle class and the poor. Whether one begins with Bultmann or with Barth, other difficulties arise which appear both formidable and more germane to the American theological enterprise.

In the United States in the past decade there has been a pronounced tendency for countless Americans to identify Christianity with "the American way of life." This identification is fostered by public officials; after a week of widespread rioting in Negro ghettoes, President Johnson called upon the nation to observe a Sunday of prayer. Such reliance upon an easily evoked sentiment, coupled with the avoidance of secular responsibilities (the Congress had just refused to pass a rat-control act aimed at one of the terrors of ghetto living), makes the Germanic distinction between a "religionless Christianity" and "religion" a tempting one. For, according to this distinction, religion is a sentiment of evasion and smugness, whereas genuine Christianity is unsettling and unsentimental; far from being an opiate, it is an agency of responsibility for shaping the future city of man.

The trouble with this distinction is that it does not take the secular saint, the humanistic atheist, into account. The social activist, the writer, the professor, the laborer whom the American theologian meets, are not likely to be "religious," but neither are they always "Christian," not even the "religionless" sort. In a perfectly good sense, in fact, without quotation marks, they may well be religious: ultimately concerned about human openness and human responsibility and moved by the vision of a city in which men are ends and never means. Thus their religion may seem wholly immanent and wholly articulable in secular, historical terms. What fascinates American theologians is that the particular kind of transcendence important to Christianity is also wholly immanent and wholly articulable in secular, historical terms. The relativity that interests the American theologian is that which links the heavily humanistic and trusting atheism so common in America to a more secular theism. According to that more secular theism, God is not to be conceived as one more object to add to the inventory of things, but rather as a kind of intelligent force or vitality *in* all things. The atheist who believes that man by his own efforts may affect the course of evolution for the better is, from the point of view of one who observes his behavior, in this belief at least very like the Christian who believes that a God whom no man sees lives in him and directs him to be cocreator of the future.

To be sure, cases may be constructed—or encouraged in experience—in which the beliefs of atheist and Christian are so divergent that their behavior, too, is opposed. But increasingly one encounters a sense of wisdom and modesty on both sides, such that the profile of belief and action of each becomes increasingly identical. Anthony Levi has argued that the behavior of a good Christian, acting as a good Christian ought to act, is from an empirical point of view indistinguishable from the behavior of a good secular humanist.[10] From personal experience, one can but concur. Thus Christian theologians are presently attempting to create a language for Christian beliefs which is, in one sense, wholly immanent. According to that sense, every word employed has at least a correlate in human experience. Meanwhile, human experience is itself envisaged as dynamic, open-ended, and at least potentially melioristic. There is nothing inevitable about human progress: Periods of decline occur and man's annihilation of his own world is all too possible. But man always finds it possible to develop beyond the stage he at present occupies; he can increase in knowledge, wisdom, power, and love. Such open-endedness might be called man's ability ever to transcend himself; but it is easily restricted to description in secular terms.

The Christian theologian sees that the old duality of "nature"

---

[10] A. Levi, *Religion in Practice* (New York, 1966), 7–30.

and "grace" was an abstraction.[11] In the concrete world of actual events, no event has ever been, is, or will be (from a Christian point of view) purely "natural"; every event takes place within the field of God's presence and love. This view might just as well be stated in the optimistic, secular language of American naturalism. From the point of view of the behavior to be expected from those who share such views, the meaning of the assertions that "grace is everywhere" and that "nature is all there is" will in certain contexts so overlap as to be virtually identical. Both Christian and naturalist might face evils and joys with virtually identical behavior, resting on virtually identical assumptions stated in different language. *In the American context*, then, the project of interpreting Christianity in a wholly immanent language has a pronounced plausibility; the orientation of American thought toward the future provides a lever of criticism against the present required of the traditional notion of the transcendent.

Thus American theology is free to reject the Germanic polarity between God and man, and to achieve the same effect by being certain that every reference to God has a secular experiential correlate. No one has ever seen God. No one save God speaks for God. From the point of view of the sociology of knowledge, moreover, men speak from within communities which rest upon given social infrastructures. Even the preachers of the gospel differ from one another according to their different communities or places within the communities. No man escapes from the conditions of human language, culture, social and economic conditions, temperament, and nervous system. There is no way, then, for men to hear the voice of God pure and limpid, but only by way of other men or through written texts or through the ambiguous deliverances of their own consciousness. God (if Christianity is to be believed) speaks *through* men and *through* instruments; he does not show himself face to face. Consequently, there is no genuine polarity between the primacy of man and the primacy of God. Instrumen-

---

[11] See J. Fuchs, *National Law: A Theological Inquiry* (New York, 1964); also, B. Lonergan, "St. Thomas' Thought on Gratia Operans," *Theological Studies*, 2 (1941), 289–324; 3 (1942), 69–88, 375–402, 533–78; O. Lottin, *Au coeur de la morale chrétienne* (Belgium, 1957).

tally and empirically, all that Christians have to deal with directly are human words and human deeds. While it may be true that Christians listen for *more* than the human word, *more* than the human deed, that "more" is neither easily discovered nor free from ambiguity and conflicting interpretations.

WHO SPEAKS FOR GOD?

If an impartial observer studies carefully the language of those who speak of God as acting in the world, he will notice that in every case of such usage the referent for "God" is actually a human deed or an historical occurrence. To talk about "God acting in the world" is to talk about the values and meaning which some persons attach to human actions or human situations. No one actually sees *God* acting in the world. They merely see things happening which, according to their interpretations, appear to gain in meaningfulness if viewed in the perspective of their tradition and their Scripture. Thus "divine revelation" is experienced as a living presence in the observer, a living light, whose resonance acts upon the concrete socially structured man to form his vision of life and its unfolding. By comparison with other elements in the infrastructure of his perceptual apparatus, this living presence may on occasion appear to be "shattering." But it is so because the Jew and the Christian allow themselves to be conditioned by yet one other social community: the historical, living church (people). That community, with its pluralistic history, offers them leverage against the biases of their present culture. When Barth wrote his revolutionary 1919 commentary on *Romans,* he gained a perspective beyond that of his immediate teachers from assiduous reading in the obscure commentaries of the four previous centuries.[12]

In one sense, no man speaks *for* God. In another sense, every man does. Yet in every man there are also countless voices of chaos, of conformity, of nervous impulse, of merely conventional wisdom. No easy theological formula teaches anyone the discernment of

[12] See Smart, *The Divided Mind of Modern Theology,* ed. *cit.,* 66f.

spirits. How, then, do we know when a man speaks for God or for the Gospels or for the people of Moses and the prophets? Here too, within the church or outside it, we have come to be aware of a fundamental relativism. Each of us chooses his favorite authors, his traditions, his teachers, his leaders, his emphases, his prior values, his "style." What we now hope is that in the concert of voices there will emerge the voice of prophecy, judgment, and creativity. Yet in the middle of the battle, at the moment when it is imperative to hear the authentic and the fruitful voice, that voice is often indistinguishable in the general clamor. Looking back into history, it is at least a little easier (but not much) to discern who was speaking most fully for the Gospels. Consequently, the fundamental battle rages in the hearts of each of us. To whose voices shall we attend? On which side ought we to throw our weight? Many are ready with good will and with energy, but lack light and certainty about which way to run. What one Christian sees as betrayal, another sees as the only hope of advance. In his own day Jesus was a sign of contradiction. Relativism is a rule of life, not only outside, but also inside, the church.

It remains true, for a Christian, that salvation comes only through Jesus. But Jesus is not only the historical figure, a Jew, who lived, died, and rose again in an underdeveloped country in the first century. He is, rather, the Word who was at the beginning, through whom, by whom, and with whom were made all the things that are made. There are, then, two sources of knowledge about Jesus. One is through the tradition of that historical community which is nourished by his living presence, through the preaching of the *kerygma* and the celebration of the meal of remembrance and unity. The other is through reflection upon the dynamism of nature and history: through faithful attention to the things made in his image and progressively through the ages revealing more about him. For not all that can be known of the Word will be known until all the things made by him have unfolded. The Eastern church—manifestly in Berdyaev and Dostoevsky, and indirectly through its influence upon Teilhard de Chardin—has kept this cosmic notion of the Christ more adequately than has the Western church.[13] Con-

---

[13] See P. Evdokomov, *The Struggle with God* (Glen Rock, 1966), 155f.

sequently, the parochialism of Christianity is properly to be "shattered" by a loving and eager study of other religions, other cultures, and the whole of nature itself, in which the Word reveals himself. To be sure, he is not there called by the name "Jesus." It is not those who cry "Lord, Lord!" who enter the kingdom of heaven, but those who do the will of the Father. Erik Erikson has pointed out that the wisdom of the "golden rule" is crosscultural.[14] Surely, the primacy of understanding and loving, the primacy of community, is given witness in other cultures besides Christian cultures, sometimes more effectively. In brief, attention to the Jesus of the Christian church and to the Word of that tradition can also be idolatrous; grace is operative in more places and in more ways than Christian theologians customarily map.

Bonhoeffer, I believe, insisted too much upon the need which other men might have for Jesus and the church. With him, one may assert that the church is a concrete, historical community of power and grace, for whose continued efficacy it is worth laboring. More extensively than he, one might also see many other communities not only of power and grace, but also of revelation, accurate interpretation, and illuminating symbols of the same Word. It will be the task of prophetic spirits in all the world religions, in the common noosphere we are already coming to share, to bring together all the wisdom about man and God that they are faithful to. The dangers of an easy syncretism will be as acute as ever. But Christians, in particular, may look to the wisdom of other peoples for further light on that Logos whose traces they track throughout the universe. Wisdom grows in concrete traditions, where it has been watered with the blood of a thousand witnesses and has brought reconciliation to ten thousand cries of anguish in ten thousand nights. It is as mistaken to abandon these concrete traditions as to stand within one of them arrogantly, unwilling to enrich one's own by learning from another.

The Christian missionary enterprise has too often consisted not of the gentle telling of parables, which learned as much from the wisdom already proper to the people as it taught dialogically, but of the preachment of an alien and one-sided monologue.

14 E. Erikson, *Insight and Responsibility* (New York, 1964), 221.

Teaching the death and resurrection of Jesus is scandal and stumbling block enough, without arrogance being added to the style of the kerygma. When the preacher is willing to die to his own feelings of superiority in order to enter into dialogue, then, perhaps, he can commend the death and resurrection of Jesus Christ as a penetrating illumination of how God manifests himself among men. In dialogue, one can and must remain faithful to oneself. Still, where such fidelity is open to the Word who speaks everywhere, one need not be afraid to learn from others.

A NEW SYSTEMATIC PRINCIPLE

Theology is inevitably conditioned by the political situation in which it takes shape. Our concrete understanding of words like "liberty," "power," "obedience," "justification," "hope," "kingdom of God," "love," "person," "community," derives from the way we concretely experience the political and social roles in which our society places us. Men who speak these words in one culture relate them to different matrices of experience than do men who speak them in another. Men in different social classes, of different economic standing, or in different political roles also use these words with a different concrete significance. The more exact a theologian tries to be in his grasp of the concrete, empirical meaning of the words he uses, the more political and socially alert he must be.

Moreover, a theology which simply *describes* the world, and does not at all set out to try to *change* the world, is inadequate on two counts. First, it would lose its chief fruit, which is its effect upon the way men actually live. But, more profoundly, a method which refuses to engage the concrete world is removed from that world and is inherently unable to grasp it or to reflect it. It may present a more detached, orderly, and clearer *hypothesis* about that world, but its fundamental mythical stance is that of a detached observer. Adherence to such a myth alienates a man from the object of his attention. The object is imagined as *over there* while he, cool and detached, stands *over here*. One may come to a certain intellectual clarity in that way, but not to a full, concrete, complex readiness for accurate judgment. It is easy to coach from the stands or on Monday morning. But the concrete human situation is not a football game at which there are seats for spectators; the theologian, like others, is on the playing field while the game is in progress.

Theology is at the present moment weakest in its ability to put into language such matters as the following: elements of personal history, attitudes, emotions, impulse, instinct, trained perception, imagination, fantasy, intuitiveness, a sense of fitness, the criterion of satisfaction with evidence, etc. But these are the very matters which enter into and constitute the most important moments of thought: perception of data, formulation of hypotheses, decision on evidence. "Symbols give rise to thought," Paul Ricoeur is fond of saying.[15] This insight needs to be read in two directions: Symbols give rise to *thought*; and, *symbols* give rise to thought. It is the function of symbols and myths to give shape to those many activities of the human person listed above from which thought *arises*. It is the function of thought to thematize, to criticize, and to send withering or fructifying light into those same concrete resources of the psyche. We cannot neglect the critical task by being content with symbol and myth. Even more necessary at the present moment, however, is our need to fashion a more adequate sensitivity to the power of symbol and myth over thought itself. Symbol and thought interact, each showing primacy over the other, and instrumentality toward the other in complimentary ways. What is commonly called an "objective method" in the best Anglo-American universities, for example, is inherently and not merely accidentally in the service of politico-social myths of great danger to the rest of the world. As an example of the opposite abuse, many theologians today evade the critical task by an appeal to uncriticized symbols like "the unique, once and forever act of God" or to an eschatological "future." They seem to be in bad faith similar to those political ideologues who speak fervently of the pure revolutionary act and the coming utopia.

Theology today needs to fashion a language for speaking of the

---

[15] *The Symbolism of Evil* (Boston, 1969), 347ff.

concrete present. Preoccupation with the future is an evasion. A language for speaking of the concrete present must grow out of a rhythm of action and reflection—out of interaction with the real, concrete world of the present. The recalcitrance of the real present induces modesty. The human enterprise, now as ever, is caught in a context of fraudulence, madness, and absurdity; images of a madhouse, hospital, prison, labyrinth, and vipers' nest are not merely contemporary. A language adequate to the complexities of the concrete present must grow out of the awareness that our perceptions, our raw, brute experience ("inner" and "outer," as if either of these metaphors were valid), and our very fantasies and instincts are given shape and form by subtle social, political, and economic arrangements. There is a politics of experience.[16] There are various types of sensibility.[17] There are a variety of standpoints, horizons, basic life stories.[18] Politics today has become the art of shaping the human psyche, and the possibilities of liberating or suppressing that psyche are political possibilities. The contexts of Freud and of Marx have been joined.[19]

If the worlds of Marx and Freud have been joined, so also the gap between existentialism and Marxism has been transcended. The experience of nothingness is a communal achievement; authenticity is the fruit of a long communal labor.[20] In a repressive society, a new man can be only marginally free or authentic. Theology must be worked out in full political and social consciousness. Here, too, theology's greatest pitfall is the rationalistic bias— the myth that an adequately concrete and complex theory can be worked out through "objective analysis," from the standpoint of a dispassionate observer. The onlooker is, by his choice of standpoint, at a distance. But a theologian is, in fact, not at a distance at all but in the middle of a politico-social system. That system is already *inside* him, in his experience, his imagination, his sensi-

[16] See R. D. Laing, *The Politics of Experience* (New York, 1967).

[17] See S. Sontag, *Against Interpretation* (New York, 1966).

[18] See J. S. Dunne, *City of the Gods* (New York, 1965); also *A Search for God in Time and Memory* (New York, 1969).

[19] Notably by Herbert Marcuse in *Eros and Civilization* (Boston, 1955) and *An Essay on Liberation* (Boston, 1969).

[20] See Novak, *The Experience of Nothingness* (New York, 1970).

bilities, his language, his criteria of reasonableness and relevance and selectivity. To view himself as an objective observer is to be in bad faith. As theology needs a swift development of tools for articulating the concrete complexity of personal subjectivity, so also it needs a swift development of tools for speaking of social and political constraints upon consciousness.

Consciousness, then, becomes the key category for theological analysis. We must learn to experience, to describe, and to understand subtle forms of consciousness—their differences and their consequences. For consciousness is not only personal and subjective, but also communal and political. Culture is constituted by consciousness. So is political legitimacy. And so, finally, is personal authenticity. At present, theology, due to a rationalistic bias, speaks weakly, confusedly, and disconnectedly to all of these dimensions.

On the other hand, theology has been, of all disciplines, the least inclined to surrender entirely to the rationalistic bias. For theology has had to respect ritual, tradition, symbol, and scripture, even when it most wished to adopt rationalistic categories in order to disarm its cultured despisers, or to show itself to be modern and critical. Today the mythical status of the nationalistic bias has become obvious to the younger generation. The present moment is auspicious. There is grave danger, however, that the reaction against the nationalistic bias (which is in part a reaction against the bureaucracy and managerial forms which flow from that bias) will carry too far over to the opposite error. It is no gain if suddenly *all* power goes to the imagination. Symbols give rise to *thought;* the critical task cannot be evaded. Hitler tried that path, to the bitter instruction of our parents' generation.

In a word, theology must become orderly and thorough. Second, any orderly and full body of inquiry acceptable to us must be concrete; it must arise out of experience and action. A theology involved in experience and action must, at the same time, develop a rich articulation of symbol and myth. Moreover, such a theology must be thoroughly social and political, since socioeconomic and political institutions shape personal consciousness with awesome subtlety and effectiveness. Theology will meet its responsibilities, in brief, when it finds a starting place deep enough to illuminate the pressing problems of personal authenticity and intelligent subjectivity, and the equally urgent but in many ways prior problems of social, economic, and political liberation. Unless it works at the latter, its efforts regarding the former are vain; unless it accomplishes the former, its efforts regarding the latter are empty.

American Historical Experience and Christian Reflection

✠

CARL BRAATEN

The American Experience. While building the future it is always risky to overlook America's formation in its own history. It has been "The New World"—an entire continent to be explored, conquered, and developed. There is a unique American historical experience: a history of why Americans think in a particular way, a history of their faith brought from England, Germany, Ireland, or heard from the Methodist preachers of the plains. Carl Braaten is Professor of Theology at Chicago Lutheran Seminary. He has edited posthumous publications of Paul Tillich and helped to found one of the first American ecumenical publications, Dialog. *His books include* History and Hermeneutics *(1966) and* The Future of God *(1969).*

When a new theology announces its arrival by claiming history as its all-embracing horizon of reflection,[1] it is not at all certain that what is meant will be understood. For "history" is not a word that arouses a lot of enthusiasm these days. If theology must always move between the poles of Christian identity and contemporary relevance, it would at first seem that by linking itself so closely to history, theology opts in favor of identity at the expense of

[1] Wolfhart Pannenberg, "Redemptive Event and History," *Essays on Old Testament Hermeneutics,* Claus Westermann, ed. (Richmond, 1963), 314.

86

relevance. For history makes us think about the past, and it is always a task for the history teacher to convince students of its relevance. To many people the study of the past is boring; to others it is an excuse for not taking the present seriously. So a theology of history, whatever can be said for it in the long run, must limp onto the stage of our present with several handicaps.

AN APOLOGY FOR HISTORY

In the first place, American experience seems to run forward to the future, and away from the past. History is thought of as the tradition which our pioneering fathers left behind in the Old World. John Dewey observed that Americans have never thrived on an apriori type of philosophy, because they do not accept a ready-made world of laws and orders that have endured long enough to have acquired a semblance of the eternal. For us history still lies in the future. Our mainspring is "opportunity," and that is something we keep looking for. This led Dewey to lay down a challenge which we have yet to take seriously enough: "An American philosophy of history must necessarily be a philosophy for the future."[2] The same thing is true of a theology of history. It can be interesting to Americans if it connects up with the American experience of history marked by openness to new possibilities that throb in the imagination, and that cannot be confined by the apriori-like structures of the past.

A second handicap that makes a theology of history somewhat difficult, even suspect, is that the progressive and militant youth of today think of the past as an unnecessary detour to action in the present. Those who plan seminary curricula can vouch for the fact that more church history is notably absent from the list of students' demands. There is no loud cry for more biblical history either. Hence, if it is thought that a theology of history is inviting a revolutionary-minded generation to release the levers of action which can change the world and instead pour themselves into a con-

---

[2] John Dewey, *German Philosophy and Politics* (New York, 1915), 145.

templation of the past, that will be rejected as a trick of thinkers who enjoy some status in the establishment of the status quo. But that would be to misunderstand the kind of theology of history we propose in this chapter.

A theology of history can be attractive to an activist generation bent on change only if it cleanly disaffiliates itself from the status quo historiography that has often arrested the minds of historians in both the church and the university. The mighty virtues of positivistic historicism—objectivity and excellence—are the rewards we are promised for the "end of ideology." But positivism is the petrification of the past; the past loses its quality as the medium of promise; then the established society can rest content in its present. The end of ideology which the hard-headed realists proclaim is itself an ideology to extinguish the signals of transcendence which history sends forth, if only we have the radar to pick them up.

Radical youth often speak as though history is irrelevant. In being so wholly immersed in the present, however, they become its slaves. The intellectual leaders of these student radicals know better. Both Ernst Bloch and Herbert Marcuse, for example, turn to history as the indispensable ally of their philosophy of revolution. And black militants know better; their demand is for black history in all the schools. Historical reason is needed to help the mind to leap to freedom, to gain enough distance from the present to be critical, and to come at it with transcendent insights and oppositional power.[3]

The revolutionary philosophy of history today can strengthen the will of theology to accept history as the horizon within which to bring to expression its own sense of identity as well as its relevance to the present situation. Therefore, while at first glance "history" seems to put theology at a disadvantage, a little more thought will show that the historical dimension is the only mode of mediation that can keep theology a potent factor in the present. Otherwise, it simply gets locked into the stagnant present, becoming a prisoner of whatever is *au courant* for the time being.

Perhaps our apology for *history* as the proper horizon of theological thought is not really necessary. But that may be wishful thinking.

[3] Herbert Marcuse, *One Dimensional Man* (Boston, 1964), 97–98.

I rather agree with Marcuse that there is "suppression of history" in our one-dimensional world.[4] I agree that there is a widespread feeling that history is the study of our dead past, that we can feel safe in leaving the historians "to do their thing." Our established society may tolerate the curiosity of antiquarians, but it does not expect it to yield great things for the real world of men and institutions. I also think that the standard case for the study of history made by positivistic historians has successfully been exposed to be ideological in character, namely, that the positivistic mind handles the past in a way that leaves the present world as it is. At best we learn how the present is the outcome of the past. But analysis as such does not lead to action. A merely analytic attitude toward history is an excellent way to stifle the imagination, the living memory, from which impulses of social truth and therapy may be released as explosives into the structures of our present.

We have suggested two elements that a theology of history must peruse as integral to itself in order to make a good case for its contemporary relevance. It must, first, take up the horizon of the future to gain continuity with American experience, and it must, secondly, release its own revolutionary potential to make contact with what is stirring the minds of the younger generation. These elements are not uncontested today. We cannot count on much support from the established theologies of recent times, for they have shared in the fight against history, the flight from the future, and the fear of the revolutionary dynamics of eschatological hope for the future. A theology of history that focuses on the power of the future for the sake of revolutionary change in the present will be resisted not only by the positivistic frame of mind, but also by the "history-is-meaningless" tendencies in existentialism and its concomitant retreat into "the interior dimension" (*Innerlichkeit*). This is a way of copping out of history, again leaving everything as it is. A theology of history goes hand in glove with an ethics of change.[5] Therefore, it finds that positivism and existentialism (objectification and subjectivism), which otherwise seem so ex-

---

[4] *Ibid.*, 97.
[5] See Wolfhart Pannenberg's article, *"Geschichtstatsachen und christliche Ethik," Evangelische Kommentare,* 1 (1968), 688–94.

tremely opposite, join hands to let things rest pretty much as they are.

We shall begin our discussion of the two elements we find integral to a contemporary theology of history—namely, the horizon of the future and the ethos of change—by a brief portrayal of America's historic sense of being on the way to a better future, often interpreted in its religious tradition as the quest for paradise, as the journey to the Promised Land, or as traveling toward the coming kingdom of God.

ÈUTOPIA AND THE COMING KINGDOM
IN AMERICA

An American theology cannot ignore American history. And the history of America from its very beginnings has happened under the sign of the future. Its drive toward the future is the key that opens up a deeper understanding of its past as well as its present. Historians are piling up evidence that an adequate interpretation of American history is possible only in light of its eschatological underpinnings.[6] The crossing of the Atlantic was the Red Sea experience of the new exodus people, whom one early writer called "God's American Israel."[7] Columbus himself, in his *Book of Prophecies*, thought he had found the spot where the new heaven and the new earth would be realized. Eliade observes that "the most popular religious doctrine in the Colonies was that America had been chosen among all the nations of the earth as the place of the Second Coming of Christ."[8] Colonizing America was a

[6] Charles Sanford, *The Quest for Paradise* (Urbana, 1961); George H. Williams, *Wilderness and Paradise in Christian Thought* (New York, 1962); Mircea Eliade, "Paradise and Utopia: Mythical Geography and Eschatology," *Utopias and Utopian Thought* (Boston, 1967); H. Richard Niebuhr, *The Kingdom of God in America* (New York, 1937).

[7] He was Edward Johnson in *Wonder Working Providence of Zion's Saviour* (1650), quoted in Reinhold Niebuhr's *The Irony of American History* (New York, 1962), 25.

[8] M. Eliade, *op. cit.*, 264.

chapter of sacred history. The pioneers were marching toward the Promised Land; they were out to regain paradise—a future Eden. Even as late as Abraham Lincoln the eschatological theme was the burning light in his political consciousness. James Sellers has pointed out how Lincoln used the phrase "the almost chosen people" to speak of America's role in the unfolding of the divine promise. To him the Declaration of Independence and the Bill of Rights were "translations of the biblical hope into political reality."[9] And Wolf-Dieter Marsch, who belongs to the new theologians of history in Germany who are attempting to politicize theology from the standpoint of eschatology, wrote and published his doctoral dissertation, *Christian Faith and Democratic Ethos,* as an exposition of Abraham Lincoln's political life and thought. He interprets Lincoln's political ideal of a new birth of freedom under God and the principle of equality as rooted in "a vision of the anticipated eschaton."[10] Elsewhere he refers to Lincoln as a "utopian realist."[11] The term is coined to indicate that Lincoln's hope for the American future envisaged a real political fulfillment of God's promise on the plane of history.

As soon as the word "utopia" is introduced, however, to characterize the hope for the future among the makers of American history, we are in danger of being misled. To many people, "utopia" is synonymous with nonsense or a make-believe world. They would use the word as a negative judgment of value. Utopianists indulge in wishful thinking, fantastic illusions, useless idealism, and escapist fairy tales. That is a common opinion among self-styled practical realists. And they seem to have the literal meaning of the word on their side. For the word "utopia" comes from the Greek *ou* (not) plus *topos* (place). "Utopia" means "no place." However, the pilgrims, pioneers, and settlers in America were in quest of the kingdom of God. In their view, they were not going nowhere. They moved beyond the frontiers to seek a

[9] James Sellers, "The Almost Chosen People: A Theological Approach to American Society," *The Journal of Religion,* 45 (1965), 276.

[10] Wolf-Dieter Marsch, *Christlicher Glaube und demokratisches Ethos* (Hamburg, 1958), 81.

[11] Wolf-Dieter Marsch, "Abraham Lincoln—ein utopischer Realist," *Die Freiheit erlernen* (Freiburg im Breisgau, 1967), 112.

better place.[12] One can call their hope utopian if one wishes, but that does not begin to grasp their own self-understanding. It would be more accurate to speak of their expectation as *eutopian. Eu* is Greek for good and blessed. A *eutopia* is a good and blessed place.

It is interesting that soon after Sir Thomas More published his *Utopia* an argument arose as to whether the underlying Greek prefix was *ou* or *eu.* The English pronunciation led some to argue that it must be *eu*, since it is sounded the same as words like eugenics, eulogy, euphoria, etc. In Thomas More's own time Peter Giles of Antwerp wrote a poem offering to clear up the ambiguity:

> Wherefore not Utopie, but rather rightely
> My name is Eutopie: a place of felicitie.[13]

Commenting on this odd etymological play, F. L. Polak says: "Ever since, there has been an acrimonious battle of pens between the *ou*-ists and the *eu*-ists."[14] There is no doubt that the main line of hope in American history would like to stand on the side of the *eu*-ists, if this is more than a game of words.

The quest for the kingdom of God in America was a creative movement involved in the workings of history. H. Richard Niebuhr has sketched for us the history of the distinctively American theology of history around the idea of the kingdom of God. He reached the conclusion "that the idea of the kingdom of God has indeed been the dominant idea in American Christianity."[15] It is not the case that this was merely a handy theological idea with which to interpret American history; rather, the kingdom of God was a powerful religious image that affected the course of history. American history has been, from the time of the Founding Fathers, a living

[12] G. H. Williams discusses the importance of the frontier concept to two American historians, Frederick Jackson Turner and William Warren Sweet. He refers particularly to Turner's address, "The Significance of the Frontier in American History," and Sweet's address, "The Churches as Moral Courts of the Frontier." G. H. Williams, *op. cit.,* 3.

[13] Quoted by F. L. Polak, *The Image of the Future* (New York, 1961), 380, n.1.

[14] *Ibid.,* 380.

[15] H. Richard Niebuhr, *op. cit.,* xii.

movement on the frontiers in tension toward the realm of the future —the coming kingdom of God. That is a generalization that one dares to make even after taking into account the many oscillations of this idea in American Christianity. It is this theme that accounts for the continuity from Puritan Theocracy through Evangelical Awakening to the Social Gospel.

The idea of the kingdom of God as the lodestar of a theology of history reaches its high point in the theology of Walter Rauschenbusch. As the tides of neo-orthodox and existentialist theologies ebb away, we might do no better than to restore the doctrine of the kingdom of God to its place of centrality in systematic theology. The doctrine of the kingdom once gave the social gospel its creative force; today it might become the source for the renewal of the Christian revolution in world history, of its radical hope for the transformation of the world. Rauschenbusch complained that theology has allowed the doctrine "to lead a decrepit, bed-ridden, and senile existence in that museum of antiquities which we call eschatology."[16] The doctrine lost its relevance when it became merely another world into which people entered one by one when they died, or when it was thought of statically as the remote end of the world. In either case it reinforced the tendency of the church to be a stationary structure in history, and to lend its influence to keep other social orders intact. Rauschenbusch saw the kingdom of God as the realm of the future, approaching with revolutionary force to bring about social righteousness and to call the church to the front line of its mission.

THE COLLAPSE OF BELIEF IN PROGRESS

A revival of the idea of the kingdom of God for a theology of history would be ill-advised without removing the serious flaw in the earlier liberal version. Even in Rauschenbusch the idea of the kingdom was often confused with the notion of progress. He could

[16] Walter Rauschenbusch, *A Theology for the Social Gospel* (Nashville, 1945), 53.

speak of "the progress of the Kingdom of God in the flow of history."[17] Sometimes he spoke of the kingdom as something which "grows" and "develops" in an organic way in history, and which can be equated with the ethical and spiritual progress of mankind.[18] In this way the kingdom quietly shifts from being a predicate of God as promise to becoming a predicate of society as process. He says, "This change from catastrophe to development is the most essential step to enable modern men to appreciate the Christian hope."[19] A half century later we can see the irony in this assertion. By identifying the promise with progress, liberal theology collapsed when catastrophe came. And with the fall of liberal theology, other theologies arose to make room for faith without hope, and for an eschatology of crisis without the kingdom. The American liberal theology of history, with its orientation to the kingdom, had invested so much in the belief in progress that when disillusionment set in, American theology had to look to Europe for new beginnings.

The nineteenth-century belief in progress was ultimately rooted in Christian eschatology. Its secularized form can hardly conceal its dependence on the Jewish-Christian view of history as reality in motion toward the kingdom of God. The question theology faces today is whether the kingdom must forever go down with progress, that is, whether hope for the kingdom in history is bound up with an evolutionary optimism based on visible progress. After all, does hope in history really go well with belief in automatic progress? Is not hope ground to bits in an automatic time machine equipped with its own self-winding mechanism? To the notion that there is an unbroken line of evolution flowing beautifully from the protozoan to the philosopher, Bertrand Russell has cleverly retorted that, unfortunately, we have only the philosopher's word for it and not that of the protozoan. The philosophy of progress was a poor model after which to pattern a theological idea of the coming of God's kingdom in history. Essentially, the one entailed the replacement of the other. The eschatological idea of God's future as the

[17] *Ibid.,* 146.
[18] *Ibid.,* 225.
[19] *Ibid.*

creative power in history was transformed into an idea of history as a developing process that can sow its own seeds of progress as it goes along. The *coming* of the kingdom was exchanged for a *becoming* of the world, meaning that it was no longer an object of hope but a matter of sight. "Now hope that is seen is not hope. For who hopes for what he sees?" (Rom. 8:24)

The theologies that cropped up during the first half of our century can be seen as emergency exits from a world that had become hopeless and meaningless. The upward curve of progress extending into an unending future snapped back upon the dead center of a futureless present. Black clouds of cultural pessimism and fatalism loomed upon the horizon. The spirit of the times unleashed a flood of anti-utopias. The horizon of the future became filled with horrors rigged up by an imagination fearing the worst that our technological skills could devise. After World War I, not one utopia with a hopeful content was produced. It would have been ridiculed. The imagination was reeling on the psychiatrist's couch or falling into the arms of death. The power of negative thinking was exploited for all its worth. It brought forth the feeling that the world is running against man; history is absurd because it is plotless and goal-less; the myth of Sisyphus becomes the story of man's self-understanding; the future will bring only more rounds of misery and meaninglessness.

Existentialism was the philosophy which published all this bad news about man and his world, and theology read it as the lesson for the day. But theology did more than that; it attempted a solution—an eschatological solution. But it was an eschatology without an eschaton for the world, for history. There is meaning *in* history or *above* history, but no meaning *to* history or *for* it. Theology can be seen straining to get away from history, going so far above it (Barth) or so deep into the existential moment (Bultmann) to find the eschatological Word, that history—in the sense of the social, political, and cultural life of mankind on earth—is left out. Bultmann spoke for a whole generation or two when he admonished us: "Do not look around yourself into universal history; you must look into your personal history."[20]

---

[20] Rudolf Bultmann, *History and Eschatology* (New York, 1957), 155.

95

RISING ABOVE AND BEYOND HISTORY

No theology of history has arisen out of the theologies of Barth and Bultmann, because they are not oriented primarily to the future of God's coming kingdom. The kingdom is absorbed into the category of the eternal lying above and beyond history; the future is contracted into a dialectical present, either in God (Barth) or in man (Bultmann), and in thus losing its own power of being over against the past and the present, the future gives man no help in his struggle to go beyond the one-dimensional world of the present. We cannot extend this critique.[21] But on the basis of what we have already stated, it is useful to pose this question: Can eschatology be meaningful for the individual if it does not embrace the future of the world? Perhaps the attempt to have eschatology without *eschaton* is but a prelude to the attempt to have a theology without *theos*. Perhaps the hope for man cannot survive while assigning the world to a hopeless future. Perhaps if man can no longer expect anything from God for the world, there is nothing for the individual to expect for himself. Perhaps the Christian hope for the future is indivisible, so that the God of personal existence is not some other than the God of world history.

To drive home the point I am suggesting here with all these "perhapses," I would like to recall an instructive debate between the Niebuhr brothers that appeared in *The Christian Century* in 1932. Japan had just invaded China. There was a widespread feeling of helplessness. What could anyone do? To this H. Richard Niebuhr answered in his rather famous article "The Grace of Doing Nothing" that there are various kinds of inactivity. There is the inactivity of the pessimist who sits back and watches the world go to pieces; there is the inactivity of the conservative who believes that by his *laissez faire* approach things will work out best. A third way of doing nothing rests on faith in the God who

[21] For an extended critique, with which I agree, see Jürgen Moltmann's *Theology of Hope* (New York, 1967), 50–57.

96

works in the actual processes of history to bring about his ends. In a given situation there may be nothing I can do, but that does not mean that nothing is being done. He calls for Christians to form themselves into cells within each nation as part of a new Christian international, which transcends the narrowing loyalties to class and nation, etc. He offers a vision of a radical Christianity that prepares for the future, full of patience and hope, even while at times appearing to do nothing.

Reinhold Niebuhr registered his disagreement with his brother's idea in an article entitled "Must We Do Nothing?" Here I am not interested in the relative merits of their views about the Sino-Japanese conflict. What is interesting is the way Reinhold Niebuhr introduces his usual note of realism based on a view of the tragic character of history. This prompts him to take issue with the way his brother has recourse to eschatology in dealing with history. It just is not realistic to expect the kingdom of God to create a new society in which the tragic conflicts will be overcome through the processes of history. But he generously admits: "I realize quite well that my brother's position both in its ethical perfectionism and in its apocalyptic note is closer to the gospel than mine."[22] Since "the history of mankind is a perennial tragedy,"[23] Reinhold Niebuhr postulates an eschatological goal "a little outside and beyond history." Then he adds, "My brother does not like these goals above and beyond history."[24] That was not the end of the exchange. H. Richard Niebuhr titled his reply, "The Only Way into the Kingdom of God."[25] The question became clarified. Is the history of mankind a perennial tragedy whose meaning lies in a goal outside of history? Or is tragedy a prelude to historical fulfillment? Is not Christian hope a way of seeing history, including its tragedies, as a zigzagging way to fulfillment. This is not the same as belief in progress; it is faith in the coming of God's kingdom as the fulfilling future of history, in spite of all appearances to the con-

[22] Reinhold Niebuhr, "Must We Do Nothing?" *The Christian Century* (1932), 417.
[23] *Ibid.*
[24] *Ibid.*
[25] *The Christian Century*, 49 (1932), 447.

trary. In Reinhold Niebuhr's eschatology there remained a remnant of the Greek vision of the eternal as a point outside of time and history. H. Richard Niebuhr stayed more on the level of the Hebraic expectation of a new time for history in the advent of God's kingdom.

The tension that appeared in this give-and-take between brothers was internalized in Paul Tillich's theology as the struggle between space and time.[26] This struggle consisted of a continuing warfare between a spatialistic ontology and a temporalistic eschatology, between nature and history, between the priestly return to origins and the prophetic advance toward the new in history, between the predominance of the past and the priority of the future, between the motion of a wheel and the flight of an arrow, between the vertical leap of mysticism into eternal life and the horizontal mission of hope toward the coming kingdom, between a transcendence shining through as a dimension of depth in the present and a transcendence breaking in as the future from ahead. There are signals of great stress between these two sides of Tillich's thinking. In this struggle for predominance between space and time, Tillich was aware that the issue is usually resolved in any one system to the advantage of one side or the other. Then he remarks, "Religion as well as philosophy must choose between these two possibilities which ultimately are exclusive. And this choice is the decision against or for Christianity."[27] This would suggest that his eschatological interpretation of history ought to have resisted being swallowed up in an essentialist ontology that originated in Neoplatonic mysticism. When Tillich offered a description of what is essentially Christian, he made clear use of the categories of history and eschatology. Christianity is essentially an historical religion with an orientation to the eschatological future. Christianity looks ahead toward a future transformation of reality, interpreting the past and acting in the present in light of the advancing future. "The New Being," he said, "is expected predominantly in a horizontal direction rather than a

[26] See Paul Tillich's "The Struggle Between Time and Space," *Theology of Culture* (Oxford, 1959), 30–39.

[27] Paul Tillich, "Historical and Nonhistorical Interpretations of History: A Comparison," *The Protestant Era* (Chicago, 1948), 17.

vertical one."[28] Tillich was aware that there is always a risk in using the categories of an essentialist ontology. "Ontology stands on the basis of the myth of origin, and is bound to space. Ontology must also make time into something spatial. It is the final and most abstract version of the myth of origin."[29] Ontology must be broken open by a theology of history, Tillich acknowledged; otherwise it leaves no room for the new and dissolves the future into the past.

Tillich's theology of history did not, however, successfully break through and outlast his suprahistorical ontology. His doctrine of "essentialization"[30] seems to me the decisive evidence that in the end he tipped the scales against history and the future. The future end of history was elevated by this idea of essentialization into the permanent presence of eternal life. The eschatological future is translated into the mystical presence of being itself. It seems that existence returns to essence, that the end is a return to the beginning, that eschatology is a little wheel that spins within the big wheel of ontology, that the magnitude of the new being is preset by an ontology of being as such.

Tillich formulated the requirements of a theology of history oriented to the kingdom of God, but he could not abide by them. He found them too confining. His spirit soared into a suprahistorical mysticism in which the eschatological future underwent a metamorphosis into the immanence of the eternal now, and thus lost all decisive relation to history. This is nowhere more clear than in one of his last articles, "The Decline and the Validity of the Idea of Progress."[31] Here he restated his famous idea of the *kairos*. A *kairos* is an epochal moment of history in which a new theonomous society might emerge, not a perfect society, but a more perfect one. This idea of the *kairos*, however, was not really aligned with the *eschatos*. In this essay Tillich uses the idea of the *kairos* to assure us that there can be meaningful *moments in history*, but not a fulfilling *future of history*. The only fulfillment there is must

[28] Paul Tillich, *Systematic Theology*, 2 (Chicago, 1957), 87.
[29] Paul Tillich, *Die sozialistische Entscheidung*, in *Christentum und Soziale Gestaltung, Gesammelte Werke*, 2 (Stuttgart, 1963), 239.
[30] Paul Tillich, *Systematic Theology*, 3 (Chicago, 1963), 400ff.
[31] Paul Tillich, "The Decline and the Validity of the Idea of Progress," *The Future of Religions* (New York, 1960).

be snatched now, and the place of fulfillment is outside of time in eternity. "As a Christian theologian I would say that fulfillment is going on in every moment here and now beyond history, not some time in the future, but here and now above ourselves. . . . Something might happen which is elevated out of time into eternity."[32] History ends in mysticism; fulfillment is not expected from the future but by a leap out of time into eternity. That is a Platonic heaven which has no use for a theology of history.

HISTORY AS THE HORIZON OF THEOLOGY

As far as I can see, Tillich's theology of history has not yet made a great impact on American theology. The chief reason perhaps is that it is internally aborted because his major notion of the kingdom of God merges with and passes over into the symbol of eternal life. By that door a transcendental, nonhistorical mysticism slips in to devour the prophetic, historical, futurist, and revolutionary side of Tillich's theology. I believe that as theology shifts to the horizon of history again, developing perspectives on secularization, revolution, and political ethics, we will rediscover a wealth of insights for a theology of history that are latent within Tillich's religious socialist period. These are insights that tended to be overshadowed during the American phase of his career by his apologetic attention to the ultimate existential questions of the individual person—*Angst* and meaninglessness.

The new stimulus to orient theology to history did not come from Tillich's theology. Rather, it came along the pathway of hermeneutics. After World War II the main drive of theology was to go beyond Barth and Bultmann, for reasons we cannot elaborate here. Pressing the hermeneutical question became the means to do it. One option was a hermeneutics of language, refined by Ebeling and Fuchs; quite another was a hermeneutics of history, emerging with Pannenberg and Moltmann. Someone who is interested in a theory of historical understanding which encompasses the future

[32] *Ibid.*, 79.

horizon and motivates an ethics of change will be more enchanted by the latter. Of course, it is not an either/or, since the hermeneutics of language is a narrower field of vision that can be included within the broader horizon of history. But the reverse is not true. The hermeneutics of language is not adequate to a theology of history, since it cannot glimpse and grasp such things as impersonal economic forces in history, sociocultural problems and challenges, political structures and trends, and everything that falls outside the interpersonal sphere. These are bread-and-butter issues that are not adequately addressable by the rubric of "word-event" favored by the hermeneutics of language.

Bultmann will be remembered in the history of hermeneutics for underscoring the existential structure of man as one who asks questions. Man asks questions because he is a question; he asks the questions about himself. This is why he undertakes historical research and digs into ancient manuscripts. When he inquires into a text, he is not standing nowhere. He himself is bound up with the question he puts. For Bultmann, one brings to the biblical text the question concerning human existence. We accept this as an indispensable element in a hermeneutic geared to a theology of history. But it is only a starting point. We have to ask whether the question concerning human existence exhausts the horizon of the human quest for historical understanding. With Pannenberg, Moltmann, and others, I have to say "no."[33] For the hermeneutical task, it is important that the interpreter's horizons be broadened in the process of inquiry to overtake the horizon of the text. The text has its own horizon within which its questions and answers stand. In the case of the biblical texts, my own existential horizon as the point from which I set out is challenged by the wider horizon of their understanding of God and his actions in the affairs of men and nations. The responses may be a broadening of my own horizon of inquiry, so that the question I ask about myself

---

[33] See especially Wolfhart Pannenberg's "Hermeneutics and Universal History," *History and Hermeneutic, Journal for Theology and the Church*, 4 (New York, 1967) and J. Moltmann's *Theology of Hope, ed. cit.*, to which the following paragraphs on hermeneutics are indebted to a great extent. For a lengthier treatment of the historical dimension of hermeneutics, see my book *History and Hermeneutics* (Philadelphia, 1966).

may become intertwined inextricably with the wider question of social and communal fulfillment, and even cosmic fulfillment. One may discover that the individualistic question of authentic existence for myself is interlocked with a longing for a healing and wholeness that embraces the city and community of which I am a part, and even the larger commonwealth of mankind out of my sight. The utopias of mankind, since Plato, offer evidence that the scope of human anticipation is seldom restricted to the existentialist narrowing of the horizon to include only possibilities of individual human existence.[34] Above all, the biblical symbol of the kingdom of God can hardly be voided of its social and political dimensions. And if it cannot be reduced to an individualistic horizon of interest, still less can it be so absorbed into the present moment as to lose its inherent futurity.

A hermeneutic that is allied to a theology of history must take seriously the historical distance and difference between the situation of the biblical millennium and the present world situation on the threshold of the third millennium A.D. It is difficult to exaggerate this distance and difference. Once we realize this, we can better cope with the current crises of faith and understanding in church and theology. Modern man seems to be alienated from the horizon of the historical situation within which the biblical authors lived and wrote. The major new movements in theology have been concerned to bridge over the distance between the "there and then" of the Bible and the "here and now" of the modern world. Bultmann's demythologizing, the post-Bultmannian new quest of the historical Jesus, the language hermeneutics of Ebeling and Fuchs, the post-Bonhoefferian vogue of secular theology, etc., have tried, without success, to bridge the gulf between the biblical texts and the present situation. What is it that could make the answers in the biblical past truly relevant to our contemporary questions, and how is it possible to release them from the limits of their own historical situation to mobilize our lives in a totally different time and place? It is at this point that I find the initiatives of Pannenberg and Moltmann, among others, to be promising for a theology of history that comprises both Christian identity and relevance to the present.

[34] *Utopias and Utopian Thought,* Frank E. Manuel, ed. (Boston, 1967).

Pannenberg speaks of hermeneutics as "fusing the horizons"[35] of the past text and the present interpreter. This is a key idea for a Christian theology of history, and I accept Pannenberg's way of turning the key as particularly useful. The horizons must be merged without submerging the particularities of the present into the sacred traditions of the past, as in orthodoxy, biblicism, or fundamentalism. Usually these sacred traditions are equated with some past apprehension of the past—the fifth, thirteenth, sixteenth, or nineteenth century's. Similarly, the theologian must be careful not to fasten on to quite peripheral matters within the horizon of the biblical texts, matters that just happen to be most easily amenable to the horizon of the present. That leads to facile and false contemporization—the classical trademark of liberalism. In this light, much so-called radical theology is also a failure, for its radicalism consists chiefly of the enormity of its denial of what counts most within the horizon of early Christianity. It is not radical enough; it begins and ends with a rigidly self-sufficient horizon of some imaginary and usually superficial fellow called "the modern man."

Following up a suggestion from H. G. Gadamer, Pannenberg has developed the insight that "it is just the temporal distance of the interpreter from the situation within which the text originated which alone makes possible the occurrence of understanding as an occurrence of interpretation."[36] This means that the distance between the biblical text and ourselves, which we usually experience in a negative way, may actually have a positive significance. If the text were to say merely what we already know or what fits neatly into our modern horizon, there would be little point to the study of history. History would only illustrate universal possibilities of human experience. The historical dimension of the hermeneutical problem would then be overcome in a psychological way.[37] On the other hand, the positive significance of the gulf between the past text and the present situation can be acknowledged and then

35 W. Pannenberg, "Hermeneutics and Universal History," *op. cit.*, 136ff.
36 *Ibid.*, 137.
37 This is ultimately the fate of Wilhelm Dilthey's projection of a critique of historical reason. See Pannenberg's critique in "Hermeneutics and Universal History," *art. cit.*, 129f.

overcome in a historical way only by a comprehensive horizon that includes the two horizons that are historically strange to each other.[38] How can such a new third horizon be conceived? As soon as the question is asked, the words for the answer almost tumble into place. The horizon of the past and the horizon of the present can be connected historically, without collapsing one into the other, only as both of them are in motion toward the horizon of the future.

Thus the attempt to develop a hermeneutical approach pointing to the interpretation of history gives rise to the problem of the future. Any past event can be understood only from its own future. The meaning of our present can be determined only by anticipating its outcome. Bultmann once affirmed this very point, but I think he failed to follow it up consistently: "One must say that a historical event is always first knowable for what it is—precisely as a historical event—in the future. And therefore one can also say that the future of a historical event belongs to that event. . . . It holds good that what a historical event means always first becomes clear in the future. It can definitely disclose itself only when history has come to an end."[39] If we follow up this suggestion we will inevitably reach the conclusion that the question about the meaning of any event in history will be connected with the question of the meaning of the whole of history. And the idea of history as a whole raises from its side the question of a possible eschatological interpretation of history. Eschatology is the answer to the quest for the meaning of history. The meaning is hidden in the mystery of the final future; it is a matter of revelation; it is an object of faith and hope. The belief that in the end there is only one history, that all history is involved in a meaningful sequence, and that it has a plot and a goal, is an affirmation of hope within the ambiguities of history. No one stands at the end, surveying the totality of history behind him in a holistic way. The oneness of history's meaning and truth is something the believer can only anticipate as long as history is still on the way. The basis of this anticipation for

[38] *Ibid.*, 137–38.
[39] Rudolph Bultmann, "Is Exegesis Without Presuppositions Possible?" *Existence and Faith* (New York, 1960), 295.

the Christian is the inbreaking of the future of God's kingdom in Jesus of Nazareth. He preached the kingdom; he represented it; he let it have complete sway in his teachings and actions; he obediently let it lead him to death on a cross; and by his resurrection he announced that the peace and righteousness of the kingdom will win in the end for all mankind. The Christian interpretation of history must, therefore, be projected in an eschatological form under a Christological norm.

THE DRIVING FORCE OF THE FUTURE

Karl Jaspers has stated that "a conception of history intending to cover the totality of human affairs must take in the future. . . . No philosophical consciousness of history is possible without consciousness of the future."[40] We have argued that this holds good especially for a theological interpretation of history. We cannot block out the vision of the future if we wish to understand the past and act meaningfully in the present. But *what* future? Not just any future, and not mere futuricity as an existential stance of openness. Rather, we have been referring to the future of God whose attributes are known through his promises, whose nature is identical with his coming kingdom,[41] whose kingdom has been opened up as our future by the intervening Messiahship of Jesus. The contents of

[40] Karl Jaspers, *The Origin and Goal of History* (New Haven, 1953), 141.

[41] Ernst Bloch defines Jahweh, the God of history, as One in whom futurity is fundamental to his being: *"Eh'je ascher eh'je dagegen stellt bereits an die Schwelle der Jahwe-Erscheinung einen Gott vom Ende der Tage, mit Futurum als Seinsbeschaffenheit"* (*Das Prinzip Hoffnung*, 3 [Frankfurt, 1959], 1457–58). Similarly, Pannenberg writes: "The primacy of the future and its newness are only assured if the coming kingdom is ontologically grounded in itself and owes its future not merely to the presently existing wishes and efforts of man. When the coming kingdom is designated in the Bible as the kingdom of *God*, it is concerned to express this ontological primacy of the future of the kingdom over everything that is presently real, including all psychic states. Thus, in fact, the being of God and of the kingdom are identical in the Bible, for the being of God is his rulership" ("Der Gott der Hoffnung," *Grundfragen systematischer Theologie* [Göttingen, 1967], 391).

this future are projected as images of hope at work in history to realize themselves. We will now, in conclusion, try to point out the significance of this futurist perspective on history for our own existential present and the mission of the church in America.

Because the eschatological future of the kingdom of God became present in Jesus without losing its element of pure futurity, Christians do not look back to the past without at the same time looking ahead to new things that have not yet become reality. They walk through hope, crossing over frontiers to meet the oncoming future which holds the key to the meaning of our existence. They are lured forward by the call of the not-yet-fully-known. The knowledge of Christian faith is not primarily an inventory of memory, a taking stock of the past; it is "the knowledge of things hoped for."[42] This means that each day Christians hope to be able to draw new boundaries to the known. The attracting power of the future is an incitement for man to expand his horizon of understanding, to flood the darkness of ignorance with light from the future. Science and philosophy both presuppose the driving force of the future upon the imagination. In religion it is the prophetic imagination that picks up signals from the future, clarifying alternatives in the present, and charting the course of responsible decision and action. A man's vision of the future will give us the best clue as to what he's made of and the way he is likely to act. Similarly, a society's picture of the future will indirectly influence the way it stacks its priorities and directs its energies. We reject the common opinion that a person is what his past has made him and that society in the future must be an extension of what it is at present. To be sure, the present of man and his culture has been shaped by the past, but in constant interaction with their foreconsciousness of the driving power of the future upon them. The future works in the present through symbols that propagate the right of that future to be. In the Christian view we are driven by symbols that proclaim the future of shalom, joy, unity, fullness, and righteousness. These are some of the reigning symbols of the future which live in the Christian imagination.

[42] See Robert William Jenson's book, *The Knowledge of Things Hoped For* (Oxford, 1969).

The church is called to exist proscopically toward the new world that is coming. "For here we have no lasting city, but we seek the city which is to come." (Heb. 13:14) This places the church in tension toward the present, since its image of the coming world is a counterimage to the established order in the present—the old age. The tension reaches a breaking point and leads to revolutionary action when the present order refuses to be fructified by the future, thereby provoking the future into a contradicting, aggressive, and retaliatory position over against the present.

The church's mission to the world is to keep it from getting bogged down in the present. The world at this historical juncture is in danger of getting mired in the present—on the one side by an existentialism which places us under the tyranny of the ecstatic moment; and on the other side, by a positivism which analyzes the world in a way that offers no clue about how to change it. Marx had a better insight when he said that philosophers only interpret the world, but the point is to change it. This is more in line with the Christian spirit that seeks the transformation of that which is, and looks upon the urge to conform to that which is as a manifestation of sin.

The church ought to be a sacrament of hope for the world's future. When the world is swallowed up by hopelessness or is bored by its stagnant present, the church can lift up public symbols of the future that generate new possibilities in the present. The church is needed as the voice of prophecy in the world to regenerate the social and political images that inspire the world to change for the better. The church cannot limit its mission in history to salvaging individuals from a meaningless world; it works not only *in* history but *for* history, not only *in* culture but *for* culture, not only for persons but for communities, not only in the present but toward the ultimate future. The church must dream vicariously for those who will dream no more. "Where there is no vision, the people perish." (Prov. 29:18)

What counts in a theology of history is not merely another theory about the world; it must champion another way of action for the world. Two themes have been circulating through these pages: the theme of the future and the theme of revolution. These are, in my view, *conditiones sine qua non* for awakening an interest in a theology of history in America. Books like Van Harvey's *The Historian and the Believer* and Gordon D. Kaufman's *Systematic Theology: A Historicist Perspective* are signs that theology in America is persistently historical. Both of them, however, are lacking precisely the dimensions which we have suggested as essential to a theology of history: an eschatology of the future and the ethics of radical change derived from it. Van Harvey's presentation of "the Christian perspective," or "the perspectival image of Jesus,"[43] lacks the eschatological sense in interpreting history; and Gordon Kaufman's sketchy references to a "metaphysics of history," or a "historicist metaphysics," seem to be equally devoid of it.[44] Therefore, both of them are insufficiently aware of and even ignore, the role of the future in analyzing the structures of historical experience and knowledge.

Finally, I believe that a theology of history oriented to the eschatological future has the potential power to close ecumenical gaps. The main lines of this kind of theology seem to me to be shared by Roman Catholics like J. B. Metz[45] and E. Schillebeeckx,[46] by Continental theologians like W. Pannenberg (Lutheran) and J. Moltmann (Reformed), by a Baptist like Harvey Cox, Presbyterian Richard Shaull, and by American Lutherans like R. W. Jenson and myself. The eschatological perspective relativizes our doctrinal and institutional traditions, so that while our past may have divided us, we can now open ourselves to a common future that frees and unites us.

[43] Van A. Harvey, *The Historian and the Believer* (New York, 1966), 268ff.

[44] Gordon D. Kaufman, *Systematic Theology: A Historicist Perspective* (New York, 1969), 25, n.10.

[45] Johann Baptist Metz, *Theology of the World* (New York, 1969).

[46] E. Schillebeeckx, *God the Future of Man* (New York, 1968).

Pragmatic Science and Man

✠

HERBERT RICHARDSON

Herbert Richardson has done what many have asked for: He has written one of the few books on American theology, Towards an American Theology *(1967). Christian faith and its articulation must radically change, for we have entered the new "sociotechnic age." It replaces separated institutional functions with the cybernetic integration of society and environments within a single rational system. Professor Richardson is a member of the Institute of Christian Thought at St. Michael's College in Toronto.*

American science is unique. It is as unique in its own way as American politics, art, or religion.

From its earliest days American science has been consistently pragmatic not simply in its goals, but also in its procedures. This orientation has frequently been contrasted with the European view of science. Slater and Bennis present a paradigm illustration of this difference. "Many observers," they note, "have been impressed with the disdain European intellectuals seem to show for practical matters. Even in Russia, where one would least expect it, there is little interest in the 'merely useful.' Harrison Salisbury of the New York *Times* was struck during his recent travels in the Soviet Union by the almost total absence of liaison between research and practical application. He saw only one agricultural experimental station on the American model. There, professors were working in the fields and told him, 'People call us Americans.'"[1]

People Call Us Americans. Of course who would not admit that culture may affect the way scientists actually view their work and go about it. But I am actually suggesting more than this. I am suggesting that American science *qua* science is different. I am suggesting that there is not simply a cultural, but a *scientific* reason why American science is more practical, more inclined to find its fulfillment in technology. The purpose of this essay is to discuss this claim and its implications for our future.

THE UNIQUENESS OF
THE AMERICAN SCIENTIFIC ENTERPRISE

The uniqueness of the American scientific enterprise includes the following distinctives: (1) a pragmatic conception of what constitutes an explanation; (2) an aspiration toward the transformation and control of the world; (3) a manipulative, or "machine-using," type of experimentation; and (4) a commitment to a democratic value orientation and to transactional communications. These distinctives are so much a part of the American scientific enterprise that neither its experimental work nor its theoretical conceptions—much less its actual achievements—can be understood without them.

We must, first, observe that the ideal of scientific knowledge in America is not identical with the ideal in Europe. In Europe, scientific investigation ends in *scientia,* i.e., in a theoretical understanding of those principles which account for observed regularities in nature. The debate that goes on between Anglo-Saxon and European philosophers of science over whether those principles are, in the last analysis, empirical (i.e., descriptive generalizations) or rational (i.e., laws constructed by the human reason) does not engage what is the real point for the American scientist. That debate is intrafamilial. Both parties assume that true science ends in a theoretical

[1] Warren G. Bennis and Philip E. Slater, *The Temporary Society* (New York, 1968), 62.

understanding—whether the form of that understanding be descriptive generalizations or rational constructions. American science aims, however, not at *scientia* but at *pragmatica*: not at those principles which account for the fact that things are the way they are, but at those principles that allow us to control and change them. The American scientist is actually looking for a different kind of explanation of things. He seeks not the reason why things are as they are, but for reasons by which he can make them be otherwise. He seeks not simply to account for a state of affairs and to predict its future, but to manipulate a state of affairs and to control its future.

The difference between these two conceptions of an explanation is the difference between "theoretical" and "pragmatic." Theoretical explanations are said to be true if they are consistent with the empirical data and can be used to predict. Pragmatic explanations are said to be true only if they can be construed as instructing a course of action or human behavior that can effect a change in the course of events. The model for confirming a theoretical explanation is *observing;* the model for confirming a pragmatic explanation is *manipulating*. Therefore, a theoretical explanation takes the form of a "law" that accounts for the way things are. But a pragmatic explanation takes the form of an "instruction" that tells what operation should be performed in order to effect a given outcome.

It is widely thought that the pragmatic attitude culminates not in knowledge but in action. (It is not interested in abstract formulations of truth.) This is a serious misunderstanding, and the failure to be clear about this matter leads to confusions about the status of "pure research" in America. It is not true that American science is less interested in "pure research" (and has done less to develop it) than European science, although it is true that a certain kind of "pure research" (that characteristic of *scientia*, theoretical science) is less highly regarded in America. Pragmatic no less than theoretical science seeks and culminates in *knowledge*. Pragmatic science is no less interested in impractical and abstract questions. The difference between the two conceptions of science is not that the one culminates in action and is concerned with the useful while the other culminates in knowledge without regard for its use. The difference lies in their conceptions of scientific knowledge itself, i.e., their disagreement about what constitutes a genuinely scientific explanation. In order to see the difference between the two conceptions, let us consider the following case.

For the past ten years the American scientific community has gathered vast statistical and experimental evidence showing a correlation between cigarette smoking and lung cancer. The statistical evidence consists of large-scale and varied studies on the incidence of lung cancer in smoking and nonsmoking groups. The experimental evidence consists in exposing living tissue to tars from cigarette smoke in order to verify the hypothesis, or prediction, that cancer forms in tissues following its exposure to tars. This gives us a theoretical knowledge of a relation between two things. Some argue, however, that the kind of knowledge gained through this statistical and laboratory investigation is not yet scientific. They contend that the experiments confirm a constant correlation between the inhalation of tars and cancer, but that they do not show that these tars are the actual agent, or efficient cause, of cancer. A scientific explanation, they contend, should demonstrate this. It should not simply show that one state of affairs follows upon another, but should show the reason, or mechanism, that explains how something is "caused," or why it necessarily follows another. Today many of us smile amusedly at those who still believe there is something like "efficient causality," that there is something in one thing that accounts for the presence of an occurrence in another thing. We know, or think we know, that efficient causality is an imagination of the mind. Perhaps so, perhaps not. But it is worth pointing out that the demand for the demonstration of an efficient causality can also be formulated as a demand for a more rigorous kind of experimental procedure, an experimental procedure that does not simply confirm a prediction, but one that allows us to control and alter an outcome. To the extent that theoretical science has not devised such an experimental procedure but has been satisfied with a procedure that is merely consistent with its notion of causality as constant conjunction, this science has not been experimentally rigorous.

Actually, the demand for a more rigorous experimental procedure follows from the pragmatic conception of a scientific explanation. We must seek an explanation in the form of an instruction telling what operation should be performed in order to control a given outcome. An experiment that merely confirms a predication, or shows *that* X follows Y, is not sufficient. What is needed, rather, is an experiment that shows *why* X follows Y. This can be done only by manipulating the materials and the process until we find a way to control the outcome. We can be sure that one thing "causes" another only if we can both allow this process to occur *and* find a way to stop it from occurring. To discover this is to discover the mechanism, the "switch" that allows us to turn the process on and off. Technically, this can be stated as follows: A true experimental verification requires that we be instructed in a procedure that can be performed to *disconfirm* as well as to *confirm* our assertion.

This more rigorous notion of an experimental verification has recently been established by the Food and Drug Administration as the new basis for licensing drugs. Previously a drug could be licensed if (1) the correlation between ingestion and cure that was affirmed (predicted) actually did take place and (2) there were no inbalancing negative effects. The FDA rejected these previous criteria as unscientific and required in their place experimental evidence showing not simply a correlation between ingestion of a drug and a cure, but an experiment that isolated the mechanism, or process, by which the drug *produced* the cure. Without such experimental evidence, there could be no certainty that the drug was more than an effective placebo.

Are we inclined to agree with this more rigorous notion of what constitutes a scientific explanation? I am sure we are; we prefer it for scientific reasons. We prefer it because it both includes all that is involved in a predictive verification and goes beyond this. Since the goal of science is to be as scientific as possible—i.e., to seek the greatest amount of knowledge that can be gained through experimental investigation—it is clear that the pragmatic-manipulative ideal of understanding is superior to the theoretical-predictive ideal.

PRAGMATIC KNOWLEDGE:
THE UNIFICATION OF MAN'S WORLD

Pragmatic science—like theoretical science—terminates in knowledge, not in action. What is gained through experiments and verified by them is a knowledge of the mechanisms of things—and not simply their conjunctions. This knowledge is expressed, therefore, in terms that can be read as *instructions* about operations to be performed in order to permit or to impede any given effect. We may call such instructions "laws" only if we keep in mind the difference in verificational procedures between assertions that intend to be understood as instructions and those that intend to be understood as descriptions. There is, too, the difference in experimental attitude implied by these different approaches. The model of the theoretical experiment is for the scientist to "stand outside" the process, observing it from an "objective" point of view, and allowing it to run its course. The model of the pragmatic experiment, on the other hand, *requires* that the scientist interfere with the process at some point, manipulating it in order to produce *both* outcomes required for experimental verification.

Let me anticipate a possible misunderstanding. When I say that theoretical and pragmatic conceptions of science generate different kinds of experimentation—one where the scientist "stands outside" and observes, and the other where the scientist interferes and manipulates—I do not mean that the experiments would necessarily appear different to, for example, a movie camera. Actually the same laboratory equipment and procedures could be used while the scientists understood what they were doing in different ways. Their attitudes directing the same procedures would differentiate the conceptions and results.

If this seems paradoxical, consider the following example: Suppose we were to isolate an object from its environment by placing it in a vacuum jar, observing its actions in this new location. Would we be standing apart from it, observing it from an objective point of view? Or would we be manipulating and interacting with it by means of a machine (the vacuum jar)? The manipulative attitude is going to generate increased interest in laboratory equipment and encourage manipulation and increased "field work." But, in the last analysis, the differences in experimental procedures are less important than the attitude, or self-understanding, that underlies those procedures. It is this that makes American science unique.

This difference in attitude is so important because it expresses and confirms a whole metaphysics of man and nature. If we think of scientific experiments as a way of standing "outside" nature and observing it as an object engaged in its own intrinsic operations, then these experiments confirm that nature is a self-contained, autonomous, nonhuman order of things having intrinsic intentionalities that are totally indifferent to man. This would hardly be a surprising discovery, because each experiment will have been conceived in such a way that this idea of nature is implicit within the understanding of the experiment itself. Man separates himself from nature through an experimental procedure and thereby discovers—through his experiment—that nature is indifferent to human intentionalities and "final causes." Whether this discovery then leads to that peculiar European reverence for nature that abhors technology or to the equally peculiar European fatalism is all the same. Both attitudes are consistent consequences of the "objective" experimental attitude.

The pragmatic conception of an explanation and the manipulative understanding of experimentation generate, therefore, a completely different perception of the world. Whereas theoretical science develops experiments that lead us to perceive nature as an autonomous order with its own intrinsic intentionalities, pragmatic experiments generate a perception of nature as open to receive human intentions, as receptive to—even inviting—technological transformation. The pragmatic experimental attitude tends to heighten the involvement between man and nature; it tends to break down the subject-object distinction. It tends to generate a process of manipulation and response through which nature and man become more and more one. The nexus of this heightened unity, or involvement, between man and nature is technology. And American science has its intrinsic fulfillment and culmination in this. Not that every scientist is involved in the direct production of technology, of course. But the whole scientific enterprise is oriented on this scope by virtue of its striving through manipulative experimentation for pragmatic explanations. American science is more available for, or further developed toward, this use than is the theoretical science characteristic of Europe.

AMERICAN SCIENCE AND
THE AMERICAN CHRISTIAN

How should the projections relating science to theology be developed? The problem includes a range of possibilities. Is it a question of forecasting areas in which scientific knowledge will soon vastly increase (e.g., knowledge of extraplanetary life, subatomic particles, brain mechanisms, and cybernetic processes) in order to suggest how theology might cope with the problems such new scientific knowledge might raise? Or is the issue the resolution of tensions between the Christian and scientific views of the world (e.g., arguing that scientific regularities are statistical and therefore not deterministic impediments to the exercise of human freedom)? Or is it a problem in imagining future technological scenarios—à la Herman Kahn—in order to determine which lines of technological development are most consistent with the Christian hope for man? All these approaches have respectable pedigrees. But the more I pondered, the more I became convinced that none of them really hit the mark. My own stance had developed from seeing that what is uniquely characteristic of America is not what she shares with modern Europe, but her faith in social technology. The vision of a wholly artificial environment, man and society together, restructured by the power of the machine, is the American dream. At that time I still distinguished sharply—in my own mind, at least—between *science* and *technology*. I had not yet come to see that there are, in the modern Western world, two different conceptions of science: One is purely theoretical, hence discontinuous with technology; the other is pragmatic, hence culminating in technology. It seemed to me that the frequent coupling of the two notions in sentences such as, "*Science* and *technology* are giving men the power to attain complete control over nature" tended to confuse our understanding of technology. It implied that technology is a mere instrument whereby Man-the-subject mastered Nature-the-object. This seemed to me to draw attention away from technology's real effect and import. What man really does through the use of technology is not transform nature, but transform *human nature;* the real effect of technology is not the reconstruction of the world, but the reconstruction of human society. And this is its import for Christianity. We fail to see this, however, because we are accustomed to think of technology as having the same orientation as (theoretical) "science." We think of it as an instrument of the subject-object relationship, a means whereby man controls the world.

In order to draw attention to the other affect of technology—namely, to the fact that in using it, man transforms not simply his world but himself—I coined the neologism "sociotechnics" (for "social technology"). This term has the effect of building into the very concept of technology the specification that it has, explicitly or implicitly, *social consequences.* It helps, I believe, to break down a false kind of braggadocio about how man masters nature through the use of technology and forces a more sober calculation about what the use of technology is doing to man. It was for this reason that I felt the neologism intellectually useful. A second set of considerations also suggested this word to me. It was the awareness that a machine is in many ways only an alternative form of social organization. One can place a sail on a ship and replace two rows of oarsmen. One can build a cannon and replace a phalanx. One can buy a computer and replace a mass of human calculators. The introduction of technology both presupposes certain social institutions and, once introduced, causes the reconstruction of those institutions. The calculus of technology must, therefore, be expressed not simply in physical terms, but in institutional and sociological terms as well. Because of this, every new technology also activates a new social process.

These reflections on technology led me to suggest that the pre-eminent sociotechnical disciplines are economics, cybernetics, polling and psychological testing, management, mass communications, and so forth. It is in these disciplines rather than in the technology associated with the development of heavy industry that the *socio*technical interest is seen most clearly—though it is also perfectly obvious that the development of machine technology also has had vast social consequences. It is in America that these explicitly sociotechnical disciplines have thrived. In Europe, the sense of separation between man and nature is such that there is general opposition to the use of technology to analyze and influence human beings. This is why sociotechnics is pre-eminently an American creation.

There was, I felt, a third reason for coining the word "sociotechnics." American universities, heir to the European distinction between "arts" and "sciences," have been uncertain how to provide an intellectual justification for the "social sciences" and for such "professional schools" as business, education, and public administration. The social sciences have, tragically, felt an obligation to justify themselves as "sciences" like the "natural sciences." (Not that even American "natural sciences" in fact operated in accordance with the ideology of *theoretical science* prepared for them by European philosophers.) And the "professional schools" had to accept an outside status—since, according to "the arts and sciences mentality," the goal of the university is to develop theoretical understanding; hence, it does not admit into its inner sanctum such practical enterprises as the training of teachers, city planners, or businessmen.

The victimization and snobbery indigenous to the American university, because it conceives what it is doing in terms of these inadequate categories ("arts" and "sciences"), can hardly be imagined by those who have not shared its life. In any case, recalling that science was able to develop an autonomous method only after it had gained a distinctive name, it seemed to me that the social sciences and professional schools engaged in the study of man and society should have their own name so that they might also develop their distinctive method. Hence, *sociotechnics*. Sociotechnical knowledge is neither an art nor a theoretical science; it is a *tertium quid,* whose methods and criteria are wholly new. "Consider, for example, how the psychologist or sociologist or historian or manager investigates his material by taking up a position within it. In this participational attitude, the 'positional' subject-object stance . . . is overthrown. The investigator actually influences his subject matter by his questions (as in the effect of pollsters on elections), yet his questions are also affected by the answers he receives. . . . Because the investigator does not stand outside the system, but is a part of it, the modern subject-object distinction does not arise. The sociotechnical disciplines, therefore, have no particular point of view. . . . This does not mean that they are arts rather than sciences. They are, rather, a wholly new discipline, one which utilizes participation in order to know."[2]

At the time I wrote this statement, I had not yet seen that in America even the natural sciences are sociotechnical. For the sociotechnical-participational investigation of materials—an investigation that sets up a process of intervention, feedback, and response —is identical with the pragmatic-manipulative method as it is applied to the study of nature. The development of the distinctive and overtly sociotechnical disciplines in America is, therefore, nothing but the natural consequence of the pragmatic mentality, as that mentality shaped all scientific investigation in America from her earliest history. The form of American science has been determined by her seventeenth-century *fons et origo:* The *technologia* of Petrus Ramus and William Ames and the inventive experimental program established by Francis Bacon in his *Novum Organum* and in the Royal Society (to which a disproportionate number of Americans belonged). The inventions of Franklin, Jefferson, and Von Humboldt in the following century are only the more obvious fruits of a distinctive mentality that has characterized American science from its earliest days.

The realization that the method of the sociotechnical disciplines is identical with that of the pragmatic-manipulative sciences leads to an extension of my earlier ideas, namely, that the fundamental sociotechnical discipline is not one of the sciences (even the "social sciences"), but is the entire enterprise of science itself. It is for this reason that American science has not remained a single institution within society, but has expanded and engulfed the total society within itself. It does so by scientifically investigating every aspect of human life. Since its investigation is not theoretical, but

[2] Herbert W. Richardson, *Toward an American Theology* (New York, 1967), 18.

pragmatic and manipulative, it initiates change in whatever it studies by the very act of studying it. In this way, it engulfs whatever it studies within the values and procedures of the scientific community and brings it within the total cybernetic process of change that is American science. Since the values and procedures of this science are democratic, American society becomes increasingly democratized. The most important impact of science upon society during the next generation will, therefore, not be any particular technological product. It will be, rather, the sociotechnical "feedback effect" upon society that occurs through the employment of science as an instrument of knowledge. It will be the speeding-up of the process of democratization. This includes:

A. The further dissolution of elites under the drive toward equality,

B. The further dissolution of tradition and authority under the drive toward experimentation,

C. The further dissolution of "minorities" under the drive toward participation and enfranchisement,

D. The further dissolution of hierarchical organization under the drive toward decentralization and pluralism,

E. The further dissolution of coercion and the drive toward persuasion and consensus.

THE HUMAN CONDITION AND TECHNOLOGY'S FEEDBACK

The usual approach to thinking about the future of science and its impact on the human condition is to focus on new technologies and possibilities for their use. Without denying the importance of such developments, I am more inclined to the view that the feedback impact of the development of such technologies on man himself will be the decisive factor in the future. For example, educational technologies increase the rate of the learning process tremendously. More importantly, however, they make use solely of positive reinforcement (or "reward") as a motivation. The introduction of such educational technologies will mean that threat and punishment will no longer be viable motivations. Children will grow up relatively free from those "fears of failure" that inhibit so many adults today. In this situation, would we really say that the greatest importance of educational technology is that it increases the rate of learning? I doubt it. A fact of far greater importance is that a generation from now society will be filled with adults who will not only know more, but be less inclined to be fearful, less inclined to accept punishment and coercion as ways of achieving goals. We already see the emergence of these new attitudes in the college revolutionaries.

In my conversations with persons belonging to my parents' generation, I have become aware that perhaps the major factor influencing our differing views about the world is that they lived through a major economic depression while I did not. That experience created in many of them a cautiousness in outlook, a defensive orientation, and a gratitude toward life in its present imperfect state that I do not share. Their feelings about life are very much the consequence of the social trauma they experienced during the depression. My feelings are no less a consequence of my experience. But I have not lived through a depression. Hence, I am less cautious about the future, less defensive in my attitudes toward life, and less inclined to be grateful for imperfect institutions. I want things to get better. Then I shall be grateful.

This indifference between my parents and myself is one of the "feedback effects" of scientific economics and computer technology. The fact that I have not lived through a depression is in large part the consequence of these new sciences. A generation ago they did not exist and, in fact, it was assumed that the economic cycle was an autonomous "law of nature" that could not (therefore, *should* not) be brought under scientific control. The bringing of the economic process under scientific control, however, is less important for this than it is for citizens in a society that employs these new sciences. They will be different kinds of persons because they will be motivated by totally new attitudes toward life.

In stressing that the sociotechnical feedback is more important than the technological product, I am simply following in the line of Marx and McLuhan. Both pointed out how technological innovations are not socially and psychologically neutral but have distinctive biases. Marx saw that the accumulation of capital to build a heavy industry created a new social class, the proletariat. McLuhan sees how the creation of electronic communications is destroying old political units and procedures, making the world a "global village." I accept *both* these arguments, for Marx and McLuhan are focusing on different stages of the same process of social transformation that occurs after new technologies are introduced into a society, causing it to shift from a static to a dynamic mode of maintaining equilibrium. That modern society maintains its equilibrium only by changing *both* its machine technologies and its social institutions is the consequence of gaining knowledge by manipulation. The change has a distinctive direction, however. It tends toward the democratization of society.

SCIENCE AND BELIEF

The first and most far-reaching effect of the scientific process is the undermining of belief based on authority. Naturally, this has ramifications for the Christian both in the spheres of personal faith and ecclesiastical and cultural systems of authority. Beliefs are personal habits or attitudes, conducive to typically expressive actions. Shared beliefs maintain the harmony of the social system. To investigate beliefs scientifically is to open human beings up to the possibility of feeling and acting differently. This creates a threat to the harmony of society. Even if it should turn out that what was believed on authority is also demonstrably true by the canons of experimental science, there is still a change in men. For they now believe *autonomously*. They now act out of what they themselves have determined. They are freed from their self-denigration and dependence on other men whom they believe to be better than they—namely, "authorities."

By pressing for an experimental justification of belief, science not only undermines authority, but also the privileged position of certain elites in whom special access to authoritative truth is vested. There is no authority that does not receive social embodiment in some elite or privileged group. The king, the priest, and "the company of educated men" (as Harvard euphoniously designates its own special community) all purport—by virtue of person, or initiation, or office—to an esoteric wisdom. This wisdom is not susceptible of scientific verification. The demand for such verification as the criterion of truth is destructive of such elites and their esoteric claims.

Not that elites are willing to risk their authority by opening their claims to inspection! Quite the contrary. They engage in a sophisticated defense purposed to explain the incapacities of science to do full justice to what they know. But this is a temporary delaying tactic. For as men become less fearful and less distrustful of their own capacities, they need authorities less and less. To the extent that they need them less, they are more willing to expose their claims to experimental scrutiny. And as this is done, the transformation of man takes place. This transformation, it should be noted, is not something I am *predicting*. It is something that is occurring within our own lifetime. We have seen the economic process demystified. More and more we see the traditional political elites who thought it within their personal province to determine the destiny of men give way to technocrats: No modern mayor could do without his "city planner" and no senator could survive without his pollster. We have seen the first steps in the scientific study of human sexuality and the debunking of authoritative myths and folklore passed down from parents and teachers over many generations. We are at the beginnings of the scientific study of religion—a study that has already demonstrated that *confessionally organized* Christian churches cause antisemitism and racism—in spite of their *professions* to the contrary. (This is the importance of scientific study. It shows what a given act *really* does; it shows that the time meaning of an act may be different from what those who do it profess as its meaning. If the Christian's denial of antisemitism itself becomes a cause of antisemitism, then may the Christian honestly say that he is denying antisemitism? This is one of the questions experimental science is forcing contemporary religion to face.)

The penetration of scientific investigation into areas previously protected by elites and by authoritative belief systems has the effect not only of disenfranchising those elites and increasing the tendency toward social equality, but also of setting in motion a process of change that then requires further scientific control. Once a given area is opened to scientific investigation, a social and psychological disequilibrium is created that can be overcome only by continuing that investigation. In this way, scientific values and procedures gradually penetrate the total society, so that pragmatic experimentation is what that society does, not simply in one of its institutions but in the totality of its life.

TECHNOLOGY AND WIDER DEMOCRATIZATION

Max Lerner has noted the tendency of technological science to pervade all strata of American life and has remarked on the uniqueness of this tendency:

> The American has been a machine-intoxicated man. . . . As by some tropism of the spirit, the Americans have followed out the logic of technology all the way. The world has seen civilizations based on very different principles: on beauty and an equipoise of living, on otherworldiness and reality of the supernatural, on close personal allegiance, on military prowess, on ascetic control of the self. But in each case the principle was embodied mainly in the life and outlook of an elite group. *Never before has the motive principle of a civilization spread so pervasively through all strata of its population,* so completely changing the lives of its ordinary people.[3]

Is this diffusion of scientific technology throughout all strata of American society—this extension of a society's motive principle beyond the confines of a single elite group—a mere accident? Or is it intrinsic to the character of technological science as such? I have presented some considerations implying that this extension has some inner necessity about it. By breaking down authoritative belief systems and undermining the elites on which they depend, pragmatic science generates democracy. This question should next

[3] Max Lerner, "Big Technology and Neutral Technicians," *The Dilemma of Organizational Society,* H. Ruitenbeek, ed. (New York, 1963), 77f.

be discussed in terms of the dynamics of American institutions and their attitude toward democratic votes.

The development of technology (in both its research and its production aspects) is neither simple nor inexpensive. Scientific research and development can be carried on only within large, complex organizations which must be socially productive in order to sustain themselves financially. The same is true in the university world. It has been obvious since the 1940s that small and middle-size universities can no longer afford the equipment needed to attract faculties and students in the natural sciences. Over the past decade it has also become clear that even the library costs in the humanities cannot be managed within the budgetary capacities of these same universities. In the universities, as in business, the larger organizational size and complexity is necessary for the maintenance of scientific research and development. The process thus resembles a squeeze play. Those institutions that are large enough to afford scientific research are then more profitably rewarded than the institutions that cannot afford it. The rich get richer and the less rich get poorer. This explains why no organization can survive in a scientific society without sustained growth.

Many have noted how this multiplicative growth of American business corporations contrasts with corporations in Europe. The size of the American organizations enables efficiencies in research and production that allow them to be economically competitive even in nations that have much lower wage scales. We should note this correlation: American success in the development of scientific technology is a consequence of the American ability to develop and sustain large, complex social organizations. But why are Americans especially competent at this? It is not, as some may think, the mere advantage of having a large national consumer market. (It should be observed, in fact, that the ability to develop a large national consumer market is itself part of what it means to be a large, complex social organization.) Rather, many studies seem to confirm that this organizational development requires (a) the introduction of nonauthoritarian "managers" in place of "bosses," (b) the creation of democratic transactional communications to replace hierarchical patterns, and (c) the decentralization of decision-making into a plurality of centers of initiative. That is, the creation of large, complex rational societies requires that they be organized in terms of democratic values and procedures.

For example, in his studies of Latin American and European businessmen, Thomas Cochran has shown their tendency, as directors of corporate enterprises, to maintain full decision-making power in their own hands.[4] Since decisions must be made on the basis of knowledge, the size of such corporations cannot *rationally* exceed the capacity of a single directorate to assimilate relevant information. This directorate cannot rationally decide about more than he can know. This sets a limit on the maximum efficient size of his corporation. It may grow beyond this size, of course. But to the extent that it does, irrationalities are introduced into its structure and it becomes inefficient. The smaller size of European and Latin American corporations, therefore, is necessitated by a tendency toward individualistic authoritarianism.

In American enterprises, on the other hand, corporations grow larger without losing efficiency. They are able to sustain the research and development costs that enhance their competitive advantage and further their multiplicative growth. They attain this greater size without becoming irrational because they broaden their decision-making base. There is a tendency within American business for decision-making to be delegated as far down in the corporate structure as possible. In this way, many people can share responsibility for decision-making. The American director seeks to multiply the rationality of his corporation while increasing its size by relinquishing his decision-making powers to others. Leadership and initiative are thereby decentralized and dispersed throughout the social organization.

In transmitting his decision-making powers to others, the director of an American organization assumes a new role and new behavior vis-à-vis its members. Instead of telling others what to do, he enables them to decide what they should do. His job is to coordinate their decisions and initiatives and assist them to work together. In a sense, he becomes the servant of his employees—asking how he can help them to do their work together better. The ethos of

[4] "Cultural Factors in Economic Development," *The Journal of Economic History*, 20 (1960), 515–30.

management becomes democratic and equalitarian. As Slater and Bennis have observed, "In order for the spirit of inquiry, the foundation of science, to grow and flourish, a democratic environment is a necessity. Science encourages a political view that is egalitarian, pluralistic, liberal. A prominent social psychologist points out: 'Men have asked for freedom, justice, and respect precisely as science has spread among them. In short, we believe that the only way in which organizations can ensure a scientific *attitude* is by providing conditions where it can flourish. Very simply, this means democratic social conditions.' "[5] These democratic social conditions must exist wherever science is to be found—that is, in every institution within a scientific society.

A leader or director cannot, however, merely *choose* to act like a manager. He cannot merely choose to relinquish authority. One cannot give up authority or allow it to be relinquished until one has learned how to act in this way. The European, educated in a traditional society that emphasizes binary "command-obey" relationships in every social institution, is characterologically incapable of suddenly becoming a manager. For him, to relinquish authority or to accept its relinquishment leads to the disintegration of that social structure in terms of which he has defined himself and his world. A lengthy and difficult educational experience is necessary. It requires, first, the experience of being granted initiative by the one who relinquishes authority, being rewarded for speaking out honestly whenever one disagrees, discovering how to risk testing personal opinions in discussion and rational conflict, and learning to discern and contribute to the rational processes of a democratic group. Through such experiences a democratic person is formed. For example, my family has recently moved to Canada—a somewhat more traditional society than the United States. After about four months, my son commented on the fact that schools here are different. "What's different, John," I asked. "Well," he said, "for one thing, the teachers don't like it if you disagree with them." I dare not allow a single school to exemplify the entire Canadian educational system; but it is instructive that my twelve-year-old son had learned, over several years in an American school, that teachers *liked* it

[5] Bennis and Slater, *op. cit.*, 6f.

when you disagreed with them. And it is worth noting as an oddity of social history that at the same time respectable Americans were being scandalized by the revelation that corporal punishment (the switch and the ruler) was being illegally used in Boston schools, a ringing public debate was underway in Toronto about the advisability of abolishing the corporal punishment of students by teachers. Why is this debate significant? Because traditional societies, or societies organized on the basis of esoteric knowledge imputed to certain elites, must—in the last analysis—maintain the authority of those elites, when their judgments are questioned, by adverting to coercion. The switch does not need to be used to make its point. It communicates the message that the court of last resort (if the students' questioning ever exceeds the tolerance of those in authority) is coercion. Ultimately, coercion rather than consensus will be the method used for maintaining community. On the other hand, the American unwillingness to use or to condone the use of corporal punishment in schools and in families conveys a commitment to a different court of last resort: the democratic process itself. The refusal to suppress dissent as the condition of social unity is the sole way to democracy, for it forces the adoption of a noncoercive method of attaining agreement. This noncoercive method is implied in the commitment to a pragmatic-scientific attitude toward life.

Religious institutions are uniquely related to authority. An increased emphasis on democratic participation in decision-making and on responsible initiative in the ethos of management certainly lies behind the various crises in church structure. The wider and deeper influence of American science and its many feedback effects is a catalyst here.

TECHNOLOGICAL CONTROL AND
THE DIGNITY OF MAN

The unique character of American science as a democratizing sociotechnical procedure has the concomitant tendency toward the creation of new technologies. These technologies create disequilibriums within society. They raise problems pertaining to their control. The sole way to cope with the problems created by the development of these new technologies is by concomitantly extending the democratization of society. Only in this way can we create an information-gathering, decision-making, experimental base large enough to cope with the magitude of problems that will be raised. The problem of control is the problem of inventing procedures whereby the men and women affected by the new technologies can increasingly participate in decisions relating to their use and further development. *We can insure that technologies are "rightly" developed and employed for what is truly "good" only by embodying such values within the institutional procedures by which such questions are decided.* If, for example, we fear that developments in biology will destroy the dignity of man, then the best protection is to insure that the procedures determining these developments are used to protect, maintain, even enhance man's dignity. Maximizing the participation of persons in all institutional decisions affecting them protects and enhances their dignity. There is no alternative guarantor.

The process of scientific development shifts the determination of values from cosmology to community, from principles to procedures. Only the radical extension of democracy into all aspects of our society can insure that technology is rightly used. It is sometimes suggested that this is impossible—that to extend participation in decision-making further will make society too cumbersome, make order and consensus too difficult to achieve, and even be unscientific. Only in the recent past have most men believed the small degree of democracy and science we enjoy today to be impossible. The inventiveness of earlier social scientists was equal to the task of creating institutional technologies sufficient to this beginning. Now it is time for us to become inventive again. It is a time for new communitarian experiments; it is a moment for new utopians. We have been living too long on the political heritage of our ancestors. Many of the political institutions we use today were created in the seventeenth and eighteenth centuries, and few new ones have been invented in the last hundred years.

Why must we become social inventors again? Because only by inventing new institutional procedures that embody the human values we seek to maintain can the new technologies be humanely deployed. The rightness of all that we do is insured in the rightness of our deciding what is to be done. This is why a society that in its social procedures deprives members of a share in those decisions affecting their destiny can *neither rightly use its technology nor sustain the science necessary for the production of that technology.* By impeding democracy, it impedes the development of its own science. A society that seeks to develop its scientific enterprise and technologies soon finds itself confronted with the demand for greater participation in social decision-making. It is confronted with protests in behalf of the enfranchisement of its minorities. It is confronted with symbolic protests against traditional authorities and their use of coercive power. This is the crossroads at which America has arrived today.

BIBLIOGRAPHICAL EXCURSUS

Such a broad range of ideas as those presented in this essay could hardly be substantiated through the device of footnotes. These ideas should, rather, be regarded as an intellectual hypothesis intended to guide further research. This proposal is on a level of generality resembling that of Frederick Jackson Turner's essay on the frontier as a factor in American history. I recognize that its adequate vindication requires much more research in primary source materials.

It may be useful to suggest certain books that have been instrumental in shaping my reflections. For understanding the unique character of American science *qua* science, there are three figures who must be read and pondered simultaneously. First, *The New Atlantis* and *Novum Organum* of Francis Bacon. Second, the *Autobiography* of Benjamin Franklin. Third, the writings of Charles Sanders Peirce on the method and purposes of science (*Collected Papers of Charles S. Peirce* [Cambridge, 1965–67], 8 vols.). While reading these three figures, certain critical questions should be kept in mind. What does Bacon mean by "hidden causes"? What is the equivalent of this notion in Peirce's thought? How does their conception of the machine and its use differ from "mechanism"? Why is invention so highly valued and what does this imply for their notion of science? Why does Bacon speak so highly of the medieval magicians? Peirce's admiration for Bacon should be noted.

Broadening the Bacon-Franklin-Peirce base are Petrus Ramus and William Ames. Ames's *Technometria* has recently been translated and fully commentated in a Harvard doctoral thesis by Lee Wayland Gibbs entitled *The Technometry of William Ames*. The *Technometria* is *the treatise on method* of seventeenth-century New England. It has been heretofore unstudied. Robert Merton's writings on Puritanism and the Royal Society are an important secondary source.

Among twentieth-century figures, let me select five who innovate within the distinctively American tradition: Arthur Bentley, John Dewey, Norbert Wiener, Harold Lasswell, and B. F. Skinner. In their writings we see the increasing identification of the values of science with the procedures of democracy. The contemporary key to this development is (a) cybernetics and (b) teaching technologies that build on positive reinforcement alone. On cybernetics, Wiener's *The Human Use of Human Beings* (New York, 1967) and Karl Deutsch's *The Nerves of Government* (London, 1963) are basic. On developments in education, two valuable writings are George Leonard's *Education and Ecstasy* (New York, 1964) and W. Randall Huntsberry's "Learning Without Authority" in *The Religious Situation—1969* (Boston, 1969).

From a vast number of sociological studies approaching science through the notion of "democracy," I have found Warren Bennis and Philip Slater's *The Temporary Society* (New York, 1968) to be most fresh and interesting. A little known but extremely important book is *The Fraternal Society* (New York, 1963) by Richard and Hephzibah Hauser. Thomas Cochran has done pioneering work in cross-cultural economic development. A representative essay is "Cultural Factors in Economic Development," which first appeared in *The Journal of Economic History*, 20 (1960). A valuable history of scientific studies of human motivation in industrial organizations is Saul Gellerman's *Motivation and Productivity* (New York, 1968).

My understanding of authority derives in large part from Yves Simon's *Authority* (Notre Dame, 1962) and the radical criticism of his view by Robert Johann entitled "Authority and Fellowship" in *Building the Human* (New York, 1968). Equally important to me is Hannah Arendt's "What Is Authority" in *Between Past and Future* (New York, 1961). Miss Arendt shows how authority legitimates itself in terms of a society's founding event. What this means when that founding event is itself a revolt against authority —i.e., a revolution—is brilliantly analyzed in Seymour Lipset's *The First New Nation* (New York, 1963). My view of Canadian society as more elitist in its practices than American society depends more on Lipset's writings than on my son's observations.

My personal view is that science and management are better described as alternative forms of authority than as alternatives to authority. In this view I differ from C. S. Peirce, whose vocabulary in "The Fixation of Belief" (in *Values in a Universe of Change*, P. Wiener, ed. [New York, 1958]) I have used in contrasting the various methods of settling belief. It seemed to me wiser to set my disagreement on this linguistic point outside the present essay and follow the well-established, though somewhat biased usage that contrasts "authority" with "science and freedom." Certain others of my ideas—especially those on the function of religious myth and religious action in a democratic-scientific society—have also been excluded from the argument. Interested readers may consult the first three chapters of my *Toward an American Theology* (New York, 1967).

The Behavioral Sciences and Christian Ethics

✠

JOHN GILES MILHAVEN

The interchange in the future between the Judaeo-Christian ethical tradition and the explosion of information in the medical and behavioral sciences will be decisive for man's destiny. John Giles Milhaven of the Society of Jesus is Professor of Pastoral Theology at Woodstock Theological College and Lecturer in Medical Ethics at Georgetown University. He has published a number of ethical studies on natural law, contraception, situation ethics, homosexuality, and the quest for new directions in Christian ethics.

Christian ethics is the attempt to understand what Christian faith means in action. Hardly anyone would deny that American Christian ethics, Catholic and Protestant, is veering off in a new direction. To chart the direction at so early a stage in its history would be a hazardous enterprise. Even the younger theologians representative of the trend, such as Gustafson, Curran, Johann, Wassmer, Springer, would give us a consensus on very few points.[1] At the beginning of an intellectual movement, there is naturally confusion and disagreement about where it should lead. And yet there are signs that

[1] For the preparation of the present trend by an older generation, see James M. Gustafson, "Christian Ethics," *Religion*, Paul Ramsey, ed. (Englewood Cliffs, N.J., 1965), 287–354; John G. Milhaven, S.J., and David J. Casey, S.J., "Introduction to the Theological Background of the New Morality," *Theological Studies*, 28 (1967), 213–44.

the general thrust of the new direction is beginning to emerge, and that its recognition would aid its progress. With this hope (and with some trepidation) the following forecast in the form of a synthesis is offered.

It might be wise to enunciate at the start three criteria I use to judge which currents will develop and which will fade away. First, in analyzing the kind of reasoning used in current publications on moral theology, we observe the emergence of a new approach, or methodology, for reaching a moral decision. It is true that one also sees new practical conclusions (for example, on abortion, on war, on disobedience to authority)—new in the sense that they are heard from Christian thinkers of respectability and number. But logical analysis, I find, shows most of the new practical conclusions to be simply the consequences of a new basic approach to Christian ethics. This approach reveals itself as remarkably similar in quite diverse ethical thinkers and writings. The approach is often implicit, and I know of no contemporary thinker who has recognized and described it with clarity and consistency. Yet the powerful effect it exercises today in practical ethical thinking indicates it will be with us for some time and can only grow in evidence and influence.

Another criterion in this forecast is that the new approach is not a phenomenon restricted to moral theology. Rather, it corresponds to a new way of thinking by Americans in general as they enter the last third of the twentieth century. When Christians gradually adopted a natural-law moral code, they were in fact taking over a way of thinking common to the educated population of the Roman Empire. There is good evidence that Christian moralists are doing something similar today, and it argues for the continuance of the trend.

A final criterion for my projection may seem a strange one for a theologian. It is the strong popular response to this new ethical approach. It will be a strange and unconvincing reason for those who conceive of theology as a science like medicine or physics. Popular support for this or that medical or physical theory is obviously no criterion for predicting the future development of the science. But popular interest is a valid criterion for those of us who believe that developments in theology are, at their origin, new ways of understanding one's faith which come into existence among the people of God dimly and confusedly. The service of the professional theologian is never more than to articulate and clarify what is going on in the people's new understanding of Christian belief, and in that way to further its growth.

So, much of the criticism of books like *Honest to God, The Secular City,* and *Situation Ethics* is academic in the bad sense of the word.[2] To concentrate on any errors or oversimplifications found in these books is to miss the point. That two million copies of them were sold in the United States evidences their serious theological significance.[3] The significance is well expressed, I believe, by a remark I have heard several times from readers of *Honest to God.* "It's a relief to know I can think the way I have been and still be a Christian." The growing use of Louis Monden's *Sin, Liberty and Law* in college theology courses testifies similarly

---

[2] John A. T. Robinson, *Honest to God* (Philadelphia, 1963); Harvey Cox, *The Secular City* (New York, 1965); Joseph Fletcher, *Situation Ethics* (Philadelphia, 1966).

[3] In writings from the last years of his life, collected in *Ethics* (New York, 1959) and *Letters and Papers from Prison* (New York, 1963), Dietrich Bonhoeffer developed the new ethical approach in a radical, provocative form. In England and America, unlike the Continent, it was the ethical import of the latter book, its implications for life and action, that drew attention (see Eberhard Bethge's foreword in the edition cited above). John Godsey reports that the English-language editions account for the majority of the 300,000 copies of the latter book that were sold by 1967 (John D. Godsey, "Reading Bonhoeffer in English Translations: Some Difficulties," in *Bonhoeffer in a World Come of Age* [Philadelphia, 1968], 123). Bonhoeffer was, of course, a Continental thinker, and my point here is simply that the widespread American interest in the ethical import of his final writings argues for something similar going on today in the United States. One recalls, however, that Bonhoeffer spent the hot evening of June 19, 1939, walking up and down Times Square, painfully coming to the decision to refuse the new work in America planned for him by friends such as Reinhold Niebuhr and to return to Germany and share the life of his people. If he had chosen to stay, he might have become an "American" theologian in the sense that Paul Tillich did. But would he have evolved his revolutionary theology? It was the decision to return to Germany and his experience in the "secular" activity he took up there that are reflected in his ethical writings and best explain the final, radical turn of his thought. (Cf. Eberhard Bethge, "Turning Points in Bonhoeffer's Life and Thought," in *Bonhoeffer in a World Come of Age. ed. cit.*)

to the growing popularity of the new approach.[4] So, too, the downgrading of code morality in high-school catechetics and the prominence given there to Christian love and social responsibility. One who listens to after-lecture questions and discussions around the country has to be struck by similar new ways of thinking about moral questions, especially among the younger members of the audience. That this way of thinking exists presently in an inchoate and groping state renders all the more striking the similarity and simultaneity of its appearance throughout the country.

There is, of course, a strong negative response by many Christians (and not merely older Christians) to the new approach. But they seem to be those who, not merely in ethical thinking, but along all lines, oppose the new trends of Christian thought and action. Without belittling their sincerity or intelligence or the value of the old way, it is hard to believe that the future belongs to them.

A NEW METHODOLOGY

What, then, is the new ethical approach which the above three criteria would identify as indicating the future of American Christian ethics? One characteristic is its methodology. The new methodology springs from a new theological vision of Christian life. Such theology is different from the theology generating the methodology of natural-law ethics, just as it is different from the fundamentalist theology that generated a good deal of American Protestant ethics. Each reacting against their own traditions, the Catholic and Protestant ethicists are effecting a confluence. Despite divergences of formulation and real theological differences, they have arrived at a common theological basis for their ethics.

Christ's love received by the Christian and made his own, remains at the heart of Christian life; it grounds the new Christian ethics as it did the best of the old. But in keeping with contemporary thinking, "love" means something new. Love is no longer basically a trusting submission that searches out God's universal

[4] Louis Monden, S.J., *Sin, Liberty and Law* (New York, 1965).

137

laws for human behavior and institutions, confident that with obedience to the laws everything will turn out well for all concerned.[5] Rather, the new trend sees God leaving it completely up to man as to how things turn out. Christian "love," therefore, comes to mean that a man takes from God into his own hands all responsibility for what happens. It is up to him, not God, to figure out what will be good for those concerned and how this good can be realized, just as it is up to him, not God, to act and make the good a reality. In this sense, it can be said that the new Christian love proceeds as it would *etsi deus non daretur*, even if there were no God. The slogans have quickly become worn, but some are still apt. Facing his responsibility, the Christian sees himself "having come of age" and now "condemned to freedom."

As theology follows the way of American thinking today, the contemporary vision of Christian responsibility is pragmatic and empirical. Responsibility means reponsibility for consequences as they take place in human experience. Consequently, a pragmatic and empirical methodology is engendered. The methodology is pragmatic in that it looks solely to consequences in order to assess morally a given action. It is empirical in that it looks solely to experience in order to predict consequences and to evaluate them.[6] The result is that it comes to rely more and more upon the behavioral sciences. Despite sundry limitations—some inherent in the objectives and methodology of the particular science, some

[5] A classic example of the view that can reduce certain moral obligations to such blind obedience is Germain G. Grisez, *Contraception and the Natural Law* (Milwaukee, 1964). A good example of contemporary questioning of such moral absolutes is Charles E. Curran's *Absolutes in Moral Theology?* (Washington, 1968).

[6] I suspect that Robert Johann might disagree with some of my presentation, but his *Building the Human* (New York, 1968), a collection of essays that appeared over a period of several years in *America,* impresses me as one of the most lucid and valuable philosophical expositions of the "pragmatic" and "empirical" tenor of the new approach. It is a sign of the times that in the writings of one man, such as Johann or Charles Curran, we see the transition from the old to the new way of ethical thinking. Forces in the evolution of Johann's thought were American thinkers such as John Dewey, H. Richard Niebuhr, and Paul Tillich, although he also owes a good deal to Gabriel Marcel.

due to the present state of research in the particular field—the behavioral sciences offer a unique and relatively well-grounded survey of the data of experience. The increasing and fundamental use Christian ethics is making, and will make, of the behavioral sciences, illustrates well its new methodology and will serve as the leitmotif of the present essay.[7]

Nevertheless, an adequate theological basis for the methodology and its use of the behavioral sciences is not reached just by recognizing that God has promulgated no moral code for man but has left him alone with responsibility for human history. An opposite question necessarily arises. How *is* God relevant to man's ethical decision? In what way has Christ's coming transformed human life and history, if man is still left with sole responsibility for it? What importance remains for Christ in Christian ethics, when man simply looks to consequences as they would take place in experience in order to decide what to do? If a homosexual's moral obligation is simply to follow the advice of the psychologist, how does Christ have any relevance for "Christian" ethics?

The question of the relevancy of Christ is rendered more acute by the secularity of the new theology. With Irenaeus, it says, "God's glory is a living man." But unlike Irenaeus, it would not go on to say, "and human life is the vision of God." Contemporary ethicists would not necessarily deny this, nor would they deny that a person's afterlife with God is the fulfillment and continuation of his human life and history. But they refrain generally from making belief in an afterlife pertinent to Christian decision in the world. This world and this life have to be dealt with on their own terms and for themselves. The emphasis on secularity gives further impetus for Christian ethics to turn to surveys of human experience found in the behavioral sciences. But it also augments the problem of relevancy. If our being with Christ after death is not relevant to Christian ethics, in what way is Christ relevant?

---

[7] One could illustrate other aspects of contemporary Christian ethics by the use the ethical makes of other forms of communicating experience, such as phenomenology or the arts. One example of this would be the interacting influence going on today—in writing, lectures, and discussion—between ethics and the science of the film.

The thinkers of the new trend wrestle with this question. It dominates James Gustafson's *Christ and the Moral Life* and Robert Johann's *The Pragmatic Meaning of God,* as well as the writings of Cox, Robinson, and Bonhoeffer.[8] Present-day pastoral experience of American Catholics suggests that the question does not preoccupy only theologians. If we are tired of the question of "relevance," it may be because we have not yet answered it adequately. Moreover, I tend to agree with drama critic Clive Barnes who writes that "a truism has to be true to be a truism, and behind every cliché lies a thought not only promiscuous, but immortal."

Today's theologians try to develop in different ways how Christ is relevant to Christian ethics. They all make the point that belief in Jesus Christ not only does not conflict with man's this-world responsibility, pragmatically and empirically conceived, but confirms this responsibility, giving man strength and light to carry it out. Christ does not merely not prevent the Christian from turning to human experience, but Christ sends him there and is there with him.

The explanations for this vary, yet have a common drift. The relevance of Christ to man's ethical responsibility is seen by many theologians simply as one example of the relevance of Christ to man's secularity in general. In this connection, we should recall that the genial synthesis of Teilhard de Chardin which has found such resonance in this country has not yet been brought to bear on Christian ethics. Would it not offer a rich theological grounding of the relevance of Christ for ethical responsibility in the current conception of man and his world? In particular, the recurring theme of

---

[8] James M. Gustafson, *Christ and the Moral Life* (New York, 1968); Robert O. Johann, *The Pragmatic Meaning of God* (Milwaukee, 1966). One exception among contemporary ethicists is Joseph Fletcher, who in his *Situation Ethics* and his *Moral Responsibility: Situation Ethics at Work* (Philadelphia, 1967) gives only limited attention to the question of the relevance of the Christian faith for ethics. Gustafson's book is particularly illuminating, since he surveys the views of many theologians on the question, before presenting his own. A good number of the thinkers he treats are from the twentieth century, either representative of the current trend or having prepared the way for it, e.g., Barth, Bonhoeffer, Bultmann, Lehmann, the two Niebuhrs, and Sittler.

Teilhard, the significance of Christ for the scientist in his labors, could be applied to the ethicist in his use of the behavioral sciences.

Much of the new theological grounding of ethics understands responsibility as response. The Good News of Jesus Christ is that God is with us in the world calling us to love: God wills that we work in the concrete situation here and now for our own and each other's fuller humanity. By accepting our solitary, pragmatic responsibility, by employing an empirical methodology, by striving for this-worldly goals, we are responding to God's concrete will for us.

> The reality of our responsiveness to God will be the humanity of our dealings with one another. It is only as working always for a fuller realization of the ideal of community that we are truly responsive to Him. Far, then, from restricting us to the actual shape of things, God's presence in our life is what continually calls us to move beyond where we are. We cannot rest until we have done all that we can to make love prevail in our world.[9]

In the Christian tradition moral responsibility was always response to God. But the theological understanding of the nature of this response has changed, and the implications of this change for moral responsibility are profound. Responsibility in sexual matters, for example, is no longer a response to God's detailed law found in the Bible or in nature, but rather to human experience, as it is reported by the behavioral sciences; the Christian consults them under God's mandate.

One element in my interpretation of the newer theological foundation for ethics would be contested by many contemporary ethicists. Christian faith reveals a radically new dimension of human life, but, as I presented it, it alters in no way the secular, humanistic dimensions. The Christian dimension reinforces the value and importance of being a fully secular man, but it in no way changes what this means. This is why all ethical goals (except for the sphere of man's direct relationship with God, such as faith itself, church life, prayer) are totally secular and all ethical methodology is totally empirical. As a result, Christian ethics is in no way different from

9 Johann, *op. cit.*, 65.

a pure humanism in the specific obligations to which it concludes. I submit that this is the direction in which the new trend is going, but some contemporary ethicists within this trend, especially from Protestant traditions, would contest the affirmation of total secularity and the denial of any distinctiveness of Christian ethics as to specific goals, methodology, and concrete moral obligations. The question is too complex to discuss here. In any case, when the ethicists in question explain what is really distinctive in Christian ethics, it does not seem to me to exclude what I present as its totally secular and empirical methodology. Rather, it leads to it!

MULTILEVELED MAN

The theological foundation contemporary ethicists provide, grounds an ethical methodology which is pragmatic and empirical, characterized by its use of human experience collated and analyzed in the behavioral sciences. Now we must probe the methodology itself and see consequences it brings about in the new ethics. Moral decision itself is now understood in the light of the contemporary social and behavioral sciences.[10] When man is seen as a multileveled being, the same decision has a different reality at different depths. Christian ethics is just starting to assimilate a scientific understanding of man that some time ago won acceptance in intellectual circles and that has even passed into an habitual way of popular thinking. Americans automatically assess decisions on different levels. A man decides to buy a new car. Superficially, he seems to himself and to his neighbors only to be choosing something of practical and aes-

[10] Behavioral scientists will hopefully pardon the vast oversimplification inevitable in an attempt to synthesize briefly the impact of the behavioral sciences upon ethics. Under the label "attitudes," I will be including what at times might better be termed "tendencies" or "myths," "cultural values" or "drives," "compulsions" or "habits," etc. What seems to be common to all the behavioral sciences is their effort to trace out empirically factors of human behavior that are most useful in predicting personal decisions. They are only simply conscious, if at all, and enjoy a certain permanence in affecting the person. This is what is meant, for convenience of terminology, by the word "attitudes" in the following pages.

thetic value. Yet anyone, including the man himself and his neighbor, knows that a stronger and more decisive motive for the man might be one that springs from an inferiority complex or from an outer-directed orientation that needs the approval of the group. He may really be choosing the support of his ego through display. Psychology, sociology, and anthropology have established that at deeper levels a man often chooses something different from what he chooses on the explicit conscious level. The multileveled view has passed into the clichés and truisms of our time, but only now is moral theology beginning to grasp the implications. One example might be the conduct of two students in the face of an organized sit-in. One chooses to participate, the other refuses. On the conscious level, the former is choosing to protest some injustice, the latter to make studies and the pursuit of his career his primary concern. Yet on a deeper level, the first student may be motivated far more by a deep hostility to all authority. The actions of authority regularly infuriate him, and he regularly chooses to oppose them. The fact of social injustice is irrelevant to his decision at the deeper level. If the university authorities had chosen on their own initiative to call on the students to work for the elimination of the injustice, this student would have had no interest and would probably have found reasons for criticizing the initiative of those in authority.

The second student might have been choosing, on the deeper level and for the thousandth time, to conform to authority rather than think for himself. In other words, it is not his career as primary concern that he is choosing, but the security that comes from being on the side of authority. What both students choose at the deeper level is to express their basic attitudes toward authority. In one case it is blind hostility; in the other, blind submission.

Any educated person today could suggest the above example. A psychiatrist would probe deeper. For him it would be possible that both attitudes regarding authority, opposite though they seem to be, really arise from the same fundamental stance: fear. Because the one is profoundly terrified of authority, he continually chooses, in panic, to attack. Because the other is equally terrified of authority, he continually chooses unconditional surrender. The above analysis leads to and demands a different moral judgment than the data of explicit consciousness. The key moral question for the two students (and for those counseling them) becomes not to what extent should a person be involved in social issues and to what extent should a person prepare his career, not when to resist authority and when to obey, but how to find and take at the deepest level an inner stance with respect to authority—a stance not based on fear but on a sense of one's own personal dignity and of the true function and value of authority. The key moral question for the students is, therefore, What is this stance and how can we achieve it? This question is the central moral question because the deeper psychological attitudes are what *consistently* determine the life of the person. To speak of deeper attitudes is simply to use a spatial metaphor that expresses the greater influence these psychological attitudes have on the decisions of a person and on his actions and life. Since the central question of morality is what a man ought to do, its central concern must be to form the attitudes through which what he does will be Christian action.

The determining attitudes in the students could be different from the attitudes suggested. The student who protests injustice might also at the deepest level simply be choosing to do precisely that. But if so, it probably arises from some basic attitude like sympathy for the oppressed. The student's present decision to protest is not as morally crucial as the process over the years which led to his now abiding sensitivity to injustice. This makes him the kind of person he now is, someone who acts the way he now does. The major battleground of life, therefore, is the "depths" where the attitudes are found which determine most decisions. If, for example, promiscuous sexual behavior is often an expression of a personal discontent with one's own sex, the discontent is a more important moral problem than the promiscuity and demands, more urgently, understanding and help.

A multilevel view of man's decision-making relocates the consequences toward which the Christian strives. In an ethics that advocates a solely pragmatic responsibility for consequences, the implication is far-reaching. The consequences now identified as prime ethical goals are those within the person himself, i.e., attitudes making him the kind of person who acts consistently in a good way. Correspondingly, there is now a serious moral obligation to work for similar consequences in other persons. The moral injustice of racism, for example, arises ultimately not from some absolute right to be treated as a man regardless of race, but ultimately from the fact that current racist practices engender or preserve in men of the demeaned race inner attitudes of shame, alienation, and hostility, and so thwart them from fully becoming men. Their right to develop in the depths and core of their person is what determines their right to just and human treatment. When social scientists note that in the United States forms of Black Power are among the more effective means of educing the sense of personal dignity lacking in many black Americans, then white and black Christians have a paramount obligation to encourage forms of Black Power. Since racial integration is not of absolute obligation, if the blacks on a certain campus should request racial segregation in dormitories and courses in order to aid their inner development, then that would be ethically obligatory in that situation. From this new point of view, the authorities of a university do not meet the ethical demands of racial justice simply by accepting black students without discrimination.

Besides their determinative influence on most of man's decisions and actions, there is a second reason why sound basic attitudes in oneself and in others become significant consequences for which the Christian should strive. The attitudes themselves do not constitute intrinsically the highest value for the new ethics. The supreme value, the absolute value that is the source of all other human values, is what the ethicist, borrowing from contemporary philosophy, describes as the unique "I": It is core freedom, the self as self-creating. Now, the basic attitudes of a person are key forces in restricting or favoring the inner freedom. A compulsive personality will be far less able to exercise his unique self-creativity than a person who possesses a basic self-confidence. Furthermore, although the self-created is primarily the self of the moment (the act of self-creation and the self-created are one), still it is also (and this is important) the self which perdures, both the self that is me and the self that I may be molding in others. An important part of a person is "who he is": the constellation of ongoing attitudes that make him the kind of person he is. How the attitudes make up the person is also evoked by the spatial metaphors of "depth" and "core."

The profound shame, alienation, and hostility of a black American is, therefore, a moral outrage for two reasons. Such emotional attitudes restrict his inner life of freedom, of personal self-possession and self-making. Secondly, with the inner freedom, they have the intrinsic value of creating or deforming the ongoing self of man. To commit hateful actions regularly is bad enough, but it does not come near the moral tragedy of having become a hating person. Within the limits of this essay we cannot develop further the value philosophy of freedom and selfhood, or show how it fuses well with the new theological foundation of ethics discussed above. It focuses the moral obligation of forming sound basic attitudes in oneself and in others and thereby reinforces the role of the behavioral sciences in ethics as they identify and illuminate these inner forces that control the person. Parenthetically, it is not clear how completely new the methodology of the behavioral sciences and their multileveled view of man is. Analogies with the scholastic theory of habits, virtues, and vices come readily to mind. And the ancient and medieval thinkers occasionally anticipated the methodology and findings of the modern behavioral sciences. The uniqueness of the sciences in their present state lies in their awareness of their own methodology, their purifying it of foreign elements, their carrying it out with concentrated efficiency, and, as a result, their gleaning of a vast and wide-ranging knowledge of human behavior. It is not surprising, then, that whatever the novelty *in principle* of the methodology of the behavioral sciences and their multileveled view of man, moral theology is *in fact* changing and will continue to change as it integrates them into its inquiry.[11]

We saw that one change was the location of the results toward which the Christian ought to strive at deeper levels within the person. New goals however introduce further changes in ethics concerning the means to be followed. Obviously, one necessary means is the discernment of a given person's basic attitudes. But they are not easy to discern. They are not conscious in the ordinary sense of the word. They can become clearly conscious, as a counselor, for example, will often try to effect. And in a sense the person has always known of them. Freud said that the sign of a successful completion of therapy would be the cry of the patient, "I always

[11] Pioneering in this respect is Robert Springer, S.J. See "Notes on Moral Theology," *Theological Studies*, 28 (1967), 308–35; 29 (1968), 275–300.

knew it." Even popular reading of psychology or sociology can bring us to realize emotional patterns that have gone on for years in a dimly conscious state, although we have never adverted to them. I now can experience clearly, let us say, the pang of anxiety I have always felt in speaking with persons of authority.

And yet the personal attitudes that make a man act in a given way are normally not clearly conscious. Nor is this the only difficulty in discussing them. Neither can they be inferred from the behavior in a simple, obvious way. The old moralist could presuppose that the man who regularly performed unchaste or unjust or gluttonous acts was acting from a habit of unchastity or injustice or gluttony. A direct correspondence presupposed between behavior and habit made it easy for the moralist to conclude from the evident behavior to the virtues and vices behind it. Incidentally, it also left him free to focus his inquiry on the morality of individual acts and not on virtues and vices, though he might admit that virtues and vices were in some ways more important in a man's moral life than the isolated acts.

With the acceptance of the contemporary understanding of man, the new ethics knows it cannot interpret so simply such patterns of behavior as those mentioned above. An unmarried girl may be sexually promiscuous mainly because of hostility toward her mother. A thief from a slum area may steal mainly out of need to prove his manhood. A man may overeat and overdrink because of anxiety. In brief, the basic attitudes that determine human behavior are difficult to discern not merely because we are usually not conscious of them, but also because they cannot be always and certainly inferred from the resulting behavior. The behavior does not correspond to them in a direct and obvious way, at least not to the eyes of the layman. The old moral questions (How often did I tell a certain lie? How often did I commit adultery?) could be easily answered. But not the new questions that are now interpreted as the important ones. Am I going to Mass out of my abiding faith in Christ and his community? Or do I go out of a need to conform socially and be respectable? The radical character of the new problematic is illustrated by Karl Rahner's "unbelieving believer." The man thinks he is a good Christian, possessing faith, hope, and charity. In fact, in his depths, he has never turned to God; his fundamental posture is concerned with self, not at all with anyone else, much less God. He is an atheist. A more easily recognizable case in the same ethical area is the young man who encounters recurrent temptations to doubt his faith. He yields to the temptations. He continues to lead an active Christian life, but wonders whether he believes at all. He is prepared to become an agnostic if this state of affairs continues. What should he do? Perhaps what lies behind his doubts are acute drives toward promiscuous sexual behavior. He doubts his faith because his faith condemns what he wants to do. On this hypothesis, his doubting is blameworthy because he is facing squarely neither the moral question of sexual behavior nor the moral question of believing. He will justify his sexual conduct by his agnosticism. The reasons for condemning sexual promiscuity are now gone. The real reason for his agnosticism is to obtain sexual license. However, what could lie behind his doubts is that he has chosen, for the first time in his life, to take Christ and his faith seriously. He wants to adopt an honest, responsible position in this regard. He finds he can do it only if he admits his doubts, accepts them, and lives with them for a while. In this hypothesis, his doubting is praiseworthy; it is at least a necessary symptom of something fine he is doing.

The difficulty of discerning basic, personal attitudes behind external behavior affects ethical methodology in several ways. Negatively, it warns against unqualified generalizations about many moral questions, e.g., against declaring from the pulpit or podium that all doubts against faith should be put away or resisted. Positively, it requires the counselor (and the person being counseled) to know well the whole person before giving ethical advice on a given problem. Again, the example of doubting one's faith illustrates the point. The difficulty of discerning attitudes behind personal behavior sometimes requires the knowledge of the professional—the psychiatrist, the trained counselor, or the social worker. Some general principles of psychology or the social sciences are not difficult to understand or to apply, although in applying psychological or sociological principles to individual cases, a little knowledge can be a dangerous thing. A knowledge of some of the hidden forces at work in the average adolescent can be communicated without great difficulty to teachers and parents and even to the adolescent. All of this is common knowledge, of course, but the point is that the acquisition and use of such knowledge are seen by the new ethics as matters of moral obligation.

THE BASES OF ETHICAL OBLIGATION

Since Christian ethics recognizes as its primary obligation the strengthening or modification or rechanneling of these determinants of behavior, the behavioral sciences have not only the role of identifying them, but the role of indicating how to deal with basic attitudes once they are discovered. The pragmatic, empirical bias of the new ethics turns it to the experience of the behavioral sciences in order to learn how to bring about the consequences it desires; i.e., given the psychic, social, and cultural forces at work in a particular person, how does the Christian ethical word lead him to be healthier, more mature, and more loving? Christian ethics learns its principles from Carl Rogers or Hans Morgenthau, from Lester Kirkendall or Margaret Mead. It recognizes an obligation to do *something* about the drug addict, the alcoholic, the alienated married couple, the casualties of war, the homosexual, the aged. But to do *something*, the Christian has to turn to professional experience. The behavioral sciences are, of course, not the only source of such experience. The social worker, Alcoholics Anonymous, Saul Alinsky, Dr. Spock, the marriage counselor, the educator, can all give practical advice drawn from their experience of actually doing something for people as well as from their communication with others engaged in the same professional field. It is not new that a fusion of professional training and experience can provide useful advice. What *is* new is that it is seen as determining moral obligations. What *ought* a homosexual to do? What his psychiatrist tells him to do. This presupposes that he has good reasons for trusting the judgment of the psychiatrist and that following his advice does not threaten serious harm to others. But since the new Christian ethics holds no absolute moral principles, even in the sexual domain, the goals it envisages for human conduct, the kind of person the Christian should make of himself, does not differ essentially from

149

the goals of a good psychiatrist. And the psychiatrist is likelier to know what the homosexual can do to draw nearer to those goals.

Similarly, there will be a moral obligation in given situations to avail oneself of the techniques or treatments elaborated by the sciences to modify and redirect the forces behind behavior. Professional counseling, psychotherapy, psychoanalysis, rehabilitation of drug addicts and alcoholics are already common in America. Now we are beginning to appreciate useful applications of group dynamics such as T-groups and sensitivity sessions.

It might be accurate to say that someday there will no longer be a "moral theologian" or a "Christian ethicist." As scientific experience is integrated into the theology of ethics, there will no longer be anyone who can enunciate pertinent principles on a wide spectrum of moral problems in the manner of a John Ford, Francis Connell, or Gerald Kelly. There will only be ethical specialists for given areas, such as race relations, student-faculty relationships, business ethics, child-rearing. (This will hopefully have the added advantage of removing sexual ethics from the domain of celibates.) These ethical specialists will need extensive formation in the pertinent behavioral sciences or in other professional fields. The purely theological elements of Christian ethics are the most important, but also—if we can speak of theological and intellectual understanding in a quantified way—the fewest in number. In order to be able to indicate usefully some ethical obligations concerning the drug addict or the high-school principal or the politician, the ethical specialist needs to have spent much more time studying secular sciences and gaining secular experience than studying theology. This is undoubtedly one reason why contemporary Christian ethicists, on the whole, restrict themselves to foundational questions or to the description of general goals, such as racial equality, peace, or conjugal love. They do not presume to spell out, for example, concrete ethical responsibilities of husband and wife. They have neither the competence nor the time to glean from the reports of sociologists, psychologists, doctors, marriage counselors, and married people what effective forms conjugal love can take in the light of the differing physiological and psychological make-up of the human male and female, the social pressures of our time, and the influence of our culture.

Correspondingly, the average Christian will find it neither possible nor necessary to make frequent use of professional treatment or advice in order to form or reform personal attitudes. However, if the Christian educates himself to some degree in the knowledge at hand, he can apply certain things to his own situation. Moreover, he can learn one truth that applies to all situations, namely, that deeper, more influential attitudes can be changed only slowly. They form, like glaciers, little by little over the years; they can be changed only in the same slow, gradual way. A good deal of the formation and change is independent of the person's own free choice. Opinions differ widely about the extent to which a person can freely mold the attitudes which determine the kind of life he leads. Moral theologians influenced by existentialism tend to accord a large place for man's freedom to create himself, to *make* himself into the kind of person he is. The proponents of the "basic option" theory appear to share this optimistic view of human freedom.[12] American moral theology, as it is influenced by the behavioral sciences, probably will see human freedom as a spark, affecting only in small part

[12] The "basic option" theology owes its origin in part to the multileveled view of psychology, and by this route the behavioral sciences may have their greatest impact on Christian ethics, since this theology affects radically practical questions such as mortal sin and return to the state of grace. I have not discussed this theory at all in the present essay, partly because it is still a raw Continental import (its main exponents, to my knowledge, are still European thinkers like Karl Rahner, Johannes B. Metz, and Louis Monden), and partly because the minimum adequate presentation of the theory (along with its undergirding of transcendental philosophy and existentialism, and its manifold practical ramifications) would require an article in itself. A useful introduction in English is Louis Monden's *Sin, Liberty and Law* or, briefer and yet much to the point as far as it goes, John W. Glaser's "Transition Between Grace and Sin: Fresh Perspectives," *Theological Studies*, 29 (1968), 260–74. The theory illustrates the fruitfulness of reconciling existentialist thought and modern science. James Collins has reminded us that in contrast to existentialism, the other existentialist, the late Karl Jaspers, devoted his life in thought and action to reconciling, on the one hand, human values, and, on the other, "a world increasingly organized around scientific methods and technology." Jaspers' own self-professed philosophizing began when he realized, as a practicing and lecturing psychiatrist, that "he had been speaking philosophical prose all along, but that his discourse was set in a new register and hence had gone undetected even by himself." "Karl Jaspers: A Tribute," *America*, 120 (1969), 328–30.

the operative determinisms of human life—although the spark of self-creating will remain the most important and precious part of human life. Practically, although the behavioral sciences do not deny human freedom, their data indicate that any efforts to change basic attitudes will be, at best, partial and gradual in effectiveness. This underscores the Christian's need to find in his faith a light and strength that helps him to accept himself peacefully, despite his abiding weakness and continuing failures. Protestant ethicists, influenced by the original Reformation experience, have contributed more toward meeting this need than have their Catholic colleagues.

There is some resistance in American churches to the way the behavioral sciences are transforming and, in good part, constituting the methodology of Christian ethics. Some of the resistance is a justified reaction to the sciences' being applied to ethical problems without due regard for their limits. They are far from infallible; in fact, by nature they are always tentative and subject to revision. On many important questions, diverse schools cannot reach a consensus. Nor can the generalizations that are agreed upon be applied to individual cases with anything like the rigor and certainty of the old moral principles. Furthermore, the generalizations of the behavioral sciences are never in themselves statements about morality or objective value. Much of the current resistance, however, to the use of behavioral sciences in ethics does not arise from their misuse. It arises rather from a general dissatisfaction, often vague and undefined, with the ethical import of using these sciences. The objection runs: We can and should use the behavioral sciences more, but this is not morality! In presenting the theological and philosophical bases of the new ethical methodology, I hope I have met this objection. By way of conclusion, I would like to reply from a different point of view.

We can state the objection differently: What good comes of attributing moral obligation to empirical methods and to the use of the behavioral sciences? Modern Americans use them anyway and need no urging to do so. The issue is not what good comes from it, but whether a moral obligation is really there. But the objection can be profitably met on its own terms. A great deal of good can come from recognizing our moral obligation to use contemporary empirical methods and sciences. Moral obligation comes to the

Christian from Christ himself, and if he is open to Christ, he energizes and encourages him to do the actions necessary. And as much as Americans take them for granted, Christians do need energy and courage, not to use sciences in general but to use them to fulfill responsibilities we do not like to face: toward the old and the problem child, toward the rebellious student and the poor, toward our own weaknesses. Bringing the sciences to bear on moral responsibility, Christian ethics will contribute in a new and important way to American Christian life.

Language in a New World

✠

JAMES M. ROBINSON

Contemporary life revolves around language, from coded signals guiding unmanned probes to Mars to verbalized interactions shaping and expressing human life. Through his work in the New Testament, Professor Robinson was led to study the problems of hermeneutic and language. In order to break down the "translation gap" between Europe and America, he coedits the series New Frontiers in Theology. He is Professor of Religion at Claremont Graduate School and a member of the Institute for Antiquity and Christianity there. He heads an international team working on the publication of the Coptic manuscripts found at Nag Hammadi.

At the time of the American Revolution, leading Roman Catholic theology existed mainly in the Latin world (especially France), and Protestant theology was largely British. For those of us accustomed to think in terms of the hegemony of German theology, it is a liberating experience to trace the roots of many a scholarly specialty regarded as distinctively German back to its French or British beginnings. One may recall that the Graf-Wellhausen theory of Pentateuch sources goes back to the Frenchman Jean Astruc, and that the Strauss-Bultmann mythological tradition goes back to the Oxford scholar and bishop Robert Lowth. When one thinks of the German quest of the historical Jesus "from Reimarus to Wrede," one's imagination may be kindled by the thought of the Jeffersonian

Bible, a scissors-and-paste job on the Gospels in the most *avant-garde* Enlightenment tradition by the resident inventor at Monticello.

To be sure, one does not wish to advocate an "Americanism" such as the papacy condemned in 1899, any more than one would advocate the "German Christian" church for which German Protestantism repented after World War II. "American" theology is as suspect of nationalism as is "black" theology of racism. To make light of their dangerous potentialities would merely expose one as prejudiced, in assuming that the chauvinistic groups in this case were harmlessly inferior. If German theology renders no other service in the era of American hegemony than to draw attention to its own burnt fingers, it will have rendered an invaluable service. Yet, in an age when internationalism has time on its side, and when Bayer Aspirin may be replaced by International Business Machines as the symbol of international wares, international theology may not only become an American export as well as import, but there may even be a favorable balance of trade.

A MEETING PLACE FOR LANGUAGE-THEORIES

Language has been the medium of philosophy and theology for millennia. But only in modern times has this "medium" itself become the "message," in that the study of language has become the subject matter of these disciplines. We may well wonder how such a development could be possible, when we consider language as the means not the end, the form not the substance. But in the case of theology, such a dichotomy had in principle long since been transcended, even in traditional theological views. The word of God is itself the revelation; revelation is man's contact with God; and this contact is man's transcendence, or authenticity, the goal of life.

This material understanding of language inherent in the concept of the *verbum Domini* has more recently taken the variant forms of a Barthian theology of the word and a Bultmannian kerygmatic theology. The latter led via demythologization into a more direct confrontation with language as such, in the development toward a "new hermeneutic." In the case of philosophy, there has been a plurality of strands, each going largely its separate way. One direction they all have shared has been the move from the European continent toward America.

Ernst Cassirer's *Philosophy of Symbolic Forms,* imbedded in the German academic tradition (three volumes, plus index volume), was imported in the form of Cassirer himself (1941–45), and was Americanized by Susanne K. Langer, who served both as translator of such popular works as his *Language and Myth,* and as author of her own *Philosophy in a New Key.* This understanding of language as symbol has become indigenous in American theology in such works as John A. Hutchison's *Language and Faith: Studies in Sign, Symbol and Meaning* (1968).

Ludwig Wittgenstein was, like Cassirer, a German-Jewish philosopher; indeed, both were central Europeans, Cassirer originating in what is now Poland, Wittgenstein in Austria. But whereas Cassirer left Germany only with the rise of Hitler, and moved rapidly via Oxford and Sweden to America, Wittgenstein moved to England (Cambridge) in 1929, where he died a British citizen. Yet his influence, in the form of logical positivism and linguistic analysis, made its way rapidly across the Atlantic to become the dominant philosophy, if not of the nation, at least of most philosophy departments. The impact on theology in this country has been considerable, most provocatively in Paul M. van Buren's *The Secular Meaning of the Gospel Based on an Analysis of Its Language* (1963).

Martin Heidegger has remained in his native Germany, and was influential outside that language area primarily as an originator of modern existentialism. More recently, the "turn" in his thought has led him to focus on language, as his *Unterwegs zur Sprache* (1959) indicates. The influence of this "later" Heidegger on theology was mediated through German theologians seeking to move beyond Bultmann, and was introduced into American theology by the first two volumes of the *New Frontiers in Theology* series, on *The Later Heidegger and Theology* (1963) and *The New Hermeneutic* (1964), and, in philosophically more comprehensive fashion, by William J. Richardson, S.J., in *Heidegger: Through Phenomenology to Thought* (1963).

One of the vital issues facing theology in the coming generation is whether these various philosophies and theologies of language can come into dialogue with sufficient rapidity and clarity to produce a coherent understanding of theological language. If such a meeting takes place, it will probably be in America. For these strands of language philosophy did not meet philosophically or theologically in their native Europe. Indeed, they hardly entered seriously into dialogue with each other as contemporaries. But they have become contemporary with each other in their American Indian summer.

Of course, any such coherent merger of these strands would be in terms of the alchemy of American culture. The effect of the largely American science of linguistics has not yet become clearly discernible in American theology. But as it works "down" via philosophy into theology, it may be met with a movement "up" from its impact on the understanding of New Testament Greek and thus on exegesis, somewhat as computer "languages" are beginning to work their way into the exegetical side of theology, with inevitable but hardly foreseeable consequences not only for method but also for the philosophical presuppositions of theology as a whole.

HISTORY AND INTERPRETATION

Such a development in terms of understandings of language would take place at a propitious moment in the history of hermeneutics. When humanistic learning, following the Renaissance, became a science, its first emphasis was the science of philology, the study of the classic texts surviving from the past. Hermeneutics was its methodology, the effort to set up the canons for correctly interpreting such foreign texts. But philology led to historiography, seeking to establish the historical matrix in which the text was written and by which it was to be interpreted, as well as attempting to reconstruct the historical facts to which many classic texts refer in conflicting versions. Hence, hermeneutics was gradually replaced by the critical-historical method as the means for understanding the religious tradition. Yet successive generations of "objective" historians produced a series of diverging reconstructions, and the divergence was not simply the gradual shift due to the cumulation of more data and new analyses. Rather, the divergences were directly correlated to the theological and ideological shifts taking place in Western civilization. It became painfully apparent that the "objective" and "disinterested" historians were the heirs to the "subjective" and "prejudiced" theologians they thought they were refuting and replacing. The scientists' own historicity came to consciousness.

This discovery was comparable to that in modern physics, in that the scientific access to the object is an ingredient in the total situation reflected in the scientific results. The results are not simply a reflection of the object in and of itself, but of the situation of the experiment: the object as conditioned by the scientific access to it. Yet if the object remains closed in a black box, and we have to do only with phenomena, symptoms resulting from experimentation, it is inappropriate to consider the object as real reality and the symptoms as a deficient mode of reality. And there is even less validity in regarding method as objective in neat distinction from subjective, when the method we construct for analyzing the object conditions the results to such an extent that a different method attains different results, without in every case thereby disproving the relative validity of the first method and its conclusions. Obviously, science, and therefore theology as an academic discipline, functions in terms of an overarching reality including "subject," and "object," and the "method" of communication between them. The effect of such considerations is that "language," the medium of communication between "subject" and "object," is a more integral part of scientific reality than had previously been assumed.

When the critical-historical method shifted the focus of attention from the interpretation of the text to the reconstruction of history, a further unexpressed result emerged. The Bible's *Heilsgeschichte* turned out to be a secondary construct, the conflation of originally independent traditions into a historical sequence that, as such, never existed except as a phenomenon of language: the *traditions* of Israel, Judaism and Christianity, the *Bible story*.

This is not to say that no facts are behind that construct. Of course, one category among the historical causes of that construct consists of facts recounted in that story, even though another category would embrace "facts" not explicitly stated, i.e., the facts of merging traditions as tribes assembled into the people "Israel," or provincial Christian groups gradually merged into one orthodox church under the hegemony of the provincial church of the Roman Empire's capital.

Modern archaeology is doing much to fill in the details of Ancient Near Eastern history and culture, and to indicate the verisimilitude of the biblical story to customs and traditions of the day. But its actual results have not conformed to the apologetic slant of "confirming the biblical record," as is often claimed. Some of archaeology's most famous "confirmations" have been deconfirmed by subsequent and more careful archaeology. Schliemann did *not* discover Homer's Troy or Agamemnon's tomb, and Garstang did *not* discover Joshua's walls of Jericho, which by Joshua's time were long since torn down. That is to say, the ancient ruins must have led, in antiquity, to an aetiological legend attached by Israelites to Joshua's conquest, and the history of this legend would replace Joshua's victory as a "fact" in Israelite history. The Bible story then reports that after the dramatic "fall of Jericho" the victorious Israelites broke through to the center of Palestine with the conquest of Ai—which had been an abandoned ruin for a millennium before the Israelite "conquest." Since "Ai" means "ruins," we may have to do here with an etymological as well as an aetiological "history," which may serve especially well to illustrate a language event.

Thus the "history of traditions" has tended to replace the "factual" history as the primary historical datum to be reconstructed from the biblical text. It is indicative of this that the reaction against Bultmann—e.g., on the part of the Pannenberg circle—for having dissolved "history" and "fact" into "kerygma" and "interpretation" has tended to come full circle, with the emergence of the history of traditions and the history of ideas as the basic sequence they themselves are now tracing. Thus the "revelation of God in history" is subject to scientific analysis less in terms of what happened "with outstretched arm" than what happened around the campfire or the cultic shrine or the ecumenical gathering by way of language event. The history to which the Bible points the scholar is hermeneutical in nature: the progressive interpretation of the striking phenomenon, such as the rainbow, the megalithic menhir, the tell in ruins; or the reinterpretation of a local Canaanite tradition in need of conversion, such as a high place or legendary personage; or a more inclusive interpretation of one tribe's tradition about its origin, in need of incorporation into the ecumenical history of Israel, such as the exodus or Sinai traditions. That is to say, the revelation of God in history has turned out to be a series of interpretations of traditions referring to the past, and yet interpretations of the past by means of which the people of God interpret themselves to be precisely that. In thus interpreting themselves, they experience God. Thus the critical historical method has tended to lead to the interpretation of interpretations as the subject matter of the theologian's historiography, and thus point to a renewal of the centrality of hermeneutic.

Meanwhile, during the century in which hermeneutics has been eclipsed by the critical-historical method, a more modern understanding of hermeneutics itself had been introduced. Schleiermacher broadened the scope of hermeneutics beyond the interpretation of texts to the interpretation of human experience as such. Dilthey sought to elevate his understanding of Schleiermacher's hermeneutic into a critique, a scientific foundation, for the humanities as such. Freud was able to interpret dreams as our subconscious interpretation of life. Existentialistic interpretation has defined myth, to the extent its intent is religious rather than scientific, as man's misleadingly objectifying way of interpreting his own existence.

With the shift from the existentialistic to the linguistic focus of hermeneutic, the text has come to be seen less as the expression of man's understanding of existence than the echo, in a prophet's individuation, of the language world of which he is part. Thus the history of world, the language trajectories in which Christian history is caught up, the deviations and proclivities emergent in such trajectories, the directionalities characteristic of Christianity, become the ultimate subject matter of the theologian's historical research. Even if one shares historicism's turn from the philological concentration on the interpretation of the text to the critical-historical reconstruction of the sequence of events, one nevertheless finds oneself in the area of hermeneutic. For one is involved in the interpretation of the ongoing interpretation of Christian tradition down through the ages, as the traditional way of expressing one's own interpretation of what it is to be Christian.

CULTURE AS LANGUAGE WORLD

Of course, the traditional way of expressing one's own interpretation of what it is to be Christian, namely credal reformulation, scriptural exegesis, dogmatic theology, etc., is far from dominant today. Even theology now is more likely to be involved in interpreting culture than in interpreting Scripture. A new hermeneutic should not be inclined to provide special pleading for tradition as what is to be interpreted, but should stem from and be part of the understanding of our world with which modern man is quite rightly engrossed. The modern language of today should be our theological language. To be sure, traditional terms do and should occur in theological literature. But the dogmatician's hoof is show ing when one moves from a modern formulation to a traditional phrase to "understand" what the modern language "really" means. For all he is doing is classifying or pigeonholing, and thereby avoiding the hermeneutical problem. For the only language one understands is the language in which one thinks and acts.

The invisibility of God should imply the indistinguishability of theological language from other modern language. Theological language involves a critical stance within and among live options of thought and action, and so can be traced or plotted within the flow of modern language. As a directionality that can be intuited within modern language, the Christian witness can be heard and God can thus be revealed. But as the incarnate God, as the word in earthen vessels, the revelation, as language, is indistinguishable from current usage. Theology should not sell out to culture, but should be a witness directed to, and at times against, the culture; and, as orthodox (i.e., right) theology, it should retain its own gyroscopic directionality within any given culture. But this orthodoxy is no given flow of language, not even biblical or credal phrases, but rather a point scored within any given language, an eddy within any stream, a variant upon any trajectory.

Some language worlds are a readier medium for a given aspect of the message, and the languages of the West have already undergone the influence of Christian theology. Yet the West may also have suppressed vital aspects of the Christian witness, because of Western language patterns uncongenial for the communication of this originally Eastern religion. Werner Elert has shown how the revelation of God in the passion of Jesus could not come to full expression in Western theology as it progressively fell under the sway of Greek philosophy, for which apathy, insufferability, was of the essence of God. The result was that even sympathy could not be attributed to God, nor even to the divine nature of Jesus. Defections from this Western language world could only be rejected as patropassion heretics. The Japanese theologian Kitamori has argued in *The Pain of God* that the cultural presuppositions of Japan make it possible for the first time adequately to bring into language this central aspect of the Christian witness to God.

The death-of-God theologies of America have been in vogue not simply because of the journalistic style of the theologians involved; nor should their paperback format be relegated to the condescending category of popularization, but should be recognized as a medium integrally related to the message. The significance of these radical theologies is that they have combined form and matter, language and its point, interpretation of culture and theological critique. Like linguistic analysts, they hold that one must be clear about what meaning (if any) the language one uses can have, if one hopes to make meaningful statements in that language. Yet their discussions of what meaning (if any) God-talk can have is itself theology, not merely propaedeutics or prolegomena to any future theology. In their view, God-talk is impossible because of the heretical doctrine of God that is prevalent inside and outside theology today. Their anathema upon or excommunication of such God-talk(ers) takes the form of witnessing that the judgment has taken place already; God has been put to death by such God-talk. Indeed, God-talk is in this view the hermeneutical translation into our situation of the cry in Jesus' time: "Crucify him!" Yet God gave himself into the hiddenness of full incarnation or death, as the modern version of "filling up what is lacking in the sufferings of Christ." The language event of the death of God is thus the saving event as it is happening in our time. In such patterns of thought the death-of-God theologies have taken with radical seriousness the language world of the secular West in which they find themselves, and identify within it, at the converging point of their understanding of culture and of the Christian tradition, the language event they interpret as the saving event.

To be sure, the death-of-God theologies seem to be passing off the stage as rapidly as they came on, and their imprecision in terms of rigorous conceptualization and historical scholarship does not call for emulation. But the seriousness with which they have taken their language world, and the radicality of their commitment to identify in it the saving event as a language event, are clearly indicative of the radical hermeneutical dimensions of any viable American theology to come.

When one turns to the most radical movements in American culture today, the hippie and black-power movements, it is relevant to observe the efforts under way there to identify a language adequate for interpreting themselves. Such movements are not a dropout into solitude, but rather from a language world not their own. They search for new language worlds that embody the meaning they inarticulately intuit. The hippie finds in the vibrations of sound and color the medium in which he happens, the language that speaks to him and makes him articulate. The flower girls, in reaction against a long series of neocultures, attest a direct experience of natural beauty and simplicity that is simply disconcerting, say, to a policeman. Yet hippie posters actually represent, in terms of the history of art, less an innovation than a revival of the neoromantic return to nature current at the turn of the century in Germany.

The black-power movement is also as radical a rejection of the Establishment's (white) culture as could be conceived; its motto, "Burn, baby, burn," is quite unambiguous and is comparable in bluntness only to the white man's slogan that the only good Indian is a dead Indian. If anywhere, we would look to find here the matrix of the truly modern man, the social scientist, the technocrat, pragmatic, future-oriented—for whom history, culture, the humanities, tradition, and the like, were too soft and slow, too inefficient for and irrelevant to his pressing needs. Yet the black student, at last emancipated from white culture, has as his most urgent demand, his most frequent ultimatum, that he be instantly given a new language world, as if his very life depended upon it. No doubt, as strong empirical evidence shows, it does!

Once the Negro students at a white college or university become bold enough to create a black students' union, they demand a black studies program, and orient the program strongly toward black history, culture, and language—the humanities! A revolutionary with a copy of neither Marx nor Mao but of Bantu grammar in which to engross himself! What more striking demonstration that man is by his very nature linguistic, and simply feels naked (with all the dehumanizing implications of that) when not clothed in a language world! Black Americans seek a new language for their world. They study African grammar because they saw that they were naked and were ashamed. And this is fleshed out, perhaps somewhat more realistically, with African cultural history. For man is the historic animal.

The theology of hope has brought to our attention forcefully that where there is no hope the people perish. This is of course true of the black-power movement. Yet it is significant that the tooling up for launching into the future consists in a crash program to attain the past: a culture as a language medium in which a black man can *be*. A future attains its velocity from the propulsion of a past; together, the past and the future comprise a trajectory which is man's path.

If the movement toward racial expression and integration has provided a remarkably illuminating case study of the shift, in group after group, from the sect type to the church type of organizational ethos, it also provides, in addition to such a sociological ecclesiology, a fascinating case study of the indispensable role of tradition, history, and language in the actual functioning of such a secularized church-equivalent. Since American theology is often more oriented to the social sciences and their analysis of contemporary experience than to the humanities and historical research, it might well find in these traits of the black-power movement insight into what it had conceived of as rather meaningless and irrelevant vestiges of the past hanging on in our religious heritage. Even the Eucharist might seem relevant, as the white equivalent to soul food.

Celebrating Change:
Communications and Theology

✠

ANTHONY SCHILLACI

The media revolution—consciously or unconsciously we are all part of it as we enter the fourth decade of television and casually watch live color transmission from the moon. This is an American revolution; it goes as deep as the structures of our minds. Anthony Schillaci is one of the leading theoreticians of the new directions in films. Participant or director in many conferences on Christianity and the mass media, he is the author of Movies and Morals *(1968).*

The communications revolution, unlike so many others which have influenced American society, did not have to be imported. It was invented here, and is in turn being exported to every part of the planet via satellite and other instruments of mass communication. It is a revolution whose effects and implications are enormously pervasive—so pervasive that the revolution receives relatively little attention. As long as that unawareness continues, we will live through this revolution more its victims than its liberators. Nowhere is this more true than in the area of theology.

Our current practice in theology and religious education has been to import movements of thought and techniques of instruction from Europe. That this practice has stimulated the American churches is undeniable. Theology, nevertheless, may be one of the last vestiges of American intellectual inferiority. Consultation with scholars from different cultures can give fresh perspectives to our own problems,

166

often too close to us. But we have too readily transferred, uncritically, European modes of thought to our own situation; this has resulted in the past fifteen years in the bewildering turnover of theological fads. In terms of the area of communications, to rely on European thinkers is to step backwards from our own mass-media environment to a world that is still largely print-oriented and reliant almost exclusively upon words. The reason such attempts fail is that changes in communications on the scale we refer to are usually irreversible processes. They involve both theologian and audience in radically different orientations. Even if we can expect Europe to pursue the directions already in progress in America, we cannot look for leadership to a culture just entering the communications age. The leadership must come from within the United States, from theologians who are men of that age and society.

Before launching an American theology of the future, however, theologians must become aware of how communications profoundly affect their basic contact with reality. Marshall McLuhan has observed that, once a communications satellite is launched around the earth, nature ceases to exist. The major thought of this statement, to be analyzed more in depth later, is that what was once our primary sphere of contact with God has been changed from nature to the man-made world of information. For theologians, this means that a whole new set of analogies must be created to maintain contact between theology and contemporary reality. For liturgists, this means that a whole new set of symbols and rituals must be developed to maintain basic contact between worship and the environment, between sacrament and world. For all Christians this means that the style of our contact with God has to change.

Theologians of great sophistication often fail to show any awareness of the effects of the communications environment. Hypersensitive to philosophical systems and world views as they affect theology, the theologian nevertheless remains insensitive to the subtle shape the media give to contemporary living. Just as an awareness of philosophical patterns in the history of theology can help detect limiting presuppositions in theology, so too an insight into communications can reveal radical changes in sense perception which profoundly affect the process of theology. Our perception of time and space, for example, is more than a cultural difference. Old

Testament writers patterned their image of God after their knowledge of the world and the modes of communication available to them. Present writers reflect a similar dependency upon mythical structures, many of them communications-based. More than a change of vocabulary, what is at stake here is the basic point of contact with God in today's world. The structures of sign and symbol, an indispensable element in theological work, reflect the human perceptual sets created by the most powerful forms of communication.

Perhaps what is needed is a new process of "demythologizing"— a continuation of this general task already begun. That process in the past concentrated on content, carefully showing how cultural accretions flavored theological sources and even Scripture. Today the work must be extended to an awareness of such unexamined presuppositions in our theology as the new "tyranny of words," the unconscious reliance upon print as the sole source and primary locus of theology. No theologian would defend the proposition that theology is something that exists in books. Many, however, proceed in their writings and teaching as if that were precisely the case. By the simple expedient of relying upon abstract symbols in phonetic alphabet representation, the point is made that this is where theological action lives. Although we shall explore later the reasons for such presuppositions, one illustration of this unexamined presupposition immediately comes to mind. Anyone who was born or has lived in the machine age tends to think of electric technology as "mechanical." The computer is a "robot," and a radio or television set is a "contraption." This confusion between machine and electronic technology is not only a source of our misuse of our instruments, but it is an unnecessary, and for today stultifying, coloration in our theology. Considered as machines, electrical instruments seem to have little significance for theology except in the morality of their use. Considered in their true nature as modes of communication, these instruments affect our very contact with reality, reducing work, money, war, and perhaps even human beings to instantaneous information. No theologian to date has even shown an awareness of this mythical structure.

I am proposing in this study that the same respectful attention given rather freely to sociology, psychology, and anthropology today by the theologian must be extended to communications. The popular conception that expertise in communications means a theologian who is "with it," or "swings a little," is ridiculous. One cannot overcome mythical structures and gain awareness simply by knowing the contents of the latest film, recording, or television show. At the same time, the theologian need not become a communications expert. What is necessary is that each theologian be a thoroughly contemporary man, one who lives in his culture as part of it, aware of it, and reflecting upon it. Increasingly, theology will work to humanize the environment in the light of revelation. This process cannot be undertaken by men who are the victims of that environment through lack of awareness. It is doubtful that any man today can afford to live at odds with his technology; for a theologian, to whom is entrusted the continuing explanation and development of revelation, such naïveté is unthinkable.

RELIGION AND ENVIRONMENTS

My basic argument is a simple one. Religion historically rose out of man's attempt to understand and control his environment. When natural catastrophe struck a culture in which the cycle of natural forces held the sole means of survival, man evolved by developing a controlling awareness of his environment. Where knowledge was primitive, man supplied myth and magic to augment his sense of control. This form of religion is as old as man. In the first stages of human development, the environment was nature, the world of natural objects, living things, and processes. The Old Testament transcended this pattern as a revealed religion, but it reflected many of the previous forms. Reflecting a growing critical awareness of the environment in the Mideastern cultures of the time, the Old Testament is in part a scientific mythology; it gave as satisfactory an explanation of natural processes and human origins as was available in each stage of its writing. As knowledge of the natural world increased, science and religion went their ways, with theology working to free Scripture from its ancient task of pro-

169

viding a scientific explanation of the world to which God's revelation had come.

Man has continued to reflect on his environment and to mature and vary his knowledge of God, but today he does so in what is no longer a natural but an informational environment. It is manmade and based on electric technology. Once we can view Earth from the moon and chart natural phenomena involving whole continents through weather satellites, we no longer live rooted to a planet. We have now extended our senses to a new sphere of pure information which holds Earth as an object for our scrutiny. That same communications environment becomes in turn the preoccupation of religion, which continues to reflect man's attempt to control and understand it. Theology cannot function today without reflecting on and using the information media in its deliberations, any more than it could operate in the past without focusing upon the natural environment or the human environment of man's relations with his fellows. Just as nature was once the primary point of contact between God and man, the communications media have now become that meeting place. Their very content, which is the human image, reflects the incarnational mode of God's continuing revelation. Theology was never purely speculative; today it may of necessity become eminently practical, taking upon itself the enormous task of making the technological environment humanly livable . . . the task of redeeming created reality.

Like the various media themselves, our encounter between theology and media described in the following pages will develop simultaneously in several directions. First, we will note that the role of theology in reflecting upon the *environment* is a traditional one, but became inoperative through theological insensitivity and unawareness. Restoration of this role demands that the communications media become an object of theological reflection. Secondly, once we consider *communications* in general as the basic contact we have with our environments and with each other, we must next consider *change* as a characteristic of all environments. This transition is from a simple awareness of communications patterns to their attempted control through the arts. The role of theology will here be viewed as the perception and study of Christ's work unfolding in the environment. When we come to the areas of theology itself, under the loose categories of belief and value (corresponding roughly to dogma and morals), its present role will be suggested as that of intensifying the environment so that human transcendence generates a divine response. Theology tomorrow is to become an agent of change; in the area of belief it accelerates revelation as process; in the area of value it accelerates man's evolution to appropriate revolutionary levels.

The stages of inquiry just described can be summed up under the headings of Communications, Control, Change. At each stage it is necessary to destroy some mythical structure affecting the existing theology. On the level of *communications* as a basic contact with the environment, the demon of language must be exorcised before the full range of human awareness can develop. On the level of *control* of the environment, it is the myth of stability, carried over from periods of less rapid change, that must be excised. As we explore the role of theology in accelerating *change*, we encounter myths that impede that role both in the area of belief and value. Unnecessary limits on faith have been placed out of fear of the demon of the profane, or the practice of removing elements of reality from theological consideration because they are not "sacred." Many of our attitudes toward the communications environment stem from this arbitrary rejection of the secular as "profane." A more subtle restraint is operative in morals, i.e., the practice of refusing to recognize man in his technology *by reason of* a false anthropomorphic bias.

COMMUNICATIONS

Our first task is to situate contemporary theology in a communications culture. We are accepting for the time being communications as our basic contact with the environment and with each other. Theology in this context is reduced to a basic form: a religious quest for understanding one's environment. Where natural forces terrify and destroy men, the primitive theologian develops magic ritual in the attempt to control the natural environment. The significance of these observations is that theology from the beginning has been involved in man's growing awareness of his environment, even when that awareness is marked by magic and superstition.

What happens when, as McLuhan suggests, nature is no longer the primary environment? The electronic information environment cradles the earth in knowledge, a man-made sphere of intelligible relationships uniting man to a different nature (now become an artifact) and to other men. A natural catastrophe like a hurricane which once inspired religious awe and terror is now an entertainment event scheduled for television. Prior to this broadcast satellites have traced the hurricane in weather patterns that cover half the globe. When it strikes, the blow is cushioned by our knowledge of its shape, force, and direction. Earth then becomes an artifact, reduced to the size of a color photograph or television image which we can watch for amusement or education in the safety of our living room.

Even more radical than our new relationship to Earth is our novel means of relating to each other. Since the information sphere has brought Earth down to scale, communications become our basic contact with the environment and with other men. Increasingly, the work of relating meaningfully to this technological human environment becomes our foremost activity and our most nagging concern. Changes in this environment cannot help but affect theology, especially in its new personalist orientation. This will be especially true of any theology which retains its basic role of helping man to understand his environment.

Complicating this role of theology is the instantaneous nature of the information environment, a world in which simultaneity has replaced staging or gradualism of any kind. Many contemporary films that make great demands on audiences are signs of the current capacity or need for simultaneity. Fellini's 8½ compresses past and present, fantasy and actuality into one simultaneous experience of its hero's interior states. Richard Lester's *Petulia* fragments a simple narrative until past and future are condensed into a single NOW. Charles Braverman and other young experimenters in film have explored and pushed back the boundaries of our image perception toward new levels of simultaneity. In the three and a half minutes of *An American Time Capsule*, Braverman presents the whole of American history in still photographs of paintings and woodcuts, bombarding the eye with images from the signing of the Declaration of Independence to the election of Richard Nixon as fast as ten images per second! In his *World of 1968,* using news photographs explored by zoom and pan, and joined by expert editing into a remarkable unity, we are given the events of a troubled year in just four and a half minutes.

What demands does the contemporary thirst for simultaneity place on theology? The first reaction is one which all studies, and education in general, have experienced—a dissatisfaction with the book as the exclusive medium of theology. The linear development of print communication, evident in its type-based format and the logical demands of grammar, make it a relatively slow, difficult, and sensorily remote mode of communication. Print theology, by mediating our contact with reality through the abstract symbols of words, loses the preconceptual impact of instantaneous information. Ideals are developed gradually in sequence, rather than being allowed to interact and bombard the learner who makes the associations himself.

Perhaps even more important than these differences is the derivation of our notion of "objectivity" in a theology-from-print, from a severance of intellect and emotion traceable to print communication. Simultaneity bespeaks a coordination of sense, emotion, and intellect into a total experience. Objectivity begins by separating our subjective reactions from the events outside us, and ends by making even these subjective states "objects" of scrutiny. The ultimate result is fragmentation, the Cartesian sensibility which has led print-oriented Western man to live outside his own experiences. Symptomatic of the reactions to this fragmentation are the hallucinogenic drugs which not only reflect the media environment, but offer some promise of total awareness rather than escape. Our confidence in "objectivity" for theology was first shaken when we began to suspect that rationalism had crept into that quest, by the very reaction in theological circles to nineteenth-century forms. In substitution for such rationalism we are offered simultaneity, which is an integrating experience, fostering wholeness through its total appeal, rather than alienation through its sensory and intellectual abstraction. Now we are no longer certain of the value of objectivity, learning as we have what price has been paid for it. For our concerns it is important to recall that the medium of print, quite independently of its content, was responsible for our concepts of objectivity. A book theology, almost in spite of itself, implies objectivity, detachment, analysis, minimal emotional reinforcement, and slight sensory involvement. This *mode* of media irrelevancy is far more serious than that which surfaces on the level of content. It is, moreover, an irrelevancy of communications style that can devitalize even the most current and dynamic content.

A theology that hopes to assist men in understanding today's environment must first exorcise the demon of language. Without becoming totally nonverbal, theology must free itself from the conceptual limitations, the unexamined mythology, of the print society in which it arose. We have already cited the notion of "objectivity" as one prejudicial to experiential totality. We should develop a similar awareness of the historical effects that two communications revolutions have worked on the theology of the time. The first is itself a two-part revolution; its first stage takes us from the oral/aural mode to that of the phonetic alphabet; the second stage takes us from the alphabet to print. The second is our current revolution from print to the new electric environment, appealing to all senses simultaneously. The significance in these examples for our remarks on theology is that each age shapes radical differences in the harmony of the senses. The print-oriented person who hugs to himself the missal or hymnal has been conditioned to look on the world in a linear, sequential way through the window of print, a one-way mirror of sorts which made possible exquisite abstractions, but rendered total involvement difficult. However beautifully one reads Scripture or pronounces the words of a traditional liturgy, for this person it must be accompanied by his own scrutiny of the printed page.

In theology we have lived through the same revolutions with similar lack of awareness. The inordinate emphasis on learning theology by memorizing was really an attempt to make learning modes of an oral/aural culture work with contemporary students. The unexamined (and almost antique) premise beneath these attempts was that one person, the professor, had the written manuscript; the others had the choice of using his copy or copying it either by memory or hand. St. Thomas' *Summa* was one of the earliest texts, i.e., a convenient collection of the encyclopedic materials contained in the master's memory and in his library. But it was only a substitute for reading the inaccessible original. The advent of print made these and similar techniques outdated, but they continue to impede education even in our own day. A good portion of the charges of irrelevancy in present campus upheavals centers unknowingly upon the university as a place where one goes to read. Students know there is more to learning than reading and feel frustrated and impeded in their education by so archaic a stance. Even the counter-arguments of the secular academic establishment add fuel to the fire, for the university as a haven for "reason" reflects the kind of subjective personal detachment from social issues that is fostered by an exclusive diet of print.

Theology texts have largely disappeared, not because there is no sure ground in the field, but because students who can read and own cheap copies of the classics do not wish to have their opinions premasticated and subjected to death by taxonomy. Ownership of one's books has made the concept of the university as a cluster of colleges around a good library hopelessly inadequate. The idea of a tutor who guides one's reading is further outdated, because the paperback revolution produces students who read more than the professors. In this situation, the student will not slow down for his mentor in class, but will demand a different role of him. The problem is no longer to record, transmit, memorize, and meditate upon classics within a field, but, having read them, to reflect upon the ideas in a challenging atmosphere of dialogue. This dialectic is marked by an ongoing comparison between the needs of today and the wisdom of the past. Not every classic will survive such an ordeal, and few students are treated to such an education. The resounding complaint is that education more and more takes place outside the school, where the mass media conduct a stimulating, delightful, involving, and profitable tutelage . . . and it's free! Lectures come under attack for lack of the feedback style which is reflected in telephone talk shows on radio and television. The more carefully the professor wraps the materials, the more completely he excludes the student from the learning process of making the relationships and associations, incorporating them into his total personality. And perhaps most damning of all, the typical classroom lacks the shared experiential involvement without which learning becomes rote absorption rather than rapt inquiry.

Theology, stalled in similar outdated communication patterns, ceases to exercise its traditional function: to help man relate to his environment through his understanding of it. Since that environment is no longer primarily natural but informational, the role of theology can only be restored by permitting the contemporary arts of communication to give it an orientation to the present. This would be the first step toward what we might call a "theology of awareness." We shall pursue the idea of the phenomenon of change raising questions of environmental control, with practical problems in the areas of belief and value. For now, however, the first step toward a theology with future promise is to make it a theology of awareness. The sensitivity to the communications environment would extend beyond its surface meanings to a level which would ultimately embody the work of Christ's redemption as it unfolds concretely in today's world. Theological response of this kind would embody both a perception in faith (belief that Christ's work continues) and a conviction of values (belief that we have a part in that ongoing work). These ultimately are the means by which theology helps man to relate to what is now a new and threatening environment.

This task will be difficult, especially as it demands freeing oneself from mythological structures and patterned contacts with reality determined by outdated modes of communication. The hold that such patterns retain on our consciousness became apparent with the appearance of Pasolini's film *The Gospel According to Saint Matthew*. The reception of this film revealed how one's entire concept of revelation, one's preconceptual portrait of Christ, was conditioned by media. The traumatic effect of the film was not merely the result of the advanced, semidocumentary style of the work. The first shock came from the initial encounter with Saint Matthew "raw." Building on recent exegetical knowledge of Matthew, Pasolini presents the specific image of Jesus as a somewhat fanatical prophet, fiercely carrying out his Father's work; a zealot who had so little time he spent his active life on the road, speaking constantly over his shoulder to the stumbling fishermen who followed him, and to whom he was to entrust his Gospel. Audiences were repelled and outraged (some asked why Pasolini had not done St. Luke's gentle Gospel!). Others were perceptive enough to note that the film did not tell a story. It was not *The Greatest Story Ever Told* but something quite different—the Gospel.

A story, in this technical sense, is a specific artistic structure reflecting the sensory modes of a culture. It was inevitable that a literary culture should fashion a story out of the radically fragmented Gospels, thereby smoothing out the different viewpoints and styles, homogenizing the image of Christ until an uneasy composite appeared, reflecting more the subjectivity of the storyteller than the knowledge of the Evangelists. To make of the Gospels a "story" is to structure the life of Jesus dramatically, to mold his life and sayings into a single pattern, packaged for consumption with an emphasis that limits the total impact of the biblical Christ. A literary culture cries, "Tell me a story," and as late as the cinema age we take the vital fragments which are the Gospels and press them into a dramatic narrative of an unrecognizable character. Of course, Pasolini's Christ offends: He is too radical, too offensively prophetic, too intolerant of fools, in short, too Jewish (as Matthew is Jewish) for many to love.

This is what we mean by saying that a mythical structure—a direct consequence of the pattern of our contact with reality—can screen even our perceptions of Christ. There is no need to wring our hands over the fact. A far more radical transformation of the Gospel came when it was first entrusted to print; it thereby lost the living development of oral catechesis. The Greeks in Plato's time complained that committing the *Iliad* and *Odyssey* to writing would destroy these epic myths. What is important, however, is that we become aware of the changes a transfer of media works in theology and its sources.

Today, if there is to be a theology of awareness it must turn to the arts for the new incarnation which will insure the vitality of the Gospel in our age, and which will enable it to speak to contemporary men. McLuhan has demonstrated that the media are not neutral channels through which the same Gospel can pass unchanged. Television, for example, is not just a better way for a priest to reach more people than he can cram into the parish church. A priest who can effectively or partially communicate in church may fail when television brings his countenance under the scrutiny of millions who are the judge of whether he believes the God-

Word that he utters. And this judgment will be based less on the words uttered than on the nonverbal ensemble of features, hesitations, gestures, shape of face, and use of eyes. If the media are not neutral, then the new theology must be media-sensitive. It will scrutinize the information environment for signs of Christ's presence there just as diligently as past theologies studied nature for God's signature. What the new theology must perceive and tell the world is the evidence for Christ's continued presence on earth in his Spirit.

This role for theology is a new one, but it is not without precedents in tradition. It transcends mere awareness of modern techniques, or sensitivity to cultural differences. The very modes of contemporary sense-contact with reality cannot be left out of theological speculation. If man today feels a need for simultaneity, it means he is most alive, most involved, most integral when absorbing many impressions and relating them personally to each other and to himself. And these reactions are appropriate to our encounter with God, which should speak of life now, rather than life after a longed-for death. The information environment (which is the contemporary world) is in reality the noosphere of Teilhard de Chardin—where redemption takes place. A theology freed of the burden of past media structures assumes a new and urgent role in this new world of man, staging a new meeting place for God and man. Man has yet to learn to live humanly in the new technological environment. It continues to destroy him on the highways and battlefields, continues to dehumanize and degrade him through poverty and disease. He is more its victim than its director. What is needed is a new awareness which can discover order in multiple change, direction in our accelerating lives, purpose in chaotic simultaneity. This order and direction cannot be imposed but must be discovered in new relationships within the environment. This approach has an appropriately strong humanistic tone. Today, less than ever, can we afford to skip the human in our eagerness to reach the divine. We are not likely, however, to make an unwarranted leap as we call upon the arts to make the environment visible to us. We are, rather, collaborating in a new incarnation of the Gospel. This aware theology must arise in the United States and can spread to the entire world. Once aware, the theologian can begin to think of his next function, which is control.

CONTROL

Control is closely allied to awareness of the environment. The pattern by which understanding leads to mastery is a familiar one and lies at the base of modern technology. We control, for example, the hurricane, because we understand its speed, force, and direction. But in the case of the information environment, any new and fresh perception can lead to control of a sort that is properly theological.

Theology began by controlling the natural environment. Primeval man chose religious leaders whose role it was to explain natural phenomena and to harness its potentially dangerous force through ritual magic. This primitive control often marked the birth of a culture's arts, which frequently rose out of religious ritual. The relation between Dionysian rites and the origins of Greek drama are well known, but something more to the point would be the cave drawings at Lascaux and Altamira. Cultural anthropologists describe them as elements of religious ceremonies in which, by representing the animals of the hunt, man hoped to gain control of his prospective prey. As we shall see, religious control of the environment has always had liturgical implications. For now, having recalled these precedents, we can go on to explore the means by which theology today might exercise an equivalent role in our society.

This exploration should take place in the context of William Kuhns's ideas on the four periods of man's relations to his environment, a process which he calls "interface." In his recent stimulating work, *Environmental Man*,[1] Kuhns analyzes the major periods of human development, characterizing them by distinct modes of awareness of the environment and of its unique effects on man. The first period, or Primeval Interface, found man dominated by his natural environment. Incapable of shaping the environment in human forms, primeval man thought only of participating in the processes of nature, ritualizing change through fertility and harvest rites. The second period, or Anthropomorphic Interface, grew with

[1] New York, 1969.

the early city civilizations, from Babylonia to Rome. Not yet in control of the environment, man was nevertheless able to detach himself from natural processes sufficiently to attend to man as man. The result was the birth of law and morality, new cultures and religions. The origin of Christianity at this time is significant, not only for the Roman legal emphasis it sometimes manifests, but by reason of the belief that God had taken on human identity. The incarnation reflected and reinforced a contemporary concentration on human values. The third period, or Power Interface, is one that we have experienced, although its origins go back as far as the tenth and eleventh centuries. Primitive technological advances, such as the stirrup or plow, gave man a taste for control over the environment of nature. For Galileo, Bacon, and Newton, the cosmos was a "vast reservoir of energies to be tapped and used according to human intentions."[2] There is a strong residue of this power complex as we reach for outer space today, a transitional confusion touching the fourth period, or Creative Interface. The difference between the two is the growth from control to the active creation of environments with a freedom that still leaves us uncomfortable.

Kuhns draws some interesting conclusions for Christianity in the new age, and we will refer to them later. First we must note how radically different our new situation of interface is from past forms. Most evident among differences is our greater consciousness of environments, as witnessed by the growth of environmental sciences, most of which study the effects of technological culture on the atmosphere, land, and sea. The discrepancy between our ability to control and our level of understanding is evident in the creation of man-made environments potentially more destructive than any found in simple nature. Unlike primeval man, we are not dominated by nature, yet we seek, like him, a new participation in nature on the basis of partnership. Former life necessities now give human satisfaction as art forms (soil cultivation gives way to gardening, the open fire becomes the charcoal broiler, etc.). A model of the new partnership is found in surfing, where the

---

[2] *Ibid.*, 129, citing Lynn White's *Mediaeval Technology and Social Change* (Oxford, 1962).

frightening wave becomes a source of beautiful, graceful control through technological cooperation. The trend is significant, for as we free ourselves from total dependence on a natural process or even an artifact, we give it aesthetic deference, thereby elevating it to a uniquely human level of perception. The objects of the old technology, such as autos, looms, coffee mills, and windup phonographs are now collectors' items. It will be some time before we can do the same with our most recent technology, because we do not consider it under our control. The route from utility to art, however, has such strong precedents that we can see implications for theology in this process.

Theologizing began in the attempt to supply reasons for the ritual control of nature through the application of the arts in magic and myth. So powerful are the traditions of natural cycle in liturgy that we are hard put to develop an urban or technological ritual for contemporary worship. Theology's vital speculation on the natural environment, as well as its insights into man during the anthropomorphic interface, have not found an equivalent in our own potentially creative relationship to the new information environment. Galileo's treatment by the Church is symptomatic of the failure to respond to growing knowledge of the environment and the control through technology apparent in the instrument of the telescope. Worse failures appeared in those ages when Christian nations casually permitted technology, in the form of factory and modern warfare, to dehumanize and destroy man. A theology arrested in development at a previous interface was unable to grow into a guiding force as the power interface modified nature through technology. As Kuhns states, Christianity's ". . . interfaces emphasize man and God, man and man, man and himself; they will not support a vision large enough to include nuclear weapons or the automobile, television commercials or mass magazines."[3]

Theology, in McLuhan's terms, failed to recognize machine and electric technology as extensions of man: limbs become wheel and wing, senses become telescope and microscope; the internal nervous system externalized in electric circuitry, transistors, radar, etc. Much of the implicit humanism in the new technology has not been

[3] *Ibid.*, 131.

released because it has not been properly understood. Theologians who are unfamiliar with this role either try to silence the experimenter or attack the discovery as "inhuman." Such attitudes give the Christian little assistance in living humanly with his machines, because they are made to seem alien or even positively evil. It is interesting to note that man is more likely to abuse an instrument he considers other than himself than one with which he identifies. The automobile has become deadly because man is unaware of acting out his subconscious conflicts with this machine. The theological significance of the automobile goes far beyond speed limits and discourteous driving; personality transformations and identity crises are related to autos. Instead of wondering how to provide sufficient parking for a new church, perhaps we should ask if the auto has not made the church structure an anachronism. This is only one of the many questions which a technological environment poses for theology.

The first priority in the age of creative interface is for theology to study the electric technology directly. We continually commit the serious mistake of speaking of "the effects of technology on man." This approach embodies the very separation which diminishes responsibility, since it represents technology as some wild beast that has leaped up to confront man. But technology did not just happen; man extended himself, cleverly and consciously, into the natural world in order to control it. McLuhan's simile relating technology to the myth of Narcissus has still not been understood. As he points out, it was precisely because Narcissus did *not* recognize himself in his reflection that he tragically fell in love with it *as other*, and perished. We constantly look into the mirror of technology without recognizing there our own face. In Stanley Kubrick's modern epic 2001: *A Space Odyssey*, we have in the phenomenon of Hal, the 9000 Series computer, a contemporary classic of electronic interface. Hal develops neurotic symptoms and eventually destroys several of the astronauts, not because man has created a ruthless machine, but because man has programed "him" with human emotions. As such, the computer is simply a mirror for the humans who rely on him for survival, as we rely on machinery for our own survival. Furthermore, Hal has been programed simultaneously with absolute truthfulness *and* the reservation of the true nature of the Jupiter mission from the astronauts. Here man has the opportunity to face himself in his technology and to learn who he is. Theology has often invited man to know himself in contemplating nature and serving his fellow man; it has yet to ask man to look into the mirror of his own technology for his identity. Whether we use this extension of ourselves for narcissistic self-congratulation or real self-discovery may depend, ultimately, upon theology's definition of this choice.

Before beginning a direct study of electric technology, theology should understand that we are no longer in the power interface primarily. The cosmos is no longer a powerhouse but a network of intelligible relationships to be understood. Christians must recognize that even war has been reduced to information, whether tactical or strategic. By games theory, computers could calculate in advance the victor of any conflict. Adhered to without atavistic longing for revenge, euphemistically called "massive retaliation," this theory would enable a nation to surrender without a shot being fired. If war, like so much else in our environment, has been reduced to information, then theology has a unique role to play. The point is not so much to harness power (e.g., movie and television censorship struggles by the Church) as to interpret the ultimate significance of processes. The overview, which is the theological viewpoint, is one that takes man through and beyond the signal surfeit of the present scene to what we will study as ultimate significance of the media for belief and value.

Ultimately, this work will involve controlling the present environment by teaching man to live humanly amid change. The work is hampered by a deep-seated fear of change, for theology often expends most of its energies either on defense of established positions or feverish searchings for the newest ideas. Perhaps we need to exorcise the demon of stability, a romantic nostalgia for "tranquil" times when theology had the task of preserving past cultures (the Benedictines storing up the riches of Greece and Rome) or synthesizing philosophical systems (the medieval scholars blending Neoplatonism and Aristotle). There are those, for example, who wait for the current passing phase of change to settle down in the Church. Others perform elaborate exegeses on the documents of Vatican II in a similar grasp at premature stability. But Vatican II is rather a mandate for change, for there is little time left for the leisurely mastication of new developments. Ours is an age of process, and the greatest gift a theology can offer the age is to enable us to live humanly amid that process.

Stability, in such a situation, becomes explosive as well as repressive. A theology bent on braking rapid change tends to react more than act. We realize now how panic shaped the seminary curriculum, multiplying new courses for each new intellectual threat, from Modernism and the Dead Sea Scrolls to God-Is-Dead theology. By refusing to act until a problem becomes intolerable, theology ends up pronouncing on crises already near solution. There is also a tendency to incorporate changes into the existing institutions, instead of immersing the institutions in the change. If theology becomes an anchor, the one stable element in a fluctuating culture, it will become as functional as the calm certitude of a monument for the dead. As we become aware that physical structures, giant schools and massive churches, are shaping our priorities with little reference to real needs, it becomes apparent that conceptual structures are creating their own equally irrelevant demands. Theology can learn from the best adjusted elements of our society, business and science, that one does not control change by restraining it but by affirming it and reading it correctly.

What may appear an impossible task seems more manageable when we realize that technology creates its own regulatory devices. The arts are now available to theology both for insights into the environment and the means of humanizing it. Without excepting any one of the arts, those which seem most helpful in this work are the environmental arts of film (the best developed), television (the greatest potential), and the new sound (the most pervasive). These arts are joined by any mixed-media combination of existing arts, because all alike create antienvironments which make the environment visible. They appeal to many senses simultaneously, inviting a high level of sensory/intellectual participation by deriving their unity and delight from audience-originated associations. Moreover, these arts are highly technological devices which nevertheless control our electric environment by the specifically human ordering which is beauty. Finally, these are arts fully immersed in change and yet dealing with it creatively.

The arts, by their very medium, can help the theologian to live in a new space/time continuum proper to the present rather than the past. They do so, not by initiating changes but by sensitively reflecting the changes that they record before we become aware of them. Change is often distasteful because it disorients us, violating the comfortable space and time references that order our existence and even our identities, as does the simultaneity earlier referred to. The Braverman films, *An American Time Capsule* and *The World of 1968*, turn centuries of history into present tense by compressing them tightly against today. What one senses is not only the continuity of human events, but profound relationships that give history significance. In the former film, for example, one is suddenly aware that at the very same time we were enslaving and dehumanizing the American Negro, we were systematically annihilating the American Indian. The implications of this technique for a theological viewpoint are evident.

Film, like all environmental art, begins by mirroring change, and then goes on to assume creative control over it. Early techniques of fast and slow motion were crude experiments which were gradually refined into subtle manipulations of changing reality. Cinema creates its own time, as intensification of real life, and yet a freedom from its limits which permits great leaps backward and forward in history. These leaps are now accepted as conventions which reflect and cause new conceptions of time itself. Cinema also treats space creatively, leaping from continent to continent without even the token "curtain" of the fade-out. The jump cut and telescoped scene transitions further reflect the shrunken dimensions of our globe. Film can, in experimental setting, abstract from time by radical expedients such as reversed motion, a practice which amazingly gives the viewer no sense of temporal reversal but only a spatial one. Although not used as creatively today (except in commercials), television can, like film, exercise creative control over space, time, and motion.

Once freed from unnecessary limits of time and space (many of which we now recognize as the perceptual heritage of print orientation), film can reflect our very knowing processes. Films such as *8½* and *Last Year at Marienbad,* which abandon all linear, sequential development of plot or character, reveal the medium's true nature as a mirror of our conscious life and the unbroken stream of living. These relationships, a web of free associations of infinite variety and profound subtlety, tell us more of ourselves than rational explanation or logical dialogue. The fantasies of Guido in *8½* hold the key to his inner struggle and personal mystery much more meaningfully than do his words and actions. Dream and fantasy are part of the environmental arts and their totality, especially in those works, like *Rachel, Rachel* or *Petulia,* which set out to explore the inner environment of the human psyche.

The environmental arts, then, can help the theologian pass out of the old into the new environment. What is significant in this passage is that the arts do so by selecting and intensifying that environment. Rapid and pervasive change may appear intolerable in life, but it is somehow made manageable, comprehensible, and perhaps even delightful when brought to the screen in accelerated form. One reason for this reversal, so instructive for theology, is that the arts order our perceptions, training our senses to perceive reality more quickly and comprehensively. An example that comes to mind is the cinematic punctuation of the dissolve. By permitting one image to remain on the screen for a time with its successor, more than a multiple image is accomplished; a metaphor of continuity in motion results, with aspects of ease, facility, and causal relationship enriching it.

The organization of environmental arts is orchestration. It replaces the preference for organic unities which is a residue of a purely "nature" orientation in theology. In a theology wherein all conclusions flow from a single source, as life from a soul, there is little incorporation of diverse opinions. Contemporary communal efforts model themselves on an orchestration of effects, each part retaining its autonomy in the over-all unity, not losing it in an organic whole. The loose structure, fragmentation, even the use of existing songs ("Mrs. Robinson," "Changes," etc.) are a case in point. Multimedia events are an orchestration of media, with radio sound, clips of film, snatches of song and narration, plus black light or strobes to make participants integral. An "orchestrated" theology would be freed of the impossible task of creating an organic unity, and opened up to divergent opinions with all their multiple options.

How radical is the transformation advocated here? It would place on theology the role of a ritual acceleration of change which we shall call celebration. Instead of restraining change in order to parcel out the new after adequate reflection, theology must become the agency which could accelerate change humanely through the arts. The artistic pattern of selection and acceleration (or intensification) seems possible to theology by reason of its native freedom. The theological perspective which is an overview of ultimate meanings gives an unexcelled vantage point for understanding control of the environment. Even the simple invitation to live fully in the new time/space milieu can become a theological preparation for a freer life and a more pronounced transcendence. Christianity brings to its encounter with the present a strongly temporal orientation, the heritage both of its historical origins and its sense of a direction to world events. If this temporal cast has taken on extrinsic linear dimensions inimical to the futurity of the Gospel, it can be corrected by the spatial primacy of the information environment. When simultaneity eradicated time, turning past and present into what we may contradictorily call an "extended *now*," it demanded constant spatial, concrete incarnations of ideas. We have been reluctant in the past to attempt any study of the present because of its ephemeral nature, but when all becomes now, then the future is not distant but all about us. Like instantaneous replay on television, theological reflection can bring instant significance to this simultaneity, satisfying contemporary needs and celebrating the release from past limits. The process is not unlike the sacramental reality which is free from temporal limits so that it can effect needed incarnations of Christ's redemptive power in any age and place. The parallel may not diminish the radical nature of the theological work being described here, but it may show the way to an important Christian sense in which *the future is now*.

Our task is to free theology for this work. We have already freed ourselves from such arcane notions as historical "Christendom." Why not relieve the burden of maintaining an organic Christian community in a pluralistic age? The theologian may have to settle for what is "less," that is, some part in orchestrating the diverse peoples and ideas, theologies and rituals, into a new kind of unity. In doing so, he will resume a traditional role, that of enabling man to live in his environment so that his native transcendence is not stifled but liberated. As we shall see, this requires that the theologian discover his materials in the environment, rather than preserve them in the past. What may achieve order in the growing chaos around us may be the act of recognition that it is not chaos at all, but Christ continuing to work in his Spirit.

The content of these general ideas may become clearer as we explore the specific areas in which theology can take up its role of accelerating change, namely, in the context of belief and value. Enter theology—tomorrow's agent of change.

CHANGE

In the above paragraphs, theology was assigned the role of helping man to live humanly in his environment. The relation between this task and acceleration of change (our present concern) is theology's ability to intensify the human until it *becomes* divine. Basically, this means accelerating the processes of revelation and of human evolution. The means by which this can become possible are the arts, since theology will perform an artistic manipulation of change, ritualizing it, for example, and reducing it to the human mode of the beautiful. The pattern of such theological functions has changed through time. In the Primeval Interface, the natural environment was intensified by elevating the significance of the yearly cycle of planting and harvest, heat and cold. Theology via liturgy was able to give mythic meaning to natural forces, even personifying them for a more human rapport on the level of art and religion. This interpretation was actually a learning process, and actual improvements based on increased knowledge (e.g., agricultural lore) were introduced as religious rite. Unfortunately, this mode of acceleration and intensification has no counterpart in the Power Interface. Nevertheless, it is possible for theology to overcome its fear of technology, and to become an agent of change both in revelation and in values.

CHANGE AND BELIEF:
ACCELERATING REVELATION-AS-PROCESS

The future role of theology in the area of belief may be to illumine the environment for men in the light of the Gospel. This task requires both an immersion in the electronic environment and an act of faith that the work of Christ in his Spririt can operate there. The futuristic profession of faith may become a living assent to evidences of Christ's continuing redemptive work in the contemporary world. Selecting and interpreting the chaos of events and impressions, theology can invite man's recognition, so essential for Christian life, of a continual incarnation of the Gospel. The Incarnation is a way of looking at the world in the light of an event which forever weds the divine to the human. The very mode of the Incarnation, however, requires only that we detect the subtle transformation, the added *significance,* the divine gives to the human. Once again, the artistic representation and intensification of the present offer a beginning awareness of significance on which theology can work and build.

As we hold the mirror of art to the world for the insights which an antienvironment can afford us, specific examples come to mind. Cinema is a ready instance of an art ripe for collaboration with theology in a revelation of God's presence. Based on photographic art, film radically differs from other graphic arts in that the object creates its own "image." Photosensitive materials react to light from the object in a manner largely beyond the control of the artist. He can change the light, speed of film, time of day, angle of the camera, but the object makes its own image, which thereafter testifies to the existence (at one time) of what it portrays. The viewer, in turn, is left free to mine the riches of the reality which the photographic artist opens up to him. In motion-picture art, this freedom of the audience extends to relating the photographs which, shot by shot, constitute the raw material of the film. The artist merely begins the associations, which can extend as far as the riches of reality and the sensitivity of the viewer's perceptions will go. Art experience, as seen in the cinema, can then become an opening up of reality to as many levels of meaning as we are able to absorb.

The use of reality as a metaphor is one sign of film's capabilities in the area of theology. Film symbols are objects or processes revealing truths far beyond their own intelligibility as they appear in the context of the film. In *La Strada*, when Fellini associates Gelsomina with the sea and Zampano with the road, he releases associations from these settings which reinforce his characters by an appeal to the archetypes of the subconscious. All the sunny, cleansing regeneration of the sea are in Gelsomina, who offers salvation to Zampano in the form of self-knowledge through love. All the isolation, pragmatism, mundane brutality, and impermanence of the road are in Zampano, whose motto is, "I don't need anyone!" Gelsomina can change the signification of *La Strada* from "the road" to "the way" for Zampano, if he will open himself to love. Symbols such as these use reality, recognizable and autonomous, to create beautiful truth. The discipline of theology invites man to live on the level of analogy. Why should it not begin with the visual metaphors which are the unique feature of cinematic art? Creative artists such as Fellini, Richardson, Truffaut, and Kurosawa are continually revealing levels of the real formerly closed to us. In symbols of caged birds (*Nights of Cabiria*) or animals (*La Dolce Vita*), swimming pools (*The Graduate*) or computers (*2001: A Space Odyssey*), the filmmaker is inviting an open response to life.

The best way to make the Incarnation a reality is to perceive continually, prophetically, the relatedness of things. This relatedness exists independently of our perception of it, but it will not work its effect without the awakening of our critical awareness. This is the revelation behind our proposal that theology take on the announcing of Christ's continued presence and triumph in a world of change. The arts provide here not only an antienvironment for perspective, but actual embodiment of the Gospel as it has, perhaps unconsciously, affected the artist and the society. Affirmation of theological belief can then become the expressed conviction that the Incarnation is continually happening as divine and human are wed through the power of the Spirit. The union may not be Church-sanctioned, but it is still evidence of the divine. The arts in medieval times painted a sweeping incarnation of the Gospel in stained glass and sculpture, Gothic arch and Gregorian chant. They do the same today, speaking of the sacred in the language of secular liberation. The Christian humanist must learn that language.

Religion increasingly takes on the role of clarifying the human, defining its limits and encouraging its continued extension and development. Even as this trend increases, some recoil from the novelty and power of the humanist culture being approached. The reaction is not only a rejection of all that is not obviously sacred as "profane," but rather a fear of the humanist environment's vitality. The media address themselves so completely to the whole man, intensifying his life as art, that they tend to make ordinary religious experience (or the lack of it) seem pale. A naïve reaction says that the media are sensual, materialistic distractions to be avoided. Whatever the truth of these criticisms, the solution is not avoidance but control through understanding, an element which theology can provide. Applied faith means belief in levels of the real which eradicate the divisions between future and present, heaven and earth. Does it mean also that we cease to believe in a personal God?

The strongest objection to humanist Christianity is that it seems to make God unnecessary. Revelation comes from the world, our gaze is always on the human image—is there need any longer for God? Does God become simply our fellow man in need? This sense of the irrelevance of God is widespread, and causes alarm in Christians. But there is another sense in which God has become "unnecessary," and that is in the sense of his playing a new, unique role in our lives. The residue of myth and magic leaves God in our conceptions with primitive nature functions. It is precisely here that secularity liberates, rinsing the useless anthropomorphisms and cultural accretions from our notion of God. This is not an escalating abstraction which takes refuge in the pure, inaccessible notion of God as Pure Act. It is rather a freedom to contact God on the highest personal level. When God is recognized not as wind and water, or even as the Old Testament Father, but rather as the full call of Person to human person, then he will become the Prime Mover in man's self-actualization. It is clear that this is not to make

God unnecessary, but more necessary than ever on a level appropriate to his nature and our needs.

The more sophisticated act of faith required for this new encounter demands recognition of the hidden presence of God in the technological as well as the human environment. This recognition makes some sense of the sacred nature of objects. When objects tend to crowd personal values from our lives, as Citizen Kane's belongings destroy him in Orson Welles's picture we come to fear the "thingedness" of our existence. Filmmakers like Antonioni are not only interested in objects, but have the power to transform them into intelligible realities. The menacing factories belching poisonous fumes in *Red Desert* terrify the neurotic woman until, at the end, like the sparrows, she has learned not to fly through the smoke. The interface with technology is even more pronounced in *Blow-Up*, where the photographer seems to give up the very means by which he could have faced reality—his photographic equipment. These are the significant objects of our culture, and for the first time they become comprehensible through art. Cinema, unlike past forms, celebrates objects, just as television commercials make of their products the heroes of sixty-second dramas. Out of its history of animation (giving life to objects through motion photography) film has developed an art of discovery, finding beauty in the objects on junk heaps, releasing the meanings of things by relieving them of their utilitarian functions.

Ultimately this requires and feeds a sacramental view of reality. The cinematic symbolism we mentioned is a recognition that objects and processes—even persons—can have greater reality in their signification than in their simple existence. The sacramental system is a similar instance of spiritual energy released through signification and recognition. Bread and wine have more reality in a eucharistic celebration than in themselves. And yet, unless they are completely themselves, they cannot become more than they are. Environmental arts continually discover the reality of things, altering our sense perceptions so that we can really see and hear all the subtle messages of the object world. Best of all, film allows things to remain themselves even when used to signify, to reinforce ideas, or to illustrate characters. This insight is not available to all, but can become the project of theological inquiry. Christ said that if

192

his disciples were silenced even the stones would cry out. Perhaps today we need theological disciples who can evoke a witnessing cry from objects and from other men who speak to us of God.

CHANGE AND VALUE:
ACCELERATING HUMAN EVOLUTION

Evolution today means self-actualization. The role of theology, then, becomes one of accelerating the process of personal realization. But here we encounter one of the chief obstacles to a new theology of values—the static view of human nature. In the past, "nature" became an absolute principle from which certain modes of behavior were "deduced," and others were classified as human or nonhuman. Basing its observations on the relative unity of Western civilization, theology accepted humanity in its Western form and projected this as the ideal. However, anthropological studies revealed a far greater range of human possibilities than we had imagined. Although these findings were perhaps overdramatized, or offered as "refutations" of moral principles, their impact on values retains objective significance. Without becoming morally indifferent to the bewildering variety in the modes of human culture, we can nevertheless incorporate these findings into our concept of an evolving humanity. It will be easier to detect changes in man if we are not overly structured in our view of human nature.

Another facet of past rigidity with regard to human nature derives in part from an exaggerated concern for human freedom, understandable at the time it developed. Human psychology, sociological pressures, effects of mass media and similar forces lead us to consider man less free than we were accustomed to assume. Once again, this is not to deny freedom but to redefine its boundaries, with more attention paid to individual susceptibility to external forces. A greater insight into our own motives demands such consideration. There was a time when it was considered sufficient to assert human freedom firmly, and to remind people they were free "by definition," as it were. Today the need has changed, and it is more necessary to remind people to choose, and to assist them in choices by which they can grow. The more powerful the pressures from without, the more necessary it becomes to evoke choices from within, on the basis of personal authenticity rather than moral code or social mores, especially since these latter may be either faulty or insufficiently assimilated into one's personality.

In the light of communications theory, a theology of values should be aware of the patterns that contemporary media impose upon our views of human nature. A structured, stable view probably derives in part from the use of words, whether in the oral tradition or that of print. In a theology concerned with precise definitions, it was easy to confuse the clarity of a definition with the arbitrary fixity of the concrete individual nature. "Man" was one of the few perfect definitions known to speculative science, and so more time was spent elucidating the content of the definition than in exploring the existential richness of the defined. Moreover, studies made of any reality tended to be more structured when aimed at the formulation of a definition.

Today the richness of human possibilities is so apparent that the tendency is toward maximum individuality and the fulfillment of "doing your own thing." This phrase, we may note here, does not signify a program of action based on our knowledge of who we are, but a process of discovery of self in action. The activist movement on college campuses is symptomatic of this tendency, especially as it appears to symbolize rather than define. When told, "We know what you're against, but what are you *for?*" the student activist points to *what he does,* even if all he does is to demonstrate against what he considers injustices on campus, in the nation, or in the world. Seizing upon symbolic issues such as university land grabs, or conversion of an empty lot into a people's park, the student will confront authority in symbolic action. The overreaction of some authorities is, in turn, a gesture of violent symbolic significance. Student impatience with bargaining sessions, policy statements by administration officials, and with university codes of student behavior may in part be a young person's distrust of print, a medium that has betrayed him into inactivity so often in the past. Book people sometimes find it almost impossible to act, taking refuge in prolonged reflection, assembly of enormous amounts of data through regular channels of research. A television generation is more inclined to define itself in action rather than speculation. We can see the implications here for living as a Christian. Teaching values in terms of "control" communicates in reality a repression inhibiting change within the person. Rather than repression, control is an expression of self that externalizes feelings and attitudes, just as mastery of a difficult sport enables one to communicate with beauty and grace. A Christian ethical stance developed through repeated acts now appears to have had its roots in past traditions where the content of a culture was communicated by committing the classics to memory through repetition. Repetition is a valid learning device (witness the television commercial!), but it assumes a linear approach of a one-line form. Today it is being replaced by a more contemporary mode of "reinforcement," i.e., simultaneity. This is a more effective conditioning because it saturates the sensibility for the purpose of creative insight. Out of the surfeit of images and impressions can come a higher level of personal involvement, which is to relate the sensations and incorporate them into the total personality. Multisensory overload can also be used to diminish consciousness—as in techniques of brainwashing. Nevertheless, it should be tried in the work of fostering awareness and involvement as habitual responses by the individual in the area of values.

Once again, theology's collaborator in this process can be the contemporary media arts. To say that man's evolution is in his own hands is to recognize a human control over environment which will either stifle personal authenticity or promote growth and maturity. As our environment becomes more and more a network of information relationships, the problem of value becomes more and more that of self-actualization by control of the very means by which man extends himself into nature. Once more, man must face himself in his technology—the theme of *2001: A Space Odyssey,* dramatized in the "person" of Hal, the 9000 Series computer. Any return to a past period of stability is a dangerous and expensive romanticism, because the shortest route to extinction in the evolutionary process is not to change.

Leadership exercised by Christianity will counteract unrealistic stabilization and encourage self-actualization through change. If the computer diminishes human freedom, as some fear, it will be because man has failed to recognize it as an extension of himself. Such failure will lead either to unthinking worship of the apparatus, or to stupid misuse of computers as "mechanical men." The latter error already exists in the form of computer-controlled processes which merely duplicate, like primitive machines incapable of anything more complex. In reality, the significance of computer control is that infinite variety is now a possibility. That uniformity which was the strength and limit of the printing press and all subsequent assembly-line machine production need not restrict man today. This realization is important because it is easier to see the computer as an extension of man's higher functions in the context of a situation where it creates an ever greater number of choices. As for theology, it should concern itself with criteria for determining whether the changes that one undergoes are a true actualization of his own potentiality, or something foreign and imposed. Technology potentially frees man for a choice that is ultimately creative of himself. This is one way of looking at the devices for controlling birth, devices which are now distrusted as technology incapable of humanizing effects. As we attempt to sensitize ourselves to occasions for choice, control of birth becomes a key instance of man's facing himself in his technology with obvious implications for control of environment.

The environmental arts offer Christian ethics one means of recognizing man in his technology by their successful initial attempts to humanize the technological environment. We saw how film creatively manipulates time, space, and motion; it can be a powerful force in the area of values as well. There is today an art-based morality which grows out of the potential which arts such as film and television have for exploring human identity. We are speaking not only of possible subjective identification and involvement, but of emotional maturity through the experience of beauty. No one can feel personally the full range of the human condition, but many can become more fully human through artistic savoring of much of that condition. Without art, the range of our human emotional and sensory response is limited. But with selective experience and reflection in the arts, we can extend the scope of our response toward a keen moral sensitivity. Previous moral training, with its imperatives and warnings, tended to make us moralistic, condemning artistic presentations out of context or twisting them to draw unwarranted lessons from them. More appropriate is an openness to the art experience, and a realization which theology can bring, namely, that art helps us face our common humanity under conditions of crucial choice. Merely to mention Ben in *The Graduate,* or the couple in *Elvira Madigan,* or the lead in *Salesman* is to recognize that all of them are portrayed as making a choice that will either destroy or create them.

Films raise moral problems in the context of experience, a situation where relevance is less rarely a factor. The artist's work detects problems long before speculative sciences are customarily aware of them. With the artist's help in making the environment visible and somewhat comprehensible, the theologian can perform his task of inviting man to reflect on his identity and to actualize it by authentic activity. The change in values described earlier can become an evolutionary change if it uncovers human values in action. Some of the most profound comments on contemporary moral problems are being made in film art today: on violence, in *Bonnie and Clyde*; on beautiful, destructive fantasies, in *Elvira Madigan*; on nuclear war, in *Dr. Strangelove*; on the use of technology, in *Blow-Up*; and on delayed maturity, in *Rachel, Rachel.* Through film we become sensitized to the full range of the human condition: to a deaf mute's agonizing need for communication, in *The Heart Is a Lonely Hunter*; to the suffocating repression experienced by youth, in *If . . .* and *The Graduate*; to the ordeal of old age, in *The Whisperers*; and to the healing power of love, in *David and Lisa.* The humanist image which film holds up to man is a mirror of his own transcendence, not merely reflecting, but causing, inviting, intensifying response. All that is needed is a reflection on the experience of himself which can be held in discussion and conversation. The relationship between the film experience and value should be one discovered by the individual and not imposed by the theologian.

The collaboration between theology and the arts in morality extends far beyond the suggestions just made. It is a collaboration long overdue, for we find ourselves still unable to live humanly in our environment. Much of the difficulty lies in a criminal reluctance to face ourselves there, and to find in confrontation that control is ours. There are dangers indigenous to the media themselves: conformity through mass communications, alienation submersion in a mass society, and noninvolvement as a desperate attempt at control through exclusion of input. There is, in addition, the fear that media can diminish our freedom by so multiplying our choices that we feel they are no longer under our control. The present mode of world news reportage, for example, brings all of humanity into our living room, but it so homogenizes the news that it comes out all the same. Giving world news equal time with local trivia makes us consider them equally unimportant. With newsreel photos of dying men in Vietnam and Biafra interspersed with commercials for sports cars and dog food "with more meat," we turn off our sensibilities lest we die of irony. The potential impact of world news, with its power to foster unity and responsibility, is offset by the media blend which reduces our response. Objectivity redefined in reductionist terms places news "coverage" higher on the priority list than "uncoverage" or useful interpretation of the significance of events. Television news analysts such as David Brinkley are popular not only for their obvious talent and wit, but for the attitude of detached irony which helps the viewer feel superior to the events they report. The over-all effect of objectivity without object is indifference, which is a greater threat than the political and economic manipulation of broadcasting.

Theology has to deal with the general response to the problems listed above—the response of apathy. The only active vibration to media ills seems to be the philosophy of consumerism, merely a reminder that depth psychology used in commercials pays off. Programing is often indistinguishable from selling, since the life style in domestic comedies, for example, consistently dramatizes objects over love, beauty, thought, and other human values. What concerns us is that these experiences will communicate values, whether we are aware of them or not. There is a value system of exclusion in the absence of Black and Puerto Rican, of the aged and the unlovely from the television screen. There is a school for indifference in the silence (except for the palliative "specials") on poverty, hunger, and disease, which jar badly alongside the entertainment fare of the TV screen. Instead of these services, there appears the suburban unreality of most domestic comedies, the historical distortions of *Hogan's Heroes,* the casual violence as a solution to human problems in western and spy series, and the caricatured sexuality of the variety and romance shows. As the examples indicate, creative interface has two sides, and one at least conceals instead of revealing the environment.

The theologian of values must make an act of faith that Christ wishes man to evolve into full humanity, into the human potential of the Incarnation. Even more, he must believe that Christ is working, in his Spirit, to effect that evolution. His work then becomes an acknowledgment of that presence, and a cooperation with its effects wherever they appear. Using the means best suited to provide controlled acceleration of man's evolution, theology takes the arts to help man understand the true nature of the process of self-actualization. Forming consciences, for example, will be closely allied to forming consciousness or awareness, since we cannot become ourselves unless we are concretely a part of our own time and place. Providing experiences in the arts, and following them up with reflection, can become the most effective training ground in moral sensitivity.

We have reason to hope that theological work in the arts and media of mass communication can help launch a new humanism. The false barrier of the two cultures is gradually giving way to a creative interface with technology in the information environment. As they help us face our instruments, the arts also remind us that we are free and we must choose. These choices are presented with concrete beauty in the arts, so that the ethic which emerges is situational and existential. All that is needed is a reminder that we continually affirm and express our identity by acting decisively and recognize clearly those actions which destroy realization of self. Theological work in this area effectively accelerates man's evolution in the light of the Gospel. As always, man will evolve by relating more perfectly to the environment, especially when it becomes an extension of himself, and a mirror in which he can study his countenance. Such an evolution is already taking place both on the level of the individual and that of society.

Individual evolution is already a fact on the level of sense perceptions, where the media are altering the balance and harmony of our senses. Among the many manifestations of this change is the generation gap. Aside from sociological and psychological factors, the generations are divided by different modes of contacting reality. The perceptive life of different age groups is radically different, even among children of the same family. As the first TV generation arrives in college, individuals find their younger brother too different to communicate with effectively, even if the greatest sympathy and tact are employed. Perceptive styles change so rapidly that our emotional maturity cannot keep up with the opening contact with reality. The result could be a generation of young who know everything but themselves. This is one reason why they should be invited to understand personal values through an open response to arts and media.

Social evolution is accelerated by media feedback, and operation by consensus. The telephone talk show, although often handled like cheap melodrama, can be an occasion for creative insight, as the feedback helps us understand what is disturbing men. Whether it is the pathetic rage of a warped individual enjoying his first captive audience, or the earnest concern of a man who has never sensed his own power before, what comes to light is a common humanity. As a mass society seeks a means of creating a sense of community, we should recognize the unifying effect of bringing others into one's home to discuss issues that concern us all. As for the consensus we mentioned, it may seem to be far from actualization, but in a form that we do not yet recognize easily it may be closer than we know. The media arts are searching for a myth which will unite modern society. The profound effect of gazing on earth from the moon caused the astronauts to speak with amazed insight of our *one* earth, a unity that makes trivial the human divisions we live with. These effects properly reinforced can extend to society at large, giving us a new perspective for solving divisive issues. Initial attempts to formulate a meaningful myth may appear a bit awkward. *Star Trek* presents an intergalactic good-will force fighting for humanist values in a bizarre variety of circumstances. Other programs cater to our fascination with gadgetry by making technology the hero in solving human problems. *Mission: Impossible,* by submerging the individual within the team and making the object its "star," unconsciously recognizes that technology represents man. Theology can have a part in the erection of such new mythical structures. The only myths that are harmful are the myths that foster unawareness or an inability to live in the present.

In a sense, the role of theology in accelerating human evolution is a revolutionary one, if we take revolution in Chalmers Johnson's sense: sweeping, fundamental change in political organization, social structure, economic property control, and the predominant myth of social order, thus indicating a major break in the continuity of development. What we might add here is a sweeping change in values accompanying all the others, and this is what will effect the major leap in human evolution. Theology should speak on issues: political groupings that destroy free participation in government; social structures and economic systems that place property and profits over personal growth; societal myths that paralyze human response. It is so easy for such structures to dominate our existence. Only after the riots following Martin Luther King's assassination did we realize that our laws and customs placed property over human life. In the agony of deciding what way to control looting, we faced our legal environment and found it to be a defense of the rich against the poor. There must be less violent ways to make such discoveries, and theology can be an instrument for such investigations.

The work of revolution is urgent—in most areas a major break is necessary. This work, however, does not necessarily mean a career of political activism for the theologian. Sometimes the most effective way to accelerate change is to affirm it, ride with it, direct it from within. A revolution in values does not seem extreme when placed next to the human ills it is designed to correct. The Gospel offers a remedy for the dehumanizing effects of alienation, and this is its character as a revolutionary document for social change and human evolution. A morality of self-actualization, a crusade for freer choice and more effective action, a fostering of values through simultaneity—all these are revolutionary concepts derived from the Gospel. After enough talk of the political Christian revolutionary (as in South America), we need to learn the capabilities of Christian revolution in the area of creative interface where man is evolving today. It may be that theology can offer contemporary man, out of the chaos of a runaway technology, the inner sources of control. If so, it will have helped man evolve according to the pattern of unlimited potential which is the Incarnation.

Educational Processes and Theology

✠

PATRICK C. ROONEY

Education is involved in every change; it is as necessary to the prophet of the future as to the builder. Patrick Rooney, O.P., is a member of an experimental team which is exploring the problem areas of contemporary religious education. Assistant Director of the Center for Studies in Religious Education, and Instructor in the Education Department of Notre Dame University, he is editor of A Social Science Approach to Religious Education *(1969).*

There can be little doubt that education occupies a central position in the phenomenon which is the American way of life. For better or worse, this country initiated a great experiment in massive education for all its citizens, and the most casual glance at the popular press will reveal the anxieties and tensions, the joys and pride this experiment is causing the American people today. Indeed, fears concerning the very survival of this nation are usually generated by, or at least closely related to, one's personal evaluation of the current educational scene. Whether or not the educational establishment of this country actually does play as significant a role in the total picture of our society as many people (particularly educationists) are inclined to think, is itself a topic open to much debate. But to say that student unrest, campus demonstrations, and riots, the apparent revolt of the present generation and the educational system which has variously encouraged and repressed these situations are of ordinary importance to the well-being of the United States is to grossly underestimate the foundational position present educational issues hold in the American context. This essay will attempt to delineate at least some of the issues presently responsible for the crisis in our schools, what they mean for the immediate future of education, and how they are significant for the Christian churches in this country.

John I. Goodlad claims that the Sputnik revolution of 1957 resulted in ten years of American history which should be denominated as the Education Decade.[1] During this time, public sentiment attempted to lay the blame for America's apparent lag in scientific and technological sophistication on the schools. It became fashionable, and still is, to criticize the school system for not producing the alert, scientifically knowledgeable, but humanly compassionate person who, according to the best American tradition(s), should have been the result of public school processes. This outcry resulted, with the aid of the National Defense Education Act and ultimately the Elementary and Secondary Education Act of 1965, in the establishment of science and technological education as the center of the school's curriculum.

In itself, the advancement of science education during the Education Decade was undoubtedly a blessing for the American people. The technological gap which was so rapidly closed enabled Americans to have once again that satisfying feeling of conquering new frontiers, this time in the world of outer space. But as with so many frontiers, great and small, in the history of the American people the satisfaction was in the process of conquering. Once the frontier was attained, we found ourselves with little or no rationale for being there in the first place. This meant that by the end of this decade an increasing number of voices were heard demanding a thorough look at American schools and questioning the advisability of such a heavy concentration on science education. Does not human life, after all, comprise something more than scientific and technological skills, and is it not the function of our schools to educate the young in this "something more" so that they might

[1] John I. Goodlad, "The Schools vs. Education," *Saturday Review*, 52 (Apr. 19, 1969), 59.

become wise humanitarians in a society which sorely needs such persons? Many Americans came to share a common complaint: "My pet peeve is that our whole educational system seems directed to discovering how, in the shortest period of time, we may turn clever children into stupid adults."[2]

The most dramatic critics of the educational establishment in the years following the Education Decade have been the students themselves. Major campus disorders have disrupted universities in every corner of the country, and at this writing there appears to be no relief on the horizon. In fact, many observers feel that the student movement—or rebellion, as some prefer to call it—will continue to grow and spread downward to the high school and junior high school levels.[3] The surface issues in campus disorders range from internal collegiate matters such as curriculum revision, grading, parietal hours, and even the quality of dining hall food, to the burning issues of the world community at large, war, racial injustice, poverty. But underlying all of these issues there seems to be a profound disgust, a dread, an *Angst*, of an increasingly complex educational system which, in the words of Kenneth Boulding, "has been quite successful in preparing people to be middle class, to the point indeed where middle-class values permeate perhaps eighty percent of our population."[4] What is apparent through most of the students' demands is that they simply do not want to be formed into the great American model of righteous middle-class life.

Contributing to the general picture of educational chaos and unrest are a number of significant factors intrinsic as well as extrinsic to the academic community. Some of these will be discussed here in order to delineate as clearly as possible the enormous task facing American education in the years to come.

[2] Rudolf Dreikus, as quoted in *Information Service,* Department of Research of the National Council of Churches, 48 (March 8, 1969), 7.

[3] Diane Divoky, "The Way It's Going To Be," *Saturday Review,* 52 (Feb. 15, 1969), 83.

[4] Kenneth E. Boulding, "Expecting the Unexpected: The Uncertain Future of Knowledge and Technology," in Edgar L. Morphet and Charles O. Ryan, eds., *Prospective Changes in Society by 1980:* Vol. 1 of *Designing Education for the Future* (New York, 1967), 212.

THE NEW AMERICAN WAY OF LIFE

Earlier, reference was made to the impact of scientific developments upon education between 1957 and 1967. The educational system of this country, however, does not exist in isolation from society at large, and in order to understand how scientific and technological advances have affected education, these advances must be seen in the larger context of American society.

Science, and its cybernated application, technology, are changing the American way of life. This is fairly obvious from a material, quantitative point of view when one considers the amazing scientific discoveries of just the past twenty-five years. Production is now at a peak, and its continued growth is expected by most experts in spite of periodic warnings that these affluent times cannot increase *ad infinitum*. Accordingly, the cash value of goods and services available to the American public will increase from $676 billion to $1¼ trillion by 1980.[5] Along with this steady growth of goods and material, there has been, as a result of technological automation, a decline in the number of people needed to keep production at peak levels. It is now believed that within fifteen years only two or three percent of the population will be needed to do the work necessary to fulfill the material needs of society.[6] This means that there will be a marked development of the so-called service industries such as education, health, recreation, and social services, which as early as 1960 already employed 55 percent of the American labor force.[7]

Note must also be taken that the above figures do not imply a sharp increase in unemployment; on the contrary, employment will

[5] Gerard Colm, "Prospective Economic Developments," in Morphet and Ryan, *op. cit.*, 92.

[6] *Ibid.*, 90.

[7] Ralph W. Tyler, "Purposes, Scope and Organization of Education," in Morphet and Ryan, eds., *Implications for Education of Prospective Changes in Society*: Vol. 2 of *Designing Education for the Future* (New York, 1967), 35.

be at an all-time high. Many economists believe that by the middle 1970s unemployment can be stabilized at only 3 percent of the labor force.[8] Projections also indicate that we may have to find a term other than "labor force," for although the United States can expect a record 97 percent of its available workers employed, the amount of time spent in work will decrease from a typical 40 hours per week at the present time to 36.7 hours per week, as a maximum, as early as 1975.[9]

What all of this seems to indicate is that Americans can expect continued and increased material affluence and leisure through the 1970s and on into the next decade. But this may not remain as pleasant a picture as it at first seems, for along with a quantitative development of the American way of life, the scientific-technological revolution is also touching the quality of our life and the values for which this country stands.

The drive toward material well-being and economic prosperity has been built into the American value system ever since colonial days and the predominant Calvinist ethic. Whether most Americans would care to admit it or not, the technological advances of the last twenty-five years have seriously threatened the Puritan religious/moral stance. One of the principal canons of the Puritan ethical code was based on the assumption that salvation is indicated for each individual to the degree that he is a materially productive member of society. This meant that work, honest hard work, held an essential place in the American value system.

The development of this principle in space and time has given a highly individualistic orientation to basic American values. Salvation came to those who worked hard and possessed much, and the ideal American became the person who started in relative poverty but attained fabulous wealth in a lifetime devoted to work. The fact that wave after wave of immigrants coming to this country were able to participate in and even succeed in this work process simply reconfirmed its fundamental position in the American way of life.

[8] Edward W. Uthe, ed., *Social Change: An Assessment of Current Trends* (Philadelpha, 1968), 92–94.
[9] *Ibid.*

Today, it is no longer necessary to work as if ultimate happiness depended on it. America is producing more and working less, thanks to science and technology. Salvation through work alone is fast approaching the level of meaningless verbiage. Indeed, for the present student generation it is already senseless, because they have not been faced with the struggle to get ahead materially, to acquire money and goods as a sign of their success as "good citizens." They can look forward to an adult life in which work *as a moral value* has an increasingly diminished role. This is undoubtedly one of the major contributing factors to the generation gap much publicized today. The gap is not simply a temporal phenomenon; it is a crisis of morals and values in which a subtle, and sometimes not so subtle, shift is occurring from an ethic of individualism to an ethic which hopefully will be characterized by a profound social concern.

The educational establishment of the United States can be seen today as both promoting change in our collective value system as well as standing in reaction to such change. If students today seem radically idealistic, open to new views and a thorough reorganization of society, their schooling has substantially aided the formation of these attitudes. Professor Charles Muscatine of Berkeley feels that in spite of all the criticisms which can justly be leveled against the American school system, at least some good has rubbed off on the students. He says, "It is as if for years we had taught Freedom, Democracy, the need for Criticism—for years had been assigning Plato, Voltaire, Jefferson, Thoreau, Emerson, Mill—and suddenly there appeared a generation of students with the temerity to take it all literally."[10]

Something similar has been happening within Christian education in the recent past. This ministry of the church, always the center of controversy, criticism, and opinionated prejudice, has perhaps had an effect which most church members fail to recognize. Within Roman Catholicism, for example, there has been a tremendous effort over the past ten years to update the teaching of religion in the Catholic school system. While the majority of Church

[10] Charles Muscatine, "The Future of University Education as an Idea," in Walter Ong, ed., *Knowledge and the Future of Man* (New York, 1968), 58.

members—students, parents, teachers, and hierarchs—would probably agree that this effort has been far from successful, the possibility exists that the countless boys and girls who have been inundated with the "new catechetics" may have actually *believed* some of it. This means that they would base their personal values upon such radical Gospel themes as individual freedom, social justice, personal authenticity, and the fundamental dignity of the human person. This is what has increasingly been taught and verbalized in Catholic schools throughout the country, yet it is definitely not the religion of simple conformity taught and learned by most adults. What happens to young people who believe that religion is a program of justice, honesty, and love when they willingly or unwillingly attend typical Sunday services or when they see the Church publicly "discipline" certain of its members for undertaking concrete actions aimed at promoting Gospel values? While the Gospel itself may remain for them a meaningful, radical, and believable ideal, the Church becomes inconsequential, irrelevant, and unbelievable. There is generated, in other words, a crisis of confidence in the Church, which claims on the one hand to be the interpreter and preserver of the true Gospel, while on the other hand not providing realistic opportunities to experience the Gospel within ecclesial structures.

If the churches can be faulted for the lack of a marked convergence between what they say they stand for and what they actually do in the concrete, so can the American school system. While Muscatine's observation is certainly true, namely, that the schools teach Freedom, Democracy, and the need for Criticism, they have also taught that the one valid way of practicing these values is by conforming to and participating in the life style of complacent, white, middle-class America. This is perhaps nowhere more apparent than on the countless college and university campuses throughout the country which have erupted in violent conflict between students and administration not so much over basic values (everyone is in favor of justice, honesty, and love) but over what kind of life styles such values allow.

The problem of pluralistic life styles, of convergence between stated belief and actual practice is no longer limited to higher education. It is rapidly becoming a key issue in American secondary schooling and will, hopefully, promote a thorough rethinking of what the American high school does. Professor Edward J. Gordon of Yale believes that

> . . . the school itself as an institution cannot contradict what it is trying to teach in the classroom. It cannot teach the value of freedom of inquiry and at the same time censor books and ideas. It cannot teach the value of individual dignity and disregard student opinion. It cannot call for responsible behavior without allowing students— and teachers—to have responsibility. It cannot be built around the governmental structure of a boss who dictates school policy and then expect to produce students who really believe in a majority rule, or even that a human being matters.[11]

At the present time there is a renaissance in the philosophy of education brought on by the need to question radically once again the meaning and purpose of American education. And although Gordon can rightly suggest that the goal of the school is today what it always has been, "to produce a free, reasoning person who can make up his own mind, who will understand his cultural tradition, and who can live compassionately with his fellow men,"[12] there is a whole new way of viewing this product and the hopeful expectation that educationists at long last have truly effective means of attaining this goal. While some may think that this is another classic example of educational euphoria, recent developments indicate that there is greater foundation in reality for these expectations today than there has been in the past.

One of the most significant advances in the philosophy of education is found in the new insights concerning the process of teaching/learning. Jerome Bruner of Harvard has pointed out that the learning process, while traditionally concerned with content and method, has not dealt adequately with the real meaning of these concepts. He believes that content, i.e., what is to be taught, ought to concern itself with the fundamental structures of a particular discipline rather then with the comprehensive body of in-

---

[11] Edward J. Gordon, "Conflicting Values in the Secondary School," in Alfred de Grazia and David A. Sohn, eds., *Revolution in Teaching: New Theory, Technology, and Curricula* (New York, 1964), 55.

[12] *Ibid.*, 51.

formation a particular discipline has accumulated through centuries of human endeavor.[13] This means that whatever content is taught ought to lead the student not merely to be intellectually aware of what a certain discipline deals with but especially to participate in the processes of that discipline. In actual school practice, this would demand that in regard to mathematics, for example, the students be taught the information necessary to be—or, better, to become— mathematicians instead of mechanically reproducing mathematical exercises.

In order to bring this about, Bruner also contends that we have been inadequate in the area of methodology, or *how* a discipline is to be taught. Traditionally, methodology has dealt with various styles, practices, and even gimmicks which the teacher would use in the course of a normal classroom period. Bruner believes that methodology ought to center more on the student rather than the teacher, so that it becomes what he calls "discovery learning."[14] Discovery learning is the process whereby a student actively participates in the unearthing of knowledge, and the key to this process is not how much, quantitatively speaking, a student knows about the discipline at hand, but rather how he views and reacts to the evidence or information which he uncovers with the aid of the teacher.

For Bruner, then, content and method are correlatives, one cannot exist without the other, and their emphasis has shifted away from the teacher toward the student. Actually, Bruner has pointed out that teaching/learning is one thing, a process which is engaged in simultaneously by teacher and pupil alike. This is certainly a fundamental redirection from previous learning theories which opted for a kind of magisterial program in which the teacher would verbally tell the students what was good for them to hear. On this basis, Bruner's theory of instruction is in reality a new philosophy of education because it centers the purpose of education on a

---

[13] Bruner's major works include *The Process of Education* (New York, 1960); *On Knowing* (Cambridge, 1963); *Toward a Theory of Instruction* (New York, 1968).

[14] J. Bruner, "The Act of Discovery," in Edwin Fenton, ed., *Teaching the New Social Studies* (New York, 1966), 125.

dynamic interaction of teacher and pupil in a continuing process of discovery instead of upon the simple imparting of factual, intellectual information.[15] In other words, Bruner's ideas redirect the basic meaning of education from a medieval *magister-auditor* relationship to a more human and, hopefully, educationally more effective, enterprise in which both teacher and pupil together embark on a quest for truth and knowledge which leads to a fuller, more rational and compassionate appreciation of this world, its human existence and its ultimate destiny. In coming generations students will be able to cope with and perhaps direct the course of their future rather than to defend incessantly the knowledges, emotions, morals, and values of previous generations. This will demand that teacher-student relationships enter a new phase characterized by a more intimate personal concern for each other, so that the process of education, which is a mutual quest, can take place. Education in the coming years ought, therefore, to be closely allied with the ancient Greek idea of the pedagogue, an adult person who *cares for* the students entrusted to him.[16]

OPTIONS FOR THE CHURCH

The Christian churches have a number of options open to them in responding to education in the coming years. In the first place, they can simply ignore educational developments and processes within American public schooling. This is possible because church functionaries are still able to argue that the church has an essentially spiritualized ministry which ought to concern itself exclusively with the particular relationship of each church member to his God. But most likely such a head-in-the-sand attitude will not characterize the church's relationship in the years to come,

---

[15] An interesting discussion of Bruner's theories as applied to religious education can be found in Janet E. Shapiro, "The Significance of Jerome Bruner's Educational Philosophy for Religious Education," *Religious Education*, 43 (1968), 462–68.

[16] Gordon categorically states that the best way to evaluate a school is to discover what its graduates *care for. Cf.* Gordon, *loc. cit.*

since education occupies the talents of roughly 30 percent of the American population, and it would be simply preposterous to imagine that the church could somehow justify a lack of concern for the educational enterprise.

More probably, the years to come will see the church continue to take a deep interest in educational developments from the traditional point of view of making use of advances in the field for her own educational ministry. Christian educators at the theoretical and practical levels will attempt to convert the findings of secular educationists into programs for religious education. While this has occurred in a rather haphazard manner in the past, recent educational discoveries indicate that it will be increasingly important for religious educators to become more and more educationally sophisticated.[17] This would be especially true concerning new proposals on the nature and purpose of education. As secular educational theorists restate the goal of American public education in humanizing and value-oriented terms, the religious educator will be forced thoroughly to rethink his own task and distinctive contribution.

An obligation of this sort will fall most heavily upon those Christian denominations which own and operate their own schools. Within Roman Catholicism, the largest operator of private schools in this country, for example, the thrust of public education toward humanization and value/moral education ought to represent the most serious threat to the existence of separate Catholic schools ever seen in this country. Catholic schools began in reaction to a public school system which was predominantly Protestant in orientation. This rationale eventually gave way to the idea that Catholics had to have a separate school system because public education, while no longer a Protestant enterprise, had become secularistic and even pagan. Although not articulated in such gross terms, this argument continues today to be the fundamental rationale for the separate Catholic system. But within Catholic *religious* education (as opposed to mere Catholic schooling) the direction is toward

17 An excellent example of how religious educators are beginning to listen to their secular colleagues can be found in the symposium, "Educational Theory and Religious Education," *Religious Education*, 43 (1968), 457–89.

a more human interpretation of the Christian Gospel with a deep concern for value, for moral, and attitudinal education. Since this direction is almost identical with the growing concerns of public education, the question of a separate system must once again be seriously considered by Catholics and those other denominations which have a large stake in their own schools. Hopefully, this questioning will occur on the level of the philosophy of education and the theology of Christian teaching and not, as at the present time, merely on the level of finances and personnel resources.

The third option, which ought to be the keynote of the church's and Christian theology's relationship to education in the future, must be discussed. If the church should not ignore education, neither should it view educational developments in this country simply as something it can use for its own purposes in religious education. This would be too narrow a relationship, and might indicate a reluctance on the part of the church to serve one of the most significant movements in the United States. The option, then, is to discover what the church can contribute in a positive and perhaps direct way to education in America.

From a traditional theological standpoint, it is extremely difficult to delineate a direct role for the Church in educational enterprise. Indeed, if theology were done today in the unchanging patterns of the past with only traditional concerns, there would be little hope that the church has anything to say to American public education. Fortunately, theology is breaking away from its historical modes and is becoming increasingly this-worldly in orientation and methodology. Theology is now a problematical activity which addresses itself to the issues of the marketplace in an effort to serve the people of this world at this time. What this orientation means in practice is that the Church can and ought to have something relevant to say about the problems and tensions faced by contemporary society. The Church should not, and theologically cannot, have the final, definitive word for the key issues of the day, but it certainly can give a supporting, sustaining, and enabling word to those engaged in the sometimes bitter endeavor of attempting to alleviate the great difficulties facing the human community.

It is in this light that the Christian churches and theology might speak to the educational community. To a great degree, the very existence of America as a nation that promotes democracy, freedom, and human dignity depends on the quality of education its citizens are able to receive. Since the founding of this country, we have been engaged in the most extensive educational experiment ever undertaken in the history of man. It is still problematical whether the experiment will work, but it is at the heart of Jeffersonian political theory—that the people can and should govern themselves provided every citizen, through education, can attain the developmental level needed for intelligent, rational, and compassionate participation in the democratic processes.

Secular educational theorists are faced today with the enormous task of creating an educational establishment which will effectively produce a free, pluralistic, and humanly sensitive citizen. They have been called to this task by their own students, who, perceiving the incongruities and lack of convergence in the American way of life, have dramatically demanded honesty, authenticity, and individual responsibility from American society in general and from the American educational system in particular. Professionally, the theorists of education may have the competence to provide such an education. But from a human, workaday point of view, they need the assistance of whatever agency contemporary society is willing to provide.

It is here that the Christian churches can render a decisive service. Just as there is concern within the church for a political theology, a theology of revolution, a theology of history, and a theology of the future, there ought to be a corresponding concern for an educational theology. Educational theology is the effort on the part of Christian theology to delineate the place of teaching/ learning in the human processes leading to salvation. This means that the churches, theologically, must concentrate on the prophetic nature of teaching. Teaching may have to stand in contradiction to the status quo, or at least assume a critical but positive role in relation to the environment in which it exists. What the churches ought to do in the near future, then, is to speak to the educational community with a saving word, one that encourages, sustains, and even enables secular educationists to continue to probe the most realistic measures needed to create a truly free human society.

In the final analysis, an educational theology may demand that the churches divest themselves of duplicating educational programs, that they give up the right to educate their own members fully, so that they might concentrate their energies within the larger community—an America existing in desperate need of some kind of good news. That Gospel insists, in a prophetic way, that justice, honesty, and love are realistic possibilities in a nation which claims to be founded upon the premises of life, liberty, and the pursuit of happiness.

Afterword: The End of Theology?

✠

THOMAS F. O'MEARA AND
DONALD M. WEISSER

The preceding pages have repeatedly shown that Christ cannot be at work in the world if his presence does not emerge out of the life and mentality of each new people and time. Christians, along with all citizens of this planet, must learn new languages, must accept unexpected ideas and aspirations gleaned from new experiences both awesome and hopeful. The future stands at the end of these projections as it did at their beginning. But for man the future is now different, for it is literally becoming eschaton—apocalypse or kingdom.

ENVIRONMENT AS CREATIVE OF THEOLOGY

The wise men of the media revolution as well as city planners recognize that the horizon of American life is now *environment*. There are environments of steel and glass, of barns and meadows, and there are new environments of television and communications satellites. Some see the city as obsolete, to be replaced by environmental systems. An American lives in a series of environments. He is surrounded by systems which both serve him and form him. The water he drinks, the air he breathes, his means of transcending space come from these systems. To travel is ultimately to submit oneself to a vast network of electronic and combustion systems spread over the globe. Entertainment and the arts, too, have turned from the object to the system. In films the story line is reduced; people are central. Realism is present, but not as a realism in the screen actors but as reality for the viewers.

> The young have discovered that film is an environment which you put on, demanding a different kind of structure, a different mode of attention than any other art. . . . By a process of intense identification, brought on by the environment created and special devices such as the subjective camera, the viewer is invited to experience himself what the actors say and do on the screen. The film idiom demands that the viewer make the associations which give the film unity and coherence, and in addition to those intended by the director, there are hundreds of associations made only by the viewer.[1]

There is a shift from the object to the environmental system. Man no longer uses things, but fashions, by means of technologies, systems which can determine him in their embrace.

> Furniture, books, cooking utensils, tools, toys and reliquaries were only some of the objects which made existence *objectively* real. . . . In contrast, the object now is a replaceable component in an interlocking system of production and need fulfillment. When we buy an automobile we no longer buy an object in the old sense of the word, but instead we purchase a three- to five-year lease for participation in the state-recognized private transportation system, a highway system, a traffic safety system, an industrial parts-replacement system, a costly insurance system, an outdoor advertising system, a state park recreation system, a drive-in eating and entertainment system—and, not least of all, the general economic system.[2]

Education also implies large systematic administrations with computers and evaluating and testing processes. This system is the ticket to others: vocation, profession, adult life. The world is becoming unified so that the economic stability of one country is affected by riots in another. Any war can be televised in color.

---

[1] Anthony Schillaci, "Film as Environment," *Saturday Review,* 51 (December 28, 1968), 8.

[2] Jack Burnham, "Introduction," *Beyond Modern Sculpture* (New York, 1968), 11.

Technology allows man to create his environment rather than fight it. "The system becomes a logical extension of the object through intellectual domination of the environment."[3] But will we bless or curse man with our environmental systems? Technology may be the means by which all societies become an interconnected living system structured to allow for maximum human communication and sharing within the whole, or technology's systems may lead to an inhuman collapse of living together. Rather than building the City, they allow the City, as in a retroactive time-machine, to become again the primitive jungle or the smoke-filled cave.

Christianity must recognize this new situation of environments. For fifteen centuries Christian churches struggled to retain a position of being *the* environment. From the century of discovery, renaissance, and religious reformation onwards, the possibility of maintaining such a unity declined. In the Middle Ages, theology was the queen of the sciences and spread over the other departments of life like a canopy; for the Protestant Hegel, theology was an aspect of a universal science-politics which included the church and the state. When these patterns declined, the Christian found himself in a split world. He left his secular life and the city where he worked and entered into the parish church, which presented briefly a sacred world. Both the movement toward a social unity-with-pluralism and urban secularization make this split between the sacred and the secular impossible. Christianity is now called upon not just to survive with toleration amid a new world of sociotechnical environments, but to find the realization and expression of its Gospel there. Secondly, it is looked to as a source of true humanity and transcendent hope in the midst of uncertainty and alienation.

The Christian Gospel can be a faithful and hopeful stimulus for accepting and rejoicing in change. Pluralism and adaptation in the churches offer an encouraging pattern for other institutions to follow. If ecclesiastical office is submitted to criteria of efficacy

[3] *Ibid.*, 18. "This is the real use of the computer, not to expedite marketing or solve technical problems, but to speed the process of discovery and orchestrate terrestrial and eventually galactic environments and energies. . . . In a Christian sense, this is merely a new interpretation of the mystical body of Christ; after all, Christ is the ultimate extension of man." "Marshall McLuhan: An Interview," *Playboy* (March, 1969), 53.

and fidelity, then political institutions can certainly be questioned. Christ does not become merely the means to an improved secular life, but he does interpret everything which touches the ultimate concerns of men. It is difficult to express this new interplay of the Christian within the environments of life, and yet the New Testament is written in these terms. Teilhard de Chardin writes of a dynamic interaction of two forward movements: "In order to match the new curve of Time, Christianity is led to discover the values of this world below the level of God, while Humanism finds room for a God above the level of this world. Inverse and complementary movements; or rather, the two faces of a single event which perhaps marks the beginning of a new era for Mankind."[4]

The churches dimly recognize the shift of life from objects to environments. Fewer institutions and church buildings are being built; ecumenical cooperation is increasing. It is important to understand what lies behind the formation of the many "floating parishes."[5] With expensive, comfortable church buildings for their use, thousands of groups flee to a classroom or to a neighbor's living room to express their Christian faith. They illustrate the need to allow Christianity to refashion envangelical community.

There is a twofold relationship of Christian community to the world of environments. It cannot find satisfaction in an artificial atmosphere on Sunday morning, a "sacred" world of large church buildings. That system of sacred buildings, ancient rites, and venerable songs is artificial, unrelated to the environments shaping our life. It gives us nothing to return with; it ignores our self and our world. There is a parallel between the religious and the scientific situations. Science no longer is content simply to receive data from an immutable world of nature, but shapes man's relationships to nature. Similarly, the Christian no longer wants simply to receive the "holy" from sacral places and persons. Rather (and here he is close to the early church), he takes seriously the incarnational and communal aspects of Christ, seeing faith as the entrance to new

[4] *The Future of Man* (New York, 1964), 18.

[5] T. M. Steeman, "The Underground Church: The Forms and Dynamics of Change in Contemporary Catholicism," *The Religious Situation–1969* (Boston, 1969), 713–748.

relationships: with himself, with other men, with God. The Christian environment, the *ecclesia,* has two directions: *It is environment-reflective and environment-creative.* It reflects and finds its own incarnation out of the life of men as lived today. But it also creates for men not a separate world or a ghetto, but an environment that discloses through the message of Jesus Christ the openness of history and life.

The first facet celebrates the Christian's life in faith and worship as he lives it. He does not leave his art or his problems behind, nor does he enter into another more religious or more Christian world of the past. Christ finds renewed incarnation within a continuity with the workaday world. Something is "Christian" not because it imitates another world but because it offers the Christian perspective. Thanksgiving, benediction, and celebration are not superimposed upon the "material" or "worldly"; rather, the latter are the stuff out of which the former come into life. From the second point of view, Christianity is not just an affirmation of the world, but a critical and decisive perspective. It is such because it is eschatological and transcendent. These last two words describe the values of the life of Jesus Christ. His resurrection is the unnerving disclosure that every human life has a destiny both within and beyond this life. Yet that destiny—in resurrection—is itself tangible and worldly. The Incarnation initiates an environment. Paul called it the mystical body of Christ. It was not exclusively a "redemption" of sinful man, but a many-sided affirmation of complex man and his future. This affirmation of man protests against every demonization, and struggles for every individual man. It tries to make dehumanizing environments void, for that is what sin is—the absence of the whole man. The environmental-creative aspect of the Christian faith remains open precisely through its celebration and reflection in its language and worship of other environments.

Theology has for some centuries meant the clear and rather abstract statement of the truths of faith. Christians originally were reluctant to use the Greek work *theologia.* Not only did it have overtones of Greek paganism but it had connotations of detached and a-historical philosophical world views. If Christian faith, worship, and community find themselves in a new "secular" (in the sense of expressing but not fashioning its hope) situation of influential and reciprocal environments, what is the role of theology?

> Man must, as a simple survival strategy, become aware of what is happening to him despite the attendant pain of such comprehension. . . . Today, in the electronic age of instantaneous communication, I believe that our survival and—at the very least—our comfort and happiness are predicated on understanding the nature of our new environment.[6]

Environment and systems mean going beyond religious words to word-in-deed. For most Christians, faith was a commitment to a set of words or to a book. Its frame was the man-object pattern; the object stands somewhat divorced from the person, who hears the word and receives the sacraments. This may be natural for less sophisticated cultures, but it is below the revolutionary freedom and mature commitment of the Gospel.

If the Christian faith contains at its very depths this openness to being an environment reflective and creative of contemporary life, then "theology" is thinking and planning and probing how this will come about. It is possible that we need a new word to express theology as the union of Christian reflection and mission, to join both the personal and communal aspects (including national worldwide harmony). "Theology," like the biblical "word," is both thoughtful and active. It is the place where the fruitful mutability of Jesus Christ encounters anew each new culture and age, each new individual with his hopes. With the unification of the sacred and the secular (a concrete social overcoming of the illusive gap between "nature" and "grace"), theology will exist as thought-in-action, creatively at work in the midst of man shaping his world. If Christ is to become present in this complex, it will not be a Christ derived from past icons nor a judge descending from on high, nor an a-historical and abstractly universal ecclesiastical administration. It will be the presence of Christ honestly but subtly active in today's environments. The "new creation," the "new Israel," the "new man" are descriptions of this Christian environment.

[6] "Marshall McLuhan: An Interview," art. cit.

THE END OF THEOLOGY?

The kind of work this book has sketched out involves *doing* as well as *thinking*. It does not demand simply a new conceptualization of Christian ideas or a new language or jargon. It looks for something which includes newness in both words and concrete structures. It can be satisfied only by efficiency and relevancy in both theory and practice. This unity is attainable by an interaction between thinking and testing. Research and action merge as have belief and witness. The conceptualization of Christian revelation will be more and more discovered in the Gospel's encounter with life. Action in society rather than solitary insight will lead the way to understanding. By discovering the articulation of Christ's preaching in doing and acting, American theology will make Christ present not through objective dogmas or liturgies drawn from folkways but by allowing him to emerge out of the patterns of human life and death. The search for a community in justice for each human being is really helped only by a faith which is lived and martyred as well as preached.

Theology is no longer simply words about God, but the word finds its voice as it extends into action. Religious truth by its nature (oscillating between the theoretical and the particular) is existentially verified in life. Faith, the medieval theologians said, finds its vital form in love. The word alone, the idea alone, is no longer enough. We are deluged with words, threatened by an inundation of information and media. The educated man is driven to specialize while the specialist struggles through mountains of printed symbols. The word flood explains why a Protestantism preaching individual justification is increasingly ineffective, and why venerable doctrines and laws are breaking down rapidly within Catholicism. This is all part of the collapse of words, and to that extent every theology remaining within words and concepts is doomed. American experiences lies in the new land of "hardware" and "software," of "happenings." Even beyond the inundation of

223

information, the spirit of celebration and the appetite of computers would destroy any overly verbalized theology—for they both exalt and destroy words. Any theology which sees Christianity as words and hopes to save theology through sophisticated new verbal systems is playing games. In the bright new world of media, sensitivity, and psychedelia, words are too limited, too dull. They are only means. And the Christian religion, moreover, was founded not on a word, but on the Word-Made-Flesh. Christianity has its own genius which is to be based on a man, on a history, on events. When it becomes only linguistics it competes with metaphysics and law. The biblical word describes itself as active. It is a word only metaphorically. The incarnate Logos, the Word of God in flesh and blood sojourning among men (John 1:1–13), was not the creative intellectual pattern of the universe nor a divine message to men. Jesus' existence is manifest in his statements and deeds so that by faith we might see how he actually is. The Logos is incarnate; the word is deed. And so too for the Christian there can be no false dichotomy between knowing and loving, between word and action (I John 4:7ff.). But when Jesus Christ is seen primarily as teacher or Word of God, he then becomes the purchased field of exegetes and historical critics. It is the genius of the Incarnation to reduce the gap between word and action. For the divine Logos is before all a person, and a person is something that happens, the event of being a man.

Is this the end of theology? Theology is no longer, certainly, *theo-logos*. Much less is it a history of Christian ideas or the phenomenology of the Judaeo-Christian tradition. It cannot be confused with metaphysics or pose as an ideology (whose only action is violence). When theology only writes commentaries on previous ideas, it is dry and static and therefore incompatible with the nature of revelation and faith. Information about and acknowledgment of the Christian doctrines is not the same as Christian faith or life. As culture and man's self-perception have become increasingly, almost unbearably anthropocentric, so the past exaltation of a text to be believed has become less meaningful. The American today must be involved in his faith. He must approach it through his business and politics, his neighborhood, schools, and city.

Afterword: The End of Theology?

CHRISTOPRAXIS

Can theology become action-oriented? What does it mean to "do theology"? It means learning from the present needs and challenges facing Christians as well as from Christ present in community and Scripture. Faith is not simply "completed" in action, but for its very understanding faith demands to be "discovered" in action. Theological method no longer means studying sources and ideas in a seminary or university and then bravely but unpreparedly facing secular city or bored parish. Like Christ's mission, theology springs up within the issues and people it addresses. The problem is no longer having a *fides quaerens intellectum* (Anselm) or even a *spes quaerens intellectum* (Moltmann), but it is man the Christ-bearer seeking the incarnation of his faith and grace-given potentiality in and for the world around him. Faith seeks realized witness.

Thinking about Christ for men in the milieu of life and the Christian mission, which includes both the stimulus to effective action and its evaluation, is "christopraxis." The prophetic word to the crisis situations of human life (not always solving and so not commanding, but with the free authority of the Word) is concretized in the renewal of social institutions through Christian community life—family, church, town and city, megalopolis. Christopraxis is not divorced from Christ as witnessed in past history, but *its orientation and source are actions for building the future.* This action should not be confused with "doing good." Nor is it an empirical and autonomous religious experience. It is the sovereign word of revelation discovered again and again in the form of secular servant. It involves being, becoming, doing. It accepts change and freedom for man to build. It sees the milieu of Christian grace to be human life.

Christopraxis names a new approach. Thinking is neither prior to nor superior to, nor independent of, action, but rather takes place in action. This action does not determine the uniqueness of Jesus Christ's life. The kerygma is present not in static "preservation," but in the very realization of Christian life and

225

community. Action judges whether Christ has been frustrated by men, whether the Spirit has been extinguished, whether God has been rendered an ungodly idol.

A methodology for christocentric action-research would transcend conceptualization and dogmatics to the planning of the holy and Christian within the evolving concentric circles of secular life. First, a factual analysis of past failures or obsolescence would presuppose the emotional freedom for change. Adequate training, personnel, and finances for experimentation and radicalization in temporary structures would be seen as necessary, the result of this intellectual and emotional openness. Next, there must be the establishment of priorities out of the crucible of continuity, tradition, and change. Finally, there must be a pluralism of approaches. Pluralism is possible only in an atmosphere which encourages experimentation, and it is the only Christian answer to the rapid rate of diversity and change in American society. This methodology is threatening, for it implies risk and uncertainty. Not *what is,* but *what must be done,* is the matrix. Action complements research. And research extends into the realization of the Christian mission, into the very life of the Christian in his family and parish. Change is the normal situation, and continuing education is the condition for survival.

Christopraxis is not pragmatism in the dogmatic or pastoral domain. Pragmatism in the sense of American political liberalism—working to modify for the better a given system—contains the same weaknesses as Bultmannism or the less sophisticated secular theologies. Doing theology cannot uncover quick universal theories, nor does it decide a priori what modern man will or will not believe. The introduction of a real action orientation into the marrow of theology implies an end to ideology, for ideology assumes its narrow generalizations only because it sees individuals and situations as manipulable to achieving a theoretical end.

The present revolutions in politics and education also stem from a realization of the necessary unity between theory and practice. John Dewey and Karl Marx pointed to the necessity of ending the gap. And this same phenomenon underlies the anger of the younger generation before the hypocrisy of all institutions which place themselves within the humanism of Western culture and yet neglect the individual and his rights in conflict with the servants of that society, e.g., the military, the police, "law and order." This includes the churches. Angry disillusionment mocks the credibility gap long allowed between Christian theory and historical practice. This becomes especially disconcerting in face of the fact that among religious events the Incarnation allows no institutionalized gap between the human ("realism") and the divine ("idealism"). The double standard is old and runs deep, so deep that many Christians cannot even see the credibility gaps in their churches and institutions. Man is learning neither to confuse nor to separate the tenuous temporal kingdom of evolving mankind and the eschatological fulfillment of beginnings. Christianity has suddenly been forced to take seriously standards of honesty, effectiveness, meaningfulness. These pressures from society find an ally in the reading of the New Testament. The Gospel itself excoriates every dehumanization and legalization carried out in the name of religion.

THIS NEW AGE

Prometheus stole fire from the gods and so began human culture and technology. He was the symbol of man in the age of Enlightenment, Romanticism, and Revolution stretching from the eighteenth to the twentieth century. Two world wars born of confidence in educated man and of the fiery products of this theft dampened man's vision. Now we stand at a new era, trying to understand something of the motions hurling us forward. Our prototype is no longer independent Prometheus but, as others have suggested, Faust. Man develops enormous power to control his environments —not only the outside world, but also his own biological and psychological worlds. This is progress, and there can be no questioning of the process of scientific discovery. Yet power over nature is ambiguous: It can be power *against* nature, but power *over* man. Whether total power can produce human integrity is unknown; it *can* produce total nothingness.

In the final decades of this century, we shall have the technological and economic power to change the world radically, but probably we will not get very much ability to restrain our strivings, let alone understand or control the results of the changes we will be making. But if we cannot learn not only to take full advantage of our increasing technological success, but also to cope with its dangerous responsibilities, we may only have thrown off one set of chains—nature-imposed—for another, ostensibly man-made, but in a deeper sense, as Faust learned, also imposed by nature.[7]

The Faust story is a question; the answer awaits our discovery. The Faustian impulse is not merely to explore and control, but to do this blindly and exclusively. Sin in the Faustian syndrome is to want something without truly human reflection, at any price, even at the price of setting aside both God and man.

Who is the Christian our faith projects into the future? It would be too slick and too disappointing to say the new man is Christ—either historical or mystical. It would be too weak to say he is a new type of man, honest like the hippies and trained like the astronauts. Both Jesus Christ and men of today are intimations. The future Christian is a man who has rediscovered the values of his self along with the great potentialities for scientific conquest and human creation. He is a man who understands, beneath the crushing burden of cybernetic driven societies, the breadth and depth of the second great commandment. He *can* exist, Isaiah and Jesus and Paul tell us. He *must* exist, Chardin, Kahn, and McLuhan demand. He will not be a Prometheus or a Faust. He will not be like Thomas More or like Dietrich Bonhoeffer. Who is this new man, this new creation? Our age is unique. The reality awaits.

[7] See H. Kahn, *The Year 2000*, 412ff.; *cf.* also J. Moltmann, *Theology of Hope* (New York, 1967), 24; E. Kahler, "Doctor Faustus from Adam to Sartre," *The Orbit of Thomas Mann* (Princeton, 1969).

Index

Index

BEAT READER

YALE UNIVERSITY

BEAT
READER

Edited by
ANN CHARTERS

I.C.C. LIBRARY

VIKING

82105

VIKING
Published by the Penguin Group
Viking Penguin, a division of Penguin Books USA Inc.,
375 Hudson Street, New York, New York 10014, U.S.A.
Penguin Books Ltd, 27 Wrights Lane,
London W8 5TZ, England
Penguin Books Australia Ltd, Ringwood,
Victoria, Australia
Penguin Books Canada Ltd, 10 Alcorn Avenue, Suite 300,
Toronto, Ontario, Canada M4V 3B2
Penguin Books (N.Z.) Ltd, 182–190 Wairau Road,
Auckland 10, New Zealand

Penguin Books Ltd, Registered Offices:
Harmondsworth, Middlesex, England

First published in 1992 by Viking Penguin,
a division of Penguin Books USA Inc.

1 3 5 7 9 10 8 6 4 2

Copyright © Viking Penguin,
a division of Penguin Books USA Inc., 1992
Copyright © Ann Charters, 1992
All rights reserved

Pages 643–649 constitute an extension of this copyright page.

LIBRARY OF CONGRESS CATALOGING IN PUBLICATION DATA
The Portable Beat Reader / edited by Ann Charters.
p.   cm.—(The Viking portable library)
Includes bibliographical references.
ISBN 0-670-83885-3
1. American literature—20th century.   2. Beat generation—
Literary collections.   I. Charters, Ann.   II. Series.
PS536.T48   1992
810.8'0054—dc20   91–16155

Printed in the United States of America
Set in Times Roman

Without limiting the rights under copyright reserved above,
no part of this publication may be reproduced, stored in or
introduced into a retrieval system, or transmitted, in any form
or by any means (electronic, mechanical, photocopying, recording or otherwise), without the prior written permission of
both the copyright owner and the above publisher of this book.

THIS BOOK IS DEDICATED

TO MY DAUGHTERS

MALLAY AND NORA

We were so many,
We were working as one,
We were miles of moiling wheat
In a sizzling summer's heat.
But now we are scattered
And flung far apart,
But you and I still live as one
Through coals in the heart.
And if anything is left
Of the coal in the soul,
Oh, flash it to me.

        —Ed Sanders, "Keeping
          the Issues Alive" (Song)

CONTENTS

PART 5
"TALES OF BEATNIK GLORY"
Memoirs and Posthumous Tributes

PART 6
"THE UNSPEAKABLE VISIONS OF THE INDIVIDUAL"
Later Work

"VARIATIONS ON A GENERATION"

> As a vast, solid phalanx the generations come on, they have the same features and their pattern is new in the world. All wear the same expression, but it is this which they do not detect in each other. It is the one life which ponders in the philosophers, which drudges in the laborers, which basks in the poets, which dilates in the love of the women.
> —Ralph Waldo Emerson, *Notebooks*

Earlier in the history of American literature, the novelist Henry James acknowledged in his biography of Nathaniel Hawthorne that "the best things come, as a general thing, from the talents that are members of a group; every man works better when he has companions working in the same line, and yielding the stimulus of suggestion, comparison, emulation." As a facet of our country's cultural history, clusters have been an outstanding feature of our literature. They can be a group of writers joined by a common geographical location who share philosophical sympathies, such as the cluster of transcendentalist writers in Concord, Massachusetts, in the mid-nineteenth century—Ralph Waldo Emerson, Henry David Thoreau, and Bronson Alcott. More often, given the sheer physical size of the United States, the writers share a temporal rather than a spatial proximity along with their literary aesthetic, for example the local-color realists Sarah Orne Jewett, Lafcadio Hearn, and Kate Chopin, all born between 1849 and 1851, or the experimental modernist poets born in the decade between 1879 and 1888—William Carlos Williams,

Ezra Pound, Hilda Doolittle, Marianne Moore, T. S. Eliot, and Wallace Stevens.

As the critic Malcolm Cowley has recognized, literary scholars have advanced rather elaborate theories about the nature of literary generations, those "clusters or constellations of writers, with their coevals in the other arts." Writers themselves have also speculated about the phenomenon, often more cogently than the critics and scholars.

F. Scott Fitzgerald, for example, gave considerable thought to what he called "My Generation"—usually referred to as the "Lost Generation" of the 1920s—those American writers such as Fitzgerald, Ernest Hemingway, Kay Boyle, and Robert McAlmon who flocked to London and Paris at the end of World War I to escape what Julian Symons described as "the puritanism and philistinism of a country run by what Mencken called the booboisie, from Prohibition and President Harding."

Looking back in the late 1930s, Fitzgerald said that "by a generation I mean that reaction against the fathers which seems to occur about three times in a century. It is distinguished by a set of ideas inherited in modified form from the madmen and the outlaws of the generation before; if it is a real generation it has its own leaders and spokesmen, and it draws into its orbit those born just before it and just after, whose ideas are less clear-cut and defiant."

Fitzgerald's definition is helpful when it comes to analyzing the qualities of a major cluster of writers who emerged after World War II in the chronicle of American literary history—the poets and novelists of the Beat Generation. There has been considerable confusion about the term, as well as the word "beat" itself, but there is no disagreement that there has been a phenomenon known as the Beat Generation writers. Its members share what Cowley described as their "own sense of life, something that might be defined as an intricate web of perceptions, judgments, feelings, and aspirations."

This shared experience for the Beat writers was historical and political, based on the tumultuous changes of their times: the historic events that began with America's dropping the atomic bomb on Japan to bring World War II to an end, and the political ramifications of the ensuing Cold War and wave of anti-Communist hysteria that followed in the United States in the late 1940s and the 1950s.

As Fitzgerald specified, the postwar literary movement was shaped by "the madmen and the outlaws of the generation before." The early Beat writers deliberately selected as their models such unlikely "Secret Heroes" (the term is Allen Ginsberg's) as the bop musicians Charlie Parker and Dizzy Gillespie, the French poet Arthur Rimbaud, the Welsh alcoholic performer-poet Dylan Thomas, the California anarchist poet Kenneth Rexroth, and others outside the canon of acceptable Anglo-American literary models.

The Beat Generation had "its own leaders and spokesmen," the early members of the cluster, writers like Jack Kerouac, Allen Ginsberg, William Burroughs, Lawrence Ferlinghetti, and Gary Snyder, who exemplified what Cowley called "new standards of conduct, a distinctive life style that was soon adopted by others of the group." While they drew into orbit "those born just before it and just after," the other writers participating in the literary generation were hardly less defiant.

The discovery of the word "beat" was essential to the formation of a sense of self-definition among the earliest writers making up the cluster that would later call itself members of a "Beat Generation." The word "beat" was primarily in use after World War II by jazz musicians and hustlers as a slang term meaning down and out, or poor and exhausted. The jazz musician Mezz Mezzrow combined it with other words, like "dead beat" or "beat-up," when he used it with humorous exaggeration in his book *Really the Blues* (1946): "Things went from bad to worse, and kept right on traveling. I was dead beat, troubled with the shorts; not penny one did I have, and I prowled around town in the only suit I had to my name, a beat-up old tuxedo with holes in the pants where I sat, and my hair so long that Louis Armstrong got the impression I was a violin player."

In 1944 the word "beat" as used by a Times Square hustler named Herbert Huncke came to the attention of William Burroughs, a Harvard graduate living in New York whom Huncke had introduced to heroin. Through Burroughs, the word was passed on to a young Columbia College freshman named Allen Ginsberg and a friend who shared his interest in writing named

Jack Kerouac, a Columbia dropout serving during the war as a merchant marine seaman based in New York. As Ginsberg remembered first hearing the word "beat," the "original street usage" in Huncke's speech meant "exhausted, at the bottom of the world, looking up or out, sleepless, wide-eyed, perceptive, rejected by society, on your own, streetwise."

Kerouac was fascinated by the tone of the word "beat" as Huncke said it hunched over a cup of coffee in a Times Square cafeteria. Kerouac heard a "melancholy sneer" in the sound of Huncke's voice that Kerouac later insisted "never meant juvenile delinquents" despite its use by drug addicts, but rather "meant characters of a special spirituality who didn't gang up but were solitary Bartlebies staring out the dead wall window of our civilization." Kerouac's insistence that the word possessed deeper allusive qualities and meant something mysterious and spiritual, suggestive of Herman Melville's story more than a century before about the archetypal American nonconformist "Bartleby the Scrivener," grew out of his conversations with Ginsberg and Ginsberg's friend Lucien Carr, another Columbia undergraduate in the New York group.

Ginsberg and Carr were only eighteen-year-old college students at the time, but they were drawn to literature and were using drugs like Benzedrine and marijuana in their dormitory rooms near the Columbia campus to inspire them to create what they called a "New Vision" of art. They were attempting to follow the example of the French poet Arthur Rimbaud, whom Carr introduced to Ginsberg as the ideal poet. Their efforts were the earliest attempts of the group later labeled "Beat writers" to define a philosophy.

Carr later remembered that "in those years at Columbia, we really did have something going. It was a rebellious group, I suppose, of which there are many on campuses, but it was one that really was dedicated to a 'New Vision.' It's practically impossible to define. Maybe it was a term we just sold ourselves. It was trying to look at the world in a new light, trying to look at the world in a way that gave it some meaning. Trying to find values . . . that were valid. And it was through literature all this was supposed to be done. And it was through Jack and Allen, principally, that it was going to be done."

Burroughs, who was older than the others, discouraged their

more extravagant antics, like their candlelit exercises writing poetry with their own blood, and urged them to read one of his favorite books, Oswald Spengler's *Decline and Fall of the West,* in an effort to help them develop a more substantial historical context for their "New Vision." At the end of the war, Kerouac (whose father was dying of cancer) and Ginsberg (whose writing reflected his obsession with atomic fallout and radiation sickness) shared a sense of what Ginsberg later called "the idea of transience of phenomena—the poignant Kewpie-doll dearness of personages vanishing in time. Not a morbid interest in death but the realization of the mortal turn." According to Ginsberg's biographer, Barry Miles, this awareness of "everybody lost in a dream world of their own making . . . was the basis of the Beat Generation."

The actual term "Beat Generation" was coined a few years later, in 1948, after Kerouac had finished his first novel, *The Town and the City.* He met another aspiring writer in New York City named John Clellon Holmes, who shared his love for bop music and enjoyed theorizing about social trends and cultural changes. In November 1948 they sat up late drinking beer and talking into the night in Holmes's Lexington Avenue apartment.

Kerouac's stories about the Times Square junkies, the Fifty-second Street bop musicians, and the "wild kids" he'd met on his cross-country trip the previous year to visit a Denver friend named Neal Cassady, fascinated Holmes. He felt Kerouac's stories "seemed to be describing a new sort of stance toward reality, behind which a new sort of consciousness lay." Holmes responded to the "restless exuberance, the quality of search" that he sensed in Kerouac's descriptions, and he urged Jack to characterize the new attitude by trying to define it in a phrase or two.

As Holmes recalled the conversation, Kerouac replied, " 'It's a kind of furtiveness. . . . Like we were a generation of furtives. You know, with an inner knowledge there's no use flaunting on that level, the level of the "public," a kind of beatness—I mean, being right down to it, to ourselves, because we all *really* know where we are—and a weariness with all the forms, all the conventions of the world. . . . So I guess you might say we're a *beat* generation,' and he laughed a conspiratorial, the Shadow-knows kind of laugh at his own words and at the look on my face."

Holmes was startled at what he felt was the appropriateness of the label. It seemed to him "to have had the subversive attraction of an image that just might contain a concept, with the added mystery of being hard to define." At the same time he recognized that the term "beat generation" was a tag that evaded close scrutiny. It was "a vision, not an idea."

A month later, at the end of December 1948, Holmes met Kerouac's and Ginsberg's Denver friend, Neal Cassady, when Cassady drove to New York. Cassady seemed to embody the spirit of "beat" so compellingly that Holmes made him a central figure in a novel he began writing about Kerouac and Ginsberg and the others in the New York group. He titled the book *Go* (after one of Cassady's favorite expressions) when the novel was published by Scribner's in 1952.

Holmes included an echo of his earlier conversation with Kerouac as the basis for a line in *Go:* "You know, everyone I know is kind of furtive, kind of beat . . . a sort of revolution of the soul, I guess you'd call it." This idea of "beat" intrigued a young book reviewer named Gilbert Millstein at *The New York Times.* After reading *Go,* Millstein commissioned an article from Holmes, "This Is the Beat Generation," which appeared in the magazine section of the Sunday *Times* on November 16, 1952. The article officially launched the term.

Holmes characterized the Beat Generation as a cultural revolution in progress, made by a post–World War II generation of disaffiliated young people coming of age into a Cold War world without spiritual values they could honor. Instead of obeying authority and conforming to traditional middle-class materialistic aspirations, these young people dealt as best they could with what Holmes called their "*will* to believe, even in the face of an inability to do so in conventional terms." Nowhere in this early article did Holmes refer to Beat Generation writers, because he did not think of himself or his friends Ginsberg and Kerouac in this way, although he shared with them the new sensibility he had described.

Holmes's article and his novel *Go* stirred what he called "a ripple of curiosity." The Beat Generation as a cultural revolution or a literary movement didn't seem evident to many readers, despite the fact that two other novels published along with *Go* in 1952 also reflected aspects of what Holmes had characterized as the new Beat consciousness—Chandler Brossard's *Who Walk in Darkness,* about a young disaffiliated Greenwich Village writer, and George Mandel's *Flee the Angry Strangers,* about a rebellious middle-class white teenager's addiction to heroin. The original Beat nucleus was a small, tightly knit group of friends, and Brossard and Mandel, although part of the New York scene, weren't part of their inner circle, didn't share their sense of total cultural rebellion, and soon distanced themselves from the group.

Three years later, Kerouac published a sketch titled "Jazz of the Beat Generation" in the paperback anthology *New World Writing* series that achieved some notice for its exuberant, experimental prose style. But it wasn't until the publication of his novel *On the Road* in 1957, following on the heels of the well-publicized censorship trial in San Francisco of Ginsberg's book *Howl and Other Poems,* that the Beat Generation and the Beat literary group became a national phenomenon. Kerouac was dubbed the spokesman for the Beat Generation, and he was besieged with requests to explain it.

In "The Philosophy of the Beat Generation," which he wrote for *Esquire* magazine in March 1958, Kerouac made clear that the group that originated the idea of a "Beat Generation" was short-lived, consisting only of a few friends in the 1940s such as Ginsberg, Carr, Burroughs, Huncke, and Holmes, who had scattered and left New York years before. But after the Korean War, in the early 1950s, according to Kerouac, the "postwar youth emerged cool and beat, had picked up the gestures and the style; soon it was everywhere, the new look . . . the bop visions became common property of the commercial, popular cultural world. . . . The ingestion of drugs became official (tranquilizers and the rest); and even the clothes style of the beat hipsters carried over to the new rock 'n' roll youth . . . and the Beat Generation, though dead, was resurrected and justified."

When the term "Beat Generation" began to be used as a label for the young people Kerouac called "hipsters or beatsters" in the late 1950s, the word "beat" lost its specific reference to a particular subculture and became a synonym for anyone living as a bohemian or acting rebelliously or appearing to advocate a revolution in manners. Other writers had their favorite label for the cultural change. Mailer's term was the "Hip Generation," Ginsberg used the name "The Subterraneans," Kerouac also referred to the "Bop Generation."

On April 2, 1958, several months after the Russians launched their "sputnik" satellite, the *San Francisco Chronicle* columnist Herb Caen coined the word "beatnik" when he wrote condescendingly that "*Look Magazine,* preparing a picture spread on San Francisco's Beat Generation (oh, no, not AGAIN!), hosted a party in a North Beach house for 50 Beatniks, and by the time word got around the sour grapevine, over 250 bearded cats and kits were on hand, slopping up Mike Cowles's free booze. They're only Beat, y'know, when it comes to work. . . ."

Kerouac tried to clarify the spiritual dimension of the word "beat" in an article for *Playboy* in June 1959 titled "The Origins of the Beat Generation," explaining that the linguistic root of the word "beat" also carried the connotations of beatitude or beatific. To the casual reader flipping the pages of the magazine in search of entertainment, his words probably carried less weight than the *Playboy* pinup centerfold. It is ironic but perhaps symptomatic of the discontinuity of the times that the medium and the message were so much at odds in Kerouac's case.

A comic poem titled "Circular from America" by the British poet George Barker, published in 1959 in a new literary magazine called *X,* summed up the opposition's point of view:

> Against the eagled
> Hemisphere
> I lean my eager
> Editorial ear
> And what the devil
> You think I hear?
> I hear the Beat
> No not of the heart
> But the dull palpitation
> Of the New Art

As, on the dead tread
Mill of no mind,
It follows its leaders
Unbeaten behind.
O Kerouac Kerouac
What on earth shall we do
If a single Idea
Ever gets through?
. . . ½ an idea
To a hundred pages
Now Jack, dear Jack,
That ain't fair wages
For labouring through
Prose that takes ages
Just to announce
That Gods and Men
Ought all to study
The Book of Zen.
If you really think
So low of the soul
Why don't you write
On a toilet roll?

The English magazine *X* preferred to champion the work of "pure" writers like James Joyce and Samuel Beckett rather than treat the Beats as anything more than what its editors called "an amusing phenomenon" that had "no more connection with literature than the men in the moon." But England also had its own cluster of young writers who were challenging postwar social values and conventions in their country, a group called "The Kitchen-Sink Writers" or "The Angry Young Men."

In the late 1950s this group of controversial writers, which included the playwright John Osborne and the novelists Colin Wilson, John Wain, and John Braine, was often linked with the American Beats, as in the 1958 anthology *Protest: The Beat Generation and the Angry Young Men,* edited by Gene Feldman and Max Gartenberg. Unlike the Beat writers, the English writers' identity as a group was short-lived. Their literary interests led them to take different paths in the development of their separate careers.

In America the Beat Generation didn't fade away or disappear. The media tumult and controversy surrounding the word "beat" and the idea of a Beat Generation literary movement climaxed in the years immediately following the publication of Kerouac's *On the Road* and Ginsberg's *Howl.* Three anthologies of Beat writing were published in New York in 1960: *The Beats,* edited by Seymour Krim; *The Beat Scene,* edited by Elias Wilentz, and *Beat Coast East: An Anthology of Rebellion,* edited by Stanley Fisher. For the introduction to his book, Fisher walked the streets of Greenwich Village and asked the "beatniks" he met there what they thought the word "beat" meant. He heard twenty definitions before he stopped writing them down, starting with:

1. A formal desperation which became a rebellion against all political and literary forms.
2. A new concept instinctively arrived at—a personal attitude that isn't in our vocabulary.
3. Very tired people—tired of living before one has started living, not being corny . . . cool.

Kerouac's efforts to convince magazine editors and television interviewers that his concept of the Beat Generation included a spiritual dimension were unavailing, but the readers of his books, which sold widely, understood him and his contribution to the cultural changes underway in America. The literary establishment was hostile, but the first small group of Beat writers in New York had found its most important supporters a few years before the hullabaloo over *On the Road* and "Howl" in 1957.

Before the Beats surfaced as a literary movement that had a sufficient number of talented and mutually sympathetic writers to cohere as a recognizable group with staying power, they had been reinforced by the addition of a critical mass—several young writers active on the West Coast in the San Francisco Poetry Renaissance.

The West Coast had a well-established alternative poetry community by 1954, when Allen Ginsberg arrived in San Francisco from New York. A decade before, George Leite's Circle Editions in Berkeley published the avant garde American writers William Carlos Williams, Kenneth Rexroth, Kenneth Patchen, Robert Duncan, William Everson, Henry Miller, Anaïs Nin, and Philip Lamantia. A radical literary community had formed during World War II in the conscientious objector camp in Waldport, Oregon, which published a militant resistance magazine called *The Illiterati,* advocating "Creation, Experiment, and Revolution to build a warless, free society." Adrian Wilson, Kermit Sheets, and William Everson were among those who ran the small press at the camp under the imprint of the Untide Press.

After the war, Wilson worked with a theater group in the East Bay and printed their programs and posters. Sheets founded Centaur Press in San Francisco and published Mary Fabilli, a Berkeley poet, and Kenneth Rexroth's translations. Everson started Equinox Press in Berkeley, where a literary group had formed around poets Robert Duncan, Jack Spicer, and Robin Blazer with ties to Josephine Miles, a poet and professor of English at the University of California at Berkeley.

Duncan, whose essay "The Homosexual in Society" appeared in *Politics* in 1944, was one of the first poets in America to express his homosexuality openly and identify himself as a member of what he considered a politically oppressed group. William Everson recalled that Duncan was "indefatigable in his arrangement of poetry readings as our key creative outlet, since the dominant centers of publication were largely closed to us." In the late 1940s the literary activities of Everson, Duncan, Spicer, and others gave rise to the term "Berkeley Renaissance."

In San Francisco, the radical poet Kenneth Rexroth was the center of another literary circle that met weekly in Rexroth's apartment and sometimes overflowed into a rented hall on Steiner Street. Rexroth remembered that this group "had by far the largest meetings of any radical or pseudo-radical group in San Francisco. The place was always crowded, and when the topic for the evening was sex and anarchy, you couldn't get in the doors. People were standing on one another's shoulders, and we had to have two meetings, one upstairs, the overflow in the downstairs meeting hall." Rexroth's group published two magazines, George Leite's *Circle* and the Anarchist Circle's publication *Ark,* which featured poetry by Duncan, Everson, Lamantia, and Thomas Parkinson.

By 1954 there was such an avid audience for poetry in San Francisco that the poet Weldon Kees organized a "Poets' Follies," a poetry vaudeville made up of readings, jazz, and satiric sketches. That same year Ruth Witt-Diamant founded the San Francisco State College Poetry Center, where "Poets' Seminars" and readings with visiting and local writers were frequently held. At the reception for W. H. Auden, who inaugurated the Poetry Center readings, Ginsberg met the young poet Michael McClure, who had come to San Francisco because of his interest in painting and literature.

Ginsberg had read *Circle* and *Ark*, and understood that unlike the conservative academic establishment and the large commercial publishing companies that dominated the literary life of New York City, San Francisco's community of writers was supported and encouraged by an ongoing tradition of experimental poetry, radical politics, and little magazines and small presses, including a more open and tolerant acceptance of homosexuality.

Moving to San Francisco with a letter of introduction to Rexroth from the New Jersey poet William Carlos Williams, Ginsberg felt himself in sympathetic company. Through Rexroth he met many "interesting types," among them Duncan, Patchen, and a young poet in Berkeley named Gary Snyder, who was studying Asian languages and philosophy. Ginsberg also met Peter Orlovsky through the San Francisco painter Robert LaVigne, and they began to live together in an apartment on Montgomery Street.

In the summer of 1955, Ginsberg decided to bring more stability to his life by enrolling in the graduate English program at the University of California in Berkeley. In July 1955 he found himself a cottage in Berkeley and signed up for classes in the fall semester, even though he knew that English departments were dominated by the New Criticism. This was an elegant classicism that admired the language of the past but was scarcely the best environment for a poet determined to create a "New Vision" in literature. As the writer Aram Saroyan understood, the times made "a difficult atmosphere for a young poet to make an approach into print. Everything had already been done, and done better. The New Criticism itself made a clear case for one's elders and betters . . . but this has nothing to do with growing up to be a poet, and wanting to write a poem. This is something which is given each successive generation of poets as a natural right."

Early in August, still on Montgomery Street, Ginsberg began to write a long poem about his life, in part influenced by Rexroth's conversation and poetry. The poem was "Howl," which gave Ginsberg the courage to give up his plans for graduate school and make poetry his full-time career. Shortly after its composition he decided to organize a poetry reading on October 13, 1955, at the Six Gallery, a cooperative art gallery in San Francisco. The reading featured himself and the four young West Coast poets Michael McClure, Gary Snyder, Philip Whalen, and Philip Lamantia. Jack Kerouac, who was visiting Ginsberg at the time, was unwilling to read with the others, but Kenneth Rexroth agreed to be master of ceremonies.

The "Six Poets at the Six Gallery" reading was the catalyst that dramatically revealed what Ginsberg later called the "natural affinity of modes of thought or literary style or planetary perspective" between the East Coast writers and the West Coast poets. Michael McClure later described the atmosphere he felt the night of the reading in 1955:

We were locked in the Cold War and the first Asian debacle—the Korean War. . . . We hated the war and the inhumanity and the coldness. The country had the feeling of martial law. An undeclared military state had leapt out of Daddy Warbucks' tanks and sprawled over the landscape. As artists we were oppressed and indeed the people of the nation were oppressed. . . . We knew we were poets and we had to speak out as poets. We saw that the art of poetry was essentially dead—killed by war, by academies, by neglect, by lack of love, and by disinterest. We knew we could bring it back to life. We could see what Pound had done—and Whitman, and Artaud, and D. H. Lawrence in his monumental poetry and prose. . . . We wanted to make it new and we wanted to invent it and the process of it as we went into it. We wanted voice and we wanted vision.

Ginsberg's "Howl" delivered the necessary "voice" and "vision" on October 13, 1955, with the now famous opening words, "I saw the best minds of my generation destroyed by madness, starving hysterical naked, dragging themselves through the negro streets at dawn looking for an angry fix. . . ." The 150 people in the audience cheered Ginsberg on to the poem's conclusion. As McClure realized, everyone knew "at the deepest level that a barrier had been broken, that a human voice and body had been hurled against the harsh wall of America and its supporting armies and navies and academies and institutions and ownership systems and power-support bases."

The poet Lawrence Ferlinghetti, who was in the Six Gallery audience that night, sent Ginsberg a telegram after the reading offering to publish "Howl" as a volume in the Pocket Poets Series recently started by his publishing company City Lights. In May 1957, a few months after its publication, *Howl and Other Poems,* number four in the series, was seized by San Francisco customs officers. Ferlinghetti and Shigeyoshi Murao, his employee at the City Lights Bookstore in North Beach, were charged with publishing and selling an obscene book. Ferlinghetti strongly defended *Howl,* saying that "it is not the poet but what he observes which is revealed as obscene. The great obscene wastes of *Howl* are the sad wastes of the mechanized world, lost among atom bombs and insane nationalisms. . . ."

The *Howl* trial in San Francisco was a widely publicized event, bringing national attention to Ginsberg and Ferlinghetti and selling thousands of copies of the little black and white paperback book throughout the country. When Judge Clayton Horn cleared it of the charge of being obscene literature, its sales swelled into the tens of thousands. The Beats, as represented by Ginsberg, had joined forces with the San Francisco poets, as represented by Ferlinghetti, and the Beat Generation literary cluster was ready to go into orbit.

The amalgam was strengthened in the public's mind with the publication of Kerouac's autobiographical novel *The Dharma Bums* (1958), which described his adventures hitchhiking on the West Coast, including an account of the Six Gallery reading, and romanticized the ideas of the West Coast poet Gary Snyder, the book's central figure. Kerouac's portrayal of Snyder's values and life-style became a blueprint for the hippie culture a decade later.

In the novel Kerouac had Snyder (named Japhy Ryder) predict a future time in America when the visions of the poets would revolutionize the country. Talking to Kerouac (Ray Smith) outside the Berkeley cottage where Ginsberg (Alvah Goldbook) had lived in the fall of 1955, Japhy says,

> "I've been reading Whitman, know what he says, *Cheer up slaves, and horrify foreign despots,* he means that's the attitude for the Bard, the Zen Lunacy bard of old desert paths, see the whole thing is a world full of rucksack wanderers, Dharma Bums refusing to subscribe to the general demand that they consume production and therefore have to work for the privilege of consuming, all that crap they didn't really want anyway such as refrigerators, TV sets, cars, at least new fancy cars, certain hair oils and deodorants and general junk you finally always see a week later in the garbage anyway, all of them imprisoned in a system of work, produce, consume, work, produce, consume, I see a vision of a great rucksack revolution, thousands or even millions of young Americans wandering around with rucksacks, going up to mountains to pray, making children laugh and old men glad, making young girls happy and old girls happier, all of 'em Zen Lunatics who go about writing poems that happen to appear in their heads for no reason and also by being kind and also by strange unexpected acts keep giving visions of eternal freedom to everybody and to all living creatures, that's what I like about you Goldbook and Smith [Ginsberg and Kerouac], you two guys from the East Coast which I thought was dead."
>
> "We thought the *West* Coast was dead!"
>
> "You've really brought a fresh wind around here. . . ."

In the late 1950s literary magazines such as the *Evergreen Review* and the *Chicago Review* strengthened the bond between the writers by featuring poetry and fiction by the San Francisco poets and the Beats. In 1959 books began to appear analyzing the effect of the new literary group on American culture. Some were sympathetic, like Lawrence Lipton's *The Holy Barbarians.* Lipton lumped together the East and West

Coast writers and called them "holy barbarians—holy in their search of Self, barbarian in their total rejection of the so-called civilized standards of success, morality and neurosis." Others were more frivolous, such as William F. Brown's *Beat Beat Beat* (1959), a "hip collection of cool cartoons about life and love among the Beatniks," and George Mandel's *Beatville U.S.A.* (1961), a "hilarious, opinionated and uncensored view of the Beat Generation by a noted author who saw it coming—and ducked!"

Encyclopedias like *The Americana 1958 Annual* represented the country's prevailing conservatism. In a review of the most significant literary events of the year, it reprimanded Kerouac for taking the wrong turn:

> The "beat" generation of postwar America, similar in essence to the heroes of the "kitchen-sink" school of contemporary English literature, was celebrated in 1957 by Jack Kerouac in his novel *On the Road*. This book, a report of the half-literate comments of a group of self-conscious delinquents, addicted to traveling at high speed between New York and San Francisco, and given to jazz, dope, and the lunatic fringe of sex and literature, received attention out of all proportion to its significance as fiction. Kerouac's first novel, *The Town and the City* (1950), was a sensitive study of a young man's growing to maturity; but his new work, describing a marginal, infinitesimally small group of posturing bohemians, was most accurately described by Herbert Gold in *The Nation* (November 16) as a "frantic tirade."

The fiction and poetry by Beat writers like Kerouac, Ginsberg, Ferlinghetti, Snyder, and McClure probably offended more Americans than it found readers over thirty years old who agreed with its attack on such cherished institutions as capitalism, consumerism, the military-industrial complex, racism, and ecological destruction. Even the older poet William Carlos Williams, who had written a sympathetic introduction to the *Howl* volume, had his reservations about Beat poetry. On March 24, 1958, he wrote the poet Joseph Renard, "Do you know any of the San Francisco gang who are making a name for themselves in the papers now-a-days? Your own poems are not an off shoot from that impetus—which is really illiterate, though I should be strung up [if] it were known."

Like the work of the radical writers of the 1930s (but without their specific political agenda), Beat poetry and fiction was an alternative literature by writers who were sweeping in their condemnation of their country's underlying social, sexual, political, and religious values. Earlier modernist poets like Ezra Pound or Lost Generation writers like Ernest Hemingway had attacked the system from the safeguard of their life abroad as expatriates, but the Beat Generation writers protested their country's excesses on the front lines. They advocated personal and social changes that made them heroes to some readers, and heretics to others.

The novelist William Burroughs understood the threat to established American values posed by the Beats:

> Once started, the Beat movement had a momentum of its own and a world-wide impact. In fact, the intelligent conservatives in America saw this as a serious threat to their position long before the Beat writers saw it themselves. A much more serious threat, say, than the Communist party. The Beat literary movement came at exactly the right time and said something that millions of people of all nationalities all over the world were waiting to hear. You can't tell anybody anything he doesn't know already. The alienation, the restlessness, the dissatisfaction were already there waiting when Kerouac pointed out the road.
>
> Artists to my mind are the real architects of change, and not political legislators, who implement change after the fact. Art exerts a profound influence on the style of life, the mode, range and direction of perception. Art tells us what we know and don't know that we know. Certainly *On the Road* performed that function in 1957 to an extraordinary extent. There's no doubt that we're living in a freer America as a result of the Beat literary movement, which is an important part of the larger picture of cultural and political change in this country during the last forty years, when a four letter word couldn't appear on the printed page, and minority rights were ridiculous.

The fiction and poetry reflecting what Hettie Jones, co-publisher of the literary magazine *Yugen,* called "the new consciousness in arts and letters" was taken seriously by a sufficient number of editors, academics, and publishers to ensure its survival in formats that made it accessible to a widening circle of readers. In 1960, the editor Donald M. Allen persuaded Grove Press to issue an anthology of experimental work titled *The New American Poetry*. It featured the most powerful poets associated with the Beat Generation literary movement along with other clusters of writers from Black Mountain College, the New York School, and the San Francisco Poetry Renaissance. Donald Allen included "Statements on Poetics" and biographical notes, and his anthology went through several editions.

In 1961, the poet Thomas Parkinson, who was also a professor at the University of California, Berkeley, prepared *A Casebook on the Beat* as a textbook for the Thomas Y. Crowell Company, which gave "the pros and cons of the beat movement—with thirty-nine pieces of beat writing—Kerouac, Ginsberg, and others." That same year, Vista Books in London published *"Beat" Poets* selected by Gene Baro in its Pocket Poets Series, along with its volumes on Shakespeare, Baudelaire, and Christina Rossetti.

At the beginning of the 1960s the Beat Generation writers were solidly established as a literary cluster with the publication of several anthologies and a stream of books by individual authors over nearly a decade. Included were Ginsberg's *Howl* (1956) and *Kaddish* (1961), Kerouac's *On the Road* (1957), *The Dharma Bums* (1958), *Doctor Sax* (1959), *Mexico City Blues* (1959), and *Book of Dreams* (1961), John Clellon Holmes's *Go* (1952) and *The Horn* (1958), Lawrence Ferlinghetti's *Pictures of the Gone World* (1955) and *Coney Island of the Mind* (1958), Gregory Corso's *Bomb* (1958), Michael McClure's *Peyote Poem* (1958) and *Dark Brown* (1961), John Wieners's *The Hotel Wentley Poems* (1958), Diane DiPrima's *This Kind of Bird Flies Backwards* (1958) and *Dinners and Nightmares* (1961), William Burroughs's *Junky* (1953) and *Naked Lunch* (1959), Gary Snyder's *Riprap* (1959) and *Myths & Texts* (1960), Philip Whalen's *Self-Portrait from Another Direction* (1959) and *Like I Say* (1960), and LeRoi Jones's *Preface to a Twenty Volume Suicide Note* (1961).

After the publication of *Howl* and *On the Road,* many

American experimental writers felt their political or spiritual affinities with the East Coast Beats and the San Francisco Renaissance poets. Scores of "fellow travelers" in New York, Boston, Chicago, New Orleans, and other cities and towns throughout the United States started their own magazines or sent off their manuscripts to be published in the proliferation of small presses (some run off on the lowly mimeograph machine) during the heyday of the movement. The scholar George Butterick listed 235 periodicals in the 1950s and 1960s inspired by the Beat Generation for the *Dictionary of Literary Biography*. Writers expressing the "new consciousness" had found a way, in the words of the critic Northrop Frye, "to produce out of the society we have to live in, a vision of the society we want to live in."

The poet Diane DiPrima recognized that the writers associated with the Beat Generation were strengthened by the looseness of the affiliation of the different people in the group. The literary movement supported the individual development of each writer and let them express what she called their "pluralism" of interests. There were no social requirements for membership or narrow literary platforms, as with the cluster of experimental Imagist poets at the beginning of the century. African-American poets, who had formed their own group as Harlem Renaissance writers before World War II, were encouraged to be part of the "new consciousness," as in the work of the Beat poets LeRoi Jones and Ted Joans in New York City, and Bob Kaufman in San Francisco.

The Beat Generation did less well for its women. Reflecting the sexism of the times, the women mostly stayed on the sidelines as girlfriends and wives, as the novelist Joyce Johnson described in her memoir *Minor Characters*. The writing of the exceptional Diane DiPrima flourished, but most women living with or married to the Beats, for example Carolyn Cassady, Bonnie Bremser (Brenda Frazer), and Hettie Jones, took care of the children, worked to support the family, and did little writing, mostly memoirs years later.

The community of males in *On the Road, Howl,* and Burroughs's *Junky* and *Naked Lunch,* works that defined Beat literature for most readers, reflected the open homosexuality of some of the members of the group. Male bonding was also crucial in the writers' determination to circumvent what they felt were the insufferable pressures of conventional family life in a consumer society. The feminist historian Barbara Ehrenreich understood that "in the Beats, the two strands of male protest—one directed against the white-collar work world and the other against the suburbanized family life that work was supposed to support—come together into the first all-out critique of American consumer culture."

Within the diversity of expression in the "new consciousness" literature there was often a recognizable "Beat" quality that distinguished it from other experimental poetry and fiction of the time. The Beat literary aesthetic welcomed experimentation and advocated what Gregory Corso characterized as "the use of mixtures containing spontaneity, 'bop prosody,' surreal-real images, jumps, beats, cool measures, long rapid vowels, long long lines, and the main content, soul." Beat literature reflected the brash assertiveness of the postwar years, insisting that the idealism of the American dream could be put to the ultimate test. Evolving naturally out of their cultural tradition, the writers reflected the staunch individualism of the nation's past, and its prosperity and optimism at mid-century.

As the 1960s progressed, the number of dissident writers and small press publishers swelled in the development of an American "counterculture." In this time of disruptive social changes, the complacency of the 1950s evaporated as the civil rights movement took on a new militancy in the South, the resistance to war in Southeast Asia grew when United States troops were sent to Vietnam, students protested adult authority on college campuses across the nation, LSD became more readily available than peyote as a "consciousness expander," and rock music developed as an art form from earlier folk roots and black rhythm and blues.

At the end of the sixties the *Random House Dictionary* included the term "Beat Generation," crediting Jack Kerouac for defining it as "members of the generation that came of age after World War II who, supposedly as a result of disillusionment stemming from the Cold War, espouse mystical detachment and relaxation of social and sexual tensions."

By the time the term made the dictionary, it was nearly

obsolete. "Beatniks" had been replaced by the "hippies" as representatives of an alternative American culture. The February 1968 *Readers' Guide to Periodical Literature* advised "See also *Hippies*" under the rubric "Beatniks," after an index of only three articles that included a review of John Clellon Holmes's collection of elegaic essays on the Beat Generation titled *Nothing More to Declare.* In 1968 fifty-three articles were listed under *Hippies* in the *Readers' Guide,* and more than one hundred articles appeared in the following year.

Like the Lost Generation writers of the 1920s, the Beat Generation writers were associated with a specific time frame. Most participating in the literary cluster weren't sorry to see the Beat and Beatnik labels go. The poet Gregory Corso understood that the words stood for a "generation of outlaws." As the years went on the careers of some of the writers developed beyond their early identification with the group. When Allen Ginsberg was awarded the National Book Award for poetry in 1974 for his book *The Fall of America,* his acceptance speech stressed the importance of recognizing what he called the sovereignty of the individual mind in post-Vietnam America. "There is no longer any hope for the Salvation of America proclaimed by Jack Kerouac and others of our Beat Generation, aware and howling, weeping and singing Kaddish for the nation decades ago, 'rejected yet confessing out the soul.' All we have to work from now is the vast empty quiet space of our own Consciousness. AH! AH! AH!"

When Gary Snyder won the Pulitzer Prize for *Turtle Island,* his 1974 collection of poetry, he said he hoped the dust wrappers for his books could finally drop the "Beat poet" label and describe him as a more honored "Pulitzer Prize–winning poet." With hindsight, Snyder felt that "the term Beat is better used for a smaller group of writers (as it was in the Don Allen anthology)—the immediate group around Allen Ginsberg and Jack Kerouac, plus Gregory Corso, and a few others. Many of us . . . belong together in the category of San Francisco Renaissance. Both categories fall within, it seems to me, a definable time frame. It would be from sometime in the early fifties up until the mid-sixties when jazz was replaced by rock and roll and marijuana by LSD and a whole new generation of youth jumped on board and the name beatnik changed to hippy. Still, beat can also be defined as a particular state of mind . . . and I was in that mind for a while. Even the state of mind belongs to that historic window."

Emerson's "vast, solid phalanx" of generations moves on, and the literary clusters inevitably disappear with the passing years. What is left is the work of the writer after the particular chemistry of the cluster has done its job. If it is successful—as shown perhaps by the City Lights paperback volume of poems by Allen Ginsberg found on a shelf with other books of American literature in Boris Pasternak's dacha in Peredelkino—the work is what survives.

"THE BEST MINDS OF A GENERATION"

East Coast Beats

The poet Gary Snyder once joked there was no Beat Generation—it consisted of only three or four people, and four people don't make up a generation. He was referring to the small group of friends in New York City who formed the first group of Beat writers, and he was right—at the beginning, there weren't many in the group. Ginsberg and Lucien Carr, both Columbia undergraduates in 1944 determined to find a "New Vision" in literature, were its nucleus, which doubled within a short time to include William Burroughs and Jack Kerouac. All four were passionately interested in literature and thought of themselves as potential writers, except for Lucien Carr, who—according to Ginsberg's journals at the time—was a perfectionist and believed he couldn't write. "He had to be a genius or nothing, and since he couldn't be creative he turned to bohemianism, eccentricity, social versatility, conquests."

The original group of Beat writers in New York City might have been small, but its members added to their ranks steadily in the next few years. First Burroughs introduced the others to Herbert Huncke, the Times Square hustler who taught them the word "beat" and was a contact for drugs. Then, in 1946, Neal Cassady, a Denver acquaintance of one of Ginsberg's friends at Columbia, rode a Greyhound to New York. Cassady became Kerouac's friend and Ginsberg's lover, and joined the group. In 1948, Kerouac met another aspiring novelist in New York, John Clellon Holmes, who helped him think up the name "Beat Generation" for the new consciousness they both sensed in the country. In 1949 Ginsberg was a patient at the Columbia Psychiatric Institute for a short time, where he met Carl Solomon, who had voluntarily committed himself for shock treatments. Solomon began to write after he got out of the psychiatric hospital and was the friend to whom Ginsberg dedicated "Howl" six years later. Finally, in a Greenwich Village bar in 1950, Ginsberg met Gregory Corso, a twenty-year-old "jail kid" who had a passionate desire to write poetry.

These writers formed lifelong friendships that survived despite their dispersion as a group in the early 1950s. As the historian Alfred Kazin understood, the Beats created a new kind of bohemian community. They were a "family of friends," to use Kazin's term, which found the strength like any family through their bonds of affection and common interests to withstand the indifference and hostility of the larger society around them. Over the years they lived in various rooms and apartments scattered throughout New York, first around Columbia University and Times Square, then on the Lower East Side, Brooklyn, Harlem, the Bronx, and Lexington Avenue. Greenwich Village was rarely in the picture. Its heyday as a center for radical literary and political activity had passed with the area's gentrification in the early 1940s. There was no radical bohemian tradition in New York City to sustain the early Beats.

They didn't identify with turn-of-the-century Greenwich Village anarchists like Alexander Berkman or World War I–era Greenwich Village literary innovators like Alfred Kreymborg. If anything, when the Beats formed as a group the Village had come to represent the commercial exploitation that prevailed in America, as Edmund Wilson recognized as early as 1929 in his novel *I Thought of Daisy:* "I did not know that I was soon to see the whole quarter fall victim to the landlords and real estate speculators, who would raise rents and wreck the old houses . . . [until] the very configuration of the streets should be wiped out . . . [and] the proportions of everything should be spoiled by the first peaks of a mountain range of modern apartment houses. . . ."

The unlikely geographical center of the early Beat group in New York was Times Square, as Kerouac's first published novel *The Town and the City* (1950) made clear. Written between 1946 and 1948, it included a fictionalized account of the earliest years of his friendship with Ginsberg, Carr, Burroughs, and Huncke, who appear under pseudonyms. The novel gave a vivid sense of their conversations in Times Square cafeterias and incorporated one of Ginsberg's early "New Vision" prose experiments describing Forty-second Street. While a Columbia freshman, Ginsberg had written a sketch of an amusement arcade in Times Square frequented by hustlers and drug addicts he called "the Pokerino." He described it as if it manifested a post-atomic bomb apocalyptic vision.

In *The Town and the City,* Kerouac called Ginsberg Leon Levinsky and presented him as a nineteen-year-old poet, an "eager, intense, sharply intelligent boy of Russian-Jewish parentage who rushed around New York in a perpetual sweat of emotional activity." In the novel Levinsky explained that when he went into the amusement arcade on Forty-second Street "among all the children of the sad American paradise, you can only stare at them, in a Benzedrine depression, don't you see, or with that sightless stare that comes from too much horror. . . . In the end, everyone looks like a Zombie, you realize that everyone is dead, locked up in the sad psychoses of themselves. It goes on all night, everyone milling around uncertainly among the ruins of bourgeois civilization, seeking each other, don't you see, but so stultified by their upbringings somehow, or by the disease of the age, that they can only stumble about. . . ."

Ginsberg's fascination with atomic contamination and radiation sickness was symptomatic of his time, shortly after the explosion of nuclear bombs in the American Southwest and on Japanese cities in the Second World War. "The disease of the age," for Ginsberg and others in the early Beat group, also drew them to drugs like marijuana, morphine, heroin, and Benzedrine, which fueled their writing and gave Kerouac the sense they were a "generation of furtives."

In their drug experiences they were looking for what Ginsberg later called "some kind of opening of mind" beyond the rationality of science that had led to nuclear bombs. As John Clellon Holmes wrote later in *Nothing More to Declare,* "The burden of my generation was the knowledge that something rational had caused all this (the feeling that something had gotten dreadfully, dangerously out of hand in our world—this vast maelstrom of death . . . the concentration camps that proved too real) and that nothing rational could end it. . . . The bombs had gotten bigger, but the politics had stayed the same. The burden of my generation was to carry this in utter helplessness—the genocide, the overkill—and still seek love in the underground where all living things hide if they are to survive our century."

Burroughs's biographer, Ted Morgan, understood that the Beats' search for an identity outside of conventional society made many of them feel at home in a "community of outlaws." Burroughs has described how he forged stolen prescriptions for drugs and robbed drunks in the New York subways to get the money he needed to support his morphine habit. Kerouac went to jail as a material witness for helping Lucien Carr destroy evidence after Carr fatally stabbed David Kammerer, another member of the early group around Columbia. Ginsberg was expelled from Columbia and spent time in the psychiatric wards of the Presbyterian Hospital after letting Herbert Huncke store stolen goods in his apartment.

The New York Beat writers were a wild group with firsthand experience of life on the fringes of society. Pushing themselves with various drugs to the emotional edge and beyond, Burroughs, Ginsberg, and Kerouac created visionary works of autobiographical fiction and poetry unprecedented in American literature. They became the spokesmen for people rejected by the mainstream, whether drug addicts, homosexuals, the emotionally dispossessed, or the mentally ill. It is significant that the first literary magazine to sponsor the writing of the early Beats was a little magazine titled *Neurotica.* This was started in 1948 by Jay Landesman, a St. Louis businessman who moved to New York soon after its first issue. Nine issues of *Neurotica* were published before it folded in 1951.

The magazine announced that its purpose was "to implement the realization on the part of people that they live in a

neurotic culture and that it is making neurotics out of them."
Neurotica kept itself aloof from other East Coast literary magazines, claiming that the "little mags that died to make verse free have been replaced by subsidized vehicles for clique poetry, critical back-scratching, and professional piddle. . . .
Having embraced the preciosity and academicism that the little mag was raised up to fight, the current types find themselves wholly without purpose. . . ."

Neurotica published early poetry by Ginsberg, essays by Holmes and Solomon, and articles, poems, and translations by Marshall McLuhan, Lawrence Durrell, Kenneth Patchen, Leonard Bernstein, Malcolm Cowley, and Anatole Broyard. Its heavy-handed satirical attacks on the American mainstream included what it called "needle-nose analysis of a culture clearly going insane" by coeditor Gershman Legman, whose articles dissected the deeper social and psychological influences behind the popularity of violence in best-sellers, murder mysteries, western pulp novels, and comic books.

America's dominant mood of optimism and complacency in its economic prosperity during the early years of the Korean War was undermined by its fear of Communist expansion during the Cold War. The contents of the Sunday *New York Times*, on November 16, 1952, which contained Holmes's article "This Is the Beat Generation," reflected the mood of the country.

Featured in the newspaper was an interview with General Matthew B. Ridgway, who felt that the NATO alliance of armies, air force, and navies in Europe was stronger than ever before, but "still too weak to counterbalance the huge growing Soviet armed menace." Another article described the Republic of Korea infantrymen training under U.S. military supervision, ready to fight the Red Chinese "even though they may lack some of the polish of Western troops." The next article in the magazine section was by a congressman who asserted that "during the last twenty years Washington has supplanted New York as the real center of America." Then came the feature article on food, titled "Men Are the Best Cooks," inspired by the recent confession of Mamie Eisenhower that her husband President Eisenhower was a better cook than she.

The complacent sexism of the *Times* in the food article was echoed by its subtle racism on the "Entertainment" page when it commended two white actors giving their ten-thousandth performance as the African-American radio characters Amos 'n' Andy. Even Holmes's article about young people growing up in a Beat Generation moved by what he called "a desperate craving for affirmative beliefs" was belied by the advertising copy that followed it, a photograph of a beautiful model in a plaid robe posed with her knitting needles before a marble fireplace. The subtext in the words over her picture, "How to live a lovely private life in Viyella," made clear that the model had no difficulty finding "affirmative beliefs" as a member of the affluent society.

After the success of Kerouac's *On the Road,* Holmes wrote a second, more sharply focused article titled "The Philosophy of the Beat Generation," published in *Esquire* in February 1958. By this time American troops had failed to achieve a clear-cut victory in Korea, and the country's confidence was not so strong as it had been in 1952. James Dean and Elvis Presley had become idolized figures in American popular culture, and Holmes noted with relief that they seemed to symbolize important social changes. America could no longer find it so easy to sweep her dust under the carpet, although conservative forces still dominated the country. Critics wanting to maintain the status quo noted with alarm "more delinquency, more excess, more social irresponsibility" in young people "than in any generation in recent years," and "less interest in politics, community activity, and the orthodox religious creeds."

Replying to the critics, Holmes supported Kerouac's assertion that "the Beat Generation is basically a religious generation." He insisted that books such as *On the Road* were harbingers of necessary change because they stripped away social hypocrisy. Holmes wrote, "What differentiated the characters in *On the Road* from the slum-bred petty criminals and icon-smashing Bohemians which have been something of a staple in much modern American fiction—what made them *beat*—was . . . Kerouac's insistence that actually they were on a quest, and that the specific object of their quest was spiritual. . . . If they seemed to trespass most boundaries, legal and moral, it was only in the hope of finding a belief on the other side."

Holmes argued for the acceptance of the Beat Generation because it was the product of the postwar world, not something foreign to the culture. "It is the first generation in American history that has grown up with peacetime military training as a fully accepted fact of life. . . . It is also the first generation that has grown up since the possibility of the nuclear destruction of the world has become the final answer to all questions."

What struck Holmes—and later generations of sympathetic readers—as the most important quality of *On the Road* was the energy of its affirmative tone. He urged readers of Kerouac's novel to celebrate it as the achievement it was, because it transcended "the cynicism and apathy which accompanies the end of ideals." In 1957 *On the Road* wasn't the first Beat novel—Holmes's *Go* (1952) and Burroughs's *Junky* (1953) preceded it—but it was the one that most people identified with the Beat literary movement when it surfaced as a part of American cultural life in the late 1950s.

Jack Kerouac

Jack Kerouac was born on March 12, 1922, in Lowell, Massachusetts, into a French Canadian immigrant family, and died in Saint Petersburg, Florida, on October 21, 1969. He came to New York City at seventeen on a football scholarship to the Horace Mann School and Columbia College. With the outbreak of World War II, he dropped out of Columbia to enlist in the navy. He was discharged with an "indifferent character" after he refused to accept navy discipline and served as a merchant seaman for the remainder of the war.

While working as a seaman Kerouac had started to write a novel titled The Sea Is My Brother *(which he finished in 1943). His decision to become a writer was encouraged by Allen Ginsberg, Lucien Carr, and William Burroughs, but in the autobiographical novel* Vanity of Duluoz *(1968), which Kerouac wrote late in life about the period 1939–1946, he expressed reservations about his friends' wild behavior. In describing their association with criminals and drug dealers, and his own Benzedrine and alcohol addictions, he acknowledged that this "clique was the most evil and intelligent buncha bastards and shits in America but had to admire in my admiring youth."*

Even at the time Kerouac said he was bored by what he called his Columbia friends' "tedious intellectualness." When he wrote On the Road *in 1951, he made his new friend Neal Cassady from Denver, Colorado, the central figure in the novel. Cassady seemed to Kerouac like a true brother, a "western kinsman of the sun." The opening pages of* On the Road *describe Cassady's arrival in New York in 1946 and his electrifying effect on the*

8

group at Columbia. In the novel Cassady is named Dean Moriarty, Kerouac is Sal Paradise, Ginsberg is Carlo Marx, Burroughs is Old Bull Lee and Huncke is Elmer Hassel.

The Town and the City *(1950), Kerouac's first published book, had been modeled on the fiction of Thomas Wolfe, then the strongest influence on aspiring novelists in America, but Kerouac found his own voice writing* On the Road. *He began planning a series of autobiographical novels that would tell his life story and completed a dozen books comprising what he called "the legend of Duluoz," his fictitious French-Canadian name for himself.* Visions of Gerard, Doctor Sax, *and* Maggie Cassidy *describe his early life growing up in Lowell.* The Subterraneans *is the book in the chronology following* On the Road, *which covers the period 1946–1950.* The Subterraneans *is the story of a love affair Kerouac (named Leo Percepied in the novel) had in New York in 1953 with a young black woman he named Mardou. To protect himself from libel, he changed the setting to San Francisco. In* The Subterraneans, *Lucien Carr is named Julien, Ginsberg is Adam Moorad, Burroughs is Frank Carmody, Gregory Corso is Yuri Gligoric, and John Clellon Holmes is Mac Jones.*

Kerouac titled his novel The Subterraneans *because that was the name Ginsberg called their group. He wrote the book in a three day and three night Benzedrine-fueled burst right after the love affair ended. His prose style so impressed Ginsberg and Burroughs that they asked him to write down his method of writing. Kerouac obliged with "Belief & Technique for Modern Prose" and "Essentials of Spontaneous Prose," his most extensive accounts of his method of spontaneous prose.*

The Dharma Bums, *another book describing Beat life in the "Duluoz" chronology, fictionalized Kerouac's adventures in California in the fall of 1955. He had spent the summer in Mexico City, where he had written the experimental book of poetry titled* Mexico City Blues, *which included a tribute to the legendary bebop saxophonist Charlie Parker, one of his early "secret heroes," who had died in the spring of that year.* The Dharma Bums *centered on Kerouac's friendship with the West Coast poet Gary Snyder. It opened with a description of the group of poets who became associated with the New York Beats after the poetry reading at the Six Gallery in San Francisco in*

October 1955. In this novel Kerouac called himself Ray Smith, Ginsberg is Alvah Goldbook, and Cassady is Cody Pomeray, while in the group of West Coast poets Gary Snyder is Japhy Ryder, Kenneth Rexroth is Rheinhold Cacoethes, Michael McClure is Ike O'Shay, Philip Whalen is Warren Coughlin, and Philip Lamantia is Francis DaPavia. Desolation Angels *and* Big Sur, *covering the years 1956–1960, are the other books in the "Duluoz" chronology where the Beat writers appear.*

from ON THE ROAD

[PART ONE]

1

I first met Dean [Neal Cassady] not long after my wife and I split up. I had just gotten over a serious illness that I won't bother to talk about, except that it had something to do with the miserably weary split-up and my feeling that everything was dead. With the coming of Dean Moriarty began the part of my life you could call my life on the road. Before that I'd often dreamed of going West to see the country, always vaguely planning and never taking off. Dean is the perfect guy for the road because he actually was born on the road, when his parents were passing through Salt Lake City in 1926, in a jalopy, on their way to Los Angeles. First reports of him came to me through Chad King [Hal Chase], who'd shown me a few letters from him written in a New Mexico reform school. I was tremendously interested in the letters because they so naïvely and sweetly asked Chad to teach him all about Nietzsche and all the wonderful intellectual things that Chad knew. At one point Carlo [Allen Ginsberg] and I talked about the letters and wondered if we would ever meet the strange Dean Moriarty. This is all far back, when Dean was not the way he is today, when he was a young jailkid shrouded in mystery. Then news came that Dean was out of reform school and was coming to New York for the first time; also there was talk that he had just married a girl called Marylou.

One day I was hanging around the campus and Chad and

Tim Gray told me Dean was staying in a cold-water pad in East Harlem, the Spanish Harlem. Dean had arrived the night before, the first time in New York, with his beautiful little sharp chick Marylou; they got off the Greyhound bus at 50th Street and cut around the corner looking for a place to eat and went right in Hector's, and since then Hector's cafeteria has always been a big symbol of New York for Dean. They spent money on beautiful big glazed cakes and creampuffs.

All this time Dean was telling Marylou things like this: "Now, darling, here we are in New York and although I haven't quite told you everything that I was thinking about when we crossed Missouri and especially at the point when we passed the Booneville reformatory which reminded me of my jail problem, it is absolutely necessary now to postpone all those leftover things concerning our personal lovethings and at once begin thinking of specific worklife plans . . ." and so on in the way that he had in those early days.

I went to the cold-water flat with the boys, and Dean came to the door in his shorts. Marylou was jumping off the couch; Dean had dispatched the occupant of the apartment to the kitchen, probably to make coffee, while he proceeded with his loveproblems, for to him sex was the one and only holy and important thing in life, although he had to sweat and curse to make a living and so on. You saw that in the way he stood bobbing his head, always looking down, nodding, like a young boxer to instructions, to make you think he was listening to every word, throwing in a thousand "Yeses" and "That's rights." My first impression of Dean was of a young Gene Autry—trim, thin-hipped, blue-eyed, with a real Oklahoma accent—a sideburned hero of the snowy West. In fact he'd just been working on a ranch, Ed Wall's in Colorado, before marrying Marylou and coming East. Marylou was a pretty blonde with immense ringlets of hair like a sea of golden tresses; she sat there on the edge of the couch with her hands hanging in her lap and her smoky blue country eyes fixed in a wide stare because she was in an evil gray New York pad that she'd heard about back West, and waiting like a long-bodied emaciated Modigliani surrealist woman in a serious room. But, outside of being a sweet little girl, she was awfully dumb and capable of doing horrible things. That night we all drank beer and pulled wrists and talked till dawn, and in the morning, while we sat around dumbly smoking butts from ashtrays in the gray light of a gloomy day, Dean got up nervously, paced around, thinking, and decided the thing to do was to have Marylou make breakfast and sweep the floor. "In other words we've got to get on the ball, darling, what I'm saying, otherwise it'll be fluctuating and lack of true knowledge or crystallization of our plans." Then I went away.

During the following week he confided in Chad King that he absolutely had to learn how to write from him; Chad said I was a writer and he should come to me for advice. Meanwhile Dean had gotten a job in a parking lot, had a fight with Marylou in their Hoboken apartment—God knows why they went there—and she was so mad and so down deep vindictive that she reported to the police some false trumped-up hysterical crazy charge, and Dean had to lam from Hoboken. So he had no place to live. He came right out to Paterson, New Jersey, where I was living with my aunt, and one night while I was studying there was a knock on the door, and there was Dean, bowing, shuffling obsequiously in the dark of the hall, and saying, "Hel-lo, you remember me—Dean Moriarty? I've come to ask you to show me how to write."

"And where's Marylou?" I asked, and Dean said she'd apparently whored a few dollars together and gone back to Denver—"the whore!" So we went out to have a few beers because we couldn't talk like we wanted to talk in front of my aunt, who sat in the living room reading her paper. She took one look at Dean and decided that he was a madman.

In the bar I told Dean, "Hell, man, I know very well you didn't come to me only to want to become a writer, and after all what do I really know about it except you've got to stick to it with the energy of a benny addict." And he said, "Yes, of course, I know exactly what you mean and in fact all those problems have occurred to me, but the thing that I want is the realization of those factors that should one depend on Schopenhauer's dichotomy for any inwardly realized . . ." and so on in that way, things I understood not a bit and he himself didn't. In those days he really didn't know what he was talking about; that is to say, he was a young jailkid all hung-up on the wonderful possibilities of becoming a real intellectual, and he liked to talk in the tone and using the words, but in a jumbled way, that he had heard from "real intellectuals"—although, mind you, he wasn't so naïve as that in all other things, and it took him just a few months with Carlo Marx to become completely *in there* with all the terms and jargon. Nonetheless we understood each other on other levels of madness, and I agreed that he could stay at my house till he found a job and furthermore we agreed to go out West sometime. That was the winter of 1947.

One night when Dean ate supper at my house—he already had the parking-lot job in New York—he leaned over my shoulder as I typed rapidly away and said, "Come on man, those girls won't wait, make it fast."

I said, "Hold on just a minute, I'll be right with you soon as I finish this chapter," and it was one of the best chapters in the book. Then I dressed and off we flew to New York to meet some girls. As we rode in the bus in the weird phosphorescent void of the Lincoln Tunnel we leaned on each other with fingers waving and yelled and talked excitedly, and I was beginning to get the bug like Dean. He was simply a youth tremendously excited with life, and though he was a con-man, he was only conning because he wanted so much to live and to get involved with people who would otherwise pay no attention to him. He was conning me and I knew it (for room and board and "how-to-write," etc.), and he knew I knew (this has been the basis of our relationship), but I didn't care and we got along fine—no pestering, no catering; we tiptoed around each other like heartbreaking new friends. I began to learn from him as much as he probably learned from me. As far as my work was concerned he said, "Go ahead, everything you do is great." He watched over my shoulder as I wrote stories, yelling, "Yes! That's right! Wow! Man!" and "Phew!" and wiped his face with his handkerchief. "Man, wow, there's so many things to do, so many things to write! How to even *begin* to get it all down and without modified restraints and all hung-up on like literary inhibitions and grammatical fears . . ."

"That's right, man, now you're talking." And a kind of holy lightning I saw flashing from his excitement and his visions, which he described so torrentially that people in buses looked

around to see the "overexcited nut." In the West he'd spent
a third of his time in the poolhall, a third in jail, and a third
in the public library. They'd seen him rushing eagerly down
the winter streets, bareheaded, carrying books to the poolhall,
or climbing trees to get into the attics of buddies where he
spent days reading or hiding from the law.

We went to New York—I forget what the situation was,
two colored girls—there were no girls there; they were supposed to meet him in a diner and didn't show up. We went to
his parking lot where he had a few things to do—change his
clothes in the shack in back and spruce up a bit in front of a
cracked mirror and so on, and then we took off. And that was
the night Dean met Carlo Marx. A tremendous thing happened
when Dean met Carlo Marx. Two keen minds that they are,
they took to each other at the drop of a hat. Two piercing
eyes glanced into two piercing eyes—the holy con-man with
the shining mind, and the sorrowful poetic con-man with the
dark mind that is Carlo Marx. From that moment on I saw
very little of Dean, and I was a little sorry too. Their energies
met head-on, I was a lout compared, I couldn't keep up with
them. The whole mad swirl of everything that was to come
began then; it would mix up all my friends and all I had left
of my family in a big dust cloud over the American Night.
Carlo told him of Old Bull Lee [William Burroughs], Elmer
Hassel [Herbert Huncke], Jane [Joan Vollmer Burroughs]:
Lee in Texas growing weed, Hassel on Riker's Island, Jane
wandering on Times Square in a benzedrine hallucination, with
her baby girl in her arms and ending up in Bellevue. And Dean
told Carlo of unknown people in the West like Tommy Snark,
the clubfooted poolhall rotation shark and cardplayer and
queer saint. He told him of Roy Johnson, Big Ed Dunkel, his
boyhood buddies, his street buddies, his innumerable girls and
sex-parties and pornographic pictures, his heroes, heroines,
adventures. They rushed down the street together, digging
everything in the early way they had, which later became so
much sadder and perceptive and blank. But then they danced
down the streets like dingledodies, and I shambled after as
I've been doing all my life after people who interest me, because the only people for me are the mad ones, the ones who
are mad to live, mad to talk, mad to be saved, desirous of

everything at the same time, the ones who never yawn or say a commonplace thing, but burn, burn, burn like fabulous yellow roman candles exploding like spiders across the stars and in the middle you see the blue centerlight pop and everybody goes "Awww!" What did they call such young people in Goethe's Germany? Wanting dearly to learn how to write like Carlo, the first thing you know, Dean was attacking him with a great amorous soul such as only a con-man can have. "Now, Carlo, let *me* speak—here's what *I'm* saying . . ." I didn't see them for about two weeks, during which time they cemented their relationship to fiendish allday-allnight-talk proportions.

Then came spring, the great time of traveling, and everybody in the scattered gang was getting ready to take one trip or another. I was busily at work on my novel and when I came to the halfway mark, after a trip down South with my aunt [mother Gabrielle Kerouac] to visit my brother Rocco [sister Caroline], I got ready to travel West for the very first time.

Dean had already left. Carlo and I saw him off at the 34th Street Greyhound station. Upstairs they had a place where you could make pictures for a quarter. Carlo took off his glasses and looked sinister. Dean made a profile shot and looked coyly around. I took a straight picture that made me look like a thirty-year-old Italian who'd kill anybody who said anything against his mother. This picture Carlo and Dean neatly cut down the middle with a razor and saved a half each in their wallets. Dean was wearing a real Western business suit for his big trip back to Denver; he'd finished his first fling in New York. I say fling, but he only worked like a dog in parking lots. The most fantastic parking-lot attendant in the world, he can back a car forty miles an hour into a tight squeeze and stop at the wall, jump out, race among fenders, leap into another car, circle it fifty miles an hour in a narrow space, back swiftly into tight spot, *hump,* snap the car with the emergency so that you see it bounce as he flies out; then clear to the ticket shack, sprinting like a track star, hand a ticket, leap into a newly arrived car before the owner's half out, leap literally under him as he steps out, start the car with the door flapping, and roar off to the next available spot, arc, pop in, brake, out, run; working like that without pause eight hours a night, evening rush hours and after-theater rush hours, in greasy wino pants with a frayed fur-lined jacket and beat shoes that flap. Now he'd bought a new suit to go back in; blue with pencil stripes, vest and all—eleven dollars on Third Avenue, with a watch and watch chain, and a portable typewriter with which he was going to start writing in a Denver rooming house as soon as he got a job there. We had a farewell meal of franks and beans in a Seventh Avenue Riker's, and then Dean got on the bus that said Chicago and roared off into the night. There went our wrangler. I promised myself to go the same way when spring really bloomed and opened up the land.

And this was really the way that my whole road experience began, and the things that were to come are too fantastic not to tell.

Yes, and it wasn't only because I was a writer and needed new experiences that I wanted to know Dean more, and because my life hanging around the campus had reached the completion of its cycle and was stultified, but because, somehow, in spite of our difference in character, he reminded me of some long-lost brother; the sight of his suffering bony face with the long sideburns and his straining muscular sweating neck made me remember my boyhood in those dye-dumps and swim-holes and riversides of Paterson and the Passaic. His dirty work-clothes clung to him so gracefully, as though you couldn't buy a better fit from a custom tailor but only earn it from the Natural Tailor of Natural Joy, as Dean had, in his stresses. And in his excited way of speaking I heard again the voices of old companions and brothers under the bridge, among the motorcycles, along the wash-lined neighborhood and drowsy doorsteps of afternoon where boys played guitars while their older brothers worked in the mills. All my other current friends were "intellectuals"—Chad the Nietzschean anthropologist, Carlo Marx and his nutty surrealist low-voiced serious staring talk, Old Bull Lee and his critical anti-everything drawl—or else they were slinking criminals like Elmer Hassel, with that hip sneer; Jane Lee the same, sprawled on the Oriental cover of her couch, sniffing at the *New Yorker*. But Dean's intelligence was every bit as formal and shining and complete, without the tedious intellectualness. And his "criminality" was not something that sulked and sneered; it was a wild yea-saying

overburst of American joy; it was Western, the west wind, an
ode from the Plains, something new, long prophesied, long a-
coming (he only stole cars for joy rides). Besides, all my New
York friends were in the negative, nightmare position of putting down society and giving their tired bookish or political or
psychoanalytical reasons, but Dean just raced in society, eager
for bread and love; he didn't care one way or the other, "so
long's I can get that lil ole gal with that lil sumpin down there
tween her legs, boy," and "so long's we can *eat,* son, y'ear
me? I'm *hungry,* I'm *starving,* let's *eat right now!*"—and off
we'd rush to *eat,* whereof, as saith Ecclesiastes, "It is your
portion under the sun."

A western kinsman of the sun, Dean. Although my aunt
warned me that he would get me in trouble, I could hear a
new call and see a new horizon, and believe it at my young
age; and a little bit of trouble or even Dean's eventual rejection
of me as a buddy, putting me down, as he would later, on
starving sidewalks and sickbeds—what did it matter? I was a
young writer and I wanted to take off.

Somewhere along the line I knew there'd be girls, visions,
everything; somewhere along the line the pearl would be
handed to me.

[PART THREE]

In no time at all we were back on the main highway and that
night I saw the entire state of Nebraska unroll before my eyes.
A hundred and ten miles an hour straight through, an arrow
road, sleeping towns, no traffic, and the Union Pacific stream-
liner falling behind us in the moonlight. I wasn't frightened at
all that night; it was perfectly legitimate to go 110 and talk
and have all the Nebraska towns—Ogallala, Gothenburg,
Kearney, Grand Island, Columbus—unreel with dreamlike
rapidity as we roared ahead and talked. It was a magnificent
car; it could hold the road like a boat holds on water. Gradual
curves were its singing ease. "Ah, man, what a dreamboat,"
sighed Dean. "Think if you and I had a car like this what we
could do. Do you know there's a road that goes down Mexico
and all the way to Panama?—and maybe all the way to the
bottom of South America where the Indians are seven feet

tall and eat cocaine on the mountainside? Yes! You and I, Sal, we'd dig the whole world with a car like this because, man, the road must eventually lead to the whole world. Ain't nowhere else it can go—right? Oh, and are we going to cut around old Chi with this thing! Think of it, Sal, I've never been to Chicago in all my life, never stopped."

"We'll come in there like gangsters in this Cadillac!"

"Yes! And girls! We can pick up girls, in fact, Sal, I've decided to make extra-special fast time so we can have an entire evening to cut around in this thing. Now you just relax and I'll ball the jack all the way."

"Well, how fast are you going now?"

"A steady one-ten I figure—you wouldn't notice it. We've still got all Iowa in the daytime and then I'll make that old Illinois in nothing flat." The boys [two passengers in the backseat] fell asleep and we talked and talked all night.

It was remarkable how Dean could go mad and then suddenly continue with his soul—which I think is wrapped up in a fast car, a coast to reach, and a woman at the end of the road—calmly and sanely as though nothing had happened. "I get like that every time in Denver now—I can't make that town any more. Gookly, gooky, Dean's a spooky. Zoom!" I told him I had been over this Nebraska road before in '47. He had too. "Sal, when I was working for the New Era Laundry in Los Angeles, nineteen forty-four, falsifying my age, I made a trip to Indianapolis Speedway for the express purpose of seeing the Memorial Day classic hitch, hiking by day and stealing cars by night to make time. Also I had a twenty-dollar Buick back in LA, my first car, it couldn't pass the brake and light inspection so I decided I needed an out-of-state license to operate the car without arrest so went through here to get the license. As I was hitchhiking through one of these very towns, with the plates concealed under my coat, a nosy sheriff who thought I was pretty young to be hitchhiking accosted me on the main drag. He found the plates and threw me in the two-cell jail with a county delinquent who should have been in the home for the old since he couldn't feed himself (the sheriff's wife fed him) and sat through the day drooling and slobbering. After investigation, which included corny things like a fatherly quiz, then an abrupt turnabout to frighten me with threats, a comparison of my handwriting, et cetera, and after I made the most magnificent speech of my life to get out of it, concluding with the confession that I was lying about my car-stealing past and was only looking for my paw who was a farmhand hereabouts, he let me go. Of course I missed the races. The following fall I did the same thing again to see the Notre Dame–California game in South Bend, Indiana—trouble none this time and, Sal, I had just the money for the ticket and not an extra cent and didn't eat anything all up and back except for what I could panhandle from all kinds of crazy cats I met on the road and at the same time gun gals. Only guy in the United States of America that ever went to so much trouble to see a ballgame."

I asked him the circumstances of his being in LA in 1944. "I was arrested in Arizona, the joint absolutely the worst joint I've ever been in. I had to escape and pulled the greatest escape in my life, speaking of escapes, you see, in a general way. In the woods, you know, and crawling, and swamps—up around that mountain country. Rubber hoses and the works and accidental so-called death facing me I had to cut out of those woods along the ridge so as to keep away from trails and paths and roads. Had to get rid of my joint clothes and sneaked the neatest theft of a shirt and pants from a gas station outside Flagstaff, arriving LA two days later clad as gas attendant and walked to the first station I saw and got hired and got myself a room and changed name (Lee Buliay) and spent an exciting year in LA, including a whole gang of new friends and some really great girls, that season ending when we were all driving on Hollywood Boulevard one night and I told my buddy to steer the car while I kissed my girl—I was at the wheel, see —and *he didn't hear me* and we ran smack into a post but only going twenty and I broke my nose. You've seen before my nose—the crooked Grecian curve up here. After that I went to Denver and met Marylou in a soda fountain that spring. Oh, man, she was only fifteen and wearing jeans and just waiting for someone to pick her up. Three days three nights of talk in the Ace Hotel, third floor, southeast corner room, holy memento room and sacred scene of my days—she was so sweet then, so *young,* hmm, ahh! But hey, look down there in the night thar, hup, hup, a buncha old bums by a fire by the rail, damn me." He almost slowed down. "You see, I never know whether my father's there or not." There were some figures by the tracks, reeling in front of a woodfire. "I never know whether to ask. He might be anywhere." We drove on. Somewhere behind us or in front of us in the huge night his father lay drunk under a bush, and no doubt about it— spittle on his chin, water on his pants, molasses in his ears, scabs on his nose, maybe blood in his hair and the moon shining down on him.

I took Dean's arm. "Ah, man, we're sure going home now." New York was going to be his permanent home for the first time. He jiggled all over; he couldn't wait.

"And think, Sal, when we get to Pennsy we'll start hearing that gone Eastern bop on the disk jockeys. Geeyah, roll, old boat, roll!" The magnificent car made the wind roar; it made the plains unfold like a roll of paper; it cast hot tar from itself with deference—an imperial boat. I opened my eyes to a fanning dawn; we were hurling up to it. Dean's rocky dogged face as ever bent over the dashlight with a bony purpose of its own.

"What are you thinking, Pops?"

"Ah-ha, ah-ha, same old thing, y'know—gurls gurls gurls."

I went to sleep and woke up to the dry, hot atmosphere of July Sunday morning in Iowa, and still Dean was driving and driving and had not slackened his speed; he took the curvy corndales of Iowa at a minimum of eighty and the straightaway 110 as usual, unless both-ways traffic forced him to fall in line at a crawling and miserable sixty. When there was a chance he shot ahead and passed cars by the half-dozen and left them behind in a cloud of dust. A mad guy in a brandnew Buick saw all this on the road and decided to race us. When Dean was just about to pass a passel the guy shot by us without warning and howled and tooted his horn and flashed the tail lights for challenge. We took off after him like a big bird. "Now wait," laughed Dean, "I'm going to tease that sonofabitch for a dozen miles or so. Watch." He let the Buick go way ahead and then accelerated and caught up with it most impolitely. Mad Buick went out of his mind; he gunned up to a hundred. We had a chance to see who he was. He seemed to be some kind of Chicago hipster traveling with a woman old enough to be—and probably actually was—his mother.

God knows if she was complaining, but he raced. His hair was dark and wild, an Italian from old Chi; he wore a sports shirt. Maybe there was an idea in his mind that we were a new gang from LA invading Chicago, maybe some of Mickey Cohen's men, because the limousine looked every bit the part and the license plates were California. Mainly it was just road kicks. He took terrible chances to stay ahead of us; he passed cars on curves and barely got back in line as a truck wobbled into view and loomed up huge. Eighty miles of Iowa we unreeled in this fashion, and the race was so interesting that I had no opportunity to be frightened. Then the mad guy gave up, pulled up at a gas station, probably on orders from the old lady, and as we roared by he waved gleefully. On we sped, Dean barechested, I with my feet on the dashboard, and the college boys sleeping in the back. We stopped to eat breakfast at a diner run by a white-haired lady who gave us extra-large portions of potatoes as church-bells rang in the nearby town. Then off again.

"Dean, don't drive so fast in the daytime."

"Don't worry, man, I know what I'm doing." I began to flinch. Dean came up on lines of cars like the Angel of Terror. He almost rammed them along as he looked for an opening. He teased their bumpers, he eased and pushed and craned around to see the curve, then the huge car leaped to his touch and passed, and always by a hair we made it back to our side as other lines filed by in the opposite direction and I shuddered. I couldn't take it any more. It is only seldom that you find a long Nebraskan straightaway in Iowa, and when we finally hit one Dean made his usual 110 and I saw flashing by outside several scenes that I remembered from 1947—a long stretch where Eddie and I had been stranded two hours. All that old road of the past unreeling dizzily as if the cup of life had been overturned and everything gone mad. My eyes ached in nightmare day.

"Ah hell, Dean, I'm going in the back seat, I can't stand it any more, I can't look."

"Hee-hee-hee!" tittered Dean and he passed a car on a narrow bridge and swerved in dust and roared on. I jumped in the back seat and curled up to sleep. One of the boys jumped in front for the fun. Great horrors that we were going to crash this very morning took hold of me and I got down on the floor and closed my eyes and tried to go to sleep. As a seaman I used to think of the waves rushing beneath the shell of the ship and the bottomless deeps thereunder—now I could feel the road some twenty inches beneath me, unfurling and flying and hissing at incredible speeds across the groaning continent with that mad Ahab at the wheel. When I closed my eyes all I could see was the road unwinding into me. When I opened them I saw flashing shadows of trees vibrating on the floor of the car. There was no escaping it. I resigned myself to all. And still Dean drove, he had no thought of sleeping till we got to Chicago. In the afternoon we crossed old Des Moines again. Here of course we got snarled in traffic and had to go slow and I got back in the front seat. A strange pathetic accident took place. A fat colored man was driving with his entire family in a sedan in front of us; on the rear bumper hung one of those canvas desert waterbags they sell tourists in the desert. He pulled up sharp, Dean was talking to the boys in the back and didn't notice, and we rammed him at five miles an hour smack on the waterbag, which burst like a boil and squirted water in the air. No other damage except a bent bumper. Dean and I got out to talk to him. The upshot of it was an exchange of addresses and some talk, and Dean not taking his eyes off the man's wife whose beautiful brown breasts were barely concealed inside a floppy cotton blouse. "Yass, yass." We gave him the address of our Chicago baron and went on.

The other side of Des Moines a cruising car came after us with the siren growling, with orders to pull over. "Now what?"

The cop came out. "Were you in an accident coming in?"

"Accident? We broke a guy's waterbag at the junction."

"He says he was hit and run by a bunch in a stolen car."

This was one of the few instances Dean and I knew of a Negro's acting like a suspicious old fool. It so surprised us we laughed. We had to follow the patrolman to the station and there spent an hour waiting in the grass while they telephoned Chicago to get the owner of the Cadillac and verify our position as hired drivers. Mr. Baron said, according to the cop, "Yes, that is my car but I can't vouch for anything else those boys might have done."

"They were in a minor accident here in Des Moines."

"Yes, you've already told me that—what I meant was, I can't vouch for anything they might have done in the past."

Everything was straightened out and we roared on. Newton, Iowa, it was, where I'd taken that dawn walk in 1947. In the afternoon we crossed drowsy old Davenport again and the low-lying Mississippi in her sawdust bed; then Rock Island, a few minutes of traffic, the sun reddening, and sudden sights of lovely little tributary rivers flowing softly among the magic trees and greeneries of mid-American Illinois. It was beginning to look like the soft sweet East again; the great dry West was accomplished and done. The state of Illinois unfolded before my eyes in one vast movement that lasted a matter of hours as Dean balled straight across at the same speed. In his tiredness he was taking greater chances than ever. At a narrow bridge that crossed one of these lovely little rivers he shot precipitately into an almost impossible situation. Two slow cars ahead of us were bumping over the bridge; coming the other way was a huge truck-trailer with a driver who was making a close estimate of how long it would take the slow cars to negotiate the bridge, and his estimate was that by the time he got there they'd be over. There was absolutely no room on the bridge for the truck and any cars going the other direction. Behind the truck cars pulled out and peeked for a chance to get by it. In front of the slow cars other slow cars were pushing along. The road was crowded and everyone exploding to pass. Dean came down on all this at 110 miles an hour and never hesitated. He passed the slow cars, swerved, and almost hit the left rail of the bridge, went head-on into the shadow of the unslowing truck, cut right sharply, just missed the truck's left front wheel, almost hit the first slow car, pulled out to pass, and then had to cut back in line when another car came out from behind the truck to look, all in a matter of two seconds, flashing by and leaving nothing more than a cloud of dust instead of a horrible five-way crash with cars lurching in every direction and the great truck humping its back in the fatal red afternoon of Illinois with its dreaming fields. I couldn't get it out of my mind, also, that a famous bop clarinetist had died in an Illinois car-crash recently, probably on a day like this. I went to the back seat again.

The boys stayed in the back too now. Dean was bent on

Chicago before nightfall. At a road-rail junction we picked up
two hobos who rounded up a half-buck between them for gas.
A moment before sitting around piles of railroad ties, polishing
off the last of some wine, now they found themselves in a
muddy but unbowed and splendid Cadillac limousine headed
for Chicago in precipitous haste. In fact the old boy up front
who sat next to Dean never took his eyes off the road and
prayed his poor bum prayers, I tell you. "Well," they said,
"we never knew we'd get to Chicaga sa fast." As we passed
drowsy Illinois towns where the people are so conscious of
Chicago gangs that pass like this in limousines every day, we
were a strange sight: all of us unshaven, the driver barechested,
two bums, myself in the back seat, holding on to a strap and
my head leaned back on the cushion looking at the countryside
with an imperious eye—just like a new California gang come
to contest the spoils of Chicago, a band of desperados escaped
from the prisons of the Utah moon. When we stopped for
Cokes and gas at a small-town station people came out to stare
at us but they never said a word and I think made mental
notes of our descriptions and heights in case of future need.
To transact business with the girl who ran the gas-pump Dean
merely threw on his T-shirt like a scarf and was curt and abrupt
as usual and got back in the car and off we roared again. Pretty
soon the redness turned purple, the last of the enchanted rivers
flashed by, and we saw distant smokes of Chicago beyond the
drive. We had come from Denver to Chicago via Ed Wall's
ranch, 1180 miles, in exactly seventeen hours, not counting
the two hours in the ditch and three at the ranch and two with
the police in Newton, Iowa, for a mean average of seventy
miles per hour across the land, with one driver. Which is a
kind of crazy record.

10

Great Chicago glowed red before our eyes. We were suddenly
on Madison Street among hordes of hobos, some of them
sprawled out on the street with their feet on the curb, hundreds
of others milling in the doorways of saloons and alleys. "Wup!
wup! look sharp for old Dean Moriarty there, he may be in
Chicago by accident this year." We let out the hobos on this

street and proceeded to downtown Chicago. Screeching trolleys, newsboys, gals cutting by, the smell of fried food and beer in the air, neons winking—"We're in the big town, Sal! Whooee!" First thing to do was park the Cadillac in a good dark spot and wash up and dress for the night. Across the street from the YMCA we found a redbrick alley between buildings, where we stashed the Cadillac with her snout pointed to the street and ready to go, then followed the college boys up to the Y, where they got a room and allowed us to use their facilities for an hour. Dean and I shaved and showered, I dropped my wallet in the hall, Dean found it and was about to sneak it in his shirt when he realized it was ours and was right disappointed. Then we said good-by to those boys, who were glad they'd made it in one piece, and took off to eat in a cafeteria. Old brown Chicago with the strange semi-Eastern, semi-Western types going to work and spitting. Dean stood in the cafeteria rubbing his belly and taking it all in. He wanted to talk to a strange middle-aged colored woman who had come into the cafeteria with a story about how she had no money but she had buns with her and would they give her butter. She came in flapping her hips, was turned down, and went out flipping her butt. "Whoo!" said Dean. "Let's follow her down the street, let's take her to the ole Cadillac in the alley. We'll have a ball." But we forgot that and headed straight for North Clark Street, after a spin in the Loop, to see the hootchy-kootchy joints and hear the bop. And what a night it was. "Oh, man," said Dean to me as we stood in front of a bar, "dig the street of life, the Chinamen that cut by in Chicago. What a weird town—wow, and that woman in that window up there, just looking down with her big breasts hanging from her nightgown, big wide eyes. Whee. Sal, we gotta go and never stop going till we get there."

"Where we going, man?"

"I don't know but we gotta go." Then here came a gang of young bop musicians carrying their instruments out of cars. They piled right into a saloon and we followed them. They set themselves up and started blowing. There we were! The leader was a slender, drooping, curly-haired, pursy-mouthed tenorman, thin of shoulder, draped loose in a sports shirt, cool in the warm night, self-indulgence written in his eyes, who picked up his horn and frowned in it and blew cool and complex and was dainty stamping his foot to catch ideas, and ducked to miss others—and said, "Blow," very quietly when the other boys took solos. Then there was Prez, a husky, handsome blond like a freckled boxer, meticulously wrapped inside his sharkskin plaid suit with the long drape and the collar falling back and the tie undone for exact sharpness and casualness, sweating and hitching up his horn and writhing into it, and a tone just like Lester Young himself. "You see, man, Prez has the technical anxieties of a money-making musician, he's the only one who's well dressed, see him grow worried when he blows a clinker, but the leader, that cool cat, tells him not to worry and just blow and blow—the mere sound and serious exuberance of the music is all *he* cares about. He's an artist. He's teaching young Prez the boxer. Now the others dig!!" The third sax was an alto, eighteen-year-old cool, contemplative young Charlie-Parker-type Negro from high school, with a broadgash mouth, taller than the rest, grave. He raised his horn and blew into it quietly and thoughtfully and elicited birdlike phrases and architectural Miles Davis logics. These were the children of the great bop innovators.

Once there was Louis Armstrong blowing his beautiful top in the muds of New Orleans; before him the mad musicians who had paraded on official days and broke up their Sousa marches into ragtime. Then there was swing, and Roy Eldridge, vigorous and virile, blasting the horn for everything it had in waves of power and logic and subtlety—leaning to it with glittering eyes and a lovely smile and sending it out broadcast to rock the jazz world. Then had come Charlie Parker, a kid in his mother's woodshed in Kansas City, blowing his taped-up alto among the logs, practicing on rainy days, coming out to watch the old swinging Basie and Benny Moten band that had Hot Lips Page and the rest—Charlie Parker leaving home and coming to Harlem, and meeting mad Thelonius Monk and madder Gillespie—Charlie Parker in his early days when he was flipped and walked around in a circle while playing. Somewhat younger than Lester Young, also from KC, that gloomy, saintly goof in whom the history of jazz was wrapped; for when he held his horn high and horizontal from his mouth he blew the greatest; and as his hair grew longer and he got lazier and stretched-out, his horn came down half-way; till it finally fell all the way and today as he wears his thick-soled shoes so that he can't feel the sidewalks of life his horn is held weakly against his chest, and he blows cool and easy getout phrases. Here were the children of the American bop night.

Stranger flowers yet—for as the Negro alto mused over everyone's head with dignity, the young, tall, slender, blond kid from Curtis Street, Denver, jeans and studded belt, sucked on his mouthpiece while waiting for the others to finish; and when they did he started, and you had to look around to see where the solo was coming from, for it came from angelical smiling lips upon the mouthpiece and it was a soft, sweet, fairy-tale solo on an alto. Lonely as America, a throatpierced sound in the night.

What of the others and all the soundmaking? There was the bass-player, wiry redhead with wild eyes, jabbing his hips at the fiddle with every driving slap, at hot moments his mouth hanging open trancelike. "Man, there's a cat who can really *bend* his girl!" The sad drummer, like our white hipster in Frisco Folsom Street, completely goofed, staring into space, chewing gum, wide-eyed, rocking the neck with Reich kick and complacent ecstasy. The piano—a big husky Italian truck-driving kid with meaty hands, a burly and thoughtful joy. They played an hour. Nobody was listening. Old North Clark bums lolled at the bar, whores screeched in anger. Secret Chinamen went by. Noises of hootchy-kootchy interfered. They went right on. Out on the sidewalk came an apparition—a sixteen-year-old kid with a goatee and a trombone case. Thin as rickets, mad-faced, he wanted to join this group and blow with them. They knew him and didn't want to bother with him. He crept into the bar and surreptitiously undid his trombone and raised it to his lips. No opening. Nobody looked at him. They finished, packed up, and left for another bar. He wanted to jump, skinny Chicago kid. He slapped on his dark glasses, raised the trombone to his lips alone in the bar, and went "Baugh!" Then he rushed out after them. They wouldn't let him play with them, just like the sandlot football team in back of the gas tank. "All these guys live with their grandmothers just like Tom Snark and our Carlo Marx alto," said Dean. We rushed after the whole gang. They went into Anita O'Day's club and there unpacked and played till nine o'clock in the morning. Dean and I were there with beers.

At intermissions we rushed out in the Cadillac and tried to pick up girls all up and down Chicago. They were frightened of our big, scarred, prophetic car. In his mad frenzy Dean backed up smack on hydrants and tittered maniacally. By nine o'clock the car was an utter wreck; the brakes weren't working any more; the fenders were stove in; the rods were rattling. Dean couldn't stop it at red lights, it kept kicking convulsively over the roadway. It had paid the price of the night. It was a muddy boot and no longer a shiny limousine. "Whee!" The boys were still blowing at Neets'.

Suddenly Dean stared into the darkness of a corner beyond the bandstand and said, "Sal, God has arrived."

I looked. *George Shearing.* And as always he leaned his blind head on his pale hand, all ears opened like the ears of an elephant, listening to the American sounds and mastering them for his own English summer's-night use. Then they urged him to get up and play. He did. He played innumerable choruses with amazing chords that mounted higher and higher till the sweat splashed all over the piano and everybody listened in awe and fright. They led him off the stand after an hour. He went back to his dark corner, old God Shearing, and the boys said, "There ain't nothin left after that."

But the slender leader frowned. "Let's blow anyway."

Something would come of it yet. There's always more, a little further—it never ends. They sought to find new phrases after Shearing's explorations; they tried hard. They writhed and twisted and blew. Every now and then a clear harmonic cry gave new suggestions of a tune that would someday be the only tune in the world and would raise men's souls to joy. They found it, they lost, they wrestled for it, they found it again, they laughed, they moaned—and Dean sweated at the table and told them to go, go, go. At nine o'clock in the morning everybody—musicians, girls in slacks, bartenders, and the one little skinny, unhappy trombonist—staggered out of the club into the great roar of Chicago day to sleep until the wild bop night again.

Dean and I shuddered in the raggedness. It was now time

to return the Cadillac to the owner, who lived out on Lake Shore Drive in a swank apartment with an enormous garage underneath managed by oil-scarred Negroes. We drove out there and swung the muddy heap into its berth. The mechanic did not recognize the Cadillac. We handed the papers over. He scratched his head at the sight of it. We had to get out fast. We did. We took a bus back to downtown Chicago and that was that. And we never heard a word from our Chicago baron about the condition of his car, in spite of the fact that he had our addresses and could have complained.

11

It was time for us to move on. We took a bus to Detroit. Our money was now running quite low. We lugged our wretched baggage through the station. By now Dean's thumb bandage was almost as black as coal and all unrolled. We were both as miserable-looking as anybody could be after all the things we'd done. Exhausted, Dean fell asleep in the bus that roared across the state of Michigan. I took up a conversation with a gorgeous country girl wearing a low-cut cotton blouse that displayed the beautiful sun-tan on her breast tops. She was dull. She spoke of evenings in the country making popcorn on the porch. Once this would have gladdened my heart but because her heart was not glad when she said it I knew there was nothing in it but the idea of what one should do. "And what else do you do for fun?" I tried to bring up boy friends and sex. Her great dark eyes surveyed me with emptiness and a kind of chagrin that reached back generations and generations in her blood from not having done what was crying to be done—whatever it was, and everybody knows what it was. "What do you want out of life?" I wanted to take her and wring it out of her. She didn't have the slightest idea what she wanted. She mumbled of jobs, movies, going to her grandmother's for the summer, wishing she could go to New York and visit the Roxy, what kind of outfit she would wear—something like the one she wore last Easter, white bonnet, roses, rose pumps, and lavender gabardine coat. "What do you do on Sunday afternoons?" I asked. She sat on her porch. The boys went by on bicycles and stopped to chat. She read the funny papers, she reclined on the hammock. "What do you do on a warm summer's night?" She sat on the porch, she watched the cars in the road. She and her mother made popcorn. "What does your father do on a summer's night?" He works, he has an all-night shift at the boiler factory, he's spent his whole life supporting a woman and her outpoppings and no credit or adoration. "What does your brother do on a summer's night?" He rides around on his bicycle, he hangs out in front of the soda fountain. "What is he aching to do? What are we all aching to do? What do we want?" She didn't know. She yawned. She was sleepy. It was too much. Nobody could tell. Nobody would ever tell. It was all over. She was eighteen and most lovely, and lost.

And Dean and I, ragged and dirty as if we had lived off locust, stumbled out of the bus in Detroit. We decided to stay up in all-night movies on Skid Row. It was too cold for parks. Hassel had been here on Detroit Skid Row, he had dug every shooting gallery and all-night movie and every brawling bar with his dark eyes many a time. His ghost haunted us. We'd never find him on Times Square again. We thought maybe by accident Old Dean Moriarty was here too—but he was not. For thirty-five cents each we went into the beat-up old movie and sat down in the balcony till morning, when we were shooed downstairs. The people who were in that all-night movie were the end. Beat Negroes who'd come up from Alabama to work in car factories on a rumor; old white bums; young longhaired hipsters who'd reached the end of the road and were drinking wine; whores, ordinary couples, and housewives with nothing to do, nowhere to go, nobody to believe in. If you sifted all Detroit in a wire basket the beater solid core of dregs couldn't be better gathered. The picture was Singing Cowboy Eddie Dean and his gallant white horse Bloop, that was number one; number two double-feature film was George Raft, Sidney Greenstreet, and Peter Lorre in a picture about Istanbul. We saw both of these things six times each during the night. We saw them waking, we heard them sleeping, we sensed them dreaming, we were permeated completely with the strange Gray Myth of the West and the weird dark Myth of the East when morning came. All my actions since then have been dictated automatically to my subconscious by this horrible osmotic experience. I heard big Greenstreet sneer a hundred times; I heard Peter Lorre make his sinister come-on; I was with George Raft in his paranoiac fears; I rode and sang with Eddie Dean and shot up the rustlers innumerable times. People slugged out of bottles and turned around and looked everywhere in the dark theater for something to do, somebody to talk to. In the head everybody was guiltily quiet, nobody talked. In the gray dawn that puffed ghostlike about the windows of the theater and hugged its eaves I was sleeping with my head on the wooden arm of a seat as six attendants of the theater converged with their night's total of swept-up rubbish and created a huge dusty pile that reached to my nose as I snored head down—till they almost swept me away too. This was reported to me by Dean, who was watching from ten seats behind. All the cigarette butts, the bottles, the matchbooks, the come and the gone were swept up in this pile. Had they taken me with it, Dean would never have seen me again. He would have had to roam the entire United States and look in every garbage pail from coast to coast before he found me embryonically convoluted among the rubbishes of my life, his life, and the life of everybody concerned and not concerned. What would I have said to him from my rubbish womb? "Don't bother me, man, I'm happy where I am. You lost me one night in Detroit in August nineteen forty-nine. What right have you to come and disturb my reverie in this pukish can?" In 1942 I was the star in one of the filthiest dramas of all time. I was a seaman, and went to the Imperial Café on Scollay Square in Boston to drink; I drank sixty glasses of beer and retired to the toilet, where I wrapped myself around the toilet bowl and went to sleep. During the night at least a hundred seamen and assorted civilians came in and cast their sentient debouchments on me till I was unrecognizably caked. What difference does it make after all?—anonymity in the world of men is better than fame in heaven, for what's heaven? what's earth? All in the mind.

Gibberishly Dean and I stumbled out of this horror-hole at dawn and went to find our travel-bureau car. After spending a good part of the morning in Negro bars and chasing gals and listening to jazz records on jukeboxes, we struggled five miles in local buses with all our crazy gear and got to the home of a man who was going to charge us four dollars apiece for the ride to New York. He was a middle-aged blond fellow with glasses, with a wife and kid and a good home. We waited in the yard while he got ready. His lovely wife in cotton kitchen dress offered us coffee but we were too busy talking. By this time Dean was so exhausted and out of his mind that everything he saw delighted him. He was reaching another pious frenzy. He sweated and sweated. The moment we were in the new Chrysler and off to New York the poor man realized he had contracted a ride with two maniacs, but he made the best of it and in fact got used to us just as we passed Briggs Stadium and talked about next year's Detroit Tigers.

In the misty night we crossed Toledo and went onward across old Ohio. I realized I was beginning to cross and recross towns in America as though I were a traveling salesman—raggedy travelings, bad stock, rotten beans in the bottom of my bag of tricks, nobody buying. The man got tired near Pennsylvania and Dean took the wheel and drove clear the rest of the way to New York, and we began to hear the Symphony Sid show on the radio with all the latest bop, and now we were entering the great and final city of America. We got there in early morning. Times Square was being torn up, for New York never rests. We looked for Hassel automatically as we passed.

In an hour Dean and I were out at my aunt's new flat in Long Island, and she herself was busily engaged with painters who were friends of the family, and arguing with them about the price as we stumbled up the stairs from San Francisco. "Sal," said my aunt, "Dean can stay here a few days and after that he has to get out, do you understand me?" The trip was over. Dean and I took a walk that night among the gas tanks and railroad bridges and fog lamps of Long Island. I remember him standing under a streetlamp.

"Just as we passed that other lamp I was going to tell you a further thing, Sal, but now I am parenthetically continuing with a new thought and by the time we reach the next I'll return to the original subject, agreed?" I certainly agreed. We were so used to traveling we had to walk all over Long Island, but there was no more land, just the Atlantic Ocean, and we could only go so far. We clasped hands and agreed to be friends forever.

Not five nights later we went to a party in New York and I saw a girl called Inez and told her I had a friend with me that she ought to meet sometime. I was drunk and told her he was a cowboy. "Oh, I've always wanted to meet a cowboy."

"Dean?" I yelled across the party—which included Angel Luz García the poet; Walter Evans; Victor Villanueva, the Venezuelan poet; Jinny Jones, a former love of mine; Carlo Marx; Gene Dexter; and innumerable others—"Come over here, man." Dean came bashfully over. An hour later, in the drunkenness and chichiness of the party ("It's in honor of the end of the summer, of course"), he was kneeling on the floor with his chin on her belly and telling her and promising her everything and sweating. She was a big, sexy brunette—as García said, "Something straight out of Degas," and generally like a beautiful Parisian coquette. In a matter of days they were dickering with Camille [Carolyn Cassady] in San Francisco by longdistance telephone for the necessary divorce papers so they could get married. Not only that, but a few months later Camille gave birth to Dean's second baby, the result of a few nights' rapport early in the year. And another matter of months and Inez had a baby. With one illegitimate child in the West somewhere, Dean then had four little ones and not a cent, and was all troubles and ecstasy and speed as ever. So we didn't go to Italy.

[PART FOUR]

Immediately outside Gregoria the road began to drop, great trees arose on each side, and in the trees as it grew dark we heard the great roar of billions of insects that sounded like one continuous high-screeching cry. "Whoo!" said Dean, and he turned on his headlights and they weren't working. "What! what! damn now what?" And he punched and fumed at his dashboard. "Oh, my, we'll have to drive through the jungle without lights, think of the horror of that, the only time I'll see is when another car comes by and there just *aren't* any cars! And of course no lights? Oh, what'll we do, dammit?"

"Let's just drive. Maybe we ought to go back, though?"

"No, never-never! Let's go on. I can barely see the road. We'll make it." And now we shot in inky darkness through the scream of insects, and the great, rank, almost rotten smell descended, and we remembered and realized that the map indicated just after Gregoria the beginning of the Tropic of Cancer. "We're in a new tropic! No wonder the smell! Smell it!" I stuck my head out the window; bugs smashed at my face; a great screech rose the moment I cocked my ear to the wind. Suddenly our lights were working again and they poked ahead, illuminating the lonely road that ran between solid walls of drooping, snaky trees as high as a hundred feet.

"Son-of-a-*bitch!*" yelled Stan in the back. "Hot *damn!*" He was still so high. We suddenly realized he was still high and the jungle and troubles made no difference to his happy soul. We began laughing, all of us.

"To hell with it! We'll just throw ourselves on the gawddamn jungle, we'll sleep in it tonight, let's go!" yelled Dean. "Ole Stan is right. Ole Stan don't care! He's so high on those women and that tea and that crazy out-of-this-world impossible-to-absorb mambo blasting so loud that my eardrums still beat to it—whee! he's so high he knows what he's doing!" We took off our T-shirts and roared through the jungle, bare-chested. No towns, nothing, lost jungle, miles and miles, and down-going, getting hotter, the insects screaming louder, the vegetation growing higher, the smell ranker and hotter until we began to get used to it and like it. "I'd just like to get naked and roll and roll in that jungle," said Dean. "No, hell, man, that's what I'm going to do soon's I find a good spot." And suddenly Limón appeared before us, a jungle town, a few brown lights, dark shadows, enormous skies overhead, and a cluster of men in front of a jumble of woodshacks—a tropical crossroads.

We stopped in the unimaginable softness. It was as hot as the inside of a baker's oven on a June night in New Orleans. All up and down the street whole families were sitting around in the dark, chatting; occasional girls came by, but extremely young and only curious to see what we looked like. They were barefoot and dirty. We leaned on the wooden porch of a broken-down general store with sacks of flour and fresh pine-apple rotting with flies on the counter. There was one oil lamp in here, and outside a few more brown lights, and the rest all black, black, black. Now of course we were so tired we had to sleep at once and moved the car a few yards down a dirt road to the backside of town. It was so incredibly hot it was impossible to sleep. So Dean took a blanket and laid it out on the soft, hot sand in the road and flopped out. Stan was stretched on the front seat of the Ford with both doors open for a draft, but there wasn't even the faintest puff of a wind. I, in the back seat, suffered in a pool of sweat. I got out of the car and stood swaying in the blackness. The whole town had instantly gone to bed; the only noise now was barking dogs. How could I ever sleep? Thousands of mosquitoes had already bitten all of us on chest and arms and ankles. Then a bright idea came to me: I jumped up on the steel roof of the car and stretched out flat on my back. Still there was no breeze, but the steel had an element of coolness in it and dried my back of sweat, clotting up thousands of dead bugs into cakes on my skin, and I realized the jungle takes you over and you become it. Lying on the top of the car with my face to the black sky was like lying in a closed trunk on a summer night. For the first time in my life the weather was not something that touched me, that caressed me, froze or sweated me, but became me. The atmosphere and I became the same. Soft infinitesimal showers of microscopic bugs fanned down on my face as I slept, and they were extremely pleasant and soothing. The sky was starless, utterly unseen and heavy. I could lie there all night long with my face exposed to the heavens, and it would do me no more harm than a velvet drape drawn over me. The dead bugs mingled with my blood; the live mosquitoes exchanged further portions; I began to tingle all over and to smell of the rank, hot, and rotten jungle, all over from hair and face to feet and toes. Of course I was barefoot. To minimize the sweat I put on my bug-smeared T-shirt and lay back again. A huddle of darkness on the blacker road showed where Dean was sleeping. I could hear him snoring. Stan was snoring too.

Occasionally a dim light flashed in town, and this was the sheriff making his rounds with a weak flashlight and mumbling to himself in the jungle night. Then I saw his light jiggling toward us and heard his footfalls coming soft on the mats of sand and vegetation. He stopped and flashed the car. I sat up and looked at him. In a quivering, almost querulous, and extremely tender voice he said, "*Dormiendo?*" indicating Dean in the road. I knew this meant "sleep."

"*Si, dormiendo.*"

"*Bueno, bueno,*" he said to himself and with reluctance and sadness turned away and went back to his lonely rounds. Such lovely policemen God hath never wrought in America. No suspicions, no fuss, no bother: he was the guardian of the sleeping town, period.

I went back to my bed of steel and stretched out with my arms spread. I didn't even know if branches or open sky were directly above me, and it made no difference. I opened my mouth to it and drew deep breaths of jungle atmosphere. It was not air, never air, but the palpable and living emanation of trees and swamp. I stayed awake. Roosters began to crow the dawn across the brakes somewhere. Still no air, no breeze, no dew, but the same Tropic of Cancer heaviness held us all pinned to earth, where we belonged and tingled. There was no sign of dawn in the skies. Suddenly I heard the dogs barking furiously across the dark, and then I heard the faint clip-clop of a horse's hooves. It came closer and closer. What kind of mad rider in the night would this be? Then I saw an apparition: a wild horse, white as a ghost, came trotting down the road directly toward Dean. Behind him the dogs yammered and contended. I couldn't see them, they were dirty old jungle dogs, but the horse was white as snow and immense and almost phosphorescent and easy to see. I felt no panic for Dean. The horse saw him and trotted right by his head, passed the car like a ship, whinnied softly, and continued on through town, bedeviled by the dogs, and clip-clopped back to the jungle on the other side, and all I heard was the faint hoofbeat fading away in the woods. The dogs subsided and sat to lick themselves. What was this horse? What myth and ghost, what spirit? I told Dean about it when he woke up. He thought I'd been dreaming. Then he recalled faintly dreaming of a white horse, and I told him it had been no dream. Stan Shephard slowly woke up. The faintest movements, and we were sweating profusely again. It was still pitch dark. "Let's start the car and blow some air!" I cried. "I'm dying of heat."

"Right!" We roared out of town and continued along the mad highway with our hair flying. Dawn came rapidly in a gray haze, revealing dense swamps sunk on both sides, with tall, forlorn, viny trees leaning and bowing over tangled bottoms. We bowled right along the railroad tracks for a while. The strange radio-station antenna of Ciudad Mante appeared ahead, as if we were in Nebraska. We found a gas station and loaded the tank just as the last of the jungle-night bugs hurled themselves in a black mass against the bulbs and fell fluttering at our feet in huge wriggly groups, some of them with wings a good four inches long, others frightful dragonflies big enough to eat a bird, and thousands of immense yangling mosquitoes and unnamable spidery insects of all sorts. I hopped up and down on the pavement for fear of them; I finally ended up in the car with my feet in my hands, looking fearfully at the ground where they swarmed around our wheels. "Lessgo!" I yelled. Dean and Stan weren't perturbed at all by the bugs; they calmly drank a couple of bottles of Mission Orange and kicked them away from the water cooler. Their shirts and pants, like mine, were soaked in the blood and black of thousands of dead bugs. We smelled our clothes deeply.

"You know, I'm beginning to like this smell," said Stan. "I can't smell myself any more."

"It's a strange, good smell," said Dean. "I'm not going to change my shirt till Mexico City, I want to take it all in and remember it." So off we roared again, creating air for our hot caked faces.

Then the mountains loomed ahead, all green. After this climb we would be on the great central plateau again and ready to roll ahead to Mexico City. In no time at all we soared to an elevation of five thousand feet among misty passes that overlooked steaming yellow rivers a mile below. It was the great River Moctezuma. The Indians along the road began to be extremely weird. They were a nation in themselves, mountain Indians, shut off from everything else but the Pan-American Highway. They were short and squat and dark, with bad teeth; they carried immense loads on their backs. Across enormous vegetated ravines we saw patchworks of agriculture on steep slopes. They walked up and down those slopes and worked the crops. Dean drove the car five miles an hour to see. "Whooee, this I never thought existed!" High on the highest peak, as great as any Rocky Mountain peak, we saw bananas growing. Dean got out of the car to point, to stand around rubbing his belly. We were on a ledge where a little thatched hut suspended itself over the precipice of the world. The sun created golden hazes that obscured the Moctezuma, now more than a mile below.

In the yard in front of the hut a little three-year-old Indian girl stood with her finger in her mouth, watching us with big brown eyes. "She's probably never seen anybody parked here before in her entire life!" breathed Dean. "Hel-lo, little girl. How are you? Do you like us?" The little girl looked away bashfully and pouted. We began to talk and she again examined us with finger in mouth. "Gee, I wish there was something I could give her! *Think of it,* being born and living on this ledge—this ledge representing all you know of life. Her father is probably groping down the ravine with a rope and getting his pineapples out of a cave and hacking wood at an eighty-degree angle with all the bottom below. She'll never, never leave here and know anything about the outside world. It's a nation. Think of the wild chief they must have! They probably, off the road, over that bluff, miles back, must be even wilder and stranger, yeah, because the Pan-American Highway partially civilizes this nation on this road. Notice the beads of sweat on her brow," Dean pointed out with a grimace of pain. "It's not the kind of sweat we have, it's oily and it's *always there* because it's *always* hot the year round and she knows nothing of non-sweat, she was born with sweat and dies with sweat." The sweat on her little brow was heavy, sluggish; it didn't run; it just stood there and gleamed like a fine olive oil. "What that must do to their souls! How different they must be in their private concerns and evaluations and wishes!" Dean drove on with his mouth hanging in awe, ten miles an hour, desirous to see every possible human being on the road. We climbed and climbed.

As we climbed, the air grew cooler and the Indian girls on the road wore shawls over their heads and shoulders. They hailed us desperately; we stopped to see. They wanted to sell us little pieces of rock crystal. Their great brown, innocent eyes looked into ours with such soulful intensity that not one of us had the slightest sexual thought about them; moreover they were very young, some of them eleven and looking almost thirty. "Look at those eyes!" breathed Dean. They were like the eyes of the Virgin Mother when she was a child. We saw in them the tender and forgiving gaze of Jesus. And they stared unflinching into ours. We rubbed our nervous blue eyes and looked again. Still they penetrated us with sorrowful and hypnotic gleam. When they talked they suddenly became frantic and almost silly. In their silence they were themselves. "They've only *recently* learned to sell these crystals, since the highway was built about ten years back—up until that time this entire nation must have been *silent!*"

The girls yammered around the car. One particularly soulful child gripped at Dean's sweaty arm. She yammered in Indian. "Ah yes, ah yes, dear one," said Dean tenderly and almost sadly. He got out of the car and went fishing around in the battered trunk in the back—the same old tortured American trunk—and pulled out a wristwatch. He showed it to the child. She whimpered with glee. The others crowded around with amazement. Then Dean poked in the little girl's hand for "the sweetest and purest and smallest crystal she has personally picked from the mountain for me." He found one no bigger than a berry. And he handed her the wristwatch dangling. Their mouths rounded like the mouths of chorister children. The lucky little girl squeezed it to her ragged breastrobes. They stroked Dean and thanked him. He stood among them with his ragged face to the sky, looking for the next and highest and final pass, and seemed like the Prophet that had come to them. He got back in the car. They hated to see us go. For the longest time, as we mounted a straight pass, they waved and ran after us. We made a turn and never saw them again, and they were still running after us. "Ah, this breaks my heart!" cried Dean, punching his chest. "How far do they carry out these loyalties and wonders! What's going to happen to them? Would they try to follow the car all the way to Mexico City if we drove slow enough?"

"Yes," I said, for I knew.

We came into the dizzying heights of the Sierra Madre Oriental. The banana trees gleamed golden in the haze. Great fogs yawned beyond stone walls along the precipice. Below, the Moctezuma was a thin golden thread in a green jungle mat. Strange crossroad towns on top of the world rolled by, with shawled Indians watching us from under hatbrims and *rebozos*. Life was dense, dark, ancient. They watched Dean, serious and insane at his raving wheel, with eyes of hawks. All had their hands outstretched. They had come down from the back mountains and higher places to hold forth their hands for something they thought civilization could offer, and they never dreamed the sadness and the poor broken delusion of it. They didn't know that a bomb had come that could crack all our bridges and roads and reduce them to jumbles, and we would be as poor as they someday, and stretching out our hands in the same, same way. Our broken Ford, old thirties upgoing America Ford, rattled through them and vanished in dust.

We had reached the approaches of the last plateau. Now the sun was golden, the air keen blue, and the desert with its occasional rivers a riot of sandy, hot space and sudden Biblical tree shade. Now Dean was sleeping and Stan driving. The shepherds appeared, dressed as in first times, in long flowing robes, the women carrying golden bundles of flax, the men staves. Under great trees on the shimmering desert the shepherds sat and convened, and the sheep moiled in the sun and raised dust beyond. "Man, man," I yelled to Dean, "wake up and see the shepherds, wake up and see the golden world that Jesus came from, with your own eyes you can tell!"

He shot his head up from the seat, saw one glimpse of it all in the fading red sun, and dropped back to sleep. When he woke up he described it to me in detail and said, "Yes, man, I'm glad you told me to look. Oh, Lord, what shall I do? Where will I go?" He rubbed his belly, he looked to heaven with red eyes, he almost wept.

The end of our journey impended. Great fields stretched on both sides of us; a noble wind blew across the occasional immense tree groves and over old missions turning salmon pink in the late sun. The clouds were close and huge and rose. "Mexico City by dusk!" We'd made it, a total of nineteen hundred miles from the afternoon yards of Denver to these vast and Biblical areas of the world, and now we were about to reach the end of the road.

"Shall we change our insect T-shirts?"

"Naw, let's wear them into town, hell's bells." And we drove into Mexico City.

A brief mountain pass took us suddenly to a height from which we saw all of Mexico City stretched out in its volcanic crater below and spewing city smokes and early dusklights. Down to it we zoomed, down Insurgentes Boulevard, straight toward the heart of town at Reforma. Kids played soccer in enormous sad fields and threw up dust. Taxi-drivers overtook us and wanted to know if we wanted girls. No, we didn't want girls now. Long, ragged adobe slums stretched out on the plain; we saw lonely figures in the dimming alleys. Soon night would come. Then the city roared in and suddenly we were passing crowded cafés and theaters and many lights. Newsboys yelled at us. Mechanics slouched by, barefoot, with wrenches and rags. Mad barefoot Indian drivers cut across us and surrounded us and tooted and made frantic traffic. The noise was incredible. No mufflers are used on Mexican cars. Horns are batted with glee continual. "Whee!" yelled Dean. "Look out!" He staggered the car through the traffic and played with everybody. He drove like an Indian. He got on a circular glorietta drive on Reforma Boulevard and rolled around it with its eight spokes shooting cars at us from all directions, left, right, *izquierda,* dead ahead, and yelled and jumped with joy. "This is traffic I've always dreamed of! Everybody *goes!*" An ambulance came balling through. American ambulances dart and weave through traffic with siren blowing; the great world-wide Fellahin Indian ambulances merely come through at eighty miles an hour in the city streets, and everybody just has to get out of the way and they don't pause for anybody or any circumstances and fly straight through. We saw it reeling out of sight on skittering wheels in the breaking-up moil of dense downtown traffic. The drivers were Indians. People, even old ladies, ran for buses that never stopped. Young Mexico City businessmen made bets and ran by squads for buses and athletically jumped them. The bus-drivers were barefoot, sneering and insane, and sat low and squat in T-shirts at the low, enormous wheels. Ikons burned over them. The lights in the buses were brown and greenish, and dark faces were lined on wooden benches.

In downtown Mexico City thousands of hipsters in floppy straw hats and long-lapeled jackets over bare chests padded along the main drag, some of them selling crucifixes and weed in the alleys, some of them kneeling in beat chapels next to

Mexican burlesque shows in sheds. Some alleys were rubble, with open sewers, and little doors led to closet-size bars stuck in adobe walls. You had to jump over a ditch to get your drink, and in the bottom of the ditch was the ancient lake of the Aztec. You came out of the bar with your back to the wall and edged back to the street. They served coffee mixed with rum and nutmeg. Mambo blared from everywhere. Hundreds of whores lined themselves along the dark and narrow streets and their sorrowful eyes gleamed at us in the night. We wandered in a frenzy and a dream. We ate beautiful steaks for forty-eight cents in a strange tiled Mexican cafeteria with generations of marimba musicians standing at one immense marimba—also wandering singing guitarists, and old men on corners blowing trumpets. You went by the sour stink of pulque saloons; they gave you a water glass of cactus juice in there, two cents. Nothing stopped; the streets were alive all night. Beggars slept wrapped in advertising posters torn off fences. Whole families of them sat on the sidewalk, playing little flutes and chuckling in the night. Their bare feet stuck out, their dim candles burned, all Mexico was one vast Bohemian camp. On corners old women cut up the boiled heads of cows and wrapped morsels in tortillas and served them with hot sauce on newspaper napkins. This was the great and final wild uninhibited Fellahin-childlike city that we knew we would find at the end of the road. Dean walked through with his arms hanging zombie-like at his sides, his mouth open, his eyes gleaming, and conducted a ragged and holy tour that lasted till dawn in a field with a boy in a straw hat who laughed and chatted with us and wanted to play catch, for nothing ever ended.

Then I got fever and became delirious and unconscious. Dysentery. I looked up out of the dark swirl of my mind and I knew I was on a bed eight thousand feet above sea level, on a roof of the world, and I knew that I had lived a whole life and many others in the poor atomistic husk of my flesh, and I had all the dreams. And I saw Dean bending over the kitchen table. It was several nights later and he was leaving Mexico City already. "What you doin, man?" I moaned.

"Poor Sal, poor Sal, got sick. Stan'll take care of you. Now listen to hear if you can in your sickness: I got my divorce from Camille down here and I'm driving back to Inez in New York tonight if the car holds out."

"All that again?" I cried.

"All that again, good buddy. Gotta get back to my life. Wish I could stay with you. Pray I can come back." I grabbed the cramps in my belly and groaned. When I looked up again bold noble Dean was standing with his old broken trunk and looking down at me. I didn't know who he was any more, and he knew this, and sympathized, and pulled the blanket over my shoulders. "Yes, yes, yes, I've got to go now. Old fever Sal, good-by." And he was gone. Twelve hours later in my sorrowful fever I finally came to understand that he was gone. By that time he was driving back alone through those banana mountains, this time at night.

When I got better I realized what a rat he was, but then I had to understand the impossible complexity of his life, how he had to leave me there, sick, to get on with his wives and woes. "Okay, old Dean, I'll say nothing."

from THE SUBTERRANEANS

So there we were at the Red Drum, a tableful of beers a few that is and all the gangs cutting in and out, paying a dollar quarter at the door, the little hip-pretending weasel there taking tickets, Paddy Cordavan floating in as prophesied (a big tall blond brakeman type subterranean from Eastern Washington cowboy-looking in jeans coming in to a wild generation party all smoky and mad and I yelled "Paddy Cordavan?" and "Yeah?" and he'd come over)—all sitting together, interesting groups at various tables, Julien [Lucien Carr], Roxanne (a woman of 25 prophesying the future style of America with short almost crewcut but with curls black snaky hair, snaky walk, pale pale junky anemic face and we say junky when once Dostoevski would have said what? if not ascetic or saintly? but not in the least? but the cold pale booster face of the cold blue girl and wearing a man's white shirt but with the cuffs undone untied at the buttons so I remember her leaning over talking to someone after having slinked across the floor with flowing propelled shoulders, bending to talk with her hand

holding a short butt and the neat little flick she was giving it
to knock ashes but repeatedly with long long fingernails an
inch long and also orient and snake-like)—groups of all kinds,
and Ross Wallenstein, the crowd, and up on the stand Bird
Parker with solemn eyes who'd been busted fairly recently and
had now returned to a kind of bop dead Frisco but had just
discovered or been told about the Red Drum, the great new
generation gang wailing and gathering there, so here he was
on the stand, examining them with his eyes as he blew his
now-settled-down-into-regulated-design "crazy" notes—the
booming drums, the high ceiling—Adam for my sake dutifully
cutting out at about 11 o'clock so he could go to bed and get
to work in the morning, after a brief cutout with Paddy and
myself for a quick ten-cent beer at roaring Pantera's, where
Paddy and I in our first talk and laughter together pulled
wrists—now Mardou cut out with me, glee eyed, between sets,
for quick beers, but at her insistence at the Mask instead where
they were fifteen cents, but she had a few pennies herself and
we went there and began earnestly talking and getting high-
tingled on the beer and now it was the beginning—returning
to the Red Drum for sets, to hear Bird [Charlie Parker], whom
I saw distinctly digging Mardou several times also myself directly into my eye looking to search if really I was that great
writer I thought myself to be as if he knew my thoughts and
ambitions or remembered me from other night clubs and other
coasts, other Chicagos—not a challenging look but the king
and founder of the bop generation at least the sound of it in
digging his audience digging his eyes, the secret eyes him-
watching, as he just pursed his lips and let great lungs and
immortal fingers work, his eyes separate and interested and
humane, the kindest jazz musician there could be while being
and therefore naturally the greatest—watching Mardou and
me in the infancy of our love and probably wondering why,
or knowing it wouldn't last, or seeing who it was would be
hurt, as now, obviously, but not quite yet, it was Mardou whose
eyes were shining in my direction, though I could not have
known and now do not definitely know—except the one fact,
on the way home, the session over the beer in the Mask drunk
we went home on the Third Street bus sadly through night
and throb knock neons and when I suddenly leaned over her

to shout something further (in her secret self as later confessed)
her heart leapt to smell the "sweetness of my breath" (quote)
and suddenly she almost loved me—I not knowing this, as we
found the Russian dark sad door of Heavenly Lane a great
iron gate rasping on the sidewalk to the pull, the insides of
smelling garbage cans sad-leaning together, fish heads, cats,
and then the Lane itself, my first view of it (the long history
and hugeness of it in my soul, as in 1951 cutting along with
my sketchbook on a wild October evening when I was discovering my own writing soul at last I saw the subterranean
Victor who'd come to Big Sur once on a motorcycle, was
reputed to have gone to Alaska on same, with little subterranean chick Dorie Kiehl, there he was in striding Jesus coat
heading north to Heavenly Lane to his pad and I followed him
awhile, wondering about Heavenly Lane and all the long talks
I'd been having for years with people like Mac Jones [John
Clellon Holmes] about the mystery, the silence of the subterraneans, "urban Thoreaus" Mac called them, as from Alfred
Kazin in New York New School lectures back East commenting on all the students being interested in Whitman from
a sexual revolution standpoint and in Thoreau from a contemplative mystic and antimaterialistic as if existentialist or whatever standpoint, the *Pierre*-of-Melville goof and wonder of it,
the dark little beat burlap dresses, the stories you'd heard
about great tenormen shooting junk by broken windows and
starting at their horns, or great young poets with beats lying
high in Rouault-like saintly obscurities, Heavenly Lane the
famous Heavenly Lane where they'd all at one time or another
the beat subterraneans lived, like Alfred and his little sickly
wife something straight out of Dostoevski's Petersburg slums
you'd think but really the American lost bearded idealistic—
the whole thing in any case), seeing it for the first time, but
with Mardou, the wash hung over the court, actually the back
courtyard of a big 20-family tenement with bay windows, the
wash hung out and in the afternoon the great symphony of
Italian mothers, children, fathers BeFinneganing and yelling
from stepladders, smells, cats mewing, Mexicans, the music
from all the radios whether bolero of Mexican or Italian tenor
of spaghetti eaters or loud suddenly turned-up KPFA sym-
phonies of Vivaldi harpsichord intellectuals performances

boom blam the tremendous sound of it which I then came to hear all the summer wrapt in the arms of my love—walking in there now, and going up the narrow musty stairs like in a hovel, and her door.

Plotting I demanded we dance—previously she'd been hungry so I'd suggested and we'd actually gone and bought egg foo young at Jackson and Kearny and now she heated this (later confession she'd hated it though it's one of my favorite dishes and typical of my later behavior I was already forcing down her throat that which she in subterranean sorrow wanted to endure alone if at all ever), ah.—Dancing, I had put the light out, so, in the dark, dancing, I kissed her—it was giddy, whirling to the dance, the beginning, the usual beginning of lovers kissing standing up in a dark room the room being the woman's the man all designs—ending up later in wild dances she on my lap or thigh as I danced her around bent back for balance and she around my neck her arms that came to warm so much the *me* that then was only hot—

And soon enough I'd learn she had no belief and had had no place to get it from—Negro mother dead for birth of her —unknown Cherokee-halfbreed father a hobo who'd come throwing torn shoes across gray plains of fall in black sombrero and pink scarf squatting by hotdog fires casting Tokay empties into the night "Yaa Calexico!"

Quick to plunge, bite, put the light out, hide my face in shame, make love to her tremendously because of lack of love for a year almost and the need pushing me down—our little agreements in the dark, the really should-not-be-tolds—for it was she who later said "Men are so crazy, they want the essence, the woman is the essence, there it is right in their hands but they rush off erecting big abstract constructions." —"You mean they should just stay home with the essence, that is lie under a tree all day with the woman but Mardou that's an old idea of mine, a lovely idea, I never heard it better expressed and never dreamed."—"Instead they rush off and have big wars and consider women as prizes instead of human beings, well man I may be in the middle of all this shit but I certainly don't want any part of it" (in her sweet cultured hip tones of new generation).—And so having had the essence of her love now I erect big word constructions and thereby betray it really—telling tales of every gossip sheet the washline of the world—and hers, ours, in all the two months of our love (I thought) only once-washed as she being a lonely subterranean spent mooningdays and would go to the laundry with them but suddenly it's dank late afternoon and too late and the sheets are gray, lovely to me—because soft.—But I cannot in this confession betray the innermosts, the thighs, what the thighs contain—and yet why write?—the thighs contain the essence—yet tho there I should stay and from there I came and'll eventually return, still I have to rush off and construct construct—for nothing—for Baudelaire poems—

from THE DHARMA BUMS

The little Saint Teresa bum was the first genuine Dharma Bum I'd met, and the second was the number one Dharma Bum of them all and in fact it was he, Japhy Ryder [Gary Snyder], who coined the phrase. Japhy Rydcr was a kid from eastern Oregon brought up in a log cabin deep in the woods with his father and mother and sister, from the beginning a woods boy, an axman, farmer, interested in animals and Indian lore so that when he finally got to college by hook or crook he was already well equipped for his early studies in anthropology and later in Indian myth and in the actual texts of Indian mythology. Finally he learned Chinese and Japanese and became an Oriental scholar and discovered the greatest Dharma Bums of them all, the Zen Lunatics of China and Japan. At the same time, being a Northwest boy with idealistic tendencies, he got interested in oldfashioned I.W.W. anarchism and learned to play the guitar and sing old worker songs to go with his Indian songs and general folksong interests. I first saw him walking down the street in San Francisco the following week (after hitchhiking the rest of the way from Santa Barbara in one long zipping ride given me, as though anybody'll believe this, by a beautiful darling young blonde in a snow-white strapless bathing suit and barefooted with a gold bracelet on her ankle, driving a next-year's cinnamonred Lincoln Mercury, who wanted benzedrine so she could drive all the way to the City and when I said I had some in my duffel bag yelled "Crazy!")—I saw Japhy loping along in that curious long stride of the mountain-climber, with a small knapsack on his back filled with books and toothbrushes and whatnot which was his small "goin-to-the-city" knapsack as apart from his big full rucksack complete with sleeping bag, poncho, and cook-pots. He wore a little goatee, strangely Oriental-looking with his somewhat slanted green eyes, but he didn't look like a Bohemian at all, and was far from being a Bohemian (a hanger-onner around the arts). He was wiry, suntanned, vigorous, open, all howdies and glad talk and even yelling hello to bums on the street and when asked a question answered right off the bat from the top or bottom of his mind I don't know which and always in a sprightly sparkling way.

"Where did you meet Ray Smith [Jack Kerouac]?" they asked him when we walked into The Place, the favorite bar of the hepcats around the Beach.

"Oh I always meet my Bodhisattvas in the street!" he yelled, and ordered beers.

It was a great night, a historic night in more ways than one. He and some other poets (he also wrote poetry and translated Chinese and Japanese poetry into English) were scheduled to give a poetry reading at the Six Gallery in town. They were all meeting in the bar and getting high. But as they stood and sat around I saw that he was the only one who didn't look like a poet, though poet he was indeed. The other poets were either hornrimmed intellectual hepcats with wild black hair like Alvah Goldbook [Allen Ginsberg], or delicate pale handsome poets like Ike O'Shay [Michael McClure] (in a suit), or out-of-this-world genteel-looking Renaissance Italians like Francis DaPavia [Philip Lamantia] (who looks like a young priest), or bow-tied wild-haired old anarchist fuds like Rheinhold Cacoethes [Kenneth Rexroth], or big fat bespectacled quiet booboos like Warren Coughlin [Philip Whalen]. And all the other hopeful poets were standing around, in various costumes, worn-at-the-sleeves corduroy jackets, scuffly shoes, books sticking out of their pockets. But Japhy was in rough workingman's clothes he'd bought secondhand in Goodwill stores to serve him on mountain climbs and hikes and for sitting in the open at night, for campfires, for hitchhiking up and down the Coast. In fact in his little knapsack he also had a funny green alpine cap that he wore when he got to the foot of a mountain, usually with a yodel, before starting to tromp up a few thousand feet. He wore mountainclimbing boots, expensive ones, his pride and joy, Italian make, in which he clomped around over the sawdust floor of the bar like an oldtime lumberjack. Japhy wasn't big, just about five foot seven, but strong and wiry and fast and muscular. His face was a mask of woeful bone, but his eyes twinkled like the eyes of old giggling sages of China, over that little goatee, to offset the rough look of his handsome face. His teeth were a little brown, from early backwoods neglect, but you never noticed that and he opened his mouth wide to guffaw at jokes. Sometimes he'd quiet down and just stare sadly at the floor, like a man whittling. He was merry at times. He showed great sympathetic interest in me and in the story about the little Saint Teresa bum and the stories I told him about my own experiences hopping freights or hitchhiking or hiking in woods. He claimed at once that I was a great "Bodhisattva," meaning "great wise being" or "great wise angel," and that I was ornamenting this world with my sincerity. We had the same favorite Buddhist saint, too: Avalokitesvara, or, in Japanese, Kwannon the Eleven-Headed. He knew all the details of Tibetan, Chinese, Mahayana, Hinayana, Japanese and even Burmese Buddhism but I warned him at once I didn't give a goddamn about the mythology and all the names and national flavors of Buddhism, but was just interested in the first of Sakyamuni's four noble truths, *All life is suffering.* And to an extent interested in the third, *The suppression of suffering can be achieved,* which I didn't quite believe was possible then. (I hadn't yet digested the Lankavatara Scripture which eventually shows you that there's nothing in the world but the mind itself, and therefore all's possible including the suppression of suffering.) Japhy's buddy was the aforementioned booboo big old good-hearted Warren Coughlin a hundred and eighty pounds of poet meat, who was advertised by Japhy (privately in my ear) as being more than meets the eye.

"Who is he?"

"He's my big best friend from up in Oregon, we've known

each other a long time. At first you think he's slow and stupid but actually he's a shining diamond. You'll see. Don't let him cut you to ribbons. He'll make the top of your head fly away, boy, with a choice chance word."

"Why?"

"He's a great mysterious Bodhisattva I think maybe a reincarnation of Asagna the great Mahayana scholar of the old centuries."

"And who am I?"

"I dunno, maybe you're Goat."

"Goat?"

"Maybe you're Mudface."

"Who's Mudface?"

"Mudface is the mud in your goatface. What would you say if someone was asked the question 'Does a dog have the Buddha nature?' and said 'Woof!' "

"I'd say that was a lot of silly Zen Buddhism." This took Japhy back a bit. "Lissen Japhy," I said, "I'm not a Zen Buddhist, I'm a serious Buddhist, I'm an old-fashioned dreamy Hinayana coward of later Mahayanism," and so forth into the night, my contention being that Zen Buddhism didn't concentrate on kindness so much as on confusing the intellect to make it perceive the illusion of all sources of things. "It's *mean,*" I complained. "All those Zen Masters throwing young kids in the mud because they can't answer their silly word questions."

"That's because they want them to realize mud is better than words, boy." But I can't recreate the exact (will try) brilliance of all Japhy's answers and come-backs and come-ons with which he had me on pins and needles all the time and did eventually stick something in my crystal head that made me change my plans in life.

Anyway I followed the whole gang of howling poets to the reading at the Six Gallery that night, which was, among other important things, the night of the birth of the San Francisco Poetry Renaissance. Everyone was there. It was a mad night. And I was the one who got things jumping by going around collecting dimes and quarters from the rather stiff audience standing around in the gallery and coming back with three huge gallon jugs of California Burgundy and getting them all piffed so that by eleven o'clock when Alvah Goldbook was reading his, wailing his poem "Wail" drunk with arms outspread everybody was yelling "Go! Go! Go!" (like a jam session) and old Rheinhold Cacoethes the father of the Frisco poetry scene was wiping his tears in gladness. Japhy himself read his fine poems about Coyote the God of the North American Plateau Indians (I think), at least the God of the Northwest Indians, Kwakiutl and what-all. "Fuck you! sang Coyote, and ran away!" read Japhy to the distinguished audience, making them all howl with joy, it was so pure, fuck being a dirty word that comes out clean. And he had his tender lyrical lines, like the ones about bears eating berries, showing his love of animals, and great mystery lines about oxen on the Mongolian road showing his knowledge of Oriental literature even on to Hsuan Tsung the great Chinese monk who walked from China to Tibet, Lanchow to Kashgar and Mongolia carrying a stick of incense in his hand. Then Japhy showed his sudden barroom humor with lines about Coyote bringing goodies. And his anarchistic ideas about how Americans don't know how to live, with lines about commuters being trapped in living rooms that come from poor trees felled by chainsaws (showing here, also, his background as a logger up north). His voice was deep and resonant and somehow brave, like the voice of oldtime American heroes and orators. Something earnest and strong and humanly hopeful I liked about him, while the other poets were either too dainty in their aestheticism, or too hysterically cynical to hope for anything, or too abstract and indoorsy, or too political, or like Coughlin too incomprehensible to understand (big Coughlin saying things about "unclarified processes" though where Coughlin did say that revelation was a personal thing I noticed the strong Buddhist and idealistic feeling of Japhy, which he'd shared with goodhearted Coughlin in their buddy days at college, as I had shared mine with Alvah in the Eastern scene and with others less apocalyptical and straighter but in no sense more sympathetic and tearful).

Meanwhile scores of people stood around in the darkened gallery straining to hear every word of the amazing poetry reading as I wandered from group to group, facing them and facing away from the stage, urging them to glug a slug from the jug, or wandered back and sat on the right side of the stage giving out little wows and yesses of approval and even whole sentences of comment with nobody's invitation but in the general gaiety nobody's disapproval either. It was a great night. Delicate Francis DaPavia read, from delicate onionskin yellow pages, or pink, which he kept flipping carefully with long white fingers, the poems of his dead chum Altman who'd eaten too much peyote in Chihuahua (or died of polio, one) but read none of his own poems—a charming elegy in itself to the memory of the dead young poet, enough to draw tears from the Cervantes of Chapter Seven, and read them in a delicate Englishy voice that had me crying with inside laughter though I later got to know Francis and liked him.

Among the people standing in the audience was Rosie Buchanan, a girl with a short haircut, red-haired, bony, handsome, a real gone chick and friend of everybody of any consequence on the Beach, who'd been a painter's model and a writer herself and was bubbling over with excitement at that time because she was in love with my old buddy Cody [Neal Cassady]. "Great, hey Rosie?" I yelled, and she took a big slug from my jug and shined eyes at me. Cody just stood behind her with both arms around her waist. Between poets, Rheinhold Cacoethes, in his bow tie and shabby old coat, would get up and make a little funny speech in his snide funny voice and introduce the next reader; but as I say come eleven-thirty when all the poems were read and everybody was milling around wondering what had happened and what would come next in American poetry, he was wiping his eyes with his handkerchief. And we all got together with him, the poets, and drove in several cars to Chinatown for a big fabulous dinner off the Chinese menu, with chopsticks, yelling conversation in the middle of the night in one of those freeswinging great Chinese restaurants of San Francisco. This happened to be Japhy's favorite Chinese restaurant, Nam Yuen, and he showed me how to order and how to eat with chopsticks and told anecdotes about the Zen Lunatics of the Orient and had me going so glad (and we had a bottle of wine on the table) that finally I went over to an old cook in the doorway of the kitchen and asked him "Why did Bodhidharma come from the West?" (Bodhidharma was the Indian who brought Buddhism eastward to China.)

"I don't care," said the old cook, with lidded eyes, and I

told Japhy and he said, "Perfect answer, absolutely perfect. Now you know what I mean by Zen."

I had a lot more to learn, too. Especially about how to handle girls—Japhy's incomparable Zen Lunatic way, which I got a chance to see firsthand the following week.

from MEXICO CITY BLUES

211TH CHORUS

The wheel of the quivering meat
                              conception
Turns in the void expelling human beings,
Pigs, turtles, frogs, insects, nits,
Mice, lice, lizards, rats, roan
Racinghorses, poxy bucolic pigtics,
Horrible unnameable lice of vultures,
Murderous attacking dog-armies
Of Africa, Rhinos roaming in the
                              jungle,

Vast boars and huge gigantic bull
Elephants, rams, eagles, condors,
Pones and Porcupines and Pills—
All the endless conception of living
                              beings
Gnashing everywhere in Consciousness
Throughout the ten directions of space
Occupying all the quarters in & out,
From supermicroscopic no-bug
To buge Galaxy Lightyear Bowell
Illuminating the sky of one Mind—
     Poor! I wish I was free
     of that slaving meat wheel
     and safe in heaven dead

239TH CHORUS

Charlie Parker looked like Buddha
Charlie Parker, who recently died

Laughing at a juggler on the TV
after weeks of strain and sickness,
was called the Perfect Musician.
And his expression on his face
Was as calm, beautiful, and profound
As the image of the Buddha
Represented in the East, the lidded eyes,
The expression that says "All Is Well"
—This was what Charlie Parker
Said when he played, All is Well.
You had the feeling of early-in-the-morning
Like a hermit's joy, or like
                    the perfect cry
Of some wild gang at a jam session
"Wail, Wop"—Charlie burst
His lungs to reach the speed
Of what the speedsters wanted
And what they wanted
Was his Eternal Slowdown.
A great musician and a great
                    creator of forms
That ultimately find expression
In mores and what have you.

240TH CHORUS

Musically as important as Beethoven,
Yet not regarded as such at all,
A genteel conductor of string
                    orchestras
In front of which he stood,
Proud and calm, like a leader
                    of music
In the Great Historic World Night,
And wailed his little saxophone,
The alto, with piercing clear
                    lament
In perfect tune & shining harmony,
Toot—as listeners reacted
Without showing it, and began talking

And soon the whole joint is rocking
And everybody talking and Charlie
                              Parker
Whistling them on to the brink of eternity
With his Irish St Patrick
                    patootle stick,
And like the holy piss we blop
And we plop in the waters of
                              slaughter
And white meat, and die
One after one, in time.

241ST CHORUS

And how sweet a story it is
When you hear Charlie Parker
                    tell it,
Either on records or at sessions,
Or at official bits in clubs,
Shots in the arm for the wallet,
Gleefully he Whistled the
                    perfect
                    horn

Anyhow, made no difference.

Charlie Parker, forgive me—
Forgive me for not answering your eyes—

For not having made an indication
Of that which you can devise—
Charlie Parker, pray for me—
Pray for me and everybody
In the Nirvanas of your brain
Where you hide, indulgent and huge,
No longer Charlie Parker
But the secret unsayable name
That carries with it merit
Not to be measured from here

To up, down, east, or west—
—Charlie Parker, lay the bane,
  off me, and every body

242ND CHORUS

The sound in your mind
  is the first sound
    that you could sing

If you were singing
  at a cash register
    with nothing on yr mind—

But when that grim reper
  comes to lay you
    look out my lady

He will steal all you got
  while you dingle with the dangle
  and having robbed you

Vanish.
  Which will be your best reward,
  T'were better to get rid o
  John O'Twill, then sit a-mortying
  In this Half Eternity with nobody
  To save the old man being hanged
  In my closet for nothing
  And everybody watches
  When the act is done—

Stop the murder and the suicide!
  All's well!
    I am the Guard

ESSENTIALS OF SPONTANEOUS PROSE

SET-UP   The object is set before the mind, either in reality, as in sketching (before a landscape or teacup or old face) or is set in the memory wherein it becomes the sketching from memory of a definite image-object.

PROCEDURE   Time being of the essence in the purity of speech, sketching language is undisturbed flow from the mind of personal secret idea-words, *blowing* (as per jazz musician) on subject of image.

METHOD   No periods separating sentence-structures already arbitrarily riddled by false colons and timid usually needless commas—but the vigorous space dash separating rhetorical breathing (as jazz musician drawing breath between outblown phrases)—"measured pauses which are the essentials of our speech"—"divisions of the *sounds* we hear"—"time and how to note it down." (William Carlos Williams)

SCOPING   Not "selectivity" of expression but following free deviation (association) of mind into limitless blow-on-subject seas of thought, swimming in sea of English with no discipline other than rhythms of rhetorical exhalation and expostulated statement, like a fist coming down on a table with each complete utterance, bang! (the space dash)—Blow as deep as you want—write as deeply, fish as far down as you want, satisfy yourself first, then reader cannot fail to receive telepathic shock and meaning-excitement by same laws operating in his own human mind.

LAG IN PROCEDURE   No pause to think of proper word but the infantile pileup of scatalogical buildup words till satisfaction is gained, which will turn out to be a great appending rhythm to a thought and be in accordance with Great Law of timing.

TIMING   Nothing is muddy that *runs in time* and to laws of *time*—Shakespearian stress of dramatic need to speak now in own unalterable way or forever hold tongue—*no revisions* (except obvious rational mistakes, such as names or *calculated* insertions in act of not writing but *inserting*).

CENTER OF INTEREST   Begin not from preconceived idea of what to say about image but from jewel center of interest in subject of image at *moment* of writing, and write outwards swimming in sea of language to peripheral release and exhaustion—Do not afterthink except for poetic or P. S. reasons. Never afterthink to "improve" or defray impressions, as, the best writing is always the most painful personal wrung-out tossed from cradle warm protective mind—tap from yourself the song of yourself, *blow!—now!—your* way is your only way—"good"—or "bad"—always honest, ("ludicrous"), spontaneous, "confessional" interesting, because not "crafted." Craft *is* craft.

STRUCTURE OF WORK   Modern bizarre structures (science fiction, etc.) arise from language being dead, "different" themes give illusion of "new" life. Follow roughly outlines in outfanning movement over subject, as river rock, so mindflow over jewel-center need (run your mind over it, *once*) arriving at pivot, where what was dim-formed "beginning" becomes sharp-necessitating "ending" and language shortens in race to wire of time-race of work, following laws of Deep Form, to conclusion, last words, last trickle—Night is The End.

MENTAL STATE   If possible write "without consciousness" in semitrance (as Yeats' later "trance writing") allowing subconscious to admit in own uninhibited interesting necessary and so "modern" language what conscious art would censor, and write excitedly, swiftly, with writing-or-typing-cramps, in accordance (as from center to periphery) with laws of orgasm, Reich's "beclouding of consciousness." *Come* from within, out—to relaxed and said.

BELIEF & TECHNIQUE
FOR MODERN PROSE

LIST OF ESSENTIALS

1. Scribbled secret notebooks, and wild typewritten pages, for yr own joy

2. Submissive to everything, open, listening
3. Try never get drunk outside yr own house
4. Be in love with yr life
5. Something that you feel will find its own form
6. Be crazy dumbsaint of the mind
7. Blow as deep as you want to blow
8. Write what you want bottomless from bottom of the mind
9. The unspeakable visions of the individual
10. No time for poetry but exactly what is
11. Visionary tics shivering in the chest
12. In tranced fixation dreaming upon object before you
13. Remove literary, grammatical and syntactical inhibition
14. Like Proust be an old teahead of time
15. Telling the true story of the world in interior monolog
16. The jewel center of interest is the eye within the eye
17. Write in recollection and amazement for yourself
18. Work from pithy middle eye out, swimming in language sea
19. Accept loss forever
20. Believe in the holy contour of life
21. Struggle to sketch the flow that already exists intact in mind
22. Dont think of words when you stop but to see picture better
23. Keep track of every day the date emblazoned in yr morning
24. No fear or shame in the dignity of yr experience, language & knowledge
25. Write for the world to read and see yr exact pictures of it
26. Bookmovie is the movie in words, the visual American form
27. In praise of Character in the Bleak inhuman Loneliness
28. Composing wild, undisciplined, pure, coming in from under, crazier the better
29. You're a Genius all the time
30. Writer-Director of Earthly movies Sponsored & Angeled in Heaven

Allen Ginsberg

Allen Ginsberg was born on June 3, 1926, in Newark, New Jersey, the son of the poet and high school teacher Louis Ginsberg. His mother Naomi Ginsberg was a member of the Communist party during the years of the Depression and suffered a series of nervous breakdowns. When Allen began to study at Columbia College in 1943 on a scholarship from the Paterson YMCA, he thought he wanted to become a labor lawyer. In his early years at Columbia he was editor of the Jester, *the literary humor magazine, and won the Woodbury Poetry Prize in 1947. He was also suspended twice from Columbia, once for writing "Butler has no balls" (a reference to Columbia University President Nicholas Murray Butler) on the dirty windows of his dormitory room and for letting Kerouac sleep in his room overnight, and another time for getting involved as an accessory in a robbery after he let Herbert Huncke store stolen goods in his apartment.*

Ginsberg's biographer, Barry Miles, understood that the great appeal of breaking the rules for Ginsberg was the "acceptance and approval of madness" in an unconventional life-style. Bohemianism gave him a framework within which to accept his mother's mental illness and his confused feelings about his homosexuality. In 1948, after a vision of the poet William Blake, Ginsberg formally dedicated himself to becoming a poet, but he was not able to express himself freely until he left New York and moved to San Francisco in 1954. There he met the older anarchist poet Kenneth Rexroth, who encouraged him to drop formal poetic forms and meters and write to please himself.

Following Rexroth's advice, Ginsberg decided he would ex-periment with a technique more like Kerouac's spontaneous prose. As Ginsberg recalled the moment, "I thought I wouldn't write a poem but just write what I wanted to without fear, let my imagination go, open secrecy, and scribble magic lines from my real mind—sum up my life—something I wouldn't be able to show anybody, writ for my own soul's ear and a few other golden ears." He used a triadic verse form he admired in the poetry of William Carlos Williams, extending the line out to the length of his own long breath, thinking of himself—as Kerouac was doing in the poems he was writing in Mexico City Blues —as a jazz musician.

Academic critics like James Breslin and Michael Davidson have pointed out that Ginsberg's preparation for the compo-sition of "Howl" extended over a number of years in notebooks and rough drafts. With the completion of the poem, he entered an inspired period, creating lyrics like "A Supermarket in Cal-ifornia," "Sunflower Sutra," and "America" in the fall and winter of 1955 through 1956, when he shared a cottage in Berke-ley with his lover, Peter Orlovsky. "Song" and "On Burroughs' Work" are earlier lyrics from 1954.

In 1958, after living in Paris, Ginsberg returned to New York City, where he found an apartment at 170 East Second Street on the Lower East Side. There he wrote a long formal elegy, "Kaddish," personalizing the traditional Jewish memorial poem for the dead in memory of his mother, who had died in the Pilgrim State Hospital on Long Island in June 1956.

Naomi Ginsberg had been one of the "best minds of my time destroyed by madness" Ginsberg had evoked in the opening line of "Howl." Writing fifty-eight pages in an inspired forty-hour stretch at his desk while taking, by his own account, heroin, liquid Methedrine and Dexedrine, Ginsberg completed "Kad-dish" in November 1958. A poem in six sections (Proem, Nar-rative, Hymmnn, Lament, Litany, and Fugue) it was the culmination of his early work, a deeply compassionate portrait of his mother's mental illness and its devastating effect on Gins-berg and his family.

HOWL

For Carl Solomon

I

I saw the best minds of my generation destroyed by madness, starving
     hysterical naked,
dragging themselves through the negro streets at dawn looking for
     an angry fix,
angelheaded hipsters burning for the ancient heavenly connection to
     the starry dynamo in the machinery of night,
who poverty and tatters and hollow-eyed and high sat up smoking in
     the supernatural darkness of cold-water flats floating across
     the tops of cities contemplating jazz,
who bared their brains to Heaven under the El and saw Mohammedan
     angels staggering on tenement roofs illuminated,
who passed through universities with radiant cool eyes hallucinating
     Arkansas and Blake-light tragedy among the scholars of war,
who were expelled from the academies for crazy & publishing obscene
     odes on the windows of the skull,
who cowered in unshaven rooms in underwear, burning their money
     in wastebaskets and listening to the Terror through the wall,
who got busted in their pubic beards returning through Laredo with
     a belt of marijuana for New York,
who ate fire in paint hotels or drank turpentine in Paradise Alley,
     death, or purgatoried their torsos night after night
with dreams, with drugs, with waking nightmares, alcohol and cock
     and endless balls,
incomparable blind streets of shuddering cloud and lightning in the
     mind leaping toward poles of Canada & Paterson, illumi-
     nating all the motionless world of Time between,
Peyote solidities of halls, backyard green tree cemetery dawns, wine
     drunkenness over the rooftops, storefront boroughs of tea-
     head joyride neon blinking traffic light, sun and moon and
     tree vibrations in the roaring winter dusks of Brooklyn,
     ashcan rantings and kind king light of mind,
who chained themselves to subways for the endless ride from Battery
     to holy Bronx on benzedrine until the noise of wheels and
     children brought them down shuddering mouth-wracked and

battered bleak of brain all drained of brilliance in the drear
light of Zoo,

who sank all night in submarine light of Bickford's floated out and
sat through the stale beer afternoon in desolate Fugazzi's,
listening to the crack of doom on the hydrogen jukebox,

who talked continuously seventy hours from park to pad to bar to
Bellevue to museum to the Brooklyn Bridge,

a lost battalion of platonic conversationalists jumping down the stoops
off fire escapes off windowsills off Empire State out of the
moon,

yacketayakking screaming vomiting whispering facts and memories
and anecdotes and eyeball kicks and shocks of hospitals and
jails and wars,

whole intellects disgorged in total recall for seven days and nights
with brilliant eyes, meat for the Synagogue cast on the
pavement,

who vanished into nowhere Zen New Jersey leaving a trail of ambiguous picture postcards of Atlantic City Hall,

suffering Eastern sweats and Tangerian bone-grindings and migraines
of China under junk-withdrawal in Newark's bleak furnished
room,

who wandered around and around at midnight in the railroad yard
wondering where to go, and went, leaving no broken hearts,

who lit cigarettes in boxcars boxcars boxcars racketing through snow
toward lonesome farms in grandfather night,

who studied Plotinus Poe St. John of the Cross telepathy and bop
kabbalah because the cosmos instinctively vibrated at their
feet in Kansas,

who loned it through the streets of Idaho seeking visionary indian
angels who were visionary indian angels,

who thought they were only mad when Baltimore gleamed in supernatural ecstasy,

who jumped in limousines with the Chinaman of Oklahoma on the
impulse of winter midnight streetlight smalltown rain,

who lounged hungry and lonesome through Houston seeking jazz or
sex or soup, and followed the brilliant Spaniard to converse
about America and Eternity, a hopeless task, and so took
ship to Africa,

who disappeared into the volcanoes of Mexico leaving behind nothing

but the shadow of dungarees and the lava and ash of poetry
   scattered in fireplace Chicago,

who reappeared on the West Coast investigating the FBI in beards
   and shorts with big pacifist eyes sexy in their dark skin passing out incomprehensible leaflets,

who burned cigarette holes in their arms protesting the narcotic tobacco haze of Capitalism,

who distributed Supercommunist pamphlets in Union Square weeping
   and undressing while the sirens of Los Alamos wailed them
   down, and wailed down Wall, and the Staten Island ferry
   also wailed,

who broke down crying in white gymnasiums naked and trembling
   before the machinery of other skeletons,

who bit detectives in the neck and shrieked with delight in policecars
   for committing no crime but their own wild cooking ped-
   erasty and intoxication,

who howled on their knees in the subway and were dragged off the
   roof waving genitals and manuscripts,

who let themselves be fucked in the ass by saintly motorcyclists, and
   screamed with joy,

who blew and were blown by those human seraphim, the sailors,
   caresses of Atlantic and Caribbean love,

who balled in the morning in the evenings in rosegardens and the
   grass of public parks and cemeteries scattering their semen
   freely to whomever come who may,

who hiccuped endlessly trying to giggle but wound up with a sob
   behind a partition in a Turkish Bath when the blond & naked
   angel came to pierce them with a sword,

who lost their loveboys to the three old shrews of fate the one eyed
   shrew of the heterosexual dollar the one eyed shrew that
   winks out of the womb and the one eyed shrew that does
   nothing but sit on her ass and snip the intellectual golden
   threads of the craftsman's loom,

who copulated ecstatic and insatiate with a bottle of beer a sweetheart
   a package of cigarettes a candle and fell off the bed, and
   continued along the floor and down the hall and ended faint-
   ing on the wall with a vision of ultimate cunt and come
   eluding the last gyzym of consciousness,

who sweetened the snatches of a million girls trembling in the sunset,
   and were red eyed in the morning but prepared to sweeten

the snatch of the sunrise, flashing buttocks under barns and naked in the lake,

who went out whoring through Colorado in myriad stolen night-cars, N.C., secret hero of these poems, cocksman and Adonis of Denver—joy to the memory of his innumerable lays of girls in empty lots & diner backyards, moviehouses' rickety rows, on mountaintops in caves or with gaunt waitresses in familiar roadside lonely petticoat upliftings & especially secret gas-station solipsisms of johns, & hometown alleys too,

who faded out in vast sordid movies, were shifted in dreams, woke on a sudden Manhattan, and picked themselves up out of basements hungover with heartless Tokay and horrors of Third Avenue iron dreams & stumbled to unemployment offices,

who walked all night with their shoes full of blood on the snowbank docks waiting for a door in the East River to open to a room full of steamheat and opium,

who created great suicidal dramas on the apartment cliff-banks of the Hudson under the wartime blue floodlight of the moon & their heads shall be crowned with laurel in oblivion,

who ate the lamb stew of the imagination or digested the crab at the muddy bottom of the rivers of Bowery,

who wept at the romance of the streets with their pushcarts full of onions and bad music,

who sat in boxes breathing in the darkness under the bridge, and rose up to build harpsichords in their lofts,

who coughed on the sixth floor of Harlem crowned with flame under the tubercular sky surrounded by orange crates of theology,

who scribbled all night rocking and rolling over lofty incantations which in the yellow morning were stanzas of gibberish,

who cooked rotten animals lung heart feet tail borsht & tortillas dreaming of the pure vegetable kingdom,

who plunged themselves under meat trucks looking for an egg,

who threw their watches off the roof to cast their ballot for Eternity outside of Time, & alarm clocks fell on their heads every day for the next decade,

who cut their wrists three times successively unsuccessfully, gave up and were forced to open antique stores where they thought they were growing old and cried,

who were burned alive in their innocent flannel suits on Madison

Avenue amid blasts of leaden verse & the tanked-up clatter of the iron regiments of fashion & the nitroglycerine shrieks of the fairies of advertising & the mustard gas of sinister intelligent editors, or were run down by the drunken taxicabs of Absolute Reality,

who jumped off the Brooklyn Bridge this actually happened and walked away unknown and forgotten into the ghostly daze of Chinatown soup alleyways & firetrucks, not even one free beer,

who sang out of their windows in despair, fell out of the subway window, jumped in the filthy Passaic, leaped on negroes, cried all over the street, danced on broken wineglasses barefoot smashed phonograph records of nostalgic European 1930s German jazz finished the whiskey and threw up groaning into the bloody toilet, moans in their ears and the blast of colossal steamwhistles,

who barreled down the highways of the past journeying to each other's hotrod-Golgotha jail-solitude watch or Birmingham jazz incarnation,

who drove crosscountry seventytwo hours to find out if I had a vision or you had a vision or he had a vision to find out Eternity,

who journeyed to Denver, who died in Denver, who came back to Denver & waited in vain, who watched over Denver & brooded & loned in Denver and finally went away to find out the Time, & now Denver is lonesome for her heroes,

who fell on their knees in hopeless cathedrals praying for each other's salvation and light and breasts, until the soul illuminated its hair for a second,

who crashed through their minds in jail waiting for impossible criminals with golden heads and the charm of reality in their hearts who sang sweet blues to Alcatraz,

who retired to Mexico to cultivate a habit, or Rocky Mount to tender Buddha or Tangiers to boys or Southern Pacific to the black locomotive or Harvard to Narcissus to Woodlawn to the daisychain or grave,

who demanded sanity trials accusing the radio of hypnotism & were left with their insanity & their hands & a hung jury,

who threw potato salad at CCNY lecturers on Dadaism and subsequently presented themselves on the granite steps of the madhouse with shaven heads and harlequin speech of suicide, demanding instantaneous lobotomy,

and who were given instead the concrete void of insulin Metrazol
electricity hydrotherapy psychotherapy occupational therapy pingpong & amnesia,

who in humorless protest overturned only one symbolic pingpong
table, resting briefly in catatonia,

returning years later truly bald except for a wig of blood, and tears
and fingers, to the visible madman doom of the wards of
the madtowns of the East,

Pilgrim State's Rockland's and Greystone's foetid halls, bickering
with the echoes of the soul, rocking and rolling in the midnight solitude-bench dolmen-realms of love, dream of life a
nightmare, bodies turned to stone as heavy as the moon,

with mother finally ******, and the last fantastic book flung out of
the tenement window, and the last door closed at 4 A.M.
and the last telephone slammed at the wall in reply and the
last furnished room emptied down to the last piece of mental
furniture, a yellow paper rose twisted on a wire hanger in
the closet, and even that imaginary, nothing but a hopeful
little bit of hallucination—

ah, Carl, while you are not safe I am not safe, and now you're really
in the total animal soup of time—

and who therefore ran through the icy streets obsessed with a sudden
flash of the alchemy of the use of the ellipsis catalog a vari-
able measure & the vibrating plane,

who dreamt and made incarnate gaps in Time & Space through images
juxtaposed, and trapped the archangel of the soul between
2 visual images and joined the elemental verbs and set the
noun and dash of consciousness together jumping with sensation of Pater Omnipotens Aeterna Deus

to recreate the syntax and measure of poor human prose and stand
before you speechless and intelligent and shaking with
shame, rejected yet confessing out the soul to conform to
the rhythm of thought in his naked and endless head,

the madman bum and angel beat in Time, unknown, yet putting down
here what might be left to say in time come after death,

and rose reincarnate in the ghostly clothes of jazz in the goldhorn
shadow of the band and blew the suffering of America's
naked mind for love into an eli eli lamma lamma sabacthani
saxophone cry that shivered the cities down to the last radio

with the absolute heart of the poem of life butchered out of their
own bodies good to eat a thousand years.

II

What sphinx of cement and aluminum bashed open their skulls and ate up their brains and imagination?

Moloch! Solitude! Filth! Ugliness! Ashcans and unobtainable dollars! Children screaming under the stairways! Boys sobbing in armies! Old men weeping in the parks!

Moloch! Moloch! Nightmare of Moloch! Moloch the loveless! Mental Moloch! Moloch the heavy judger of men!

Moloch the incomprehensible prison! Moloch the crossbone soulless jailhouse and Congress of sorrows! Moloch whose buildings are judgment! Moloch the vast stone of war! Moloch the stunned governments!

Moloch whose mind is pure machinery! Moloch whose blood is running money! Moloch whose fingers are ten armies! Moloch whose breast is a cannibal dynamo! Moloch whose ear is a smoking tomb!

Moloch whose eyes are a thousand blind windows! Moloch whose skyscrapers stand in the long streets like endless Jehovahs! Moloch whose factories dream and croak in the fog! Moloch whose smokestacks and antennae crown the cities!

Moloch whose love is endless oil and stone! Moloch whose soul is electricity and banks! Moloch whose poverty is the specter of genius! Moloch whose fate is a cloud of sexless hydrogen! Moloch whose name is the Mind!

Moloch in whom I sit lonely! Moloch in whom I dream Angels! Crazy in Moloch! Cocksucker in Moloch! Lacklove and manless in Moloch!

Moloch who entered my soul early! Moloch in whom I am a consciousness without a body! Moloch who frightened me out of my natural ecstasy! Moloch whom I abandon! Wake up in Moloch! Light streaming out of the sky!

Moloch! Moloch! Robot apartments! invisible suburbs! skeleton treasuries! blind capitals! demonic industries! spectral nations! invincible madhouses! granite cocks! monstrous bombs!

They broke their backs lifting Moloch to Heaven! Pavements, trees, radios, tons! lifting the city to Heaven which exists and is everywhere about us!

Visions! omens! hallucinations! miracles! ecstasies! gone down the American river!

Dreams! adorations! illuminations! religions! the whole boatload of
sensitive bullshit!

Breakthroughs! over the river! flips and crucifixions! gone down the
flood! Highs! Epiphanies! Despairs! Ten years' animal
screams and suicides! Minds! New loves! Mad generation!
down on the rocks of Time!

Real holy laughter in the river! They saw it all! the wild eyes! the
holy yells! They bade farewell! They jumped off the roof!
to solitude! waving! carrying flowers! Down to the river!
into the street!

III

Carl Solomon! I'm with you in Rockland
  where you're madder than I am
I'm with you in Rockland
  where you must feel very strange
I'm with you in Rockland
  where you imitate the shade of my mother
I'm with you in Rockland
  where you've murdered your twelve secretaries
I'm with you in Rockland
  where you laugh at this invisible humor
I'm with you in Rockland
  where we are great writers on the same dreadful typewriter
I'm with you in Rockland
  where your condition has become serious and is reported
  on the radio
I'm with you in Rockland
  where the faculties of the skull no longer admit the worms
  of the senses
I'm with you in Rockland
  where you drink the tea of the breasts of the spinsters of
  Utica
I'm with you in Rockland
  where you pun on the bodies of your nurses the harpies of
  the Bronx
I'm with you in Rockland
  where you scream in a straightjacket that you're losing the
  game of the actual pingpong of the abyss

I'm with you in Rockland

> where you bang on the catatonic piano the soul is innocent and immortal it should never die ungodly in an armed madhouse

I'm with you in Rockland

> where fifty more shocks will never return your soul to its body again from its pilgrimage to a cross in the void

I'm with you in Rockland

> where you accuse your doctors of insanity and plot the Hebrew socialist revolution against the fascist national Golgotha

I'm with you in Rockland

> where you will split the heavens of Long Island and resurrect your living human Jesus from the superhuman tomb

I'm with you in Rockland

> where there are twentyfive thousand mad comrades all together singing the final stanzas of the Internationale

I'm with you in Rockland

> where we hug and kiss the United States under our bedsheets the United States that coughs all night and won't let us sleep

I'm with you in Rockland

> where we wake up electrified out of the coma by our own souls' airplanes roaring over the roof they've come to drop angelic bombs the hospital illuminates itself   imaginary walls collapse   O skinny legions run outside   O starry-spangled shock of mercy the eternal war is here   O victory forget your underwear we're free

I'm with you in Rockland

> in my dreams you walk dripping from a sea-journey on the highway across America in tears to the door of my cottage in the Western night

San Francisco, 1955–1956

FOOTNOTE TO HOWL

Holy! Holy! Holy! Holy! Holy! Holy! Holy! Holy! Holy! Holy! Holy! Holy! Holy! Holy! Holy!

The world is holy! The soul is holy! The skin is holy! The nose is holy! The tongue and cock and hand and asshole holy!

Everything is holy! everybody's holy! everywhere is holy! everyday
is in eternity! Everyman's an angel!

The bum's as holy as the seraphim! the madman is holy as you my
soul are holy!

The typewriter is holy the poem is holy the voice is holy the hearers
are holy the ecstasy is holy!

Holy Peter holy Allen holy Solomon holy Lucien holy Kerouac holy
Huncke holy Burroughs holy Cassady holy the unknown
buggered and suffering beggars holy the hideous human
angels!

Holy my mother in the insane asylum! Holy the cocks of the grandfathers of Kansas!

Holy the groaning saxophone! Holy the bop apocalypse! Holy the
jazzbands marijuana hipsters peace peyote pipes & drums!

Holy the solitudes of skyscrapers and pavements! Holy the cafeterias
filled with the millions! Holy the mysterious rivers of tears
under the streets!

Holy the lone juggernaut! Holy the vast lamb of the middleclass!
Holy the crazy shepherds of rebellion! Who digs Los Angeles
IS Los Angeles!

Holy New York Holy San Francisco Holy Peoria & Seattle Holy Paris
Holy Tangiers Holy Moscow Holy Istanbul!

Holy time in eternity holy eternity in time holy the clocks in space
holy the fourth dimension holy the fifth International holy
the Angel in Moloch!

Holy the sea holy the desert holy the railroad holy the locomotive
holy the visions holy the hallucinations holy the miracles
holy the eyeball holy the abyss!

Holy forgiveness! mercy! charity! faith! Holy! Ours! bodies! suffering!
magnanimity!

Holy the supernatural extra brilliant intelligent kindness of the soul!

Berkeley, 1955

A SUPERMARKET IN
CALIFORNIA

What thoughts I have of you tonight, Walt Whitman, for I
walked down the sidestreets under the trees with a headache self-
conscious looking at the full moon.

In my hungry fatigue, and shopping for images, I went into the neon fruit supermarket, dreaming of your enumerations!

What peaches and what penumbras! Whole families shopping at night! Aisles full of husbands! Wives in the avocados, babies in the tomatoes!—and you, García Lorca, what were you doing down by the watermelons?

I saw you, Walt Whitman, childless, lonely old grubber, poking among the meats in the refrigerator and eyeing the grocery boys.

I heard you asking questions of each: Who killed the pork chops? What price bananas? Are you my Angel?

I wandered in and out of the brilliant stacks of cans following you, and followed in my imagination by the store detective.

We strode down the open corridors together in our solitary fancy tasting artichokes, possessing every frozen delicacy, and never passing the cashier.

Where are we going, Walt Whitman? The doors close in an hour. Which way does your beard point tonight?

(I touch your book and dream of our odyssey in the supermarket and feel absurd.)

Will we walk all night through solitary streets? The trees add shade to shade, lights out in the houses, we'll both be lonely.

Will we stroll dreaming of the lost America of love past blue automobiles in driveways, home to our silent cottage?

Ah, dear father, graybeard, lonely old courage-teacher, what America did you have when Charon quit poling his ferry and you got out on a smoking bank and stood watching the boat disappear on the black waters of Lethe?

Berkeley, 1955

SUNFLOWER SUTRA

I walked on the banks of the tincan banana dock and sat down under
     the huge shade of a Southern Pacific locomotive to look at
     the sunset over the box house hills and cry.
Jack Kerouac sat beside me on a busted rusty iron pole, companion,
     we thought the same thoughts of the soul, bleak and blue

and sad-eyed, surrounded by the gnarled steel roots of trees
of machinery.

The oily water on the river mirrored the red sky, sun sank on top of
final Frisco peaks, no fish in that stream, no hermit in those
mounts, just ourselves rheumy-eyed and hung-over like old
bums on the riverbank, tired and wily.

Look at the Sunflower, he said, there was a dead gray shadow against
the sky, big as a man, sitting dry on top of a pile of ancient
sawdust—

—I rushed up enchanted—it was my first sunflower, memories of
Blake—my visions—Harlem

and Hells of the Eastern rivers, bridges clanking Joes Greasy Sandwiches, dead baby carriages, black treadless tires forgotten
and unretreaded, the poem of the riverbank, condoms &
pots, steel knives, nothing stainless, only the dank muck and
the razor-sharp artifacts passing into the past—

and the gray Sunflower poised against the sunset, crackly bleak and
dusty with the smut and smog and smoke of olden locomotives in its eye—

corolla of bleary spikes pushed down and broken like a battered
crown, seeds fallen out of its face, soon-to-be-toothless
mouth of sunny air, sunrays obliterated on its hairy head
like a dried wire spiderweb,

leaves stuck out like arms out of the stem, gestures from the sawdust
root, broke pieces of plaster fallen out of the black twigs,
a dead fly in its ear,

Unholy battered old thing you were, my sunflower O my soul, I loved
you then!

The grime was no man's grime but death and human locomotives,

all that dress of dust, that veil of darkened railroad skin, that smog
of cheek, that eyelid of black mis'ry, that sooty hand or
phallus or protuberance of artificial worse-than-dirt—industrial—modern—all that civilization spotting your crazy
golden crown—

and those blear thoughts of death and dusty loveless eyes and ends
and withered roots below, in the home-pile of sand and
sawdust, rubber dollar bills, skin of machinery, the guts and
innards of the weeping coughing car, the empty lonely tin-
cans with their rusty tongues alack, what more could I name,
the smoked ashes of some cock cigar, the cunts of wheel-

barrows and the milky breasts of cars, wornout asses out of chairs & sphincters of dynamos—all these

entangled in your mummied roots—and you there standing before me in the sunset, all your glory in your form!

A perfect beauty of a sunflower! a perfect excellent lovely sunflower existence! a sweet natural eye to the new hip moon, woke up alive and excited grasping in the sunset shadow sunrise golden monthly breeze!

How many flies buzzed round you innocent of your grime, while you cursed the heavens of the railroad and your flower soul?

Poor dead flower? when did you forget you were a flower? when did you look at your skin and decide you were an impotent dirty old locomotive? the ghost of a locomotive? the specter and shade of a once powerful mad American locomotive?

You were never no locomotive, Sunflower, you were a sunflower!

And you Locomotive, you are a locomotive, forget me not!

So I grabbed up the skeleton thick sunflower and stuck it at my side like a scepter,

and deliver my sermon to my soul, and Jack's soul too, and anyone who'll listen,

—We're not our skin of grime, we're not our dread bleak dusty imageless locomotive, we're all golden sunflowers inside, blessed by our own seed & hairy naked accomplishment-bodies growing into mad black formal sunflowers in the sunset, spied on by our eyes under the shadow of the mad locomotive riverbank sunset Frisco hilly tincan evening sit-down vision.

Berkeley, 1955

AMERICA

America I've given you all and now I'm nothing.

America two dollars and twentyseven cents January 17, 1956.

I can't stand my own mind.

America when will we end the human war?

Go fuck yourself with your atom bomb.

I don't feel good don't bother me.

I won't write my poem till I'm in my right mind.

America when will you be angelic?

When will you take off your clothes?

When will you look at yourself through the grave?

When will you be worthy of your million Trotskyites?

America why are your libraries full of tears?

America when will you send your eggs to India?

I'm sick of your insane demands.

When can I go into the supermarket and buy what I need with my good looks?

America after all it is you and I who are perfect not the next world.

Your machinery is too much for me.

You made me want to be a saint.

There must be some other way to settle this argument.

Burroughs is in Tangiers I don't think he'll come back it's sinister.

Are you being sinister or is this some form of practical joke?

I'm trying to come to the point.

I refuse to give up my obsession.

America stop pushing I know what I'm doing.

America the plum blossoms are falling.

I haven't read the newspapers for months, everyday somebody goes on trial for murder.

America I feel sentimental about the Wobblies.

America I used to be a communist when I was a kid I'm not sorry.

I smoke marijuana every chance I get.

I sit in my house for days on end and stare at the roses in the closet.

When I go to Chinatown I get drunk and never get laid.

My mind is made up there's going to be trouble.

You should have seen me reading Marx.

My psychoanalyst thinks I'm perfectly right.

I won't say the Lord's Prayer.

I have mystical visions and cosmic vibrations.

America I still haven't told you what you did to Uncle Max after he came over from Russia.

I'm addressing you.

Are you going to let your emotional life be run by Time Magazine?

I'm obsessed by Time Magazine.

I read it every week.

Its cover stares at me every time I slink past the corner candystore.

I read it in the basement of the Berkeley Public Library.

It's always telling me about responsibility. Businessmen are serious.
Movie producers are serious. Everybody's serious but me.

It occurs to me that I am America.
I am talking to myself again.

Asia is rising against me.
I haven't got a chinaman's chance.
I'd better consider my national resources.
My national resources consist of two joints of marijuana millions of genitals
     an unpublishable private literature that jetplanes 1400 miles an hour
     and twentyfive-thousand mental institutions.
I say nothing about my prisons nor the millions of underprivileged who live
     in my flowerpots under the light of five hundred suns.
I have abolished the whorehouses of France, Tangiers is the next to go.
My ambition is to be President despite the fact that I'm a Catholic.

America how can I write a holy litany in your silly mood?
I will continue like Henry Ford my strophes are as individual as his automo-
     biles more so they're all different sexes.
America I will sell you strophes $2500 apiece $500 down on your old strophe
America free Tom Mooney
America save the Spanish Loyalists
America Sacco & Vanzetti must not die
America I am the Scottsboro boys.
America when I was seven momma took me to Communist Cell meetings
     they sold us garbanzos a handful per ticket a ticket costs a nickel and
     the speeches were free everybody was angelic and sentimental about
     the workers it was all so sincere you have no idea what a good thing
     the party was in 1835 Scott Nearing was a grand old man a real
     mensch Mother Bloor the Silk-strikers' Ewig-Weibliche made me cry
     I once saw the Yiddish orator Israel Amter plain. Everybody must
     have been a spy.
America you don't really want to go to war.
America it's them bad Russians.
Them Russians them Russians and them Chinamen. And them Russians.
The Russia wants to eat us alive. The Russia's power mad. She wants to take
     our cars from out our garages.
Her wants to grab Chicago. Her needs a Red *Reader's Digest.* Her wants our
     auto plants in Siberia. Him big bureaucracy running our fillingsta-
     tions.
That no good. Ugh. Him make Indians learn read. Him need big black
     niggers. Hah. Her make us all work sixteen hours a day. Help.
America this is quite serious.

America this is the impression I get from looking in the television set.
America is this correct?
I'd better get right down to the job.
It's true I don't want to join the Army or turn lathes in precision parts
    factories, I'm nearsighted and psychopathic anyway.
America I'm putting my queer shoulder to the wheel.

Berkeley, January 17, 1956

KADDISH

For Naomi Ginsberg, 1894–1956

I

Strange now to think of you, gone without corsets & eyes, while I
    walk on the sunny pavement of Greenwich Village.
downtown Manhattan, clear winter noon, and I've been up all night,
    talking, talking, reading the Kaddish aloud, listening to Ray
    Charles blues shout blind on the phonograph
the rhythm the rhythm—and your memory in my head three years
    after—And read Adonais' last triumphant stanzas aloud—
    wept, realizing how we suffer—
And how Death is that remedy all singers dream of, sing, remember,
    prophesy as in the Hebrew Anthem, or the Buddhist Book
    of Answers—and my own imagination of a withered leaf—
    at dawn—
Dreaming back thru life, Your time—and mine accelerating toward
    Apocalypse,
the final moment—the flower burning in the Day—and what comes
    after,
looking back on the mind itself that saw an American city
a flash away, and the great dream of Me or China, or you and a
    phantom Russia, or a crumpled bed that never existed—
like a poem in the dark—escaped back to Oblivion—
No more to say, and nothing to weep for but the Beings in the Dream,
    trapped in its disappearance,
sighing, screaming with it, buying and selling pieces of phantom,
    worshipping each other,
worshipping the God included in it all—longing or inevitability?—
    while it lasts, a Vision—anything more?
It leaps about me, as I go out and walk the street, look back over

my shoulder, Seventh Avenue, the battlements of window
office buildings shouldering each other high, under a cloud,
tall as the sky an instant—and the sky above—an old blue
place.

or down the Avenue to the south, to—as I walk toward the Lower
East Side—where you walked 50 years ago, little girl—from
Russia, eating the first poisonous tomatoes of America—
frightened on the dock—

then struggling in the crowds of Orchard Street toward what?—toward Newark—

toward candy store, first home-made sodas of the century, hand-
churned ice cream in backroom on musty brownfloor
boards—

Toward education marriage nervous breakdown, operation, teaching
school, and learning to be mad, in a dream—what is this
life?

Toward the Key in the window—and the great Key lays its head of
light on top of Manhattan, and over the floor, and lays down
on the sidewalk—in a single vast beam, moving, as I walk
down First toward the Yiddish Theater—and the place of
poverty

you knew, and I know, but without caring now—Strange to have
moved thru Paterson, and the West, and Europe and here
again,

with the cries of Spaniards now in the doorstoops doors and dark
boys on the street, fire escapes old as you

—Tho you're not old now, that's left here with me—

Myself, anyhow, maybe as old as the universe—and I guess that dies
with us—enough to cancel all that comes—What came is
gone forever every time—

That's good! That leaves it open for no regret—no fear radiators,
lacklove, torture even toothache in the end—

Though while it comes it is a lion that eats the soul—and the lamb,
the soul, in us, alas, offering itself in sacrifice to change's
fierce hunger—hair and teeth—and the roar of bonepain,
skull bare, break rib, rot-skin, braintricked Implacability.

Ai! ai! we do worse! We are in a fix! And you're out, Death let you
out, Death had the Mercy, you're done with your century,
done with God, done with the path thru it—Done with
yourself at last—Pure—Back to the Babe dark before your
Father, before us all—before the world—

There, rest. No more suffering for you. I know where you've gone,
it's good.

No more flowers in the summer fields of New York, no joy now, no
more fear of Louis,

and no more of his sweetness and glasses, his high school decades,
debts, loves, frightened telephone calls, conception beds,
relatives, hands—

No more of sister Elanor,—she gone before you—we kept it secret
—you killed her—or she killed herself to bear with you—
an arthritic heart—But Death's killed you both—No
matter—

Nor your memory of your mother, 1915 tears in silent movies weeks
and weeks—forgetting, agrieve watching Marie Dressler address humanity, Chaplin dance in youth,

or Boris Godunov, Chaliapin's at the Met, halling his voice of a
weeping Czar—by standing room with Elanor & Max—
watching also the Capitalists take seats in Orchestra, white
furs, diamonds,

with the YPSL's hitch-hiking thru Pennsylvania, in black baggy gym
skirts pants, photograph of 4 girls holding each other round
the waste, and laughing eye, too coy, virginal solitude of
1920

all girls grown old, or dead, now, and that long hair in the grave—
lucky to have husbands later—

You made it—I came too—Eugene my brother before (still grieving
now and will gream on to his last stiff hand, as he goes thru
his cancer—or kill—later perhaps—soon he will think—)

And it's the last moment I remember, which I see them all, thru
myself, now—tho not you

I didn't foresee what you felt—what more hideous gape of bad mouth
came first—to you—and were you prepared?

To go where? In that Dark—that—in that God? a radiance? A Lord
in the Void? Like an eye in the black cloud in a dream?
Adonoi at last, with you?

Beyond my remembrance! Incapable to guess! Not merely the yellow
skull in the grave, or a box of worm dust, and a stained
ribbon—Deaths-head with Halo? can you believe it?

Is it only the sun that shines once for the mind, only the flash of
existence, than none ever was?

Nothing beyond what we have—what you had—that so pitiful—yet
Triumph,

to have been here, and changed, like a tree, broken, or flower—fed
to the ground—but mad, with its petals, colored, thinking
Great Universe, shaken, cut in the head, leaf stript, hid in
an egg crate hospital, cloth wrapped, sore—freaked in the
moon brain, Naughtless.

No flower like that flower, which knew itself in the garden, and fought
the knife—lost

Cut down by an idiot Snowman's icy—even in the Spring—strange
ghost thought—some Death—Sharp icicle in his hand—
crowned with old roses—a dog for his eyes—cock of a
sweatshop—heart of electric irons.

All the accumulations of life, that wear us out—clocks, bodies, consciousness, shoes, breasts—begotten sons—your Communism—'Paranoia' into hospitals.

You once kicked Elanor in the leg, she died of heart failure later.
You of stroke. Asleep? within a year, the two of you, sisters
in death. Is Elanor happy?

Max grieves alive in an office on Lower Broadway, lone large mustache over midnight Accountings, not sure. His life passes
—as he sees—and what does he doubt now? Still dream of
making money, or that might have made money, hired
nurse, had children, found even your Immortality, Naomi?

I'll see him soon. Now I've got to cut through—to talk to you—as I
didn't when you had a mouth.

Forever. And we're bound for that, Forever—like Emily Dickinson's
horses—headed to the End.

They know the way—These Steeds—run faster than we think—it's
our own life they cross—and take with them.

Magnificent, mourned no more, marred of heart, mind behind, married dreamed, mortal changed—Ass and face done with
murder.

In the world, given, flower maddened, made no Utopia,
shut under pine, almed in Earth, balmed in Lone, Jehovah, accept.

Nameless, One Faced, Forever beyond me, beginningless,
endless, Father in death. Tho I am not there for this Prophecy, I am
unmarried, I'm hymnless, I'm Heavenless, headless in blisshood I
would still adore

Thee, Heaven, after Death, only One blessed in Nothingness, not light or darkness, Dayless Eternity—

Take this, this Psalm, from me, burst from my hand in a day, some of my Time, now given to Nothing—to praise Thee—But Death

This is the end, the redemption from Wilderness, way for the Wonderer, House sought for All, black handkerchief washed clean by weeping—page beyond Psalm—Last change of mine and Naomi—to God's perfect Darkness—Death, stay thy phantoms!

II

Over and over—refrain—of the Hospitals—still haven't written your history—leave it abstract—a few images

run thru the mind—like the saxophone chorus of houses and years—remembrance of electrical shocks.

By long nites as a child in Paterson apartment, watching over your nervousness—you were fat—your next move—

By that afternoon I stayed home from school to take care of you—once and for all—when I vowed forever that once man disagreed with my opinion of the cosmos, I was lost—

By my later burden—vow to illuminate mankind—this is release of particulars—(mad as you)—(sanity a trick of agreement)—

But you stared out the window on the Broadway Church corner, and spied a mystical assassin from Newark,

So phoned the Doctor—'OK go way for a rest'—so I put on my coat and walked you downstreet—On the way a grammar-school boy screamed, unaccountably—'Where you goin Lady to Death'? I shuddered—

and you covered your nose with motheaten fur collar, gas mask against poison sneaked into downtown atmosphere, sprayed by Grandma—

And was the driver of the cheesebox Public Service bus a member of the gang? You shuddered at his face, I could hardly get you on—to New York, very Times Square, to grab another Greyhound—

where we hung around 2 hours fighting invisible bugs and jewish sickness—breeze poisoned by Roosevelt—

out to get you—and me tagging along, hoping it would end in a quiet room in a Victorian house by a lake.

Ride 3 hours thru tunnels past all American industry, Bayonne preparing for World War II, tanks, gas fields, soda factories, diners, locomotive roundhouse fortress—into piney woods New Jersey Indians—calm towns—long roads thru sandy tree fields—

Bridges by deerless creeks, old wampum loading the streambed—down there a tomahawk or Pocahontas bone—and a million old ladies voting for Roosevelt in brown small houses, roads off the Madness highway—

perhaps a hawk in a tree, or a hermit looking for an owl-filled branch—

All the time arguing—afraid of strangers in the forward double seat, snoring regardless—what busride they snore on now?

'Allen, you don't understand—it's—ever since those 3 big sticks up my back—they did something to me in Hospital, they poisoned me, they want to see me dead—3 big sticks, 3 big sticks—

'The Bitch! Old Grandma! Last week I saw her, dressed in pants like an old man, with a sack on her back, climbing up the brick side of the apartment

'On the fire escape, with poison germs, to throw on me—at night—maybe Louis is helping her—he's under her power—

'I'm your mother, take me to Lakewood' (near where Graf Zeppelin had crashed before, all Hitler in Explosion) 'where I can hide.'

We got there—Dr. Whatzis rest home—she hid behind a closet—demanded a blood transfusion.

We were kicked out—tramping with Valise to unknown shady lawn houses—dusk, pine trees after dark—long dead street filled with crickets and poison ivy—

I shut her up by now—big house REST HOME ROOMS —gave the landlady her money for the week—carried up the iron valise—sat on bed waiting to escape—

Neat room in attic with friendly bedcover—lace curtains—spinning wheel rug—Stained wallpaper old as Naomi. We were home.

I left on the next bus to New York—laid my head back in the last seat, depressed—the worst yet to come?—abandoning her, rode in torpor—I was only 12.

Would she hide in her room and come out cheerful for breakfast? Or lock her door and stare thru the window for sidestreet spies? Listen at keyholes for Hitlerian invisible gas? Dream in a chair—or mock me, by—in front of a mirror, alone?

12 riding the bus at nite thru New Jersey, have left Naomi to Parcae in Lakewood's haunted house—left to my own fate bus—

sunk in a seat—all violins broken—my heart sore in my ribs—mind was empty—Would she were safe in her coffin—

Or back at Normal School in Newark, studying up on America in a black skirt—winter on the street without lunch—a penny a pickle—home at night to take care of Elanor in the bedroom—

First nervous breakdown was 1919—she stayed home from school and lay in a dark room for three weeks—something bad—never said what—every noise hurt—dreams of the creaks of Wall Street—

Before the gray Depression—went upstate New York—recovered—Lou took photo of her sitting crossleg on the grass—her long hair wound with flowers—smiling—playing lullabies on mandolin—poison ivy smoke in left-wing summer camps and me in infancy saw trees—

or back teaching school, laughing with idiots, the backward classes—her Russian specialty—morons with dreamy lips, great eyes, thin feet & sicky fingers, swaybacked, rachitic—

great heads pendulous over Alice in Wonderland, a blackboard full of C A T.

Naomi reading patiently, story out of a Communist fairy book—Tale of the Sudden Sweetness of the Dictator—Forgiveness of Warlocks—Armies Kissing—

Deathsheads Around the Green Table—The King & the Workers—Paterson Press printed them up in the '30s till she went mad, or they folded, both.

O Paterson! I got home late that nite. Louis was worried. How could I be so—didn't I think? I shouldn't have left her. Mad in Lakewood. Call the Doctor. Phone the home in the pines. Too late.

Went to bed exhausted, wanting to leave the world (probably that year newly in love with R——my high school mind hero, jewish boy who came a doctor later—then silent neat kid—

I later laying down life for him, moved to Manhattan—followed him to college—Prayed on ferry to help mankind if admitted—vowed, the day I journeyed to Entrance Exam—

by being honest revolutionary labor lawyer—would train for that—inspired by Sacco Vanzetti, Norman Thomas, Debs, Altgeld, Sandburg, Poe—Little Blue Books. I wanted to be President, or Senator.

ignorant woe—later dreams of kneeling by R's shocked

knees declaring my love of 1941—What sweetness he'd have shown me, tho, that I'd wished him & despaired—first love—a crush—

Later a mortal avalanche, whole mountains of homosexuality, Matterhorns of cock, Grand Canyons of asshole—weight on my melancholy head—

meanwhile I walked on Broadway imagining Infinity like a rubber ball without space beyond—what's outside?—coming home to Graham Avenue still melancholy passing the lone green hedges across the street, dreaming after the movies—)

The telephone rang at 2 A.M.—Emergency—she'd gone mad—Naomi hiding under the bed screaming bugs of Mussolini—Help! Louis! Buba! Fascists! Death!—the landlady frightened—old fag attendant screaming back at her—

Terror, that woke the neighbors—old ladies on the second floor recovering from menopause—all those rags between thighs, clean sheets, sorry over lost babies—husbands ashen—children sneering at Yale, or putting oil in hair at CCNY—or trembling in Montclair State Teachers College like Eugene—

Her big leg crouched to her breast, hand outstretched Keep Away, wool dress on her thighs, fur coat dragged under the bed—she barricaded herself under bedspring with suitcases.

Louis in pajamas listening to phone, frightened—do now? —Who could know?—my fault, delivering her to solitude?—sitting in the dark room on the sofa, trembling, to figure out—

He took the morning train to Lakewood, Naomi still under bed—thought he brought poison Cops—Naomi screaming—Louis what happened to your heart then? Have you been killed by Naomi's ecstasy?

Dragged her out, around the corner, a cab, forced her in with valise, but the driver left them off at drugstore. Bus stop, two hours' wait.

I lay in bed nervous in the 4-room apartment, the big bed in living room, next to Louis' desk—shaking—he came home that nite, late, told me what happened.

Naomi at the prescription counter defending herself from the enemy—racks of children's books, douche bags, aspirins, pots, blood—'Don't come near me—murderers! Keep away! Promise not to kill me!'

Louis in horror at the soda fountain—with Lakewood girlscouts—Coke addicts—nurses—busmen hung on schedule—Police from country precinct, dumbed—and a priest dreaming of pigs on an ancient cliff?

Smelling the air—Louis pointing to emptiness?—Customers vomiting their Cokes—or staring—Louis humiliated—Naomi triumphant—The Announcement of the Plot. Bus arrives, the drivers won't have them on trip to New York.

Phonecalls to Dr. Whatzis, 'She needs a rest,' The mental hospital—State Greystone Doctors—'Bring her here, Mr. Ginsberg.'

Naomi, Naomi—sweating, bulge-eyed, fat, the dress unbuttoned at one side—hair over brow, her stocking hanging evilly on her legs—screaming for a blood transfusion—one righteous hand upraised—a shoe in it—barefoot in the Pharmacy—

The enemies approach—what poisons? Tape recorders? FBI? Zhdanov hiding behind the counter? Trotsky mixing rat bacteria in the back of the store? Uncle Sam in Newark, plotting deathly perfumes in the Negro district? Uncle Ephraim, drunk with murder in the politician's bar, scheming of Hague? Aunt Rose passing water thru the needles of the Spanish Civil War?

till the hired $35 ambulance came from Red Bank—— Grabbed her arms—strapped her on the stretcher—moaning, poisoned by imaginaries, vomiting chemicals thru Jersey, begging mercy from Essex County to Morristown—

And back to Greystone where she lay three years—that was the last breakthrough, delivered her to Madhouse again—

On what wards—I walked there later, oft—old catatonic ladies, gray as cloud or ash or walls—sit crooning over floorspace— Chairs—and the wrinkled hags acreep, accusing—begging my 13-year-old mercy—

'Take me home'—I went alone sometimes looking for the lost Naomi, taking Shock—and I'd say, 'No, you're crazy Mama,— Trust the Drs.'—

And Eugene, my brother, her elder son, away studying Law in a furnished room in Newark—

came Paterson-ward next day—and he sat on the broken-down couch in the living room—'We had to send her back to Greystone'—

—his face perplexed, so young, then eyes with tears—then crept weeping all over his face—'What for?' wail vibrating in his cheekbones, eyes closed up, high voice—Eugene's face of pain.

Him faraway, escaped to an Elevator in the Newark Library, his bottle daily milk on windowsill of $5 week furn room downtown at trolley tracks—

He worked 8 hrs. a day for $20/wk—thru Law School years—stayed by himself innocent near negro whorehouses.

Unlaid, poor virgin—writing poems about Ideals and politics letters to the editor Pat Eve News—(we both wrote, denouncing Senator Borah and Isolationists—and felt mysterious toward Paterson City Hall—

I sneaked inside it once—local Moloch tower with phallus spire & cap o' ornament, strange gothic Poetry that stood on Market Street—replica Lyons' Hotel de Ville—

wings, balcony & scrollwork portals, gateway to the giant city clock, secret map room full of Hawthorne—dark Debs in the Board of Tax—Rembrandt smoking in the gloom—

Silent polished desks in the great committee room—Aldermen? Bd of Finance? Mosca the hairdresser aplot—Crapp the gangster issuing orders from the john—The madmen struggling over Zone, Fire, Cops & Backroom Metaphysics—we're all dead—outside by the bus stop Eugene stared thru childhood—

where the Evangelist preached madly for 3 decades, hardhaired, cracked & true to his mean Bible—chalked Prepare to Meet Thy God on civic pave—

or God is Love on the railroad overpass concrete—he raved like I would rave, the lone Evangelist—Death on City Hall—)

But Gene, young,—been Montclair Teachers College 4 years—taught half year & quit to go ahead in life—afraid of Discipline Problems—dark sex Italian students, raw girls getting laid, no English, sonnets disregarded—and he did not know much—just that he lost—

so broke his life in two and paid for Law—read huge blue books and rode the ancient elevator 13 miles away in Newark & studied up hard for the future

just found the Scream of Naomi on his failure doorstep, for the final time, Naomi gone, us lonely—home—him sitting there—

Then have some chicken soup, Eugene. The Man of Evangel wails in front of City Hall. And this year Lou has poetic loves of suburb middle age—in secret—music from his 1937 book—Sincere —he longs for beauty—

No love since Naomi screamed—since 1923?—now lost in

Greystone ward—new shock for her—Electricity, following the 40 Insulin.

And Metrazol had made her fat.

So that a few years later she came home again—we'd much advanced and planned—I waited for that day—my Mother again to cook &—play the piano—sing at mandolin—Lung Stew, & Stenka Razin, & the communist line on the war with Finland—and Louis in debt—suspected to be poisoned money—mysterious capitalisms

—& walked down the long front hall & looked at the furniture. She never remembered it all. Some amnesia. Examined the doilies—and the dining room set was sold—

the Mahogany table—20 years love—gone to the junk man—we still had the piano—and the book of Poe—and the Mandolin, tho needed some string, dusty—

She went to the backroom to lie down in bed and ruminate, or nap, hide—I went in with her, not leave her by herself—lay in bed next to her—shades pulled, dusky, late afternoon—Louis in front room at desk, waiting—perhaps boiling chicken for supper—

'Don't be afraid of me because I'm just coming back home from the mental hospital—I'm your mother—'

Poor love, lost—a fear—I lay there—Said, 'I love you Naomi,'—stiff, next to her arm. I would have cried, was this the comfortless lone union?—Nervous, and she got up soon.

Was she ever satisfied? And—by herself sat on the new couch by the front windows, uneasy—cheek leaning on her hand—narrowing eye—at what fate that day—

Picking her tooth with her nail, lips formed an O, suspicion—thought's old worn vagina—absent sideglance of eye—some evil debt written in the wall, unpaid—& the aged breasts of Newark come near—

May have heard radio gossip thru the wires in her head, controlled by 3 big sticks left in her back by gangsters in amnesia, thru the hospital—caused pain between her shoulders—

Into her head—Roosevelt should know her case, she told me—Afraid to kill her, now, that the government knew their names—traced back to Hitler—wanted to leave Louis' house forever.

One night, sudden attack—her noise in the bathroom—like croaking up her soul—convulsions and red vomit coming out of her mouth—diarrhea water exploding from her behind—on all fours in front of the toilet—urine running between her legs—left retching on the tile floor smeared with her black feces—unfainted—

At forty, varicosed, nude, fat, doomed, hiding outside the apartment door near the elevator calling Police, yelling for her girlfriend Rose to help—

Once locked herself in with razor or iodine—could hear her cough in tears at sink—Lou broke through glass green-painted door, we pulled her out to the bedroom.

Then quiet for months that winter—walks, alone, nearby on Broadway, read Daily Worker—Broke her arm, fell on icy street—

Began to scheme escape from cosmic financial murder plots—later she ran away to the Bronx to her sister Elanor. And there's another saga of late Naomi in New York.

Or thru Elanor or the Workmen's Circle, where she worked, addressing envelopes, she made out—went shopping for Campbell's tomato soup—saved money Louis mailed her—

Later she found a boyfriend, and he was a doctor—Dr. Isaac worked for National Maritime Union—now Italian bald and pudgy old doll—who was himself an orphan—but they kicked him out— Old cruelties—

Sloppier, sat around on bed or chair, in corset dreaming to herself—'I'm hot—I'm getting fat—I used to have such a beautiful figure before I went to the hospital—You should have seen me in Woodbine—' This in a furnished room around the NMU hall, 1943.

Looking at naked baby pictures in the magazine—baby powder advertisements, strained lamb carrots—'I will think nothing but beautiful thoughts.'

Revolving her head round and round on her neck at window light in summertime, in hypnotize, in doven-dream recall—

'I touch his cheek, I touch his cheek, he touches my lips with his hand, I think beautiful thoughts, the baby has a beautiful hand.'—

Or a No-shake of her body, disgust—some thought of Buchenwald—some insulin passes thru her head—a grimace nerve shudder at Involuntary (as shudder when I piss)—bad chemical in her cortex—'No don't think of that. He's a rat.'

Naomi: 'And when we die we become an onion, a cabbage,

a carrot, or a squash, a vegetable.' I come downtown from Columbia and agree. She reads the Bible, thinks beautiful thoughts all day.

'Yesterday I saw God. What did he look like? Well, in the afternoon I climbed up a ladder—he has a cheap cabin in the country, like Monroe, N.Y. the chicken farms in the wood. He was a lonely old man with a white beard.

'I cooked supper for him. I made him a nice supper—lentil soup, vegetables, bread & butter—miltz—he sat down at the table and ate, he was sad.

'I told him, Look at all those fightings and killings down there, What's the matter? Why don't you put a stop to it?

'I try, he said—That's all he could do, he looked tired. He's a bachelor so long, and he likes lentil soup.'

Serving me meanwhile, a plate of cold fish—chopped raw cabbage dript with tapwater—smelly tomatoes—week-old health food—grated beets & carrots with leaky juice, warm—more and more disconsolate food—I can't eat it for nausea sometimes—the Charity of her hands stinking with Manhattan, madness, desire to please me, cold undercooked fish—pale red near the bones. Her smells—and oft naked in the room, so that I stare ahead, or turn a book ignoring her.

One time I thought she was trying to make me come lay her—flirting to herself at sink—lay back on huge bed that filled most of the room, dress up round her hips, big slash of hair, scars of operations, pancreas, belly wounds, abortions, appendix, stitching of incisions pulling down in the fat like hideous thick zippers—ragged long lips between her legs—What, even, smell of asshole? I was cold—later revolted a little, not much—seemed perhaps a good idea to try—know the Monster of the Beginning Womb—Perhaps—that way. Would she care? She needs a lover.

Yisborach, v'yistabach, v'yispoar, v'yisroman, v'yisnaseh, v'yishador, v'yishalleh, v'yishallol, sh'meh d'kudsho, b'rich hu.

And Louis reestablishing himself in Paterson grimy apartment in negro district—living in dark rooms—but found himself a girl he later married, falling in love again—tho sere & shy—hurt with 20 years Naomi's mad idealism.

Once I came home, after longtime in N.Y., he's lonely—sitting in the bedroom, he at desk chair turned round to face me—weeps, tears in red eyes under his glasses—

That we'd left him—Gene gone strangely into army—she

out on her own in N.Y., almost childish in her furnished room. So
Louis walked downtown to postoffice to get mail, taught in
highschool—stayed at poetry desk, forlorn—ate grief at Bickford's
all these years—are gone.

Eugene got out of the Army, came home changed and
lone—cut off his nose in jewish operation—for years stopped girls
on Broadway for cups of coffee to get laid—Went to NYU, serious
there, to finish Law.—

And Gene lived with her, ate naked fishcakes, cheap, while
she got crazier—He got thin, or felt helpless, Naomi striking 1920
poses at the moon, half-naked in the next bed.

bit his nails and studied—was the weird nurse-son—Next
year he moved to a room near Columbia—though she wanted to live
with her children—

'Listen to your mother's plea, I beg you'—Louis still sending
her checks—I was in bughouse that year 8 months—my own visions
unmentioned in this here Lament—

But then went half mad—Hitler in her room, she saw his
mustache in the sink—afraid of Dr. Isaac now, suspecting that he
was in on the Newark plot—went up to Bronx to live near Elanor's
Rheumatic Heart—

And Uncle Max never got up before noon, tho Naomi at
6 A.M. was listening to the radio for spies—or searching the
windowsill,

for in the empty lot downstairs, an old man creeps with his
bag stuffing packages of garbage in his hanging black overcoat.

Max's sister Edie works—17 years bookkeeper at Gimbels
—lived downstairs in apartment house, divorced—so Edie took in
Naomi on Rochambeau Ave—

Woodlawn Cemetery across the street, vast dale of graves
where Poe once—Last stop on Bronx subway—lots of communists
in that area.

Who enrolled for painting classes at night in Bronx Adult
High School—walked alone under Van Cortlandt Elevated line to
class—paints Naomiisms—

Humans sitting on the grass in some Camp No-Worry sum-
mers yore—saints with droopy faces and long-ill-fitting pants, from
hospital—

Brides in front of Lower East Side with short grooms—lost
El trains running over the Babylonian apartment rooftops in the
Bronx—

Sad paintings—but she expressed herself. Her mandolin gone, all strings broke in her head, she tried. Toward Beauty? or some old life Message?

But started kicking Elanor, and Elanor had heart trouble —came upstairs and asked her about Spydom for hours,—Elanor frazzled. Max away at office, accounting for cigar stores till at night.

'I am a great woman—am truly a beautiful soul—and because of that they (Hitler, Grandma, Hearst, the Capitalists, Franco, Daily News, the '20s, Mussolini, the living dead) want to shut me up—Buba's the head of a spider network—'

Kicking the girls, Edie & Elanor—Woke Edie at midnite to tell her she was a spy and Elanor a rat. Edie worked all day and couldn't take it—She was organizing the union.—And Elanor began dying, upstairs in bed.

The relatives call me up, she's getting worse—I was the only one left—Went on the subway with Eugene to see her, ate stale fish—

'My sister whispers in the radio—Louis must be in the apartment—his mother tells him what to say—LIARS!—I cooked for my two children—I played the mandolin—'

Last night the nightingale woke me / Last night when all was still / it sang in the golden moonlight / from on the wintry hill. She did.

I pushed her against the door and shouted 'DON'T KICK ELANOR!'—she stared at me—Contempt—die—disbelief her sons are so naive, so dumb—'Elanor is the worst spy! She's taking orders!'

'—No wires in the room!'—I'm yelling at her—last ditch, Eugene listening on the bed—what can he do to escape that fatal Mama—'You've been away from Louis years already—Grandma's too old to walk—'

We're all alive at once then—even me & Gene & Naomi in one mythological Cousinesque room—screaming at each other in the Forever—I in Columbia jacket, she half undressed.

I banging against her head which saw Radios, Sticks, Hitlers—the gamut of Hallucinations—for real—her own universe —no road that goes elsewhere—to my own—No America, not even a world—

That you go as all men, as Van Gogh, as mad Hannah, all the same—to the last doom—Thunder, Spirits, Lightning!

I've seen your grave! O strange Naomi! My own—cracked grave! Shema Y'Israel—I am Svul Avrum—you—in death?

Your last night in the darkness of the Bronx—I phone-called—thru hospital to secret police

that came, when you and I were alone, shrieking at Elanor in my ear—who breathed hard in her own bed, got thin—

Nor will forget, the doorknock, at your fright of spies,—Law advancing, on my honor—Eternity entering the room—you running to the bathroom undressed, hiding in protest from the last heroic fate—

staring at my eyes, betrayed—the final cops of madness rescuing me—from your foot against the broken heart of Elanor,

your voice at Edie weary of Gimbels coming home to broken radio—and Louis needing a poor divorce, he wants to get married soon—Eugene dreaming, hiding at 125 St., suing negroes for money on crud furniture, defending black girls—

Protests from the bathroom—Said you were sane—dressing in a cotton robe, your shoes, then new, your purse and newspaper clippings—no—your honesty—

as you vainly made your lips more real with lipstick, looking in the mirror to see if the Insanity was Me or a carful of police.

or Grandma spying at 78—Your vision—Her climbing over the walls of the cemetery with political kidnapper's bag—or what you saw on the walls of the Bronx, in pink nightgown at midnight, staring out the window on the empty lot—

Ah Rochambeau Ave.—Playground of Phantoms—last apartment in the Bronx for spies—last home for Elanor or Naomi, here these communist sisters lost their revolution—

'All right—put on your coat Mrs.—let's go—We have the wagon downstairs—you want to come with her to the station?'

The ride then—held Naomi's hand, and held her head to my breast, I'm taller—kissed her and said I did it for the best—Elanor sick—and Max with heart condition—Needs—

To me—'Why did you do this?'—'Yes Mrs., your son will have to leave you in an hour'—The Ambulance

came in a few hours—drove off at 4 A.M. to some Bellevue in the night downtown—gone to the hospital forever. I saw her led away—she waved, tears in her eyes.

Two years, after a trip to Mexico—bleak in the flat plain near Brentwood, scrub brush and grass around the unused RR train track to the crazyhouse—

new brick 20 story central building—lost on the vast lawns of madtown on Long Island—huge cities of the moon.

Asylum spreads out giant wings above the path to a minute black hole—the door—entrance thru crotch—

I went in—smelt funny—the halls again—up elevator—to a glass door on a Women's Ward—to Naomi—Two nurses buxom white—They led her out, Naomi stared—and I gaspt—She'd had a stroke—

Too thin, shrunk on her bones—age come to Naomi—now broken into white hair—loose dress on her skeleton—face sunk, old! withered—cheek of crone—

One hand stiff—heaviness of forties & menopause reduced by one heart stroke, lame now—wrinkles—a scar on her head, the lobotomy—ruin, the hand dipping downwards to death—

O Russian faced, woman on the grass, your long black hair is crowned with flowers, the mandolin is on your knees—

Communist beauty, sit here married in the summer among daisies, promised happiness at hand—

holy mother, now you smile on your love, your world is born anew, children run naked in the field spotted with dandelions,

they eat in the plum tree grove at the end of the meadow and find a cabin where a white-haired negro teaches the mystery of his rainbarrel—

blessed daughter come to America, I long to hear your voice again, remembering your mother's music, in the Song of the Natural Front—

O glorious muse that bore me from the womb, gave suck first mystic life & taught me talk and music, from whose pained head I first took Vision—

Tortured and beaten in the skull—What mad hallucinations of the damned that drive me out of my own skull to seek Eternity till I find Peace for Thee, O Poetry—and for all humankind call on the Origin

Death which is the mother of the universe!—Now wear your nakedness forever, white flowers in your hair, your marriage sealed behind the sky—no revolution might destroy that maidenhood—

O beautiful Garbo of my Karma—all photographs from 1920 in Camp Nicht-Gedeiget here unchanged—with all the teachers from

Newark—Nor Elanor be gone, nor Max await his specter—nor Louis retire from this High School—

Back! You! Naomi! Skull on you! Gaunt immortality and revolution come—small broken woman—the ashen indoor eyes of hospitals, ward grayness on skin—

'Are you a spy?' I sat at the sour table, eyes filling with tears—'Who are you? Did Louis send you?—The wires—'

in her hair, as she beat on her head—'I'm not a bad girl—don't murder me!—I hear the ceiling—I raised two children—'

Two years since I'd been there—I started to cry—She stared—nurse broke up the meeting a moment—I went into the bathroom to hide, against the toilet white walls

'The Horror' I weeping—to see her again—'The Horror'—as if she were dead thru funeral rot in—'The Horror!'

I came back she yelled more—they led her away—'You're not Allen—' I watched her face—but she passed by me, not looking—

Opened the door to the ward,—she went thru without a glance back, quiet suddenly—I stared out—she looked old—the verge of the grave—'All the Horror!'

Another year, I left N.Y.—on West Coast in Berkeley cottage dreamed of her soul—that, thru life, in what form it stood in that body, ashen or manic, gone beyond joy—

near its death—with eyes—was my own love in its form, the Naomi, my mother on earth still—sent her long letter—& wrote hymns to the mad—Work of the merciful Lord of Poetry.

that causes the broken grass to be green, or the rock to break in grass—or the Sun to be constant to earth—Sun of all sunflowers and days on bright iron bridges—what shines on old hospitals—as on my yard—

Returning from San Francisco one night, Orlovsky in my room—Whalen in his peaceful chair—a telegram from Gene, Naomi dead—

Outside I bent my head to the ground under the bushes near the garage—knew she was better—

at last—not left to look on Earth alone—2 years of solitude—no one, at age nearing 60—old woman of skulls—once long-tressed Naomi of Bible—

or Ruth who wept in America—Rebecca aged in Newark
—David remembering his Harp, now lawyer at Yale

or Svul Avrum—Israel Abraham—myself—to sing in the
wilderness toward God—O Elohim!—so to the end—2 days after
her death I got her letter—

Strange Prophecies anew! She wrote—'The key is in the
window, the key is in the sunlight at the window—I have the key—
Get married Allen don't take drugs—the key is in the bars, in the
sunlight in the window.

Love,

your mother'

which is Naomi—

HYMMNN

In the world which He has created according to his will Blessed
Praised

Magnified Lauded Exalted the Name of the Holy One Blessed is He!

In the house in Newark Blessed is He! In the madhouse Blessed is
He! In the house of Death Blessed is He!

Blessed be He in homosexuality! Blessed be He in Paranoia! Blessed
be He in the city! Blessed be He in the Book!

Blessed be He who dwells in the shadow! Blessed be He! Blessed be
He!

Blessed be you Naomi in tears! Blessed be you Naomi in fears! Blessed
Blessed Blessed in sickness!

Blessed be you Naomi in Hospitals! Blessed be you Naomi in solitude!
Blest be your triumph! Blest be your bars! Blest be your
last years' loneliness!

Blest be your failure! Blest be your stroke! Blest be the close of your
eye!
Blest be the gaunt of your cheek! Blest be your withered
thighs!

Blessed be Thee Naomi in Death! Blessed be Death! Blessed be
Death!

Blessed be He Who leads all sorrow to Heaven! Blessed be He in
the end!

Blessed be He who builds Heaven in Darkness! Blessed Blessed
Blessed be He! Blessed be He! Blessed be Death on us All!

III

Only to have not forgotten the beginning in which she drank cheap
sodas in the morgues of Newark,
only to have seen her weeping on gray tables in long wards of her
universe
only to have known the weird ideas of Hitler at the door, the wires
in her head, the three big sticks
rammed down her back, the voices in the ceiling shrieking out her
ugly early lays for 30 years,
only to have seen the time-jumps, memory lapse, the crash of wars,
the roar and silence of a vast electric shock,
only to have seen her painting crude pictures of Elevateds running
over the rooftops of the Bronx
her brothers dead in Riverside or Russia, her lone in Long Island
writing a last letter—and her image in the sunlight at the
window
'The key is in the sunlight at the window in the bars the key is in the
sunlight,'
only to have come to that dark night on iron bed by stroke when the
sun gone down on Long Island
and the vast Atlantic roars outside the great call of Being to its own
to come back out of the Nightmare—divided creation—with her head
lain on a pillow of the hospital to die
—in one last glimpse—all Earth one everlasting Light in the familiar
blackout—no tears for this vision—
But that the key should be left behind—at the window—the key in
the sunlight—to the living—that can take
that slice of light in hand—and turn the door—and look back see
Creation glistening backwards to the same grave, size of universe,
size of the tick of the hospital's clock on the archway over the white
door—

IV

O mother
what have I left out
O mother
what have I forgotten
O mother

farewell
with a long black shoe
farewell
with Communist Party and a broken stocking
farewell
with six dark hairs on the wen of your breast
farewell
with your old dress and a long black beard around the vagina
farewell
with your sagging belly
with your fear of Hitler
with your mouth of bad short stories
with your fingers of rotten mandolins
with your arms of fat Paterson porches
with your belly of strikes and smokestacks
with your chin of Trotsky and the Spanish War
with your voice singing for the decaying overbroken workers
with your nose of bad lay with your nose of the smell of the pickles
    of Newark
with your eyes
with your eyes of Russia
with your eyes of no money
with your eyes of false China
with your eyes of Aunt Elanor
with your eyes of starving India
with your eyes pissing in the park
with your eyes of America taking a fall
with your eyes of your failure at the piano
with your eyes of your relatives in California
with your eyes of Ma Rainey dying in an aumbulance
with your eyes of Czechoslovakia attacked by robots
with your eyes going to painting class at night in the Bronx
with your eyes of the killer Grandma you see on the horizon from
    the Fire-Escape
with your eyes running naked out of the apartment screaming into
    the hall
with your eyes being led away by policemen to an ambulance
with your eyes strapped down on the operating table
with your eyes with the pancreas removed
with your eyes of appendix operation

with your eyes of abortion
with your eyes of ovaries removed
with your eyes of shock
with your eyes of lobotomy
with your eyes of divorce
with your eyes of stroke
with your eyes alone
with your eyes
with your eyes
with your Death full of Flowers

V

Caw caw caw crows shriek in the white sun over grave stones in Long
        Island
Lord Lord Lord Naomi underneath this grass my halflife and my own
        as hers
caw caw my eye be buried in the same Ground where I stand in Angel
Lord Lord great Eye that stares on All and moves in a black cloud
caw caw strange cry of Beings flung up into sky over the waving trees
Lord Lord O Grinder of giant Beyonds my voice in a boundless field
        in Sheol
Caw caw the call of Time rent out of foot and wing an instant in
        the universe
Lord Lord an echo in the sky the wind through ragged leaves the
        roar of memory
caw caw all years my birth a dream caw caw New York the bus the
        broken shoe the vast highschool caw caw all Visions of
        the Lord
Lord Lord Lord caw caw caw Lord Lord Lord caw caw caw Lord

                                        Paris, December 1957–New York, 1959

SONG

            The weight of the world
                    is love.
            Under the burden
                    of solitude,

under the burden
    of dissatisfaction

    the weight,
the weight we carry
    is love.

Who can deny?
    In dreams
it touches
    the body,
in thought
    constructs
a miracle,
    in imagination
anguishes
    till born
in human—

looks out of the heart
    burning with purity—
for the burden of life
    is love,

but we carry the weight
    wearily,
and so must rest
in the arms of love
    at last,
must rest in the arms
    of love.

No rest
    without love,
no sleep
    without dreams
of love—
    be mad or chill
obsessed with angels
    or machines,

the final wish
　　　　is love
—cannot be bitter,
　　　　cannot deny,
cannot withhold
　　　　if denied:

the weight is too heavy

　　　　—must give
for no return
　　　　as thought
is given
　　　　in solitude
in all the excellence
　　　　of its excess.

The warm bodies
　　　　shine together
in the darkness,
　　　　the hand moves
to the center
　　　　of the flesh,
the skin trembles
　　　　in happiness
and the soul comes
　　　　joyful to the eye—

yes, yes,
　　　　that's what
I wanted,
　　　　I always wanted,
I always wanted,
　　　　to return
to the body
　　　　where I was born.

San Jose, 1954

ON BURROUGHS' WORK

The method must be purest meat
    and no symbolic dressing,
actual visions & actual prisons
    as seen then and now.

Prisons and visions presented
    with rare descriptions
corresponding exactly to those
    of Alcatraz and Rose.

A naked lunch is natural to us,
    we eat reality sandwiches.
But allegories are so much lettuce.
    Don't hide the madness.

San Jose, 1954

William Burroughs

William Burroughs was born on February 5, 1914, in St. Louis, Missouri, the grandson of the inventor of the Burroughs adding machine. After his graduation from Harvard, he lived in Chicago and New York on an income of two hundred dollars a month from his parents. He met Lucien Carr and Allen Ginsberg in New York City around Christmas 1943, shortly after Ginsberg began studying at Columbia, and Burroughs impressed them with his erudition, as well as his sardonic humor and reserved poise. Older than the others in the group, he took on the role of teacher, encouraging Kerouac and Ginsberg in their attempts to write fiction and poetry.

Although Burroughs collaborated on a humorous sketch with a classmate, Kells Elvins, at Harvard and completed a short novel written in the style of Dashiell Hammett with Kerouac, both works were rejected by publishers, and Burroughs did not think of himself as a writer. Instead, his search for an identity led him to deliberately seek out a criminal life.

In the hope that he would feel at home in a "community of outlaws," Burroughs began buying stolen goods, including morphine Syrettes, and became addicted to morphine. In 1947 he began to live with Joan Vollmer, another member of the group around the Columbia campus, and they had a son William S. Burroughs, Jr. Joan was addicted to Benzedrine, and they moved to New Orleans, Texas, and Mexico City where drugs were more easily obtainable.

In the spring of 1950, Burroughs's old Harvard friend Kells Elvins visited him in Mexico City and talked him into writing a factual book about his drug experience as a "memory exercise." Burroughs set himself a daily schedule, helped by injections of morphine. He finished the project in December, titled his book Junk, *and sent the manuscript to Lucien Carr in New York. Acting as an agent for both Burroughs and Kerouac, Ginsberg was able to get the book published as a pulp paperback in 1953 under the pseudonym "William Lee" with the lurid subtitle* Confessions of an Unredeemed Drug Addict.

On September 6, 1951, Burroughs accidentally killed his wife and was charged in Mexico City with criminal imprudence. His parents took over the care of Billy Junior and brought him to their home in Florida. Released on bail, Burroughs left Mexico and traveled in South America looking for a drug called yage. His letters to Ginsberg describing his experiences in the cities, jungles, and mountains of Ecuador and Peru were collected in the volume later published by City Lights as The Yage Letters *(1963), which Burroughs thought would interest readers after the success of Aldous Huxley's* The Doors of Perception *in 1954.*

After Burroughs left South America, he settled in Tangier, where he could live cheaply and obtain the drugs he needed. Burroughs has said that the death of his wife gave him a literary vocation. He felt that he had been possessed by an invader, "the Ugly Spirit," who controlled him at the time of the accident and maneuvered him into a lifelong struggle, "in which I have had no choice except to write my way out."

In February 1957 Kerouac came to visit him in Tangier and began to type the hundreds of handwritten pages of Burroughs's new book that Kerouac titled Naked Lunch. *Writing it, Burroughs said he was "shitting out my educated Middlewest background once and for all. It's a matter of catharsis, where I say the most horrible things I can think of. Realize that—the most horrible dirty slimy awful niggardliest posture possible. . . ."*

Burroughs continued to work on the book until its publication in 1959, thinking of it as a picaresque novel narrated by an alter ego, "William Lee." As his biographer, Ted Morgan, understood, Burroughs shared Ginsberg and Carr's "New Vision" of the writer as an outlaw creating a "literature of risk." The compression and urgency of Naked Lunch *in "the fragmentation of the text is like the discontinuity of the addict's life between fixes. . . . For Burroughs sees addiction as a general condition not limited to drugs. Politics, religion, the family, love, are all forms of addiction. In the post-Bomb society, all the mainstays of the social order have lost their meaning, and bankrupt nation-states are run by 'control addicts.' " Burroughs's essay "Deposition: Testimony Concerning a Sickness," describing an experimental cure for heroin addiction developed by a London doctor, was published in the* Evergreen Review *in 1960.*

from JUNKY

My first experience with junk was during the War, about 1944 or 1945. I had made the acquaintance of a man named Norton who was working in a shipyard at the time. Norton, whose real name was Morelli or something like that, had been discharged from the peacetime Army for forging a pay check, and was classified 4-F for reasons of bad character. He looked like George Raft, but was taller. Norton was trying to improve his English and achieve a smooth, affable manner. Affability, however, did not come natural to him. In repose, his expression was sullen and mean, and you knew he always had that mean look when you turned your back.

Norton was a hard-working thief, and he did not feel right unless he stole something every day from the shipyard where he worked. A tool, some canned goods, a pair of overalls, anything at all. One day he called me up and said he had stolen a Tommy gun. Could I find someone to buy it? I said, "Maybe. Bring it over."

The housing shortage was getting under way. I paid fifteen dollars a week for a dirty apartment that opened onto a companionway and never got any sunlight. The wallpaper was flaking off because the radiator leaked steam when there was any steam in it to leak. I had the windows sealed shut against the cold with a caulking of newspapers. The place was full of roaches and occasionally I killed a bedbug.

I was sitting by the radiator, a little damp from the steam, when I heard Norton's knock. I opened the door, and there he was standing in the dark hall with a big parcel wrapped in brown paper under his arm. He smiled and said, "Hello."

I said, "Come in, Norton, and take off your coat."

He unwrapped the Tommy gun and we assembled it and snapped the firing pin.

I said I would find someone to buy it.

Norton said, "Oh, here's something else I picked up."

It was a flat yellow box with five one-half grain syrettes of morphine tartrate.

"This is just a sample," he said, indicating the morphine. "I've got fifteen of these boxes at home and I can get more if you get rid of these."

I said, "I'll see what I can do."

At that time I had never used any junk and it did not occur to me to try it. I began looking for someone to buy the two items and that is how I ran into Roy and Herman [Herbert Huncke].

I knew a young hoodlum from upstate New York who was working as a short-order cook in Riker's, "cooling off," as he explained. I called him and said I had something to get rid of, and made an appointment to meet him in the Angle Bar on Eighth Avenue near 42nd Street.

This bar was a meeting place for 42nd Street hustlers, a peculiar breed of four-flushing, would-be criminals. They are always looking for a "setup man," someone to plan jobs and tell them exactly what to do. Since no "setup man" would have anything to do with people so obviously inept, unlucky, and unsuccessful, they go on looking, fabricating preposterous lies about their big scores, cooling off as dishwashers, soda jerks, waiters, occasionally rolling a drunk or a timid queer, looking, always looking, for the "setup man" with a big job who will say, "I've been watching you. You're the man I need for this setup. Now listen . . ."

Jack—through whom I met Roy and Herman—was not one of these lost sheep looking for the shepherd with a diamond ring and a gun in the shoulder holster and the hard, confident voice with overtones of connections, fixes, setups that would make a stickup sound easy and sure of success. Jack was very successful from time to time and would turn up in new clothes and even new cars. He was also an inveterate liar who seemed to lie more for himself than for any visible audience. He had a clean-cut, healthy country face, but there was something curiously diseased about him. He was subject to sudden fluctuations in weight, like a diabetic or a sufferer from liver trouble. These changes in weight were often accompanied by an uncontrollable fit of restlessness, so that he would disappear for some days.

The effect was uncanny. You would see him one time a fresh-faced kid. A week or so later he would turn up so thin, sallow and old-looking, you would have to look twice to recognize him. His face was lined with suffering in which his eyes did not participate. It was a suffering of his cells alone. He himself—the conscious ego that looked out of the glazed, alert-calm hoodlum eyes—would have nothing to do with this suffering of his rejected other self, a suffering of the nervous system, of flesh and viscera and cells.

He slid into the booth where I was sitting and ordered a shot of whiskey. He tossed it off, put the glass down and looked at me with his head tilted a little to one side and back.

"What's this guy got?" he said.

"A Tommy gun and about thirty-five grains of morphine."

"The morphine I can get rid of right away, but the Tommy gun may take a little time."

Two detectives walked in and leaned on the bar talking to the bartender. Jack jerked his head in their direction. "The law. Let's take a walk."

I followed him out of the bar. He walked through the door sliding sideways. "I'm taking you to someone who will want the morphine," he said. "You want to forget this address."

We went down to the bottom level of the Independent Subway. Jack's voice, talking to his invisible audience, went on and on. He had a knack of throwing his voice directly into your consciousness. No external noise drowned him out. "Give me a thirty-eight every time. Just flick back the hammer and let her go. I'll drop anyone at five hundred feet. Don't care what you say. My brother has two 30-caliber machine guns stashed in Iowa."

We got off the subway and began to walk on snow-covered sidewalks between tenements.

"The guy owed me for a long time, see? I knew he had

it but he wouldn't pay, so I waited for him when he finished work. I had a roll of nickels. No one can hang anything on you for carrying U.S. currency. Told me he was broke. I cracked his jaw and took my money off him. Two of his friends standing there, but they kept out of it. I'd've switched a blade on them."

We were walking up tenement stairs. The stairs were made of worn black metal. We stopped in front of a narrow, metal-covered door, and Jack gave an elaborate knock inclining his head to the floor like a safecracker. The door was opened by a large, flabby, middle-aged queer, with tattooing on his fore-arms and even on the backs of his hands.

"This is Joey," Jack said, and Joey said, "Hello there."

Jack pulled a five-dollar bill from his pocket and gave it to Joey. "Get us a quart of Schenley's, will you, Joey?"

Joey put on an overcoat and went out.

In many tenement apartments the front door opens directly into the kitchen. This was such an apartment and we were in the kitchen.

After Joey went out I noticed another man who was standing there looking at me. Waves of hostility and suspicion flowed out from his large brown eyes like some sort of television broadcast. The effect was almost like a physical impact. The man was small and very thin, his neck loose in the collar of his shirt. His complexion faded from brown to a mottled yellow, and pancake make-up had been heavily applied in an attempt to conceal a skin eruption. His mouth was drawn down at the corners in a grimace of petulant annoyance.

"Who's this?" he said. His name, I learned later, was Herman.

"Friend of mine. He's got some morphine he wants to get rid of."

Herman shrugged and turned out his hands. "I don't think I want to bother, really."

"Okay," Jack said, "we'll sell it to someone else. Come on, Bill."

We went into the front room. There was a small radio, a china Buddha with a votive candle in front of it, pieces of bric-a-brac. A man was lying on a studio couch. He sat up as we entered the room and said hello and smiled pleasantly, showing discolored, brownish teeth. It was a Southern voice with the accent of East Texas.

Jack said, "Roy, this is a friend of mine. He has some morphine he wants to sell."

The man sat up straighter and swung his legs off the couch. His jaw fell slackly, giving his face a vacant look. The skin of his face was smooth and brown. The cheekbones were high and he looked Oriental. His ears stuck out at right angles from his asymmetrical skull. The eyes were brown and they had a peculiar brilliance, as though points of light were shining behind them. The light in the room glinted on the points of light in his eyes like an opal.

"How much do you have?" he asked me.

"Seventy-five half grain syrettes."

"The regular price is two dollars a grain," he said, "but syrettes go for a little less. People want tablets. Those syrettes have too much water and you have to squeeze the stuff out and cook it down." He paused and his face went blank: "I could go about one-fifty a grain," he said finally.

"I guess that will be okay," I said.

He asked how we could make contact and I gave him my phone number.

Joey came back with the whiskey and we all had a drink. Herman stuck his head in from the kitchen and said to Jack, "Could I talk to you for a minute?"

I could hear them arguing about something. Then Jack came back and Herman stayed in the kitchen. We all had a few drinks and Jack began telling a story.

"My partner was going through the joint. The guy was sleeping, and I was standing over him with a three-foot length of pipe I found in the bathroom. The pipe had a faucet on the end of it, see? All of a sudden he comes up and jumps straight out of bed, running. I let him have it with the faucet end, and he goes on running right out into the other room, the blood spurting out of his head ten feet every time his heart beat." He made a pumping motion with his hand. "You could see the brain there and the blood coming out of it." Jack began to laugh uncontrollably. "My girl was waiting out in the car. She called me—ha-ha-ha!—she called me—ha-ha-ha!—a cold-blooded killer."

He laughed until his face was purple.

A few nights after meeting Roy and Herman, I used one of the syrettes, which was my first experience with junk. A syrette is like a toothpaste tube with a needle on the end. You push a pin down through the needle; the pin punctures the seal; and the syrette is ready to shoot.

Morphine hits the backs of the legs first, then the back of the neck, a spreading wave of relaxation slackening the muscles away from the bones so that you seem to float without outlines, like lying in warm salt water. As this relaxing wave spread through my tissues, I experienced a strong feeling of fear. I had the feeling that some horrible image was just beyond the field of vision, moving, as I turned my head, so that I never quite saw it. I felt nauseous; I lay down and closed my eyes. A series of pictures passed, like watching a movie: A huge, neon-lighted cocktail bar that got larger and larger until streets, traffic, and street repairs were included in it; a waitress carrying a skull on a tray; stars in the clear sky. The physical impact of the fear of death; the shutting off of breath; the stopping of blood.

I dozed off and woke up with a start of fear. Next morning I vomited and felt sick until noon.

Roy called that night.

"About what we were discussing the other night," he said. "I could go about four dollars per box and take five boxes now. Are you busy? I'll come over to your place. We'll come to some kind of agreement."

A few minutes later he knocked at the door. He had on a Glen plaid suit and a dark, coffee-colored shirt. We said hello. He looked around blankly and said, "If you don't mind, I'll take one of those now."

I opened the box. He took out a syrette and injected it into his leg. He pulled up his pants briskly and took out twenty dollars. I put five boxes on the kitchen table.

"I think I'll take them out of the boxes," he said. "Too bulky."

He began putting the syrettes in his coat pockets. "I don't think they'll perforate this way," he said. "Listen, I'll call you again in a day or so after I get rid of these and have some more money." He was adjusting his hat over his asymmetrical skull. "I'll see you."

Next day he was back. He shot another syrette and pulled out forty dollars. I laid out ten boxes and kept two.

"These are for me," I said.

He looked at me, surprised. "You use it?"

"Now and then."

"It's bad stuff," he said, shaking his head. "The worst thing that can happen to a man. We all think we can control it at first. Sometimes we don't want to control it." He laughed. "I'll take all you can get at this price."

Next day he was back. He asked if I didn't want to change my mind about selling the two boxes. I said no. He bought two syrettes for a dollar each, shot them both, and left. He said he had signed on for a two-month trip.

During the next month I used up the eight syrettes I had not sold. The fear I had experienced after using the first syrette was not noticeable after the third; but still, from time to time, after taking a shot I would wake up with a start of fear. After six weeks or so I gave Roy a ring, not expecting him to be back from his trip, but then I heard his voice on the phone.

I said, "Say, do you have any to sell? Of the material I sold you before?"

There was a pause.

"Ye-es," he said, "I can let you have six, but the price will have to be three dollars per. You understand I don't have many."

"Okay," I said. "You know the way. Bring it on over."

It was twelve one-half grain tablets in a thin glass tube. I paid him eighteen dollars and he apologized again for the retail rate.

Next day he bought two grains back.

"It's mighty hard to get now at any price," he said, looking for a vein in his leg. He finally hit a vein and shot the liquid in with an air bubble. "If air bubbles could kill you, there wouldn't be a junky alive."

Later that day Roy pointed out to me a drugstore where they sold needles without any questions—very few drugstores will sell them without a prescription. He showed me how to make a collar out of paper to fit the needle to an eyedropper. An eyedropper is easier to use than a regular hypo, especially for giving yourself vein shots.

Several days later Roy sent me to see a doctor with a story about kidney stones, to hit him for a morphine prescription. The doctor's wife slammed the door in my face, but Roy finally got past her and made the doctor for a ten-grain script.

The doctor's office was in junk territory on 102nd, off Broadway. He was a doddering old man and could not resist the junkies who filled his office and were, in fact, his only patients. It seemed to give him a feeling of importance to look out and see an office full of people. I guess he had reached a point where he could change the appearance of things to suit his needs and when he looked out there he saw a distinguished and diversified clientele, probably well-dressed in 1910 style, instead of a bunch of ratty-looking junkies come to hit him for a morphine script.

Roy shipped out at two- or three-week intervals. His trips were Army Transport and generally short. When he was in town we generally split a few scripts. The old croaker on 102nd finally lost his mind altogether and no drugstore would fill his scripts, but Roy located an Italian doctor out in the Bronx who would write.

I was taking a shot from time to time, but I was a long way from having a habit. At this time I moved into an apartment on the Lower East Side. It was a tenement apartment with the front door opening into the kitchen.

I began dropping into the Angle Bar every night and saw quite a bit of Herman. I managed to overcome his original bad impression of me, and soon I was buying his drinks and meals, and he was hitting me for "smash" (change) at regular intervals. Herman did not have a habit at this time. In fact, he seldom got a habit unless someone else paid for it. But he was always high on something—weed, benzedrine, or knocked out of his mind on "goof balls." He showed up at the Angle every night with a big slob of a Polack called Whitey. There were four Whities in the Angle set, which made for confusion. This Whitey combined the sensitivity of a neurotic with a psychopath's readiness for violence. He was convinced that nobody liked him, a fact that seemed to cause him a great deal of worry.

One Tuesday night Roy and I were standing at the end of the Angle bar. Subway Mike was there, and Frankie Dolan. Dolan was an Irish boy with a cast in one eye. He specialized in crummy scores, beating up defenseless drunks, and holding out on his confederates. "I got no honor," he would say. "I'm a rat." And he would giggle.

Subway Mike had a large, pale face and long teeth. He looked like some specialized kind of underground animal that preys on the animals of the surface. He was a skillful lush-worker, but he had no front. Any cop would do a doubletake at sight of him, and he was well known to the subway squad. So Mike spent at least half of his time on the Island doing the five-twenty-nine for jostling.

This night Herman was knocked out on "nembies" and his head kept falling down onto the bar. Whitey was stomping up and down the length of the bar trying to promote some free drinks. The boys at the bar sat rigid and tense, clutching their drinks, quickly pocketing their change. I heard Whitey say to the bartender, "Keep this for me, will you?" and he passed his large clasp knife across the bar. The boys sat there silent and gloomy under the fluorescent lights. They were all afraid of Whitey, all except Roy. Roy sipped his beer grimly. His eyes shone with their peculiar phosphorescence. His long asymmetrical body was draped against the bar. He didn't look at Whitey, but at the opposite wall where the booths were located. Once he said to me, "He's no more drunk than I am. He's just thirsty."

Whitey was standing in the middle of the bar, his fists doubled up, tears streaming down his face. "I'm no good," he said. "I'm no good. Can't anyone understand I don't know what I'm doing?"

The boys tried to get as far away from him as possible without attracting his attention.

Subway Slim, Mike's occasional partner, came in and ordered a beer. He was tall and bony, and his ugly face had a curiously inanimate look, as if made out of wood. Whitey slapped him on the back and I heard Slim say, "For Christ's sake, Whitey." There was more interchange I didn't hear. Somewhere along the line Whitey must have got his knife back from the bartender. He got behind Slim and suddenly pushed his hand against Slim's back. Slim fell forward against the bar, groaning. I saw Whitey walk to the front of the bar and look around. He closed his knife and slipped it into his pocket.

Roy said, "Let's go."

Whitey had disappeared and the bar was empty except for Mike, who was holding Slim up on one side. Frankie Dolan was on the other.

I heard next day from Frankie that Slim was okay. "The croaker at the hospital said the knife just missed a kidney."

Roy said, "The big slob. I can see a real muscle man, but a guy like that going around picking up dimes and quarters off the bar. I was ready for him. I was going to kick him in the belly first, then get one of those quart beer bottles from the case on the floor and break it over his sconce. With a big villain like that you've got to use strategy."

We were all barred from the Angle, which shortly afterwards changed its name to the Roxy Grill. . . .

One day Herman told me about a kilo of first-class New Orleans weed [marijuana] I could pick up for seventy dollars. Pushing weed looks good on paper, like fur farming or raising frogs. At seventy-five cents a stick, seventy sticks to the ounce, it sounded like money. I was convinced, and bought the weed.

Herman and I formed a partnership to push the weed. He located a Lesbian named Marian who lived in the Village and said she was a poetess. We kept the weed in Marian's apartment, turned her on for all she could use, and gave her fifty percent on sales. She knew a lot of tea heads. Another Lesbian moved in with her, and every time I went to Marian's apartment, there was this huge red-haired Lizzie watching me with her cold fish eyes full of stupid hate.

One day, the red-haired Lizzie opened the door and stood there, her face dead white and puffy with nembutal sleep. She shoved the package of weed at me. "Take this and get out," she said. "You're both mother fuckers." She was half asleep. Her voice was matter-of-fact as if referring to actual incest.

I said, "Tell Marian thanks for everything."

She slammed the door. The noise evidently woke her up. She opened the door again and began screaming with hysterical rage. We could still hear her out on the street.

Herman contacted other tea heads. They all gave us static. In practice, pushing weed is a headache. To begin with, weed is bulky. You need a full suitcase to realize any money. If the cops start kicking your door in, it's like being with a bale of alfalfa.

Tea heads are not like junkies. A junky hands you the money, takes his junk and cuts. But tea heads don't do things that way. They expect the peddler to light them up and sit around talking for half an hour to sell two dollars' worth of weed. If you come right to the point, they say you are a "bring down." In fact, a peddler should not come right out and say he is a peddler. No, he just scores for a few good "cats" and "chicks" because he is viperish. Everyone knows that he himself is the connection, but it is bad form to say so. God knows why. To me, tea heads are unfathomable.

There are a lot of trade secrets in the tea business, and tea heads guard these supposed secrets with imbecilic slyness. For example, tea must be cured, or it is green and rasps the throat. But ask a tea head how to cure weed and he will give you a sly, stupid look and come-on with some double-talk. Perhaps weed does affect the brain with constant use, or maybe tea heads are naturally silly.

The tea I had was green so I put it in a double boiler and set the boiler in the oven until the tea got the greenish-brown look it should have. This is the secret of curing tea, or at least one way to do it.

Tea heads are gregarious, they are sensitive, and they are paranoiac. If you get to be known as a "drag" or a "bring down," you can't do business with them. I soon found out I couldn't get along with these characters and I was glad to find someone to take the tea off my hands at cost. I decided right then I would never push any more tea.

In 1937, weed was placed under the Harrison Narcotics Act. Narcotics authorities claim it is a habit-forming drug, that its use is injurious to mind and body, and that it causes the people who use it to commit crimes. Here are the facts: Weed is positively not habit-forming. You can smoke weed for years and you will experience no discomfort if your supply is suddenly cut off. I have seen tea heads in jail and none of them showed withdrawal symptoms. I have smoked weed myself off and on for fifteen years, and never missed it when I ran out. There is less habit to weed than there is to tobacco. Weed does not harm the general health. In fact, most users claim it gives you an appetite and acts as a tonic to the system. I do not know of any other agent that gives as definite a boot to the appetite. I can smoke a stick of tea and enjoy a glass of California sherry and a hash house meal.

I once kicked a junk habit with weed. The second day off junk I sat down and ate a full meal. Ordinarily, I can't eat for eight days after kicking a habit.

Weed does not inspire anyone to commit crimes. I have never seen anyone get nasty under the influence of weed. Tea heads are a sociable lot. Too sociable for my liking. I cannot understand why the people who claim weed causes crimes do not follow through and demand the outlawing of alcohol. Every day, crimes are committed by drunks who would not have committed the crime sober.

There has been a lot said about the aphrodisiac effect of weed. For some reason, scientists dislike to admit that there is such a thing as an aphrodisiac, so most pharmacologists say there is "no evidence to support the popular idea that weed possesses aphrodisiac properties." I can say definitely that weed is an aphrodisiac and that sex is more enjoyable under the influence of weed than without it. Anyone who has used good weed will verify this statement.

You hear that people go insane from using weed. There is, in fact, a form of insanity caused by excessive use of weed. The condition is characterized by ideas of reference. The weed available in the U.S. is evidently not strong enough to blow your top on and weed psychosis is rare in the States. In the Near East, it is said to be common. Weed psychosis corresponds more or less to delirium tremens and quickly disappears when the drug is withdrawn. Someone who smokes a few cigarettes a day is no more likely to go insane than a man who takes a few cocktails before dinner is likely to come down with the D.T.'s.

One thing about weed. A man under the influence of weed

is completely unfit to drive a car. Weed disturbs your sense of time and consequently your sense of spatial relations. Once, in New Orleans, I had to pull over to the side of a road and wait until the weed wore off. I could not tell how far away anything was or when to turn or put on the brakes for an intersection.

from THE YAGE LETTERS

March 3
Hotel Nueva Regis, Bogota

Dear Al:

Bogota horrible as ever. I had my papers corrected with the aid of U.S. Embassy. Figure to sue the truss off PAA for fucking up the tourist card.

I have attached myself to an expedition—in a somewhat vague capacity to be sure—consisting of Doc Schindler, two Colombian Botanists, two English Broom Rot specialists from the Cocoa Commission, and will return to the Putumayo in convoy. Will write full account of trip when I get back to this town for the third time.

As Ever,
Bill

April 15
Hotel Nuevo Regis, Bogota

Dear Al:

Back in Bogota. I have a crate of Yage. I have taken it and know more or less how it is prepared. By the way you may see my picture in *Exposure.* I met a reporter going in as I was going out. Queer to be sure but about as appetizing as a hamper of dirty laundry. Not even after two months in the brush, my dear. This character is shaking down the South American continent for free food and transport, and discounts on everything he buys with a "We-got-like-two-kinds-of-publicity-favorable-and-unfavorable-which-do-you-want-Jack?" Routine. What a shameless mooch. But who am I to talk?

Flashback: Retraced my journey through Cali, Popayan and Pasto to Macoa. I was interested to note that Macoa dragged Schindler and the two Englishmen as much as it did me.

This trip I was treated like visiting royalty under the misapprehension I was a representative of the Texas Oil Company travelling incognito. (Free boat rides, free plane rides, free chow; eating in officers' mess, sleeping in the governor's house.)

The Texas Oil Company surveyed the area a few years ago, found no oil and pulled out. But everyone in the Putumayo believes the Texas Company will return. Like the second coming of Christ. The governor told me the Texas Company had taken two samples of oil 80 miles apart and it was the same oil, so there was a pool of the stuff 80 miles across under Macoa. I heard this same story in a back water area of East Texas where the oil company made a survey and found no oil and pulled out. Only in Texas the pool was 1000 miles across. The beat town psyche is joined the world over like the oil pool. You take a sample anywhere and it's the same shit. And the governor thinks they are about to build a railroad from Pasto to Macoa, and an airport. As a matter of fact the whole of Putumayo region is on the down grade. The rubber business is shot, the cocoa is eaten up with broom rot, no price on rotenone since the war, land is poor and there is no way to get produce out. The dawdling psychophrenia of small town boosters. Like I should think some day soon boys will start climbing in through the transom and tunneling under the door.

Several times when I was drunk I told some one, "Look. There is no oil here. That's why Texas pulled out. They won't ever come back. Understand?" But they couldn't believe it.

We went out to visit a German who owned a finca near Macoa. The British went looking for wild coca with an Indian guide. I asked the German about Yage.

"Sure," he said, "My Indians all use it." A half hour later I had 20 pounds of Yage vine. No trek through virgin jungle and some old white haired character saying, "I have been expecting you my son." A nice German 10 minutes from Macoa.

The German also made a date for me to take Yage with the local Brujo (at that time I had no idea how to prepare it.)

The medicine man was around 70 with a baby smooth face. There was a sly gentleness about him like an old time junkie. It was getting dark when I arrived at this dirt floor thatch shack for my Yage appointment. First thing he asked did I have a bottle. I brought a quart of aguardiente out of my knapsack and handed it to him. He took a long drink and passed the bottle to his assistant. I didn't take any as I wanted straight Yage kicks. The Brujo put the bottle beside him and squatted down by a bowl set on a tripod. Behind the bowl was a wood shrine with a picture of the Virgin, a crucifix, a wood idol, feathers and little packages tied with ribbons. The Brujo sat there a long time without moving. He took another long swig on the bottle. The women retired behind a bamboo partition and were not seen again. The Brujo began crooning over the bowl. I caught "Yage Pintar'" repeated over and over. He shook a little broom over a bowl and made a swishing noise. This is to whisk away evil spirits who might slip in the Yage. He took a drink and wiped his mouth and went on crooning. You can't hurry a Brujo. Finally he uncovered the bowl and dipped about an ounce more or less of black liquid which he handed me in a dirty red plastic cup. The liquid was oily and phosphorescent. I drank it straight down. Bitter foretaste of nausea. I handed the cup back and the medicine man and the assistant took a drink.

I sat there waiting for results and almost immediately had the impulse to say, "That wasn't enough. I need more." I have noticed this inexplicable impulse on the two occasions when I got an overdose of junk. Both times before the shot took effect I said, "This wasn't enough. I need more."

Roy told me about a man who came out of jail clean and nearly died in Roy's room. "He took the shot and right away said, 'That wasn't enough' and fell on his face out cold. I dragged him out in the hall and called an ambulance. He lived."

In two minutes a wave of dizziness swept over me and the hut began swimming. It was like going under ether, or when you are very drunk and lie down and the bed spins. Blue flashes passed in front of my eyes. The hut took on an archaic far-Pacific look with Easter Island heads carved in the support posts. The assistant was outside lurking there with the obvious intent to kill me. I was hit by violent, sudden nausea and rushed for the door hitting my shoulder against the door post. I felt the shock but no pain. I could hardly walk. No coordination. My feet were like blocks of wood. I vomited violently leaning against a tree and fell down on the ground in helpless misery. I felt numb as if I was covered with layers of cotton. I kept trying to break out of this numb dizziness. I was saying over and over, "All I want is out of here." An uncontrollable mechanical silliness took possession of me. Hebrephrenic meaningless repetitions. Larval beings passed before my eyes in a blue haze, each one giving an obscene, mocking squawk (I later identified this squawking as the croaking of frogs)—I must have vomited six times. I was on all fours convulsed with spasms of nausea. I could hear retching and groaning as if I was some one else. I was lying by a rock. Hours must have passed. The medicine man was standing over me. I looked at him for a long time before I believed he was really there saying, "Do you want to come into the house?" I said, "No," and he shrugged and went back inside.

My arms and legs began to twitch uncontrollably. I reached for my nembutals with numb wooden fingers. It must have taken me ten minutes to open the bottle and pour out five capsules. Mouth was dry and I chewed the nembutals down somehow. The twitching spasms subsided slowly and I felt a little better and went into the hut. The blue flashes still in front of my eyes. Lay down and covered myself with a blanket. I had a chill like malaria. Suddenly very drowsy. Next morning I was all right except for a feeling of lassitude and a slight back-log nausea. I paid off the Brujo and walked back to town.

We all went down to Puerto Assis that day. Schindler kept complaining the Putumayo had deteriorated since he was there ten years ago. "I never made a Botanical expedition like this before," he said. "All these farms and *people*. You have to walk miles to get to the jungle."

Schindler had two assistants to carry his luggage, cut down trees and press specimens. One of them was an Indian from the Vaupes region where the method of preparing Yage is different from the Putumayo Kofan method. In Putumayo the Indians cut the vines into 8 inch pieces using about five sections to a person. The pieces of vine are crushed with a rock and boiled with a double handful of leaves from another plant—tentatively identified as ololiqui—the mixture is boiled all day

with a small amount of water and reduced to about two ounces
of liquid.

In the Vaupes the bark is scraped off about three feet of
vine to form a large double handful of shavings. The bark is
soaked in a liter of cold water for several hours, and the liquid
strained off and taken over a period of an hour. No other plant
is added.

I decided to try some Yage prepared Vaupes method. The
Indian and I started scraping off bark with machetes (the inner
bark is the most active). This is white and sappy at first but
almost immediately turns red on exposure to air. The landlady's daughters watched us pointing and giggling. This is
strictly against Putumayo protocol for the preparation of Yage.
The Brujo of Macoa told me if a woman witnesses the preparation the Yage spoils on the spot and will poison anyone
who drinks it or at least drive him insane. The old women-
are-dirty-and-under-certain-circumstances-poisonous routine.
I figured this was a chance to test the woman pollution myth
once and for all with seven female creatures breathing down
my neck, poking sticks in the mixture fingering the Yage and
giggling.

The cold water infusion is a light red color. That night I
drank a quart of infusion over a period of one hour. Except
for blue flashes and slight nausea—though not to the point of
vomiting—the effect was similar to weed. Vividness of mental
imagery, aphrodisiac results, silliness and giggling. In this dos-
age there was no fear, no hallucinations or loss of control.
I figure this dose as about one third the dose that Brujo
gave me.

Next day we went on down to Puerto Espina where the
governor put us up in his house. That is we slung our hammocks
in empty rooms on the top floor. A coolness arose between
the Colombians and the British because the Colombians refused to get up for an early start, and the British complained
the Cocoa Commission was being sabotaged by a couple of
"lazy spics."

Every day we plan to get an early start for the jungle. About
11 o'clock the Colombians finish breakfast (the rest of us waiting around since 8) and begin looking for an incompetent
guide, preferably someone with a finca near town. About 1
we arrive at the finca and spend another hour eating lunch.

Then the Colombians say, "They tell us the jungle is far. About 3 hours. We don't have time to make it today." So we start back to town, the Colombians collecting a mess of plants along the way. "So long as they can collect any old weed they don't give a ruddy fuck," one of the Englishmen said to me after an expedition to the nearest finca.

There was supposed to be plane service out of Puerto Espina. Schindler and I were ready to go back to Bogota at this point, so there we sit in Puerto Espina waiting on this plane and the agent doesn't have a radio or any way of finding out when the plane gets there if it gets there and he says, "Sure as shit boys one of these days you'll look up and see the Catalina coming in over the river flashing in the sun like a silver fish."

So I says to Doc Schindler, "We could grow old and simple-minded sitting around playing dominoes before any sonofabitching plane sets down here and the river getting higher every day and how to get back up it with every motor in Puerto Espina broke?"

(The citizens who own these motors spend all the time fiddling with their motors and taking the motors apart and leaving out pieces they consider non-essential so the motors never run. The boat owners do have a certain Rube Goldberg ingenuity in patching up the stricken motor for one last more spurt— but this was a question of going up the river. Going down river you will get there eventually motor or no, but coming up river you gotta have some means of propulsion.)

Sure you think it's romantic at first but wait til you sit there five days onna sore ass sleeping in Indian shacks and eating yoka and same hunka nameless meat like the smoked pancreas of a two toed sloth and all night you hear them fiddle fucking with the motor—they got it bolted to the porch—"buuuuurt spluuuu . . . ut . . . spluuuu . . . ut," and you can't sleep hearing the motor start and die all night and then it starts to rain. Tomorrow the river will be higher.

So I says to Schindler, "Doc, I'll float down to the Atlantic before I start back up that fuckin river."

And he says, "Bill, I haven't been 15 years in this sonofabitch country and lost all my teeth in the service without picking up a few angles. Now down yonder in Puerto Leguisomo —they got like military planes and I happen to know the commandante is Latah." (Latah is a condition occurring in South East Asia. Otherwise normal, the Latah cannot help doing whatever anyone tells him to do once his attention has been attracted by touching him or calling his name.)

So Schindler went on down to Puerto Leguisomo while I stayed in Puerto Espina waiting to hitch a ride with the Cocoa Commission. Every day I saw that plane agent and he came on with the same bullshit. He showed me a horrible looking scar on the back of his neck. "Machete," he said. No doubt some exasperated citizen who went berserk waiting on one of his planes.

The Colombians and the Cocoa Commission went up the San Miguel and I was alone in Puerto Espina eating in the Commandante's house. God awful greasy food. Rice and fried platano cakes three times a day. I began slipping the platanos in my pocket and throwing them away later. The Commandante kept telling me how much Schindler liked this food— (Schindler is an old South American hand. He can really put down the bullshit)—did I like it? I would say, "Magnificent," my voice cracking. Not enough I have to eat his greasy food. I have to say I like it.

The Commandante knew from Schindler I had written a book on "marijuana." From time to time I saw suspicion seep into his dull liverish eyes.

"Marijuana degenerates the nervous system," he said looking up from a plate of platanos.

I told him he should take Vitamin B1 and he looked at me as if I had advocated the use of a narcotic.

The Governor regarded me with cold disfavor because one of the gasoline drums belonging to the Cocoa Commission had leaked on his porch. I was expecting momentarily to be evicted from the governmental mansion.

The Cocoa Commission and the Colombians came back from the San Miguel in a condition of final estrangement. It seems the Colombians had found a finca and spent three days there lolling about in their pajamas. In the absence of Schindler I was the only buffer between the two factions and suspect by both parties of secretly belonging to the other (I had borrowed a shot gun from one of the Colombians and was riding in the Cocoa Commission boat).

We went on down the river to Puerto Leguisomo where the Commandante put us up in a gun boat anchored in the Putumayo. There were no guns on it actually. I think it was the hospital ship.

The ship was dirty and rusty. The water system did not function and the W.C. was in unspeakable condition. The Colombians run a mighty loose ship. It wouldn't surprise me to see someone shit on the deck and wipe his ass with the flag. (This derives from dream that came to me in 17th century English. "The English and French delegates did shit on the floor, and tearing the Treaty of Seville into strips with such merriment did wipe their backsides with it, seeing which the Spanish delegate withdrew from the conference.")

Puerto Leguisomo is named for a soldier who distinguished himself in the Peruvian War in 1940. I asked one of the Colombians about it and he nodded, "Yes, Leguisomo was a soldier who did something in the war."

"What did he do?"

"Well, he did *something.*"

The place looks like it was left over from a receding flood. Rusty abandoned machinery scattered here and there. Swamps in the middle of town. Unlighted streets you sink up to your knees in.

There are five whores in town sitting out in front of blue walled cantinas. The young kids of Puerto Leguisomo cluster around the whores with the immobile concentration of tom cats. The whores sit there in the muggy night under one naked electric bulb in the blare of juke box music, waiting.

Inquiring in the environs of Puerto Leguisomo I found the use of Yage common among both Indians and whites. Most everybody grows it in his backyard.

After a week in Leguisomo I got a plane to Villavencenio, and from there back to Bogota by bus.

So here I am back in Bogota. No money waiting for me (check apparently stolen), I am reduced to the shoddy expedient of stealing my drinking alcohol from the university laboratory placed at disposal of the visiting scientist.

Extracting Yage alcoloids from the vine, a relatively simple process according to directions provided by the Institute. My experiments with extracted Yage have not been conclusive. I do not get blue flashes or any pronounced sharpening of mental imagery. Have noticed aphrodisiac effects. The extract makes me sleepy whereas the fresh vine is a stimulant and in overdose convulsive poison.

Every night I go into a cafe and order a bottle of pepsi-cola and pour in my lab alcohol. The population of Bogota lives in cafes. There are any number of these and always full. Standard dress for Bogota cafe society is a gabardine trench coat and of course suit and tie. A South American's ass may be sticking out of his pants but he will still have a tie.

Bogota is essentially a small town, everybody worrying about his clothes and looking as if he would describe his job as responsible. I was sitting in one of these white collar cafes when a boy in a filthy light gray suit, but still clinging to a frayed tie asked me if I spoke English.

I said, "Fluently," and he sat down at the table. A former employee of the Texas Company. Obviously queer, blond, German looking, European manner. We went to several cafes. He pointed people out to me saying, "He doesn't want to know me any more now that I am without work."

These people, correctly dressed and careful in manner, did in fact look away and in some cases call for the bill and leave. I don't know how the boy could have looked any less queer in a $200 suit.

One night I was sitting in a Liberal cafe when three civilian Conservative gun men came in yelling "Viva los Conservadores" hoping to provoke somebody so they could shoot him. There was a middle aged man of the type who features a loud mouth. The others sat back and let him do the yelling. The other two were youngish, ward heelers, corner boys, border-line hoodlums. Narrow shoulders, ferret faces and smooth, tight, red skin, bad teeth. It was almost too pat. The two hoodlums looked a little hang dog and ashamed of themselves like the young man in the limerick who said, "I'll admit I'm a bit of a shit."

Everybody paid and walked out leaving the loud mouthed character yelling "Viva El Partido Conservador" to an empty house.

As Ever,
Bill

May 5
930 Jose Leal, Lima

Dear Allen:

This finds me in Lima which is enough like Mexico City to make me homesick. Mexico is home to me and I can't go there. Got a letter from my lawyer—I am sentenced in absentia. I feel like a Roman exiled from Rome. Plan to hit Peru jungle for additional Yage material. Will spend a few weeks digging Lima.

Went through Ecuador fast as possible. What an awful place it is. Small country national inferiority complex in most advanced stage.

Ecuadorian Miscellanea: *Esmeraldas* hot and wet as a turkish bath and vultures eating a dead pig in the main drag and everywhere you look there is a Nigra scratching his balls. The inevitable Turk who buys and sells everything. He tried to cheat me on every purchase and I spent an hour arguing with this bastard. The Greek shipping agent with his dirty silk shirt and no shoes and his dirty ship that left Esmeraldas seven hours late.

On the boat I talked to a man who knows the Ecuador jungle like his own prick. It seems jungle traders periodically raid the Auca (a tribe of hostile Indians. Shell lost about twenty employees to Auca in two years) and carry off women they keep penned up for purposes of sex. Sounds interesting. Maybe I could capture an Auca boy.

I have precise instructions for Auca raiding. It's quite simple. You cover both exits of Auca house and shoot everybody you don't wanna fuck.

Arriving in Manta a shabby man in a sweater started opening my bags. I thought he was a brazen thief and gave him a shove. Turns out he was customs inspector.

The boat gave out with a broken propeller at Las Playas half way between Manta and Guayaquil. I rode ashore on a balsa raft. Arrested on the beach suspect to have floated up from Peru on the Humboldt Current with a young boy and a tooth brush (I travel light, only the essentials) so we are hauled before an old dried up fuck, the withered face of cancerous control. The kid with me don't have paper one. The cops keep saying plaintively:

"But don't you have any papers *at all?*"

I talked us both out in half an hour using the "We-got-like-two-types-publicity-favorable-and-unfavorable-which-do-you-want?" routine. I am down as writer on tourist card.

Guayaquil. Every morning a swelling cry goes up from the kids who sell Luckies in the street—"A ver Luckies," "Look here Luckies"—will they still be saying "A ver Luckies" a hundred years from now? Nightmare fear of stasis. Horror of being finally *stuck* in this place. This fear has followed me all over South America. A horrible sick feeling of final desolation.

"La Asia," a Chinese restaurant in Guayaquil, looks like 1890 whorehouse opium den. Holes eaten by termites in the floor, dirty tasselled pink lamps. A rotting teak-wood balcony.

Ecuador is really on the skids. Let Peru take over and civilize the place so a man can score for the amenities. I never yet lay a boy in Ecuador and you can't buy any form of junk.

As Ever,
W. Lee

P.S. Met a Pocho cab driver—the Pocho is type found in Mexico who dislikes Mexico and Mexicans. This cab driver told me he was Peruvian but he couldn't stand Peruvians. In Ecuador and Colombia no one will admit anything is wrong with his jerk water country. Like small town citizens in U.S. I recall an army officer in Puerto Leguisomo telling me:

"Ninety percent of the people who come to Colombia never leave."

He meant, presumably, they were overcome by the charms of the place. I belong to the ten percent who never come back.

As Ever,
Bill

from NAKED LUNCH

I can feel the heat closing in, feel them out there making their moves, setting up their devil doll stool pigeons, crooning over my spoon and dropper I throw away at Washington Square Station, vault a turnstile and two flights down the iron stairs, catch an uptown A train. . . . Young, good looking, crew cut, Ivy League, advertising exec type fruit holds the door back for me. I am evidently his idea of a character. You know the type comes on with bartenders and cab drivers, talking about right hooks and the Dodgers, call the counterman in Nedick's by his first name. A real asshole. And right on time this narcotics dick in a white trench coat (imagine tailing somebody in a white trench coat—trying to pass as a fag I guess) hit the platform. I can hear the way he would say it holding my outfit in his left hand, right hand on his piece: "I think you dropped something, fella."

But the subway is moving.

"So long flatfoot!" I yell, giving the fruit his B production. I look into the fruit's eyes, take in the white teeth, the Florida tan, the two hundred dollar sharkskin suit, the button-down Brooks Brothers shirt and carrying *The News* as a prop. "Only thing I read is Little Abner."

A square wants to come on hip. . . . Talks about "pod" [marijuana], and smoke it now and then, and keeps some around to offer the fast Hollywood types.

"Thanks, kid," I say, "I can see you're one of our own." His face lights up like a pinball machine, with stupid, pink effect.

"Grassed on me he did," I said morosely. (Note: Grass is English thief slang for inform.) I drew closer and laid my dirty junky fingers on his sharkskin sleeve. "And us blood brothers in the same dirty needle. I can tell you in confidence he is due for a hot shot." (Note: This is a cap of poison junk sold to addict for liquidation purposes. Often given to informers. Usually the hot shot is strychnine since it tastes and looks like junk.)

"Ever see a hot shot hit, kid? I saw the Gimp catch one in Philly. We rigged his room with a one-way whorehouse mirror and charged a sawski to watch it. He never got the needle out of his arm. They don't if the shot is right. That's the way they find them, dropper full of clotted blood hanging out of a blue arm. The look in his eyes when it hit—Kid, it was tasty. . . .

"Recollect when I am traveling with the Vigilante, best Shake Man in the industry. Out in Chi. . . . We is working the fags in Lincoln Park. So one night the Vigilante turns up for work in cowboy boots and a black vest with a hunka tin on it and a lariat slung over his shoulder.

"So I says: 'What's with you? You wig already?'

"He just looks at me and says: 'Fill your hand stranger' and hauls out an old rusty six shooter and I take off across Lincoln Park, bullets cutting all around me. And he hangs three fags before the fuzz nail him. I mean the Vigilante earned his moniker. . . .

"Ever notice how many expressions carry over from queers to con men? Like 'raise,' letting someone know you are in the same line?

" 'Get her!'

" 'Get the Paregoric Kid giving that mark the build up!'

" 'Eager Beaver wooing him much too fast.'

"The Shoe Store Kid (he got that moniker shaking down fetishists in shoe stores) say: 'Give it to a mark with K.Y. and he will come back moaning for more.' And when the Kid spots a mark he begin to breathe heavy. His face swells and his lips turn purple like an Eskimo in heat. Then slow, slow he comes on the mark, feeling for him, palpating him with fingers of rotten ectoplasm.

"The Rube has a sincere little boy look, burns through him like blue neon. That one stepped right off a *Saturday Evening Post* cover with a string of bullheads, and preserved himself in junk. His marks never beef and the Bunko people are really carrying a needle for the Rube. One day Little Boy Blue starts to slip, and what crawls out would make an ambulance attendant puke. The Rube flips in the end, running through empty automats and subway stations, screaming: 'Come back, kid!! Come back!!' and follows his boy right into the East River, down through condoms and orange peels, mosaic of floating newspapers, down into the silent black ooze with gangsters in concrete, and pistols pounded flat to avoid the probing finger of prurient ballistic experts."

And the fruit is thinking: "What a character!! Wait till I tell the boys in Clark's about this one." He's a character collector, would stand still for Joe Gould's seagull act. So I put it on him for a sawski and make a meet to sell him some "pod" as he calls it, thinking, "I'll catnip the jerk." (Note: Catnip smells like marijuana when it burns. Frequently passed on the incautious or uninstructed.)

"Well," I said, tapping my arm, "duty calls. As one judge said to another: 'Be just and if you can't be just, be arbitrary.' "

I cut into the automat and there is Bill Gains huddled in someone else's overcoat looking like a 1910 banker with paresis, and Old Bart, shabby and inconspicuous, dunking pound cake with his dirty fingers, shiny over the dirt.

I had some uptown customers Bill took care of, and Bart knew a few old relics from hop smoking times, spectral janitors, grey as ashes, phantom porters sweeping out dusty halls with a slow old man's hand, coughing and spitting in the junk-sick dawn, retired asthmatic fences in theatrical hotels, Pantopon Rose the old madam from Peoria, stoical Chinese waiters never show sickness. Bart sought them out with his old junky walk, patient and cautious and slow, dropped into their bloodless hands a few hours of warmth.

I made the round with him once for kicks. You know how old people lose all shame about eating, and it makes you puke to watch them? Old junkies are the same about junk. They gibber and squeal at the sight of it. The spit hangs off their chin, and their stomach rumbles and all their guts grind in peristalsis while they cook up, dissolving the body's decent skin, you expect any moment a great blob of protoplasm will flop right out and surround the junk. Really disgust you to see it.

"Well, my boys will be like that one day," I thought philosophically. "Isn't life peculiar?"

So back downtown by the Sheridan Square Station in case the dick is lurking in a broom closet.

Like I say it couldn't last. I knew they were out there powowing and making their evil fuzz magic, putting dolls of me in Leavenworth. "No use sticking needles in that one, Mike."

I hear they got Chapin with a doll. This old eunuch dick just sat in the precinct basement hanging a doll of him day and night, year in year out. And when Chapin hanged in Connecticut, they find this old creep with his neck broken.

"He fell downstairs," they say. You know the old cop bullshit.

Junk is surrounded by magic and taboos, curses and amulets.

I could find my Mexico City connection by radar. "Not this street, the next, right . . . now left. Now right again," and there he is, toothless old woman face and cancelled eyes.

I know this one pusher walks around humming a tune and everybody he passes takes it up. He is so grey and spectral and anonymous they don't see him and think it is their own mind humming the tune. So the customers come in on *Smiles,* or *I'm in the Mood for Love,* or *They Say We're Too Young to Go Steady,* or whatever the song is for that day. Sometime you can see maybe fifty ratty-looking junkies squealing sick, running along behind a boy with a harmonica, and there is The Man on a cane seat throwing bread to the swans, a fat queen drag walking his Afghan hound through the East Fifties, an old wino pissing against an El post, a radical Jewish student giving out leaflets in Washington Square, a tree surgeon, an exterminator, an advertising fruit in Nedick's where he calls the counterman by his first name. The world network of junkies, tuned on a cord of rancid jissom, tying up in furnished rooms, shivering in the junk-sick morning. (Old Pete men suck the black smoke in the Chink laundry back room and Melancholy Baby dies from an overdose of time or cold turkey withdrawal of breath.) In Yemen, Paris, New Orleans, Mexico City and Istanbul—shivering under the air hammers and the steam shovels, shrieked junky curses at one another neither of us heard, and The Man leaned out of a passing steam roller and I coped in a bucket of tar. (Note: Istanbul is being torn down and rebuilt, especially shabby junk quarters. Istanbul has more heroin junkies than NYC.) The living and the dead, in sickness or on the nod, hooked or kicked or hooked again, come in on the junk beam and the Connection is eating Chop Suey on Dolores Street, Mexico D.F., dunking pound cake in the automat, chased up Exchange Place by a baying pack of People. (Note: People is New Orleans slang for narcotic fuzz.)

The old Chinaman dips river water into a rusty tin can, washes down a yen pox hard and black as a cinder. (Note: Yen pox is the ash of smoked opium.)

Well, the fuzz has my spoon and dropper, and I know they are coming in on my frequency led by this blind pigeon known as Willy the Disk. Willy has a round, disk mouth lined with sensitive, erectile black hairs. He is blind from shooting in the eyeball, his nose and palate eaten away sniffing H, his body a mass of scar tissue hard and dry as wood. He can only eat the shit now with that mouth, sometimes sways out on a long tube of ectoplasm, feeling for the silent frequency of junk. He follows my trail all over the city into rooms I move out already, and the fuzz walks in some newlyweds from Sioux Falls.

"All right, Lee!! Come out from behind that strap-on! We know you" and pull the man's prick off straightaway.

Now Willy is getting hot and you can hear him always out there in darkness (he only functions at night) whimpering, and feel the terrible urgency of that blind, seeking mouth. When they move in for the bust, Willy goes all out of control, and his mouth eats a hole right through the door. If the cops weren't there to restrain him with a stock probe, he would suck the juice right out of every junky he ran down.

I knew, and everybody else knew they had the Disk on me. And if my kid customers ever hit the stand: "He force me to commit all kinda awful sex acts in return for junk" I could kiss the street good-bye.

So we stock up on H, buy a second-hand Studebaker, and start West.

The Vigilante copped out as a schizo possession case:

"I was standing outside myself trying to stop those hangings with ghost fingers. . . . I am a ghost wanting what every ghost wants—a body—after the Long Time moving through odorless alleys of space where no life is only the colorless no smell of death. . . . Nobody can breathe and smell it through pink convolutions of gristle laced with crystal snot, time shit and black blood filters of flesh."

He stood there in elongated court room shadow, his face torn like a broken film by lusts and hungers of larval organs stirring in the tentative ectoplasmic flesh of junk kick (ten days on ice at time of the First Hearing) flesh that fades at the first silent touch of junk.

I saw it happen. Ten pounds lost in ten minutes standing with the syringe in one hand holding his pants up with the other, his abdicated flesh burning in a cold yellow halo, there in the New York hotel room . . . night table litter of candy boxes, cigarette butts cascading out of three ashtrays, mosaic of sleepless nights and sudden food needs of the kicking addict nursing his baby flesh. . . .

The Vigilante is prosecuted in Federal Court under a lynch bill and winds up in a Federal Nut House specially designed for the containment of ghosts: precise, prosaic impact of objects . . . washstand . . . door . . . toilet . . . bars . . . there they are . . . this is it . . . all lines cut . . . nothing beyond . . . Dead End . . . And the Dead End in every face. . . .

The physical changes were slow at first, then jumped forward in black klunks, falling through his slack tissue, washing away the human lines. . . . In his place of total darkness mouth and eyes are one organ that leaps forward to snap with transparent teeth . . . but no organ is constant as regards either function or position . . . sex organs sprout anywhere . . . rectums open, defecate and close . . . the entire organism changes color and consistency in split-second adjustments. . . .

The Rube is a social liability with his attacks as he calls them. The Mark Inside was coming up on him and that's a rumble nobody can cool; outside Philly he jumps out to con a prowl car and the fuzz takes one look at his face and bust all of us.

Seventy-two hours and five sick junkies in the cell with us. Now not wishing to break out my stash in front of these hungry coolies, it takes maneuvering and laying of gold on the turnkey before we are in a separate cell.

Provident junkies, known as squirrels, keep stashes against a bust. Every time I take a shot I let a few drops fall into my vest pocket, the lining is stiff with stuff. I had a plastic dropper in my shoe and a safety-pin stuck in my belt. You know how this pin and dropper routine is put down: "She seized a safety pin caked with blood and rust, gouged a great hole in her leg which seemed to hang open like an obscene, festering mouth waiting for unspeakable congress with the dropper which she now plunged out of sight into the gaping wound. But her hideous galvanized need (hunger of insects in dry places) has broken the dropper off deep in the flesh of her ravaged thigh (looking rather like a poster on soil erosion). But what does she care? She does not even bother to remove the splintered glass, looking down at her bloody haunch with the cold blank eyes of a meat trader. What does she care for the atom bomb, the bed bugs, the cancer rent, Friendly Finance waiting to repossess her delinquent flesh. . . . Sweet dreams, Pantopon Rose."

The real scene you pinch up some leg flesh and make a quick stab hole with a pin. Then fit the dropper *over, not in* the hole and feed the solution slow and careful so it doesn't squirt out the sides. . . . When I grabbed the Rube's thigh the flesh came up like wax and stayed there, and a slow drop of pus oozed out the hole. And I never touched a living body cold as the Rube there in Philly. . . .

I decided to lop him off if it meant a smother party. (This is a rural English custom designed to eliminate aged and bed-fast dependents. A family so afflicted throws a "smother party" where the guests pile mattresses on the old liability, climb up on top of the mattresses and lush themselves out.) The Rube is a drag on the industry and should be led out into the skid rows of the world. (This is an African practice. Official known as the "Leader Out" has the function of taking old characters out into the jungle and leaving them there.)

The Rube's attacks become an habitual condition. Cops, doormen, dogs, secretaries snarl at his approach. The blond God has fallen to untouchable vileness. Con men don't change, they break, shatter—explosions of matter in cold interstellar space, drift away in cosmic dust, leave the empty body behind. Hustlers of the world, there is one Mark you cannot beat: The Mark Inside. . . .

I left the Rube standing on a corner, red brick slums to the sky, under a steady rain of soot. "Going to hit this croaker I know. Right back with that good pure drugstore M. . . . No, you wait here—don't want him to rumble you." No matter how long, Rube, wait for me right on that corner. Good-bye, Rube, good-bye kid. . . . Where do they go when they walk out and leave the body behind?

Chicago: invisible hierarchy of decorticated wops, smell of atrophied gangsters, earthbound ghost hits you at North and Halstead, Cicero, Lincoln Park, panhandler of dreams, past invading the present, rancid magic of slot machines and roadhouses.

Into the Interior: a vast subdivision, antennae of television to the meaningless sky. In lifeproof houses they hover over the young, sop up a little of what they shut out. Only the young bring anything in, and they are not young very long. (Through the bars of East St. Louis lies the dead frontier, riverboat days.) Illinois and Missouri, miasma of mound-building peoples, groveling worship of the Food Source, cruel and ugly festivals, dead-end horror of the Centipede God reaches from Moundville to the lunar deserts of coastal Peru.

America is not a young land: it is old and dirty and evil before the settlers, before the Indians. The evil is there waiting.

And always cops: smooth college-trained state cops, practiced, apologetic patter, electronic eyes weigh your car and luggage, clothes and face; snarling big city dicks, soft-spoken country sheriffs with something black and menacing in old eyes color of a faded grey flannel shirt. . . .

And always car trouble: in St. Louis traded the 1942 Studebaker in (it has a built-in engineering flaw like the Rube) on an old Packard limousine heated up and barely made Kansas City, and bought a Ford turned out to be an oil burner, packed it in on a jeep we push too hard (they are no good for highway driving)—and burn something out inside, rattling around, went back to the old Ford V-8. Can't beat that engine for getting there, oil burner or no.

And the U.S. drag closes around us like no other drag in the world, worse than the Andes, high mountain towns, cold wind down from postcard mountains, thin air like death in the throat, river towns of Ecuador, malaria grey as junk under black Stetson, muzzle loading shotguns, vultures pecking through the mud streets—and what hits you when you get off the Malmo Ferry in (no juice tax on the ferry) Sweden knocks all that cheap, tax free juice right out of you and brings you all the way down: averted eyes and the cemetery in the middle of town (every town in Sweden seems to be built around a cemetery), and nothing to do in the afternoon, not a bar not a movie and I blasted my last stick of Tangier tea and I said, "K.E. let's get right back on that ferry."

But there is no drag like U.S. drag. You can't see it, you don't know where it comes from. Take one of those cocktail lounges at the end of a subdivision street—every block of houses has its own bar and drugstore and market and liquorstore. You walk in and it hits you. But where does it come from?

Not the bartender, not the customers, nor the cream-colored plastic rounding the bar stools, nor the dim neon. Not even the TV.

And our habits build up with the drag, like cocaine will build you up staying ahead of the C bring-down. And the junk was running low. So there we are in this no-horse town strictly from cough syrup. And vomited up the syrup and drove on and on, cold spring wind whistling through that old heap around our shivering sick sweating bodies and the cold you always come down with when the junk runs out of you. . . . On through the peeled landscape, dead armadillos in the road and vultures over the swamp and cypress stumps. Motels with beaverboard walls, gas heater, thin pink blankets.

Itinerant short con and carny hyp men have burned down the croakers of Texas. . . .

And no one in his right mind would hit a Louisiana croaker. State Junk Law.

Came at last to Houston where I know a druggist. I haven't been there in five years but he looks up and makes me with one quick look and just nods and says: "Wait over at the counter. . . ."

So I sit down and drink a cup of coffee and after a while he comes and sits beside me and says, "What do you want?"

"A quart of PG and a hundred nembies."

He nods, "Come back in half an hour."

So when I come back he hands me a package and says, "That's fifteen dollars. . . . Be careful."

Shooting PG is a terrible hassle, you have to burn out the alcohol first, then freeze out the camphor and draw this brown liquid off with a dropper—have to shoot it in the vein or you get an abscess, and usually end up with an abscess no matter where you shoot it. Best deal is to drink it with goof balls. . . . So we pour it in a Pernod bottle and start for New Orleans past iridescent lakes and orange gas flares, and swamps and garbage heaps, alligators crawling around in broken bottles and tin cans, neon arabesques of motels, marooned pimps scream obscenities at passing cars from islands of rubbish. . . .

New Orleans is a dead museum. We walk around Exchange Place breathing PG and find The Man right away. It's a small place and the fuzz always knows who is pushing so he figures what the hell does it matter and sells to anybody. We stock up on H and backtrack for Mexico.

Back through Lake Charles and the dead slot-machine country, south end of Texas, nigger-killing sheriffs look us over and check the car papers. Something falls off you when you cross the border into Mexico, and suddenly the landscape hits you straight with nothing between you and it, desert and mountains and vultures; little wheeling specks and others so close you can hear wings cut the air (a dry husking sound), and when they spot something they pour out of the blue sky, that shattering bloody blue sky of Mexico, down in a black funnel. . . . Drove all night, came at dawn to a warm misty place, barking dogs and the sound of running water.

DEPOSITION: TESTIMONY
CONCERNING A SICKNESS

I awoke from The Sickness at the age of forty-five, calm and sane, and in reasonably good health except for a weakened liver and the look of borrowed flesh common to all who survive The Sickness. . . . Most survivors do not remember the delirium in detail. I apparently took detailed notes on sickness and delirium. I have no precise memory of writing the notes which have now been published under the title *Naked Lunch*. The title was suggested by Jack Kerouac. I did not understand what the title meant until my recent recovery. The title means exactly what the words say: NAKED Lunch—a frozen moment when everyone sees what is on the end of every fork.

The Sickness is drug addiction and I was an addict for fifteen years. When I say addict I mean an addict to *junk* (generic term for opium and/or derivatives including all synthetics from demerol to palfium). I have used junk in many forms: morphine, heroin, dilaudid, eukodal, pantapon, diocodid, diosane, opium, demerol, dolophine, palfium. I have smoked junk, eaten it, sniffed it, injected it in vein-skin-muscle, inserted it in rectal suppositories. The needle is not important. Whether you sniff it smoke it eat it or shove it up your ass the result is the same: addiction. When I speak of drug addiction I do not refer to keif, marijuana or any preparation of hashish, mescaline, Bannisteria Caapi, LSD6, Sacred Mushrooms or any other drug of the hallucinogen group. . . . There is no evidence that the use of any hallucinogen results in physical dependence. The action of these drugs is physiologically opposite to the action of junk. A lamentable confusion between the two classes of drugs has arisen owing to the zeal of the U.S. and other narcotic departments.

I have seen the exact manner in which the junk virus operates through fifteen years of addiction. The pyramid of junk, one level eating the level below (it is no accident that junk higher-ups are always fat and the addict in the street is always thin) right up to the top or tops since there are many junk pyramids feeding on peoples of the world and all built on basic principles of monopoly:

1. Never give anything away for nothing.
2. Never give more than you have to give (always catch the buyer hungry and always make him wait).
3. Always take everything back if you possibly can.

The Pusher always gets it all back. The addict needs more and more junk to maintain a human form . . . buy off the Monkey.

Junk is the mold of monopoly and possession. The addict stands by while his junk legs carry him straight in on the junk beam to relapse. Junk is quantitative and accurately measurable. The more junk you use the less you have and the more you have the more you use. All the hallucinogen drugs are considered sacred by those who use them—there are Peyote Cults and Bannisteria Cults, Hashish Cults and Mushroom Cults—"the Sacred Mushrooms of Mexico enable a man to see God"—but no one ever suggested that junk is sacred. There are no opium cults. Opium is profane and quantitative like money. I have heard that there was once a beneficent non-habit-forming junk in India. It was called *soma* and is pictured as a beautiful blue tide. If *soma* ever existed the Pusher was there to bottle it and monopolize it and sell it and it turned into plain old time JUNK.

Junk is the ideal product . . . the ultimate merchandise. No sales talk necessary. The client will crawl through a sewer and beg to buy. . . . The junk merchant does not sell his product to the consumer, he sells the consumer to his product. He does not improve and simplify his merchandise. He degrades and simplifies the client. He pays his staff in junk.

Junk yields a basic formula of "evil" virus: *The Algebra of Need.* The face of "evil" is always the face of total need. A dope fiend is a man in total need of dope. Beyond a certain frequency need knows absolutely no limit or control. In the words of total need: *"Wouldn't you?"* Yes you would. You would lie, cheat, inform on your friends, steal, do *anything* to satisfy total need. Because you would be in a state of total sickness, total possession, and not in a position to act in any other way. Dope fiends are sick people who cannot act other than they do. A rabid dog cannot choose but bite. Assuming a self-righteous position is nothing to the purpose unless your purpose be to keep the junk virus in operation. And junk is a big industry. I recall talking to an American who worked for the Aftosa Commission in Mexico. Six hundred a month plus expense account:

"How long will the epidemic last?" I enquired.

"As long as we can keep it going. . . . And yes . . . maybe the aftosa will break out in South America," he said dreamily.

If you wish to alter or annihilate a pyramid of numbers in a serial relation, you alter or remove the bottom number. If we wish to annihilate the junk pyramid, we must start with the bottom of the pyramid: *the Addict in the Street,* and stop tilting quixotically for the "higher-ups" so called, all of whom are immediately replaceable. *The addict in the street who must have junk to live is the one irreplaceable factor in the junk equation.* When there are no more addicts to buy junk there will be no junk traffic. As long as junk need exists, someone will service it.

Addicts can be cured or quarantined—that is allowed a morphine ration under minimal supervision like typhoid carriers. When this is done, junk pyramids of the world will collapse. So far as I know, England is the only country to apply this method to the junk problem. They have about five hundred quarantined addicts in the U.K. In another generation when the quarantined addicts die off and pain killers operating on a non-junk principle are discovered, the junk virus will be like smallpox, a closed chapter—a medical curiosity.

The vaccine that can relegate the junk virus to a land-locked past is in existence. This vaccine is the Apomorphine Treatment discovered by an English doctor whose name I must withhold pending his permission to use it and to quote from his book covering thirty years of apomorphine treatment of addicts and alcoholics. The compound apomorphine is formed by boiling morphine with hydrochloric acid. It was discovered years before it was used to treat addicts. For many years the only use for apomorphine which has no narcotic or pain-killing properties was as an emetic to induce vomiting in cases of poisoning. It acts directly on the vomiting center in the back brain.

I found this vaccine at the end of the junk line. I lived in one room in the Native Quarter of Tangier. I had not taken a bath in a year nor changed my clothes or removed them except to stick a needle every hour in the fibrous grey wooden flesh of terminal addiction. I never cleaned or dusted the room. Empty ampule boxes and garbage piled to the ceiling. Light and water long since turned off for non-payment. I did absolutely nothing. I could look at the end of my shoe for eight hours. I was only roused to action when the hourglass of junk ran out. If a friend came to visit—and they rarely did since who or what was left to visit—I sat there not caring that he had entered my field of vision—a grey screen always blanker and fainter—and not caring when he walked out of it. If he had died on the spot I would have sat there looking at my shoe waiting to go through his pockets. Wouldn't you? Because I never had enough junk—no one ever does. Thirty grains of morphine a day and it still was not enough. And long waits in front of the drugstore. Delay is a rule in the junk business. The Man is never on time. This is no accident. There are no accidents in the junk world. The addict is taught again and again exactly what will happen if he does not score for his junk ration. Get up that money or else. And suddenly my habit began to jump and jump. Forty, sixty grains a day. And it still was not enough. And I could not pay.

I stood there with my last check in my hand and realized

that it was my last check. I took the next plane for London.

The doctor explained to me that apomorphine acts on the back brain to regulate the metabolism and normalize the blood stream in such a way that the enzyme system of addiction is destroyed over a period of four or five days. Once the back brain is regulated apomorphine can be discontinued and only used in case of relapse. (No one would take apomorphine for kicks. *Not one case of addiction to apomorphine has ever been recorded.*) I agreed to undergo treatment and entered a nursing home. For the first twenty-four hours I was literally insane and paranoid as many addicts are in severe withdrawal. This delirium was dispersed by twenty-four hours of intensive apomorphine treatment. The doctor showed me the chart. I had received minute amounts of morphine that could not possibly account for my lack of the more severe withdrawal symptoms such as leg and stomach cramps, fever and my own special symptom, The Cold Burn, like a vast hive covering the body and rubbed with menthol. Every addict has his own special symptom that cracks all control. There was a missing factor in the withdrawal equation—that factor could only be apomorphine.

I saw the apomorphine treatment really work. Eight days later I left the nursing home eating and sleeping normally. I remained completely off junk for two full years—a twelve year record. I did relapse for some months as a result of pain and illness. Another apomorphine cure has kept me off junk through this writing.

The apomorphine cure is qualitatively different from other methods of cure. I have tried them all. Short reduction, slow reduction, cortisone, antihistamines, tranquilizers, sleeping cures, tolserol, reserpine. None of these cures lasted beyond the first opportunity to relapse. I can say definitely that I was never *metabolically* cured until I took the apomorphine cure. The overwhelming relapse statistics from the Lexington Narcotic Hospital have led many doctors to say that addiction is not curable. They use a dolophine reduction cure at Lexington and have never tried apomorphine so far as I know. In fact, this method of treatment has been largely neglected. No research has been done with variations of the apomorphine formula or with synthetics. No doubt substances fifty times stronger than apomorphine could be developed and the side effect of vomiting eliminated.

Apomorphine is a metabolic and psychic regulator that can be discontinued as soon as it has done its work. The world is deluged with tranquilizers and energizers but this unique regulator has not received attention. No research has been done by any of the large pharmaceutical companies. I suggest that research with variations of apomorphine and synthesis of it will open a new medical frontier extending far beyond the problem of addiction.

The smallpox vaccine was opposed by a vociferous lunatic group of anti-vaccinationists. No doubt a scream of protest will go up from interested or unbalanced individuals as the junk virus is shot out from under them. Junk is big business; there are always cranks and operators. They must not be allowed to interfere with the essential work of inoculation treatment and quarantine. *The junk virus is public health problem number one of the world today.*

Since *Naked Lunch* treats this health problem, it is necessarily brutal, obscene and disgusting. Sickness is often repulsive details not for weak stomachs.

Certain passages in the book that have been called pornographic were written as a tract against Capital Punishment in the manner of Jonathan Swift's *Modest Proposal.* These sections are intended to reveal capital punishment as the obscene, barbaric and disgusting anachronism that it is. As always the lunch is naked. If civilized countries want to return to Druid Hanging Rites in the Sacred Grove or to drink blood with the Aztecs and feed their Gods with blood of human sacrifice, let them see what they actually eat and drink. Let them see what is on the end of that long newspaper spoon.

I have almost completed a sequel to *Naked Lunch.* A mathematical extension of the Algebra of Need beyond the junk virus. Because there are many forms of addiction I think that they all obey basic laws. In the words of Heiderberg: "This may not be the best of all possible universes but it may well prove to be one of the simplest." If man can *see.*

Post Script . . . Wouldn't You?

And speaking *Personally* and if a man speaks any other way we might as well start looking for his Protoplasm Daddy or Mother Cell. . . . *I Don't Want To Hear Any More Tired Old Junk Talk And Junk Con.* . . . The same things said a million times and more and there is no point in saying anything because *NOTHING Ever Happens* in the junk world.

Only excuse for this tired death route is THE KICK when the junk circuit is cut off for the non-payment and the junk-skin dies of junk-lack and overdose of time and the Old Skin has forgotten the skin game simplifying a way under the junk cover the way skins will. . . . A condition of total exposure is precipitated when the Kicking Addict cannot choose but see smell and listen. . . . Watch out for the cars. . . .

It is clear that junk is a Round-the-World-Push-an-Opium-Pellet-with-Your-Nose-Route. Strictly for Scarabs—stumble bum junk heap. And as such report to disposal. Tired of seeing it around.

Junkies always beef about *The Cold* as they call it, turning up their black coat collars and clutching their withered necks . . . pure junk con. A junky does not want to be warm, he wants to be Cool-Cooler-COLD. But he wants The Cold like he wants His Junk—NOT OUTSIDE where it does him no good but INSIDE so he can sit around with a spine like a frozen hydraulic jack . . . his metabolism approaching Absolute ZERO. TERMINAL addicts often go two months without a bowel move and the intestines make with sit-down-adhesions—Wouldn't you?—requiring the intervention of an apple corer or its surgical equivalent. . . . Such is life in The Old Ice House. Why move around and waste TIME?

Room for One More Inside, Sir.

Some entities are on thermodynamic kicks. They invented thermodynamics. . . . Wouldn't you?

And some of us are on Different Kicks and that's a thing out in the open the way I like to see what I eat and visa versa mutatis mutandis as the case may be. *Bill's Naked Lunch Room.* . . . Step right up. . . . Good for young and old, man and bestial. Nothing like a little snake oil to grease the wheels and get a show on the track Jack. Which side are you on? Fro-

Zen Hydraulic? Or you want to take a look around with Honest Bill?

So that's the World Health Problem I was talking about back in The Article. The Prospect Before Us Friends of MINE. Do I hear muttering about a personal razor and some bush league short con artist who is known to have invented The Bill? Wouldn't You? The razor belonged to a man named Occam and he was not a scar collector. Ludwig Wittgenstein *Tractatus Logico-Philosophicus* "If a proposition is NOT NECESSARY it is MEANINGLESS and approaching MEANING ZERO."

"And what is More UNNECESSARY than junk if You Don't NEED it?"

Answer: "Junkies, if you are not ON JUNK."

I tell you boys, I've heard some tired conversation but no other OCCUPATION GROUP can approximate that old thermodynamic junk Slow-DOWN. Now your heroin addict does not say hardly anything and that I can stand. But your Opium "Smoker" is more active since he still has a tent and a Lamp . . . and maybe 7-9-10 lying up in there like hibernating reptiles keep the temperature up to Talking Level: How low the other junkies are "whereas We—WE have this tent and this lamp and this tent and this lamp and this tent and nice and warm in here nice and warm nice and IN HERE and nice and OUT-SIDE ITS COLD. . . . ITS COLD OUTSIDE where the dross eaters and the needle boys won't last two years not six months hardly won't last stumble bum around and there is no class in them. . . . But WE SIT HERE and never increase the DOSE . . . never—never increase the dose never except TONIGHT is a SPECIAL OCCASION with all the dross eaters and needle boys out there in the cold. . . . And we never eat it never never never eat it. . . . Excuse please while I take a trip to The Source Of Living Drops they all have in pocket and opium pellets shoved up the ass in a finger stall with the Family Jewels and the other shit.

Room for one more inside, Sir.

Well when that record starts around for the billionth light year and never the tape shall change us non-junkies take drastic action and the men separate out from the Junk boys.

Only way to protect yourself against this horrid peril is come over HERE and shack up with Charybdis. . . . Treat you right kid. . . . Candy and cigarettes.

I am out after fifteen years in that tent. In and out in and out in and OUT. *Over* and *Out.* So listen to Old Uncle Bill Burroughs who invented the Burroughs Adding Machine Regulator Gimmick on the Hydraulic Jack Principle no matter how you jerk the handle result is always the same for given co-ordinates. Got my training early . . . wouldn't you?

Paregoric Babies of the World Unite. We have nothing to lose but Our Pushers. And THEY are NOT NECESSARY.

Look down LOOK DOWN along that junk road before you travel there and get in with the Wrong Mob. . . .

STEP RIGHT UP. . . . Only a three Dollar Bill to use BILL's telescope.

A word to the wise guy.

Herbert Huncke

Herbert Huncke was born on January 9, 1915, in Greenfield, Massachusetts. He grew up in Chicago, where his father owned H.S. Huncke and Company, a business that sold machine parts. Huncke first hitchhiked to New York when he was about seventeen, but he returned to Chicago and then moved to New York permanently in 1939. Addicted to drugs as a teenager, Huncke said that he couldn't work so "I just started hustling, just knocking around, you know, scrounging, learning I guess."

He first met William Burroughs in 1944, when Burroughs was trying to sell a sawed-off shotgun and some morphine Syrettes. Burroughs took Huncke, according to biographer Ted Morgan, as a "sort of Virgilian guide to the lower depths. . . . [He] was the first hipster . . . an antihero pointing the way to an embryonic counterculture, which would arise from this Times Square world of hustlers. . . ."

Huncke turned Burroughs on to heroin, and Burroughs introduced him to Ginsberg and Kerouac, who encouraged Huncke to become a writer, as they later encouraged their friends Carl Solomon and Neal Cassady. "Elsie John" and "Joey Martinez" are two of Huncke's early stories.

Huncke's output as a writer is modest, and he says that he just tries "to tell the truth." Ginsberg has made greater claims in promoting his work, saying that Huncke's "prose proceeds from his midnight mouth, that is, literal storytelling, just talking—for that reason it is both awkward and pure. . . . In his anonymity & holy Creephood in New York he was the sensitive vehicle for a veritable new con-

*sciousness which spread to others sensitized by their disloca-
tion from History and then to entire generations."*

ELSIE JOHN

Sometimes I remember Chicago and my experiences while growing up. I remember in particular the people I knew and, as frequently happens, I associate whole periods of time as indicative of certain changes within myself. But mostly I think about the people, and I recall one person rather vividly, not only because he was obviously out of the ordinary, but also because I now recognize what a truly beautiful creature he was.

He was a giant, well over six and one-half feet tall with a large egg-shaped head. His eyes were enormous and of a very deep sea blue with a hidden expression of sadness as though contemplating the tragedy of his life. Also there were times when they appeared gay and sparkling and full of great understanding. They were alive eyes always and had seen much and were ever questing. His hair was an exquisite shade of henna red, which he wore quite long like a woman's. He gave it special care. I can see it reflecting the light from an overhead bulb which hung shadeless in the center of his room while he sat cross-legged in the middle of a big brass bed fondling his three toy Pekes whom he loved, and who were his constant companions. His body was huge with long arms which ended with thin hands and long, tapering fingers whose nails were sometimes silver or green or scarlet. His mouth was large and held at all times a slightly idiot smile and was always painted bright red. He shaded his eyelids green or blue and beaded the lashes with mascara until they were often a good three quarters of an inch long. He exhibited himself among freaks in sideshows as the only true hermaphrodite, and he called himself Elsie-John. When I met him, he was in his early thirties.

He came originally from somewhere in Germany and, before coming to this country, had traveled—or travailed if you prefer—over much of Europe and could talk for hours of strange experiences he'd had. He was a user of drugs and, although he liked cocaine best, he would shoot-up huge amounts of heroin, afterward sitting still like a big, brooding idol.

When I first knew him, he was living in a little theatrical hotel on North State Street. It was an old hotel and in all probability is no longer in existence. Apparently at one time it had been a sort of hangout for vaudeville actors. It was shabby and run-down, and the rooms were small and in need of fresh paint. He lived in one of these rooms with his three dogs and a big wardrobe trunk. One of the things I remember distinctly was his standing in front of a long, thin mirror which hung on the wall opposite his bed applying make-up, carefully working in the powder bases and various cosmetics creating the mask which he was seldom without.

When I met him, I was coming out of a Lesbian joint with a couple of friends and, upon seeing him for the first time, was struck dumb. He was so big and strange. It happened that one of the girls knew him, and he invited us all up to his room to smoke pot—tea it was called in those days. His voice was rather low and pleasant with a slight accent which gave everything he said a meaning of its own. When we were leaving, he suggested I come back; it was not too long until I became a constant visitor and something of a friend.

He liked being called Elsie, and later when I introduced him, it was always as Elsie.

We began using junk together, and sometimes I would lie around his place for two or three days at a time. A friend of mine named Johnie joined us, and we became a sort of threesome. Johnie was later shot to death by narcotic bulls in a hotel while making a junk delivery; they grabbed him as he was handing the stuff over, and he broke free and ran down the hall, and they shot him. But as I say, at this time we were all together.

Elsie was working an arcade show on West Madison Street and, though junk was much cheaper then than now, he wasn't really making enough to support his habit as he wanted to. He decided to begin pushing. As a pusher he wasn't much of a success. Everybody soon got wise; he wouldn't let you go sick, and as a result, much more was going out than coming in. Eventually one of the cats he'd befriended got caught shooting up and, when asked where he scored, turned in Elsie's name. I will never forget the shock and the terror of the moment when the door was thrust open and the big red-faced cop, shouting "Police," shoved into the room followed by two more. Upon seeing Elsie he turned to one of the others saying, "Get a load of this degenerate bastard. We sure hit the jackpot this time. This is a queer sonofabitch if I ever saw one. And what the hell are these?" The dogs had gathered around Elsie and were barking and yipping. "God-damned lap dogs. What do they lap on you?" he said, as he thrust himself toward Elsie.

Elsie had drawn himself up to his full height. "I'm a hermaphrodite, and I've papers to prove it." He tried to shove a couple of pamphlets which he used in his sideshow act toward the cop. Meanwhile, one of the others had found our works and the stash of junk, about half an ounce, and was busy tearing apart Elsie's trunk, pulling out the drawers and dumping their contents in the center of the bed. It was when one of the cops stepped on a dog that Elsie began to cry.

They took us all down to the city jail on South Street, and since Johnie and I were minors, they let us go the next morning.

The last time I saw Elsie was in the bullpen. He was cowering in the corner surrounded by a group of young Westside hoods who had been picked up the same night we were. They were exposing themselves to him and yelling all sorts of obscenities.

JOEY MARTINEZ

Joseph Martinez is a twenty-four-year-old Brooklyn man who was born in Puerto Rico. He is a drug addict and a thief. He is proud and full of vitality and is a sensitive and fully wide awake young man. Recently while in the hospital, we met and became good friends. We first saw each other in the waiting room of the hospital on the morning of our admittance. We looked at each other and flirted a little with our eyes, but we didn't speak to each other until later when we were upstairs and had settled down to the daily routine of our withdrawal program. We were waiting in line to pick up our last Methadone shot for the first day. I had been in line ahead of him and, after stepping up to the nurses' station and taking my shot (I use the word *shot* loosely; what I mean is that I drank a small glass of Methadone, supposedly fifteen milligrams), I turned away and looked directly into his eyes. He was three men behind me in the line. Still looking at each other, I began easing past the men, saying, "How are you doing? Do you feel bad?" He answered, "What room are you in? I'll stop by as soon as I've copped, and we can rap until time for sleeping medication."

I told him my room number and said, "Boss Baby, I'll expect you. I'm doing O.K., but it sure would be great to hit the cooker about now."

We both laughed, and I continued on to my room where I stretched out on my bed and waited for him to show. My mind was full of curiosity and speculation. I had just started comparing him in my thoughts to Whitey, when he came into the room, a big smile on his face and holding a couple of candy bars in his hand. He walked up and sat down on the edge of the bed, offering one of the candy bars to me. "You dig candy when you kick? I do, man, I can do up some candy when I kick. You look better already. Man, when I saw you downstairs, you looked wasted. What's that rash on your face? You take bombitas? My name Joe, in Spanish it is Jose; my full name is Joseph Martinez."

I liked him. There was something at once physical and of the essence of living and energy and soul. His eyes were full of light and expression, communicating constantly, and I imagined I could detect a glimmer of love. I opened up to him a little, and soon we were beginning to know one another. He began telling me stories of his life, of his first love, and he told it with feeling and sensitivity.

Supposedly, she was ten when he first made an approach toward her, and he was fourteen. He spoke of her in tones of tenderness and always with a certain awareness of her physical being. It was almost the classic romantic love story of the shy and poor young Puerto Rican mountain boy in the city alone and on the defensive—not yet part of the scene but sure to prove his worth—when he would eventually fall by in his convertible—he would be draped in a fine suit and wearing a neat, sharp tie with one of those English collars—the very

latest style and a boss hat—the brim snapped down in front
and sort of tilted a bit over one eye—really looking good and
with a pocket full of money—and then her parents won't object
to him anymore or interfere with their seeing each other and
of her putting down the man her family forced her into
marrying—and of course she respects her husband but her
heart is for Joey. He said, "Me, Joey Martinez, I'd show
everybody, Huncke. Everybody would see how sharp I am
and not bad. I'd even go back to her church, although I've
had a chance to see that's full of shit, also hypocritical. I don't
believe in their kind of God, if I believe in any. Anyway, her
priest sold out to her old man, because he attends the church
functions and kicks in steadily to the pot, fives and tens.

"There were some wild scenes, Huncke. There was one
where the priest told me he understood, and he would speak
to her parents, and he did but not helpfully. He agreed with
her father that it would be better to send her back to Puerto
Rico for a while. I called them all punk mother fuckers, and
I held myself up tight to keep from smashing something over
their heads. Even the priest, who kept trying to calm me,
wouldn't let me talk. And her punk father pulled her away
from me, telling her I was a no good junky—a hoodlum—
hanging around corners—probably out sticking people up—
taking their money and using it to buy filthy dope to shoot
into my arm—nodding and full of the stuff—and I'd always
be no good and should be in jail.

"She and I had talked about my quitting for good, and I
had almost made her the promise I'd stop, if we could only
go on seeing each other and her family wouldn't interfere. I'd
gone to this church affair just to speak to her mother and
father and ask them to let us see each other—and I'd get a
job—and maybe he could help me—but all hell broke loose
when they saw me walk through the door. It hurt me so much
all I wanted to do was kill somebody. And I don't like to hurt
people; I don't like fights, and baby I can fight. Finally, a cop
who knows me came in, and he calmed me down. He took
me out with him and bought me a few shots at the bar. He
talked to me, telling me he saw things my way, and they were
all full of crap. I should remember nothing was worth going
through all that kind of thing in the church, and I should wait.

Maybe, after I had lost my crazy feelings, I should try and see her again and then talk to her people.

"I fucked everybody. I left him and went and saw a friend who turned me on and gave me sixty bags on consignment, and I became a dealer and made a lot of money."

I had listened intently and had watched him, his movements, the hand gestures, the lifting of the head, the fierce expression in the eye, when he had spoken of defending himself; and the sly twinkle when he had spoken of some point where he had gotten the upper hand, or when he had evolved some scheme, and his slightly boastful tone when he had been clever or his frown when someone else had pulled a cutey. I had known all along, even though he retained his sense of humor, that he was telling me a tragic experience, and I recognized all the fine points. I was fairly sure, while he was enlightening me about himself, he was still very much aware of me, and not a word or gesture of mine had gone unnoticed.

We became fairly steady companions and made a sort of comrade-like love scene, full of the promise of becoming even more intense in the future. Frankly, I was attracted by the idea, but I wasn't at all sure I wanted things to take that turn between us. Joey wasn't Whitey. He had much the same interest, but he wasn't as full of guile as Whitey and would be hurt more easily simply because he was already aware of loneliness in a manner Whitey had never been and therefore was more honest about his feelings.

He made me happy with his charm and brightness, and I only wish I could have done some beautiful thing for him. Instead, I signed out, leaving him behind for the medical discharge in order to meet the demand of his parole officer and fulfill the required behavior pattern. He didn't want me to split, and I had to be unkind, but under the circumstances I had very little choice in the matter. He had asked me to meet him the morning of his release, and I thought of doing so but, unfortunately, was unable to keep the appointment.

One thing he did tell me made him rather special. He had been speaking at length of his neighborhood and his junk habits; he told of a couple of his capers, of the money he'd gotten and how he'd spent it and also of how he felt he was thought of by his neighbors. He had been very open, showing no embarrassment at some of the revelations, and as we were strolling down the corridor toward the nurses' station for the final medication of that day, he suddenly began telling me of a dream, and of what message the dream had given him. Looking at me he said, "Nothing bad will ever happen to me because someone looks over me and takes care of me." I asked who he thought it was. He answered, "My guardian angel."

John Clellon Holmes

John Clellon Holmes was born on March 12, 1926, in Holyoke, Massachusetts, and died on March 2, 1988, in Old Saybrook, Connecticut. In 1944 he was drafted into the United States Navy and served in the Hospital Corps. After the war he studied literature and philosophy at Columbia University. He and his first wife lived in New York City, where he began writing poetry and fiction, publishing in the Chicago Review, Poetry, *and the* Saturday Review of Literature.

In August 1948 Holmes met Jack Kerouac and Allen Ginsberg, and in November of that year he and Kerouac had the "half-serious" conversation in which Kerouac coined the term "the Beat Generation." He and Kerouac enrolled in American literature classes at the New School on the GI Bill, but in 1949 Holmes stayed home when Kerouac went on the road with Neal Cassady. Holmes began writing a roman à clef he originally titled The Daybreak Boys, *alluding to a nineteenth-century river gang in New York City that he thought paralleled the "furtive" underground culture of his new friends. The novel was retitled* Go *when it was published in 1952.*

Holmes called himself Paul Hobbes in his book, presenting himself as an intellectual struggling to find new values in his efforts to begin a career as a novelist, forging friendships with another aspiring novelist, Gene Pasternak (Jack Kerouac), the visionary poet David Stofsky (Allen Ginsberg), and their Denver friend Hart Kennedy (Neal Cassady). Unlike the others in the group, who were emotionally and sexually involved with each other, Holmes was critical of what he considered his friends' destructive activities—drug addiction, alcoholism, and petty crime.

Kerouac and Ginsberg were not surprised to find themselves made into characters in Holmes's novel—Kerouac had done the same in The Town and the City, *which Holmes read in manuscript in 1948—but Kerouac was jealous of the large advance of twenty thousand dollars that Holmes received from Bantam Books for the paperback edition of* Go, *and Ginsberg was unhappy at what he considered Holmes's caricature of himself as an aspiring poet. The publisher withheld the paperback, fearing legal action, but Holmes was commissioned by* The New York Times *for the article "This Is the Beat Generation" in November 1952. He remained good friends with Kerouac and Ginsberg, and went on to publish two more novels and several books of essays.*

from GO

Three days later, in another early summer dusk, Hart Kennedy [Neal Cassady] arrived at their apartment with an eager entourage made up of Pasternak [Jack Kerouac], Stofsky [Allen Ginsberg] and a fellow called Ed Schindel, who had driven from the coast with him.

Hobbes [John Clellon Holmes] had learned of their arrival in New York earlier that afternoon with a call from Stofsky:

"Yes, yes, they came around but I was out, so they left a note . . . Have they gotten in touch with you? I've been calling madly everywhere. They were at Verger's too, leaving notes . . . You see, I haven't seen Hart for almost two years, and now notes, notes, phantom notes and that's all!"

Soon after that, after Hobbes had tried to get back into the chapter he was retyping, and when that failed, to get off a letter to Liza which had still not been written, Ketcham had called to say that they had been at his place the night before; Hart, Pasternak, Schindel, and Hart's first wife, Dinah, whom they had picked up in Denver on the way from San Francisco.

Then Stofsky had called again, on his way to Agatson's to check there: "If they come or phone you, hold onto them until I get in touch with you. It's very important! Bye-bye," and he rang off to continue his restless search in all the various places in which his hopes located them, finally to meet them accidentally on Columbus Circle near an automat they had all frequented when Hart had lived in New York two years before.

When Kathryn got home, Hobbes excitedly told her of all this, and because her day had been relatively uneventful, she said with amusement: "Don't be so jumpy. They'll come here soon enough as it is. Don't worry about that!"

But, nevertheless, everyone stumbled during the first, awkward moments, except Ed Schindel, whose rangy height and flushed boyish face contrasted oddly to the small, wiry Hart, who moved with itchy calculation and whose reddish hair and broken nose gave him an expression of shrewd, masculine ugliness.

"Say, this is a real nice place you got here," Schindel said politely, shifting his Redwood of a body easily. "Yes, sir!"

"What do you think of all those books, Hart?" Pasternak asked, with an exuberant grin.

Hart nodded briefly, shrugging muscular shoulders. "Yes, yes. That's fine."

"My mother fixed us a big dinner, Paul," Pasternak went on, refusing to sit down. "That's where Dinah is now, washing clothes and stuff like that. You know, they drove all the way from Frisco in four days!"

"Christ," Hobbes replied uneasily. "That's terrific time. Was it a tough trip?"

"Oh, you know, man. We got our kicks."

Hart was the only one, but for the secretive Stofsky lounging in a corner, who was not blundering into uncertain formalities, but he kept moving most of the time, looking out the windows, reading book titles, tapping out clusters of pattering beats with his foot.

Hobbes put on a bop record, hoping it would relax everyone, and after only a few seconds of the honking, complex tenor sax, Hart broke into a wild eyed, broad grin and exclaimed:

"Well, yes, man, yes! Say, that's great stuff!"

He stood by the phonograph in a stoop, moving back and forth on the spot in an odd little shuffle. His hands clapped before him, his head bobbed up and down, propelled, as the music got louder, in ever greater arcs, while his mouth came grotesquely agape as he mumbled: "Go! Go!"

Hobbes wandered about nervously, feeling he should not

stare at Hart, but when he saw Stofsky looking at the agitated figure with an adoring solemnity, he stared frankly with him, remembering Ketcham's description:

"This Hart is phenomenal. I've never seen such enormous nervous energy, and Gene gets just like him, in a kind of way. Hart and Dinah kept dancing and smoking and playing my radio all night. I didn't get to bed until six, and I was sure the neighbors were going to complain."

Pasternak sat next to Kathryn, both feeling a slight tension which led him to speak haltingly and without intimacy, and Kathryn to josh him boldly to cover her consternation. Each looked anxiously in Hobbes' direction, though talking about Hart.

"Really, he's tremendous," Pasternak said with dark belligerency. "Really . . . You know, at these bop clubs, Hart sits around and yells 'go, go!' at the musicians, but all the people around him are yelling 'go!' at Hart!"

"Sure," Ed put in with a meandering drawl. "He's real hung up on music. Everyone knows him around Frisco."

Hart was suddenly impatient, came up to Hobbes decisively, put an impersonal hand on his arm, and started talking rapidly.

"Now, we came over tonight, you know, to meet you and everything—Gene told us all about you—, but you see, we've got to get ten bucks somewhere to keep going. You understand, for food and things. Now if you can let us have it, that'll be great! Ed, here . . . Ed Schindel," and he reached for Schindel's arm without shifting his gaze from Hobbes, "he's getting a check, see. Back pay on the railroad where we were working in Frisco. Positively be here by Friday. So you'll have it back in just a couple of days. We've been everywhere, all of Gene's connections and everyone, but we couldn't raise it."

"Well . . ." Hobbes stumbled.

"It's just a loan, see. We're just borrowing. You know, I've got my first wife along, and we've got to get located. You understand."

Pasternak had turned to Kathryn. "My mother gets paid on Friday, so we can get it back to you by then."

"All right," she said evenly. "We were broke just yesterday, but I got my check this morning."

"That's great!" Hart said, a brief, easy smile relaxing his

lips. "Now, look, man, we ought to be cutting out," and he swung on Pasternak. "See if we can pick up Ancke [Herbert Huncke] on the Square. He's out of jail, isn't he? Isn't that what you said, David? Maybe he could get us a connection for some weed."

Stofsky slid into the conversation like a department head making a report at a board meeting.

"Verger saw him two days ago, right after the party, in fact. Ancke came in about four one morning, slept on the floor, and then stole fifty dollars worth of Verger's books. He said he hadn't had any junk for three months."

"He stole Verger's books!" Hobbes exclaimed.

"Yes, like a Tartuffe in rags! Two Oxfords of Dryden, and a complete set of Calvin and Luther . . . the English ones Verger got at school . . . He's probably lurking somewhere on the Square, Hart, trying to set something up . . . I've absolutely *got* to get hold of him."

"And that's a friend of Verger's!" Kathryn interjected with crisp candor.

"Oh, he's not angry with Albert, just sad about the Calvin. Ancke doesn't like to steal from friends, so he must have been broke and desperate . . . I once told him all about his stealing, I mean the real inner drama of *why* he steals, but he didn't take any heed. I guess I'll have to have another *long* talk with him!"

"Well, come on then," Hart said hurriedly, and with such impatience that it brought everyone to their feet before it was hardly out. "Now, we'll go down there and find him, see. Dig all the bars and that Riker's he used to hang out in when he was peddling. Maybe he'll know some real great pad we can get, too . . . Say, why don't you come along, man?" and he looked at Hobbes sharply. "Sure, come on. That's fine!"

Kathryn didn't seem to mind; in fact, she hoped that causing him no trouble about it would still her tiny remorse about Pasternak, who had remained at a distance from them both since their arrival, and so Hobbes left with them.

Hart drove the new Cadillac with a reckless precision, manipulating it in the sluggish midtown traffic as though the axle was somehow attached to his body. He talked steadily and yet managed, while cutting in and out of the snarls created by less agile machines, to lavish his attention on whoever else spoke up. While Stofsky amplified the news about Ancke, mentioning the robbery with serious concern, Hart's mouth widened in an intense smile, and he wagged his head violently, saying over and over again:

"Sure, sure . . . I know, man! . . . Yes, of course . . . That's right! That's right!"

Whenever they paused in the thronging light of street crossings, he would doodle on the dashboard with both hands, beating out little rhythms, his eyes continually sizing everything up. Pasternak would take up the beat on his end of the board, varying it somewhat. Hart would respond, the action seeming no longer just a time-killer but something secretly edifying and communicative. He would lean across Stofsky, who sat with coy confidence between them, and his round, sharp eyes would burn hotly at Pasternak and his hands pound on relentlessly. They would increase the beat, bouncing up and down in their excitement until the car rocked and people in neighboring ones craned out toward them curiously, and Hart would yell at each crescendo: "Yes, yes! . . . *That's* right!"

They cruised slowly down the block between Broadway and Eighth Avenue, and as they passed a Riker's, Pasternak leaped out of the moving car, shouting: "I'll cut in and look around and pick you up at the corner." He disappeared between two parked cars and was lost among the streaming crowds that flowed along in front of brightly lit movie theaters and amusement arcades.

At the corner of Forty-second Street and Eighth, Hart said: "I'll get it parked and we'll search the bars." They all piled out and he drove off.

Stofsky glanced absently around the busy corner with a strange, benevolent satisfaction in everything, sympathizing with all the rush and hurry, but not approving of it in his present seriousness. Ed Schindel gazed every which way, not afraid to gawk, as though this was the axis around which all else that he had ever known actually swung. And Hobbes stood nervously, looking up and down.

Pasternak hurried up to them, his head lowered furtively: "I couldn't find him. Where's Hart? We can try the Paradise."

And so, in a straggling group, they walked up the street to

a large dark bar where they began many of their journeys in quest of one or another of their "underground" acquaintances; people who wandered around Times Square in its crystal nighttime hours as though it were their preserve, their club, and their place of business rolled into one.

But Ancke was not there, and the five of them stood about, eying the collection of swarthy individuals who filled the place and drank and smoked with an indolence which somehow suggested a temporarily relaxed stealthiness. Everyone seemed to be observing the five of them with idle, professional glances, and Hart moved about the bar, as though efficiently inspecting some shady merchandise.

"Order just one beer," he said, and Hobbes did so uneasily. "Say, that cat's got tea!" he went on in low tones. "In the booth, with the fairies," and they all looked guardedly toward a simpering young man in a turtle neck sweater, who sat tightly squeezed between two other young men very much like him.

"Sure, man, that cat's *real* high on tea! Look at those big, staring eyes. Get that! Dig those hands. Why hell, man!" He was all but licking his lips with a kind of hungry, giggling anticipation. "Catch his eye, Gene . . . No, no, look, I'll cut back past him to the can, see. If he doesn't pick up on me, you do the same thing! You got it?" Like a harried but understanding manager, who inwardly feels he must do everything himself and takes a certain pride in the fact, Hart rattled out these instructions and then darted off.

Sure enough, after Hart passed him the young man in the sweater edged out of the booth and ambled toward the back of the bar in the direction of the men's room into which Hart had disappeared.

The bar was filled with the drone of low conversation, and while they waited the beefy bartender waddled crossly up and down behind the counter mixing drinks for newcomers. Hobbes looked apprehensively toward the doors, outside of which flowed the myriad, flashing lights of the street; the gay, cool groups of chattering high school girls, and the constantly preoccupied, nattily dressed little men, inevitably sucking on cigarettes as if their last, and padding along, hatless, on guard.

Those doors swung with quick, oiled swishes and anyone might walk through them. But once inside, the hazy dimness, the jukebox which (as though part of a wry satire) ground out the same optimistic show tunes that spun in other bars, and the blank barrage of dozens of calculating eyes: all this bespoke some deeper, more essential community of those who drank and waited here night after night, than could be found in neighborhood bars elsewhere in the city. Snatches of aimless talk between two slick haired drinkers, the affected gibberish of a dwarfish fairy who could barely reach his glass atop the bar, or the occasional surly snarl from someone who would have been considered merely drunk elsewhere all seemed heavy with hidden meanings. While waiting for Hart, the other four peered about, like children who have been told not to stare at a relative's eccentricities.

Hart was back. "Let's cut out. No, he didn't have any left. Oh, he was high, okay . . . and he said a friend of his is coming in later—his connection, I guess—but, hell, we can't wait around for that. He wants two bucks a stick! What a drag! He gave me the address of a guy that peddles goof balls, though, but kee-rist, who wants to get hungup that way? Hell, no, man, none of that goof for me! Not any more! But, come on, we'll dig Lee's for Ancke . . ."

Moving down Forty-second Street in a restless platoon, they darted into bars and coffee stands and penny arcades, Hart deploying them with quick, enthusiastic commands, and pausing often to comment joyfully on the sad ragged drunks who wove weary figurines down the pavement; or the flushed, wet mouthed old men, who stood quivering, heads thrust avidly downward, before stereopticans they painfully cranked, as though unaware that others gaped at their lewd contortions with amusement, or uncaring if they were. The whole surging street glittered brightly with its countless, gaudy neons, as though it was covered by some vast roof of white light. Beneath it, the five vainly searched and finally wandered into Lee's, the huge, teeming cafeteria on the corner of Broadway, where steam tables fouled the air with a wild conflict of smells, and servers, presiding over them like unshaven wizards, imprecated the shuffling crowds indifferently, while the greasy, beardless busboys, like somnambulists, moved among the littered tables mechanically.

They got coffee, which Hobbes and Stofsky paid for because

Hart did not want to break the ten, and then they gathered around one table against a sweating wall. Hart could not keep still and he and Ed jumped up and down, talking excitedly, digging everything. Stofsky drifted off with stern aloofness to get a frankfurter, leaving Hobbes and Pasternak fidgeting over the cups, unable to talk.

To Hobbes, whose gaze roved ceaselessly, the place looked like some strange social club for drifters, dope passers, petty thieves, cheap, aging whores and derelicts: the whole covert population of Times Square that lived only at night and vanished as the streets went grey with dawn. To all this crowded room, there was an underground urgency, as though it was some limbo in the night's wanderings, an oasis which all these people inhabited at one hour as part of their shady, secret routine. Hobbes recalled the early, golden dusk out the windows of the apartment, that had been alive for him with as yet unknown excitements. And now he sat, not sad though oddly unnerved, thinking to himself that here, two scant hours later, he was watching some confraternity of the lost and damned assemble. And yet somehow he was not repulsed, but rather yearned to know it in its every aspect, the lives these people led, the emotions they endured, the fate into which they stumbled, perhaps not unawares. He longed to know it all, and for a moment hated his own uneasiness while sitting there.

Pasternak was still moody and would not take a cigarette when Hobbes offered him one.

"I was depressed for three days," he began abruptly, not looking up but obviously very serious. "You know that, Paul? I sat for three days at home, thinking about friends, and why I was a writer, and even why I was alive and everything. And about death and other enigmas."

"David must have told you about his visions."

"Sure, isn't that crazy? Hearing Blake that way?" And he gave a perplexed laugh, shaking his head slowly. "But it was really Hart who got me out of it. And my own pride. You know, I brooded about it for three whole days. Why, I even wrote big dialogues in which I asked people what it meant—"

"What what meant?"

"Oh, life and everything. You know. This whole thing with

Christine got me thinking. But in these dialogues I ran around yelling: 'What are we going to *do* about it? We've got to *do* something!' Like some silly Myshkin . . . But I said, 'What am I trying to write for? Why do I think I can win love that way?' It's just another justification I'm attempting . . . for myself, for my existence. When I wrote the book I was bitter, full of concern and everything. But you know, Paul, all that's hassles, complaints we make about life, which is really magical and crazy and nothing more."

"Well, the writer's job is to find out why, isn't it? There's nothing wrong with that, it's decent work."

"But that's another bitterness, a complaint, 'finding out why'! I think death is the only important problem, and it's really no problem at all, just a grisly amusement. You know what I mean? . . . So I've decided that life is holy in itself, life itself! All the details, everything. Just loving all things, all ways! . . . It took me three whole days. Oh, I wouldn't have committed suicide or anything like that. My pride always told me, what does it really matter? Only the holy details of life matter! Do you see?"

Hobbes bent forward eagerly, and yet also fearful lest Pasternak see his eagerness and draw back. "But what made you so depressed, Gene? I know exactly what you mean, but what caused it?"

"Oh, you know, I get like that every once in a while, everyone does. And, well, Christ, MacMurry's turned down my book, the bastards! After almost two months, they send it back with a rejection slip about paper costs and the risks of first novels! What do I care about all that! . . . But, you know, when I ran up to Hart, asking him, 'What are we going to do about it?' . . . Not the book, because that really doesn't matter, I've decided I wrote that for myself, my own soul, a sort of plea and nothing more . . . but death and the unsolvable mysteries of life . . . When I asked Hart that, do you know what he said? He said, 'Don't worry, man! Don't worry about it. Everything's fine, and life is only digging everything and waiting, just waiting and digging!' . . . And that's what he does. Look at him! Everything's perfect for him . . . Oh, he has his miseries, worse than ours sometimes, believe me . . . But he knows everything is perfect, and so it is . . . You remember Kirillov in *The Possessed?* The guy who couldn't stand ecstasy for more than a split second? Well, Hart's Kirillov, only he can stand it all the time, and all of life is ecstasy to him!"

"Well, forget about MacMurry's. Keep sending it out. You're going to get it published, and just because a few editors can't seem to understand a really honest book, don't you lose faith in it."

"Oh, I don't really care about it any more. Last night I told myself, while I was watching Hart, that I'd have to choose between the drawing rooms full of Noel Cowards and the rattling trucks on the American highways, that's all. I can't have both, and I might as well get used to it."

Amid the whirl and stir of the cafeteria, they sat talking of such things, alternately earnest and silent. Each was touchy lest the other might, at any moment, make some reference to the party or Kathryn, and each wondered how they might convey to the other that it did not matter, that it was to both (although they did not know it) a simple occurrence, nothing more, and need create no void.

Neither saw, as they conversed, that Stofsky had attached himself to a ragged, shivering old man, whose soiled alpaca jacket hung around his shoulders like a shroud, and whose wispy hair straggled over a lean sorrowful countenance. His eyes wandered pitifully and so drunk was he that he did not know what to make of the intense, grave young man who ran back and forth between his table and the counter, bringing cups of coffee, guiding them to his quivering old mouth, talking all the time with words of encouragement, and occasionally laughing to himself. But Hart and Ed, who had covered the place thoroughly, did notice and came up to him.

"Say, look, let's cut out of here. Ancke's not coming and nobody's seen him. I talked to a guy over there but he didn't even know he was out of jail. He used to peddle with Ancke out in Chicago. Imagine that! A real beat character!"

Hart, once more bent on getting things organized toward a common objective, was not curious about the old man on whom Stofsky had been fastening himself. "Come on, we've got to get some *stuff,* man! Don't you know anybody who might have some? How about that cat up in Harlem? Or this guy Verger?"

"Ask Gene about Verger. I don't think so. Go ahead, I'll

be right with you." He leaned closer to Hart eagerly, whispering so the drunk would not overhear. "This old man's a
beggar, you know that! And he knows a-l-l about grace! Do
you know what he just said to me? 'Everything's getting better
all the time!' Just like that . . . But go ahead, I'll be right over
. . ." And he turned back to the confused old fellow, and
exclaimed weightily: "Grace is come by works and deeds,
though . . . But then, of course, *you* would know that. Would
you like a cruller or a Danish or something?"

Pasternak was sure Verger would have no more marijuana
and they all stood about mulling the problem, Hart making
endless suggestions with such restless energy that Pasternak
seemed loath to point out that they would lead nowhere.
Hobbes, who cared little whether Ancke was found or tea
procured, watched Stofsky saying goodbye to the bewildered
old man.

Then he rushed up to them excitedly: "Gene, Gene, that's
what we must become! Beggars on Times Square! As soon as
I saw that man I knew he was on the bottom, looking up,
noticing the sky at last! I asked him, 'What does it feel like
to be Job?' and he said, 'Everything's getting better all the
time!' "

He could not resist the snorting, feverish laugh that beat in
his throat, but then, seeing that the others were disinterested,
he checked himself for a moment, and then began in a totally
different tone:

"But there just might be a chance, about that tea, that is if
you want to cut up to Columbia. I've still got a mailbox in my
old dorm, and Will Dennison [William Burroughs]—you remember old Will Dennison from New Orleans, Hart—well,
old Will Dennison wrote me a big letter last week and said he
was sending along a can of Orange Pekoe and he hoped I'd
enjoy it . . . So we might try up there, although he's never
sent one before even when he said he would . . ."

"Well, come on, man! Why didn't you say so before? Yes,
that'll be fine! We were going to stop in and see Dennison on
the way across, see, but we didn't because I thought he'd be
in jail or retired or something, you know? But come on, let's
ball up there and take a look in that little box of yourn!"

They roared up the West Side Drive at eighty miles an hour,

anticipation bringing silence. The river-girdled length of the island slipped by them and the George Washington Bridge up ahead hung across the dark throat of the river like some sparkling, distant necklace.

At one point, Hobbes asked Pasternak if he had seen Christine since the party, and Pasternak tightened, as at an unpleasant reminder, and said "No." Hart was curious about her.

"So you're getting a steady piece now. Well, that's fine, man! There's nothing like a big dull routine stretch of laying once in a while, you know what I mean?"

Presented in this light, Pasternak, who had been half afraid that Hart would disapprove, laughed nervously and agreed.

The streets around the University were soft with night and quite empty, and the car rolled smoothly through them to the dorm on One Hundred and Fourteenth Street where David had his mailbox. He got out without a word and vanished into the building.

They sat, itchily waiting, Ed watching out the rear windows. They joked irrelevantly, as though on some underground mission too crucial to be spoken about. There was a party going on in one of the dorms, and they could hear shrill laughter and dance music, and so peered up at the windows that were gay with light. Once a pretty little Negro girl rushed by the car, crying: "Bill! Ah, Bill, whyn't you come on back inside?"

Hart craned his head out after her, with a wide, appreciative grin, and called: "Listen, honey, I ain't Bill, but I'll do!"

"Here he comes," Ed drawled finally. "Yes, I do believe he's got a parcel. Yes!"

"No! . . . No!" Hart shouted with disbelief jumping up and down with joy and with his effort to see Stofsky coming; searching for a term to express his relief and excitement, and finding only a negative one strong enough.

They looked at the package while they sat there, but they did not open the Lipton's tea box in which the weed had been sent. It felt like almost two ounces, enough for a long time.

They whirled off, heading for Stofsky's place to smoke it. They flashed across town, cutting down one way streets, beating the dashboard and bursting into exclamations or song at every traffic light, like children released to the nursery after the ordeal of holiday relations.

"If you can let me out on Lexington, I'll grab a subway," Hobbes began. "I really should get home."

They all tried to inveigle him into coming along, but he was firm.

"Okay," Hart said, assuming a smooth suavity again. "We'll cut on down to Fifty-ninth and drop you. Hell, you should come along though and blast with us! Sure! . . . But this way, there'll be more for us, right?" And he laughed at his own frankness, and then went on as though clearing up a loose end. "We've been all excited tonight, man. You understand! I'm not coherent anymore; I mean, in any intellectual way, see. But I dig you, I dig you going home and all! Yes, sir!"

Stofsky twisted around to face the back seat as they reached Hobbes' corner. "I'll be down to see you in the next couple of days, Paul. I'm thinking of looking for a job, you see . . . I'll be a big d-u-l-l working man, maybe on a newspaper or something."

Everyone was surprised.

"Yes, you see, I'm going to pay Verger back for those books," he announced to everyone. "I introduced him to Albert, after all, and Verger doesn't understand about his stealing. But it's really my debt."

Hart jumped out of the car with Hobbes and said, flashing a smile: "Sure, we'll be seeing you over the weekend, and we'll blast some of this tea, okay? We'll be around!"

And so Hobbes climbed his stairs, half regretful that he had not gone along, knowing that the new season had indeed arrived for all of them.

Carl Solomon

Carl Solomon was born on March 30, 1928, in the Bronx, New York. After his father's death in 1939, he became deeply depressed. He remembered, "I drifted into indiscipline and intellectual adventure that eventually became complete confusion."

Solomon graduated high school at the age of fifteen and enrolled at City College of New York but dropped out of school in 1944 to join the United States Maritime Service. As a seaman, he traveled to Poland, Greece, Italy, and France, where he encountered the surrealist exposition of André Breton, attended the first play of Jean Genet, and heard Antonin Artaud read poetry. Solomon began reading Dada and Surrealist poetry; then after identifying with Kafka's hero K, he decided he was insane. In 1949, when he turned twenty-one, he presented himself to the Psychiatric Institute in New York City and voluntarily committed himself to shock treatment.

As Solomon told the story to his biographer, Tom Collins, one day, while being wheeled out after an insulin shock treatment, he saw someone he took to be a new patient. "I'm Kirillov," Solomon mumbled as he returned to consciousness, naming the nihilist of Dostoevski's The Possessed. *"I'm Myshkin," was Allen Ginsberg's reply, alluding to the saintly hero of* The Idiot. *Ginsberg noted down what Solomon said after his shock treatments, and later incorporated many of his phrases—like "pubic beards" and "lunatic saint"—into "Howl for Carl Solomon," the full title of Ginsberg's famous poem.*

After leaving the hospital, Solomon worked for his uncle A. A. Wyn, who published Ace paperback books. Solomon signed Burroughs's Junky *but rejected Kerouac's* On the Road *after Kerouac submitted it in 1951 on a 120-feet-long single-spaced typed roll of drafting paper and refused to make changes. In 1966 Solomon published his first book,* Mishaps, Perhaps, *a collection that included "Pilgrim State Hospital," "Suggestions to Improve the Public Image of the Beatnik," and "The Class of '48."*

from MISHAPS, PERHAPS

PILGRIM STATE HOSPITAL

One enters Pilgrim as though it is the death-house. One sits down in the ward and waits. 5 doctors approach, the patient weeps.

Shock treatment is prepared. One wakes dazed.

Allen comes, he says, "Don't argue with them, do as they say."

Time asserts itself again. You go home. You tire yourself out sleeping with women. Then you pause. You think, "You are a writer, you should do something again."

It is tiring to understand what they are saying to you, you talk about Nerval and you talk about Proust.

A young man comes up to you. He is of Arabian descent. He mentions Nasser and begins an anti-semitic diatribe.

Dr. Rath is a young man. Of Rumanian-Jewish descent. A background more brilliant than any doctor in the institution so far as I am concerned.

You mention Tristan Tzara to him and he understands what you mean. He works through group therapy. Patients come together and remorselessly cut each other to pieces. Fights break out during the course of the group therapy session.

"Solomon, you don't want to get well. You're just looking for a big dick." I fight back I knock the boy down. He screams, "I'll kill him even if they send me to Matteawan."

He had disclosed to me in an earlier conversation that he knew Weinberg, slayer of Bodenheim. "Bodenheim was a boy," asserts Davis.

I disagree, not being quite sure of my facts.

Come back to Village years later and find Bodenheim's reputation as a man was quite good. Davis escaped from Pilgrim. I don't know what happened to him, hard-bitten and bitter, I have never forgotten that face. Dehumanized.

Confused him in my mind with Corso since both had reformatory qualities. Met Corso again—changed my mind. Corso is a littérateur and a Catholic with a strong religious sense of right and wrong.

The tendency toward crime among the young men of my generation is impossible to surmount. We are all guttersnipes. Gratuitousness is the spirit of the age. Gide and Cocteau have made us what we are. The big dick or "BITE" if you prefer me to use Genet's French, this is all that matters. Make another man submit to you and you are God.

Ah! Ludicrous ribaldry. Hein blowing his beautiful understand face to ruins with a bullet. Camus dead in an auto accident.

Of all things, Artaud becomes vogue ten years after his death as a ridiculous nut.

Berchtesgaden. The Fuehrer and his blond boys, who is this man Castro? Very late on the scene. New young Communist intellectuals in the Village, a new group, a new element very much involved in politics.

Why, I don't understand them. They are good men.

Kennedy seems quite human after all that has occurred. Maybe he will restore some kind of dignity to my life. He has begun already. He appointed a Jew to the Cabinet.

He himself is a Catholic, an enormous advance in democratic thinking on the part of the American public. Democracy versus Nihilism in daily life. Motivation or despair.

SUGGESTIONS TO IMPROVE THE PUBLIC IMAGE OF THE BEATNIK

It is most important now to change the smell of the beatnik. Instead of using, for example, the word "shit" so often in their poems, I suggest that they tactfully substitute the word "roses" wherever the other word occurs.

This is a small adjustment.

It is just as AVANT GARDE so art will suffer no loss.

Instead of saying "MERDE" they will be saying "A rose is a rose is a rose is a rose." Just as AVANT GARDE, you see, with considerable improvement in the effect created.

THE CLASS OF '48

It was a bizarre group. Decadent in many ways, I thought. They seemed to feel that the war was over and that they would never be faced with any major challenges again. They are still with me. I meet them here and there, in the New School, in a mental hospital, on 42nd Street, in a bar. They were called then "The Silent Generation," later on "The Beat Generation." They were the precursors of the rock n' roll youngsters, but somehow neither sane enough nor mad enough, too young to have been in the war and too old to be Cold War products, a between-wars group.

Will any new influences ever jar them and me from their perpetual rut? From the boring indifference and insufficiently bleak pessimism that has been their heritage, I doubt whether anything ever will. Endless experimentation with the senses, endless metaphysical rambling. I am back in the Bronx, among the moulding influences. On the subway twice a week, I pass and can see the High School I graduated from, James Monroe, and am recalled to the early heroic, pre-decadent days of my generation. When we were busy with scrap drives, orienting ourselves toward being public-minded citizens rather than hopped-up, disoriented nuts. The reaction was a hatred of regimentation, and when the reaction set in it was bitter and fatal to some. Perhaps, now that the fifties are forgotten, another reaction will set in, in the interests of self-preservation and order. The nihilistic period is past. The time for sincere creativity, I think is here.

Gregory Corso

Gregory Corso was born on March 26, 1930, in Greenwich Village in New York City. Placed with several foster parents when his eighteen-year-old mother went back to Italy, he was sent to the Youth House after he stole a radio at the age of twelve. Corso ended his formal schooling in the sixth grade. When he was sixteen, he robbed a Household Finance office and was sent to the state prison in Dannemora, New York, to serve a three-year sentence after his partners turned him in.

Corso began to read literature and write poetry in prison. At his release he has said he was "in love with Chatterton, Marlowe, and Shelley" and aspired to be a poet. Ginsberg, whom he met in 1950 in a Greenwich Village bar, encouraged him to continue writing and showed his prison poetry to Mark Van Doren, one of Ginsberg's professors at Columbia. Corso's seduction of Kerouac's girlfriend "Mardou" during the summer of 1953 was the plot of Kerouac's novel The Subterraneans. *He fit easily into the group, having in common with them—as one critic has observed—"that he was a misfit, self-invented, rebellious, and blessed by the Muse."*

Corso began publishing in 1955, when his early poems, first published in the Harvard Advocate, *were printed in a volume titled* The Vestal Lady on Brattle and Other Poems, *financed by Harvard and Radcliffe students in Cambridge, Massachusetts. Three years later, City Lights Books of San Francisco published* Gasoline, *which included the poems "I Am 25," "The Mad Yak," and "Vision of Rotterdam."* Bomb, *published as a broadside by City Lights in 1958, was written at the Beat Hotel* in Paris. "Marriage" is an early poem that is one of his most frequently reprinted works. "Variations on a Generation" was first published in the little magazine Gemini in the spring of 1959.

I AM 25

With a love a madness for Shelley
Chatterton   Rimbaud
and the needy-yap of my youth
            has gone from ear to ear:
        I HATE OLD POETMEN!
Especially old poetmen who retract
who consult other old poetmen
who speak their youth in whispers,
saying:—I did those then
            but that was then
            that was then—
O I would quiet old men
say to them:—I am your friend
                what you once were, thru me
                you'll be again—
Then at night in the confidence of their homes
rip out their apology-tongues
            and steal their poems.

THE MAD YAK

I am watching them churn the last milk
        they'll ever get from me.
They are waiting for me to die;
They want to make buttons out of my bones.
Where are my sisters and brothers?
That tall monk there, loading my uncle,
        he has a new cap.
And that idiot student of his—
        I never saw that muffler before.
Poor uncle, he lets them load him.

How sad he is, how tired!
I wonder what they'll do with his bones?
And that beautiful tail!
How many shoelaces will they make of that!

VISION OF ROTTERDAM

September 1957 summoned by my vision-agent
via ventriloquial telegram
delivered by the dumb mouths stoned upon Notre Dame
    given golden fare & 17th Century diagram
I left the gargoyle city
And
Two suitcases filled with despair
        arrived in Rotterdam

Rotterdam is dying again
            steamers & tankers
        unload an awful sight
May 1940 stevedors lead forth a platoon of lukemia
Pleasure ships send metalvoiced rats teeheeing a propa-
    ganda of ruin
A cargo of scream deafens the tinhorn of feeble War
Bombers overhead
            Young blond children in white blouses
            crawl in the streets gnawing their houses
The old the sick the mad leave their wheelchairs & cells
    and kneel in adoration before the gentle torpedo of
    miracles
Bombers unanswerable to the heart
            vitalize a Sunday afternoon dream
Bombs like jewels surprise

Explosion explosion explosion
Avalanche on medieval stilts brought down 1940
Mercy leans against her favorite bombardment
            and forgives the bomb

Alone
Eyes on the antique diagram
    I wander down the ruin and see
        amid a madness of coughing bicycles
the scheme of a new Rotterdam humming in the vacancy

BOMB

Budger of history   Brake of time   You   Bomb
Toy of universe   Grandest of all snatched-sky   I cannot hate you
Do I hate the mischievous thunderbolt   the jawbone of an ass
The bumpy club of One Million B.C.   the mace   the flail   the axe
Catapult Da Vinci   tomahawk Cochise   flintlock Kidd   dagger Rathbone
Ah and the sad desperate gun of Verlaine   Pushkin   Dillinger   Bogart
And hath not St. Michael a burning sword   St. George a lance   David a sling
Bomb   you are as cruel as man makes you   and you're no crueller than cancer
All man hates you   they'd rather die by car-crash   lightning   drowning
Falling off a roof   electric-chair   heart-attack   old age   old age   O Bomb
They'd rather die by anything but you   Death's finger is free-lance
Not up to man whether you boom or not   Death has long since distributed its
categorical blue   I sing thee Bomb   Death's extravagance   Death's jubilee
Gem of Death's supremest blue   The flyer will crash   his death will differ
with the climber who'll fall   To die by cobra is not to die by bad pork
Some die by swamp   some by sea   and some by the bushy-haired man in the nigh
O there are deaths like witches of Arc   Scarey deaths like Boris Karloff
No-feeling deaths like birth-death   sadless deaths like old pain Bowery
Abandoned deaths   like Capital Punishment   stately deaths like senators
And unthinkable deaths like Harpo Marx   girls on Vogue covers   my own
I do not know just how horrible Bombdeath is   I can only imagine
Yet no other death I know has so laughable a preview   I scope
a city   New York City   streaming   starkeyed   subway shelter
Scores and scores   A fumble of humanity   High heels bend
Hats whelming away   Youth forgetting their combs
Ladies not knowing what to do   with their shopping bags
Unperturbed gum machines   Yet dangerous 3rd rail
Ritz Brothers   from the Bronx   caught in the A train
The smiling Schenley poster will always smile
Impish Death   Satyr Bomb   Bombdeath
Turtles exploding over Istanbul

The jaguar's flying foot
soon to sink in arctic snow
Penguins plunged against the Sphinx
The top of the Empire State
arrowed in a broccoli field in Sicily
Eiffel shaped like a C in Magnolia Gardens
St. Sophia peeling over Sudan
O athletic Death   Sportive Bomb
The temples of ancient times
their grand ruin ceased
Electrons   Protons   Neutrons
gathering Hesperean hair
walking the dolorous golf of Arcady
joining marble helmsmen
entering the final amphitheater
with a hymnody feeling of all Troys
heralding cypressean torches
racing plumes and banners
and yet knowing Homer with a step of grace
Lo the visiting team of Present
the home team of Past
Lyre and tuba together joined
Hark the hotdog soda olive grape
gala galaxy robed and uniformed
commissary   O the happy stands
Ethereal root and cheer and boo
The billioned all-time attendance
The Zeusian pandemonium
Hermes racing Owens
The Spitball of Buddha
Christ striking out
Luther stealing third
Planetarium Death   Hosannah Bomb
Gush the final rose   O Spring Bomb
Come with thy gown of dynamite green
unmenace Nature's inviolate eye
Before you the wimpled Past
behind you the hallooing Future   O Bomb
Bound in the grassy clarion air
like the fox of the tally-ho

thy field the universe thy hedge the geo
Leap Bomb   bound Bomb   frolic zig and zag
The stars a swarm of bees in thy binging bag
Stick angels on your jubilee feet
wheels of rainlight on your bunky seat
You are due and behold you are due
and the heavens are with you
hosannah incalescent glorious liaison
BOMB O havoc antiphony molten cleft BOOM
Bomb mark infinity a sudden furnace
spread thy multitudinous encompassed Sweep
set forth awful agenda
Carrion stars   charnel planets   carcass elements
Corpse the universe   tee-hee finger-in-the-mouth hop
over its long long dead Nor
From thy nimbled matted spastic eye
exhaust deluges of celestial ghouls
From thy appellational womb
spew birth-gusts of great worms
Rip open your belly Bomb
from your belly outflock vulturic salutations
Battle forth your spangled hyena finger stumps
along the brink of Paradise
O Bomb   O final Pied Piper
both sun and firefly behind your shock waltz
God abandoned mock-nude
beneath His thin false-talc'd apocalypse
He cannot hear thy flute's
happy-the-day profanations
He is spilled deaf into the Silencer's warty ear
His Kingdom an eternity of crude wax
Clogged clarions untrumpet Him
Sealed angels unsing Him
A thunderless God   A dead God
O Bomb   thy BOOM His tomb
That I lean forward on a desk of science
an astrologer dabbling in dragon prose
half-smart about wars   bombs   especially bombs
That I am unable to hate what is necessary to love
That I can't exist in a world that consents

a child in a park   a man dying in an electric-chair
That I am able to laugh at all things
all that I know and do not know   thus to conceal my pain
That I say I am a poet and therefore love all man
knowing my words to be the acquainted prophecy of all men
and my unwords no less an acquaintanceship
That I am manifold
a man pursuing the big lies of gold
or a poet roaming in bright ashes
or that which I imagine myself to be
a shark-toothed sleep   a man-eater of dreams
I need not then be all-smart about bombs
Happily so   for if I felt bombs were caterpillars
I'd doubt not they'd become butterflies
There is a hell for bombs
They're there   I see them there
They sit in bits and sing songs
mostly German songs
and two very long American songs
and they wish there were more songs
especially Russian and Chinese songs
and some more very long American songs
Poor little Bomb that'll never be
an Eskimo song   I love thee
I want to put a lollipop
in thy furcal mouth
A wig of Goldilocks on thy baldy bean
and have you skip with me Hansel and Gretel
along the Hollywoodian screen
O Bomb in which all lovely things
moral and physical anxiously participate
O fairyflake plucked from the
grandest universe tree
O piece of heaven which gives
both mountain and anthill a sun
I am standing before your fantastic lily door
I bring you Midgardian roses   Arcadian musk
Reputed cosmetics from the girls of heaven
Welcome me   fear not thy opened door
nor thy cold ghost's grey memory

nor the pimps of indefinite weather
their cruel terrestrial thaw
Oppenheimer is seated
in the dark pocket of Light
Fermi is dry in Death's Mozambique
Einstein his mythmouth
a barnacled wreath on the moon-squid's head
Let me in   Bomb   rise from that pregnant-rat corner
nor fear the raised-broom nations of the world
O Bomb I love you
I want to kiss your clank   eat your boom
You are a paean   an acme of scream
a lyric hat of Mister Thunder
O resound thy tanky knees
BOOM   BOOM   BOOM   BOOM   BOOM
BOOM ye skies and BOOM ye suns
BOOM BOOM ye moons   ye stars BOOM
nights ye BOOM   ye days ye BOOM
BOOM BOOM ye winds   ye clouds ye rains
go BANG ye lakes   ye oceans BING
Barracuda BOOM and cougar BOOM
Ubangi BANG   orangoutang
BING BANG BONG BOOM   bee bear baboon
ya BANG ye BONG ye BING
the tail the fin the wing
Yes   Yes   into our midst a bomb will fall
Flowers will leap in joy their roots aching
Fields will kneel proud beneath the halleluyahs of the wind
Pinkbombs will blossom   Elkbombs will perk their ears
Ah many a bomb that day will awe the bird a gentle look
Yet   not enough to say a bomb will fall
or even contend celestial fire goes out
Know that the earth will madonna the Bomb
that in the hearts of men to come more bombs will be born
magisterial bombs wrapped in ermine   all beautiful
and they'll sit plunk on earth's grumpy empires
fierce with moustaches of gold

MARRIAGE

Should I get married? Should I be good?
Astound the girl next door with my velvet suit and faustus hood?
Don't take her to movies but to cemeteries
tell all about werewolf bathtubs and forked clarinets
then desire her and kiss her and all the preliminaries
and she going just so far and I understanding why
not getting angry saying You must feel! It's beautiful to feel!
Instead take her in my arms lean against an old crooked tomb-
    stone
and woo her the entire night the constellations in the sky—

When she introduces me to her parents
back straightened, hair finally combed, strangled by a tie,
should I sit knees together on their 3rd degree sofa
and not ask Where's the bathroom?
How else to feel other than I am,
often thinking Flash Gordon soap—
O how terrible it must be for a young man
seated before a family and the family thinking
We never saw him before! He wants our Mary Lou!
After tea and homemade cookies they ask What do you do for
    a living?

Should I tell them? Would they like me then?
Say All right get married, we're losing a daughter
but we're gaining a son—
And should I then ask Where's the bathroom?

O God, and the wedding! All her family and her friends
and only a handful of mine all scroungy and bearded
just wait to get at the drinks and food—
And the priest! he looking at me as if I masturbated
asking me Do you take this woman for your lawful wedded wife?
And I trembling what to say say Pie Glue!
I kiss the bride all those corny men slapping me on the back
She's all yours, boy! Ha-ha-ha!
And in their eyes you could see some obscene honeymoon going
    on—

Then all that absurd rice and clanky cans and shoes
Niagara Falls! Hordes of us! Husbands! Wives! Flowers! Choco-
lates!
All streaming into cozy hotels
All going to do the same thing tonight
The indifferent clerk he knowing what was going to happen
The lobby zombies they knowing what
The whistling elevator man he knowing
The winking bellboy knowing
Everybody knowing! I'd be almost inclined not to do anything!
Stay up all night! Stare that hotel clerk in the eye!
Screaming: I deny honeymoon! I deny honeymoon!
running rampant into those almost climactic suites
yelling Radio belly! Cat shovel!
O I'd live in Niagara forever! in a dark cave beneath the Falls
I'd sit there the Mad Honeymooner
devising ways to break marriages, a scourge of bigamy
a saint of divorce—

But I should get married I should be good
How nice it'd be to come home to her
and sit by the fireplace and she in the kitchen
aproned young and lovely wanting my baby
and so happy about me she burns the roast beef
and comes crying to me and I get up from my big papa chair
saying Christmas teeth! Radiant brains! Apple deaf!
God what a husband I'd make! Yes, I should get married!
So much to do! like sneaking into Mr Jones' house late at night
and cover his golf clubs with 1920 Norwegian books
Like hanging a picture of Rimbaud on the lawnmower
like pasting Tannu Tuva postage stamps all over the picket fence
like when Mrs Kindhead comes to collect for the Community
Chest
grab her and tell her There are unfavorable omens in the sky!
And when the mayor comes to get my vote tell him
When are you going to stop people killing whales!
And when the milkman comes leave him a note in the bottle
Penguin dust, bring me penguin dust, I want penguin dust—

Yet if I should get married and it's Connecticut and snow
and she gives birth to a child and I am sleepless, worn,

up for nights, head bowed against a quiet window, the past be-
    hind me,
finding myself in the most common of situations a trembling man
knowledged with responsibility not twig-smear nor Roman coin
    soup—
O what would that be like!
Surely I'd give it for a nipple a rubber Tacitus
For a rattle a bag of broken Bach records
Tack Della Francesca all over its crib
Sew the Greek alphabet on its bib
And build for its playpen a roofless Parthenon

No, I doubt I'd be that kind of father
not rural not snow no quiet window
but hot smelly tight New York City
seven flights up, roaches and rats in the walls
a fat Reichian wife screeching over potatoes Get a job!
And five nose running brats in love with Batman
And the neighbors all toothless and dry haired
like those hag masses of the 18th century
all wanting to come in and watch TV
The landlord wants his rent
Grocery store Blue Cross Gas & Electric Knights of Columbus
Impossible to lie back and dream Telephone snow, ghost park-
    ing—
No! I should not get married I should never get married!
But—imagine If I were married to a beautiful sophisticated
    woman
tall and pale wearing an elegant black dress and long black
    gloves
holding a cigarette holder in one hand and highball in the other
and we lived high up a penthouse with a huge window
from which we could see all of New York and even farther on
    clearer days
No, can't imagine myself married to that pleasant prison dream—

O but what about love? I forget love
not that I am incapable of love
it's just that I see love as odd as wearing shoes—
I never wanted to marry a girl who was like my mother
And Ingrid Bergman was always impossible

And there's maybe a girl now but she's already married
And I don't like men and—
but there's got to be somebody!
Because what if I'm 60 years old and not married,
all alone in a furnished room with pee stains on my underwear
and everybody else is married! All the universe married but me!

Ah, yet well I know that were a woman possible as I am possible
then marriage would be possible—
Like SHE in her lonely alien gaud waiting her Egyptian lover
so I wait—bereft of 2,000 years and the bath of life.

VARIATIONS ON A GENERATION

1

The most outstanding of all the great services the Beat Generation has thus far rendered is in connection with the use of "measure" in poetry. When the Beat Generation came into existence, poets, with prophetic insight, were already insisting upon the overwhelming importance of supplementing their supplies of old iambics by the use of mixtures containing spontaniety "bop prosody" surreal-real images jumps beats cool measures long rapidic vowels, long long lines, and, the main content, soul. In 1950 these poets gave name to the generation, calling it the Beat Generation; they did not know when they created that stupid name what the vast extent of the future demand would be.

2

—What do you think about the Beat Generation?—
—I don't think it's anything. I don't think it exists. There's no such thing as the Beat Generation.—
—You don't consider yourself beat?—
—Hell no! I don't consider myself beat, or beatified.—
—What are you if not beat?—
—An individual, nothing.—
—They say to be beat is to be nothing.—

—I don't care what they say, there's no Beat Generation.—

—Don't you care about the existence of the beat?—

—Hell no! man!—

—Don't you love your fellow men?—

—No I don't love my fellow man in fact I dislike them very much, except the individual if I get to know him; I don't want to govern or be governed.—

—But you are governed by laws of society.—

—But I'm trying to avoid that.—

—Ah, by avoiding society you become separate from society and being separate from society is being BEAT.—

—Oh, yeah?—

—Yeah.—

—I don't understand. I don't want to be in the society at all, I want to be outside it.—

—Face it, man, you're beat.—

—I am not! It's not even a conscious desire on my part, it's just the way I am, I am what I am.—

—Man, you're so beat you don't know.—

—Oh, yeah?—

—Yeah.—

—Crazy, man.—

—Cool, here, light a joint.—

3

There was no mention of the use of "measure" in poetry; not one of them said a thing about the death of the iambic pentameter in America; they spoke about themselves, not about poetry. The Beat Generation is no longer about poetry. The Beat Generation is now about everything.

4

—And what do you think of the Beat Generation?—

—A generation is a human generation. Beat means to have all the blather knocked out of you by experience, suddenly seeing things as they are. Beat doesn't mean a broken spirit, on the contrary, it's scourged of external blather! Wallace Stevens said the greatest misfortune is not to live in the physical world to feel that one's desire is too difficult to tell from one's despair.—

—But what do you think about the Beat Generation?—

—A certain style, when you look back on it, old photos, Fitzgerald in Paris, 1920, high society, prohibition, jazz; that's more what characterized a generation than what they believed in. The fundamental facts are always the same, the style changes, but the facts, my boy, the facts remain.—

—Are you beat?—

—Well I'm not a square, you see a square is some guy who forces himself arbitrarily into a square auto-life mold, because squareness is not a shape that any living creature occurs in. There are all varieties of squares in America. Take for instance a sharecropper, only thing he'd share would be his manure, now that's kind of square, ain't it?—

—You're beat, then?—

—Beatness may result from any sort of fundamental experience, a particular form of insight whereby your realize that nine tenths of everything that moves and operates people is ——!—

11

—Sir, would you care to comment on the general impression that the Beat Generation stands for promiscuous, even perverted, sex, and the use of narcotics, drugs which have been outlawed by the United States of America and every other civilized country in the world today?—

—I would say that the Beat Generation challenges as any generation must challenge everything that has been done and acted before. We will not force ourselves into any hand-me-down-inherited straight-jacket of all cast-off moral concepts mixed with beastly superstition derived from the primitive mythology which is found in the bible—not that I have any objection to mythology in its proper place. We are human. And we are many. And we will have our voice in changing and making the laws which govern so-called civilized countries today; laws which have covered the earth with secret police, concentration camps, oppression, slavery, wars, death.—

—Is the Beat Generation a generation of outlaws? On what

grounds do you presume to declare yourself exempt from your fellow humans?—

—Was the father of our country an outlaw? Yes. Was Galileo an outlaw for saying the world was round?—I say the world is round! not square! This is a fact.—

13

—Hey, what do you know about the Beat Generation?—

—What we are witnessing is a delicate shift of total consciousness in America—It won't be done through publicity or propaganda, articles or any form of—brainwashing persuasion—it will occur as response to altered history scene. Statue of Liberty standing surrounded by the garbage of materialism, a sea of humanity starves in the water outside her. Love puts pressure—humanity forced into the brain and Congress. New fact, Sputnik, Heisenberg, China, Soul, Angels (the image of man)—these latter apparitions of what was sensed before. The shift and new recognition can only be incarnated and commenced thru great works of Art (as Whitman rightly demanded from poets to come)—Art to stand beacon like Statue naked and courageous, individual statement of private actual, uncensored individual perception. Always assuming as did Whitman and the early democrats—that free will is not destructive. An inspiration contrary to the teachings of the evil religions. It was the atheistical enlightment which first framed the ideal democratic declaration of independence. Therefore a new art whose objectivity will be the accuracy of its introspection—the bringing forth of heretofore hidden materials, lusts, spiritual ambitions, experiences—in the new forms in which they will necessarily arrive—rather than the cringing self-consciousness of the psyche whose individuality has been so thwarted—that it masks itself and deceives others—under a guise of a received system of thought, of a system of thought at all, a received mode of feeling (which is never received but constantly occurs on its own) (when true) (when at all) or measure, stanzaic or structural, as far as its poesy is concerned. O fear of the fury of subjective revolution, death and new beat insight!—

PART TWO

"HEART BEAT"

Enter Neal Cassady

Neal Cassady, the central character Dean Moriarty in *On the Road,* was born on February 8, 1926, in Salt Lake City, Utah. His parents were en route to Hollywood, California, where his father planned to open a barbershop. The barbershop failed, and the family moved to Denver, where Cassady's parents separated when he was six years old. As he described his childhood in his posthumously published autobiography, *The First Third* (1971), he lived with his alcoholic father in a series of rooms in skid row hotels on Larimer Street and grew up with considerable freedom. Before he was twenty-one, by his own count, he had stolen five hundred cars to go joyriding with girlfriends and served fifteen months in reform schools.

In 1945, Cassady met a young Columbia University anthropology student named Hal Chase, who had returned to his home in Denver for the summer. Chase had shared a communal apartment with Joan Vollmer the previous spring and gotten to know Jack Kerouac, William Burroughs, Allen Ginsberg, Herbert Huncke, and other Times Square characters who were friends of Huncke's. When Chase went back to Columbia, Cassady wrote him letters that Chase showed the others in the group. In December 1946, after Cassady got out of the reformatory, he rode a Greyhound bus to New York City with his teenage wife, LuAnne Henderson, and Chase introduced him to Ginsberg and Kerouac. Kerouac described their meeting in the opening chapter of *On the Road* and in his second book about Cassady, *Visions of Cody.*

At first Kerouac was put off by Cassady's hustle and opportunism, associating Cassady with the French Canadian punks he'd avoided as a boy in Lowell. Then Cassady won him over by what Kerouac called "his madness," and they began to hang out in bars together. As Kerouac wrote in the first draft of *On the Road,* "He was conning me, so-called, and I knew it, and he knew I knew (this has been the basis of our relation) but I didn't care and we got along fine."

Jack also listened while Neal began "attacking Allen with a great amorous soul such as only a conman can have. I was in the same room. I heard them across the darkness and I mused and said to myself, 'Hmm, now something's started, but I don't want anything to do with it.' " Kerouac stayed aloof from Cassady and Ginsberg's love affair, but he described them in one of the most memorable passages in the opening of *On the Road,* when he wrote that Neal and Allen "danced down the streets like dingledodies, and I shambled after as I've been doing all my life after people who interest me, because the only people for me are the mad ones, the ones who are mad to live, mad to talk, mad to be saved, desirous of everything at the same time, the ones who never yawn or say a commonplace thing, but burn, burn, burn like fabulous yellow roman candles exploding like spiders across the stars and in the middle you see the blue centerlight pop and everybody goes 'Awww!' "

Kerouac and Ginsberg both encouraged Cassady to become a writer, but Cassady was a much more important influence on Kerouac than Kerouac was on him. Cassady's letters to Kerouac started immediately after he boarded the bus from New York City back to Denver in 1947. He told Jack "when it comes to letters I show up most badly," but Kerouac was immediately impressed by his friend's uninhibited rush of words and his explicit description of his sexual exploits. He called Cassady's letter of March 7, 1947, from Kansas City describing his Greyhound bus seduction of two girls, one named Pat and the other an unnamed virgin, a "Great Sex Letter." Kerouac was struggling to finish *The Town and the City* at this time, and Cassady urged him to "just write Jack, write! forget everything else."

Cassady's belief that writing should be read as "a continuous chain of undisciplined thought," communicated in hundreds of letters to Kerouac over the next few years, became the basis of Kerouac's literary aesthetic of spontaneous prose. In mid-December 1950, Kerouac was suffering from an acute writer's block, unable to find a way to write a book he'd been trying to write for years, that he was tentatively calling "On the Road." A letter from Cassady once again got him past the logjam. This was the great "Joan Anderson" letter from Cassady in December 1950 that rambled on for thousands of words, describing his hospital visit to his girlfriend Joan after her suicide attempt, and his escape out the bathroom window after he was caught making love with another girlfriend he called "Cherry Mary" in a Denver apartment where she was baby-sitting.

The "Joan Anderson" letter convinced Kerouac that the best way to write his own novel was to tell the story of his trips cross-country with Cassady as if he were writing a letter to a friend, using first-person narration. Kerouac called Neal's prose "kickwriting," and encouraged him to "write only what kicks you and keeps you overtime awake from sheer mad joy." Later he told Cassady that he was writing a book about their road adventures as if it were a long letter explaining them to his wife Joan Haverty, and would hide nothing about what they did together, and explain only what was "painfully necessary."

Cassady's letters and Burroughs's first book, *Junky,* which Kerouac read in manuscript early in 1951, were the inspiration for Kerouac's remarkable portrayal of Cassady and their cross-country trips in *On the Road* when he finally broke through and wrote the book as an autobiographical novel in a three-week burst of typing in April 1951. The poet Gary Snyder understood that "what got Kerouac and Ginsberg about Cassady was the energy of the archetypal West, the energy of the frontier, still coming down. Cassady is the cowboy crashing. The whole thing is of that order."

According to biographer Gerald Nicosia, Cassady began his own autobiography shortly after meeting Kerouac and Ginsberg. He planned it in three parts, beginning with a prologue about his family background. He only completed the prologue and three chapters of the first volume of his life story, which he called *The First Third,* describing the first nine years of his life in Denver. Kerouac saw these chapters in manuscript while living with Neal and his wife Carolyn in San Francisco in 1952.

Cassady's earnest efforts to tell his life story gave Kerouac the idea of writing his own "Visions of Neal" about Cassady's family and childhood in Denver, which became part of the book Kerouac started after *On the Road* and published posthumously as *Visions of Cody.* As Jack admitted in the early days of his friendship with Neal, "I began to learn from him as much as he probably learned from me."

Lawrence Ferlinghetti published *The First Third* three years after Cassady's death on February 4, 1968, in San Miguel de Allende, Mexico. As Ferlinghetti understood in his "Editor's Note" in the City Lights edition of Cassady's autobiography,

> The West that Cassady grew up in—the skidrows, hobo jungles, barbershops and back streets of Denver—is a time and place as remote as the Gold Rush—a 1930s America that exists today only in forlorn bus stations in small, lost towns. . . .
>
> The homespun, primitive prose has a certain naive charm, at once antic and antique, often awkward and doubling back upon itself, like a fast talker (which is what Cassady was rather than a "writer"—in person, he moved and talked like a speeded-up Paul Newman in *The Hustler*).
>
> So hear his hustling voice as you read. . . .

Letter to Jack Kerouac, March 7, 1947 (Kansas City, Mo.)

Dear Jack:

I am sitting in a bar on Market St. I'm drunk, well, not quite, but I soon will be. I am here for 2 reasons; I must wait 5 hours for the bus to Denver & lastly but, most importantly, I'm here (drinking) because, of course, because of a woman & *what* a *woman!* To be chronological about it:

I was sitting on the bus when it took on more passengers at Indianapolis, Indiana—a perfectly proportioned beautiful, intellectual, passionate, personification of Venus De Milo asked me if the seat beside me was taken!!! I gulped, (I'm drunk) gargled & stammered NO! (Paradox of expression, after all, how can one stammer No!!?) She sat—I sweated—She started to speak, I knew it would be generalities, so to tempt her I remained silent.

She (her name Patricia) got on the bus at 8 PM (Dark!) I didn't speak until 10 PM—in the intervening 2 hours I not only of course, determined to make her, but, how to *DO IT*.

I naturally can't quote the conversation verbally, however, I shall attempt to give you the gist of it from 10 PM to 2 AM.

Without the slightest preliminaries of objective remarks (what's your name? where are you going? etc.) I plunged into a completely knowing, completely subjective, personal & so to speak "penetrating her core" way of speech; to be shorter, (since I'm getting unable to write) by 2 AM I had her swearing eternal love, complete subjectivity to me & immediate satisfaction. I, anticipating even more pleasure, wouldn't allow her to blow me on the bus, instead we played, as they say, with each other.

Knowing her supremely perfect being was completely mine (when I'm more coherent, I'll tell you her complete history & psychological reason for loving me) I could conceive of no obstacle to my satisfaction, well, "the best laid plans of mice & men go astray" and my nemesis was her sister, the bitch.

Pat had told me her reason for going to St. Louis was to see her sister; she had wired her to meet her at the depot. So, to get rid of the sister, we peeked around the depot when we arrived at St. Louis at 4 AM to see if she (her sister) was present. If not, Pat would claim her suitcase, change clothes in the rest room & she and I proceed to a hotel room for a night (years?) of perfect bliss. The sister was not in sight, so She (note the capital) claimed her bag & retired to the toilet to change———long dash———

This next paragraph must, of necessity, be written completely objectively—

Edith (her sister) & Patricia (my love) walked out of the pisshouse hand in hand (I shan't describe my emotions). It seems Edith (bah) arrived at the bus depot early & while waiting for Patricia, feeling sleepy, retired to the head to sleep on a sofa. That's why Pat & I didn't see her.

My desperate efforts to free Pat from Edith failed, even

Pat's terror & slave-like feeling toward her rebelled enough to state she must see "someone" & would meet Edith later, *all* failed. Edith was wise; she saw what was happening between Pat & I.

Well, to summarize: Pat & I stood in the depot (in plain sight of the sister) & pushing up to one another, vowed to never love again & then I took the bus for Kansas City & Pat went home, meekly, with her dominating sister. Alas, alas————

In complete (try & share my feeling) dejection, I sat, as the bus progressed toward Kansas City. At Columbia, Mo. a young (19) completely passive (my meat) *virgin* got on & shared my seat . . . In my dejection over losing Pat, the perfect, I decided to sit on the bus (behind the driver) in broad daylight & seduce her, from 10:30 AM to 2:30 PM I talked. When I was done, she (confused, her entire life upset, metaphysically amazed at me, passionate in her immaturity) called her folks in Kansas City, & went with me to a park (it was just getting dark) & I banged her; I screwed as never before; all my pent up emotion finding release in this young virgin (& she was) who is, by the by, a *school teacher!* Imagine, she's had 2 years of Mo. St. Teacher's College & now teaches Jr. High School. (I'm beyond thinking straightly).

I'm going to stop writing. Oh, yes, to free myself for a moment from my emotions, you must read "Dead Souls" parts of it (in which Gogol shows his insight) are quite like you.

I'll elaborate further later (probably?) but at the moment I'm drunk & happy (after all, I'm free of Patricia already, due to the young virgin. I have no name for her. At the happy note of Les Young's "jumping at Mesners" (which I'm hearing) I close till later.

To my Brother
Carry On!
N. L. Cassady

*Letter to Jack Kerouac, July 3, 1949 (some lines later used
by Kerouac in Part Three of* On the Road *as Dean's
account of his "twenty-dollar Buick.")*

Dear Jack:

I feel like a remembering of things past. So, here's a brief history of arrests. A case history.

My first job was on a bike delivery around Denver. I meet a lad named Ben with whom I used to steal anything we saw as we cruised in the early A.M. in his 27 Buick. One of the things we did was smash the high school principal's car, another was steal chickens from a man he disliked, another was strip cars and sell the parts. I bought the Buick from him for $20. My first car; it couldn't pass the brake and light inspection, so I decided I needed an out of state license to operate the car without arrest. I went to Wichita, Kansas to get the plates. As I was hitchhiking home with the plates concealed under my coat I passed thru Russell, Kansas. Walking down the main drag I was accosted by a nosey sheriff who must have thought I was pretty young to be hiking. He found the plates and threw me in the two cell jail with a county delinquent who should have been in the home for the old since he couldn't feed himself (The sheriff's wife fed him) and sat thru the day drooling and slobbering. After investigation, which included corny things like a fatherly quiz, then an abrupt turnabout to frighten me with threats, a comparison of my handwriting etc. I was released and hiked back to Denver. As I think back, I can recall much of my crimes and little of my next arrest, but, I believe this was my second arrest. I had been to Indianapolis for the 39 Auto classic and to South Bend to see Notre Dame and to Calif. to live in L.A. and all this hitchhiking on my own had made me see the wisdom of hiking in the day and stealing a car when nite fell to make good time. Well, when I returned to Denver this became a habit and every nite I'd sleep in some apt. house bathtub and get up and find some friends place to eat then steal a car to pick up girls at school when they got out. I might change cars in midafternoon, but at any rate I'd get some girl and spend the night in the mountains, returning at daybreak to my bathtub. I got tired of this and decided to go back to Calif. I knew a fellow named Bill Smith and he wanted to come along. One day in the spring of 41, I was just 15, we stole a Plymouth on Stout and 16th Sts. We ran out of gas just as we pulled into Colo. Springs. I walked a block or so and saw a 38 Buick at the curb, got in, picked up Bill on the corner and we were off again.

Passing thru Pueblo I saw a cop's car behind and suggested we cut and run, but Bill was adamant, Sure enough they stopped us, disbelieved our story, and took us down. At the police station I found they had caught us so quickly because it happened I'd picked up the D.A.'s car. An hour later the C. Springs D.A. came to regain his car and take us back to be tried. They wouldn't believe Bill's name was really Bill Smith for it sounded so like an alias. They wouldn't believe he was a hitchhiker too, as I told them. I had some Vaseline for my chapped lips and the desk copper leered and asked if we punked each other. We were confined in the Springs County jail for thirty days, then taken to trial. Smith's father was there and got us off. Again, I returned to Denver.

The next arrest was a year later. During that time I'd returned to my brother's to sleep, but didn't work and kept up the car stealing routine with the girls each nite. I left my brother, lived with one Bill Matley (I had before). We started to Calif. again. This time Matley and I had no trouble until we got to Albuquerque. We were washed out in a really disasterous flood (knocked out water supply, etc). We were stranded for two days, getting no rides and finding no cars to steal. We spent the night in a RR roundhouse. Bill wanted to return, me too. I finally saw a doctor park his Buick for a minute in front of the hospital. I dashed up, got in and picked up Bill, and we were off for Denver. After a 100 miles or so we were drunk from the pint we'd found on the floor, and Bill wanted to drive. He did, at 80 MPH he skidded in the still raining weather and we hit the ditch. We walked and etc. to get back. I was flirting with Justin that fall of 41 and living at his Aunt & Uncle's. I was stealing cars with Ben again and strippin them. One night, we were cruising about and just happened to drive by a lot where I'd parked a hot car some months before, in the summer. I glanced at the spot and, believe it or not, my eyes saw the same car. We couldn't believe it and creep warily up to it. As you know, Jack, a hot car, if left on a lot in the lower downtown section was sure to be found in a few days. (The lot was, since you're in Denver, on Lawrence St. between 19th & 20th) Well, somehow this car had been sitting there for 5 months and still wasn't found. Were we elated! This meant the car was cool by now and we could disguise it and keep it for our own. The local kids had played in it and pulled apart some, damaged the radio etc. but we got it going, put air in the tires at a station and were. . . . I just paused to reread this—too hastily done, silly: I stop. I been arrested 10 times and served an aggravated total of 15 months on six convictions. . . .

Letter to Jack Kerouac, July 20, 1950 (fragment)

On my first R.R. trip another brakeman I knew well & myself were standing between a morning freight & a passenger we were to board. As the end of the freight passed, an overwide boxcar approached us, (as the engine of the stopping passenger arrived) & seeing how really close it was, I extended my nerves & put all my effort into facing the wide car & turning my body sidewise; my nose grazed the car door, but I escaped.

He didn't; when I turned around as the caboose passed, he was lying under the passenger kicking & twitching like a dying rabbit. I lifted him to a bench 2 tracks away & told the passenger conductor to get an ambulance & doctor.

His head was bashed in, the area from the back of the neck to the midpoint of the skull, & from ear almost to ear, was flattened; blood was matted; in his hand he held the hat; he refused to part his fingers. It took me at least 10 minutes to fall asleep, after I had boarded the passenger train, I was so affected. You gotta watch your step in the West. . . .

Letter to Jack Kerouac, September 10, 1950 (after their trip to Mexico City described in On the Road)

Dear Jack: (Writing on engine of train)

My great wonderful friend. I have done you the justice of reading your letter from Richmond Hill high and gone to inner-inner land.

I must say you are M'boy, you beauty—well, ammit, Listen. I'm going to begin from the moment I left you & Frank & go to Now. This is such a gigantic task, I feel like Proust & you must indulge me.

Left M. City, "tightening my belt" for long drive ahead. Became more engrossed in landscape & noting people as I drove. Being alone, I was not called upon to make summaries to any other mind & since I was not responding to other voices calling my attention to other views of countryside or otherwise, did not notice what I may have missed seeing as I drove, because there was no one to call my attention to it and thus having only my own mad thoughts to contend with, I responded to each emotion perfectly as it came.

The arduous climb thru the mountain passes with the extreme beauty of handling the car so as to function perfectly on the road's surface while my mind was thinking such thoughts that soon I actually thought of how at last I could tell you on paper perhaps the knowledge of action—But later—anyway —I must emphasize how wonderful it was.

Now, eyeball kicks are among the world's greatest, second to none actually in terms of abstract thought, because it is thru the way you handle these kicks that is what determines your particular conclusion (in abstraction in the mind) to each moment's outlook. Remembrance of your life & your eyeball view are actually the only 2 immediate first hand things your mind can carry instantly.

One's mind carries at all times the pressure of its own existence, and remembers previous eyeball views to recall what its previous life has been & feeding on this stuff, carries a heavy understanding of things it is capable of knowing & this knowing is blocked from coming out, because while one's mind carries one's life's past constantly, it also carries before it all day the world which comes in thru the eyeball.

I became so engrossed in my eyeballs & what they brought me over each ridge & thru each town that I looked out into the world as one looks into a picture. My field of vision then became like the canvas, and as I looked, I saw 4 corners of the frame which held the picture. Since then, at any moment when I feel the slightest ennui, I simply look up from what

I'm doing & note carefully the particular scene before my eyes.

(Right now—to my left the fat greasy neck of the blubbery fireman carefully picking his nose.)

from
"Joan Anderson"
letter to Jack Kerouac

[*Dec. 17(?), 1950*]

To have seen a specter isn't everything, and there are death-masks piled, one atop the other, clear to heaven. Commoner still are the wan visages of those returning from the shadow of the valley. This means little to those who have not lifted the veil.

The ward nurse cautioned me not to excite her (how can one prevent that?) and I was allowed only a few minutes. The headnurse also stopped me to say I was permitted to see her just because she always called my name and I must cheer her. She had had a very near brush and was not rallying properly, actually was in marked decline, and still much in danger. Quite impressed to my duties, I entered and gazed down on her slender form resting so quietly on the high white bed. Her pale face was whiter; like chalk. It was pathetically clear how utterly weak she was, there seemed absolutely no blood left in her body. I stared and stared, she didn't breath, didn't move; I would never have recognized her, she was a waxed mummy. White is the absence of all color, she was white; all white, unless beneath the covers, whose top caressed her breasts, was still hidden a speck of pink. The thin ivory arms tapered inward until they reached the slight outward bulge of narrow palms, and the hands in turn bent inward with a more sharp taper only to quickly end in long fingers curled to a point. These things, and her head, with its completely matted hair so black and contrasting with all the whiteness, were the only parts of her visible. Quite normal, I know, but I just couldn't get over how awfully dead she looked. I had so arranged my head above hers that when her eyes opened, after about ten minutes, they were in direct line with mine; they showed no surprise, nor changed their position in the slightest. The faintest of smiles, the merest of voices, "hello." I placed my hand on her arm, it was all I could do to restrain myself from jumping on the bed to hold her. I saw she was too weak to talk and told her not to, I, however, rambled on at a great rate.

There was no doubt she was over-joyed to see me, her eyes said so. It was as though the gesture of self-destruction had, in her mind, equalized all the guilt. The courage of committing the act seemed to have justified her to herself. This action on her conviction, no matter how neurotic, had called for all her strength and she was now released. Free from the urge, since the will-for-death needs a strong concentration of pressure to fulfill itself and once accomplished via attempt, is defeated until another period of buildup is gone through; unless, of course, one succeeds in reaching death the first shot, or is really mad. Gazing down on her, with a grin of artificial buoyancy, I sensed this and felt an instant flood of envy. She had escaped, at least for some time, and I knew I had yet to make my move. Being a coward I had postponed too long and I realized I was further away from commitment than ever. Would hesitancy never end? She shifted her cramped hand, I looked down and for the first time noticed the tight sheet covering a flat belly. It was empty, sunken; she had lost her baby. For a moment I wondered if she knew it, then thought she must know—even now she was almost touching her stomach, and she'd been in the hospital ten days—surely a stupid idea. I resolved to think better. The nurse glided up and said I'd better go; promising to return the next visiting day, I leaned over and kissed Joan's clear forehead and left.

Off to the poolhall, back to the old grind; I seemed to have a mania. From the way I loafed there all day one would scarcely believe I'd never been in a poolhall two short years before; why, less than six months ago I still couldn't bear to play more than one game at a time. Well, what is one to say about things he has done? I never again went back to the hospital to bless Joan, oh, that's what I felt like; blessing her. Each day I lacerated myself thinking on her, but I didn't go back. "Sometimes I sits and thinks. Other times I sits and drinks, but mostly I just sits." I must have been in a pretty bad way.

Anyhow, two more weeks went by in this fashion, my inability to stir from my poolhall prison became a joke, even to me. It was the night before Christmas, about five PM, when a handsome woman near forty came inside the gambling gaol's gates and asked for me. I went up front to meet her, as I came closer I saw she was better than handsome, a real good-looker and despite her age, making quite a stir among the boys. She introduced herself, said she was a friend of Joan and invited me to dinner. My heart bounced with guilty joy, I accepted and we walked the five blocks to this fine-though-forty lady's apartment without talking. The fatherly taxidriver opened the door, my hostess said it was her husband and that Joan would be out in a minute. Preparations for a huge dinner were in the making, I sat on the sofa and waited. The bathroom—ugly word—door swung out and before my eyes was once again the gorgeous Joan, "second" of Jennifer Jones. Fresh from the shower, mirror-primped, stepped my heroine resplendent in her new friend's housecoat. Just when you think you've learned your lesson and swear to watch your step, a single moment offguard will pop up and hope springs high as ever. One startled look and I knew I was right back where I started; I felt again that choking surge flooding me as when first I'd seen her. I started talking to myself, determined to whip the poolhall rut and drag my stinking ass out of the hole.

Over the prosperous supper on which we soon pounced hung an air of excitement. Joan and I were leaping with lovelooks across the roastbeef, while cabby and wife beamed on us. And we planned, yessir, all four of us, and right out loud too. I was kinda embarrassed at first when the host began without preamble, "Alright, you kids have wasted enough time, I see you love each other and you're going to settle down right now. In the morning Joan is starting at St. Luke's as a student nurse, she's told me that's what she would like to do. As for you, Neal, if you're serious I'll get up a little early tomorrow and before I go to work we'll see if my boss will give you a job. If you can't get away with telling them you're 21—the law says you gotta be 21, you're not that old yet are you? (I said no) so that you can drive taxi, you can probably get a job servicing the cabs. That okay with you?" I said certainly it was and thanked him; and everybody laughed and was happy. It was further decided that Joan and I stay with them until we got our first paycheck; we would sleep on the couch that opened out into a bed. Gorged with the big meal, I retired to the bathroom as the women did the dishes and the old man read the paper. (By golly, it seems everything I write about happens in a bathroom, don't think I'm hungup that way, it's just the incidents exactly as they occurred, and here is another one, because—) A knock on the toilet door and I rose to let in my resurrected beauty. She was as coy as ever, but removed was much fear and embarrassment. We did a bit of smooching, then, seated on the edge of the tub she asked if I wanted to see her scar. I kneeled before her to observe better as she parted the bathrobe to reveal an ugly red wound, livid against her buttermilk belly, stretching nearly from naval to the clitoris. She was worried I wouldn't think her as beautiful, or love her as much now that her body had been marred by the surgeon's knife performing a Caesarean. There might have been a partial hysterectomy too and she fretted that the production of more babies—"when we get the money"—would prove difficult. I reassured her on all counts, swore my love (and meant it) and finally we returned to the livingroom.

Oh, unhappy mind; trickster! O fatal practicality! I was wearing really filthy clothes but had a change promised me by a friend who lived at 12th and Ogden Sts. So as not to hangup my dwarf cabbie savior when we went to see his buddyboss next A.M., my foolish head thought to make a speedrun and get the necessary clean impediments now. Acting on this obvious need—if I was to impress my hoped-for employer into hiring me—I promised to hurry back, and left. Where is wisdom? Joan offered to walk with me, and I turned down the suggestion reasoning it was very cold and I could make better time alone, besides, she was still pretty weak, and if she was to work tomorrow the strain of the fairly long walk might prove too much,—no sense jeopardizing her health. Would that I'd made her walk with me, would that she'd collapsed rather than let me go alone, would anything instead of what happened! Not only did the new promise for happiness go down the drain, and I lost Joan forever, but her peace was to evaporate once and for all, and she herself was to sink into the iniquity reserved for a certain type of beaten women!

I rushed my trip to the clothes depot, made good connections and was quickly on my way back to the warm apartment and my Joan. The route from 12th and Ogden to 16th and Lincoln Sts. lies for the most part, if one so desires, along East Colfax Ave. Horrible mistake, stupid moment; I chose that path just to dig people on the crowded thoroughfare as I hustled by them. At midblock between Pennsylvania and Pearl Sts. is a tavern whose plateglass front ill-conceals the patrons of its booths. I was almost past this bar when I glanced up to see my younger blood-brother inside drinking beer alone. I had made good time and the hard habit of lushing that I was then addicted to pushed me through the door to bum a quickie off him. Surprise, surprise, he was loaded with loot and, more surprising, gushed all over me. He ordered as fast as I could drink, and I didn't let the waitress stop, finishing the glass in a gulp; one draught for the first few, then two for the next several and so on until I was sipping normally by the time an hour had fled. First off he wanted a phone number—the reason for his generosity I suspect—and I was the only one who could give it to him. He claimed to have been sitting there actually brooding over the very girl on the other end of this phone number, and I believed him; had to take it true, because for the last five months it had become increasingly clear that he was hot-as-hell for this chick—who was my girl. I gave him the number and he dashed from one booth to the other. I had cautioned him not to mention my name, nor to tell her I was there, and he said he wouldn't. But he did, although he denied it later. The reason for his disloyalty, despite the fact it cost me Joan, was justifiable since as one might when about to be denied a date of importance while drinking, he had used my whereabouts as a lastditch lure to tempt her out. He came back to the booth from the phonebooth crestfallen, she had said she couldn't leave the house just now, but to call her back in a half-hour or so; this didn't cheer him as it would have me, he's richer and less easily satisfied. He called her again, about forty five minutes after I had first been pulled into the dive by my powerful thirst, and she said for him to wait at this joint and she'd be down within an hour. This length of time didn't seem unreasonable, she lived quite a ways further out in East Denver. I thought everything was going perfectly. Bill got the Girl, I got my drinks and still had a short period of grace in which to slop up more before she showed (I certainly didn't intend to be there when she arrived) and I'd only be a little late returning to Joan where I'd plead hassel in getting the clothes. O sad shock, O unpleasant time; had I just not guzzled that last beer all the following would not be written and I could end this story with "And they lived happily ever after."

Whoa, read slowly for a bit and have patience with my verbosity. There are two things I've got to say here, one is a sidepoint and it'll come second, the first is essential to the understanding of this story; so, I gotta give you one of my Hollywood flashbacks.

I'll leave out the most of it and be as brief as possible to make it tight, although, by the nature of it, this'll be hard— especially since I'm tired.

Number 1: On June 23, 1945 I was released from New Mexico State Reformatory, after doing eleven months and 10 days (know the song?) of hard labor. Soon after returning to Denver I had the rare luck to meet a 16-year-old East Hi beauty who had well-to-do parents; a mother and pretty older sister to be exact. Cherry Mary (Mary Ann Fairland) was her name because she lived on Cherry Street and was a cherry when I met her. That condition didn't last long. I ripped into her like a maniac and she loved it. A tremendous affair, countless things to be said about it—I can hardly help from blurting out twenty or thirty statements right now despite resolution to condense. I'm firm (ha) and won't tell the story of our five months' intercourse—with its many incidents that are percolating this moment in my brain; about carnival-night we met (Elitch's), the hundreds of mountain trips in her new Mercury, rented trucks with the mattress in back, at her cabin, cabins I broke into, day I got her to bang Hal Chase, time I gave her clap after momentous meeting between her and mother of my second child (only boy before Diana's), time I knocked her up; and knocked it, mad nights and early A.M.'s at Goodyear factory I worked alone in from 4 P.M. to anytime I wanted to go home, doing it on golfcourses, roofs, parks, cemeteries (you know, dead peoples' homes), snowbanks, schools and schoolyards, hotel bathrooms, her mother's vacant houses (she was a realtor), doing it every way we could think of any-old-place we happened to be, in fact, we did it in so many places that Denver was covered with our peckertracks; so many different ones that I can't possibly remember, often we'd treck clear from one side of town to another just to find a spot to drop to it, on ordinary occasions, however, I'd just pull it out and shove—to her bottom if we were secluded, to her mouth if not, the greatest most humorous incident of the lot: to please her mother she'd often babysit for some of their socially prominent and wealthy friends several times a week, I drove out to that particular evening's assignment, after she called to give the address and say the coast was clear, (funny English joke; man and wife in livingroom, phone rings, man answers and says he wouldn't know, better call the coast guard, and hangs up, wife says, "Who was it, dear?" and man says, "I don't know, some damn fool who wanted to know if the coast was clear," har-har-har) and we quickly tear-off several goodies, then, I go back to work; in Goodyear truck, don't you know. We'd done this numerous times when the "most humorous" evening came up. It was a Sunday night, so no work, I waited outside 16th and High Street apartment till parents left and then went in and fell to it. I had all my clothes off and in livingroom as she was washing my cock in bathroom, (let this be a lesson to you, men, never become separated from your clothes, at least keep your trousers handy, when doing this sort of thing in a strange house—oops, my goodness, I forgot for a second that some of you are out of circulation and certainly not in any need of "Lord Chesterfield's" counseling— don't show this to your wives, or tell them that I only offer this advice to pass on to your sons, or, if that's too harsh, to your dilettante friends, whew!, got out of that) there's a rattling of the apartment door and into the front room walks the mother of one of the parents of the baby Cherry Mary is watching, so fast did this old bat come in that we barely had time to shut the bathroom door before she saw us. Here I was, nude, no clothes, and all exits blocked. I couldn't stay there for what if the old gal wanted to pee, and most old women's bladders and kidneys are not the best in the world. There was no place in the bathroom to hide, nor could I sneak out due to the layout of the apartment. Worse, Mary suddenly remembered the fact that this intruder was expected to stay the night. We consulted in whispers, laughing and giggling despite all, and it was decided Mary would leave the bathroom and keep the old lady busy while suggesting a walk or coffee down the street and still try to collect my clothes and get them to me; no mean feat. My task was to, as quietly as a mouse, remove all the years-long collection of rich peoples' bath knick-knacks that blocked the room's only window, then, impossible though it looked, I must climb up the tub to it and with a fingernail file pry loose the outside screen. Now, look at this window, it had four panes of glass 6″ long and 4″ wide, it formed a rectangle of about 12 or 13″ high and 8 or 9″ across, difficult to squeeze through at best, but, being modern as hell, the way it was hooked to its frame was by a single metal bar in direct center! which when opened split the panes of glass down the middle and made two windows.

I could hardly reach outside to work on the screen—since the window opened outward—but I pushed and making a hell-ova noise, split the screen enough to open the window. Now the impossible compressing of my frame for the squeeze. I thought if I could get my head through I could make it; I just was able to, by bending the tough metal bar the slightest cunt-hair (in those days I cleaned and jerked 220 lbs.) and of course, I almost tore off my pride-and-joy as I wiggled out into the cold November air. I was damn glad I was only on the second floor, if I'd been higher I would have been hungup in space for sure. So I dropped into the bushes bordering the walk along the side of the building, and hid there shivering and gloating with glee. There was a film of snow on the ground, but this didn't bother anything except my feet until some man parked his car in the alley garage and came walking past my hideaway, then, much of my naked body got wet as I pressed against the icy ground so he wouldn't see me. This made me seek better shelter since it was about 9 P.M.—I'd been in the cold an hour—and a whole string of rich bastards with cars might start putting them away. I waited until no one was in sight then dashed down the walk to the alley and leaped up and grabbed the handy drainpipe of a garage and pulled myself up. The window I'd broken out of overlooked my new refuge and if anyone went in that bathroom they'd see the havoc wrought the place and be looking out to see me. This fear had just formed—I was too cold to be jolly now—when I saw Mary at last come into view. She had my pants, shoes and coat, but not my T-shirt and socks, having skipped these small items as she bustled about in front of the cause of my predicament "straightening up." The woman had only noticed my belt and Mary had said she had a leather class at school and was engraving it. When I'd bashed out the window Mary had heard the crashing about, (the old lady must have been deaf; while I was escaping kept talking about Thanksgiving turkey!)***and had come in the bathroom to clean up, close the window and otherwise coverup. I put on my clothes and chattering uncontrollably from my freezeout walked with Mary to the Oasis Cafe for some hot coffee. And so it goes, tale after tale revolving around this Cherry Mary period; here's just a couple more:

At first the mother of this frantic fucking filly confided in me and, to get me on her side, asked me to take care of Mary, watch her and so forth. After awhile, as Mary got wilder, the old bitch decided to give me a dressing down, (I can't remember the exact little thing that led up to this, offhand anyhow) and since she wasn't the type to do it herself—and to impress me, I guess—she got the pastor of the parish to give me a lecture. Now, her home was in one of the elite parishes and so she got the monseigneur—it was a Catholic church—to come over for dinner the same evening she invited me. I arrived a little before him and could at once smell something was cooking. The slut just couldn't hold back her little scheme, told Mary to listen closely and began preaching a little of her own gospel to warm me up for the main event. The doorbell rang and her eyes sparkled with anticipation as she sallied forth from the kitchen to answer it. The priest was a middlesized middleaged pink featured man with extremely thick glasses covering such poor eyes he couldn't see me until our noses almost touched. Coming toward me across the palatial livingroom he had his handshake extended and was in the midst of a normal greeting, the mother escorting him by elbow all the while and gushing introduction. Then it happened, he saw me; what an expression! I've never seen a chin drop so far so fast, it literally banged his breastbone. "Neal!! Neal!, my boy!, at last I've found my boy!" his voice broke as he said the last word and his Adam's apple refused to articulate further because all it gave out was a strangled blubber. Choked with emotion, he violently clasped me to him and flung his eyes to heaven fervently thanking his God. Tremendous tears rolled down his cheeks, poured over his upthrust jaw, and disappeared inside his tight clerical collar. I had trouble deciding whether to leave my arms hanging limp or throw them around him and try to return the depth of his goodness by turning to it. Golly and whooooeee!, what a sight!! The priest's emotion had been one of incredulous joyous recognition, Mary's mother's emotion was a gem of frustrated surprise; startled wonder at such an unimaginable happening left her gaping at us with the most foolish looking face I've ever seen. She didn't know whether to faint or flee, never had she been so taken aback, and, I'm sure, didn't think she ever would be, it was really a perfect farce. Mary and her sister—who was there to lend dignity to her mother's idea—were as slackjawed as any of us. Depend on sweet Mary to recover first, she did, with a giggle; which her sister took as a cue to frown upon, thereby regaining her senses. The mother's composure came with a gasp of artificial goo, "Well! what a pleasant surprise!!" she gurgled with strained smile, feeling lucky that she'd snuck out from under so easily. Oho!, but wait, aha! she'd made a mistake! Her tension was so unbearable—and she had succeeded so well with her first words—that she decided to speak again, "Let's all go into supper, shall we?" she said in a high-pitched nervous urge. The false earnestness of her tone struck us all as a most incongruous concern and she'd given herself away by being too quick—since her guest was still holding me tightly.

The ecstatic priest was Harlan Fischer, my Godfather when I was baptized at age 10 in 1936. He had also taught me Latin for some months and saw me occasionally during the following three years I served at Holy Ghost Church as altar boy. At our last meeting I was engrossed in the lives of the Saints and determined to become a priest or Christian brother, then, I abruptly disappear down the pleasanter path of evil. Now, six and a half years later, he met me again in Mary's house as a youth he'd come to lecture. Well, he didn't get around to the lecture, it never seemed to enter his head because it was too full of blissful joy at finding his lost son. He told me how he'd never had another Godson—it just so happened that way—

and how he'd prayed night and day for my soul and to see me again. He could hardly contain himself at the dinner-table, fidgeted and twittered and didn't touch his food. He dragged the whole story of the long wait for this moment out into the open and before the sullen-hearted (she gave me piercing glances of pure hate when Father Fischer wasn't looking) mother actually waxed moistly eloquent. When the meal was over the dirty old bitch knew her sweet little scheme had backfired completely for Fischer at once excused himself, saying he was sure everyone understood, because he wanted to talk to me alone, and we left. We drove to his church and then sat in his car for two hours before I got out and walked away, never to see him to this very day, now five years since. He started in with the old stuff, and I, knowing there could be no agreement and not wanting to use him unfairly, came down right away and for once I didn't hesitate as I told him not to bother; I was sorry for it, but we were worlds apart and it would now do no good for him to try and come closer. Oh we did a lot of talking, it wasn't quite that short and simple, but as I say, I finally left him when he realized there was nothing more to be said, and that was that.

The other incident I wanted to tell you about can wait, I must cut this to the bone from here on out because I haven't the money for paper. Anyhow, the reason for this little glimpse into the months just prior to meeting Joan was to show there was some cause for what happened to me in the bar with my younger blood brother. Mind you, I hadn't seen Mary's mother for at least a month before this night in the bar, although I'd seen Mary about two weeks earlier. Ah, what's another few lines, I gotta break in here and tell you that other funny little thing about C. Mary. It is this; she was such a hypochondriac that she often played at Blindness. Now wait a minute, this was unusual, because she never complained of illness or anything else, in fact, she didn't complain about her eyes either, just the opposite, she played at having a true martyr complex toward them. Often we'd spend 12–16 hours in a hotel room while she was "blind." I'd wait on her hand and foot (and cock) during these times. They'd begin casually enough, she'd simply announce that she couldn't see and that would go on until she'd just as quietly say she could see again. This happened while she was driving—I'd grab the wheel—while we were walking—I'd lead her—while we were loving—I'd finish anyhow—in fact, this happened any old place she felt like it happening. It was a great little game, she didn't have to worry, if she smacked up the car, or anything, the old lady would come to the rescue with lots of dough, wouldn't she? Oh enough!

Continuing then, from about 1,500 words ago, as to why Joan and I didn't live Happily Ever After; Very simple, we were given no chance.

You see, as I drank the last Blood-Brother beer—I remember deciding in all seriousness that it was definitely the last one—2 plainclothesmen approached, asked if I was Neal C. and promptly hauled me away! It seems Cherry Mary's Mother, listening on the phone extension to my friend give my whereabouts, had called the police—and she was politically powerful! Why, why, after release on statutory rape with testifying flatly refused by panicky Mary and not a shred of evidence otherwise—flatly panicky, I continued to be held in jail charged with suspicion of Burglary! Of my poolhall hangout yet. Because the charge had a superficial plausibility, since I racked balls there a couple of times and knew the layout—I knew a lot of fearful moments before Capt. of Dicks admitted he knew I was clear all along, released me finally weeks later.

Joan had disappeared completely!

Jack Kerouac
Letter to Neal Cassady,
early 1951

Just a word, now, about your wonderful 13,000 word letter about Joan Anderson and Cherry Mary. I thought it ranked among the best things ever written in America and ran to Holmes & Harrington & told them so; I said it was almost as good as the unbelievably good "Notes From Underground" of Dostoevsky. It was with some surprise I saw they weren't as impressed. I think it's because Holmes is really not hip to anything until it begins to sink in much later. I'm going to show it to Giroux if he will. Giroux is a man influenced in his work by personal feelings, therefore he may be prejudiced and blinded. Have no fear, there are others who will dig this for what it is besides me; Morley of England for one & even especially I think. You gather together all the best styles . . . of Joyce, Celine, Dusty & Proust . . . and utilize them in the muscular rush of your own narrative style & excitement. I say truly, no Dreiser, no Wolfe has come too close to it; Melville was never truer. I know that I don't dream. It can't possibly be sparse & halting, like Hemingway, because it hides nothing; the material is painfully necessary . . . the material of Scott Fitz was so sweetly unnecessary. It is the exact stuff upon which American Lit is still to be founded. You must and will go on at all costs including comfort & health & kicks; but keep it kickwriting at all costs too, that is, write only what kicks you and keeps you overtime awake from sheer mad joy. I used to think that Harrington & Fitzgerald were the only good practicing writers I knew; you have so far overshadowed them it's positively humiliating. I told Ed White in a letter that a great man had risen from his home-town. I think all this sincerely. I know I don't dream. A lot of people say I don't know what I'm doing, but of course, I do. Burroughs & Allen said I didn't know what I was doing in the years of Town & City; now they know I did. They revert & start in, re-saying, "He doesn't know," but then it will be proven all over again with disastrous boring regularity, of course I know what I'm doing. Holmes, Giroux, Harrington—all think I don't know what I'm doing. Boring regularity, etc. Because of this my judgment concerning your value is completely sound. I say this to reassure you in case you think I'm cracked, or don't think I'm cracked. You and I will be the two most important writers in America in 20 years at the least. Think that. That's why I see no harm in addressing my next ten novels & possible lifework to you and you alone. Who else? Robt. Penn Warren? This established, that you are a great writer now and have only begun, let me get into details about the letter itself.

Of course you wrote it with painful rapidity & can patch it up later for the benefit of . . . and don't have to if you don't want. It will be published. It was a moment in lit. history when I received that thing & only sweetwife & I read it & knew. Ah man it's great. Don't undervalue your poolhall musings, your excruciating details about streets, appointment times, hotel rooms, bar locations, window measurements, smells, heights of trees. I wait for you to send me the entire thing in disorderly chronological order anytime you say and anytime it comes, because I've just got to read every word you've got to say and take it all in. If that ain't life nothing ain't. Do so, do so. I'm having Joan [Kerouac's second wife] write hers in utter detail from beginning to end, including wonderful moments with old exil sexmen in L.A. who lures little kids (I mean, wonderful reading moments for lascivious lads like me & you); she has just today written a glowingly pure account of her favorite momings and fantasized them into something further & lovely. She really knows how to write from instinct & innocence. Few women can do this. Joan Kerouac . . . a new writer on this old horizon. I see me & her cutting around the world in tweeds, yass . . . Mierschom pipes with you-knowwhat in them, he he. Then consider, listen to what I say, you're the greatest; I have reason to believe that if I am to go on priding myself in my work I will have to hustle to catch you; let anybody scoff at this, I ought to know better than anybody else . . . except you.

Neal, a word or two about my plans. Joan and I have decided to get fulltime jobs till March to save several hundred bucks. In March, if I get a Guggenheim (decided around last week) we will at once buy an old panel truck, load gear, and take off for 3 wonderful lazy years perhaps in provincial Mexico (cheaper than Mexcity.) Texcoco, 30 miles away, 24¢ bus into town that I rode, pissing from the back, with Jeff, under shadow of the snowtopt volcanoes; 1¢ buys waterglass of raw tequila. Can live there off $400 or $500 a year. Guggenheim is $2500 or even 3 grand;—however, not to depend on such a dream of possibilities, if we don't get this dough, we intend to buy old car or truck, pack gear, and drive to Frisco; where we work till I get $1000 from Harcourt if ever they publish me again, if not we will work & live in Frisco, saving best we can, for eventual date in Mexico. This being case, when you get here, I hope you have car so I can get driver's license with you (also few lessons for sharpup). If only you weren't so hung up and could yourself save a few Texcoco's worth of years and come with us, or with the wife & kids . . . if we ever run out of $ together we could ride bus to Texas border and in few months rake up at construction or oilfield work and come back to year of life with kicks & wives. I wish in fact you could do this with all my heart, as with Joan I will be completely happy, but with you, I would also be completely befriended and need nothing; we'd live on same street and meet in dusty alley and go down to teafields to see Jose and hang around sun. Nights, write. I'd have me wife, and me near friend nearby, and you too. $500 a year I say. No foolishness like La Vie Parisienne, but purchase of eggs from country Indians, strict haggling purchases of bread and tortilla mix and pinto beans & cheese; buy bottles water; etc. go to big city for connection as small-town too obvious, and take great care as Bill did with odor as I say big city is hour away in car, 1 and a half in old bus. Texcoco, which you never saw, is south of Mexcity; it is hot and fine, same altitude but somehow drowsier and finer; crazy Gregors all over; Mambo in little doorway joints. It is a town with one square in middle surrounded by crumbling Spanish masonry; 3 old beautiful churches with lovely bells; fiestas almost every day and attendant fireworks; no fancy Americans like at Oaxaca and Taxco and such. We'd hang on to every cent, give the Mexes no quarter, let them get sullen at the cheap Americans and stand side by side in defense, and make friends in the end when they saw we was poor too. Comes another Mex revolution, we stands them off with our Burroughsian arsenal bought cheap on Madero St. and dash to big city in car for safety shooting and pissing as we go; whole Mex army follows hi on weed; now no worries any more. Just sit on roof hi enjoying hot dry sun and sound of kids yelling and have us wives & American talk of our own as well as exotic kicks and regular old honest Indian kicks. Become Indians . . . I personally play mambo in local catband, because of this we get close to them and go to town. Wow. How's about it? Hurry to N.Y. so we can plan and all take off in big flying boat '32 Chandler across crazy land. Bring juke, bop records, mambo records and dixieland records; typewriters, clothes, toasters, percolators, etc.

Until I see you . . . let me know when . . . I got to work now on script so I can pay Uncle Sam his bloody tax & landlord's bloody old rent & all the bloody shits together.

Neal Cassady
from **THE FIRST THIRD**

PROLOGUE

The country club of that small midwestern American city, Des Moines, contained a secluded corner table over which, on Saturday nights in the winter of 1924–25, was enacted a courtship of restraint. Short, well-built, bachelor Neal, who with his smashed nose now looked rather like a middleweight pug, was in cautious pursuit of the slim attractive middle-aged widow, Maude, she with the auburn hair and above-average height. The atmosphere of the room, with its fireplace and high-fashionable styling combined with the fine cuisine and liquors, enhanced the romance. Among other things, this cloak of surroundings which was to be her last link with days of leisure and which was the guise under which Neal was received by Maude, helped to produce the emotion of delight so strongly that she was to commit herself and her children rather willy-nilly into the care of this drink-susceptible man.

Besides these Saturday nights, always spent at the place they had met, Neal was with Maude and her family only one other time each week—those Sunday afternoons. What had begun when he escorted her home after their first concert continued after the band's last concerts, as times of romantic habit during the winter. On these occasions he tried to ingratiate himself with the older boys, played with the smaller children, and in every respect behaved like a gentleman. After these amities he would take Maude riding about the town and nearby countryside in his new Star automobile. As the winter passed and the progression of Spring lent further beauty to nature and more mud to the road, they would park in an appropriate spot to appreciate the view and avoid getting the car stuck. During one of these idyllic times Neal proposed and was accepted. They were married May 1, 1925.

Soon after their marriage they started the first of almost countless subsequent moves, created by one circumstance or another, that was to make their household a forever-fluid one. Whatever may have been the reason—perhaps it began simply as just the idea of a "honeymoon"—the newlyweds took to the hills, that is; a disbanding of Maude's family began blindly, as it were. Neal bought a Ford truck and built by himself (an unaccountable constructiveness, neither anticipated nor repeated) a top-heavy house with a sloping roof on the truck's two-ton bed. It took months to finish. Maude showed an earnest appreciation for these first consistent days of work. The youngest son and daughter, Betty, aged five, and Jimmy, aged three, were to accompany the lovers. Maude, now pregnant with her ninth child and Neal's first (the embryo, me), were all to embark on a leisurely western trip "to see the world." Thus, in the dead of winter, some ten months after their marriage, they headed for Hollywood in Neal's unique vehicle.

The five other children, despite their youth, were to stay in Des Moines and shift for themselves until the tourists returned. The three older boys, in particular, seemed eminently capable of this. William, now 18, Ralph, 15 and John, 13, had a common trait of aggressive confidence—perhaps developed by caring for Maude in the three-year period since the death of their heavy-handed father. He, being a lawyer with an honest and decisive mind, had settled everything from the most minute of domestic decisions to the largest financial matters. His passing on transferred this responsibility to them while removing the pressure of his strict ways from their formative minds, which thus unleashed, had sprung strongly outward with the youthful quality of cocksureness.

When Maude delivered en route, our travelers added to their healthy brood. Nearby the Mormon Tabernacle and the rotund and stately Temple with its 78 points of upward thrust balanced evenly atop the twin towers, is the L.D.S. Hospital, where was born on February 8, 1926, at 2:05 A.M., Maude's last son. It was to be Neal's only boy and was named after him, except that Neal had no middle name; so as compensative remedy they gave the child the additional name of "Leon," which ironically spoiled what Neal Sr. was most proud of—a "junior" Neal.

They stayed on in Salt Lake City for several weeks while Maude recuperated; then, still driving the weird truck, completed the journey to Los Angeles. On the exact corner of Hollywood and Vine streets was a barber shop which Neal bought with the last of their savings. They didn't prosper, for right from the start, and often, Neal began closing the shop to spend several days drunk. He somehow, firmly and suddenly, fixed upon an idea that no one could run the shop when he was not there, and so laid off his helper-barbers whenever the increasingly frequent urge to drink came over him. Within a year this practice, despite the shop's fabulous location, had cut the trade so drastically that one day while soberly stupid and in a black mood, Neal acted in disgust and sold the shop and figures for a pittance of the purchase price he had paid.

What to do? Then came a letter from Maude's brother, Charles, who still worked for the Railway Express Company but had been recently transferred to the Denver, Colorado, office. He suggested Maude and Neal come to beautiful Denver and settle permanently, largely because he loved the great number of green lawns so much that he thought this, in itself, was enough reason to advise relations to live there forever and manicure one of their own. Or, at least stay until they had planned with more surety a definite next step. Reluctantly, because they had no real goal, but somewhat excited and relieved since their natural naiveté was still not fully overcome by middle age, they about-faced again and drove to Denver in 1928.

There, on 23rd Street between Welton and Glenarm next to the alleyway, was a brown brick building of miniature dimensions. It housed an incredibly cluttered shoe-repair shop, the accumulation of a half-century's leather-litter. The old repairman who squatted daily before the ceiling-high barrier of sweepings that choked this shop, was Neal's new landlord. His two-chair barber shop that shared the building with the shoe stall was acquired on a one-year's lease. Neal, Maude, Jimmy, Betty and little Neal moved into the crowded quarters in the rear of the shop. Then the other children in Des Moines were sent for, and soon by train Bill, Ralph, Jack and Mae arrived in Denver. Thirteen-year-old Evelyn, as hotblooded as the boys, took an offer from an old maid Sioux City friend of Maude's and stayed there until her 21st year when she married her first cousin and went with him to California permanently.

Still, with seven children, conditions in the shop's two small rooms were intolerable. There were not beds enough; clothes lay everywhere; they could not squeeze together into the kitchen and so ate in two groups. The independent older boys had no patience with these inadequate household provisions of their stepfather and almost immediately struck out on their own. This move left Maude with but three of Daly's offspring and, of course, little Neal.

Bill, the oldest, was now twenty-one and nobody's fool. Within a month or so after arriving in this strange town, he met and married a pretty young widow whose considerable income came from her recently dead husband's "Dine and Dance" place just outside the West city limits of Denver. Bill managed this tavern with her and, while about these duties, became adept at the requisites of bartending. Picking up these fundamentals put him in good stead to become an ace barkeep, and he never again worked another trade. In later years it was his pride that he had worked the biggest, busiest and best of all the clubs from New York to Los Angeles—a slight exaggeration, of course, but true in essence.

Ralph, next in line, was the handsomest and most rugged of the lot. He was soon bootlegging liquor for one "Sam" at 11th and Larimer in downtown Denver, although at this time he was only eighteen. Among his varied tasks was making deliveries to the city from several stills some twenty to thirty miles away. In the mountains near Denver, perhaps the largest and certainly the most pretentiously and carefully-housed of these illegal whiskey-makers, was one "Blackie Barlowe." Ralph saw him regularly and before long wrangled a job for younger-brother Jack, 16, as a guard on this beautiful "ranch."

A short while later, as Jack was at his post, Barlowe's place was raided. The Federal agents making the arrests caught Jack first, then another unaware lookout. They handcuffed the two together and left them with one Oscar Dirks, while the main group advanced to nab those in the now-unguarded house. The apprehended men locked eyes for a brief moment, and each read the same thought. Still handcuffed, they suddenly raced furiously down the forested mountain slope. Agent Dirks unholstered his gun without hesitation and fired a few unproductive shots, even as the dense growth hid his prey from view. Jack and his running mate had a good headstart toward at least temporary freedom when they made the mistake of not choosing to pass a tree on the same side. This intervening tree did them in; its unyielding trunk came between, and they were flung around to crash heads in so vicious a manner that Jack fell to the ground unconscious. His dazed buddy had unwound himself and was staggering over to Jack's side by the time Dirks scrambled down on them. The government man pulled Jack to knee-height by his shirt collar; then, disregarding the boy's closed eyes and pale face, he whipped his gun arm around in a vicious blow to Jack's mouth. The heavy gun barrel did instant damage but only broke off four upper teeth. Afterwards, shiny gold was exposed every time he spoke.

Jack did some jail time, but he took up bootlegging again when released. Ralph had no police trouble and was accumulating a good deal of cash, as did Bill, coasting along on the advantage of his wife's income property while on the side selling liquor to preferred customers. Along about the time they bought twin new Model-A's, Jack and Ralph entered into business for themselves, supplying alcoholic beverages to Bill, among others.

Meantime, Neal and Maude struggled on as marriage partners. Although Neal's drink-caused poverty made Maude turn more and more to her sons for financial help, she still loved him enough to endure. Respect for their mother was all that kept the boys (Jack and Ralph, in particular—Bill was somewhat disinterested) from kicking Neal out on his ear. There were countless arguments over him, but they always gave in to Maude's wishes—if she promised not to give Neal any of the money she received from them.

In the summer of 1929 Jack and Ralph together made the down payment on a new house at West Colfax and Stuart Streets. Things were looking up for sure, since Neal, about this time also, got down to the business of being a better father—a last flurry, as it were. He made good money across town at the plush barber shop near the stockyards pavilion and even took the burden of making the house payments off the boys for a couple of months. All the family lived in this new house in reasonable harmony for the rest of that year. Bill and his wife perhaps stayed there only because it was so close to their restaurant; Ralph and Jack, both continuing to bootleg; Mae, 10, Betty, just 9, commuted across town to

Sacred Heart School; Jimmy, 7, and little Neal, 3, played every afternoon in the schoolyard directly across the street; which school Jimmy started attending in September.

Collapse came sooner than it might otherwise have. If the crash of October 1929 had not occurred, it can be supposed that the family could have continued to be moderately secure for a few years, at least. But no, everyone in Denver seemed to go broke at once, not so much as in other parts of the country, and perhaps hardly at all in reality. Still, the fact remains they all tightened up on their money doubly firm. The boys' liquor business fell to pieces, Neal got fired, and even ever-lucky Bill had all he could do to break even every month. It was to be ten years, and longer for some, before any of the family actually had enough to eat or in any way hardly escaped living from hand to mouth each day.

In 1930 many things happened, for early in the year the home was lost. Bill and his wife moved into an auto-court in West Denver and drifted from the rest almost entirely. Ralph surprised everyone by getting married. Her name was Mitch, a student nurse two years from graduation. Jack stayed any place he could hang his hat. Since he made a practice of seeing his mother daily, despite obnoxious Neal's presence, he usually came home for at least a few hours of sleep every night.

This new "home" Neal provided was really a depression dilly. It was a cheaply rented two-room apartment above a noisy creamery at 20th and Court Place. Because there was no money to care for them, Maude arranged with Catholic charities for Mae and Betty to be put in Queen of Heaven Orphanage until Neal provided a suitable house again, or until the girls reached 16.

A new difficulty arose which helped Maude to face parting with Mae and Betty temporarily; i.e., she was pregnant again. On May 22, 1930 at the age of forty, Maude gave birth to her tenth and last child, a girl named Shirley Jean.

For a long time they were really up against it. Neal could often only find work for Saturdays, and they had to live all week on this one day's barbering wage. Of course, Jack always helped as much as he could, and Ralph too gave a few dollars now and then, but it was not enough. Finally, in the last month of this hectic year, Neal got a two-chair shop near the corner of 26th and Champa Streets. In this sad little shop so filled with contention, Neal and Maude shared the last year of their pitiful marriage.

Although food was short, at least there was always dessert, for in the middle of the next block was the Puritan Pie Company, and on many an illegal Sunday the shop shades were drawn as Neal cut an employee's hair in exchange for a pie or two. Other Sundays when he had carfare, Neal would go to North Denver and barber brother-in-law Charles, the lawn-lover, who was now a near-helpless paralytic living on a small pension and cared for by a kindly landlady. Charles later died in the same hospital and on the same day as his sister, Maude; yet neither of them knew of this coincidence.

Neal's non-sobriety persisted as did the dwindling of customers, so that they just couldn't make ends meet, and Neal lost the shop, the last of several, early in 1932. He also lost his wife, who moved into an apartment at 22nd and Stout Streets that Jack paid for, taking with her Jimmy and baby Shirley. Little Neal went with his wino father into the lowest slums of Denver.

CHAPTER 1

For a time I held a unique position: among the hundreds of isolated creatures who haunted the streets of lower downtown Denver there was not one so young as myself. Of these dreary men who had committed themselves, each for his own good reason, to the task of finishing their days as pennyless drunkards, I alone, as the sharer of their way of life, presented a replica of childhood to which their vision could daily turn, and in being thus grafted onto them, I became the unnatural son of a few score beaten men.

It was my experience to be constantly meeting new cronies of my father's, who invariably introduced me with a proud, "This is my boy." Whereupon the pat on my head was usually followed by the quizzical look the eye reserved for uncertainty, which here conveyed the question, "Shall I give him a little drink?" Sensing the offer, backed by a half-extended bottle, my father would always say, "You'll have to ask him," and I would coyly answer, "No thank you, sir." Of course, this occurred only on those memorable occasions when an acceptable drink like wine was available. The unhappy times when there was none, with only denatured alcohol ("canned heat") or bay rum at hand, I did not have to go through my little routine.

Many times, after normal adult catering with questions to show interest in the child, (such gestures of talkative comradeship was their token parenthood, for these secondary fathers had nothing else to give) I would be ignored while the talk of my father and his new friend turned to recalling the past. These tête-à-têtes were full of little asides which carried with them facts establishing that much of the life they had known was in common: types of mutual friends, cities visited, things done there, and so on. Their conversation had many general statements about Truth and Life, which contained the collective intelligence of all America's bums. They were drunkards whose minds, weakened by liquor and an obsequious manner of existence, seemed continually preoccupied with bringing up short observations of obvious trash, said in such a way as to be instantly recognizable by the listener, who had heard it all before, and whose own prime concern was to nod at everything said, then continue the conversation with a remark of his own, equally transparent and loaded with generalities. The simplicity of this pattern was marvelous, and there was no limit to what they could agree on in this fashion, to say nothing of the abstract ends that could be reached. Through sheer repetitious hearing of such small talk speculation, I came to know their minds so intimately that I could understand as they understood, and there was soon no mystery to the conversation of any of them. I assumed all men thought the same, and so knew these things, because like any child, I correlated all adult action without actual regard for type.

All his fellow alcoholics called my father "the barber" since he was about the only one of them who had practiced that trade, and I was "the barber's boy." They all said I looked just like him, but I didn't think this was true in the least. And they watched me grow with comments like "Why, look there—his head is higher than your belt already!" It wasn't such a feat, I thought, to stand that tall, because my father had awfully short legs.

Jack Kerouac
from VISIONS OF CODY

Around the poolhalls of Denver during World War II a strange looking boy began to be noticeable to the characters who frequented the places afternoon and night and even to the casual visitors who dropped in for a game of snooker after supper when all the tables were busy in an atmosphere of smoke and great excitement and a continual parade passed in the alley from the backdoor of one poolroom on Glenarm Street to the backdoor of another—a boy called Cody Pomeray [Neal Cassady], the son of a Larimer Street wino. Where he came from nobody knew or at first cared. Older heroes of other generations had darkened the walls of the poolhalls long before Cody got there; memorable eccentrics, great pool-sharks, even killers, jazz musicians, traveling salesmen, anonymous frozen bums who came in on winter nights to sit an hour by the heat never to be seen again, among whom (and not to be remembered by anyone because there was no one there to keep a love check on the majority of the boys as they swarmed among themselves year by year with only casual but sometimes haunted recognition of faces, unless strictly local characters from around the corner) was Cody Pomeray, Sr. who in his hobo life that was usually spent stumbling around other parts of town had somehow stumbled in here and sat in the same old bench which was later to be occupied by his son in desperate meditations on life.

Have you ever seen anyone like Cody Pomeray?—say on a streetcorner on a winter night in Chicago, or better, Fargo, any mighty cold town, a young guy with a bony face that looks like it's been pressed against iron bars to get that dogged rocky look of suffering, perseverance, finally when you look closest, happy prim self-belief, with Western sideburns and big blue flirtatious eyes of an old maid and fluttering lashes; the small and muscular kind of fellow wearing usually a leather jacket and if it's a suit it's with a vest so he can prop his thick busy thumbs in place and smile the smile of his grandfathers; who walks as fast as he can go on the balls of his feet, talking excitedly and gesticulating; poor pitiful kid actually just out of reform school with no money, no mother, and if you saw him dead on the sidewalk with a cop standing over him you'd walk on in a hurry, in silence. Oh life, who is that? There are some young men you look at who seem completely safe, maybe just because of a Scandinavian ski sweater, angelic, saved; on a Cody Pomeray it immediately becomes a dirty stolen sweater worn in wild sweats. Something about his tigerish out-jutted raw facebone could be given a woedown melancholy if only he wore a drooping mustache (a famous bop drummer who looked just like Cody at this time wore such a mustache and probably for those reasons). It is a face that's so suspicious, so energetically upward-looking like people in passport or police lineup photos, so rigidly itself, looking like it's about to do anything unspeakably enthusiastic, in fact so much the opposite of the rosy Coke-drinking boy in the Scandinavian ski sweater ad, that in front of a brick wall where it says *Post No Bills* and it's too dirty for a rosy boy ad you can imagine Cody standing there in the raw gray flesh manacled between sheriffs and Assistant D.A.'s and you wouldn't have to ask yourself who is the culprit and who is the law. He looked like that, and God bless him he looked like that Hollywood stunt man who is fist-fighting in place of the hero and has such a remote, furious, anonymous viciousness (one of the loneliest things in the world to see and we've all seen it a thousand times in a thousand B-movies) that everybody begins to be suspicious because they know the hero wouldn't act like that in real unreality. If you've been a boy and played on dumps you've seen Cody, all crazy, excited and full of glee-mad powers, giggling with the pimply girls in back of fenders and weeds till some vocational school swallows his ragged blisses and that strange American iron which later is used to mold the suffering manface is now employed to straighten and quell the long wavering spermy disorderliness of the boy. Nevertheless the face of a great hero—a face to remind you that the infant springs from the great Assyrian bush of a man, not from an eye, an ear or a forehead—the face of a Simón Bolívar, Robert E. Lee, young Whitman, young Melville, a statue in the park, rough and free.

The appearance of Cody Pomeray on the poolroom scene in Denver at a very early age was the lonely appearance of a boy on a stage which had been trampled smooth in a number of crowded decades, Curtis Street and also downtown; a scene that had been graced by the presence of champions, the Pensacola Kid, Willie Hoppe, Bat Masterson re-passing through town when he was a referee, Babe Ruth bending to a side-pocket shot on an October night in 1927, Old Bull Balloon who always tore greens and paid up, great newspapermen traveling from New York to San Francisco, even Jelly Roll Morton was known to have played pool in the Denver parlors for a living; and Theodore Dreiser for all we know upending an elbow in the cigarsmoke, but whether it was restaurateur kings in private billiard rooms of clubs or roustabouts with brown arms just in from the fall Dakota harvest shooting rotation for a nickel in Little Pete's, it was in any case the great serious American poolhall night and Cody arrived on the scene bearing his original and sepulchral mind with him to make the poolhall the headquarters of the vast excitement of the early Denver days of his life becoming after awhile, a permanent musing figure before the green velvet of table number one where the intricate and almost metaphysical click and play of billiard balls became the background for his thoughts; till later the sight of a beautifully reverse-Englished cueball leaping back in the air, after a cannonading shot at another ball belted straight in, bam, when it takes three soft bounces and settles back on the green, became more than just the background for daylong daydreams, plans and schemes but the unutterable realization of the great interior joyful knowledge of the world that he was beginning to discover in his soul. And at night, late, when poolhalls turn white and garish and eight tables are going fullblast with all the boys and businessmen milling with cues, Cody knew, he knew everything like mad, sitting as though he wasn't noticing anything and not thinking anything on the hard onlooker's bench and yet noticing the special excellence of any good shot within the aura of his eyeball and not only that, the peculiarities and pitiful typehood of every player whether some over-flamboyant kid with his eleventh or twelfth cigarette dangling from his mouth or some old pot-bellied rotation wizard who's left his lonely wife in a varnished studio room above a *Rooms* sign in the dark of Pearl Street, he knew it all.

The first to notice him was Tom Watson. Tom was a hunchbacked poolshark with the great moon blue eyes of a saint, an extremely sad character, one of the smartest well-known shots of the younger generation in the locality. Cody couldn't have been more than fifteen years old when he wandered in from the street. It was only that many years before, in 1927, that Cody was born, in Salt Lake City; at a time when for some Godforsaken reason, some forgotten, pitiably American, restless reason his father and mother were driving in a jalopy from Iowa to L.A. in search of something, maybe they figured to start an orange grove or find a rich uncle, Cody himself never found out, a reason long buried in the sad heap of the night, a reason that nevertheless in 1927 caused them to fix their eyes anxiously and with throat-choking hope over the sad swath of brokendown headlamps shining brown on the road . . . the road that sorrowed into the darkness and huge unbelievable American nightland like an arrow. Cody was born in a charity hospital. A few weeks later the jalopy clanked right on; so that now there were three pairs of eyes watching the unspeakable road roll in on Pa's radiator cap as it steadfastly penetrated the night like the poor shield of themselves, the little Pomeray family, lost, the gaunt crazy father with the floppy slouched hat that made him look like a brokendown Okie Shadow, the dreaming mother in a cotton dress purchased on a happier afternoon in some excited Saturday five-and-ten, the frightened infant. Poor mother of Cody Pomeray, what were your thoughts in 1927? Somehow or other, they soon came back to Denver over the same raw road; somehow or other nothing worked out right the way they wanted; without a doubt they had a thousand unspecified troubles and knotted their fists in despair somewhere outside a house and under a tree where something went wrong, grievously and eternally wrong, enough to kill people; all the loneliness, remorse and chagrin in the world piled on their heads like indignities from heaven. Oh mother of Cody Pomeray, but was there secretly in you a lovely memory of a Sunday afternoon back home when you were famous and beloved among friends and family, and young?—when maybe you saw your father standing among the men, laughing, and you crossed the celebrated human floor of the then-particular beloved stage to him. Was it from lack of life, lack of haunted pain and memories, lack of sons and trouble and humiliated rage that you died, or was it from excess of death? She died in Denver before Cody was old enough to talk to her. Cody grew up with a childhood vision of her standing in the strange antique light of 1929 (which is no different than the light of today or the light when Xerxes' fleets confused the waves, or Agamemnon wailed) in some kind of livingroom with beads hanging from the door, apparently at a period in the life of old Pomeray when he was making good money at his barber trade and they had a good home. But after she died he became one of the most tottering bums of Larimer Street, making futile attempts to work and periodically leaving Cody with his wife's people to go to Texas to escape the Colorado winters, beginning a lifetime swirl of hoboing into which little Cody himself was sucked later on, when at intervals, childlike, he preferred leaving the security of his Ma's relatives which included sharing a bedroom with his stepbrother, going to school, and altar-boying at a local Catholic church, for going off to live with his father in flophouses. Nights long ago on the brawling sidewalks of Larimer Street when the Depression hobo was there by the thousands, sometimes in great sad lines black with soot in the rainy dark of Thirties newsreels, men with sober downturned mouths huddled in old coats waiting in line for misery, Cody used to stand in front of alleys begging for nickels while his father, red-eyed, in baggy pants, hid in the back with some old bum crony called Rex who was no king but just an American who had never outgrown the boyish desire to lie down on the sidewalk which he did the year round from coast to coast; the two of them hiding and sometimes having long excited conversations until the kid had enough nickels to make up a bottle of wine, when it was time to hit the liquor store and go down under ramps and railroad embankments and light a small fire with cardboard boxes and naily boards and sit on overturned buckets or oily old treestumps, the boy on the outer edges of the fire, the men in its momentous and legendary glow, and drink the wine. "Wheeoo! Hand me that damn bottle 'fore I knock somebody's head in!"

And this of course was just the chagrin of bums suddenly becoming wild joy, the switchover from all the poor lonely woe of the likes of Pomeray having to count pennies on streetcorners with the wind blowing his dirty hair over his snarling, puffy, disgruntled face, the revulsion of bums burping and scratching lonely crotches at flophouse sinks, their agony waking up on strange floors (if floors at all) with their mad minds reeling in a million disorderly images of damnation and strangulation in a world too unbearably disgusting to stand and yet so full of useless sweet and nameless moments that made them cry that they couldn't say no to it completely without committing some terrified sin, attacked repeatedly by every kind of horrible joy making them twitch and marvel and gasp as before visions of heart-wrenching hell penetrating up through life from unnumberable hullabalooing voices screaming in insanity below, with piteous memories, the sweet and nameless ones, that reached back to fleecy cradle days to make them sob, finally bound to sink to the floor of brokendown pisshouses to wrap around the bowl and maybe die—this misery with a bottle of wine was twisted around like a nerve in old man Pomeray's brain and the tremendous joy of the really powerful drunk filled the night with shouts and wild bulging power-mad eyes. On Larimer Street Cody's father was known as The Barber, occasionally working near the Greeley Hotel in a really terrible barbershop that was notable for its great unswept floor of bums' hair, and a shelf sagging under so many bottles of bay rum that you'd think the shop was on an ocean-going vessel and the boys had it stocked for a six months' siege. In this drunken tonsorial pissery called a barbershop because hair was cut off your head from the top of the ears down old Pomeray, with the same tender befuddlement with which he sometimes lifted garbage barrels to city disposal trucks during blizzards or passed wrenches in the most tragic, becluttered, greasedark auto body shop west of the Mississippi (Arapahoe Garage by name where they even hired him), tiptoed around a barber chair with scissor and comb, razor and mug to make sure not to stumble, and cut the hairs off black-necked hoboes who had such vast lugubrious personalities that they sometimes sat stiffly at attention for this big event for a whole hour. Cody, Sr. was a fine gentleman.

PART THREE

"CONSTANTLY RISKING ABSURDITY"

Some San Francisco Renaissance Poets

On September 9, 1955, Allen Ginsberg wrote a friend in New York about the people he was meeting in California, in particular "a bearded interesting Berkeley cat name of Snyder, I met him yesterday (via Rexroth suggestion) who is studying oriental and leaving in a few months on some privately put up funds to go be a Zen monk (a real one). He's a head, peyoteist, laconist, but warmhearted, nice looking with a little beard, thin, blond, rides a bicycle in Berkeley in red corduroy and levis and hungup on indians . . . Interesting person." Shortly afterward, Ginsberg invited Gary Snyder and four other local poets to participate in a reading he organized at the Six Gallery in San Francisco on October 13, 1955.

That evening was the first time Ginsberg read "Howl." He and his poem were a resounding success, but the reading did more than launch his career as a poet. It was also the inauguration of the San Francisco Poetry Renaissance, awakening a new awareness in the audience of the large group of talented young poets in the city, and giving the poets themselves a new sense of belonging to a community. The Six Poets at the Six Gallery reading was the first event in which the East Coast Beat writers joined forces with their West Coast counterparts and emerged as a literary movement that was no longer a few close friends sharing ideas about literature in New York City, but a national phenomenon.

Lawrence Ferlinghetti has characterized what happened in 1954 through 1956, when the East Coast Beat writers Ginsberg, Kerouac, and Corso met the West Coast writers Kenneth Rexroth, Lawrence Ferlinghetti, Gary Snyder, Michael McClure, Philip Whalen, Philip Lamantia, and others, as the time "when poetry went public in the city." Literature had flourished in San Francisco, Berkeley, and Oakland during and immediately after the Second World War with the activity of writers like Henry Miller, Anaïs Nin, Robert Duncan, Josephine Miles, William Everson, Mary Fabilli, and Kenneth Rexroth. This generation of the avant garde had sown the seeds for younger writers like Snyder, McClure, Whalen, and Lamantia, representatives of what Ferlinghetti called the "future rebellious decades."

Literary magazines like *Circle* (published in Berkeley from 1944 to 1948) featured local "Berkeley Renaissance" writers and European Surrealist poets expressing anarchist or anti-authoritarian attitudes. The last issue of the magazine included an ad for a "New Writers' Group" that could have been used as a Beat manifesto a decade later:

WRITERS

There is a struggle going on for the minds of the American people. Every form of expression is subject to the attack of reaction. This attack comes in the shape of silence, persecution, and censorship: three names for fear. In the face of this fear, the writer can speak. We believe in the possibility of a culture which fights for its freedom, which protects the economic interests of its workers in all fields including the arts, and which can create for itself new forms and new voices, against reaction and the threat of war.

The little magazine *Ark* (started in 1947 in San Francisco on a small hand press) was even more militant than *Circle*. Its leading editorial proclaimed that "in direct opposition to the debasement of human values made flauntingly evident by the war, there is rising among writers in America, as elsewhere, a social consciousness which recognizes the integrity of the personality as the most substantial and considerable of values. . . . Today, at this catastrophic point in time, the validity if not the future of the anarchist position is more than ever established. It has become a polished mirror in which the falsehoods of political modes stand naked."

The career of the writer Kenneth Rexroth was representative of the "intensely libertarian character" of the group of radical writers on the West Coast. Rexroth was the dominant force in the cultural life of San Francisco for more than half a century. He was one of the founders of KPFA, the local radio station in Berkeley, where he had weekly programs discussing books and various cultural topics, and he tried to organize a union of the artists and writers in San Francisco.

In 1957, when Rexroth read his poetry with Lawrence Ferlinghetti to jazz accompaniment at a club called The Cellar, the jazz critic Ralph J. Gleason understood Rexroth's passionate conviction that poetry readings could transform people's lives:

> Rexroth was the prime mover in The Cellar series. He had experimented with jazz and poetry recitals in Chicago two decades ago but then put it aside. . . . Rexroth was motivated in his activity with jazz by an attempt to broaden the audience for modern poetry. "It's very important to get poetry out of the hands of the professors and out of the hands of the squares," he says. "If we can get poetry out into the life of the country it can be creative. . . ."

At first, as in the 1957 *Evergreen Review* issue featuring the new San Francisco poetry, Rexroth championed the Beats, sympathizing with the writers because he felt they shared his radical views and were united with him in their cultural "disaffiliation" from what he called the mainstream "convergence of interest—the business community, military imperialism, political reaction, the hysterical, tear and mud drenched guilt of the ex-Stalinist, ex-Trotskyist American intellectuals."

After Kerouac gave what Rexroth considered an unflattering

portrait of him as the character "Rheinhold Cacoethes" in *The Dharma Bums,* Rexroth attacked the East Coast Beats for what he saw as their opportunism in seeking the public spotlight, describing them as "simply comical bogies conjured up by the Luce publications." A decade later, in his book *American Poetry in the Twentieth Century* (1971), Rexroth gave a more measured appraisal of the Beat writers, crediting them with what he called the most important development in American poetry since 1955. This was their promotion of a "change of medium—poetry as voice not as printing. The climacteric was not the publication of a book, it was the famous Six Gallery reading, the culmination of twenty years of the oral presentation of poetry in San Francisco."

What was most important to Rexroth about the Six Gallery reading was the sense of community, his belief that the poets shared "a quest for direct, interpersonal communication. Speech from one human to another." Rexroth also noted that although the poets had this quality in common, they all had very different literary styles and subject matter. For Rexroth, whose career in literature began in the 1920s, the East and West Coast poets were "more unlike each other than were T. S. Eliot and William Carlos Williams."

The center of activity in San Francisco for the new literary movement was a bookshop called City Lights at 261 Columbus Avenue in North Beach. Founded in 1953, it was the first all-paperback bookshop in the United States, started by Peter D. Martin and Lawrence Ferlinghetti. As Ferlinghetti described the bookshop, "City Lights itself is generally in an anarchist, civil libertarian, antiauthoritarian tradition. Martin named . . . the bookstore after the film by Chaplin, whose Little Man has always been a symbol of the subjective man against the world. . . . In the tradition of great literary bookstores on the East Coast and especially in Europe, City Lights began publishing its own books in 1955 and now has about a hundred books in print, none federally financed by grants from the National Endowment for the Arts. (Its editors, in the Anarchist/Surrealist tradition, like it that way.)"

The East Bay had a long tradition of fine press books, but Ferlinghetti published the City Lights Pocket Poets series as a deliberate attempt to attract more readers to new American poetry by bringing out a series of inexpensive paperback books with "generic" black and white covers that would fit in the pocket of a jacket or a pair of jeans. After hearing Ginsberg read "Howl" at the Six Gallery in October 1955, Ferlinghetti was so impressed that he copied Emerson's message to Whitman a century earlier and sent Ginsberg a telegram: "I greet you at the beginning of a great career. When do I get the manuscript?"

Published as number four in the Pocket Poets series, *Howl and Other Poems* was seized by the U.S. Customs in San Francisco on March 25, 1957. Ferlinghetti staunchly defended the poem against the charges of obscenity, believing that "Ginsberg chooses to walk on the wild side of this world, along with Nelson Algren, Henry Miller, Kenneth Rexroth, Kenneth Patchen, not to mention some great American dead, mostly in the tradition of philosophical anarchism."

In October 1957, Judge Clayton Horn ruled that "Howl" was not an obscene poem. His decision established judicial precedent by stating that if the printed material has social importance, it is protected by the First and Fourteenth amendments of the United States Constitution. After City Lights won its lawsuit, Grove Press went ahead with its plans to bring out D. H. Lawrence's *Lady Chatterley's Lover* and Henry Miller's *Tropic of Cancer* soon afterward.

What had been a cultural rebellion of a small literary group in New York was energized and given political focus by the contact of the East Coast Beats with the West Coast poets, who were sustained by a flourishing tradition of radical expression. When East Coast met West Coast, the whole was suddenly larger than the sum of its parts. The formation of a broad new poetry front entered the course of American literature at midcentury.

Kenneth Rexroth

Kenneth Rexroth was born on December 22, 1905, in South Bend, Indiana, and died on June 6, 1982, in Montecito, California. He moved to San Francisco from Chicago in 1927 to become involved in leftist politics and began by helping to organize maritime labor unions. During World War II Rexroth was a conscientious objector, a political stance he shared with his friend, the California poet William Everson, who later summarized Rexroth's predominant influence on local writers in the essay "Rexroth: Shaker and Maker."

An anarchist poet, critic, translator and playwright, Rexroth also wrote regular columns as the West Coast literary correspondent for The Nation *and the* Saturday Review. *In particular, Rexroth's interest in Asian literature and philosophy contributed to the Beat writers' study of what Ginsberg later called "Buddha consciousness." Rexroth's translations of Asian poetry published by New Directions were a seminal influence on Gary Snyder and other young poets.*

It was at one of Rexroth's weekly "seminars" in his apartment at 250 Scott Street above Jack's Record Cellar that Ginsberg heard him read an early mimeographed version of his eulogy for the popular Welsh poet Dylan Thomas titled "Thou Shalt Not Kill." Rexroth wrote the poem shortly after Thomas's death from alcoholism on November 9, 1953. In "Thou Shalt Not Kill," Rexroth's scathing charge that capitalism had vanquished the century's most promising writers in its materialistic pursuit of power and its worship of the destructive god Mammon would reverberate in Ginsberg's later poem "Howl."

THOU SHALT NOT KILL

A Memorial for Dylan Thomas

AUTHOR'S NOTE . . . . . .
This Poem was written in one sitting, a few hours after a phone
call came from New York with the news that Dylan [Thomas]
had died. It was circulated widely, mimeo'd, to all my friends.
The copies were all plainly labelled "NOT FOR PUBLICA-
TION." Nevertheless it has been printed, without my permission, in Japanese, Greek, French, English and several other
languages, in a shortened form. In most cases I believe it was
thought to be effective ammunition in the Cold War. After
seeing the last section in print a friend wrote me "You have
a point, powerfully put, but the other side is much worse."
The "other side"? Dylan and I are the "other side." The poem
is directed against the twentieth, the Century of Horror. It
says the same thing Holderlin or Baudelaire said of the nineteenth century, but it has the benefit of what the philosophers
call "an inclusion series"; one hundred more years. I am well
aware that there are no longer the suicides east of the Iron
Curtain there used to be. The first wave was thorough and
effective.

Kenneth Rexroth

I

They are murdering all the young men.
For half a century now, every day,
They have hunted them down and killed them.
They are killing them now.
At this minute, all over the world,
They are killing the young men.
They know ten thousand ways to kill them.
Every year they invent new ones.
In the jungles of Africa,
In the marshes of Asia,
In the deserts of Asia,
In the slave pens of Siberia,
In the slums of Europe,

In the nightclubs of America,
The murderers are at work.

They are stoning Stephen.
They are casting him forth from every city
            in the world.
Under the Welcome sign,
Under the Rotary emblem,
On the highway in the suburbs,
His body lies under the hurling stones.
He was full of faith and power.
He did great wonders among the people.
They could not stand against his wisdom.

They could not bear the spirit with which
            he spoke.
He cried out in the name
Of the tabernacle of witness in the wilderness.
They were cut to the heart.
They gnashed against him with their teeth.
They cried out with a loud voice.
They stopped their ears.
They ran on him with one accord.
They cast him out of the city and stoned him.
The witnesses laid down their clothes
At the feet of a man whose name was your name—
You.

You are the murderer.
You are killing the young men.
You are broiling Lawrence on his gridiron.
When you demanded he divulge
The hidden treasures of the spirit,
He showed you the poor.
You set your heart against him.
You seized him and bound him with rage.
You roasted him on a slow fire.
His fat dripped and spurted in the flame.
The smell was sweet to your nose.
He cried out,

"I am cooked on this side,
Turn me over and eat,
You
Eat of my flesh."

You are murdering the young men.
You are shooting Sebastian with arrows.
He kept the faithful steadfast under
        persecution.

First you shot him with arrows.
Then you beat him with rods.
Then you threw him in a sewer.
You fear nothing more than courage.
You who turn away your eyes
At the bravery of the young men.

You,
The hyena with polished face and bow tie,
In the office of a billion dollar
Corporation devoted to service;
The vulture dripping with carrion,
Carefully and carelessly robed in imported
        tweeds,
Lecturing on the Age of Abundance;
The jackal in double-breasted gabardines,
Barking by remote control,
In the United Nations;
The vampire bat seated at the couch head,
Notebook in hand, toying with his decerebrator;
The autonomous, ambulatory cancer,
The Superego in a thousand uniforms;
You,
The finger man of behemoth,
The murderer of the young men.

II

What happened to Robinson,[1]
Who used to stagger down Eighth Street,

[1] Edwin Arlington Robinson (1869–1935)

Dizzy with solitary gin?
Where is Masters,[2] who crouched in
His law office for ruinous decades?
Where is Leonard who thought he was
A locomotive? And Lindsay,[3]
Wise as a dove, innocent
As a serpent, where is he?
      Timor mortis conturbat me.
What became of Jim Oppenheim?
Lola Ridge alone in an
Icy furnished room? Orrick Johns,
Hopping into the surf on his
One leg? Elinor Wylie
Who leaped like Kierkegaard?
Sara Teasdale, where is she?
      Timor mortis conturbat me.

Where is George Sterling, that tame fawn?
Phelps Putnam who stole away?
Jack Wheelright who couldn't cross the bridge?
Donald Evans with his cane and
Monocle, where is he?
      Timor mortis conturbat me.

John Gould Fletcher who could not
Unbreak his powerful heart?
Bodenheim[4] butchered in stinking
Squalor? Edna Millay who took
Her last straight whiskey? Genevieve[5]
Who loved so much; where is she?
      Timor mortis conturbat me.

Harry who didn't care at all?
Hart[6] who went back to the sea?
      Timor mortis conturbat me.

---

[2] Edgar Lee Masters (1869–1950)
[3] Vachel Lindsay (1879–1931)
[4] Maxwell Bodenheim (1893–1954)
[5] Genevieve Taggard (1894–1948)
[6] Hart Crane (1899–1932)

Where is Sol Funaroff?
What happened to Potamkin?
Isidor Schneider? Claude McKay?
Countee Cullen? Lowenfels?[7]
Who animates their corpses today?
    Timor mortis conturbat me.

Where is Ezra,[8] that noisy man?
Where is Larsson whose poems were prayers?
Where is Charles Snider, that gentle
Bitter boy? Carnevali,[9]
What became of him?
Carol who was so beautiful, where is she?
    Timor mortis conturbat me.

III

Was their end noble and tragic,
Like the mask of a tyrant?
Like Agammemnon's secret golden face?
Indeed it was not. Up all night
In the focsle, bemused and beaten,
Bleeding at the rectum, in his
Pocket a review by the one
Colleague he respected, "If he
Really means what these poems
Pretend to say, he has only
One way out—." Into the
Hot acrid Carribean sun,
Into the acrid, transparent,
Smoky sea. Or another, lice in his
Armpits and crotch, garbage littered
On the floor, grey greasy rags on
The bed. "I killed them because they
Were dirty, stinking Communists.
I should get a medal." Again,
Another, Simenon foretold,

[7] Walter Lowenfels (1897–1976)
[8] Ezra Pound (1885–1972)
[9] Emanuel Carnevali, Avant-garde Italian poet; dates unknown.

His end at a glance. "I dare you
To pull the trigger." She shut her eyes
And spilled gin over her dress.
The pistol wobbled in his hand.
It took them hours to die.
Another threw herself downstairs,
And broke her back, it took her years.
Two put their heads under water
In the bath and filled their lungs.
Another threw himself under
The traffic of a crowded bridge.
Another, drunk, jumped from a
Balcony and broke her neck.
Another soaked herself in
Gasoline and ran blazing
Into the street and lived on
In custody. One made love
Only once with a beggar woman.
He died years later of syphilis
Of the brain and spine. Fifteen
Years of pain and poverty,
While his mind leaked away.
One tried three times in twenty years
To drown himself. The last time
He succeeded. One turned on the gas
When she had no more food, no more
Money, and only half a lung.
One went up to Harlem, took on
Thirty men, came home and
Cut her throat. One sat up all night
Talking to H. L. Mencken and
Drowned himself in the morning.

How many stopped writing at thirty?
How many went to work for Time?
How many died of prefrontal
Lobotomies in the Communist Party?
How many are lost in the back wards
Of provincial madhouses?
How many on the advice of

Their psychoanalysts, decided
A business career was best after all?
How many are hopeless alcoholics?

Rene Crevel!
Jacques Ricgaut!
Antonin Artaud!
Mayakofsky!
Essenin!
Robert Desnos!
Saint Pol Roux!
Max Jacob!
All over the world
The same disembodied hand
Strikes us down.
Here is a mountain of death.
A hill of heads like the Khans piled up.
The first born of a century
Slaughtered by Herod.
Three generations of infants
Stuffed down the maw of Moloch

IV

He is dead.
The bird of Rhiannon.
He is dead.
In the winter of the heart.
He is Dead.
In the canyons of death,
They found him dumb at last,
In the blizzard of lies.
He never spoke again.
He died.
He is dead.
In their antiseptic hands,
He is dead.
The little spellbinder of Cader Idris.
He is dead.
The sparrow of Cardiff.

He is dead.
The canary of Swansea.
Who killed him?
Who killed the bright-headed bird?
You did, you son of a bitch.
You drowned him in your cocktail brain.
He fell down and died in your synthetic heart.
You killed him,
Oppenheimer the Million-Killer.
You killed him,
Einstein the Grey Eminence.
You killed him.
Havanahavana, with your Nobel Prize.
You killed him, General,
Through the proper channels.

You strangled him, Le Mouton,
With your mains étendus.
He confessed in open court to a pince-nezed skull.
You shot him in the back of the head
As he stumbled in the last cellar.
You killed him,
Benign Lady on the postage stamp.
He was found dead at a liberal weekly luncheon.
He was found dead on the cutting room floor.
He was found dead at a Time policy conference.
Henry Luce killed him with a telegram to the Pope.
Mademoiselle strangled him with a padded brassiere.
Old Possum sprinkled him with a tea ball.
After the wolves were done, the vaticides
Crawled off with his bowels to their classrooms
          and quarterlies.
When the news came over the radio
You personally rose up shouting, "Give us
          Barrabas!"
In your lonely crowd you swept over him.
Your custom built brogans and your ballet slippers
Pummelled him to death in the gritty street.

You hit him with an album of Hindemith.
You stabbed him with stainless steel by Isamu

Noguchi.
He is dead.
He is Dead.
Like Ignacio the bullfighter,
At four o'clock in the afternoon.
At precisely four o'clock.
I too do not want to hear it.
I too do not want to know it.
I want to run into the street,
Shouting, "Remember Vanzetti!"
. . . And all the birds of the deep sea rise up
Over the luxury liners and scream,
"You killed him! You killed him.
In your God damned Brooks Brothers suit,
You son of a bitch."

POEMS FROM THE JAPANESE

I wish I were close
To you as the wet skirt of
A salt girl to her body.
I think of you always.

                    AKAHITO

The white chrysanthemum
Is disguised by the first frost.
If I wanted to pick one
I could find it only by chance.

               OSHIKOCHI NO MITSUNE

The deer on pine mountain,
Where there are no falling leaves,
Knows the coming of autumn
Only by the sound of his own voice.

               ONAKATOMI NO YOSHINOBU

William Everson
REXROTH: *Shaker and Maker*

I first heard of Kenneth Rexroth in the late Thirties when friends in Fresno told me about this radical poet on the picket lines in San Francisco. I didn't meet him, however, till World War II, when I headed up an arts program in a conscientious objector's camp at Waldport, Oregon. He wrote praising what we were doing and invited me to visit when next I came south. I found him a very winning personality and instantly fell under his spell. For his part he presented my work to James Laughlin of New Directions which led to my first national publication. Though I was neither the first nor the last to benefit by his discernment, it goes without saying that it was for me the most telling instance of what I would naturally come to recognize as a remarkable nose for talent!

After the War I moved to the Bay Area when Kenneth was welding together the nucleus of the movement that would surface ten years later as the San Francisco Renaissance, ushering in the Beat Generation which would itself usher in the Sixties, decade of confrontations and revolt, and change the lifestyle of American youth as radically as it changed the practice of contemporary poetry.

This movement did not take at its inception because the country was too preoccupied with post war problems: the cold war was freezing down and the McCarthy era was warming up. Though we did gain some national notoriety from a blast in *Harper's* called "The New Cult of Sex and Anarchy," there was no real recognition, and the movement dissolved before it could jell. It would take the passing of world crisis and the arrival of the bland Eisenhower years to provide the complacency for its revolt to be effective. It would also take the arrival in San Francisco of East Coast voices like Ginsberg and Kerouac to deepen the combustibility and extend the range. Then the media, always on the lookout for the sensational, would finally take notice. The Beat Generation was picked up by *Time* and *Life* magazines and assiduously promulgated. *Life's* feature on the Beats was called "The Only Rebellion Around," as if its editors were praying for some sign, any sign, of youthful dissent. The Sixties were the answer to that prayer, and with an awesome vengeance. People had scoffed when Rexroth called *Howl* "the confession of faith of a generation," but ten years later they were not scoffing anymore, and their prayers were choking in their throats.

All this was the product of an intense group dynamic, but it could never have happened but for the presence of a single man. That honor is usually accorded to William Carlos Williams, who is the ranking poet of open form in this country, whereas Rexroth has never received his due as a poet. But there are many reasons why Williams could not have engineered the revolt that Rexroth did, though Williams sought it, at least in literature, every bit as long.

For Williams was too exclusively literary. True, he was a professional physician who identified with his caste, simply not having the time for extracurricular activity except for his own writing. But his instincts were essentially apolitical, where Rexroth's were gut-level political. Rexroth was a radical from his youth and had earned his spurs on the picket lines of San Francisco, which brings up another important difference. Williams' region, Rutherford and the Passaic, lacks the charisma of San Francisco and Big Sur: it is too urbanized to evoke the inceptive environmental passion. Also Rexroth is a profoundly religious man while Williams was doggedly agnostic. Rexroth caught the awakening religious vibration and espoused it—the first time I ever heard the name of Martin Buber was from Kenneth's lips. Also San Francisco is the gateway to the Orient and Rexroth extolled Pacific Basin culture, translating Chinese and Japanese poetry into the vital American verse idiom. Moreover, Rexroth is erotic in a way Williams never was. His graphic imagination was on the wavelength of the future sexual liberation. Then too his pacificism and anarchism prefigured the anti-war and anti-establishment Sixties, and helped bring them into being. This summation shows that no one standing on the threshold as elder statesman sums up in his person so much of what was approaching as Rexroth did. He needed only to express it with sufficient force to initiate the wave of the future.

And the gifts of expression were not lacking in him. He is a powerful spokesman for any cause he espouses. A born journalist, he has a flair for vigorous public speech and the guts to speak out in unequivocal terms. He has fantastic intellectual and moral courage, taking on the establishment and throwing it on the defensive through the sheer force of his invective. His rhetoric is savage, sometimes shockingly so, but it is never ineffectual.

Consequently, his career has been stormy. His faults are the excesses of his virtues and he quarrels with his friends as readily as he clobbers his enemies. He demands unwavering loyalty and, poets being what they are, that is not always forthcoming. He tends to drop the movement he has fostered as soon as it shows signs of fragmenting. His precipitate departure for Europe in 1949 insured the eclipse of the first wave of the Renaissance, and it is well known how he turned against the Beat Generation when he returned from his second sojourn in Europe a decade later, enabling Charles Olson of the Black Mountain group to capture the new literary incentive with a questionable dialectic.

But his constitutional restlessness could not jeopardize the work he actually accomplished. He touched the nerve of the future and more than any other voice in the movement called it into being. Though others picked up his mantle and received the plaudits, it remains true that today we enjoy the freedom of expression and lifestyle we actually possess largely because he convinced us that it was not only desirable but possible, and inspired us to make it be.

Lawrence Ferlinghetti

Lawrence Ferlinghetti was born in Yonkers, New York, on March 24, 1919. He went to San Francisco in 1951 after finishing his doctoral dissertation at the Sorbonne on "The City as Symbol in Modern Poetry: In Search of a Metropolitan Tradition." A few years later he started City Lights with Peter Martin, who returned to New York shortly afterward.

Possessing a sound business sense in addition to a robust sense of humor, Ferlinghetti listed his dog Homer annually in Bowker's Literary Market Place *as "Homer Ferlinghetti, Publicity & Public Relations." Ferlinghetti remembers that Homer "received mail regularly, although he expressed himself a bit too candidly to be a success in that field. He peed on a policeman's leg and was immortalized for it in a poem." "Dog," conceived for jazz accompaniment as a spontaneously spoken "oral message" rather than as a poem written for the printed page, appeared in* A Coney Island of the Mind *(1958), as did Ferlinghetti's other early poems, "Constantly Risking Absurdity" and "In Goya's greatest scenes." "Horn on Howl," Ferlinghetti's account of the landmark* Howl *obscenity case, was published in the* Evergreen Review *in 1957.*

Ferlinghetti's career as a writer includes more than ten books of poetry, two volumes of plays, and two novels. His poem "One Thousand Fearful Words for Fidel Castro" was written after his visit to Cuba in December 1960. Ferlinghetti supported Castro's revolution and was dismayed at what he called the "U.S. Beats" self-centeredness, as in Jack Kerouac's comment before Ferlinghetti left for Cuba, "I got my own Revolution out here in Northport—the American Revolution."

DOG

The dog trots freely in the street
and sees reality
and the things he sees
are bigger than himself
and the things he sees
are his reality
Drunks in doorways
Moons on trees
The dog trots freely thru the street
and the things he sees
are smaller than himself
Fish on newsprint
Ants in holes
Chickens in Chinatown windows
their heads a block away
The dog trots freely in the street
and the things he smells
smell something like himself
The dog trots freely in the street
past puddles and babies
cats and cigars
poolrooms and policemen
He doesn't hate cops
He merely has no use for them
and he goes past them
and past the dead cows hung up whole
in front of the San Francisco Meat Market
He would rather eat a tender cow
than a tough policeman
though either might do
And he goes past the Romeo Ravioli Factory
and past Coit's Tower
and past Congressman Doyle
He's afraid of Coit's Tower
but he's not afraid of Congressman Doyle
although what he hears is very discouraging
very depressing

very absurd
to a sad young dog like himself
to a serious dog like himself
But he has his own free world to live in
His own fleas to eat
He will not be muzzled
Congressman Doyle is just another
fire hydrant
to him
The dog trots freely in the street
and has his own dog's life to live
and to think about
and to reflect upon
touching and tasting and testing everything
investigating everything
without benefit of perjury
a real realist
with a real tale to tell
and a real tail to tell it with
a real live
        barking
                democratic dog
engaged in real
                free enterprise
with something to say
                about ontology
something to say
            about reality
                      and how to see it
                            and how to hear it
with his head cocked sideways
                at streetcorners
as if he is just about to have
                his picture taken
                      for Victor Records
            listening for
                  His Master's Voice
        and looking
                like a living questionmark

                              into the
                              great gramaphone
                              of puzzling existence
              with its wondrous hollow horn
                which always seems
              just about to spout forth
                              some Victorious answer
                              to everything

CONSTANTLY RISKING
ABSURDITY

    Constantly risking absurdity
                              and death
          whenever he performs
                              above the heads
                                        of his audience
        the poet like an acrobat
                          climbs on rime
                              to a high wire of his own making
    and balancing on eyebeams
                              above a sea of faces
          paces his way
                      to the other side of day
      performing entrechats
                          and sleight-of-foot tricks
    and other high theatrics
                          and all without mistaking
                  any thing
                          for what it may not be
        For he's the super realist
                              who must perforce perceive
                  taut truth
                          before the taking of each stance or step
      in his supposed advance
                          toward that still higher perch
    where Beauty stands and waits
                              with gravity

                    to start her death-defying leap
And he
        a little charleychaplin man
                        who may or may not catch
        her fair eternal form
                        spreadeagled in the empty air
            of existence

IN GOYA'S GREATEST SCENES

In Goya's greatest scenes we seem to see
                                the people of the world
        exactly at the moment when
            they first attained the title of
                            "suffering humanity"
            They writhe upon the page
                            in a veritable rage
                                of adversity
            Heaped up
                    groaning with babies and bayonets
                                under cement skies
                in an abstract landscape of blasted trees
                bent statues bats wings and beaks
                        slippery gibbets
                cadavers and carnivorous cocks
                and all the final hollering monsters
                    of the
                            "imagination of disaster"
                they are so bloody real
                            it is as if they really still existed
    And they do

            Only the landscape is changed
    They still are ranged along the roads
            plagued by legionaires
                        false windmills and demented roosters

They are the same people
                              only further from home
        on freeways fifty lanes wide
                        on a concrete continent
                                spaced with bland billboards
                                illustrating imbecile illusions of happiness

The scene shows fewer tumbrils
                        but more maimed citizens
                                        in painted cars
        and they have strange license plates
        and engines
                        that devour America

ONE THOUSAND FEARFUL
WORDS FOR FIDEL CASTRO

I am sitting in Mike's Place trying to figure out
                        what's going to happen
                        without Fidel Castro
        Among the salami sandwiches and spittoons
                        I see no solution
                        It's going to be a tragedy
                        I see no way out
                among the admen and slumming models
                and the brilliant snooping columnists
                who are qualified to call Castro psychotic
                        because they no doubt are doctors
                        and have examined him personally
                and are also qualified to call him Communist
                        with a capital C
        because they know the difference between Soviet Communism
                (which put the "slave" back in Slavic)
                        and socialism with a small c
        and also know a paranoid hysterical tyrant when they see one
                because they have it on first hand

from personal observation by the CIA
and the great disinterested news services
And Hearst is dead but his great Cuban wire still stands:
"You get the pictures, I'll make the War"
I see no answer
I see no way out
among the paisanos playing pool
it looks like Curtains for Fidel
They're going to fix his wagon
in the course of human events

In the back of Mike's the pinball machines
shudder and leap from the floor
when Cuban Charlie shakes them
and tries to work his will
on one named "Independence Sweepstakes"
Each pinball wandered lonely as a man
siphons thru and sinks
no matter how he twists and turns
A billiardball falls in a felt pocket
like a peasant in a green landscape
You're whirling around in your little hole
Fidel
and you'll soon sink
in the course of human events

On the nickelodeon a cowboy ballad groans
"Got myself a Cadillac" the cowhand moans
He didn't get it in Cuba, baby
Outside in the night of North Beach America
the new North American cars flick by
from Motorama
their headlights never bright enough
to dispel this night
in the course of human events

Three creepy men come in
One is Chinese
One is Negro
One is some kind of crazy Indian

They look like they may have been
walking up and down in Cuba
but they haven't
All three have hearing aids
It's a little deaf brotherhood of Americans
The skinny one screws his hearing aid
in his skinny ear
He's also got a little transistor radio
the same size as his hearing aid box
For a moment I confuse the two
The radio squawks
some kind of memorial program:
"When in the course of human events
it becomes necessary for one people
to dissolve the political bonds
which have connected them with another—"
I see no way out
no escape
He's tuned in on your frequency, Fidel
but can't hear it
There's interference
It's going to be
a big evil tragedy
They're going to fix you, Fidel
with your big Cuban cigar
which you stole from us
and your army surplus hat
which you probably also stole
and your Beat beard

History may absolve you, Fidel
but we'll dissolve you first, Fidel
You'll be dissolved in history
We've got the solvent
We've got the chaser
and we'll have a little party
somewhere down your way, Fidel
It's going to be a Gas
As they say in Guatemala

Outside of Mike's Place now
an ambulance sirens up
It's a midnight murder or something
Some young bearded guy stretched on the sidewalk
with blood sticking out
Here's your little tragedy, Fidel
They're coming to pick you up
and stretch you on their Stretcher
That's what happens, Fidel
when in the course of human events
it becomes necessary for one people to dissolve
the bonds of International Tel & Tel
and United Fruit
Fidel
How come you don't answer anymore
Fidel
Did they cut you off our frequency
We've closed down our station anyway
We've turned you off, Fidel

I was sitting in Mike's Place, Fidel
waiting for someone else to act
like a good Liberal
I hadn't quite finished reading Camus' *Rebel*
so I couldn't quite recognize you, Fidel
walking up and down your island
when they came for you, Fidel
"My Country or Death" you told them
Well you've got your little death, Fidel
like old Honest Abe
one of your boyhood heroes
who also had his little Civil War
and was a different kind of Liberator
(since no one was shot in his war)
and also was murdered
in the course of human events

Fidel . . . Fidel . . .
your coffin passes by
thru lanes and streets you never knew

thru day and night, Fidel
While lilacs last in the dooryard bloom, Fidel
your futile trip is done
yet is not done
and is not futile
I give you my sprig of laurel

San Francisco, January, 1961

HORN ON HOWL

Fahrenheit 451, the temperature at which books burn, has finally been determined not to be the prevailing temperature at San Francisco, though the police still would be all too happy to make it hot for you. On October 3 last [1957], Judge Clayton Horn of Municipal Court brought in a 39-page opinion finding Shigeyoshi Murao and myself not guilty of publishing or selling obscene writings, to wit Allen Ginsberg's *Howl and Other Poems* and issue 11&12 of *The Miscellaneous Man.*

Thus ended one of the most irresponsible and callous police actions to be perpetrated west of the Rockies, not counting the treatment accorded Indians and Japanese.

When William Carlos Williams, in his Introduction to *Howl,* said that Ginsberg had come up with "an arresting poem" he hardly knew what he was saying. The first edition of *Howl,* Number Four in the Pocket Poets Series, was printed in England by Villiers, passed thru Customs without incident, and was published at the City Lights bookstore here in the fall of 1956. Part of a second printing was stopped by Customs on March 25, 1957, not long after an earlier issue of *The Miscellaneous Man* (published in Berkeley by William Margolis) had been seized coming from the same printer. Section 305 of the Tariff Act of 1930 was cited. The San Francisco *Chronicle* (which alone among the local press put up a real howl about censorship) reported, in part:

Collector of Customs Chester MacPhee continued his campaign yesterday to keep what he considers obscene literature away from the children of the Bay Area. He confiscated 520 copies of a paperbound volume of poetry entitled *Howl and Other Poems*. . . . "The words and the sense of the writing is obscene," MacPhee declared. "You wouldn't want your children to come across it."

On April 3 the American Civil Liberties Union (to which I had submitted the manuscript of *Howl* before it went to the printer) informed Mr. MacPhee that it would contest the legality of the seizure, since it did not consider the book obscene. We announced in the meantime that an entirely new edition of *Howl* was being printed within the United States, thereby removing it from Customs jurisdiction. No changes were made in the original text, and a photo-offset edition was placed on sale at City Lights bookstore and distributed nationally while the Customs continued to sit on the copies from Britain.

On May 19, book editor William Hogan of the San Francisco *Chronicle* gave his Sunday column to an article by myself, defending *Howl* (I recommended a medal be made for Collector MacPhee, since his action was already rendering the book famous. But the police were soon to take over this advertising account and do a much better job—10,000 copies of *Howl* were in print by the time they finished with it.) In the defense of *Howl* I said I thought it to be "the most significant single long poem to be published in this country since World War II, perhaps since T. S. Eliot's *Four Quartets.*" To which many added "Alas." Fair enough, considering the barren, polished poetry and well-mannered verse which had dominated many of the major poetry publications during the past decade or so, not to mention some of the "fashionable incoherence" which has passed for poetry in many of the smaller, avant-garde magazines and little presses. *Howl* commits many poetic sins; but it was time. And it would be very interesting to hear from critics who can name another single long poem published in this country since the War which is as significant of its time and place and generation. (A reviewer in the *Atlantic Monthly* recently wrote that *Howl* may well turn out to be *The Waste Land* of the younger generation.) The central part of my article said: . . . It is not the poet but what he observes which is revealed as obscene. The great obscene wastes of *Howl* are the sad wastes of the mechanized world, lost among atom

bombs and insane nationalisms. . . . Ginsberg chooses to walk
on the wild side of this world, along with Nelson Algren, Henry
Miller, Kenneth Rexroth, Kenneth Patchen, not to mention
some great American dead, mostly in the tradition of philosophical anarchism. . . . Ginsberg wrote his own best defense
of *Howl* in another poem called "America." Here he asks:

> What sphinx of cement and aluminum bashed open their skulls
>   and ate up their brains and imagination?
> Moloch! Solitude! Filth! Ugliness! Ashcans and unobtainable
>   dollars! Children screaming under the stairways!
>   Boys sobbing in armies! Old men weeping in the parks!

A world, in short, you wouldn't want your children to come
across. . . . Thus was Goya obscene in depicting the Disasters
of War, thus Whitman an exhibitionist, exhibiting man in his
own strange skin.

On May 29 Customs released the books it had been holding,
since the United States Attorney at San Francisco refused to
institute condemnation proceedings against *Howl*.

Then the police took over and arrested us, Captain William
Hanrahan of the juvenile department (well named, in this case)
reporting that the books were not fit for children to read. Thus
during the first week in June I found myself being booked and
fingerprinted in San Francisco's Hall of Justice. The city jail
occupies the upper floors of it, and a charming sight it is, a
picturesque return to the early Middle Ages. And my enforced
tour of it was a dandy way for the city officially to recognize
the flowering of poetry in San Francisco. As one paper reported, "The Cops Don't Allow No Renaissance Here."

The ACLU posted bail. Our trial went on all summer, with
a couple of weeks between each day in court. The prosecution
soon admitted it had no case against either Shig Murao or
myself as far as the *Miscellaneous Man* was concerned, since
we were not the publisher of it, in which case there was no
proof we knew what was inside the magazine when it was sold
at our store. And, under the California Penal Code, the willful
and lewd *intent* of the accused had to be established. Thus the
trial was narrowed down to *Howl*.

The so-called People's Case (I say so-called, since the People seemed mostly on our side) was presented by Deputy District Attorney Ralph McIntosh whose heart seemed not in it nor his mind on it. He was opposed by some of the most formidable legal talent to be found, in the persons of Mr. Jake ("Never Plead Guilty") Ehrlich, Lawrence Speiser (former counsel for the ACLU), and Albert Bendich (present counsel for the ACLU)—all of whom defended us without expense to us.

The critical support for *Howl* (or the protest against censorship on principle) was enormous. Here is some of what some said:

Henry Rago, editor of Poetry *(Chicago):*
. . . I wish only to say that the book is a thoroughly serious work of literary art. . . . There is absolutely no question in my mind or in that of any poet or critic with whom I have discussed the book that it is a work of the legitimacy and validity contemplated by existing American law, as we know it in the statement of Justice Woolsey in the classic *Ulysses* case, and as we have seen it reaffirmed just recently by the Supreme Court in the Butler case. . . . I would be unworthy of the tradition of this magazine or simply of my place as a poet in the republic of letters . . . if I did not speak for the right of this book to free circulation, and against this affront not only to Allen Ginsberg and his publishers, but to the possibilities of the art of poetry in America. . . .

Robert Duncan and Director Ruth Witt-Diamant of the San Francisco (State College) Poetry Center:
. . . *Howl* is a significant work in American poetry, deriving both a spirit and form from Walt Whitman's *Leaves of Grass,* from Jewish religious writing. . . . It is rhapsodic, highly idealistic and inspired in cause and purpose. Like other inspired poets, Ginsberg strives to include all of life, especially the elements of suffering and dismay from which the voice of desire rises. Only by misunderstanding might these tortured outcryings for sexual and spiritual understanding be taken as salacious. The poet gives us the most painful details; he moves us toward a statement of experience that is challenging and finally noble.

Thomas Parkinson (University of California):
. . . *Howl* is one of the most important books of poetry published in the last ten years. Its power and eloquence are obvious, and the talent of Mr. Ginsberg is of the highest order. Even people who do not like the book are compelled to testify to its force and brilliance. . . .

James Laughlin (New Directions):
I have read the book carefully and do not myself consider it offensive to good taste, likely to lead youth astray, or be injurious to public morals. I feel, furthermore, that the book has considerable distinction as literature, being a powerful and artistic expression of a meaningful philosophical attitude. . . .

Kenneth Patchen:
The issue here—as in every like case—is not the merit or lack of it of a book but of a Society which traditionally holds the human being to be by its very functional nature a creature of shameful, outrageous, and obscene habits. . . .

Barney Rosset and Donald Allen, editors of the Evergreen
Review *(in which* Howl *was reprinted during the trial):*
The second issue of *Evergreen Review,* which was devoted to the work of writers in the San Francisco Bay Area, attempted in large part to show the kinds of serious writing being done by the postwar generation. We published Allen Ginsberg's poem *Howl* in that issue because we believe that it is a significant modern poem, and that Allen Ginsberg's intention was to sincerely and honestly present a portion of his own experience of the life of his generation. . . . Our final considered opinion was that Allen Ginsberg's *Howl* is an achieved poem and that it deserves to be considered as such. . . .

At the trial itself, nine expert witnesses testified in behalf of *Howl.* They were eloquent witnesses, together furnishing as good a one-sided critical survey of *Howl* as could possibly be got up in any literary magazine. These witnesses were: Mark Schorer and Leo Lowenthal (of the University of California faculty), Walter Van Tilburg Clark, Herbert Blau, Arthur Foff, and Mark Linenthal (all of the San Francisco State College faculty), Kenneth Rexroth, Vincent McHugh (poet and novelist), and Luther Nichols (book editor of the San Francisco *Examiner*). A few excerpts from the trial transcript—

DR. MARK SCHORER: The theme of the poem is announced very clearly in the opening line, "I saw the best minds of my generation destroyed by madness, starving hysterical naked." Then the following lines that make up the first part attempt to create the impression of a kind of nightmare world in which people representing "the best minds of my generation," in the author's view, are wandering like damned souls in hell. That is done through a kind of series of what one might call surrealistic images, a kind of state of hallucinations. Then in the second section the mood of the poem changes and it becomes an indictment of those elements in modern society that, in the author's view, are destructive of the best qualities in human nature and of the best minds. Those elements are, I would say, predominantly materialism, conformity and mechanization leading toward war. And then the third part is a personal address to a friend, real or fictional, of the poet or of the person who is speaking in the poet's voice—those are not always the same thing— who is mad and in a madhouse, and is the specific representative of what the author regards as a general condition, and with that final statement the poem ends. . . .

DR. LEO LOWENTHAL: In my opinion this is a genuine work of literature, which is very characteristic for a period of unrest and tension such as the one we have been living through the last decade. I was reminded by reading *Howl* of many other literary works as they have been written after times of great upheavals, particularly after World War One, and I found this work very much in line with similar literary works. With regard to the specific merits of the poem *Howl,* I would say that it is structured very well. As I see it, it consists of three parts, the first of which is the craving of the poet for self-identification, where he roams all over the field and tries to find allies in similar search for self-identification. He then indicts, in the second part, the villain, so to say, which does not permit him to find it, the Moloch of society, of the world as it is today. And in the third part he indicates the potentiality of fulfillment by friendship and love, although it ends on a sad and melancholic note actually indicating that he is in search for fulfillment he cannot find.

KENNETH REXROTH: . . . The simplest term for such writing is prophetic, it is easier to call it that than anything else because we have a large body of prophetic writing to refer to. There are the prophets of the Bible, which it greatly resembles in purpose and in language and in subject matter. . . . The theme is the denunciation of evil and a pointing out of the way out, so to speak. That is prophetic literature. "Woe! Woe! Woe! The City of Jerusalem! The Syrian is about to come down or has already and you are to do such and such a thing and you must repent and do thus and so." And *Howl,* the four parts of the poem—that is including the "Footnote to *Howl*" as one additional part—do this very specifically. They take up these various specifics seriatim, one after the other. . . . And "Footnote to *Howl*," of course, again, is Biblical in reference. The reference is to the Benedicite, which says over and over again, "Blessed is the fire, Blessed is the light, Blessed are the trees, and Blessed is this and Blessed is that," and he is saying, "Everything that is human is Holy to me," and that the possibility of salvation in this terrible situation which he reveals is through love and through the love of everything Holy in man. So that, I would say, that this just about covers the field of typically prophetic poetry. . . .

The prosecution put only two "expert witnesses" on the stand—both very lame samples of academia—one from the Catholic University of San Francisco and one a private elocution teacher, a beautiful woman, who said, "You feel like you are going through the gutter when you have to read that stuff. I didn't linger on it too long, I assure you." The University of San Francisco instructor said: "The literary value of this poem is negligible. . . . This poem is apparently dedicated to a long-dead movement, Dadaism, and some late followers of Dadaism. And, therefore, the opportunity is long past for any significant literary contribution of this poem." The critically devastating things the prosecution's witnesses could have said, but didn't, remain one of the great Catholic silences of the day.

So much for the literary criticism inspired by the trial. . . .

Legally, a layman could see that an important principle was certainly in the line drawn between "hard core pornography" and writing judged to be "social speech." But more important still was the court's acceptance of the principle that if a work is determined to be "social speech," the question of obscenity may not even be raised. Or, in the words of Counsel Bendich's argument: "The first amendment to the Constitution of the United States protecting the fundamental freedoms of speech and press prohibits the suppression of literature by the application of obscenity formulae unless the trial court first determines that the literature in question is utterly without social importance." (*Roth* v. *U.S.*)

. . . What is being urged here is that the majority opinion in *Roth* requires a trial court to make the constitutional determination; to decide in the first instance whether a work is utterly without redeeming social importance, *before* it permits the test of obscenity to be applied. . . .

. . . The record is clear that all of the experts for the defense identified the main theme of *Howl* as social criticism. And the prosecution concedes that it does not understand the work, much less what its dominant theme is.

Judge Horn agreed, in his opinion:

I do not believe that *Howl* is without even "the slightest redeeming social importance." The first part of *Howl* presents a picture of a nightmare world; the second part is an indictment of those elements in modern society destructive of the best qualities of human nature; such elements are predominantly identified as materialism, conformity, and mechanization leading toward war. The third part presents a picture of an individual who is a specific representation of what the author conceives as a general condition. . . . "Footnote to *Howl*" seems to be a declamation that everything in the world is holy, including parts of the body by name. It ends in a plea for holy living. . . .

And the judge went on to set forth certain rules for the guidance of authorities in the future:

1. If the material has the slightest redeeming social importance it is not obscene because it is protected by the First and Fourteenth Amendments of the United States Constitution, and the California Constitution.

2. If it does not have the slightest redeeming social importance it *may* be obscene.

3. The test of obscenity in California is that the material must have a tendency to deprave or corrupt readers by exciting lascivious thoughts or arousing lustful desire to the point that it presents a clear and present danger of inciting to anti-social or immoral action.

4. The book or material must be judged as a whole by its effect on the *average adult* in the community.

5. If the material is objectionable only because of coarse and vulgar language which is not erotic or aphrodisiac in character it is not obscene.

6. Scienter must be proved.

7. Book reviews may be received in evidence if properly authenticated.

8. Evidence of expert witnesses in the literary field is proper.

9. Comparison of the material with other similar material previously adjudicated is proper.

10. The people owe a duty to themselves and to each other to preserve and protect their constitutional freedoms from any encroachment by government unless it appears that the allowable limits of such protection have been breached, and then to take only such action as will heal the breach.

11. Quoting Justice Douglas: "I have the same confidence in the ability of our people to reject noxious literature as I have in their capacity to sort out the true from the false in theology, economics, politics, or any other field."

12. In considering material claimed to be obscene it is well to remember the motto: *Honi soit qui mal y pense* (Evil to him who thinks evil).

At which the Prosecution was reliably reported to have blushed.

Under banner headlines, the *Chronicle* reported that "the Judge's decision was hailed with applause and cheers from a packed audience that offered the most fantastic collection of beards, turtle-necked shirts and Italian hair-dos ever to grace the grimy precincts of the Hall of Justice." The decision was hailed editorially as a "landmark of law." Judge Horn has since been re-elected to office, which I like to think means that the People agree it was the police who here committed an obscene action.

Michael McClure

Michael McClure was born on October 20, 1932, in Marysville, Kansas. He moved to San Francisco in 1954 to study art and enrolled in courses at San Francisco State College, attending readings at Ruth Witt-Diamant's Poetry Center there. In the mid-1950s, the San Francisco poet Robert Duncan's writing workshop was "one of the most brilliant things" that happened to him, and McClure took part in a reading of Duncan's play Faust Foutu *at the Six Gallery, a garage turned art gallery with a plywood platform and black walls, attracting an audience of artists, students, and local bohemians. Soon afterward McClure gave his first poetry reading at the Six Gallery with Snyder, Whalen, Lamantia, and Ginsberg. McClure wrote a full account of the 1955 "Six Poets at the Six Gallery" reading in his book* Scratching the Beat Surface *(1982).*

In 1956 McClure's first book, Passage, *was issued by the small press publisher Jonathan Williams. Two years later McClure wrote his "Peyote Poem" while experimenting with psychedelics as a means of psychic liberation. In his autobiography,* The Mad Cub *(1970), McClure explained the connection between his interest in ecology and his early peyote experiments, which taught him "the separate consciousness of my being . . . I am aware of the creature that is stomach and the one that is solar plexus and the one that is brain and chest and all the fragmented creatures of my being that form the totality. . . . In reading biology I hope to make the discoveries that will liberate man to exist in timelessness and a state of superconsciousness."*

PEYOTE POEM

Clear—the senses bright—sitting in the black chair—Rocker—
    the white walls reflecting the color of clouds
    moving over the sun. Intimacies! The rooms

  not important—but like divisions of all space
    of all hideousness and beauty. I hear
    the music of myself and write it down

  for no one to read. I pass fantasies as they
    sing to me with Circe-Voices. I visit
among the peoples of myself and know all
    I need to know.
I KNOW EVERYTHING! I PASS INTO THE ROOM

    there is a golden bed radiating all light

the air is full of silver hangings and sheathes

    I smile to myself. I know

all that there is to know. I see all there

is to feel. I am friendly with the ache
    in my belly. The answer

to love is my voice. There is no Time!
No answers. The answers to feeling is my feeling.

    The answer to joy is joy without feeling.

    The room is a multicolored cherub
of air and bright colors. The pain in my stomach
is warm and tender. I am smiling. The pain
    is many pointed, without anguish.

Light changes the room from yellows to violet!

The dark brown space behind the door is precious
    intimate, silent and still. The birthplace
      of Brahms. I know

  all that I need to know. There is no hurry.

I read the meanings of scratched walls and cracked ceilings.

I am separate. I close my eyes in divinity and pain.

I blink in solemnity and unsolemn joy.

I smile at myself in my movements. Walking
I step higher in carefulness. I fill

space with myself. I see the secret and distinct
patterns of smoke from my mouth

I am without care part of all. Distinct.
I am separate from gloom and beauty. I see all.

———————————

(SPACIOUSNESS
And grim intensity—close within myself. No longer
a cloud
but flesh real as rock. Like Herakles

of primordial substance and vitality.
And not even afraid of the thing shorn of glamor

but accepting.
The beautiful things are not of ourselves

but I watch them. Among them.

———————————

And the Indian thing. It is true!
Here in my Apartment I think tribal thoughts.)

———————————

STOMACHE!!!

There is no time. I am visited by a man
who is the god of foxes
there is dirt under the nails of his paw
fresh from his den.
We smile at one another in recognition.

I am free from Time. I accept it without triumph

—a fact.

Closing my eyes there are flashes of light.

My eyes won't focus but leap. I see that I have three feet.
I see seven places at once!
The floor slants—the room slopes

things melt
into each other. Flashes
of light

and meldings. I wait.

seeing the physical thing pass.

I am on a mesa of time and space.

!STOM—ACHE!

Writing the music of life
in words.
Hearing the round sounds of the guitar
as colors.
Feeling the touch of flesh.

Seeing the loose chaos of words
on the page.
(ultimate grace)
(Sweet Yeats and his ball of hashish.)

My belly and I are two individuals
joined together
in life.

THIS IS THE POWERFUL KNOWLEDGE

we smile with it.

At the window I look into the blue-gray
gloom of dreariness.
I am war. Into the dragon of space.
I stare into clouds seeing
their misty convolutions.

The whirls of vapor

I will small clouds out of existence.

They become fish devouring each other.

And change like Dante's holy spirits

becoming an osprey frozen skyhigh

to challenge me.

II

The huge bird with bug eyes. Caught in dynamic profile.
        Feet stretched out forward
              glaring at me.
        Feathery cloudtips of feathers
        dark gray on gray against blue.

———————————————

From the cliff of the park—the city—a twilight
        foggy vista. Green grass over the stone,
              pink auras of neon. The spires lean

into the clouds. I remember the window, wonder.

Out over the rooftops from the window.

I am at the top of the park. I look

for the clouds in the calm sky.

Tendrils and wisps. I see 180 degrees.

MY STOMACH IS SWOLLEN AND NUMB!

I have entered the essential-barrenness
there is no beauty the exotic has come to an end I face the facts
of emptiness, I recognize that time is a measurement is arbitrary,
I look for the glamor of metamorphosis, for the color of transmu-
                                    [tation,
I wait to become the flask of a wonder to see diamonds, there is no
purpose. Pain without anguish space without loveliness. The pure
facts of vision are here there is the City! There is the wonder
as far as the eye can see the close buildings I see them so close.

Oh and I am so glad to see them. This is the change

that I do not care but know.

THE GIANT, COMIC, FIERCE, BIRD FROM MY WINDOW!
        The spirits, souls rising to form it need no explanation
              in the world.
        Vast expanse without interest—undrab.

Here is the light full of grains and color
the pink auras and fresh orange. The rasping sounds,

hideous buildings leaning into emptiness.

The fact of my division is simple I am a spirit
of flesh in the cold air. I need no answer

I do not lean on others. I am separate, distinct.

There is nothing to drag me down.

Back at the window again I look for the Osprey

I remember the flow of blood, the heat
and the cold almost-fear beneath it. There is nothing

in the night but fast clouds. No stars. Smokey gray
and black the rooms are the color of blue Mexican glass
and white. I see to the undercoats of paint

to the green and brown. I am caught in reveries of love.

The tassles of the shag rug are lace.

I am in the Park above all and cold.

I am in the room in light Hell and warm Heaven.

I am lost in memories. I move feeling the pleasant bulk
of my body. I am pleased with my warm pain

I think of its cessation with pleasure.

I know it will not change. I know I am here, beyond all

in myself.

The passage—my eyes ache with joy in the warmth.

'The edge of the cloth like tassles—a shag rug

white—the loops lace over your shoulder—

the white wall behind—green showing through
lace again a sweet memory in the gloom.

The smells clear in my head over your shoulder.
Your brown arm on the tick cloth. Blue stripes

on white the smell of smoke and the smell of bodies.

Oh and the void again with space and no Time.
Our breath moving in the corners of the room!

III

I AM MOVING IN THE YELLOW KITCHEN
    high never to come down—the ceiling brown.

    I am looking at the face of the red clock—
          meaningless.

    I know of the sky from my window and I do not turn
          to look, I am
    motionless forever standing unmoving—
    a body of flesh in the empty air.

    I am in the barren warm universe of no Time.
      The ache in my belly is a solid thing.
    There is no joy or tremor, I smoke a cigarette in the small
  room elbow to the stove seeing what is new—
barren as my cigarette and hand in the air hearing the whir of
                    [unheard
    sounds, seeing the place of new things to the air. In
no relation, feeling the solid blankness of all things having
    my stomach solid and aching, I am aloof
        and we are one,
in the bare room my stomach and I held together by dry
      warmth in space.
    There is no reason for this! There is nothing but forms
      in emptiness—unugly
      and without beauty. It is that.

I AM STANDING HERE MYSELF BY THE STOVE
    without reason or time.
    I am the warmth and it is within me.

BELLY BELLY BELLY! UNENDING AND BLANK.

    I am in the instant of space, I see all I am aware of all
I am curious but knowing that there is no more than this—the

[happenings
of the world continue about me there are worls and wisps
[of smoke
there are the sounds of late afternoon and early evening
with forever between them I see it passing between them
I cannot be surprised—there is no news to me it has always
[been
this way—going into a memory would be to go into a long
black tunnel. The room is huge and spacious without
PATTERN OR REASON. IT HAS ALWAYS BEEN THIS
[WAY. THERE ARE THE COLORS
of early evening as they have always been. I am as I shall
always be. Standing feeling myself in the inert.

I raise my head with the beauty of final knowledge
I step high in pride benevolence and awareness. The
[pain

is part of me. The pain in my belly. The clouds
are passing and I will not stop them.

COLOR IS REALITY! THE EYE IS A MATCHFLAME!

The pain is a solid lump—all of the anguish
I am freed from.

The answer to joy is joy without feeling. The answer to
[love

is my voice.

The room is a solid of objects and air.

I KNOW EVERYTHING, I AM FILLED WITH WEARINESS

I close my eyes in divinity and pain.

I blink in solemnity and unsolemn joy.

I am free of the instant there is no Time!

I have lived out the phases of life from patterned opu-
[lence

to stark and unheeding.

My stomach is gentle love, gentle love.

I AM AT THE POINT OF ALL HUGENESS AND MEANING

The pain of my stomach has entered my chest
throat and head.

The enormous leap! I look from the precipice

of my window.
I watch from my warmth, feeling.

THERE ARE NO CATEGORIES!!!

(OH WONDER, WONDER, IN DREARINESS AND BEAUTY
aloof in perpetual unamazed astonishment
[warm
as stone in the emptiness of vast space
seeing the small and limitless scale
of vastness. My hand before me. Seeing

all reachable and real. The answer to love
is my voice.
I am sure. This is the ultimate
about me. My feelings real to me. Solid

as walls.—I see the meaning
of walls—divisions of space,
backgrounds of color.)

HEAVEN AND HELL THIS IS REACHABLE I AM SICK IN
[LACK OF JOY

and joyful in lack of joy and sick
in sickness of joy. Oh dry
stomach! And not ecstatic in knowledge.

I KNOW ALL THAT THERE IS TO KNOW,

feel all that there is to feel.

Piteously clear air. Radiance without glow.

Perfection.

I hear all that there is to hear.
There is no noise but a lack of sound.
I am on the plain of Space.

There are no spirits but spirits.

The room is empty of all but visible things.

THERE ARE NO CATEGORIES! OR JUSTIFICATONS!

I am sure of my movements I am a bulk
in the air.

from SCRATCHING THE
BEAT SURFACE

Three years before the peyote experience just described, I had given my first poetry reading with Allen Ginsberg, the Zen poet Philip Whalen, Gary Snyder, and the American surrealist poet Philip Lamantia. The reading was in October 1955 at the Six Gallery in San Francisco. The Six Gallery was a cooperative art gallery run by young artists who centered around the San Francisco Art Institute. They were fiery artists who had either studied with Clyfford Still and Mark Rothko or with the newly emerging figurative painters. Their works ranged from huge drip and slash to minute precision smudges turning into faces. Earlier in the year poet Robert Duncan had given a staged reading of his play *Faust Foutu* (Faust Fucked) at the Six Gallery and, with the audacious purity of an Anarchist poet, he had stripped off his clothes at the end of the play.

On this night Kenneth Rexroth was master of ceremonies. This was the first time that Allen Ginsberg read *Howl*. Though I had known Allen for some months preceding, it was my first meeting with Gary Snyder and Philip Whalen. Lamantia did not read his poetry that night but instead recited works of the recently deceased John Hoffman—beautiful poems that left orange stripes and colored visions in the air.

The world that we tremblingly stepped out into in that decade was a bitter, gray one. But San Francisco was a special place. Rexroth said it was to the arts what Barcelona was to

Spanish Anarchism. Still, there was no way, even in San Francisco, to escape the pressures of the war culture. We were locked in the Cold War and the first Asian debacle—the Korean War. My self-image in those years was of finding myself—young, high, a little crazed, needing a haircut—in an elevator with burly, crew-cutted, square-jawed eminences, staring at me like I was misplaced cannon fodder. We hated the war and the inhumanity and the coldness. The country had the feeling of martial law. An undeclared military state had leapt out of Daddy Warbucks' tanks and sprawled over the landscape. As artists we were oppressed and indeed the people of the nation were oppressed. There were certain of us (whether we were fearful or brave) who could not help speaking out—we had to speak. We knew we were poets and we had to speak out as poets. We saw that the art of poetry was essentially dead—killed by war, by academies, by neglect, by lack of love, and by disinterest. We knew we could bring it back to life. We could see what Pound had done—and Whitman, and Artaud, and D. H. Lawrence in his monumental poetry and prose.

The Six Gallery was a huge room that had been converted from an automobile repair shop into an art gallery. Someone had knocked together a little dais and was exhibiting sculptures by Fred Martin at the back of it—pieces of orange crates that had been swathed in muslin and dipped in plaster of paris to make splintered, sweeping shapes like pieces of surrealist furniture. A hundred and fifty enthusiastic people had come to hear us. Money was collected and jugs of wine were brought back for the audience. I hadn't seen Allen in a few weeks and I had not heard *Howl*—it was new to me. Allen began in a small and intensely lucid voice. At some point Jack Kerouac began shouting "GO" in cadence as Allen read it. In all of our memories no one had been so outspoken in poetry before—we had gone beyond a point of no return—and we were ready for it, for a point of no return. None of us wanted to go back to the gray, chill, militaristic silence, to the intellective void—to the land without poetry—to the spiritual drabness. We wanted to make it new and we wanted to invent it and the process of it as we went into it. We wanted voice and we wanted vision.

HOWL
for Carl Solomon

1

I saw the best minds of my generation destroyed by madness, starving
    hysterical naked,
dragging themselves through the negro streets at dawn looking for
    an angry fix,
angelheaded hipsters burning for the ancient heavenly connection to
    the starry dynamo in the machinery of night. . . .

Ginsberg read on to the end of the poem, which left us standing in wonder, or cheering and wondering, but knowing at the deepest level that a barrier had been broken, that a human voice and body had been hurled against the harsh wall of America and its supporting armies and navies and academies and institutions and ownership systems and power-support bases.

A week or so later I told Allen that *Howl* was like *Queen Mab*—Shelley's first long poem. *Howl* was Allen's metamorphosis from quiet, brilliant, burning bohemian scholar trapped by his flames and repressions to epic vocal bard. Shelley had made the same transformation.

Also that night Gary Snyder, bearded and neat, a rugged young man of nature at age twenty-five, read his scholarly and ebullient nature poem, *A Berry Feast*.

A BERRY FEAST
For Joyce and Homer Matson

I

Fur the color of mud, the smooth loper
Crapulous old man, a drifter,
Praises! of Coyote the Nasty, the fat
Puppy that abused himself, the ugly gambler,
Bringer of goodies.

In bearshit find it in August,
Neat pile on the fragrant trail, in late
August, perhaps by a Larch tree
Bear has been eating the berries.
      high meadow, late summer, snow gone
Blackbear
      eating berries, married
To a woman whose breasts bleed
From nursing the half-human cubs.

    Somewhere of course there are people
    collecting and junking, gibbering all day,

"Where I shoot my arrows
"There is the sunflower's shade
      —song of the rattlesnake
      coiled in the boulder's groin
"K'ak, k'ak, k'ak!
      sang Coyote. Mating with
      humankind—

    The Chainsaw falls for boards of pine,
    Suburban bedrooms, block on block
    Will waver with this grain and knot,
    The maddening shapes will start and fade
    Each morning when commuters wake—
    Joined boards hung on frames,
      a box to catch the biped in.
    and shadow swings around the tree
Shifting on the berrybush
    from leaf to leaf across each day
The shadow swings around the tree.

II

Three, down, through windows
Dawn leaping cats, all barred brown, grey
Whiskers aflame
      bits of mouse on the tongue

Washing the coffeepot in the river
         the baby yelling for breakfast,
Her breasts, black-nippled, blue-veined, heavy,
Hung through the loose shirt
        squeezed, with the free hand
           white jet in three cups.
Cats at dawn
        derry derry down

Creeks wash clean where trout hide
We chew the black plug
Sleep on needles through long afternoons
        "you shall be owl
        "you shall be sparrow
        "you will grow thick and green, people
        "will eat you, you berries!
Coyote: shot from the car, two ears,
A tail, bring bounty.

    Clanks of tread
        oxen of Shang
        moving the measured road

Bronze bells at the throat
Bronze balls on the horns, the bright Oxen
Chanting through sunlight and dust
        wheeling logs down hills
        into heaps,

                the yellow
    Fat-snout Caterpillar, tread toppling forward
    Leaf on leaf, roots in gold volcanic dirt.

When
Snow melts back
        from the trees
Bare branches   knobbed pine twigs
        hot sun on wet flowers
Green shoots of huckleberry
Breaking through snow.

III

Belly stretched taut in a bulge
Breasts swelling as you guzzle beer, who wants
                    Nirvana?
Here is water, wine, beer
Enough books for a week
A mess of afterbirth,
A smell of hot earth, a warm mist
Steams from the crotch

"You can't be killers all your life
"The people are coming—
                —and when Magpie
Revived him, limp rag of fur in the river
Drowned and drifting, fish-food in the shallows,
"Fuck you," sang Coyote
                    and ran.

Delicate blue-black, sweeter from meadows
Small and tart in the valleys, with light blue dust
Huckleberries scatter through pine woods
Crowd along gullies, climb dusty cliffs,
Spread through the air by birds;
Find them in droppings of bear.

  "Stopped in the night
  "Ate hot pancakes in a bright room
  "Drank coffee, read the paper
  "In a strange town, drove on,

        singing, as the drunkard swerved the car
  "Wake from your dreams, bright ladies!
  "Tighten your legs, squeeze demons from
        the crotch with rigid thighs
  "Young red-eyed men will come
  "With limp erections, snuffling cries
  "To dry your stiffening bodies in the sun!

Woke at the beach. Grey dawn,
Drenched with rain. One naked man
Frying his horsemeat on a stone.

IV

Coyote yaps, a knife!
Sunrise on yellow rocks.
People gone, death no disaster,
Clear sun in the scrubbed sky
                    empty and bright
Lizards scurry from darkness
We lizards sun on yellow rocks.

See, from the foothills
Shred of river glinting, trailing,
To flatlands, the city:
            glare of haze in the valley horizon
Sun caught on glass gleams and gocs.
From cool springs under cedar
On his haunches, white grin,
            long tongue panting, he watches:

Dead city in dry summer,
Where berries grow.

Snyder's gloss on the poem reads: "The berry feast is a first-fruits celebration that consumes a week of mid-August on the Warm Springs Indian Reservation in Oregon. Coyote is the name of the Trickster-Hero of the mythology of that region."

What I hear in the poem is Snyder's concern that we must, as Charles Olson proposed in "Call Me Ishmael," change time itself into space through an alchemic act. Then we may move in it and step outside of the disaster that we have wreaked upon the environment and upon our phylogenetic selves. Snyder looks back to the Indians with their hunting and gathering Paleolithic culture—and recounts the joy of their berry feast in a song that is like those of ancient Greece. It is dancelike and reminds me of how the Chorus dithyrambed in the wine feast to another Trickster-God, Dionysus. Snyder also looks to the measured, eudaemonic semistasis—the slow-moving post-Neolithic history of the Shang Dynasty in China with its tinkle of ox bells. To these he compares the machine harvesting of our forests—trees being mowed down to make boxes for bipeds, with no feelings for Nature. Throughout the poem there is the solidity of a physical romance with a woman and the joy in the warmth of the flesh of her arms around him— and the sight and sense and taste of the berries.

Even in those days Philip Whalen was a big man. As I watched him read, the meaning of his metamorphic poem gradually began to sink in. We laughed as the poem's intent clarified. Here was a poem by a poet-scholar (who is now a Zen priest) with a multiple thrust. Whalen was using the American speech that William Carlos Williams instructed us to use, but he put it to a different use. Whalen's poems were not only naturalistic portrayals of objects and persons transformed by poetry—they also used American speech for the naked joy of portraying metamorphosis and of exemplifying and aiding change in the universe. They manifested a positive Whiteheadian joy in shifting and in processes. Whalen read this poem with a mock seriousness that was at once biting, casual, and good natured.

"PLUS ÇA CHANGE . . ."

What are you doing?

    I am coldly calculating

I didn't ask for a characterization.
Tell me what we're going to do.

    That's what I'm coldly calculating.

You had better say "plotting" or "scheming"
You never could calculate without a machine.

    Then I'm brooding. Presently
    A plot will hatch.

Who are you trying to kid?

    Be nice.
(SILENCE)

Listen. Whatever we do from here on out
Let's for God's sake not look at each other
Keep our eyes shut and the lights turned off—
We won't mind touching if we don't have to see.

    I'll ignore those preposterous feathers.

Say what you please, we brought it all on ourselves
But nobody's going out of his way to look.

    Who'd recognize us now?

We'll just pretend we're used to it.
(Watch out with that goddamned tail!)

Pull the shades down. Turn off the lights.
Shut your eyes.

    (SILENCE)

There is no satisfactory explanation.
You can talk until you're blue

    Just how much bluer can I get?

Well, save breath you need to cool

    Will you please shove the cuttlebone a little closer?

All right, until the perfumes of Arabia

    Grow cold. Ah! Sunflower seeds!

Will you listen, please? I'm trying to make
A rational suggestion. Do you mind?

Certainly not. Just what *shall* we tell the children?

"Plus Ça Change . . ." hangs in space making a shape like a
sculpture. Each reading of it is a little different. You can see
them changing into parakeets. The poem is created like a Goya
engraving or a Sung Dynasty landscape painting with the
proper number of strokes, not too many and not too few. It
is concise, powerful, and humorous. It exhibits faith in change
to the extent of desiring change. Exuberant. Olson said in
paraphrase of Herakleitos:

What does not change / is the will to change.

The Six Gallery reading was open to the world and the world
was welcome. There were poets and Anarchists and Stalinists
and professors and painters and bohemians and visionaries and
idealists and grinning cynics.

I had been fascinated by the thought and the poetry of the
French maudite, antiphysical, mystic poet Antonin Artaud,
who had died toothless and, it is said, mad in Paris in 1948,
only seven years before our Six Gallery reading. One of my
first exchanges with Philip Lamantia on meeting him in 1954
was to ask where I could find more works by Artaud. I was
fascinated by Artaud's visionary gnosticism. I was looking for
a way beyond the objectism of American poetry and the post-
Symbolism of French poetry and I sensed that Artaud's poetry,
a breakthrough incarnate, was a way into the open field of
poetry and into the open shape of verse and into the physicality
of thought. I was looking for a verbal and physical athletics
where poetry could be achieved. In their direct statement to
my nerves, lines of Artaud's were creating physical tensions,
and gave me ideas for entries into a new mode of verse.

One phrase of Artaud's fascinated me: "It is not possible
that in the end the miracle will not occur." I replied with a
poem I read at the Six Gallery.

POINT LOBOS: ANIMISM

It is possible my friend,
If I have had a fat belly
That the wolf lives on fat
Gnawing slowly
Through a visceral night of rancor.
It is possible that the absence of pain
May be so great
That the possibility of care
May be impossible.

Perhaps to know pain.
Anxiety, rather than the fear
Of the fear of anxiety.
This talk of miracles!

Of Animism:
I have been in a spot so full of spirits
That even the most joyful animist
Brooded
When all in sight was less to be cared about
Than death
And there was no noise in the ears
That mattered.
(I knelt in the shade
By a cold salt pool
And felt the entrance of hate
On many legs,
The soul like a clambering
Water vascular system.

No scuttling could matter
Yet I formed in my mind
The most beautiful
Of maxims.
How could I care
For your illness or mine?)
This talk of bodies!

It is impossible to speak
Of lupine or tulips
When one may read
His name
Spelled by the mold on the stumps
When the forest moves about one.
Heel. Nostril.
Light. Light! Light!
This is the bird's song
You may tell it
to your children.

I did not fear obscurity in my poetry because I had come to believe that the way to the universal was by means of the most intensely personal. I believed that what we truly share with others lies in the deepest, most personal, even physiological core—and not in the outer social world of speech that is used for grooming and transactions. Further, as Clyfford Still, a contemporary of Jackson Pollock and a heroic Abstract Expressionist, said, "Demands for communication are presumptuous and irrelevant." Jazz and bop had convinced me that poets might also communicate by music, by sound, like Thelonius Monk, Charlie Parker, Miles Davis.

Point Lobos: Animism has a tight, small sound—not entirely different from the sound of a Romantic sonnet. Its intent is personal and specific. I hoped to alter the lyric form into a new shape and to allow a subject to create the exterior shape as well as the sound and music. I wanted to tell of my feelings of hunger, of emptiness, and of epiphany. I hoped to state the sharpness of a demonic joy that I found in a place of incredible beauty on the coast of Northern California. I wanted to say how I was overwhelmed by the sense of animism—and how everything (breath, spot, rock, ripple in the tidepool, cloud, and stone) was alive and spirited. It was a frightening and joyous awareness of my undersoul. I say *undersoul* because I did not want to join Nature by my mind but by my viscera—my belly. The German language has two words, *Geist* for the soul of man and *Odem* for the spirit of beasts. Odem is the undersoul. I was becoming sharply aware of it. . . .

At the Six Gallery I also read a poem that sprang from an

article in *Time* magazine (April 1954). Excerpts from the article used to preface the poem say:

> Killer whales. . . . Savage sea cannibals up to thirty feet long with teeth like bayonets . . . one was caught with fourteen seals and thirteen porpoises in its belly . . . often tear at boats and nets . . . destroyed thousands of dollars worth of fishing tackle. . . . Icelandic government appealed to the U.S., which has thousands of men stationed at a lonely NATO airbase on the subarctic island. Seventy-nine bored G.I.'s responded with enthusiasm. Armed with rifles and machine guns one posse of Americans climbed into four small boats and in one morning wiped out a pack of 100 killers. . . .
>
> First the killers were rounded up into tight formation with concentrated machine gun fire, then moved out again one by one, for the final blast which would kill them . . . as one was wounded, the others would set upon it and tear it to pieces with their jagged teeth.

I was horrified and angry when I read about the slaughter and I wrote:

FOR THE DEATH OF 100 WHALES

Hung midsea
Like a boat mid-air
The Liners boiled their pastures:
The Liners of flesh,
The Arctic steamers.

Brains the size of a football
Mouths the size of a door.

The sleek wolves
Mowers and reapers of sea kine.
THE GIANT TADPOLES
(Meat their algae)
Lept

Like sheep or children.
Shot from the sea's bore.

Turned and twisted
(Goya!!)
Flung blood and sperm.
Incense.
Gnashed at their tails and brothers,
Cursed Christ of mammals,
Snapped at the sun,
Ran for the sea's floor.

Goya! Goya!
Oh Lawrence
No angels dance those bridges.
OH GUN! OH BOW!
There are no churches in the waves,
No holiness,
No passages or crossings
From the beasts' wet shore.

The slaughter of the whales was a murder that I thought only
Goya could have portrayed in his *Horrors of War*. I called on
D. H. Lawrence at the end to be the tutelary figure of the
poem because of his description of the copulation of whales
and his imaginings of the angels moving from body to body in
the mammoth act.

And over the bridge of the whale's strong phallus, linking the
  wonder of whales
the burning archangels under the sea keep passing, back and
  forth, keep passing archangels of bliss
from him to her, from her to him, great Cherubim
that wait on whales in mid-ocean, suspended in the waves of
  the sea
great heaven of whales in the waters, old hierarchies.

from *Whales Weep Not*

Years later, at the United Nations Environmental Conference
in Stockholm in 1972, Gary Snyder and I were among the

contingent of independent lobbyists (led by Project Jonah and Stewart Brand) who took it upon themselves to represent whales, Indians, and the freedom of the diversity of the environment. We participated in whale demonstrations in Stockholm and immediately following the conference I returned to San Francisco and staged a pro-whale demonstration. At the Stockholm conference Snyder wrote and distributed a poem, *Mother Earth: Her Whales.* . . .

Gary Snyder

Gary Snyder was born on May 8, 1930, in San Francisco, California, and was raised in Washington state and Oregon. At Reed College he was part of a bohemian group that included Philip Whalen and Lew Welch, who joined him in San Francisco in the early 1950s. Snyder entered the Asian language program of the University of California in Berkeley, where he lived in a small cottage near the Young Buddhist Association and saved his money to study Buddhism in Japan. His friend Will Petersen recalls that Snyder wore blue jeans to read his poetry at the Six Gallery, whereas Ginsberg wore a charcoal gray suit, white shirt, and tie. Snyder was, according to his friend, "somehow certain of immortality, back then. In an impoverished Taoist unpublished poet sort of way. 'Save the invitation [to the Six Gallery reading],' Gary confided, 'Some day it will be worth something.' "

In Japan, Snyder wrote Petersen that he had come to realize "that I am firstmost a poet, doomed to be shamelessly silly, undignified, curious, cuntstruck, & considering (in the words of Rimbaud) the disorder of my own mind sacred. So I don't think I'll ever commit myself to the roll of Zen monk. . . ." "Higashi Hongwanji" and "Tōji" were early poems from Japan.

Snyder's first book of poems, Riprap, *was published by Origin Press in 1959 and reflect his experience in Yosemite in 1955 as a trail crew laborer laying "riprap," a kind of rock pavement set into an eroding trail. "Mid-August at Sourdough Mountain Lookout" and "Milton by Firelight" were inspired by his earlier summer jobs as a lookout ranger in the mountains of Washington. "Night Highway Ninety-nine" described various trips hitchhiking from Seattle to San Francisco early in 1956, accompanied at times by Allen Ginsberg. "Note on the Religious Tendencies" appeared in* Liberation *magazine in 1959.*

MID-AUGUST AT SOURDOUGH MOUNTAIN LOOKOUT

Down valley a smoke haze
Three days heat, after five days rain
Pitch glows on the fir-cones
Across rocks and meadows
Swarms of new flies.

I cannot remember things I once read
A few friends, but they are in cities.
Drinking cold snow-water from a tin cup
Looking down for miles
Through high still air.

MILTON BY FIRELIGHT

Piute Creek, August 1955

"Oh hell, what do mine eyes
      with grief behold?"
Working with an old
Singlejack miner, who can sense
The vein and cleavage
In the very guts of rock, can
Blast granite, build
Switchbacks that last for years
Under the beat of snow, thaw, mule-hooves.
What use, Milton, a silly story
Of our lost general parents,
      eaters of fruit?

The Indian, the chainsaw boy,
And a string of six mules
Came riding down to camp
Hungry for tomatoes and green apples.
Sleeping in saddle-blankets
Under a bright night-sky
Han River slantwise by morning.
Jays squall
Coffee boils

In ten thousand years the Sierras
Will be dry and dead, home of the scorpion.
Ice-scratched slabs and bent trees.
No paradise, no fall,
Only the weathering land
The wheeling sky,
Man, with his Satan
Scouring the chaos of the mind.
Oh Hell!

Fire down
Too dark to read, miles from a road
The bell-mare clangs in the meadow
That packed dirt for a fill-in
Scrambling through loose rocks
On an old trail
All of a summer's day.

RIPRAP

Lay down these words
Before your mind like rocks.
            placed solid, by hands
In choice of place, set
Before the body of the mind
            in space and time:
Solidity of bark, leaf, or wall
            riprap of things:

Cobble of milky way,
　　　　　straying planets,
These poems, people,
　　　　　lost ponies with
Dragging saddles—
　　　　　and rocky sure-foot trails.
The worlds like an endless
　　　　　four-dimensional
Game of *Go*.
　　　　　ants and pebbles
In the thin loam, each rock a word
　　　　　a creek-washed stone
Granite: ingrained
　　　　　with torment of fire and weight
Crystal and sediment linked hot
　　　　　all change, in thoughts,
As well as things.

PRAISE FOR SICK WOMEN

I

The female is fertile, and discipline
(contra naturam) only
　　　　　confuses her
Who has, head held sideways
Arm out softly, touching,
A difficult dance to do, but not in mind.

Hand on sleeve:　she holds leaf turning
　　　　　in sunlight on spiderweb;
Makes him flick like trout through shallows
Builds into ducks and cold marshes
Sucks out the quiet:　bone rushes in
Behind the cool pupil a knot grows
Sudden roots sod him and solid him
Rain falls from skull-roof mouth is awash
　　　　　with small creeks
Hair grows, tongue tenses out—and she

Quick turn of the head: back glancing, one hand
Fingers smoothing the thigh, and he sees.

II

Apples will sour at your sight.
Blossoms fail the bough,
Soil turn bone-white: wet rice,
Dry rice, die on the hillslope.

All women are wounded
Who gather berries, dibble in mottled light,
Turn white roots from humus, crack nuts on stone
High upland with squinted eye
            or rest in cedar shade.
Are wounded
In yurt or frame or mothers
Shopping at the outskirts in fresh clothes.
Whose sick eye bleeds the land,
Fast it!   thick throat shields from evil,
                        you young girls
First caught with the gut-cramp
Gather punk wood and sour leaf
Keep out of our kitchen.
Your garden plots, your bright fabrics,
Clever ways to carry children
Hide
        a beauty like season or tide,
                        sea cries
Sick women
Dreaming of long-legged dancing in light
No, our Mother Eve: slung on a shoulder
Lugged off to hell.
                        kali/shakti
Where's hell then?
In the moon.
In the change of the moon:
In a bark shack
Crouched from sun, five days,
Blood dripping through crusted thighs.

NIGHT HIGHWAY
NINETY-NINE

. . . only the very poor, or eccentric, can surround
themselves with shapes of elegance (soon to be
demolished) in which they are forced by poverty
to move with leisurely grace. We remain alert so
as not to get run down, but it turns out you only
have to hop a few feet, to one side, and the whole
huge machinery rolls by, not seeing you at all.
—LEW WELCH

I

We're on our way
>   man
>   out of town
>   go hitching down
>   that highway ninety-nine

Too cold and rainy to go out on the Sound
Sitting in Ferndale drinking coffee
Baxter in black, been to a funeral
Raymond in Bellingham—Helena Hotel—
Can't go to Mexico with that weak heart
Well you boys can go south. I stay here.
Fix up a shack—get a part-time job—
>   (he disappeared later
>   maybe found in the river)
In Ferndale & Bellingham
Went out on trailcrews
Glacier and Marblemount
There we part.

>   tiny men with moustaches
>   driving ox-teams
>   deep in the cedar groves.
>   wet brush, tin pants, snoose
Split-shake roof barns
>   over berryfields
>   white birch chickencoop

Put up in Dick Meigs cabin
            out behind the house—
Coffeecan, PA tin, rags, dirty cups,
Kindling fell behind the stove
                        miceshit
            old magazines,

                    winter's coming in the mountains
                    shut down the show
                    the punks go back to school
                    & the rest hit the road

        strawberries picked, shakeblanks split
        fires all out and the packstrings brought
        down to the valleys
                    set to graze

Gray wharves and hacksaw gothic homes
Shingle mills and stump farms
                    overgrown.

II

Fifty drunk Indians   *Mt. Vernon*
Sleep in the bus station
Strawberry pickers speaking Kwakiutl
            turn at Burlington for Skagit
                        & Ross Dam

        under appletrees by the river
        banks of junkd cars

            B. C. drivers give hitch-hikers rides

    "The sheriff's posse stood in double rows   *Everett*
            flogged the naked Wobblies down
            with stalks of Devil's Club
            & run them out of town"
While shingle-weavers lost their fingers

in the tricky feed and take
of double saws.

Dried, shrimp   *Seattle*
        smoked,   salmon
    —before the war old indian came
& sold us hard-smoked Chinook
From his truck-bed model T
                Lake City,

        waste of trees & topsoil, beast, herb,
        edible roots, Indian field-farms & white men
        dances   washed, leached, burnt out
        Minds blunt, ug! talk twisted

        A night of the long poem
        and the mined guitar . . .
        "Forming the new society
        within the shell of the old"
            mess of tincan camps and littered roads

The Highway passes straight through
                every town
At Matsons washing blujeans
            hills and saltwater
                ack, the woodsmoke in my brain

High Olympics—can't go there again

        East Marginal Way the hitch-hike zone
        Boeing down across Duwamish slough
& angle out
        & on.

Night rain wet concrete headlights
                blind   *Tacoma*

    Salt air/   Bulk cargo/   Steam cycle

            AIR REDUCTION

eating peanuts I don't give a damn
if anybody ever stops   I'll walk
to San Francisco   what the hell

          "that's where you're going?
          "why you got that pack?

Well man I just don't feel right
Without something on my back

          & this character in milkman overalls
          "I have to come out here
          every onct in a while, there's a guy
          blows me here"

                    way out of town.

Stayed in Olympia with Dick Meigs
     —this was a different year & he had moved—
     sleep on a cot in the back yard
     half the night watch falling stars

These guys got babies now
                    drink beer, come back from wars
          "I'd like to save up all my money
          get a big new car, go down to Reno
          & latch onto one of those rich girls—
          I'd fix their little ass"—nineteen yr old
          N. Dakota boy fixing to get married next month
To Centralia in a purple ford.

               carstruck dead doe
               by the Skookumchuck river

Fat man in a Chevrolet
                    wants to go back to L.A.
               "too damnd poor now"
Airbrakes on the log trucks hiss and whine
Stand in the dark by the stoplight.
               big fat cars tool by

Drink coffee, drink more coffee
                    brush teeth back of Shell
        hot shoes
                    stay on the rightside of that
                            yellow line

Marys Corner, turn for Mt. Rainier
        —once caught a ride at night for Portland here
Five Mexicans, ask me "chip in on the gas"
            I never was more broke & down.
            got fired that day by the USA
            (the District Ranger up at Packwood
            thought the wobblies had been dead for
                                    forty years
            but the FBI smelled treason
                            —my red beard)
That Waco Texas boy
            took A. G. & me through miles of snow
            had a chest of logger gear
            at the home of an Indian girl
            in Kelso, hadn't seen since Fifty-four

Toledo, Castle Rock, free way
                four lane
            no stoplights & no crossings, only cars
                & people walking, old hitch-hikers
            break the law. How do I know.
                            the state cop
                            told me so.

Come a dozen times into
                    Portland
        on the bum or
                    hasty lover
            late   at   night

III

Portland

dust kicking up behind the trucks—night rides—
who waits in the coffee shop

night highway 99

Sokei-an met an old man on the banks of the
Columbia river growing potatoes & living all alone,
Sokei-an asked him the reason why he lived there,
he said

Boy, no one ever asked me the reason why.
I like to be alone.
I am an old man.
I have forgotten how to speak human words.

All night freezing
in the back of a truck
dawn at Smith river
battering on in loggers pickups
prunes for lunch
The next right, Siuslaw.

Portland sawdust   down town
Buttermilk corner,   all you want for a nickel
(now a dime)
—Sujata gave Gautama
buttermilk,
(No doubt! says Sokei-an, that's all it was
plain buttermilk)
rim of mountains. pulp bark chewd snag
papermill
tugboom in the river
—used to lean on bridgerails
dreaming up eruptions and quakes—

Slept under Juniper in the Siskiyou   (Yreka)
a sleeping bag, a foot of snow
black rolled umbrella
ice slick asphalt

Caught a ride the only car come by
  at seven in the morning
  chewing froze salami

Riding with a passed-out LA whore
  glove compartment full of booze,
  the driver a rider, nobody cowboy,
  sometime hood,
Like me picked up to drive,
  & drive the blues away.
      we drank to Portland
        & we treated that girl good.

I split my last two bucks with him in town
  went out to Carol & Billy's in the woods.

  —foggy morning in Newport
   housetrailers
    under the fir.

An old book on Japan at the Goodwill
  unfurld umbrella in the sailing snow
   sat back in black wood
      barber college
    chair, a shave
On Second Street in Portland
    what elegance. What a life.

    bust my belly with a quart of
        buttermilk
   & five dry heels of French bread
   from the market cheap
      clean shaved, dry feet.

We're on our way
    man
     out of town
Go hitching down that
    highway ninety-nine.

IV

Oil-pump broken, motor burning out   *Salem*

Ex-logger selling skidder cable
  wants to get to San Francisco,
  fed and drunk   *Eugene*

Guy just back from Alaska—don't like
  the States, there's too much law   *Sutherlin*

A woman with a kid & two bales of hay.   *Roseburg*

Sawmill worker, young guy thinking of
  going to Eureka for redwood logging
  later in the year   *Dillard*

Two Assembly of God Pentecostal boys in
  a Holy Roller High School. One had
     spoken in
       tongues.   *Canyonville*

LASME   Los-Angeles—Seattle Motor Express

     place on highway 20:   LITTLE ELK
                               badger & badger

South of Yoncalla burn the engine
         run out of oil

Yaquina fishdocks
         candlefish & perch
         slant-faced woman fishing
       tuna stacked like cordwood
       the once-glimpsed-into door
             company freezer shed
        a sick old seagull settles
        down to die.
        the ordinary, casual, ruffle of the

tail & wings.
(Six great highways; so far only one)

freshwater creeks on the beach sand
at Kalaloch I caught a bag of water
at Agate Beach
made a diversion with my toe

Jumpoff Joe Creek &
a man carrying nothing, walking sort of
stiff-legged along, blue jeans & denim jacket,
wrinkled face, just north of
Louse Creek

—Abandon really means it
—the network womb stretched loose all
things slip
through

Dreaming on a bench under newspapers
I woke covered over with Rhododendron blooms
Alone in a State Park in Oregon.

V

"I had a girl in Oakland who worked
for a doctor, she was a nurse, she let him
eat her. She died of tuberculosis   *Grants*
& I drove back that night   *Pass*
to Portland
non stop, crying all the way."

"I picked up a young mother with two
children once, their house had just
burned down"
"I picked up an Italian tree-surgeon
in Port Angeles once, he had all his
saws and tools all screwed & bolted on
a beat up bike"

Oxyoke, Wolf Creek,

A guy coming off a five-day binge, to   *Phoenix*

An ex-bartender from Lebanon, to   *Redding*

Man & wife on a drinking spree, to   *Anderson*

Snow on the pines & firs around Lake Shasta
        —Chinese scene of winter hills & trees
        us "little travellers" in the bitter cold

            six-lane highway slash & DC twelves
           bridge building   squat earth-movers
   —yellow bugs

             I speak for hawks.
The road that's followed goes forever;
In half a minute crossed and left behind.

Out of the snow and into red-dirt plains

           blossoming plums

Each time you go that road it gets more straight
   curves across the mountains lost in fill
     towns you had to slow down all four lane
        Azalea, Myrtle Creek
        WATCH OUT FOR DEER

At Project City Indian hitcher
Standing under single tarpole lamp
      nobody stopped
           Ginsberg & I walked
           four miles & camped by an oak fire
           left by the road crew

Going to San Francisco
Yeah San Francisco
Yeah we came from Seattle

Even farther north
Yeah we been working in the mountains
     in the Spring
     in the Autumn
              always go this highway ninety-nine—

     "I was working in a mill three weeks there
     then it burned down & the guy didn't even
     pay us off—but I can do anything—
     I'll go to San Francisco—tend bar"

Standing in the night.
In the world-end winds
By the overpass bridge

       Junction US 40 and Highway Ninety-nine

Trucks, trucks   roll by
Kicking up dust—dead flowers—

Sixteen speeds forward
Windows open
Stoppd at the edge of Willows for a bite

          grass shoots on the edge of
          drained rice plains

              —cheap olives—

Where are the Sierras.

    level, dry,
Highway turns west

       miles gone, speed
               still
       pass through lower hills
        heat dying
        toward Vallejo
gray on the salt baywater

    brown grass ridges
        blue mesquite

One leggd Heron in the tideflats

        State of Cars.

Sailor getting back to ship
      —I'm sick of car exhaust

     City
  gleaming far away

we make it into town tonight
get clean & drink some wine—

    SAN FRANCISCO
      NO
     body
   gives a shit
       man
     who you are or
      whats your car
    there IS no
            ninety-nine

TŌJI

Shington temple,
Kyoto

Men asleep in their underwear
Newspapers under their heads
Under the eaves of Tōji,
Kobo Daishi solid iron and ten feet tall
Strides through, a pigeon on his hat.

Peering through chickenwire grates
At dusty gold-leaf statues

A cynical curving round-belly
Cool Bodhisattva—maybe Avalokita—
Bisexual and tried it all, weight on
One leg, haloed in snake-hood gold
Shines through the shadow
An ancient hip smile
Tingling of India and Tibet.

Loose-breasted young mother
With her kids in the shade here
Of old Temple tree,
Nobody bothers you in Tōji;
The streetcar clanks by outside.

HIGASHI HONGWANJI

Shinshu temple

In a quiet dusty corner
       on the north porch
Some farmers eating lunch on the steps,
Up high behind a beam: a small
       carved wood panel
Of leaves, twisting tree trunk,
Ivy, and a sleek fine-haired Doe.
       a six-point Buck in front
Head crooked back, watching her.
The great tile roof sweeps up
& floats a grey shale
Mountain over the town.

NOTE ON THE RELIGIOUS TENDENCIES

This religiosity is primarily one of practice and personal experience, rather than theory. The statement commonly heard in some circles, "All religions lead to the same goal," is the result of fantastically sloppy thinking and no practice. It is good to remember that all religions are nine-tenths fraud and are responsible for numerous social evils.

Within the Beat Generation you find three things going on:

1. Vision and illumination-seeking. This is most easily done by systematic experimentation with narcotics. Marijuana is a daily standby and peyote is the real eye-opener. These are sometimes supplemented by dips into yoga technique, alcohol, and Subud. Although a good deal of personal insight can be obtained by the intelligent use of drugs, being high all the time leads nowhere because it lacks intellect, will, and compassion; and a personal drug kick is of no use to anyone else in the world.

2. Love, respect for life, abandon, Whitman, pacifism, anarchism, etc. This comes out of various traditions including Quakers, Shinshu Buddhism, Sufism. And from a loving and open heart. At its best this state of mind has led people to actively resist war, start communities, and try to love one another. It is also partly responsible for the mystique of "angels," the glorification of skidroad and hitch-hiking, and a kind of mindless enthusiasm. If it respects life, it fails to respect heartless wisdom and death; and this is a shortcoming.

3. Discipline, aesthetics, and tradition. This was going on well before the Beat Generation got into print. It differs from the "All is one" stance in that its practitioners settle on one traditional religion, try to absorb the feel of its art and history, and carry out whatever ascesis is required. One should become an Aimu bear-dancer or a Yurok shaman as well as a Trappist monk, if he put himself to it. What this bit often lacks is what 2 and 3 have, i.e. real commitment to the stewpot of the world and real insight into the vision-lands of the unconscious.

The unstartling conclusion is that if a person cannot comprehend all three of these aspects—contemplation (and not by use of drugs), morality (which usually means social protest to me), and wisdom—in his beat life, he just won't make it. But even so he may get pretty far out, and that's probably better than moping around classrooms or writing books on Buddhism and Happiness for the masses, as the squares (who will shortly have succeeded in putting us all down) do.

Philip Whalen

Philip Whalen, an ordained Zen priest since 1973, was born on October 20, 1923, in Portland, Oregon. He began reading Gertrude Stein and experimenting with imagistic poetry while serving in the United States Army Air Corps during World War II. Afterward at Reed College he roomed with Gary Snyder and Lew Welch. Whalen had no plans to be a poet when he accepted Snyder's invitation to read his work at the Six Gallery in October 1955, but meeting Kerouac and Ginsberg reaffirmed his idea "that it was great being a writer." As Whalen said, they were "the first people I thought of as being really literary, not literary literary, but then they were doing the same kind of thing I was, living and writing and picking it up out of the air, out of books, out of other people."

Whalen broke free from his obsession with imagist poetry and the formal academic poetry of T. S. Eliot and Wallace Stevens after taking peyote in 1955: "all my dopey theories and hangups and things about writing . . . suddenly disappeared." Ginsberg's "Howl" manuscript also made him understand it was "possible for a poem to be its own shape and size."

"Sourdough Mountain Lookout" was based on Whalen's seasons in a fire lookout tower in the mountains of Washington state. "A Dim View of Berkeley in the Spring" was published in the East Bay magazine Ark III *in 1957. In "Prose Take-Out Portland," Whalen tried to capture a "graph of the mind's movement" on September 13, 1958, including his memory of drinking with Kerouac, referred to affectionately by his French-Canadian name, Jean-Louis Kerouac.*

SOURDOUGH MOUNTAIN
LOOKOUT

Tsung Ping (375–443): "Now I am old and infirm.
I fear I shall no more be able to roam among
the beautiful mountains. Clarifying my mind, I
meditate on the mountain trails and wander
about only in dreams."
—in *The Spirit of the Brush*,
tr. by Shio Sakanishi, p. 34.

FOR KENNETH REXROTH

I always say I won't go back to the mountains
I am too old and fat there are bugs mean mules
And pancakes every morning of the world

Mr. Edward Wyman (63)
Steams along the trail ahead of us all
Moaning, "My poor old feet ache, my back
Is tired and I've got a stiff prick"
Uprooting alder shoots in the rain

Then I'm alone in a glass house on a ridge
Encircled by chiming mountains
With one sun roaring through the house all day
& the others crashing through the glass all night
Conscious even while sleeping

Morning fog in the southern gorge
Gleaming foam restoring the old sea-level
The lakes in two lights green soap and indigo
The high cirque-lake black half-open eye

Ptarmigan hunt for bugs in the snow
Bear peers through the wall at noon
Deer crowd up to see the lamp
A mouse nearly drowns in the honey
I see my bootprints mingle with deer-foot
Bear-paw mule-shoe in the dusty path to the privy

Much later I write down:
    "raging. Viking sunrise
    The gorgeous death of summer in the east"
(Influence of a Byronic landscape—
Bent pages exhibiting depravity of style.)

Outside the lookout I lay nude on the granite
Mountain hot September sun but inside my head
Calm dark night with all the other stars
HERACLITUS: "The Waking have one common world
But the sleeping turn aside
Each into a world of his own."

I keep telling myself what I really like
Are music, books, certain land and sea-scapes
The way light falls across them, diffusion of
Light through agate, light itself . . . I suppose
I'm still afraid of the dark

      "Remember smart-guy there's something
      Bigger something smarter than you."
      Ireland's fear of unknown holies drives
      My father's voice (a country neither he
      Nor his great-grandfather ever saw)

      A sparkly tomb a plated grave
      A holy thumb beneath a wave

Everything else they hauled across Atlantic
Scattered and lost in the buffalo plains
Among these trees and mountains

From Duns Scotus to this page
A thousand years

      (" . . . a dog walking on his hind legs—
      not that he does it well but that he
      does it at all.")

Virtually a blank except for the hypothesis
That there is more to a man
Than the contents of his jock-strap

EMPEDOCLES: "At one time all the limbs
Which are the body's portion are brought together
By Love in blooming life's high season; at another
Severed by cruel Strife, they wander each alone
By the breakers of life's sea."

Fire and pressure from the sun bear down
Bear down centipede shadow of palm-frond
A limestone lithograph—oysters and clams of stone
Half a black rock bomb displaying brilliant crystals
Fire and pressure Love and Strife bear down
Brontosaurus, look away

My sweat runs down the rock

HERACLITUS: "The transformations of fire
are, first of all, sea; and half of the sea
is earth, half whirlwind. . . .
It scatters and it gathers; it advances
and retires."

I move out of a sweaty pool
          (The sea!)
And sit up higher on the rock

Is anything burning?

The sun itself! Dying
Pooping out, exhausted
Having produced brontosaurus, Heraclitus
This rock, me,
To no purpose
I tell you anyway (as a kind of loving) . . .
Flies & other insects come from miles around
To listen

I also address the rock, the heather,
The alpine fir

BUDDHA: "All the constituents of being are
Transitory: Work out your salvation with diligence."

(And everything, as one eminent disciple of that master
Pointed out, has been tediously complex ever since.)

There was a bird
Lived in an egg
And by ingenious chemistry
Wrought molecules of albumen
To beak and eye
Gizzard and craw
Feather and claw

My grandmother said:
"Look at them poor bed-
raggled pigeons!"

And the sign in McAlister Street:

IF YOU CAN'T COME IN
SMILE AS YOU GO BY
L♡VE
THE BUTCHER

I destroy myself, the universe (an egg)
And time—to get an answer:
There are a smiler, a sleeper, and a dancer
We repeat our conversation in the glittering dark
Floating beside the sleeper.
The child remarks, "You knew it all the time."
I: "I keep forgetting that the smiler is
Sleeping; the sleeper, dancing."

From Sauk Lookout two years before
Some of the view was down the Skagit

To Puget Sound: From above the lower ranges,
Deep in forest—lighthouses on clear nights.

This year's rock is a spur from the main range
Cuts the valley in two and is broken
By the river; Ross Dam repairs the break,
Makes trolley buses run
Through the streets of dim Seattle far away.

I'm surrounded by mountains here
A circle of 108 beads, originally seeds
    of *ficus religiosa*
        Bo-Tree
A circle, continuous, one odd bead
Larger than the rest and bearing
A tassel (hair-tuft) (the man who sat
        under the tree)
In the center of the circle,
A void, an empty figure containing
All that's multiplied;
Each bead a repetition, a world
Of ignorance and sleep.

Today is the day the goose gets cooked
Day of liberation for the crumbling flower
Knobcone pinecone in the flames
Brandy in the sun

Which, as I said, will disappear
Anyway it'll be invisible soon
Exchanging places with stars now in my head
To be growing rice in China through the night.
Magnetic storms across the solar plains
Make Aurora Borealis shimmy bright
Beyond the mountains to the north.

Closing the lookout in the morning
Thick ice on the shutters
Coyote almost whistling on a nearby ridge
The mountain is THERE (between two lakes)

I brought back a piece of its rock
Heavy dark-honey color
With a seam of crystal, some of the quartz
Stained by its matrix
Practically indestructible
A shift from opacity to brilliance
(The Zenbos say, "Lightning-flash & flint-spark")
Like the mountains where it was made
What we see of the world is the mind's
Invention and the mind
Though stained by it, becoming
Rivers, sun, mule-dung, flies—
Can shift instantly
A dirty bird in a square time

Gone
Gone
REALLY gone
Into the cool
O MAMA!

Like they say, "Four times up,
Three times down." I'm still on the mountain.

> *Sourdough Mountain 15:viii:55*
> *Berkeley 27–28:viii:56*

NOTE: The quotes of Empedocles and Heraclitus are from John
Burnet's *Early Greek Philosophy,* Meridian Books, New York.

A DIM VIEW OF BERKELEY IN
THE SPRING

A graduated row of children, the biggest
Old enough to feel the boredom
Leading the rest, tearing up flowers in the driveway

The boredom, the tension

Fraternity men crowded into the wire cage—
A volley-ball court—jumping, hollering, laughing

           (only one is headed down the hill with his books to the
                     campus, smoothing his crewed-down hair)
Too loud.
TENSION: The flying ball an indeterminate
Future, the Army? The Navy? Marriage before
Or later?

Leap, shout, a pattern of release that actually comes
Much later in some parked car
Trying to make out with some chick who
WON'T, she wants a home of her own to do it in
     (Who can blame her?)
Then going back to the house with a stone-ache
Or gooey underwear, the tension
Relieved so they can sleep or built high enough
To be dreamed off or jacked away in the shower at 3 A.M.

Where's the action? What's going on?

The Suez is not at home to anyone.
Mr. Dullness says, 'War is no longer profitable.'
Daddy Warbucks in the White House says
'Everything is going to be just dandy.'

What are we going to do?

In Hungary they had a good idea
They all got together to kill the government
But the government mowed them down . . . who cares
About revolutions, the old corpses in the street routine?
Who cares?

Several hundred of us crowded in to watch a student
Gassed to death at Q
Later, a lot of other students went to peek at the body
Preserved in the basement of the University
     THE MURDERER ON ICE
So we all saved the trouble and expense of a trip
To Central Europe

Charley Olson told me, ' "Intolerable" is all right, a very
Dramatic word, but that isn't it at all.'
What I mean is, nobody

Can stand it, the tension, the boredom, whatever . . .
Mama and Papa scream at each other about the new deep-freeze,

    (' . . . and sometimes I just turn the TV off & go do
                         something else, I get so tired of it.'—that
Was the egg-lady speaking) and
The children continue destroying the flowers,
Being too young to go to the show at night alone.

PROSE TAKE-OUT, PORTLAND
13:ix:58

I shall know better next time than to drink with any but cer-
tified drunks (or drinker) that is to say like J-L. K. who don't
fade away with the first false showing of dawn through the
Doug-fir & hemlock now here Cornell Road First of Autumn
Festival
    a mosquito-hawk awakened by my borrowed kitchen light
    scrabbles at the cupboard door
& the rain (this is Portland) all over the outdoor scene—let
it—I'm all in favor of whatever the nowhere grey overhead
sends—which used (so much, so thoroughly) to bug me
               Let it (Shakespeare) come down
                    (& thanks to Paul Bowles for
reminding me)
there it rains & here—long after rain has stopped—continues
from the sodden branch needles—to rain, equated, identified
with nowhere self indulgence drip off the eaves onto stone
drizzle mist among fern puddles—so in a manner of speaking
(Henry James tells us)   "There we are."
the booze (except for a hidden inch or so of rosé in the kitchen
jug) gone & the cigarets few—I mean where IS everybody &
they are (indisputably) very sensibly abed & asleep—
               one car slops by fast on overhead Cornell
Road the fireplace pops I wouldn't have anything else just now
except the rest of the wine & what am I trying to prove & of
course nothing but the sounds of water & fire & refusing to
surrender to unconsciousness as if that were the END of
everything—Goodbye, goodbye, at last I'm tired of this &

leave you wondering why anybody has bothered to say "The sun is rising" when there's a solar emphemeris newly printed, it makes no difference—but you will be less than nowhere without this pleasurable & instructive guide.

13:ix:58

Philip Lamantia

Philip Lamantia was born in San Francisco on October 23, 1927, the son of Sicilian immigrants. He began writing poetry in elementary school and was briefly expelled from junior high for "intellectual delinquency" when he immersed himself in the work of Edgar Allan Poe and H. P. Lovecraft. At age sixteen, after being introduced to surrealism by the Miró and Dalí retrospectives at the San Francisco Museum of Art, he began to write surrealist poetry, realizing that "the purely revolutionary nature" of surrealism, "even before my knowledge of Surrealist theory, was part of my own individual temperament." Shortly afterward Lamantia left home to join the Surrealists in New York City and was welcomed by André Breton as "a voice that rises once in a hundred years."

Lamantia's poems were published in 1943 by André Breton as VVV. *His first book,* Erotic Poems, *was published in Berkeley in 1946. His second book,* Ekstasis, *appeared after the Six Poets at the Six Gallery reading, and City Lights published his* Selected Poems 1943–1966. *"High," "The night is a space of white marble," "I have given fair warning" and "There is this distance between me and what I see" are from that volume. "Fud at Foster's" describes Foster's Cafeteria, a popular hangout for San Francisco poets and artists, the place where Ginsberg met Robert LaVigne, who took him home and introduced him to Peter Orlovsky.*

Like the work of many of his Beat colleagues, Lamantia's poetry demonstrates the tension between what his biographer calls "the exaltation of reality and an omnipresent sense of the pain and terror inherent in life." Lamantia is the only American poet of his generation to embrace fully the discoveries of surrealism, and is a contributing editor of Arsenal: Surrealist Subversion.

HIGH

O beato solitudo! where have I flown to?
stars overturn the wall of my music
as flight of birds, they go by, the spirits
opened below the lark of plenty
ovens of neant overflow the docks at Veracruz
This much is time
summer coils the soft suck of night
lone unseen eagles crash thru mud
I am worn like an old sack by the celestial bum
I'm dropping my eyes where all the trees turn on fire!
I'm mad to go to you, Solitude—who will carry me there?
I'm wedged in this collision of planets/Tough!
I'm ONGED!
I'm the trumpet of King David
the sinister elevator tore itself limb by limb

You can not close
you can not open
you break yr head
you make bloody bread!

The night is a space of white marble

The night is a space of white marble
This is Mexico
I'm sitting here, slanted light fixture, pot, altitudinous silence
your voice, Dionysius, telling of darkness, superessential light
In the silence of holy darkness I'm eating a tomato
I'm weak from the altitude
something made my clogged head move!
Rutman a week at beach at Acapulco

Carol Francesca waiting till Christmas heroin rain on them!
I see New York upside down
your head, Charlie Chaplin—in a sling
it's all in the courts of war

                              sign here—the slip of dung
technically we are all dead
this is my own thought! a hail of hell!
Saint Dionysius reminds us of flight to unknowable Knowledge
the doctrine of initiates completes the meditation!

I have given fair warning

I have given fair warning
Chicago New York Los Angeles have gone down
I have gone to Swan City where the ghost of Maldoror may still
    roam
The south is very civilized
I have eaten rhinoceros tail
It is the last night among crocodiles
Albion opens his fist in a palm grove
I shall watch speckled jewel grow on the back of warspilt horses
Exultation rides by
A poppy size of the sun in my skull
I have given fair warning
at the time of corpses and clouds I can make love here as
    anywhere

There is this distance between me and what i see

There is this distance between me and what I see
everywhere immanence of the presence of God
no more ekstasis
a cool head
watch watch watch
I'm here
He's over there . . . It's an Ocean . . .
sometimes I can't think of it, I fail, fall

This IS this look of love
there IS the tower of David
there IS the throne of Wisdom
there IS this silent look of love
Constant flight in air of the Holy Ghost
I long for the luminous darkness of God
I long for the superessential light of this darkness
another darkness I long for the end of longing
I long for the

        it is Nameless what I long for
a spoken word caught in its own meat saying nothing
This nothing ravishes beyond ravishing
There IS this look of love Throne Silent look of love

Fud at Foster's

Bowl of cold turkie fool
A roast chicken liver louie
My cigarillo's going out in a spanish bedroom
Jazz is for free
Coke is for free
Junk's unlimited and sold by Agents
      that I can make poems that I spin the day to
      Tim Buck Two that I lose tension and head
      floats forever a far inscape of lemon trees AND
NO MORE REALITY SANDWICHES!!!

Can I ever get up from this table?
Can I ever stop thunder?
Can I make it to windows of fur?
Can I soup up her eyes in a can of star milk and shoot it for
                              light?

Can I read in the park?
Can I sit on the Moon? Can I?
Oh, stop it! Oh start! Oh, make music
Though your arm is too thin
  and the jails are too small, sweaty AND STINK!

Lew Welch

Lew Welch was born in Phoenix, Arizona, on August 16, 1926, and disappeared with his 30-30 rifle into the mountains near Gary Snyder's house north of Nevada City, California, in May 1971. A roommate of Whalen and Snyder at Reed College, he completed a senior thesis on the writing of Gertrude Stein that was praised by the poet William Carlos Williams, whom Welch later visited in New Jersey. He dropped out of the graduate program of the University of Chicago after a nervous breakdown, which he referred to obliquely in "Chicago Poem."

Welch then moved to San Francisco, where he drove a cab in 1959, using the experience as the background for a group of poems titled "Taxi Suite." Soon afterward Welch met Kerouac in San Francisco and offered to drive him and his friend Albert Saijo back to New York, writing poetry together on the journey later published as Trip Trap *(1973).*

In 1960, when Kerouac returned to California, Welch lived with him in Ferlinghetti's cabin at Big Sur. Kerouac described the experience in his novel Big Sur, *calling Welch Dave Wain. Later, alone in the cabin after what he called a "wine drunk," Welch wrote the poem "I Saw Myself," a haunting vision of himself on the verge of another breakdown. As the writer Aram Saroyan understood, Welch's "continuing dilemma was how to remain a poet and at the same time support himself. . . . The farther afield he went in terms of the society of his time, the more remarkable and authentic was the poetry that came out of his life."*

"The Basic Con," "Not Yet 40, My Beard Is Already White,"

and "The Image, as in a Hexagram" are poems from Ring of Bone: Collected Poems 1950–1971, *edited by Donald M. Allen.*

CHICAGO POEM

I lived here nearly 5 years before I could
    meet the middle western day with anything approaching
Dignity. It's a place that lets you
    understand why the Bible is the way it is:
Proud people cannot live here.

The land's too flat. Ugly sullen and big it
    pounds men down past humbleness. They
Stoop at 35 possibly cringing from the heavy and
    terrible sky. In country like this there
Can be no God but Jahweh.

In the mills and refineries of its south side Chicago
    passes its natural gas in flames
Bouncing like bunsens from stacks a hundred feet high.
    The stench stabs at your eyeballs.
The whole sky green and yellow backdrop for the skeleton
    steel of a bombed-out town.

Remember the movies in grammar school? The goggled men
    doing strong things in
Showers of steel-spark? The dark screen cracking light
    and the furnace door opening with a
Blast of orange like a sunset? Or an orange?

It was photographed by a fairy, thrilled as a girl, or
    a Nazi who wished there were people
Behind that door (hence the remote beauty), but Sievers,
    whose old man spent most of his life in there,
Remembers a "nigger in a red T-shirt pissing into the
    black sand."

It was 5 years until I could afford to recognize the ferocity.
    Friends helped me. Then I put some

Love into my house. Finally I found some quiet lakes
   and a farm where they let me shoot pheasant.

Standing in the boat one night I watched the lake go absolutely
   flat. Smaller than raindrops, and only
Here and there, the feeding rings of fish were visible 100 yards
   away—and the Blue Gill caught that afternoon
Lifted from its northern lake like a tropical! Jewel at its ear
   Belly gold so bright you'd swear he had a
Light in there. His color faded with his life. A small
   green fish . . .

All things considered, it's a gentle and undemanding
   planet, even here. Far gentler
Here than any of a dozen other places. The trouble is
   always and only with what we build on top of it.

There's nobody else to blame. You can't fix it and you
   can't make it go away. It does no good appealing
To some ill-invented Thunderer
   Brooding above some unimaginable crag . . .

It's ours. Right down to the last small hinge it
   all depends for its existence
Only and utterly upon our sufferance.

Driving back I saw Chicago rising in its gases and I
   knew again that never will the
Man be made to stand against this pitiless, unparallel
   monstrocity. It
Snuffles on the beach of its Great Lake like a
   blind, red, rhinoceros.
It's already running us down.

You can't fix it. You can't make it go away.
   I don't know what you're going to do about it,
But I know what I'm going to do about it. I'm just
   going to walk away from it. Maybe
A small part of it will die if I'm not around

   feeding it anymore.

THE BASIC CON

Those who can't find anything to live for,
always invent something to die for.

Then they want the rest of us to
die for it, too.

from TAXI SUITE

1. AFTER ANACREON

When I drive cab
    I am moved by strange whistles and wear a hat.

When I drive cab
    I am the hunter. My prey leaps out from where it
    hid, beguiling me with gestures.

When I drive cab
    all may command me, yet I am in command of all who do.

When I drive cab
    I am guided by voices descending from the naked air.

When I drive cab
    A revelation of movement comes to me. They wake now.
    Now they want to work or look around. Now they want
    drunkenness and heavy food. Now they contrive to love.

When I drive cab
    I bring the sailor home from the sea. In the back of
    my car he fingers the pelt of his maiden.

When I drive cab
    I watch for stragglers in the urban order of things.

When I drive cab
    I end the only lit and waitful thing in miles of
    darkened houses.

NOT YET 40, MY BEARD IS ALREADY WHITE

Not yet 40, my beard is already white.
Not yet awake, my eyes are puffy and red,
               like a child who has cried too much.

What is more disagreeable
than last night's wine?

I'll shave.
I'll stick my head in the cold spring and
look around at the pebbles.
Maybe I can eat a can of peaches.

Then I can finish the rest of the wine,
write poems till I'm drunk again,
and when the afternoon breeze comes up

I'll sleep until I see the moon
and the dark trees
and the nibbling deer

and hear
the quarreling coons

THE IMAGE, AS IN A HEXAGRAM

The image, as in a Hexagram:

The hermit locks his door against the blizzard.
He keeps the cabin warm.

All winter long he sorts out all he has.
What was well started shall be finished.
What was not, should be thrown away.

In spring he emerges with one garment
and a single book.

The cabin is very clean.

Except for that, you'd never guess
anyone lived there.

I SAW MYSELF

I saw myself
a ring of bone
in the clear stream
of all of it

and vowed,
always to be open to it
that all of it
might flow through

and then heard
"ring of bone" where
ring is what a

bell does

Bob Kaufman

Bob Kaufman was born on April 18, 1925, in New Orleans, Louisiana, and died in San Francisco on January 12, 1986. The third youngest of thirteen children born to a German Orthodox Jew and a Catholic woman from Martinique, Kaufman's religious education was, as his biographer A. D. Winans asserts, a "spiritual mosaic." At the age of thirteen he joined the United States Merchant Marines and served for twenty years before settling in San Francisco and living as a poet.

In the late 1950s and early 1960s Kaufman so often fended off police while insisting on free speech at his poetry readings at the Co-Existence Bagel Shop and other coffee houses in North Beach that he became a symbol to the bohemian community of the poet's resistance to all forms of authority. He took a vow of silence in 1963 after the John F. Kennedy assassination that lasted for twelve years, and he withdrew into solitude in 1978 for four years.

Kaufman's early poetry was in the form of "vituperative visionary broadsides" published by City Lights in 1959, the year he and his wife Eileen joined Allen Ginsberg and others to found the long-lived San Francisco avant garde literary magazine Beatitude, *named in honor of Kerouac's religious derivation of the term "beat." New Directions published Kaufman's first book of early poetry in 1965. Two years later City Lights published* Golden Sardine, *from which collection "On" and "O-Jazz-O" are taken. Poems like "Round About Midnight," titled after a Thelonious Monk song, and "Jazz Chick," were intended to be freely improvisational when read with jazz accompaniment.*

ROUND ABOUT MIDNIGHT

Jazz radio on a midnight kick,
Round about Midnight.

Sitting on the bed,
With a jazz type chick
Round about Midnight,

Piano laughter, in my ears,
Round about Midnight.

Stirring laughter, dying tears,
Round about Midnight.

Soft blue voices, muted grins,
Exciting voices, Father's sins,
Round about Midnight.

Come on baby, take off your clothes,
Round about Midnight.

JAZZ CHICK

Music from her breast vibrating
Soundseared into burnished velvet.
Silent hips deceiving fools.
Rivulets of trickling ecstasy
From the alabaster pools of Jazz
Where music cools hot souls.
Eyes more articulately silent
Than Medusa's thousand tongues.
A bridge of eyes, consenting smiles
Reveal her presence singing
Of cool remembrance, happy balls
Wrapped in swinging
Jazz
Her music . . .
Jazz.

ON

On yardbird corners of embryonic hopes, drowned in a heroin tear.
On yardbird corners of parkerflights to sound filled pockets in space.
On neuro-corners of stripped brains & desperate electro-surgeons.
On alcohol corners of pointless discussions & historical hangovers.
On television corners of literary corn flakes & rockwells impotent
     America.
On university corners of tailored intellect & greek letter openers.
On military corners of megathon deaths & universal anesthesia.
On religious corners of theological limericks and
On radio corners of century-long records & static events.
On advertising corners of filter-tipped ice-cream & instant instants.
On teen-age corners of comic book seduction & corrupted guitars.
On political corners of wanted candidates & ritual lies.
On motion picture corners of lassie & other symbols.
On intellectual corners of conversational therapy & analyzed fear.
On newspaper corners of sexy headlines & scholarly comics.
On love divided corners of die now pay later mortuaries.
On philosophical corners of semantic desperadoes & idea-mongers.
On middle class corners of private school puberty & anatomical revolts.
On ultra-real corners of love on abandoned roller-coasters.
On lonely poet corners of low lying leaves & moist prophet eyes.

O-JAZZ-O

Where the string
At
Some point,
Was some umbilical jazz,
Or perhaps,
In memory,
A long lost bloody cross,
Buried in some steel calvary.
In what time
For whom do we bleed,
Lost notes, from some jazzman's
Broken needle.
Musical tears from lost

Eyes.
Broken drumsticks, why?
Pitter patter, boom dropping
Bombs in the middle
Of my emotions
My father's sound
My mother's sound,
Is love,
Is life.

PART FOUR

"A FEW BLUE WORDS TO THE WISE"

Other Fellow Travelers

After the publication of *Howl* and *On the Road,* many young writers aligned themselves with the Beats. Often the writers called themselves Beat or Beatnik in deliberate self-mockery, like Diane DiPrima in her half-serious, half-pornographic *Memoirs of a Beatnik* in 1969, humorously exploiting the media's sense that anything associated with beatniks would get the public's attention. The strongest young talents, like Bob Dylan, learned from Beat writing but kept their own identity. Others were affiliated with the Beats through poetry readings and publishing ventures and then moved on in their work to establish other identities as they contributed to later literary or political movements, like the African-American writer LeRoi Jones/Amiri Baraka. "Beat" was a slang word for bohemian in the late 1950s and 1960s, so that anyone publishing counterculture work at midcentury—Ed Sanders and Tuli Kupferberg, for example—could be lumped together into the Beat camp.

In the mid-1950s, the cultural ferment in America came of age in a great bohemian flowering. One evening in 1956, Diane DiPrima, an aspiring poet who had dropped out of Swarthmore College and was living in a rat-infested abandoned building near Columbus Circle in New York, was handed a book by a friend who had come to supper, saying, "You might be interested in this." She remembers that "I took it and flipped it open idly, still intent on dishing out beef stew, and found myself in the middle of *Howl* by Allen Ginsberg."

DiPrima had an acute sense that the book marked an important change in her life and the life of her friends. As she wrote in *Memoirs of a Beatnik,* up to *Howl*'s appearance, she had thought there were "only a small handful" of people like herself living a bohemian life in the city,

> who raced about in Levis and work shirts, smoked dope, dug the new jazz, and spoke a bastardization of the black argot. We surmised that there might be another fifty living in San Francisco, and perhaps a hundred more scattered throughout the country: Chicago, New Orleans, etc., but our isolation was total and impenetrable, and we did not try to communicate even with this small handful of our confreres. Our chief concern was to keep our integrity (much time and energy went into defining the concept of the "sellout") and to keep our cool: a hard, clean edge and definition in the midst of the terrifying indifference and sentimentality around us—"media mush." We looked to each other for comfort, for praise, for love, and shut out the rest of the world.

DiPrima characterized America as a "post–Korean war society" enjoying a time of economic prosperity in the early and mid-1950s while silently enduring the political suppression under President Eisenhower that led to the execution of the Rosenbergs as Communist spies and the rise of Senator Joseph McCarthy as the chairman of a Committee on Un-American Activities, staging "witch hunts" against alleged communists. This was the society that Ginsberg addressed in his poem "America" when he teased, "Are you going to let your emotional life be run by *Time* Magazine?"

DiPrima was honest enough to admit that she felt a sense of loss along with her excitement over the success of *Howl.* Ginsberg's book had drawn attention to the writers like herself who were rebelling against what they felt as the repressive conformity of American life. While she felt "we had come of age" with the book's publication, she understood that the old days of "easy, unself-conscious Bohemianism" were over, threatening the solidarity of her "unspoken sense that we were alone in a strange world, a sense that kept us proud and together."

To her surprise, DiPrima found that her sense of community was strengthened after the publication of *Howl*. She soon realized that "if there was one Allen, there must be more, other people writing. . . . For I sensed that Allen was only, could only be, the vanguard of a much larger thing. All the people who, like me, had hidden and skulked, writing down what they knew for a small handful of friends, waiting with only a slight bitterness for the thing to end, for man's era to draw to a close in a blaze of radiation—all these would now step forward and say their piece. Not many would hear them, but they would, finally, hear each other. I was about to meet my brothers and sisters."

In the late 1950s so many writers in the avant garde literary community flourished in America that they could be grouped loosely into several categories. In 1960, when the editor Donald Allen assembled *The New American Poetry* for Grove Press, he described the different literary groups as sharing one important characteristic: "a total rejection of all those qualities typical of academic verse. Following the practice and precepts of Ezra Pound and William Carlos Williams, [the new poetry] has built on their achievements and gone on to evolve new conceptions of the poem. The poets have already created their own tradition, their own press, and their public. They are our avant-garde, the true continuers of the modern movement in American poetry." Donald Allen also saw the new poets strengthened by being "closely allied to modern jazz and abstract expressionist painting, today recognized throughout the world to be America's greatest achievements in contemporary culture."

Accepting the poet Charles Olson's assertion that American literature was fundamentally geographical, Allen divided the writers into five loose groups, starting with the poets originally identified with Black Mountain College, the experimental arts college in North Carolina run by Charles Olson in the early 1950s, that included the poets Robert Creeley, Joel Oppenheimer, and Fielding Dawson, among others. The second group were the poets in the San Francisco Renaissance, some of whom—such as Lawrence Ferlinghetti, Philip Lamantia, and Lew Welch—were also associated with the Beats.

The Beat poets were the third group, writers who defied a simple geographical location. Allen described them as "originally associated with New York, but they first attracted national attention in San Francisco in 1956 when Allen Ginsberg, Jack Kerouac, and Gregory Corso joined Gary Snyder, Philip Whalen, and others in public readings." As LeRoi Jones understood, "the people tied to that name [Beats] by specific identification were every which place—in San Francisco, Paris, Tangier, Mexico, London, New Mexico, and points north, west, east, and central."

Allen's fourth group were New York poets Frank O'Hara, Kenneth Koch, and John Ashbery, who first met at Harvard but then migrated to New York. His fifth and final category was a mixed group of the younger poets Philip Whalen, Gary Snyder, Michael McClure, John Wieners, LeRoi Jones, and several others who Donald Allen described as having "evolved their own original styles and new conceptions of poetry."

Most of the writers accepted Donald Allen's five categories in the spirit in which he offered them, as arbitrary labels justified in his anthology because the groupings functioned as a "handle" that immediately suggested the poets' different backgrounds to new readers unfamiliar with their work. The writers didn't feel pigeonholed by the categories because they were confident of their own individuality and knew their various literary circles were interconnected. The original handful of Beat writers "aligned their work" with the poetry of the other groups by giving public readings and publishing together in little magazines.

One of the longest lived and most widely circulated of the little magazines was the *Floating Bear* newsletter, which Diane DiPrima and LeRoi Jones founded in New York City in 1961. It furnished an example of the interconnectedness of the various literary circles and the vigorous cross-fertilization between the writers. By publishing together, each "Beat" or "Black Mountain" or "New York School" or "San Francisco Renaissance" writer stepped outside the circle of a single category to sound an individual voice, yet each continued to be united with the others through a shared literary stance.

When Jones and DiPrima started *Floating Bear,* neither considered themselves Beat poets, yet they admired the work of Kerouac, Ginsberg, and Corso and felt themselves to be fellow travelers with them and the San Francisco Renaissance poets who were being published by small press publishers and magazines. DiPrima and Jones sympathized with the Beat writers' literary and social rebellion and attempted to further their ideals with *Floating Bear.*

Jones had experience editing several issues of another magazine that featured experimental writing, *Yugen,* which he published with his wife Hettie from 1958 to 1962. *Floating Bear* was printed in a cheaper format than *Yugen,* presented as a mimeographed newsletter instead of an offset printed magazine so that it could come out more frequently and promote a livelier contact between the experimental writers and their audience. It was designed to be a way to publish new work that was as spontaneous as the work itself.

The mimeograph machine was the ideal tool for their purposes. The editors George Montgomery and Erik Kiviat, who put out *Blue Beat* magazine in a mimeographed format after the success of *Floating Bear,* explained that "a mimeo can experiment with new ideas and expose new poets because it can afford to fail. . . . Also, the competitive scramble for excellence is less important than that much more rare quality: development for its own sake—development of the magazine itself, and the development of the poets in it, instead of the full-blown, drop-dead sell-out of a public and topical success . . . [of] a textbook-and-archive culture, or a money-economy-culture."

Jones first had the idea that the newsletter should be mimeographed and distributed free to writers; DiPrima thought up the name to reflect its improvisational quality, a half kidding reference to the boat that Winnie-the-Pooh made out of a honey pot. As she explained, "It had a characteristic I was really fond of: 'Sometimes it's a Boat, and sometimes it's more of an Accident.' "

DiPrima later remembered that when she and Jones put together the newsletter, he liked strong, "politically aware poetry, and a lot of prose and criticism. I reacted more intuitively to what I read—didn't always intellectually 'understand' the poems I was into. I had no particular poetic theory at all, and I learned a lot from Roi. We didn't really agree about a lot of the poets, and this gave rise to a very healthy tension." She was the organizing force behind the physical production of the 8½-by-11-inch newsletter. After she and Jones agreed on an issue's contents, she typed the material directly onto mimeograph stencils, laying out the pages to correspond as much as possible to the authors' pages.

At first DiPrima gave 50 of the 250 copies of each issue to the Phoenix Bookshop in exchange for the use of their mimeograph machine. Later Jones and DiPrima bought their own machine and sold fifty copies to the Phoenix to get the money they needed for paper. Every other Sunday she invited "whole bunches of people" to her apartment on Fourth Street in the East Village to run the mimeograph machine, collate the pages, and staple and address the newsletter. Anybody who asked for a copy got put on the mailing list at no charge except for an initial contribution for postage.

Early in 1961 the first issue of The *Floating Bear* opened with Michael McClure's poem "THE SMILE SHALL NOT BE MORE MUTABLE THAN THE FINAL EXTINCTION OF MEAT." Jones remembered that after running off several issues of the newsletter, it "became the talk of our various interconnected literary circles. It was meant to be 'quick, fast and in a hurry.' Something that could carry the zigs and zags of the literary scene as well as some work of the general New York creative ambiance." The newsletter had a regular circulation of about three hundred people, and "those three hundred were sufficiently wired for sound to project the *Bear*'s presence and 'message' (of a new literature and a new criticism) in all directions."

In the fall of 1961, the "message" of *Floating Bear 9* met with an unexpectedly hostile response. The issue included selections from Jones's *The System of Dante's Hell* about a homosexual rape in the army, and an excerpt from William Burroughs's *Naked Lunch*. Jones and DiPrima had sent the issue to a subscriber who was in prison, and the authorities intercepted the newsletter and reported the editors for obscenity.

Jones and DiPrima were arrested on October 18, 1961, on the charge of sending obscenity through the mails. The case never went to court, because Jones requested a grand jury hearing and spent two days on the stand. He brought in a pile of books that had been labeled "obscene," ranging from Catullus to James Joyce's *Ulysses,* and read aloud for hours to the grand jury. They refused to return an indictment.

Beat writing was often controversial, but the ease with which writers and editors could start their own literary magazines could circumvent the restrictions of censorship. In November 1958 the administrators at the University of Chicago refused to let the staff of the *Chicago Review,* the student literary magazine, publish their Winter 1959 issue. It was to include sections of Burroughs's *Naked Lunch* and Kerouac's *Old Angel Midnight.* Both works contained explicitly sexual material, and a columnist in the *Chicago Daily News* had alerted the University trustees that the *Review* intended to publish "filthy writing on the Midway." Within four months, a new magazine called *Big Table* published its first issue, its cover proclaiming that it contained "THE COMPLETE CONTENTS OF THE SUPPRESSED WINTER 1959 CHICAGO REVIEW." Copies of *Big Table* were seized by the U.S. Post Office for alleged obscenity, but the magazine was fully exonerated.

Hundreds of other little magazines publishing Beat writing flourished in the 1960s. Perhaps the best known was Ed Sanders's *Fuck You: A Magazine of the Arts,* published like *Floating Bear* in the East Village in New York, and intended as a "Total Assault on the Culture." In its first issue in 1963, Sanders announced his editorial policy, representative of the idealism of the mimeographed magazine movement:

> Send me your banned manuscripts, your
> peace-grams, your cosmic data,
> your huddled masses yearning to be free,
> your collections of
> freak-beams,
> plans for the pacifist holocaust,
> I lift my Speedoprint mimeo
> beside the Golden Door.

The contents of the Beat magazines chart an increasing politicalization as America drifted into the Vietnam War. But there were always more pages of open form poetry, spontaneous prose, projective verse, and literary reviews than political manifestos. The variety and range of the work of the various writers is a tribute to their individual talent and suggests the spontaneous alliances and survival skills of the various fellow travelers who were members of the group.

Amiri Baraka

*Amiri Baraka was born LeRoi Jones in Newark, New Jersey,
on October 7, 1934. He adopted his new name after embracing
the Kawaida branch of the Muslim faith in 1966. Baraka's father
was a postal worker, his mother a social worker, and he grew
up, as he later wrote in his autobiography, with an acute feeling
of being victimized by the racism and "cultural aggression that
is the norm of US cultural life." He moved to Greenwich Village
as a young poet in 1957, married Hettie Cohen and with her
started* Yugen *magazine and Totem Press. After the assassination of Malcolm X in 1965, he left his white wife and friends
and founded the Black Arts Repertory Theatre in Harlem as a
black cultural nationalist, believing that "moral earnestness . . .
ought to be transformed into action." In 1966 Baraka moved
back to Newark and has been active in politics there ever since,
defining himself as a Marxist-Leninist Third World Socialist.*

"In Memory of Radio" and "Way Out West" are poems from
Preface to a Twenty-Volume Suicide Note *(1961). In their
references to Kerouac and Snyder, the poems suggest what
Baraka has described as "a sense of community growing among
some of the young writers, and I was one of them as well as
the editor of one of their magazines." "The Screamers" is a
story that Baraka included in his anthology* The Moderns *(1963)
with the note that "Burroughs's addicts, Kerouac's mobile
young voyeurs, my own Negroes, are literally not included in
the mainstream of American life. These characters are people
whom Spengler called* Fellaheen, *people living on the ruins of
a civilization. They are Americans no character in a John Up-*

dike novel would be happy to meet, but they are nonetheless
Americans, formed out of the conspicuously tragic evolution of
modern American life." Baraka's discussion of Kerouac's
"Spontaneous Prose" was written as a letter to the editor of
Evergreen Review *in 1961.*

IN MEMORY OF RADIO

Who has ever stopped to think of the divinity of Lamont Cranston?
(Only Jack Kerouac, that I know of: & me.
The rest of you probably had on WCBS and Kate Smith,
Or something equally unattractive.)

What can I say?
It is better to have loved and lost
Than to put linoleum in your living rooms?

Am I a sage or something?
Mandrake's hypnotic gesture of the week?
(Remember, I do not have the healing powers of Oral Roberts . . .
I cannot, like F. J. Sheen, tell you how to get saved & *rich!*
I cannot even order you to gaschamber satori like Hitler or
     Goody Knight

& Love is an evil word.
Turn it backwards/see, see what I mean?
An evol word. & besides
who understands it?
I certainly wouldn't like to go out on that kind of limb.

Saturday mornings we listened to *Red Lantern* & his undersea folk.
At 11, *Let's Pretend*/& we did/& I, the poet, still do, Thank God!

What was it he used to say (after the transformation, when he was safe
& invisible & the unbelievers couldn't throw stones?) "Heh, heh, heh,
Who knows what evil lurks in the hearts of men? The Shadow knows."

O, yes he does
O, yes he does.

An evil word it is,
This Love.

WAY OUT WEST

for Gary Snyder

As simple an act
as opening the eyes. Merely
coming into things by degrees.

Morning: some tear is broken
on the wooden stairs
of my lady's eyes. Profusions
of green. The leaves. Their
constant prehensions. Like old
junkies on Sheridan Square, eyes
cold and round. There is a song
Nat Cole sings . . . This city
& the intricate disorder
of the seasons.

Unable to mention
something as abstract as time.

Even so, (bowing low in thick
smoke from cheap incense; all
kinds questions filling the mouth,
till you suffocate & fall dead
to opulent carpet.) Even so,

shadows will creep over your flesh
& hide your disorder, your lies.

There are unattractive wild ferns
outside the window
where the cats hide. They yowl
from there at nights. In heat
& bleeding on my tulips.

Steel bells, like the evil
unwashed Sphinx, towing in the twilight.
Childless old murderers, for centuries
with musty eyes.

I am distressed. Thinking
of the seasons, how they pass,
how I pass, my very youth, the
ripe sweet of my life; drained off . . .

Like giant rhesus monkeys;
picking their skulls,
with ingenious cruelty
sucking out the brains.

No use for beauty
collapsed, with moldy breath
done in. Insidious weight
of cankered dreams. Tiresias'
weathered cock.

Walking into the sea, shells
caught in the hair. Coarse
waves tearing the tongue.

Closing the eyes. As
simple an act. You float

THE SCREAMERS

    Lynn Hope adjusts his turban under the swishing red green yellow shadow lights. Dots. Suede heaven raining, windows yawning cool summer air, and his musicians watch him grinning, quietly, or high with wine blotches on four dollar shirts. A yellow girl will not dance with me, nor will Teddy's people, in line to the left of the stage, readying their *Routines*. Haroldeen, the most beautiful, in her pitiful dead sweater. Make it yellow, wish it whole. Lights. Teddy, Sonny Boy, Kenney & Calvin, Scram, a few of Nat's boys jamming long washed handkerchiefs in breast pockets, pushing shirts into homemade cummerbunds, shuffling lightly for any audience.

"The Cross-Over," Deen laughing at us all. And they perform in solemn unison a social tract of love. (With no music till Lynn finishes 'macking' with any big-lipped Esther screws across the stage. White and green plaid jackets his men wear, and that twisted badge, black turban/on red string conked hair. (OPPRESSORS!) A greasy hipness, down-ness, nobody in our camp believed (having social worker mothers and postman fathers; or living squeezed in light skinned projects with adulterers and proud skinny ladies with soft voices). The theory, the spectrum, this sound baked inside their heads, and still rub sweaty against those lesser lights. Those niggers. Laundromat workers, beauticians, pregnant short haired jail bait separated all ways from 'us,' but in this vat we sweated gladly for each other. And rubbed. And Lynn could be a common hero, from whatever side we saw him. Knowing that energy, and its response. That drained silence we had to make with our hands, leaving actual love to Nat or Al or Scram.

He stomped his foot, and waved one hand. The other hung loosely on his horn. And their turbans wove in among those shadows. Lynn's tighter, neater, and bright gorgeous yellow stuck with a green stone. Also, those green sparkling cubes dancing off his pinkies. A-boomp bahba bahba, A-boomp bahba bahba, A-boomp bahba bahba, A-boomp bahba bahba, the turbans sway behind him. And he grins before he lifts the horn, at deen or drunk becky, and we search the dark for girls.

Who would I get?

(Not anyone who would understand this.) Some light girl who had fallen into bad times and ill-repute for dating Bubbles. And he fixed her later with his child, now she walks Orange st. wiping chocolate from its face. A disgraced white girl who learned to calypso in vocational school. Hence, behind halting speech, a humanity as paltry as her cotton dress. (And the big hats made a line behind her, stroking their erections, hoping for photographs to take down south.) Lynn would oblige. He would make the most perverted hopes sensual and possible. Chanting at that dark crowd. Or some girl, a wino's daughter, with carefully vaselined bow legs would drape her filthy angora against the cardboard corinthian, eyeing past any greediness a white man knows, my soft tyrolean hat, pressed corduroy suit, and "B" sweater. Whatever they meant, finally to her, valuable shadows barely visible. Some stuck-up boy with "good" hair. And as a naked display of America, for I meant to her that same oppression. A stunted head of greased glass feathers, orange lips, brown pasted edge to the collar of her dying blouse. The secret perfume of poverty and ignorant desire. Arrogant too, at my disorder, which calls her smile mysterious. Turning to be eaten by the crowd. That mingled foliage of sweat and shadows: *Night Train* was what they swayed to. And smelled each other in The Grind, The Rub, The Slow Drag. From side to side, slow or jerked staccato as their wedding dictated. Big hats bent tight skirts, and some light girls' hair swept the resin on the floor. Respectable ladies put stiff arms on your waist to keep some light between, looking nervously at an ugly friend forever at the music's edge.

I wanted girls like Erselle, whose father sang on television, but my hair was not straight enough, and my father never learned how to drink. Our house sat lonely and large on a half-italian street, filled with important Negroes. (Though it is rumored they had a son, thin with big eyes, they killed because he was crazy.) Surrounded by the haughty daughters of depressed economic groups. They plotted in their projects for mediocrity, and the neighborhood smelled of their despair. And only the wild or the very poor thrived in Graham's or could be roused by Lynn's histories and rhythms. America had choked the rest, who could sit still for hours under popular songs, or be readied for citizenship by slightly bohemian social workers. They rivaled pure emotion with wind-up record players that pumped Jo Stafford into Home Economics rooms. And these carefully scrubbed children of my parents' friends fattened on their rhythms until they could join the Urban League or Household Finance and hound the poor for their honesty.

I was too quiet to become a murderer, and too used to extravagance for their skinny lyrics. They mentioned neither cocaine nor Bach, which was my reading, and the flaw of that society. I disappeared into the slums, and fell in love with violence, and invented for myself a mysterious economy of need. Hence, I shambled anonymously thru Lloyd's, The Nite-cap, The Hi-Spot, and Graham's desiring everything I felt. In a new english overcoat and green hat, scouring that town for my peers. And they were old pinch faced whores full of snuff and weak dope, celebrity fags with radio programs, mute bass players who loved me, and built the myth of my intelligence. You see, I left America on the first fast boat.

This was Sunday night, and the Baptists were still praying in their "faboulous" churches. Though my father sat listening to the radio, or reading pulp cowboy magazines, which I take in part to be the truest legacy of my spirit. God never had a chance. And I would be walking slowly towards The Graham, not even knowing how to smoke. Willing for any experience, any image, any further separation from where my good grades were sure to lead. Frightened of post offices, lawyer's offices, doctor's cars, the deaths of clean politicians. Or of the imaginary fat man, advertising cemeteries to his "good colored friends." Lynn's screams erased them all, and I thought myself intrepid white commando from the West. Plunged into noise and flesh, and their form become an ethic.

Now Lynn wheeled and hunched himself for another tune. Fast dancers fanned themselves. Couples who practiced during the week talked over their steps. Deen and her dancing clubs readied avant-garde routines. Now it was *Harlem Nocturne,* which I whistled loudly one saturday in a landromat, and the girl who stuffed in my khakis and stiff underwear asked was I a musician. I met her at Graham's that night and we waved, and I suppose she knew I loved her.

Nocturne was slow and heavy and the serious dancers loosened their ties. The slowly twisting lights made specks of human shadows, the darkness seemed to float around the hall. Any meat you clung to was yours those few minutes without interruption. The length of the music was the only form. And the idea was to press against each other hard, to rub, to shove the hips tight, and gasp at whatever passion. Professionals wore jocks against embarassment. Amateurs, like myself, after the music stopped, put our hands quickly into our pockets, and retreated into the shadows. It was as meaningful as anything else we knew.

All extremes were popular with that crowd. The singers shouted, the musicians stomped and howled. The dancers ground each other past passion or moved so fast it blurred intelligence. We hated the popular song, and any freedman could tell you if you asked that white people danced jerkily, and were slower than our champions. One style, which developed as italians showed up with pegs, and our own grace moved towards bellbottom pants to further complicate the cipher, was the honk. The repeated rhythmic figure, a screamed riff, pushed in its insistence past music. It was hatred and frustration, secrecy and despair. It spurted out of the dipthong culture, and re-inforced the black cults of emotion. There was no compromise, no dreary sophistication, only the elegance of something that is too ugly to be described, and is diluted only at the agent's peril. All the saxophonists of that world were honkers, Illinois, Gator, Big Jay, Jug, the great sounds of our day. Ethnic historians, actors, priests of the unconscious. That stance spread like fire thru the cabarets and joints of the black cities, so that the sound itself became a basis for thought, and the innovators searched for uglier modes. Illinois would leap and twist his head, scream when he wasn't playing. Gator would strut up and down the stage, dancing for emphasis, shaking his long gassed hair in his face and coolly mopping it back. Jug, the beautiful horn, would wave back and forth so high we all envied him his connection, or he'd stomp softly to the edge of the stage whispering those raucous threats. Jay first turned the mark around, opened the way further for the completely nihilistic act. McNeeley, the first Dada coon of the age, jumped and stomped and yowled and finally sensed the only other space that form allowed. He fell first on his knees, never releasing the horn, and walked that way across the stage. We hunched together drowning any sound, relying on Jay's contorted face for evidence that there was still music, though none of us needed it now. And then he fell backwards, flat on his back, with both feet stuck up high in the air, and he kicked and thrashed and the horn spat enraged sociologies.

That was the night Hip Charlie, the Baxter Terrace Romeo, got wasted right in front of the place. Snake and four friends mashed him up and left him for the ofays to identify. Also the night I had the grey bells and sat in the Chinese restaurant all night to show them off. Jay had set a social form for the poor, just as Bird and Dizzy proposed it for the middle class. On his back screaming was the Mona Lisa with the mustache, as crude and simple. Jo Stafford could not do it. Bird took the language, and we woke up one Saturday whispering Ornithology. Blank verse.

And Newark always had a bad reputation, I mean, everybody could pop their fingers. Was hip. Had walks. Knew all about The Apple. So I suppose when the word got to Lynn what Big Jay had done, he knew all the little down cats were waiting to see him in this town. He knew he had to cook. And he blasted all night, crawled and leaped, then stood at the side of the stand, and watched us while he fixed his sky, wiped his face. Watched us to see how far he'd gone, but he was tired and we weren't, which was not where it was. The girls rocked slowly against the silence of the horns, and big hats pushed each other or made plans for murder. We had not completely come. All sufficiently eaten by Jay's memory, "on his back, kicking his feet in the air, Ga-ud Dam!" So he moved cautiously to the edge of the stage, and the gritty muslims he played with gathered close. It was some mean honking blues, and he made no attempt to hide his intentions. He was breaking bad. "Okay, baby," we all thought, "Go for yourself." I was standing at the back of the hall with one arm behind my back, so the overcoat could hang over in that casual gesture of fashion. Lynn was moving, and the camel walkers were moving in the corners. The fast dancers and practicers making the whole hall dangerous. "Off my suedes, motherfucker." Lynn was trying to move us, and even I did the one step I knew, safe at the back of the hall. The hippies ran for girls. Ugly girls danced with each other. Skippy, who ran the lights, made them move faster in that circle on the ceiling, and darkness raced around the hall. Then Lynn got his riff, that rhythmic figure we knew he would repeat, the honked note that would be his personal evaluation of the world. And he screamed it so the veins in his face stood out like neon. "Uhh, yeh, Uhh, yeh, Uhh, yeh," we all screamed to push him further. So he opened his eyes for a second, and really made his move. He looked over his shoulder at the other turbans, then marched in time with his riff, on his toes across the stage. They followed; he marched across to the other side, repeated, then finally he descended, still screaming, into the crowd, and as the sidemen followed, we made a path for them around the hall. They were strutting, and all their horns held very high, and they were only playing that one scary note. They moved near the back of the hall, chanting and swaying, and passed right in front of me. I had a little cup full of wine a murderer friend of mine made me drink, so I drank it and tossed the cup in the air, then fell in line behind the last wild horn man, strutting like the rest of them. Bubbles and Rogie followed me, and four eyed Moselle Boyd. And we strutted back and forth pumping our arms, repeating with Lynn Hope, "Yeh, Uhh, Yeh, Uhh." Then everybody fell in behind us, yelling still. There was confusion and stumbling, but there were no real fights. The thing they wanted was right there and easily accessible. No one could stop you from getting in that line. "It's too crowded. It's too many people on the line!" some people yelled. So Lynn thought further, and made to destroy the ghetto. We went out into the lobby and in perfect rhythm down the marble steps. Some musicians laughed, but Lynn and some others kept the note, till the others fell back in. Five or six hundred hopped up woogies tumbled out into Belmont Avenue. Lynn marched right in the center of the street. Sunday night traffic stopped, and honked. Big Red yelled at a bus driver, "Hey, baby, honk that horn in time or shut it off!" The bus driver cooled it. We screamed and screamed at the clear image of ourselves as we should always be. Ecstatic, completed, involved in a secret communal expression. It would be the form of the sweetest revolution, to hucklebuck into the fallen capitol, and let the oppressors lindy hop out. We marched all the way to Spruce, weaving among the stalled cars, laughing at the dazed white men who sat behind the wheels. Then Lynn turned and we strutted back towards the hall. The late show at the National was turning out, and all the big hats there jumped right in our line.

Then the Nabs came, and with them, the fire engines. What was it a labor riot? Anarchists? A nigger strike? The paddy wagons and cruisers pulled in from both sides, and sticks and billies started flying, heavy streams of water splattering the marchers up and down the street. America's responsible immigrants were doing her light work again. The knives came out, the razors, all the Biggers who would not be bent, counterattacked or came up behind the civil servants smashing at them with coke bottles and aerials. Belmont writhed under the dead economy and splivs floated in the gutters, disappearing under cars. But for awhile, before the war had reached its peak, Lynn and his musicians, a few other fools, and I, still marched, screaming thru the maddened crowd. Onto the sidewalk, into the lobby, half-way up the stairs, then we all broke our different ways, to save whatever it was each of us thought we loved.

LETTER TO THE *EVERGREEN REVIEW* ABOUT KEROUAC'S SPONTANEOUS PROSE

Editors:

Jack Kerouac's essay, "The Essentials of Spontaneous Prose," is an amazing document because it not only outlines exactly how he writes (and is therefore unattackable), but also offers a general description of the processes involved in spontaneous writing. And for this last reason, it is more than just an *apologia pro* his writings, it has genuine *creative* as well as literary value. Also, what is not at all strange is that Kerouac is at his best when he adheres strictly to this outline (which I believe was also largely spontaneous, and therefore quite "honest"). When he is describing (which is all any artist can do anyway . . . though the *described* can be of many diverse natures), and describing spontaneously from the "jewel center" as he calls it, i.e., the physical event and/or the concrete emotional image, he is superb, a giant of swift exacting poetic insight. It is only when he encounters lags in his insight or spontaneity that he is duped, when he tries painstakingly and often painfully to *conjure* intellectually . . . and writes these conjurings down (instead of what they are supposed to conjure), that his prose becomes stiff, awkward and *untrue*. Intellectual conjuring has nothing to do with the creative act as such, though it may certainly be concomitant with it.

In Kerouac's spontaneous writing (which is usually very easy to recognize) one is constantly aware of the key image or "jewel center." A particularly good example is in *On the Road,* where the narrator and Dean Moriarty & Co. are leaving Louisiana and "Old Bull Lee" and heading west. He begins the section (pt. 2, sec. 8), "What is that feeling when you're driving away from people and they recede on the plain till you see their specks dispersing?—it's the too-huge world vaulting us, and it's good-by. But we lean forward to the next crazy venture beneath the skies." . . . which is poetry. But in this part he is still almost *conscious,* almost conscious of the words' *meanings* . . . and the result is that the writing is somewhat conjured (though not contrived). In the next paragraph, however, he begins the journey, and after the first *primer* sentence ("the scatological buildup"), he reaches the key word and jewel center of this association and he is off and "unconscious": "We wheeled through the sultry old light of Algiers, back on the ferry, back toward the mud-splashed, crabbed old ships across the river, back on Canal, and out; on a two-lane highway to Baton Rouge in purple darkness; swung west there, crossed the Mississippi at a place called Port Allen." (NOW) "Port Allen—where the river's all rain and roses in a misty pinpoint darkness and where we swung around a circular drive in yellow foglight and suddenly saw the great black body below a bridge and crossed eternity again." Notice how the word "back" is used as a primer throughout: "*back* on the ferry, *back* toward the mud-splashed," . . . "back on Canal," etc.

The second part of the paragraph, which is even stronger, has a very simple and effective primer. He asks himself a question, "What is the Mississippi River?" The answer rushes forth: "—a washed clod in the rainy night, a soft plopping from drooping Missouri banks, a dissolving, a riding of the tide down the eternal waterbed, a contribution to brown foams, a voyaging past endless vales and trees and levees, down along, down along" (primers) "by Memphis, Greenville, Eudora, Vicksburg, Natchez, Port Allen, and Port Orleans, and Port of the Deltas, by Potash, Venice, and the Night's Great Gulf, and out."

The statement Kerouac makes about writing *without* consciousness, i.e., "MENTAL STATE. If possible write 'without consciousness in semi-trance (as Yeats' later 'trance writing') . . ." is the most paradoxical but perhaps the most instructive statement in the whole essay. This is not to be interpreted as "clinical unconsciousness" (which hardly exists . . . but that is a philosophical question), but as *other* consciousness, that is, the "writer's voice" or the "painter's eye." This is the level or stratum of the psyche that *is* the creative act. The "writer's voice" dictates the writing just as the "painter's eye" dictates the strokes the painter makes for his picture. This is the consciousness that supersedes or usurps the *normal* consciousness of the creator (though even the usual or uninspired consciousness of the creator can hardly be called normal). For it is during this so-called normal state that the artist's peculiar and/or latent impressions are gathered; but it is only during this "unconscious" state that the *writer's voice* becomes his only voice . . . and the creative act itself is accomplished. And whether this state is largely intellectually conjured or just drops through the artist's eyes or fingers "like a brick angel," when the result is "high art," the method is, all things considered, not the point.

In the section from *On the Road* quoted above, notice that after the *trigger-inference* (jewel center) is reached, there is a quick spurt and added drive to the prose; an untangling of the intellect, as it were. The name "Port Algiers" is the instrument that unravels the whole association, noun studded though it is: all legitimate spontaneous prose is full of nouns since these are the simplest and most uncomplex parts of speech, i.e., unfettered by the need of complex definitions to explain them. Port Algiers is Port Algiers . . . it exists in a definite geographical location. It is a *thing*. The noun has not the necessary semantic dichotomy and complexity that is encountered in, say, adjectives, adverbs, etc., (i.e., what does "small" mean? Is it not relative, relative, relative, needing a relative definition, etc. The mind works best with *things,* the unabstract . . . even though it does abstract them).

In one scene of the old Howard Hughes' film *Outlaw,* the hero, Billy the Kid, whips out his gun, and from the hip shoots a hole through a thin reed (to make a whistle 25 yards away). The astonished heroine asks Billy how he does this without even aiming. Billy replies, "I aim before I pull out the gun."

I think this is also true, not only of Kerouac's writing, but of any good writer whose work is largely spontaneous. He aims before even drawing the gun. That is, the spontaneous writer has to possess a particularly facile and amazingly impressionable mind, one that is able to collect and store not just snatches or episodic bits of events, but whole and elaborate associations: the whole impression *intact,* so that at the *trigger inference* the entire impression and association comes flooding through the writer's mind almost *in toto.* The resultant impression, of course, has been thoroughly incorporated and translated into the supraconsciousness or *writing voice* of the writer. The *external event* is now the internal or psychical event which is a combination of interpretation and pure reaction.

Of course, a prose writer like Kerouac, whose best output is spontaneous, is liable to produce some very uneven novels. This is true of *On the Road* as well as of *The Subterraneans.* These novels have almost as many great stretches of mucky morass and stiff quasi-philosophical whining as of triumphant, poetic tour de force. But a novel is by its very nature addicted to such goings on. All novelists must indulge in long passages of dreary pseudodescription and "literary lying" to arrive at the physical proportions of the novel in the first place. (Almost half of *The Brothers Karamazov* is windy Slavic perversity, and it is just about a "perfect" novel.) I, personally, favor short stories as opposed to the novel, especially in the case of a writer like Kerouac, whose highest poetic force is usually not sustained for long periods. In *Dharma Bums* Kerouac has reached a critical point in his writing, where he seems finally to be taking the essentials of his method into consideration and learning to pad and coat the novel's dull passages with the device, subtlety and surprise which are the novelist's only weapons.

Finally, in the last part of his essay Kerouac says that (the writer) should "write excitedly, swiftly . . . in accordance (as from center to periphery) with laws of orgasm, Reich's beclouding of consciousness. *Come* from within, out—to relaxed and said." And while this is certainly true for the writer, the pure ecstatic power of the creative climax can never be the reader's; even though he has traced and followed frantically the writer's steps, to that final "race to the wire of time." The *actual* experience of this "race" is experienced *only* by the writer, whose entire psyche is involved and from whence the work is extracted. And no matter how much we "identify" or are extended by the work, it remains always a *work* and not *ourselves*. It is (in this case) Jack Kerouac's self. That is, only the writer is "relaxed and said"; the reader is finished, stopped, but his mind still lingers, sometimes frantically, between the essential and the projected, i.e., what we are and what the work has *made* us, which is the writer's triumph.

LeRoi Jones

Ray Bremser

Ray Bremser was born on February 22, 1934, in Jersey City, New Jersey. His father was a pianist at the Palace Theater in New York, and his mother was a factory worker. At the age of seventeen Bremser enlisted in the United States Air Force, but went AWOL on his fourth day of basic training and was discharged after a short stint in the stockade. The following year he began a six-year stretch in Bordentown Reformatory for armed robbery. While in prison Bremser began writing poetry, which he sent to Ginsberg and Corso in Paris. They gave him LeRoi Jones's New York address. Jones published Bremser's poems in Yugen *and threw a party for him when he got out of prison in 1958 to introduce him to other writers on the scene.*

The New York Beats so impressed Bremser that the next time he went to prison he wrote the long poem "Angel," a tribute to his wife, Bonnie Bremser. It was "the work of one night in the dark/solitary confinement, New Jersey State Prison, Trenton" and scribbled on "light brown toilet paper." Bremser felt he had been accepted into what he called in "Angel" "the literary life in America . . . tradition . . . starts from Poe & Whitman up thru mr. Melville into Williams & Jack & Allen & Gregory & Roi & John & Mike & Phil (both of 'em) & me . . . & all them cats living around us making the original noise. . . ."

Bremser has published five books of poetry. The relaxed "sinewy" lyricism of his work is influenced by the jazz rhythms of Kerouac's Mexico City Blues. *The poem "Funny Lotus Blues . . ." is a later jazz poem from his book* Blowing Mouth *(1978).*

FUNNY LOTUS BLUES . . .

sinister maryjane: the man sits
with tears/deluge his face with their
heap o' salt
make you understand
                                why
-so:
        when Nat King Cole is
singing
People
who needs People
is the luckiest People
in the world . . .
                        like Dial Soap,
                        very suspect—

he being 30 who listens
reveal or betray those rollerskates at 16
he sat upon his early porches, feint-
fondling the fantastic superficial beauty
of the girl beside him
put him beside himself
it too stern & brilliant
& hot to touch
& he finally cry at his groggy
image he watch fumbling funny grounders
even Buster Keaton field
                        (whch, in itself, like that song,
                        like King Cole himself
                        , either of whch
                        be too pretentious
                        to acknowledge
                                        or one of them
                        be cruel; & like
                        this poem is / either/or

this fact that makes the
maryjane

i say *sinister*

        (& come to *terms even moreso*
        with; a face that say / how
        it hardly matter anyway! for example
                MONK: "cant
        nobody tell you no different anyhow."
        Melodious Thunk!
                & then sit
        astounding even hisself
        with the density of tongue
        he transform in the cheek of the
        piano/metamorphos
        into music make you erupt into
        any effect he choose
        in some spontaneous
        emotion whch wants to re-
        ciprocate improvisationally
        , & in kind, i say:
who there is
that can do this/must make (because WANT to)
an exemplary effort to (i think) DIG (is the word).

(*or else smoke a reefer*
& that clear everything up / i shld hope so!
who wants to be embarrassed
                crying at a movie?)

O, SING THE SONG, ROSIE CLOONEY
Jack Kerouac probably understands this epoch better than any-
who got *both* his ill advised ultimately/*rather*
utterance
        neither thin (or) than famous . . .
he too fat!

or Ray Charles
who sing both the hippest
& corniest
versions together . . .
of even the same song . . .

like an afterthought . . .

(which i like / & is somehow not because
the grass
but serve anyway to reason
in favor all three the reefer-Jack K.-& Ray C. -
always—
          they speak,
neither of 'em
              , bad of any either/other ever,
& that's cooler than actual icy-disapproval &
prettier than you'll be apt to discover if you
dont already know . . .

                    as all
difficult beauty, rewards only
her uncoverer—a certain & most devoted
lover, indeed / i indeed do like!

AH, THIS POEM HAS A FORTIES-HAIRDO
swaying to the Modernaires slowly swinging
Moonlight Seranade
—& remind me now of a Yo Yo;
and legend has it that's Zen!
                    ie. Moe hammers a railroad spike
                        into the top of Curley's head
                        : who gets so angry he puts pacify aside
                        & protest with heft enuf
                        remind you of a woody-woodpecker haiku

                        'crosseyed Siamese kitty hang
                        ten feet up the tapestry,
                        rebut you!
                                SESHU
                        (whch somebody name Gregory!)
    but now,
    nothing Tanu Tuva,
    Ishkabibble, Henry Hudson

, Pubic Hair or other such
improbable immortalities

who say Phui & turn back
to read
   the rest of
      Nero Wolfe,
puff on a reefer - Phui . . .

sinister changes
     from the giggle-flower;
weeping & wolocking . . .

ha ha ha *ha* ha

ha ha ha *ha* ha

ha ha ha ha ha ha ha ha ha ha ha ha ha ha . . .

Diane DiPrima

Diane DiPrima was born in New York on August 6, 1934, the granddaughter of Italian immigrants. After she dropped out of Swarthmore College to become a writer, she took a series of jobs to support herself while she learned how, in the words of her biographer, George Butterick, to "raise her rebellion into art." DiPrima became part of the bohemian community of young writers, artists, musicians, and dancers in Manhattan, an experience she described in Memoirs of a Beatnik *(1969).*

Hettie and LeRoi Jones's Totem Press published DiPrima's first poetry collection, This Kind of Bird Flies Backward, *in 1958. The dustwrapper for her next book,* Dinners and Nightmares *(1961), announced that her "honesty will shock the romantic illusions of even the 'beat' generation." "Three Laments" and "Song for Baby-O, Unborn" are what she called "more or less love poems" from that book.*

"Poetics" and "The Practice of Magical Evocation" are other poems from the 1950s, the latter DiPrima's ironic response to Snyder's poem "Praise for Sick Women." As the critic Michael Davidson understood, "The more DiPrima asserts woman's passivity, the less we believe her and thus recognize her ability to use rhetoric to her own advantage. . . . We could see her poem as an indication of what directions her [feminist] peers have taken in poetry, appropriating the coercive rhetoric of the masculine tradition and using it against itself."

DiPrima, the mother of five children, has said she is dismayed that her eloquent meditation on her early abortion, "Brass Furnace Going Out," originally published as a broadside, has been read by anti-abortion groups as supporting their cause.

"A Few Blue Words to the Wise"

THREE LAMENTS

I

Alas
I believe
I might have become
a great writer
but
the chairs
in the library
were too hard

II

I have
the upper hand
but if I keep it
I'll lose the circulation
in one arm

III

So here I am the coolest in New York
what dont swing I dont push.

In some Elysian field
by a big tree
I chew my pride
like cud.

SONG FOR BABY-O, UNBORN

Sweetheart
when you break thru
you'll find
a poet here
not quite what one would choose.

I won't promise
you'll never go hungry
or that you won't be sad
on this gutted
breaking
globe

but I can show you
baby
enough to love
to break your heart
forever

THE PRACTICE OF MAGICAL EVOCATION

The female is fertile, and discipline
(contra naturam) only
                confuses her
                    —Gary Snyder

i am a woman and my poems
are woman's: easy to say
this.   the female is ductile
and
     (stroke after stroke)
built for masochistic
calm.   The deadened nerve
is part of it:
awakened sex, dead retina
fish eyes;   at hair's root
minimal feeling

and pelvic architecture functional
assailed inside & out
(bring forth) the cunt gets wide
and relatively sloppy
bring forth men children only
                                female

                    is
                    ductile

woman, a veil thru which the fingering Will
twice torn
twice torn
            inside & out
the flow
what rhythm add to stillness
what applause?

POETICS

I have deserted my post, I cdnt hold it
rearguard/to preserve the language/lucidity:
let the language fend for itself.
it turned over god knows enough carts in the city streets
its barricades are my nightmares

preserve the language!—there are
            enough fascists &
            enough socialists
on both sides
so that no one will lose this war

the language shall be my element, I plunge in
I suspect that I cannot drown
like a fat brat catfish, smug
            a hoodlum fish
I move more & more gracefully
            breathe it in,
success written on my mug till the fishpolice
corner me in the coral & I die

BRASS FURNACE GOING OUT:
Song, after an Abortion

I

to say I failed, that is walked out
and into the arctic
        How shd I know where I was?
A man chants in the courtyard
        the window is open
someone else drops a pecan pie
        into the yard
two dogs down there play trumpet
        there is something disturbed
about the melody.

and what of the three year old girl who poisoned her mother?
that happens, it isn't just us, as you can see—
what you took with you when you left
remains to be seen.

II

I want you in a bottle to send to your father
with a long bitter note. I want him to know
I'll not forgive you, or him for not being born
for drying up, quitting
        at the first harsh treatment
as if the whole thing were a rent party
& somebody stepped on your feet

III

send me your address a picture, I want to
keep in touch, I want to know how you
are, to send you cookies.

do you have enough sweaters, is the winter bad,
do you know what I've done, what I'm doing
do you care

write in detail of your day, what time you get up,
what you are studying, when you expect
to finish & what you will do.
is it chilly?

IV

your face dissolving in water, like wet clay
washed away, like a rotten water lily
rats on the riverbank barking at the sight
do they swim?
the trees here walk right down to the edge
conversing
your body sank, a good way back
I hear the otters will bring it to the surface

and the wailing mosquitoes even stop to examine
the last melting details of eyelid & cheekbone
the stagnant blood
who taught you not to tangle your hair in the seaweed
to disappear with finesse

the lion pads
                along the difficult path
in the heart of the jungle
and comes to the riverbank
he paws your face
I wish he would drink it up
in that strong gut it would come
to life.
        but he waits till it floats
a distance
        drinks clean water
dances a little
        starts the long walk
again

        the silent giraffe lets loose
a mourning cry
        fish surface

      your mouth and the end of your nose
disappear.

the water was cold the day you slipped into the river
wind ruffled the surface, I carried you on my back
a good distance, then you slipped in
red ants started up my leg & changed their minds
I fed my eyeballs to a carnivorous snake
& chained myself to a tree to await your end.
your face no sooner dissolved than I thought I saw
a kneecap sticking up where the current is strongest
a turtle
      older than stars
walked on your bones

V

who forged this night, what steel
clamps down?
like grey pajamas on an invalid
if I knew the names of flowers, the habits
of quadrupeds, the 13 points of the compass . . .
an aged mapmaker who lived on this street
just succumbed to rheumatism

I have cut the shroud to measure
      bought the stone
a plot in the cemetery set aside
      to bury your shadow
take your head & go!
& may the woman that you find know better
than talk to me about it

VI

your goddamned belly rotten, a home for flies.
blown out & stinking, the maggots curling your hair
your useless neverused cock, the pitiful skull
the pitiful shell of a skull, dumped in the toilet

the violet, translucent folds
                    of beginning life

VII

what is it that I cannot bear to say?
that if you had turned out mad, a murderer
a junkie pimp hanged & burning in lime
                    alone & filled w/the rotting dark
if you'd been frail and a little given to weirdness
or starved or been shot, or tortured in hunger camps
it wd have been frolic & triumph compared to this—

I cant even cry for you, I cant hang on
that long

VIII

forgive, forgive
that the cosmic waters do not turn from me
that I should not die of thirst

IX

oranges & jade at the shrine
my footprints
wet on the stone
the bells in that clear air
wind from the sea
your shadow
flat on the flat rocks
the priestess (sybil)
spelling your name
crying out, behind copper doors
giving birth
atone
                    , silence, the air
moving outside
the door to the temple blowing on its hinges

that was the spirit she said
it passed above you

the branch I carry home is mistletoe
& I walk backwards, with my eyes on the sea

X

here in my room I sit at a drawing table
as I have sat all day, or walked
from drawing table to bed,
or stopped at window
considering the things to be done
weighing them in the hand & putting them down
hung up as the young Rilke.
here in my room all day on my couch a stranger
who does not speak
who does not take his eyes
off me as I walk & walk from table to bed.

and I cannot stop thinking I would be three months pregnant
we would be well out of here & in the sun
even our telephone would be polite.
we would laugh a lot, in the morning.

XI

your ivory teeth bare in the half-light
your arms
flailing about. that is, you
age 9 months,
        sitting up & trying to stand
cutting teeth.
        your diaper trailing, a formality
elegant as a loincloth, the sweet stench
of babyshit in the house: the oil
rubbed into your hair.
blue off the moon your ghostshape
        mistaken as a broken tooth
your flesh rejected

                    never to grow—your hands
that should have closed around my finger

what moonlight
                    will play in your hair?
I mean to say
        dear fish, I hope you swim

in another river.
I hope that wasnt
rebuttal, but a transfer, an attempt
that failed, but to be followed
        quickly by another
suck your thumb somewhere
Dear silly thing, explode
make someone's colors.

the senses (five)
                a gift
to hear, see, touch, choke on & love
this life
this rotten globe
to walk in shoes
what apple doesnt get
            at least this much?

a caramel candy sticking in your teeth
you, age three
bugged
        bearing down on a sliding pond.
your pulled tooth in my hand
                    (age six)
your hair with clay in it,
                        your goddamn grin

XII

sun on the green plants, your prattle
among the vines.
that this possibility is closed to us.

my house is small, my windows look out on grey courtyard
there is no view of the sea.
will you come here again? I will entertain you
as well as I can—I will make you comfortable
in spite of new york.

will
you
come here
again

my breasts prepare
to feed you: they do what they can

Bob Dylan

Bob Dylan was born Robert Zimmerman on May 24, 1941, in Duluth, Minnesota. By the time he entered the University of Minnesota in 1960, he had changed his name to reflect his admiration for the poet Dylan Thomas. After a semester of college he dropped out to travel to New Jersey, where he visited another idol, the folksinger and songwriter Woody Guthrie, who was hospitalized for Huntington's chorea. Dylan settled in Greenwich Village and began to earn his living as a folksinger. In 1962 Columbia records released his first album, Bob Dylan. *In the recording studio Dylan preferred not to do retakes, explaining, "I can't see myself singing the same song twice in a row. That's terrible."*

The critic Joseph Wenke has interpreted Dylan's insistence on spontaneity as a link between him and the Beats, along with his sharing "the Beats' attitudes toward social authority, politics, and drugs, emphasizing the primacy of the self and rejecting institutionally prescribed norms." Over the next decade Dylan continued to be influenced by the Beats—through his reading, through his association with such Beat writers as Allen Ginsberg and Michael McClure, and by his vision of himself as a solitary creative artist in the rebellious and liberating atmosphere of the 1960s, which the Beats partly inspired and helped sustain.

"Blowin' in the Wind," "The Times They Are A-Changin'," and "A Hard Rain's A-Gonna Fall" (all from 1962–1963) suggest the Beat influence as Dylan's early lyrics developed to express a vivid and personal apocalyptic vision. As he says, "Not protest for protest's sake but always in the struggle for people's

freedom, individual or otherwise. I hate oppression." The two excerpts from Tarantula *(1971) are indebted to the collage or "kitchen garden" surrealist method of William Burroughs.*

BLOWIN' IN THE WIND

How many roads must a man walk down
Before you call him a man?
Yes, 'n' how many seas must a white dove sail
Before she sleeps in the sand?
Yes, 'n' how many times must the cannon balls fly
Before they're forever banned?
The answer, my friend, is blowin' in the wind,
The answer is blowin' in the wind.

How many times must a man look up
Before he can see the sky?
Yes, 'n' how many ears must one man have
Before he can hear people cry?
Yes, 'n' how many deaths will it take 'till he knows
That too many people have died?
The answer, my friend, is blowin' in the wind,
The answer is blowin' in the wind.

How many years can a mountain exist
Before it's washed to the sea?
Yes, 'n' how many years can some people exist
Before they're allowed to be free?
Yes, 'n' how many times can a man turn his head
Pretending he just doesn't see?
The answer, my friend, is blowin' in the wind,
The answer is blowin' in the wind.

THE TIMES THEY ARE A-CHANGIN'

Come gather 'round people
Wherever you roam

And admit that the waters
Around you have grown
And accept it that soon
You'll be drenched to the bone.
If your time to you
Is worth savin'
Then you better start swimmin'
Or you'll sink like a stone
For the times they are a-changin'.

Come writers and critics
Who prophesize with your pen
And keep your eyes wide
The chance won't come again
And don't speak too soon
For the wheel's still in spin
And there's no tellin' who
That it's namin'.
For the loser now
Will be later to win
For the times they are a-changin'.

Come senators, congressmen
Please heed the call
Don't stand in the doorway
Don't block up the hall
For he that gets hurt
Will be he who has stalled
There's a battle outside
And it is ragin'.
It'll soon shake your windows
And rattle your walls
For the times they are a-changin'.

Come mothers and fathers
Throughout the land
And don't criticize
What you can't understand
Your sons and your daughters
Are beyond your command

Your old road is
Rapidly agin'.
Please get out of the new one
If you can't lend your hand
For the times they are a-changin'.

The line it is drawn
The curse it is cast
The slow one now
Will later be fast
As the present now
Will later be past
The order is
Rapidly fadin'.
And the first one now
Will later be last
For the times they are a-changin'.

A HARD RAIN'S A-GONNA FALL

Oh, where have you been, my blue-eyed son?
Oh, where have you been, my darling young one?
I've stumbled on the side of twelve misty mountains,
I've walked and I've crawled on six crooked highways,
I've stepped in the middle of seven sad forests,
I've been out in front of a dozen dead oceans,
I've been ten thousand miles in the mouth of a graveyard,
And it's a hard, and it's a hard, it's a hard, and it's a hard,
And it's a hard rain's a-gonna fall.

Oh, what did you see, my blue-eyed son?
Oh, what did you see, my darling young one?
I saw a newborn baby with wild wolves all around it,
I saw a highway of diamonds with nobody on it,
I saw a black branch with blood that kept drippin',
I saw a room full of men with their hammers a-bleedin',
I saw a white ladder all covered with water,
I saw ten thousand talkers whose tongues were all broken,
I saw guns and sharp swords in the hands of young children,

And it's a hard, and it's a hard, it's a hard, it's a hard,
And it's a hard rain's a-gonna fall.

And what did you hear, my blue-eyed son?
And what did you hear, my darling young one?
I heard the sound of a thunder, it roared out a warnin',
Heard the roar of a wave that could drown the whole world,
Heard one hundred drummers whose hands were a-blazin',
Heard ten thousand whisperin' and nobody listenin',
Heard one person starve, I heard many people laughin',
Heard the song of a poet who died in the gutter,
Heard the sound of a clown who cried in the alley,
And it's a hard, and it's a hard, it's a hard, it's a hard,
And it's a hard rain's a-gonna fall.

Oh, who did you meet, my blue-eyed son?
Who did you meet, my darling young one?
I met a young child beside a dead pony,
I met a white man who walked a black dog,
I met a young woman whose body was burning,
I met a young girl, she gave me a rainbow,
I met one man who was wounded in love,
I met another man who was wounded with hatred,
And it's a hard, it's a hard, it's a hard, it's a hard,
It's a hard rain's a-gonna fall.

Oh, what'll you do now, my blue-eyed son?
Oh, what'll you do now, my darling young one?
I'm a-goin' back out 'fore the rain starts a-fallin',
I'll walk to the depths of the deepest black forest,
Where the people are many and their hands are all empty,
Where the pellets of poison are flooding their waters,
Where the home in the valley meets the damp dirty prison,
Where the executioner's face is always well hidden,
Where hunger is ugly, where souls are forgotten,
Where black is the color, where none is the number,
And I'll tell it and think it and speak it and breathe it,
And reflect it from the mountain so all souls can see it,
Then I'll stand on the ocean until I start sinkin',
But I'll know my song well before I start singin',

And it's a hard, it's a hard, it's a hard, it's a hard,
It's a hard rain's a-gonna fall.

from TARANTULA
I Found the Piano Player Very Crosseyed
But Extremely Solid

he came with his wrists taped & he carried his own coat
hanger—i could tell at a glance that he had no need for Sonny
Rollins but i asked him anyway "whatever happened to gregory
corso?" he just stood there—he took out a deck of cards &
he replied "wanna play some cards?" to which i answered "no
but whatever happened to jane russell?" he flapped the cards
& they went sailing all over the room "my father taught me
that" he said "it's called 52 pickup but i call it 49 pickup cause
i'm shy three cards—haw haw aint that a scream & which
one's the piano?" at this gesture, i was relieved to see that he
was human—not a saint mind you—& he wasnt very likable
—but nevertheless—he was human—"that's my piano over
there" i say "the one with the teeth" he immediately rambled
over & he stomped hard across the floor "shhhhhh" i said
"you'll wake up my No Pets Allowed sign" he shrugged his
shoulders & took out a piece of chalk—he began to draw a
picture of his kid on my piano "hey now look—that aint what's
wrong with my piano—i mean now dont take it personally—
it's got nothing to do with you, but my piano is out of tune—
now i dont care how you go about it but fix it—fix it right"
"my kid's gonna be an astronaut" "i should hope so" says me
"& by the way—could you tell me what happened to julius
larosa?" a picture of abraham lincoln falls from the ceiling
"that guy looks like a girl—i saw him on Shindig—he's a fag"
"how wise you are" says i "hurry & fix my piano willya—i
have this geisha girl coming over at midnight & she digs to
jump on it" "my kid's gonna be an astronaut" "c'mon—get
to work—my piano—my piano—c'mon it's out of tune" at
this time, he takes out his tool & starts to tinkle on a few high
notes—"yeah it's out of tune" he says "but it's also 5:30" "so
what?" i say most melancholy "so it's quitting time—that's so
what" "quitting time?" "look buddy i'm a union man . . ."

"look yourself—you ever heard of woody guthrie? he was a union man too & he fought to organize unions like yers & he dug people's needs & do you know what he'd say if he knew that a union man—an honest-to-God union man—was walking out on a poor hard traveling cat's needs—do you know what he'd say d'yuh know what he'd think?" "all right i'm getting sick of you sprouting out names at me—i never hearda no boody guppie & anyway . . ." "woody guthrie not boody guppie!" "yeah well anyway i dont know what he'd say, but tomorrow—now if you want a new man tomorrow—like you can just call up & the union'll send you over one gladly—like i dont care—it's just another job to me buddy—just another job to me" "WHAT! you dont even take any pride in your work? i cant believe this! do you know what boody guppie would do to you man? i mean do you know what he'd think of you?" "i'm going home—i hate it here—it's just not my style at all & anyway i never heard of any coody puppie" "boody guppie, you miserable bosom—not coody puppie & get out of my house—get out this instant!" "my kid's gonna be an astronaut" "i dont care—you cant bribe me—i'm bigger'n that—get out—get out" . . . after he leaves i try playing my piano—no use—it sounds like a bowling alley—i change my No Pets Allowed sign to a Home Sweet Home sign & wonder why i havent any friends . . . it starts to rain—the rain sounds like a pencil sharpener—i look out the window & everybody's walking around without a hat—it is 5:31—time to celebrate someone's birthday—the piano tuner has left his coat hanger behind . . . which really brings me down

> unfortunately my friend, you shall not get
> the information you seek out of me—i, my
> good man, am not a fink! none of my relatives
> are or have been related to benedict arnold
> & i myself despise john wilkes booth—i dont
> smoke marijuana & my family hates italian
> food—none of my friends like black & white
> movies & again myself, i have never seen a
> russian ballet—also, i have started an organization
> to turn in all people that laugh at
> newsreels—so: could you please stop those

letters to the district attorney saying that
i know who murdered my wife—my principles are
at stake here—i would NOT sacrifice them for
one moment of pleasure—i am an honest man
                              yours in growth,
                              ivan the bloodburst

A Blast of Loser Take Nothing

jack of spades—vivaldi of the coin laundry—wearing a hipster's dictionary—we see him brownnosing around the black-
belts & horny racing car drivers—dashing to & fro like a
frightened uncle remus . . . on days that he gets no mail he
rises early, sticks paper up the pay phones & cons the bubble
gum machines . . . "the world owes me a living" he says to
his half-hawaiian cousin, the half-wit, joe the head who is also
planning to marry a folksinger next month—"round & round,
old joe clark" is being recited from the steps of the water &
light building as jack ambles by with a case full of plastic
bubbles—things look well for him: he can imitate cary grant
pretty good. he knows all the facts why mabel from utah
walked out on horace, the lightingman from Theatre Altitude.
he has even stumbled onto a few hairy secrets of mrs. Cunk,
who sells fake blisters at the world's fair—plus being able to
play a few foreign legion songs on the yoyo & always managing
to look like a grapefruit in case of emergency . . . he brags
about his collection of bruises & corks & the fact that he pays
no attention to the business world. he would rather show his
fear of the bomb & say what have you done for freedom than
to praise an escaped mental patient who pisses on the floor of
junior's delicatessen—jack of spades, with his axe, the record
player. with his companion, the menu. & his destination, a
piece of kleenex—never touches the cracks on the sidewalk
—"jack" says his other cousin, Bodeguard, half danish & half
surfer, "how come you always act like Crazy, jackie gleason's
friend? i mean wow! aint there enough sadness in the world?"
jack walks by in a flash—he wears ear plugs—from the steps
of the water & light building, the band, after knocking all the
juice out of their horns, begin to play on my papa . . . jack,
shocked, takes a second look, raises his hand in a nazi salute.

a woodsman, walking by with an axe, drops it. a D.A.R.
woman flies off the handle. looks at jack. says "in some places,
you'd be arrested for obscenity" she doesnt even hear the band
. . . she falls down a sidewalk crack/ the band leader, paying
no attention, does a slight curtsy, sneezes. points his wand at
the classical guitar . . . a street cleaner bumps into jack & says
& i quote "o.k. so i bumped into you. i dont even care. i got
me a little woman at home. i know a good radiator down the
block. man, i aint never gonna starve. would you like to buy
a pail?" jack, amazed, rearranges his collar & heads off to the
bell telephone hour. which is located beyond the next cop car
. . . he passes a hot dog stand. a sauerkraut hits him in the
face . . . the band is playing malaguena salerosa—the D.A.R.
woman pops out of the sidewalk, hears the band, screams,
starts doing the jerk. the street cleaner steps on her . . . jack
hasnt eaten all day. his mouth tastes funny—he has his unpublished novel in his hand—he wants to be a star—but he
gets arrested anyway

> hi y'all. not much new happening.
> sang at the vegetarian convention
> my new song against meat. everybody
> dug it except for the plumbers neath
> the stage. this one little girl,
> fresh out of college & i believe
> president of the Dont Stomp Out the
> Cows division of the society. she tried
> to push me into one of the plumbers.
> starts a little chaos going, but you
> know me, i didnt go for that not one
> little bit. i say "look baby, i'll sing
>
> for you & all that, but just you dont
> go pushing me, y'hear?" i understand
> that theyre not gonna invite me back
> cause they didnt like the way i came on
> to the master of ceremony's old lady, all
> in all, i'm making it tho. got a new song
> against cigarette lighters. this matchbook
> company offered me free matches for the rest
> of my life, plus my picture on all the

matchbooks, but you know me, it'd take a
helluva lot more'n that before i'd sell out—
see you around nomination time

> your fellow rebel
> kid tiger

Brenda Frazer

Brenda Frazer, who published under the name Bonnie Bremser, was born on July 23, 1939, in Washington, D.C. She is best known as the author of an autobiography, Troia: Mexican Memoirs, *published by Tompkins Square Press in 1969. This was a description of the difficult first five years of her marriage to Ray Bremser, whom she followed to Mexico in 1960 when he attempted to evade prison.*

Bonnie Bremser's "Poem to Lee Forest" appeared in 1964 in the little magazine Blue Beat. *Like DiPrima and Jones's* The Floating Bear *and Ed Sanders's* Fuck You: A Magazine of the Arts, Blue Beat *was issued in an 8½-by-11-inch mimeographed format in an edition of about two hundred copies. The magazine was subtitled* A Collection Of Recent Sounds *to emphasize the open poetic form of the contributions from members of "the independent poetry movement in the Lower East Side of New York, who rejected any preconceived notion of what a poem ought to be."*

Brenda Frazer has written that she "met Lee Forest only once, the encounter in [Tompkins] park, and never really spoke with her, perhaps because I am shy, or perhaps because she too was completely encapsulated in her own experience. At that point in my life not talking was probably more meaningful than conversation could have been. I was able to let my imagination answer all the questions. I began creating a mythology for myself which included her and other people I met in the street community. We were all living in various crash pads on the Lower East Side. . . . I think the poem is an attempt to rationalize the fact that I was curious about her and unable to converse. I had been told that she was an interesting person, maybe a writer, but I had only my intuition to substantiate it."

POEM TO LEE FOREST

/a commemoration/or recourse to Elemental Beauty

i had envisioned you
                    before
                    on spontaneous pilgrimages
to Mexico
            quick flight to the border of reality
                        to beyond time journey
                    across
            dispossessed farmlands
deep into mountain passes of darkness and no
                                    actual
                                        habitation
            between live
                    and dead volcanic forms
                                    prehistoric
                    draped in foggy dew
                        and smell of rotting
                                vegetation
                                        (hiss of a
                                        lizard)

to Mexico
            in quest of seclusion
                        where blue ether touches everywhere
                    on
                        the infinite horizon
                                        and
            return
                    was a thought which
                            /alone/
                                followed DEATH

thrown back into
            this seething/
                        formless reality by
            reverberating series of planetary disturbances/////
actual surprise return/ created again to
                        create/again
                                    /and again
                                    (form of the 1st
                                                born child/bathed
                                                in black and white/ new
                                                            moonlite
                                                /blood of a lamb at
                                                PASSOVER)

and encountered your physical
                        shape
                        in the park
                                    beauty moves in
                                        /infinite measure/
                                    among the blades of
                                                grass

strains of
        liquid music
                    waft out from
behind your
        nebulous approach
                        how
                                    double swift
                        rush the
                                    torrential pulses
                                                toward
no resistance
            your
                        lovely and placid countenance

hard
    mortal shell skin burnt brown with
                        many days in the sun
broken teeth no longer chew

much hair as a token
startled your eyes open
>> on me
>>> ringed with salt of
>>>> old tears
>>>>> bleaching away the flesh
>>>>>> around
>>>>>>> them

> how gracefully
>> still
>>> you turn away
>>> too full of
>>>> LOVE
>>>>> to reject

we
> turn to our places
>>> too
>>> suspended in
>>>> this energy of love

>> and feel your white
>>>>> substance sift
>>>> quietly
>>>>> away
>>>>> /as Helen
>>>>>>> from Faust's fevered
>>>>>>>>> hand/

> /you return
>> to weaving/

Ted Joans

Ted Joans was born on a riverboat in Cairo, Illinois, on July 4, 1928, just as the holiday street parade ended. He grew up on the riverboat, where his father was an entertainer, and he told the anthologist Arna Bontemps that when he was twelve his father gave him a trumpet and put him off the boat in Memphis. Joans earned a Bachelor of Fine Arts degree from Indiana University in 1951 and then came east to become a painter in what he called "the Bohemia of Greenwich Village, U.S.A."

In New York the writer Langston Hughes encouraged Joans to read his poems like a jazz soloist, and Allen Ginsberg persuaded him to make his living from his poetry. As Joans described their meeting, "I'm not really a poet except for Allen Ginsberg who grabbed me one November day in 1958 and said he was bored stiff with reading in the coffee shop and why didn't I do it because I was great. He insisted I go with him and try. I tell you I was scared silly at first but it all worked out and now I'm making more money than I ever made from my painting. At least now I have enough coming in steady to keep the family on Staten Island well off. And I still paint too you know in my studio at Astor Place. As for all the show-off stunts well hell that's just part of the job and making a living."

The "show-off stunts" were Joans's "Rent-A-Beatnik" scheme in the late 1950s, when he hired himself out to read poems like "The Sermon" at Beatnik parties given by middle-class New Yorkers. "Afrique Accidentale" is from his later book Afrodisia *(1970). "A Few Blue Words to the Wise" is from* A Black Pow-Wow of Jazz Poems *(1969). Both were written after he left America to travel in Africa and Europe on the "Beat bread" he made from reading his earlier poetry.*

THE SERMON

So you want to be hip little girls
You want to learn to swing
You want to learn to be with it
You want to be able to dig
And take in everything
Yes, dig everything as poet Ginsberg said
Now dig me, pretty babies
I want you chicks to be real hip
I want you babes to learn the truth
I want you chicklets to get up off your lovely behinds
and participate in creative activity
I want you to find yourselves by doing
I want you to live it up
Action!
Jazz action!
If you want to be hip
Dig this sermon:

Get rid of the umbilical cord that your
Dragass prejudiced parents have around your neck
You don't need them to lay their
Antique Anglo-Saxon puritanical philosophy on you now
No, pretty chicks, you're too slick
To dig their late ungreat sick scene
But love 'em for bringing you here
All you need is you—real you—and
People that are hip enough to dig what's happening
So if your neighborhood ain't hip—split
Leave it for swinging surroundings
If you want to be a beautiful non-square angel
Sleep with everybody that's necessary
But don't make it with nobody but
Santa Claus and other cats you dig
Don't ball, pretty baby, without a

Diagram or diaphragm for what you're gonna do
If you want to be a swinger
Drink and get high, but be cool about it
If you want to be popular with the real hipsters
Don't talk so much and please don't argue
If you wish to be a sweet child of god-like intelligence
Dig jazz, support its musicians
Buy or cop dixieland as well as bop
Ball to the music of Jelly Roll Morton
At least once in your life, your grandfathers did
Dance to rhythm and blues, but
Sit down and listen to jazz
If you want to be hip, my cute hens
You must own a copy of HOWL
A copy of ON THE ROAD, and
All the MAD comics series
Read Norman Mailer's WHITE NEGRO, all the
French dada and surrealist literature, and all the
Far out classics, even UNCLE TOM
Visit all museums in the city and
Dig every zoo in the vicinity
You must not let squares bug you
Have missionary eyes for them because
They know not what they do
You must help free
The people behind our cotton curtain as well as
Those unfortunates behind the iron one

You must not live in Greenwich Village and
Pay highass rent to greedy landlords
Either take in one hundred roommates or
Move to the East Village
Wear lipstick for kissing only
Never wear a phony brassiere
Never commit adultery and get caught
Eat as much as your belly can hold
Forget about square diets and dig foods
Wear blue jeans and shorts as an article of clothing
Not a badge of courage
Keep your openings and closings clean

Never lay the claps on any chap (not even a square)
Learn to kiss cats hello as well as good-bye
With your sweet mouths wide open
Go to all parties alone and dance like mad with everyone
Dig all the old movies
Applaud in the wrong places at the new ones
Sit in the coffee houses and beer bars
Spend some money on a far out cat of the fine arts
Walk around home nude more often
Dig yourself in a full view mirror—see the truth
There should be nothing in that mirror
To be ashamed of except old virginity
Don't wait for that mythological right guy to come along
Read Gregory Corso's MARRIAGE
Before ever doing that bit
Dig the Bible, Koran and Torah once each year
Learn everything you can in school then
Come out and use it against them
Visit your psychiatrist as often as you visit your dentist
Once each year—starve those bastards
Love your life and live loving every minute in it

Say yes more often

So if you want to be hip
And you want to learn to swing
And you do want to be able to dig
And take in everything and avoid being a square
And be an in chick with an out crowd
And be hip enough to be cool without being cold
And remain young forever and never grow old
Dig my sermon, pretty babies
Pick up on what I've just said
But don't flip your wig while doing so
Be hip and be happy—and behave
For I dig you all
Sweet, angelic
Chicklets, chicks, and hens

AFRIQUE ACCIDENTALE

To Hoyt Fuller

back on the boat, now bound for Afrique, I float
land in Dakar, destination Timbuctu, not so very far
Dakar/Niger chemin de fer, Tombouctou, très loin from here
Thies, Diourbel, Kaffrine and sad Tambacounda
there's a sign to remember, "Vive Notre Frère Lumumba!"
show aint no Chattanooga Choo Choo
passengers wearing grigris and Western voodoo
Wow! a cheetah chasing the giraffe
going faster than this train, now aint that a laff?
customs here in Senegal Kidira
staying in Kayes Mali tonight, Timbuctu is nearer
fastass cheetahs usually chase gazelles
ah ha! theres a skin for sell
market place jumpin
guess I'll buy sumpin
Hello, little blackdoll can I be your man?
Oh no? You know I'm a jiving Afroamerican
Gotta ketch dis train rite-a-way
passing through the town of Bafoulabé
Fangala, Toukete, Baulouli and Kita
Timbuctu, How far, How far?
It's hot in this train & everybody sweats with me
vultures up there something must be dead, yep phew wee!
road sign reads, "Gue en saison seche"
also limonade, and fried African peche
Wow! my first hot April scene
ant hills, giants that pick you clean
Negala, Kati . . . and now Bamako
accommodations? in the capital? why no!
Russians, Chinese Reds, and some Poles
Karl Marx sent 'em here, sun bakes their souls
air-conditioned U.S. Embassy
The big white country being "real nice" to me?
visit chamber of commerce for map
buying African art, but no tourist crap
studying map with Frenchman laying out our plans
he's the guide and chauffeur, works for Trans Africane

week in Bamako, up the river by canoe and motor pirogue we go
women washing bright clothes
my how their nude bodies glows
River Niger like the Mississippi
dig that broad, show is hippy!
Koulikore first stop changing to paddlewheel slow and hot
sleep on the riverboat, just like U.S.A. South
just mosquitoes biting everywhere, even inside my mouth
roasted goat with French imported cuisine
I'm going to Tombouctou, Je suis king & vous êtes queen!
wasn't that lion drinking over there?
isn't that a vulture hoisting a snake in the air?
paddlewheeling steamboat to Timbuktu
but first we stop off, in the hot town of Segou
Bambara, Bozo people both give me masks
perhaps my ancestors lived here in the past
sleeping in mud hut Hollywood style
digging the true sound, wow they're wild
balling a chicklet on my second night here
smoking gangha with the chief, drinking later cold beer
morning sunrise tearful goodbyes
up the Niger river aint no millstream
hippos, crocodiles and many reptilian dream
Niger river wide but not always so deep
Malinké children singing me to sleep
endless sahel vistas running from riverbanks
only inhabited by the Peuls, whose goats smell so rank
big surreal trees grow upside down
Baobabs they're called some 40 feet around
Timbucktwo three days, they say
Tell the Tuaregs I'm on my way
Ké-Macina, it's evening wow, thirsty I am
one dollar for beer? I don't give a damn!
that guy there looks like Humphrey Bogart
pointing is a bad omen in Africa, so now the boat won't start
Man, I show am hot and still real thirsty
Lord wont that sun of yours show a little cooler mercy
Moslems saying their prayers, facing eastward they try
ostriches in the distant, magnificently strutting by
yonder is a wild buck and what kinda bugs are they?

Timbuktou, when I get there, gosh I'm gonna stay
Now to close my eyes for a peaceful night of sleep
I count African rhinos not American sheep
Good morning, Mopti, Niger river Venice town
where the Bani river runs into the Niger brown
dog-gone-it, a Dogon! from Bandiagara I bet
down there by the riverside, bathing, all wet
animism and Islam, even Christianity thrown in
that cat's really covered (like life insurance) when death drops in
goodby Mopti, river's getting rough
got a bit of dysentery, life can be tough
taking medical tablets, big ugly pills
daily doses of malaria drugs to drive away the chills
sun bright in the morning, so's my health
when body's O.K., that is true wealth
ten thousand crocodiles waiting for Godot?
all playing it cool? or asleep? you'd never live to know
What a beautiful leopard skin, that Senufo wants to sell
if the fuzz catches him poaching, he'll be put in jail
Ambolore-Youvarou close by Lake Debo
we change from boat to Land Rover, "safari car, you know"
dustheat, dysentery and my eternal insatiable thirst
yet its not Sahara, they tell me it would be worst
so bounce, bruise and bump along we drive
Tombouctou I hope I reach it alive
Look, at that snake crossing the road!
we run it down with our heavy load
water taste terrible, hot and chloride
have to drink sumpin, burning up inside
dry dusty savannah, show aint like my home Indiana
thorny bushes and flattop trees
now and then in the shade . . . 110 degrees
aint no body living way out here
Man, if I wouldn't pay two dollars for a beer
next town reminds me of Horace Silver's Funky band
'cause it has a gassy name, like Niafounke, man!
I lay in this bed, I'll stay in this bed
until someone pours a gallon of cold water on my head
no mosquitoes tonight, thanks to the net
yet it's still hot, sleeping gear's sweaty wet

up in the morning, out by the car
ride hard, on the range all day
I'm a lucky s.o.b. to get this far
Timbukktuu, hallelujah, I'm on my way
road pretty good as far as piste go
twenty foot ant hill, how those things do grow
we cross the river by ferry car almost too heavy to carry
Timbocktoo, just so many hours ahead
Timbucktoo, where the canoe and the camel wed
another Sudanese village, people with a smile
calabashes of goat's milk, ugh it's rank and wild
driving getting difficult and road's really rougher
thick dust in your throats & your behinds getting tougher
as we crush another snake, misfortune drops right in
the Land Rover's axle broke as tho made of tin
pile out into the blazing sun
put on our packs but have to shoulder NO GUNS!
hire few porters for trip to Kabara
we should arrive there sometime tomorrow
single file, S.V.P., and please do watch your step!
"Safari to Timbuctoo," to hear it gives me pep
damn this pack is heavy, why'd I bring all this jive
well everything I brought is essential, helps keep me alive
the elegant porters always sing as they walk
we do nothing but complain & talk, talk, talk
Kabara, at last, just before evening sun goes down
take a bath, eat and drink, then relax in this town
as I lay here in a tent & write as I think
Greenwich Village is a long way off, with its coldwater flat & sink
I have traveled a long long way on the Beat bread I made
now I'm deep in the heart of Africa, the only Afroamerican spade
TOMBOUCTOU ....tomorrow, visions in my head
TIMBUKTU ....tomorrow, unless I wake up dead
TIMBUCTOO ....tomorrow, where no beatniks ever been
TIMBUQTEW ....tomorrow, gonna make my own scene
TIMBOEKTOE ....tomorrow, thank Allah & all the rest
TIMBUCKTO ....tomorrow, overjoyed I must confess

        so now lay me down to sleep
        to count black rhinos, not white sheep

Timbukto, Timbucktoo, Thymbaktou!
I do dig you!
Timbuctu, Tombouctou
I finally made you
Timbuctoo
Yeah!!

A FEW BLUE WORDS TO THE WISE

to SHOUT / RAVE / RANT / and RAGE   is being militant
                                        as hell but not very brave
   /Especially when you're before an all Black audience)

to SCREAM / SNEER / BELLOW / and even fart   is being
                                        excited/worked-up but
      all that won't stop a Honky heart

to curse / and call him names (all true) is not really bad   Yet
                                        it makes our black
         poetry look sad (You know, like we aint got nothing better to
                                        poet about)

Then: or thus:
We must write poems black brothers about our own black
                                        relations
We must fall in love and glorify our beautiful black nation
We must create black images   give the world
      a black education

Tuli Kupferberg

Tuli Kupferberg was born on September 28, 1923, in New York. He graduated cum laude from Brooklyn College in 1944 and began his more than thirty years as a Greenwich Village publisher, poet, and anti-war activist with the magazine Birth *in 1958, featuring the work of Allen Ginsberg, Diane DiPrima, LeRoi Jones, Ted Joans, and others in the Beat circle.*

Birth *ran for three issues, most notably featuring Kupferberg's "Notes Toward a Theory of Bohemianism," which he expanded in 1961 in his book* Beatniks; or, The War Against the Beats, *published by Birth Press. There he argued that after World War II Americans suffered from a fear of a nuclear holocaust and a breakdown of traditional beliefs, resulting in what he described as "panic, confusion, failure of nerve and . . . the war against the Beatniks." Kupferberg saw the Beats used as scapegoats, but he concluded optimistically by asserting, "Listen Square . . . You may kill the Beatnik but you will not kill the Beatnik in yourself."*

In 1964 Kupferberg began performing and recording with Ed Sanders and Ken Weaver in the group called The Fugs that soon attracted a following nationwide with satirical songs like "Slum Goddess of the Lower East Side" and "Kill for Peace," a protest song against America's participation in the war in Vietnam. Kupferberg's anti-war masterpiece was 1001 Ways to Beat the Draft *(1966), in collaboration with his friend Robert Bashlow. It was originally published as a pictorial collage designed by Kupferberg to illustrate his pacifist convictions. All income from the sale of this work has been donated to the peace movement.*

from 1001 WAYS TO BEAT THE DRAFT

1. Grope J. Edgar Hoover in the silent halls of Congress.
2. Get thee to a nunnery.
3. Fly to the moon and refuse to come home.
4. Die.
5. Become Secretary of Defense.
6. Become Secretary of State.
7. Become Secretary of Health, Education and Welfare.
8. Show a li'l tit.
9. Castrate yourself.
10. Invent a time machine and go back to the 19th century.
11. Start to menstruate. (Better red than dead.)
12. Attempt to overthrow the Government of the United States by force and violence.
13. Advocate sexual freedom for children.
14. Shoot up for a day.
15. Refuse to speak to them at all.
16. Enroll at the Jefferson School of Social Science.
17. Replace your feet with wheels.
18. Rent a motel room with a ewe.
19. Rent a motel room with a ram.
20. Say you're crazy.
21. Say they're crazy.
22. Get muscular dystrophy when you're a kid.
23. Marry J. Edgar Hoover.
24. Take up residence in Albania.

> "We like 'em young,"
> says an Army major in Vietnam
> "The young ones
> take more chances."

25. Stretch yourself on a rack so that you become over 6½ feet tall.
26. Marry your mother.
27. Marry your father.
28. Blow up the Statue of Liberty.
29. Marry your sister.
30. Marry your brother.
31. Marry your daughter.
32. Join the Abraham Lincoln Brigade.
33. Marry your son.
34. Marry Lassie.
35. Marry President Johnson.
36. Marry Mao Tse-tung.
37. Proclaim that Mao Tse-tung is the Living God.
38. Proclaim that *you* are the Living God.
39. Stamp your foot in the earth like Rumpelstiltskin and refuse to eat until our boys return from Viet Nam.
40. Get elected Pope.
41. Get elected to the Supreme Soviet.
42. Get lost.
43. Shoot A for one month.
44. Grow seven toes on your head.
45. Commit an unnatural act with Walter Jenkins.
46. Make the world go away.

47. Wear pants made of jello.
48. Say you are a wounded veteran of the *lutte des classes.*
49. Solder your eyelids shut.
50. Ride naked through the streets on a white horse.
51. Declare war on Germany.
52. Tell the draft board that you will send your mother to fight in Viet Nam in your place.
53. Study Selective Service reports on malingering and military medicine, and/or military psychiatry texts or journal articles on the same subject, and use the clever methods they describe.
54. Organize your own army and advance on Washington.
55. Tell the psychiatrist that if he doesn't let you into the Army you'll kill him.
56. Turn yellow.
57. Infiltrate your local board.
58. Don't agree to anything.
59. Contract Addison's disease.
60. Contract Parkinson's disease.
61. Contract Bright's disease.
62. Contract Hodgkin's disease.

The Nineteenth Lesson

THE FIRST OF MAY.

It is a warm spring morning—the morning of the First of May. Banners are flying over the Red Square in Moscow. Comrade Stalin, the leader and teacher of the workers of the world, is standing on the tribune.

The bands are playing joyfully. The military parade begins. The square is covered with tanks and guns and soldiers. Silver airplanes are flying in the sky.

The parade is over, and the demonstration begins. Comrade Stalin raises his hand to greet the columns of happy Soviet citizens. "Long Live the First of May!" is written in golden letters on the banners. And over the columns of workers we can see the portraits of Marx and Engels, Lenin and Stalin.

How happy people are to march to the tribune, singing merry songs and greeting their beloved leader!

(After E. Ilyina.)

Could Win in a Flash, U.S. Air Chief Says

63. Contract Cushing's disease.
64. Contract Fröhlich's syndrome.
65. Announce that you have become the bridegroom of the Virgin Mary.
66. Announce that you have become the bridegroom of Jesus Christ.
67. Get your friends to crucify you.
68. Counterfeit money and omit the motto *In God We Trust.*
69. Become a publisher of smut and filth.
70. Become the publisher of the Little Mao Tse-tung Library.
71. Prove that Brezhnev is a Trotskyite wrecker.
72. Burn down the building located at 39 Whitehall Street.
73. . . . 450 Golden Gate Ave.
74. . . . 536 South Clark Street.
75. . . . 55 Tremont Street.
76. . . . 916 G Street NW.
77. Burn down the Pentagon.
78. Burn baby burn.
79. Write a best-selling novel which portrays the CIA as incompetent.
80. Catch St. Anthony's fire.
81. Say you'd be happy to serve because it'll be easier to kill

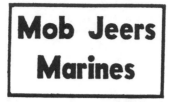

the fucken Americans who are interfering with the freedom of Viet Nam.

82. Recite the Pledge of Allegiance 2400 times a day.
83. Cut off your ears. In ancient times no animal was sacrificed unless it was a perfect specimen.
84. Cut off your left ear and send it to the draft board.
85. Grow a tail.
86. Learn to talk with your anus.
87. Become a graduate student in a subject vital to the national security, such as the epistemology of phenomenological methodology. Achieve your degree only after fifteen years of 2-S.
88. Grow old fast, or
89. When you reach the age of 17 don't get any older.
90. Drink an elixir that will cause you to shrink to a height of 2 feet 3 inches.
91. Buy a slave and send him in your place.
92. Take your girlfriend with you when you get called and insist that you will not serve unless you can sleep with her at night.
93. Take your boyfriend with you when you get called and insist that you will not serve unless you can sleep with him at night.
94. Take your mother with you when you get called and insist you will not serve unless you can sleep with *her* at night.
95. Take your chihuahua with you when you get called and insist you will not serve unless you can sleep with *it* at night.
96. Wet your bed.
97. When the doctor tells you to spread your cheeks, let him see the firecracker you have planted there beforehand.
98. Handcuff yourself to Lenin's tomb.

*"We like 'em young," says an Army major in
Vietnam. "The young ones take more chances."*

99. Handcuff yourself to Nicholas Katzenbach and shout: "We shall not be moved!"
100. Travel to Havana.
101. Grow a long straggly black beard with maggots crawling all over it.
102. Travel to Hanoi.
103. Travel to Pyongyang.
104. Travel to Peking.
105. Travel to Washington and tell them you intend to travel to one or more of the above.
106. Publish a satirical pamphlet purporting to advise young men how to beat the draft.
107. Tell the psychiatrist that you are a closet queen.
108. Tell the security officer that you are a brother of Allen Ginsberg.
109. Tell the security officer that you are a brother of Ralph Ginzburg.
110. Hand out copies of this book at the induction center. When they tell you you cannot do this, ask if it's all right if you sell them.
111. Make sure that by one method or another you get to see the psychiatrist. Do not let them rush you through without your chance. If necessary you should faint, scream, or start crying.
112. Give the psychiatrist your standard three-minute lecture in favor of bisexuality, being sure to mention again and again that animals do it.
113. Tell them that you will leap into your grave laughing.
114. Run for the House of Representatives on the platform that Red China should be invited to send its surplus population to colonize New York and Arizona.
115. Commence psychotherapy with Dr. Robert Soblen.
116. Ask Gus Hall to go down to the induction center for you the day you are called.
117. Write a letter to the New York *Daily News* stating that the Viet Cong are nothing more than peace-loving agrarian reformers.

118. Use an American flag for a breechclout.
119. Contract tertiary syphilis.
120. Steal a laser and fight it out with the CIA.
121. Develop bleeding stigmata.
122. Cop out.
123. Conspire with a known homosexual in the Soviet embassy in Ankara.
124. Conspire with a known heterosexual in the U.S. embassy in Ankara.
125. Become chairman of the Committee to Legalize Marijuana.
126. Develop an otherworldly metaphysical system and live by its precepts.
127. Cut off your head.
128. Cut off your sergeant's head. (NAPA)*
129. Walk into the induction center carrying an octopus.

---

* Not a pacifist act.

Jack Micheline

Jack Micheline was born in the Bronx on November 6, 1929, as Harvey Martin Silver. After quarreling with his father, he changed his first name to "Jack" in honor of the socialist writer Jack London, and created "Micheline" by adding an "e" to the maiden name of his mother, Helen Michelin. Informally educated, he identified closely with the tradition of American vagabond poets like Vachel Lindsay and Maxwell Bodenheim, and he moved to Greenwich Village in the 1950s to find an outlet for his poetry.

The biographer Gerard Nicosia has told how Micheline showed a collection of his work in 1957 to Rainy Cass, who ran Troubadour Press, which published a jazz and poetry magazine called Climax. *Cass agreed to bring out a book if Micheline would stagger the lines of each poem to make his verse look more unconventional, and if he would get a "famous person" to write the introduction. Jack Kerouac was sharing an apartment in the building where Micheline was living. Kerouac liked Micheline's work and did him the favor, referring to him as "Doctor Johnson Zen Master Magee of Innisfree," punning on the title of Yeats's famous poem and "in us free," meaning that Micheline was free inside of himself.*

Proclaiming himself unaffiliated with any group, including the Beats—whom he characterized as a product of the media's hustle—Micheline appeared frequently with Beat writers at poetry readings. His work is meant to be read aloud, in the tradition of Beat poetry. "Poet of the Streets" is from North of Manhattan: Collected Poems, Ballads and Songs 1954–1975.

POET OF THE STREETS

I walk east of Bleecker
the sky is blue
on this Sunday evening

there is something deeper than the earth
there is something deeper than the stone cities
there is something deeper than our existence
than all the robes of power

power and the night bleeding gutters with crutches
power and the night and the neon vibrating
the night and thirty moons and sharpies
the night and the railroad yards gleaming
the night and the sky
the night and billboards and darkness

across a nation skeletons and machinery
jaundice, joints and lips of connivers
burnt Christmas trees
jazz horns and drummers

above concrete
above whimpering voices
above calculators
riders with tokens in their hands
riders to the sea

a nation of cowards
cowards wrapped in academic cloth

over all in darkness
over all who live in deserts
over all shells covering
over all that are wasted

burying all in nothingness
burying all that is soul
burying all with layers of armour

burying herds with still voices
burying all in the nowhere of silence

herring and fish in cans
turkey and chicken in cans
humans in cells of unknowing
there is more to life than the lights of savage civilizations
there is more to life than all the words spoken
there is more to life than the eye can see

I see the sun of angels
hemp and sugar and wheat
blood and sinew within the flesh
ticker tapes, grey hair, jowls on faces
dollars and gods and people sold and traded

people dying for nothing
people selling their minds and bodies
people without courage
people with no teeth in drug stores

death loaded with goods
givers of death and more death
cranes and deep hookers
cutting shears for the young
newspapers stunting the mind
dollars the spoiler of ships of bananas

I see your faces as I stroll through the cities
the wind touching the faces of whores
the vision of poets encompassing all
songs of children outside the brick houses

there is nothing deeper than life and the livers of life
mankind raped in the bank vaults of steel
dead soldiers, battlefields surrounded by iron and ironies

a million lost sunsets
a poet unconquered with the legacy of Whitman and Lorca
a poet unconquered by stone, by glass, by greed, by madness

the lights blaze on in the night
lights and the cold wind
visions above all death
cows milked dry, golden crosses
the sky blazing with miracles

a poet walks in the cold wind
his head raised humble and unafraid
death around him filled with waste and banners
death all around him
walking alone with birds above the canoe shaped moons
sounds are heard and the sky glows in darkness
I am not afraid.

January 31, 1960   This poem turned the tide of my death,
East Bleecker   written on First Avenue off the Bowery
                           in an alley of great souls.

Frank O'Hara

Frank O'Hara was born on June 27, 1926, in Baltimore, Maryland, and died on July 25, 1966, after being run over by a beach-buggy on Fire Island. As an undergraduate at Harvard, he became friends with John Ashbery and Kenneth Koch. The three later became the nucleus of what Donald Allen called the New York School of poetry.

O'Hara worked as an associate curator at the Museum of Modern Art, and while he was close to the Beat writers in New York City, he was not actually part of their movement. As the critic Bill Berkson said, "O'Hara's most obvious distinction from the Beat aesthetic was a socioeconomic one. While espousing much the same poetic tradition and many similar personal attitudes, O'Hara went neither 'on the road' nor, indeed, on any programmatic quest; he was skeptical of almost all the publicized Beat paraphernalia—psychedelics, jazz, pronouncements on prosody, activist politics, occult or formal religious studies."

But O'Hara was sympathetic to the work and interests of many Beat writers, and he referred to them in several of his elegant, lively poems. In "Les Luths" he speculated on what Gary Snyder was reading in Kyoto and on the worth of John Wieners's The Hotel Wentley Poems. *In "Post the Lake Poets Ballad" he humorously compared the degree of self-pity in his poetry with what he felt was Allen Ginsberg's moral self-righteousness. In "Personal Poem" he described lunching with LeRoi Jones and gossiping about various literary matters. And in "The Day Lady Died," he eloquently listed what he was*

doing in Manhattan on the Friday in July 1959 just before he
learned in the afternoon newspaper about the death of the great
jazz singer Billie Holiday.

LES LUTHS

Ah nuts! It's boring reading French newspapers
in New York as if I were a Colonial waiting for my gin
somewhere beyond this roof a jet is making a sketch of the sky
where is Gary Snyder I wonder if he's reading under a dwarf pine
stretched out so his book and his head fit under the lowest branch
while the sun of the Orient rolls calmly not getting through to him
not caring particularly because the light in Japan respects poets

while in Paris Monsieur Martory and his brother Jean the poet
are reading a piece by Matthieu Galey and preparing to send a *pneu*
everybody here is running around after dull pleasantries and
wondering if *The Hotel Wentley Poems* is as great as I say it is
and I am feeling particularly testy at being separated from
the one I love by the most dreary of practical exigencies money
when I want only to lean on my elbow and stare into space feeling
the one warm beautiful thing in the world breathing upon my right rib

what are lutes they make ugly twangs and rest on knees in cafés
I want to hear only your light voice running on about Florida
as we pass the changing traffic light and buy grapes for wherever
we will end up praising the mattressless sleigh-bed and the
Mexican egg and the clock that will not make me know
    how to leave you

POST THE LAKE POETS
BALLAD

Moving slowly sweating a lot
I am pushed by a gentle breeze
outside the Paradise Bar on
    St. Mark's Place and I breathe

and bourbon with Joe he says
did you see a letter from Larry
in the mailbox what a shame I didn't
     I wonder what it says

and then we eat and go to
The Horse Riders and my bum aches
from the hard seats and boredom
     is hard too we don't go

to the Cedar it's so hot out
and I read the letter which says
in your poems your gorgeous self-pity
     how do you like that

that is odd I think of myself
as a cheerful type who pretends to
be hurt to get a little depth into
     things that interest me

and I've even given that up
lately with the stream of events
going so fast and the movingly
     alternating with the amusingly

the depth all in the ocean
although I'm different in the winter
of course even this is a complaint
     but I'm happy anyhow

no more self-pity than Gertrude
Stein before Lucey Church or Savonarola
in the pulpit Allen Ginsberg at the
     Soviet Exposition am I Joe

PERSONAL POEM

Now when I walk around at lunchtime
I have only two charms in my pocket

an old Roman coin Mike Kanemitsu gave me
and a bolt-head that broke off a packing case
when I was in Madrid the others never
brought me too much luck though they did
help keep me in New York against coercion
but now I'm happy for a time and interested

I walk through the luminous humidity
passing the House of Seagram with its wet
and its loungers and the construction to
the left that closed the sidewalk if
I ever get to be a construction worker
I'd like to have a silver hat please
and get to Moriarty's where I wait for
LeRoi and hear who wants to be a mover and
shaker the last five years my batting average
is .016 that's that, and LeRoi comes in
and tells me Miles Davis was clubbed 12
times last night outside BIRDLAND by a cop
a lady asks us for a nickel for a terrible
disease but we don't give her one we
don't like terrible diseases, then

we go eat some fish and some ale it's
cool but crowded we don't like Lionel Trilling
we decide, we like Don Allen we don't like
Henry James so much we like Herman Melville
we don't want to be in the poets' walk in
San Francisco even we just want to be rich
and walk on girders in our silver hats
I wonder if one person out of the 8,000,000 is
thinking of me as I shake hands with LeRoi
and buy a strap for my wristwatch and go
back to work happy at the thought possibly so

THE DAY LADY DIED

It is 12:20 in New York a Friday
three days after Bastille day, yes

it is 1959 and I go get a shoeshine
because I will get off the 4:19 in Easthampton
at 7:15 and then go straight to dinner
and I don't know the people who will feed me

I walk up the muggy street beginning to sun
and have a hamburger and a malted and buy
an ugly NEW WORLD WRITING to see what the poets
in Ghana are doing these days
                        I go on to the bank
and Miss Stillwagon (first name Linda I once heard)
doesn't even look up my balance for once in her life
and in the GOLDEN GRIFFIN I get a little Verlaine
for Patsy with drawings by Bonnard although I do
think of Hesiod, trans. Richmond Lattimore or
Brendan Behan's new play or *Le Balcon* or *Les Nègres*
of Genet, but I don't, I stick with Verlaine
after practically going to sleep with quandariness

and for Mike I just stroll into the PARK LANE
Liquor Store and ask for a bottle of Strega and
then I go back where I came from to 6th Avenue
and the tobacconist in the Ziegfeld Theatre and
casually ask for a carton of Gauloises and a carton
of Picayunes, and a NEW YORK POST with her face on it

and I am sweating a lot by now and thinking of
leaning on the john door in the 5 SPOT
while she whispered a song along the keyboard
to Mal Waldron and everyone and I stopped breathing

Peter Orlovsky

Peter Orlovsky was born on July 8, 1933, in the Lower East Side, New York City, the son of a Russian White Army soldier who had emigrated to America the previous decade. Growing up in poverty, Orlovsky dropped out of high school in his senior year and was drafted into the United States Army in 1953 during the Korean War. After telling a lieutenant that "an army is an army against love," he was sent to work as a medic in a San Francisco hospital for the duration of the war.

The following year he met the painter Robert LaVigne in San Francisco. LaVigne introduced him to Allen Ginsberg. Ginsberg fell in love with Orlovsky and they stayed together in an open marriage for the next thirty years.

Encouraged by Ginsberg, Orlovsky wrote occasional poetry by his own "spontaneous prose" method, which he described as "Just follow the mind out like this, when you have a hunch working in your mind or see a picture that has already expressed its self in the mind, then let that come out and not some other fast thought or idea that just jumped into the main one—but just write out what you feel the most at one moment and you can't go wrong for you can just write out forever—the pen knows its job—"

Traveling with Ginsberg in India in 1961, Orlovsky tried to help a beggar woman dying of leprosy on the streets of Benares. His poem "Lepers Cry" was included in his collection Clean Asshole Poems & Smiling Vegetable Songs, *number 37 in the City Lights Pocket Poets Series (1978).*

LEPERS CRY

When in Banaras
India in 1961 Summer I was
flooded on my morphine mattress.
So a bit shyly fitting for me to
go see how the poor sick
week thin no legs no hands no
fingers, only stubbs of joints
with the finger bones pokeing thru.
A bit like pigs feet in clean store jars.
Only these were the Lowest of
the Low of India the Leppers
or a fraction of the fractions
in this one small Lane near

Dasadsumad Ghat—this, maybe
32 yr old woman rapped in pure dirt
Burlap string strip around waist—whear
the Tips of her Toes should be were
her bone Toe stubs protruding out
still infessted with active
Leprocy growing by eating
away the flesh that surrounds
her extremites—she
could only crall on her rear
she can not walk and to
eat she has to use her rotten
sore Lepper fingers—

I gave some helpfull Indian soul
to go get her a new fresh Clean
sarrie a few ruppies
and began to help her change
her apparel when there to
my Eyes on her Left behind
I saw a 4 inch ring of open—
saw infection full of magots
cralling and happiley alive—I
was so supprised I dident know

what to do for a second—then
I hide tailed it to a doctor
in his office a bit across the street

asking him what to do
No I asked him to come down and examin
this street Lepper & that I would pay
him good for his expert servace—
He said he had to stay in his office
and told me to get some
Hydrogen Peroxide—cotton and
I think some sulpher ointment
to first clean out the infection
& kill the maybe, 30 or 50 maggots
in her side above the thigh—you
know that big round mussle
that is divided into two sphears.

Well on her Left sphear (ass)
played these maggots and as I
poured the Hydrogen Peroxide—I had to
turn her over on her side—the
maggots became more alive and
active & danced into the air
above her side more. It was
difficult to get all the maggots out
so after a few
pourings and cotton cleanings I
covered it with sulpher ointment of
I dont quite remember because its
been 10 years ago and I have

been so scattered fingers to write
This real sad tail—which is
another discusting disease in its self,
and Toped it with 5 × 5 inch compress pads—
and had some one bring her some
food and a clean mat for her to
sit on—for all this took place
in the poor beggers sick alley decked
with watery shit plops and I

finally got into the swing of
cleaning it up with my hands—that
the first problem was to clean up
all this free Floating Shit splashings all about

(I even went to Water Pipe Commissioner local office
to see if they would install a water forcet at
this disentary dispensing spot, but no luck.)
and it was on the next day I saw
her again and this Time I looked
on her right side behind and there
was another maggot soupe dish
big and eaten down
to her thigh bone I saw the
muscles getting eaten & sucked thin
jucey human sore magget puss—
have you ever smelt magot
puss on the body of a poor Human
Being—dont bother—it may make
you vommit—keep away—
Let the Prows attend the Nose.

I just dident expect to see the same
horrible infested condition on the
exact opposite side of her body—
I was now more suprissed and
taken aback—and now I Looked
into her eyes & she had very
dark olive calm eyes peasefull sweet sad
eyes that seemed to tell me
I am okay—its nice of you
to have some food brought to me
and I want to thank you
but I dont know yr Language
so I say silently with my

eyes—I gave her friends
food money for a varried diet
for a week & told them to get
her yougart & they got some
& spoon fed her—

and then I disappeared for a week
or a month and I saw her
again—in a bigger Square—up
above Dasadsumed Ghat—she—I
saw her from a distance of about
70 feet—(or someone else looking like her)
she was on her back—
in rigamaroartus I could Tell
by the ways her knees

& arms were sticking up into the
air—it looked like—I forgot her
name—I think I asked
or I forgot—I steared away
I could see the problem of
Burreying her or Burning her at
the Funeral Pire at Manikarneka Ghat—
it was—I figured
the proper Government Banaras workers job
would come and gather her up—
I was sad to see her end this way,
I dident think she would go so soon.
what fooled me was her calm eyes,

living so peasefulley
above her hip woe—

her hip infection
and then I thought that maybe me
by killing the maggots
it opened the Blood Veins
or something to cause premature
death—its all so sad—and
now to this day I feel all
the more Lazzey & Dumb
and all the more domb & Lazzey
Lazzey Bastard of a selfish
Human Creap Sleep

Halloween Night 1971

Ed Sanders

Ed Sanders was born on August 17, 1939, in Kansas City, Missouri. After reading On the Road *and "Howl," he dropped out of the University of Missouri and hitchhiked to New York to join the Beat Generation. In 1963 he completed his undergraduate degree in Greek at New York University, leaving it in 1961 and 1962 to participate in a San Francisco–to–Moscow Walk for Peace where he walked a 650-mile stretch between Ohio and New York. He also took part in two nonviolent demonstrations at the nuclear submarine base in New London, Connecticut, and an eight-week Walk for Peace from Nashville to Washington, D.C. In 1962 Sanders opened his Peace Eye Bookstore on East Tenth Street in the East Village above a kosher butcher store and began publishing the journal* Fuck You: A Magazine of the Arts.*

"The Cutting Prow" was written for Henri Matisse. Sanders imagined how the French painter at the end of his life "was confined to a wheelchair and gripped with timor mortis. *From his bed at night he'd draw on the ceiling with a long stick with crayon attached. Yet somehow he adjusted his creativity, finding a new mix of the muses, so that from the spring of 1952 through the spring of 1953, in his final creative months, he was able to produce some of the finest art of the century, a group of wall-sized works of painted paper cutouts. . . . He thought he could scissor the essence of a thing, its 'sign' as he termed it, as if he had vision in Plato's world of Forms."*

Poem from Jail, *Sanders's first published book in 1963, was written on "cigarette pack guts" while he was imprisoned in the*

*Montville State Jail in Connecticut as a "witness for peace." It
was smuggled out of the prison in the sole of his shoe.*

from POEM FROM JAIL

> Montville State Jail
> Uncasville, Connecticut
> August 8–24, 1961
> having attempted to board the
> Polaris-missile submarine
> the *Ethan Allen*, as a witness for peace

I

Redeem Zion!
Stomp up over
the Mountain!

To live as "beatific
Spirits welded
            together,"
To live with
        a fierce pacifism,
To love in haste,
as a beetle
entering bark,

To dance with
flaming mane,

All these, a man,
I, steaming, proud,
have sought
as a harlot
her jewels & paint,
as belly seeks out
belly;

And we have
demanded that

they ban the bomb,
mouth of death
convulsing upon the earth,
and the bomb gores

the guts of earth
like a split nail
in a foot fetish,
and the salt domes
rumble
as the arse
of a politician,
and Nevada
is a kangaroo
with its pouch
chopped open
by the A.E.C.

And at my ear
was the whirr
of wings,
"red wing,
 black wing,
 black wing
      shot with crimson,"
 and the Bird Flock
 stared to my eye,
 and always the Birds
 flap overhead
      shrieking
      like a "berserk
      tobacco auction":
Pains! Neverbirth! Dieness!

And we have
seen the failure
of Stassen
& the Teller
intervention
& Radford
in there wailing,

also,
for Death.

  And Madame
Chiang Kai-shek
too old now
to fuck for the
            China Lobby,

And we have learned
the Hidden History
of the Korean War,
and MacArthur
who retreated
                before
nonexistent
Chinese Hordes,

And we have seen denied
Mao's creation,
And we have denied
Van Gogh's Crow
shrieking on the
            horizon,
and Rouault's Jesus.
Chant   Chant
        O American!
lift up the Stele
            anti   bomb;
O American
        is there
an Eagle of Pacifism?
            Is there
a bevy of symbolic
        Birds?

The Rot Bird,
        The Claw Hawk,
The Sexy Dove,
        The Cormorant

of Oceanus,
The Sea Crow
of bloody claws,

Pigeon of the dance
of the belly,

Birds
Birds
Shrieks and furry assemblage
Birds
Birds
Blurred birds in flight
Birds
Birds
da Vinci's tail feathers,
Dream of Youth
Birds
Birds
Ginsberg's birds Ginsberg's
sacred scroll to Naomi,
Birds of the fluttering eyes,
Birds never asleep,
diaphanous eyelids.

Between the
Bevy of Birds
& the Sexy Lamb
there is nothing Else.

The Father negative
The Son negative
The Holy Ghost negative.

Aphrodite
Kallipugos
remains, the
hieroglyphs remain,
"Trees die

but the Dream
remains,"
Van Gogh & Ginsberg,
The Burning Bush,
The Trembling Flank,
    All remain.
Anubis & the
        power of Amulets,
The Beetle of Endlessness,
        they remain.
My flesh abides.
My electrical meat
        chatters for
a wink of eternity
between dark cunt
        and the grave.

II

Trembling   Trembling
murderous flank
of Now,

Napoleon
        is Now
& was
    & shall,
Napoleon
  stomping all
  over Europe; &
Europa has an
older meaning,
        Europa fucked
        for centuries
        by the Bull of Zeus;
        &
        Pasiphaë
        Pasiphaë, also,
        what contortions
        had you

to writhe thru
to receive
the prick
of the Bull!
you O Pasiphaë
inside the
sacred cow-skin
of Crete,
as the long tool
of the Bull arched
and gored its way
to your snatch,
O Pasiphaë
what thrill
& thunder
you felt,
& what nutty
offspring,
ah the Karma
of that fuck;
"No man who has spent
a month in the death cells
believes in capital punishment

No man who has spent
a month in the death cells
believes in cages for beasts"

No man.
　　　fucking in the sheaves,
　　　leaping in the aether,
　　　lusting for the sun,
　　　I, a man, my skull
　　　lined with bird-roosts,
　　　a man, disjunctive
　　　coalescence of thoughts,
　　　trembly, bristling,
　　　tense beyond belief,
　　　wandering, relating

thing to thing,
balling the All,

hands twisting in
                Moistness,
heart bubbling in

                Vasthood,
eyes boucing to th'
                Glaze,
brain pucking in th'
                Word-steam,
legs sucked in to
                Oceanus.

Anubis grins slyly
at the dock,
O American,
O Traveler.
The Sun boat
enters the Vastness,
Anubis stomps
with the Sun shafts,
& the man awaits,
the sun, the
eye of the
Trembling Lamb.
Move onward
O Traveler
of thick sandals
& matted hair,
flouting your
choice patterns,
for you shall
enter the
Mountain,
& the warmth
of the living
darkness, the
warmth as the warmth

between bellies,
& the closeness
as the closeness
                there.
Carve a staff
traveler, carve
it with the days,
notch it with
the ways and paths,
in the journey,
under the corn furrow,
where Persephone
is ravished by
her gloomy lover,
Dis, Pluto,
& Persephone is Darkness
also;

You shall Enter,
Traveler,
   in the myriad
directions of the
                prepositions,

            & bounce in
            & bounce over
The Trembling Flank

            & enter in
            & enter over
The Sexy Lamb
            & shriek in
            & shriek over
The Sun-shafts
            and Sun-barge.

THE CUTTING PROW

FOR HENRI MATISSE

The genius was 81
Fearful of blindness
Caught in a wheelchair
Staring at death

But the Angel of Mercy
gave him a year
to scissor some shapes
to soothe the scythe

and shriek!   shriek!

     became

    swawk!   swawk!
     the peace of
      scissors.

There was something besides
the inexpressible

     thrill

of cutting a beautiful shape—

     for
     Each thing had a "sign"
     Each thing had a "symbol"
     Each thing had a cutting form

       —swawk swawkk—

    to scissor seize.

"One must study an object a long time,"
 the genius said,
"to know what its sign is."

The scissors were his scepter
The cutting
was as the prow of a barque
to sail him away.

There's a photograph
        which shows him
sitting in his wheelchair
bare foot touching the floor
drawing with crisscross steel
a shape in the gouache

His helper sits near him
till he hands her the form
to pin to the wall

He points with a stick
how he wants it adjusted
This way and that,
        minutitudinous

The last blue iris blooms at
the top of its stalk

        scissors/sceptor
        cutting/prow

(*sung*)

Ah, keep those scissors flashing in the
World of Forms, Henri Matisse

The cutting of the scissors
was the prow of a boat
        to take him away
The last blue iris
    blooms at the top
        on a warm spring day

Ah, keep those scissors flashing in the
World of Forms, Henri Matisse

Sitting in a wheelchair
bare feet touching the floor
Angel of Mercy
        pushed him over
            next to Plato's Door

        Scissor scepter cutting prow
        Scissor scepter cutting prow
        Scissor scepter cutting prow
        Scissor scepter cutting prow

            ✂
            ahh
        swawk swawk

                ✂
                ahh
                swawk swawk

                    ✂
                    ahh
                        swawk swawk

Anne Waldman

Anne Waldman was born on April 2, 1945, in Millville, New Jersey. Her father taught journalism at Pace College and her mother was active in the New York theater. Waldman grew up in Greenwich Village, where she remembered "there was so much going on in the Village at that time—a lot of music and poetry. I used to see Bob Dylan. I used to pass Gregory Corso on Sixth Avenue when I was only twelve. He was an idol in some sense. Like Rimbaud, he was the epitome of the 'damned' poet, and so gorgeous!"

After her graduation from Bennington College in 1966, Waldman moved into an apartment on St. Mark's Place on the Lower East Side and started the literary magazine Angel Hair. *Two years later her first collection of poetry was published,* On the Wing. *She also became the director of the Poetry Project at the nearby St. Mark's Church in the Bowery, a community arts project funded by a grant from the Office of Economic Opportunity that sponsored a poetry newsletter and frequent readings and workshops in a program that continues to the present.*

Waldman says that she felt herself part of the Lower East Side community of younger New York poets rather than as one of the older generation of Beat poets. In 1974 she joined Allen Ginsberg and Diane DiPrima in setting up and teaching at the Jack Kerouac School of Disembodied Poetics at the Buddhist Naropa Institute in Boulder, Colorado, modeled after the experimental arts program of the legendary Black Mountain College in North Carolina. "Our Past" is a poem from Waldman's collection of "travel pieces," Blue Mosque *(1988).*

OUR PAST

You said my life was meant to run from yours as
    streams from the river.
You are the ocean I won't run to you
We were standing on Arapahoe in front of the Silver
    Saddle Motel
They had no rooms for us
I wore the high red huaraches of Mexico & a long skirt
    of patches
You had traveled back from Utah
I thought of the Salt Lakes, seeing them once from a
    plane they were like blank patches in the mind or
    bandaged places of the heart
I felt chilly
I had just ridden down the mountain with a car full of
    poets, one terrified of the shifting heights, the
    dark, the mountains, he said, closing in
I said Wait for me, but I have to go here first, or, it's too
    complicated, some kind of stalling because I
    wanted you
You were direct, you were traveling light, your feet
    were light, your hair was light, you were attentive
Were you rushing me?
We walked by the stream, you held me, I said I have to
    get back soon because he's waiting, maybe he's
    suffering
I think the moon was waning
You walked me back along 9th Street under dark trees
The night we'd met, June 6, we'd come out of the New
    York Church to observe a performer jumping over
    signposts
I was with my friend, a mentor, much older
You were introduced to him, to me
You said you'd followed me out from that night to where
    the continent divides, where my heart divided
I wrote poems to you in Santa Fe
You followed me all the way to Kitkitdizze
I waited for you, when you came I was away
I drove miles to speak with you on the telephone

I met you in Nevada City after nearly turning back to
    put out a fire
We went to Alta, the lake of your childhood
I wanted to stay forever in the big room with all the
    little white beds, like a nursery
You were like first love
All the impossibilities were upon us
We never had enough time
In Palo Alto where they name the streets after poets I
    admired your mother's pretty oriental things
In San Francisco we ate hurriedly at the joint near the
    opera house
I lied about going to Chicago for your birthday in New York
I lied about spending Christmas with you in Cherry Valley
I will never forget the dance you did to the pipes of
    Finbar Furey on New Year's day. You kept your
    torso bent to protect your heart
Then I moved to Colorado
We met and sat in the yard of a friend's brother's house in
    Missoula, Montana
It's wonderful the way this city turns serenely into
    country with no fuss, the city is shed, or is it the
    other way around, the country falls off into the
    city?
It was how I wanted us to shed our other lives at least
    when we were together
In that yard you made me feel our situation was
    intolerable
We seemed to be in constant pain
When we parted at the small airport early that morning
    my heart finally ripped
In the spring back in New York, things got darker
I was sick, my head was swollen
I remember reading to you about the Abidharma on a
    mattress
I had trouble speaking
I behaved badly and embarrassed you at the uptown
    party
A part of you had left me for good
You'd given your loft over to weekly parties

You were having a public life. I felt you were turning
   into me
I wanted our private romance
Was I being straight with you, I wondered?
I let you think things of me that weren't true. You
   thought I was wise & couldn't be hurt
      Then I had the person I lived with and what could
   be said about that?
That summer you visited my hotel in Boulder. We
   slept on separate mattresses. I felt I was trying to
   imprison you and after you left I couldn't go back
   there for days. When I did I found a dead bird had
   gotten entrapped, struggled fiercely to get out
The following winter I waited for you in sub zero cold,
   wearing black. I was told you'd come & gone. You
   didn't return. We spoke on the phone a long time.
I said I was going home and falling in love with someone
   else. You said It sounds like you want to
My mother heard me crying and came to me in the
   bathtub and said O don't, it breaks my heart! I
   told her I was going to the hell for a while I'd often
   made for others, karma works that way. Bosh
   karma she said
We've met briefly in Portland, Oregon and New York
We've corresponded all this time, following the details
   of each other's lives and work
Your father has recently died
My baby son grows stronger
The last time I saw you you were standing on my
   street corner
As I came toward you you said What a youthful gait
   you have

John Wieners

John Wieners was born on January 6, 1934, in Boston, Massachusetts, and graduated from Boston College in 1954. The fall of that year he heard the poet Charles Olson reading poetry and he was so impressed that he enrolled at Black Mountain College, near Asheville, North Carolina, where Olson was rector and taught poetry. After a year at Black Mountain, Wieners returned to Boston to start Measure, *a literary magazine that published poets affiliated with Black Mountain.*

In 1957 Wieners moved to San Francisco, took a job sweeping the floor at the Coffee Gallery, a favorite Beat hangout in North Beach, established contact with the poet Robert Duncan, who had also taught at Black Mountain, took a room at the Hotel Wentley, and joined the artistic community in the city, becoming close to the painter Robert LaVigne and the collage artist Wallace Berman.

"A poem for record players," "A poem for tea heads," "A poem for museum goers," and "A poem for the insane" were included in The Hotel Wentley Poems, *Wieners's first book, published by Auerhahn Press of San Francisco in 1958. He later revised them extensively. These poems contain elements of both Beat and "Projective Verse," what Olson called his method of "composition by field," an open poetic line attuned to "the smallest particle of all, the syllable" instead of the "inherited line, stanza, over-all form."*

The biographer Raymond Foye understood that Wieners's confessional style read "like a résumé of Beat poetry and of late romanticism as a whole: urban despair, poverty, madness, homosexual love, narcotics and drug addiction, the fraternity of thieves and loveless transients. Wieners is now speaking as the poete maudit, *whose true place is among the wretched who inhabit the underworld of cities."*

A POEM FOR RECORD PLAYERS

The scene changes

Five hours later and
I come into a room
where a clock ticks.
I find a pillow to
muffle the sounds I make.
I am engaged in taking away
from God his sound.

The pigeons somewhere
above me, the cough a
man makes down the hall,
the flap of wings
below me, the squeak
of sparrows in the alley.
The scratches I itch
on my scalp, a landing
of birds under the bay
window out my window.

Details
but which are here and
I hear and shall never
give up again, shall carry
with me over the streets
of this seacoast city,
forever,
oh clack your
metal wings, god, you are
mine now in the morning.

I have you by the ears
thousand cars, gunning
in the exhaust pipes of a
their motors turning over
all over town.

6.15.58

A POEM FOR TEA HEADS

I sit in Lees.   At 11:40 PM with
Jimmy the pusher. He teaches me
Ju Ju.

Hot on the table before us
shrimp foo yong, rice and mushroom
chow yuke.

Up the street under the wheels
of a strange car is his stash—The ritual.
We make it.   And have made it.
for months now together after midnight.
Soon I know the fuzz will inter-
rupt will arrest Jimmy and
I shall be placed on probation.

The poem
does not lie to us. We lie under its
law, alive in the glamour of this hour
able to enter into the sacred places
of his dark people, who carry secrets
glassed in their eyes and hide words
under the roofs of their mouth.

6.16.58

A POEM FOR MUSEUM GOERS

I walk down a long
passageway with a
red door waiting for me.
It is Edward Munch.

Turn right turn
right. And I see
                    sister
hanging on the wall,
heavy breasts and hair

Tied to a tree in the garden
with the full moon
are the ladies of the street.
Whipped for whoring.
Their long hair binds them,

They have lain long
hours in bed, blood
on their mouths, arms
reaching down for
ground not given them.

They are enveloped
in pain.   Bah.
There is none. Munch
knew it. Put the
Shriek in their ears
to remove it from his own.

Open thy mouth, tell us
the landscape you have
escaped from, Fishing
boats are in the bay, no
outgoing tides for you
who he anchored to
                    Hell.

Even here the young lovers
cast black shadows.
The nets are down.
Huge seasnakes
squirm on shore
taking away even

the beach from us.
Move on. Moonlight

I see the garden women
in their gravy days
when hair hung golden or
black to the
floor & the walls
were velvet.

An old sailor his face like wood
his chin splintered
by many shipwrecks
keeps their story
in his eyes. How the house
at the top of the drive
held them all, and their lovers,
with Munch the most
obsessed. His face
carved by knife blades.

Lover leaves lover,
1896, 62 years
later, the men
sit, paws and
jagged depths
under their heads,

Now the season of
the furnished room. Gone
the Grecian walls & the
cypress trees,
plain planks and spider
webs, a bed
only big enough for one,
it looks like a
casket. Death
death on every
wall, guillotined

and streaming in
flames.

6.21.58

A POEM FOR THE INSANE

The 2nd afternoon I come
back to the women of Munch.
Models with god over

their shoulders, vampires,
the heads are down and
blood is the water—
color they use to turn on.
The story is not done.
There is one wall
left to walk. Yeah

Afterwards—Nathan
gone, big Eric busted,
Swanson down. It is
right, the Melancholy
on the Beach. I do not
                    split

I hold on to the demon
tree, while shadows drift
around me. Until at last
there is only left the
Death Chamber. Family Reunion
in it. Rocking chairs and

who is the young man
who sneaks out thru
the black curtain, away
from the bad bed.

Yeah stand now
on the new road, with the
huge mountain on your
right out of the mist

the bridge before me,
the woman waiting
with no mouth, waiting
for me to kiss it on.

I will. I will walk with
my eyes up on you for
ever.   We step into
the Kiss, 1897.
The light streams.

Melancholy carries
a red sky and our dreams
are blue boats
no one can bust or
blow out to sea.
We ride them
and Tingel-Tangel
in the afternoon.

PART FIVE

"TALES OF BEATNIK GLORY"

Memoirs and Posthumous Tributes

Beat literature is predominantly autobiographical fiction and poetry, as in Kerouac's narrative of his cross-country trips with Neal Cassady in *On the Road,* Ginsberg's account of his mother's mental breakdowns in "Kaddish", Ferlinghetti's poetic address in a North Beach cafe to his buddy Fidel Castro, McClure's description of his peyote-induced visions in his San Francisco apartment, and DiPrima's birthday salute to her radical Socialist grandfather. The Beats insisted on writing directly about events in their own lives in part because their literary models—Arthur Rimbaud, Thomas Wolfe, William Carlos Williams—relied on autobiography, but also because the writers often felt so far outside the margins of society that they insisted on the validity of their own experience instead of accepting conventional opinions and the country's common myths.

This reliance on direct personal experience for the content of their poetry and fiction does not imply that the Beat writers suffered from a dearth of imagination or that their dominant emotion was sentimental nostalgia. Rather the autobiographical mode suggests the strength of the Beat writers' perceptions and convictions in the 1950s and 1960s, when they felt estranged from the predominantly conservative society engulfing them in America.

That the Beats could describe their individual experiences so compellingly that they transformed them from personal memories into enduring works of literature is testimony to their creative ability. That they intensely believed, as Ginsberg has said (and Emerson before him), that society is in conspiracy against its members, is shown in their autobiographical fiction and poetry, demonstrating their belief that the best way to break through the social hypocrisy they felt surrounding them was to demonstrate in their writing that "private is public." As McClure understood, the writers "had come to believe that the way to the universal was by means of the most intensely personal."

The Beats also relied heavily on personal experience for their writing because they believed, like Whitman, in the "literature of the common man." Following this point of view, ideally everyone could be a writer. In the 1940s and early 1950s the Beats inexhaustibly encouraged each other to write, just as in the late 1950s and early 1960s they tirelessly started and ran small presses and little magazines. Neal Cassady began the story of the "first third" of his life on a stolen typewriter in Denver at the urging of his friends Kerouac and Ginsberg. Cassady's performance proved, if nothing else, that memoirs are the most democratic of literary forms.

As occasional literature, memoirs can be a newspaper column like the "Notes of a Dirty Old Man" that Charles Bukowski dashed off each week for the Los Angeles *Open City* paper. Or they can be an introduction to a friend's book, like the few paragraphs of reminiscences by Brion Gysin about a famous Paris hotel that no longer existed after 1963 but was captured for all time in a photographer's lens.

With the Beats, memoirs took various forms, most written as literary experiments rather than as attempts to present a straightforward account of the past. They were undertaken as projects conceived to test the range of the writers' creative abilities, as when Diane DiPrima published her first book of poetry and then tried her hand in *Dinners and Nightmares* at prose sketches about the most memorable dinners she'd eaten. Accounts of the past were also taken up in the spirit of a deliberate personal challenge, as when Brenda Frazer read *On the Road* and then decided to tell the story of her adventures on the road in Mexico with her husband and baby daughter from a woman's point of view in *Troia: Mexican Memoirs*.

Memoirs can be a deliberate imitative exercise that takes a different turn from the instinctive bent of the writer, like McClure's Kerouac-inspired autobiography, *The Mad Cub*. In the sketchiness of its details about the people and the chronology of events in his life, the book is probably less of a memoir than a long prose-poem experiment in which McClure took his own consciousness as his subject.

Memoirs can present characters and settings so vividly that they read like fiction, like William Burroughs, Jr.'s autobiographical novel, *Kentucky Ham*. They can also masquerade as fiction, such as Ken Kesey's story "The Day After Superman Died," fleshed out with the narrator's hyperbolic dramatization of his emotions and elaborate crafting of his factual material.

Like William Burroughs, Jr., Jan Kerouac's memoir *Baby Driver* was marketed as a novel rather than as a disguised autobiography. But most often the women writers told their personal stories in a straightforward manner and did not think of themselves as novelists. Carolyn Cassady's story of her life with her husband Neal Cassady and her love affair with Kerouac, was one of the earliest Beat memoirs. Later women writers explored an awakening feminist consciousness in their autobiographies, like Joyce Johnson's prize-winning *Minor Characters* and Hettie Jones's *How I Became Hettie Jones*.

Finally, at their most fanciful, memoirs can be presented so that they masquerade as a detached vision of someone else's experience. Ed Sanders's recast his own response to Ginsberg's "Howl," an encounter that changed his life, into a wacky short story "A Book of Verse."

Regardless of the original impulse behind them, the memoirs in this section tell a plain, unvarnished tale of what life was like in the Beat Generation—as if a door opened to reveal an even more candid view of actual life itself.

Charles Bukowski

Charles Bukowski wrote a brief article for the underground paper Open City *about his meeting with Neal Cassady in West Los Angeles a few days before Cassady's death in Mexico on February 4, 1968. Bukowski contributed a weekly column to the Los Angeles newspaper under the heading "Notes of a Dirty Old Man," welcoming the freedom to write as he pleased for immediate publication. He later remembered, "There was not the tenseness or the careful carving with a bit of a dull blade, that was needed to write something for* The Atlantic Monthly." *The collected* Notes of a Dirty Old Man *columns were published by City Lights in 1973. Talking to Cassady, Bukowski referred to Cassady's long "Joan Anderson letter" to Ginsberg and Kerouac on December 17, 1950, that had appeared in the little magazine* Notes from Underground, *containing "that bit about climbing out the bathroom window and hiding in the bushes naked." Bukowski was so bowled over by Cassady's performance behind the wheel of a car that he made Cassady the center of his piece, instead of his customary self-presentation.*

from NOTES OF A DIRTY OLD MAN

I met Kerouac's boy Neal C. shortly before he went down to lay along those Mexican railroad tracks to die. his eyes were sticking out on ye old toothpicks and he had his head in the speaker, jogging, bouncing, ogling, he was in a white t-shirt and seemed to be singing like a cuckoo bird along with the music, *preceding* the beat just a shade as if he were leading the parade. I sat down with my beer and watched him. I'd brought in a six pack or two. Bryan was handing out an assignment and some film to two young guys who were going to cover that show that kept getting busted. [Michael McClure's play *The Beard*] whatever happened to that show by the Frisco poet, I forget his name. anyhow, nobody was noticing Neal C. and Neal C. didn't care, or he pretended not to. when the song stopped, the 2 young guys left and Bryan introduced me to the fab. Neal C.

"have a beer?" I asked him.

Neal plucked a bottle out, tossed it in the air, caught it, ripped the cap off and emptied the half-quart in two long swallows.

"have another."

"sure."

"I thought I was good on the beer."

"I'm the tough young jail kid. I've read your stuff."

"read your stuff too. that bit about climbing out the bathroom window and hiding in the bushes naked. good stuff."

"oh yeah." he worked at the beer. he never sat down. he kept moving around the floor. he was a little punchy with the action, the eternal light, but there wasn't any hatred in him. you liked him even though you didn't want to because Kerouac had set him up for the sucker punch and Neal had bit, kept biting. but you know Neal was o.k. and another way of looking at it, Jack had only written the book, he wasn't Neal's mother. just his destructor, deliberate or otherwise.

Neal was dancing around the room on the Eternal High. his face looked old, pained, all that, but his body was the body of a boy of eighteen.

"you want to try him, Bukowski?" asked Bryan.

"yeah, ya wanta go, baby?" he asked me.

again, no hatred. just going with the game.

"no, thanks. I'll be forty-eight in August. I've taken my last beating."

I couldn't have handled him.

"when was the last time you saw Kerouac?" I asked.

I think he said 1962, 1963. anyhow, a long time back.

I just about stayed with Neal on the beer and had to go out and get some more. the work at the office was about done and Neal was staying at Bryan's and B. invited me over for dinner. I said, "all right," and being a bit high I didn't realize what was going to happen.

when we got outside a very light rain was just beginning to fall. the kind that really fucks up the streets. I still didn't know. I thought Bryan was going to drive. but Neal got in and took the wheel. I had the back seat anyhow. B. got up in front with Neal. and the ride began. straight along those slippery streets and it would seem we were past the corner and then Neal would decide to take a right or a left. past parked cars, the dividing line just a hair away. it can only be described as hairline. a tick the other way and we were all finished.

after we cleared I would always say something ridiculous like, "well, suck my dick!" and Bryan would laugh and Neal would just go on driving, neither grim or happy or sardonic, just there—doing the movements. I understood. it was necessary. it was his bull ring, his racetrack. it was *holy* and necessary.

the best one was just off Sunset, going north toward Carlton. the drizzle was good now, ruining both the vision and the streets. turning off of Sunset, Neal picked up his next move, full-speed chess, it had to be calculated in an instant's glance. a left on Carlton would bring us to Bryan's. we were a block off. there was one car ahead of us and two approaching. now, he could have slowed down and followed the traffic in but he would have lost his *movement.* not Neal. he swung out around the car ahead of us and I thought, this is it, well, it doesn't matter, really it doesn't matter at all. that's the way it goes through your brain, that's the way it went through my brain. the two cars plunged at each other, head-on, the other so close that the headlights flooded my back seat. I do think that at the last second the other driver touched his brake. that gave us the hairline. it must have been figured in by Neal. that movement. but it wasn't over. we were going very high speed now and the other car, approaching slowly from Hollywood Blvd. was just about blocking a left on Carlton. I'll always remember the color of that car. we got that close. a kind of gray-blue, an old car, coupe, humped and hard like a rolling steel brick thing. Neal cut left. to me it looked as if we were going to ram right through the center of the car. it was obvious. but somehow, the motion of the other car's forward and our movement left coincided perfectly. the hairline was there. once again. Neal parked the thing and we went on in. Joan brought the dinner in.

Neal ate all of his plate and most of mine too. we had a bit of wine. John had a highly intelligent young homosexual baby-sitter, who I now think has gone on with some rock band or killed himself or something. anyhow, I pinched his buttocks as he walked by. he loved it.

I think I stayed long past my time, drinking and talking with Neal. the baby-sitter kept talking about Hemingway, somehow equating me with Hemingway until I told him to shove it and he went upstairs to check Jason. it was a few days later that Bryan phoned me:

"Neal's dead, Neal died."

"oh shit, no."

then Bryan told me something about it. hung up.

that was it.

all those rides, all those pages of Kerouac, all that jail, to die alone under a frozen Mexican moon, alone, you understand? can't you see the miserable puny cactii? Mexico is not a bad place because it is simply oppressed; Mexico is simply a bad place. can't you see the desert animals watching? the frogs, horned and simple, the snakes like slits of men's minds crawling, stopping, waiting, dumb under a dumb Mexican moon. reptiles, flicks of things, looking across this guy in the sand in a white t-shirt.

Neal, he'd found his movement, hurt nobody. the tough young jail kid laying it down alongside a Mexican railroad track.

the only night I met him I said, "Kerouac has written all your other chapters. I've already written your last one."

"go ahead," he said, "write it."

end copy.

William Burroughs, Jr.

*William Burroughs, Jr., described his trip to Tangier in 1961
when he was fourteen to visit his father, the "odd-looking man
on the other side of Lisbon customs." His account was included
in his second book,* Kentucky Ham *(1973). At the time of the
visit Burroughs, Sr., who had lived in Tangier for long periods
over several years, was sharing his house with two English
friends, Mikey Portman and Ian Sommerville. Burroughs continued to give more of his attention to his writing and to his
friends than to his teenage son. Burroughs, Jr., stoically stood
off the two Englishmen's sexual advances and managed to hold
his own with the apparently unlimited supply of drugs in Burroughs's household, but his father's indifference to him was
impossible to bear. Shortly after Billy's return to his grandparents' home in Palm Beach, Florida, his grandfather died and
Billy ran away to New York City, where he became addicted
to Methedrine. This was the subject of his first autobiographical
novel,* Speed *(1970), like* Kentucky Ham *a remarkable testimony to Billy Burroughs's literary talent.*

from KENTUCKY HAM

Then, two years after his last visit, I was fourteen, and my
father wanted me back.

Tangier, Morocco. My grandparents stood at the airport
gate in Miami and waved good-bye to the wrong window of
the plane as I, square, pink, fourteen, and American, settled

into my seat to watch them. Riffling through my science-fiction anthology, I watched them slide away as the big jet wallowed down the runway-bare ribbon devoid of foxprints. A blast of power, for some reason planes didn't bother me then, and there I was a few hours later waving to an odd-looking man on the other side of Lisbon customs. Fifteen minutes before it was time to board the next plane, a strangely accented voice came over the PA system to announce that it was imperative for a mister somebody to report to the customs desk immediately. I wouldn't have noticed the name sounded like ours if Bill hadn't tensed instantly and very slightly. He'd already relaxed by the time I caught the resemblance. "Is that us?" I asked. "Nope. We're cool, man." He chuckled as he settled back to digest a canary. The words seemed strangely incongruous coming from a man who could have passed as an English bank clerk. He took a long deep drag on a Players Medium cigarette and I noticed that his fingers were stained a very un-British dark nicotine yellow.

Moroccan customs officials were bored and indifferent (who would smuggle anything *into* Morocco?) and waved us past their lidded eyes into a tiny rundown taxi driven by a stoned-out hashhead who scared the daylights out of me. Tangier at that time had no traffic lights at all and the cabbies would careen through intersections playing an eternal game of chicken that *was* a game of chicken, and every time we would avoid a hair-breadth apocalypse, my father would mutter a word of appreciation like a calm bullfight aficionado. "Bueno"—even though the language spoken was French.

But finally we pulled up to the curb by the Parade Bar. Just off the European section, and out of nowhere one of the people who shared our house on the Marshan appeared to shake my hand: It was Michael Paltman. "Michael, this is my son."

An unaccustomed attempt at fatherly pride and then we were in the bar and I was apart, being accosted by an aging fag. "I know I'm old, but I really *haven't* lost my figure, dear. You know, half the old Tangerines knew you were coming and wondered what you looked like. Well Baby! I mean if you ever want your nuts blowed???" I was a little nervous, but I told him if it ever came to that I'd let him know. He looked overly hurt and gave me one of those pitying looks, like perhaps someday the poor child will see the light, as he slid off the stool caressing my thigh. "Bad medicine," I thought, and I mean to say the old fart was definitely not my type.

After something to eat and a small glass of rum (the Parade is the only place in Tangier where you can get a decent hamburger. "You needn't *insist* you're fresh from Amercah," says Michael later.), we took another Kamikaze cab to the Marshan. Most of the Tangerine cabbies speak French and my father's French is abominable. He has a very respectable working vocabulary but his accent is enough to instigate a riot. When we got to the number of our house on Calle Larache, he went to say "*ici*" but it came out southern Texas style, "eechee." The driver, understandably did not understand and drove on. Bill was livid. "EECHEE! GODDAMN IT! EE-CHEE!" His tone of voice got through and the driver backed up to stop.

Inside: total disorganization. Bill had known I was coming but he had to search the house to find a place for me to sleep. With a flashlight because something had happened to the electricity. "Wait for Ian," he said, another tenant, who came home later and fixed the electricity by going outside and striking a power pole with a broomstick.

I didn't sleep well that night. I beg you to remember that the last time I had slept was in Palm Beach on a mahogany dragon bed from the seventeenth century. And now here I lay listening to strange sounds and Arabic mutterings outside the window.

But I slept nonetheless and awoke the next morning to find Ian sitting on my bed looking at me like a loving mother. We talked for a few minutes and then he took my hand gently, ever so gently, and tried to draw it to his groin. But the attempt was premature and I pulled away. He didn't take it as hard as the old swish in the Parade though, and we were all friends that evening as he, my father, and Michael lit up their pipes. Very long pipes with clay bowls. I was curious about their contents. . . . "Kif." I remembered the word from *Naked Lunch* and asked if I could try it out. "All in good time, Billy," said Ian. But the next day the good times rolled when Bill said, "Ian, take Billy down the Grande Socco and help him pick out a pipe."

That night, I took my first draw on the celebrated medicinal herb. Problem is, that in Morocco so many people smoke dope that it has become a social thing. So they mix it with a cruel and unusual tobacco that makes Gauloises taste like ambulance oxygen. "Goddamn!" I thought. "This is worse than whiskey." But as it happened, my father had some tasty little hashish candies on hand of which I consumed quite a number not knowing what they were, and then dipped into a Mason jar of homemade *majoun,* which is grass fixed up to eat and will stone you into the middle of next week, my friend.

Off the subject for a moment, *majoun* can be dangerous if prepared stupidly. I understand that about a month before I arrived in Tangier, Gregory Corso had dropped by for a visit. And that he, Bill, Ian, and Mike had all got together after a few drinks and rather drunkenly decided to consume a bit of *majoun.* So Michael went out to buy some tea, and damned if he didn't buy the tobacco-infiltrated variety. When he got back he just went ahead and cooked it all up replete with raisins and honey. About twenty minutes after ingestion, my father sensed something amiss and immediately repaired to the bathroom to vomit up the entire dose. Everyone else followed suit except Mr. Corso who stubbornly refused to believe there was anything wrong with the stuff, or that he couldn't handle it, if there was. So about an hour later he quietly excuses himself from the room and rushes back in red-eyed as a charging ostrich, flailing at Michael and shrieking, "Poisonerrr! Poisoner-r-r!" He chased him out of the house and all the way to the medina before he calmed down, a distance of some two and a half miles, but never caught him because he had to stop every few minutes to vomit. Dynamite cat.

You will hear people say that one never gets stoned the first time but I was so far gone that I couldn't even remember the onset. Only visions of the entire course of human history, from the apeman all asteam on the hostile plains on through the blessed virgin and plunging into the abyss of technology. After two million years, Ian nudged me gently and said that he'd like to go to sleep. "Oh! Sure man," I said and went downstairs to sleep very well.

Hash dream under the influence of earphones: I see two ruined buildings, their backs blown away; naked girders grope in a smoking twilit sky. On the tenth floor of each building, leaning out the window, is a pale man with a sheet of metal. They are playing a dreadful and hyenic game of Ping-Pong with something dark and indiscernible, perhaps a human head. Below them, as far as the eye can see, is a multitude of people on their knees, some with flaming hair. They rock from side to side, hands clasped, and follow the indiscernible object; and their wailing merges with the crashing of the sheet metal to shake the girders that grind and sway as technical fingers in the darkening sky. I have the feeling that the man who misses the object first, loses and no matter who loses all the people die. . . . Michael Portman stirred me from this dream with a look of concern on his face. When I told him what I had seen, he went and told Bill about it. Bill was at work, and when Michael was through he stopped typing long enough to say "very accurate" without looking up and then resumed business.

Our house in the Marshan was very fine. Two stories and consumed by mosaics. My father's room was austere to say the least. Spotlessly clean with an army-type bunk and a cabinet and that was all besides an incredibly haunting picture of a brooding moon done by his good friend Brion Gysin. I might mention that Mr. Gysin invented the cut-up method as applied to words or at least he was one of the first to take it seriously. The cut-up method enables the writer to achieve the same effect as the artist can with picture montage. The effect can be and often is shattering to the receptive reader because words are images in a much more personalized and internal sense than pictures. I recollect one mind-blowing ditty that my father had on his tape recorder. It was a word montage by Brion Gysin and consisted of one phrase: "I come to free the words." repeated over and over in different order. That is, "The words are free to come, I come freely to the words, The free come to the words . . ." And while the words were repeated, the speed of the tape was increased gradually until it became a supersonic whine. But because of the rhythm, and after the cartoon laughter stage, some part of the listener would keep pace until he was virtually transported. To where, I don't know, or cannot report.

There was also an orgone box in the upstairs hall in which

my father would sit for hours at a time smoking kif and then rush out and attack his typewriter without warning.

The rooftops, by custom, are the women's province in Tangier because that's where they do all the washing and gossiping and whatnot. I made the mistake once of going up there during the day and the Arabs threw little pieces of mud at our door for the next week. But Bill would be on the roof every night to watch the colors in the sky as soon as the sun was starting to set. I would stumble to the roof occasionally, stoned out of my squash and would see him transfixed in his favorite spot. Transfixed and absolutely motionless, right hand holding the perpetual cigarette, lips parting to the sun, and himself stirring only to drop it when it burned his fingers. When it was finally, absolutely night, again, the sudden rush to the typewriter.

I tell you one thing though, he and everybody in that house had an appetite. Bunch of goddamn hashheads and I recollect one time I came back from the main part of town (stoned obviously) with an apple pie and a roasted chicken intent upon retiring to my room and plumbing the joys of the taste. But I was met at the door by the entire population. Zapo! One piece of pie left over and I went to my room to scarf up my angry piece of apple. Old Bill used the leftover chicken bones, scant and gnawed as they were, to make a soup that he cooked for two days using such an incredible amount of pepper that the stuff went down like whiskey. But he was so proud of the finished product that any visitor, including myself, was instantly overcome with compassion and "enjoyed" a cup and sometimes two under his imploring eyes. It would sometimes take a few minutes before the victim was able to express his appreciation.

Tangier was still pretty wild then. There was a café on a cliff called the Dancing Boy that Ian took me to my first time. Smells of hashish, kif, and mint tea. Beautiful music. The violinist sat cross-legged and played his violin upright before him like a cello. As we came in some European existentialist-type hippies whispered among themselves. They looked as if they hadn't seen daylight for years and were dressed entirely in black. They all had dark hair, underbelly skin, and black circles under their eyes.

The dancer wore long robes and a cork inner-tube affair

with tassels around his hips, and did swirling routines with trays of water-filled glasses or with lit candles, which he somehow managed not to extinguish. Something to see.

The café closed about three A.M. and sometimes Ian and I or a fellow named Peter would laugh down the street with the musicians and dart into a strange house there to continue clapping and dancing and listening and smoking until everyone dropped. Pick ourselves up at dawn and rush to the bakery to catch the boy wheeling out the new loaves in a barrow on his way to deliver to the shops. Buy a huge round loaf too hot to handle without wrapping it in a shirt and stop before home for a pound of fresh butter from a clay urn at the neighborhood 7–11.

These were pleasant times, but I couldn't make it; I was too young and found it difficult to get involved. I took to wandering the ocean cliffs with my pipe and quarter pound of unadulterated grass that Michael had very kindly gone out and got when he saw me choking one night on the other shit. I'd sit on trees that grew sideways out of the cliffs and smoke until I was unable or unwilling to make the climb back. Wait a while and then walk through the alleys admiring the colored broken glass placed on top of the rich folks' walls to keep out the riffraff. I went to cafés, movies (try watching a French movie dubbed into Arabic sometime), beaches, but I couldn't figure out what was wrong until one night Ian came to my room and told me I wanted to go home. He was on the verge of tears when he said that I didn't want to live with a houseful of "fags." The quotation marks were in his tone of voice and I wondered how my father felt. He was in his room. Was he trying to read?

Carolyn Cassady

Carolyn Cassady first published her reminiscences of her life with her husband Neal and his friend Jack Kerouac in the magazine Rolling Stone *and the book* Heart Beat: My Life With Jack & Neal *(1976), an account that became the basis of a fanciful Hollywood film a few years later.* Off the Road: My Years *with Cassady, Kerouac, and Ginsberg* (1990), *from which this excerpt is taken, gives a fuller account of her relationship with Jack and Neal in the spring of 1952, when Kerouac lived with the Cassadys and their three young children in a small rented house on Russian Hill in San Francisco. During these months, Jack revised* On the Road *and continued writing* Visions of Cody *in the Cassady's attic room while Neal worked as a brakeman for the Southern Pacific railroad. In August 1952 the Cassadys moved to a suburban house located in a place they called Nowheresville outside San Jose, where they continued their ménage à trois with Kerouac when he came to visit them in California in his times "off the road."*

from OFF THE ROAD

CHAPTER TWENTY-NINE

The old pattern thus broken, the climate of the household warmed, and there began, for me, a new life, or at least a new perspective on the old life. When Jack wasn't at work or busy writing, he'd now sit and talk to me, telling me of his childhood in Lowell, Massachusetts and of his mother's tenacity in working at the shoe factory; or he would voice his regrets at his sister Caroline's intolerance of him. Jack had a loyal affection for her, and felt it was an odd coincidence our names were so similar. She was married with a son and felt Jack should get a job, support their mother and stop wasting his time playing around with writing.

Here with us, Jack was trying to finish *On the Road*. I had only read random passages of the manuscript; I was too close to the pain of the events he described, and the more Neal chortled over it, the more fearful I became that I'd feel a necessity to start something again. The only details I'd heard of their trips were those Helen had revealed, and I was blissful in my ignorance. Jack was still writing additional scenes, and he became excited with the possibilities offered by the tape recorder to capture spontaneous discussions or stories. I was beginning to think the *Road* might become an interminable highway. Jack had found that he had an audience that believed he could do no wrong, and he was happy to share his daily efforts with us. He still carried a little five-cent notebook in his shirt pocket wherever he went to note impressions or new ideas which he would type up within a few days. One notebook he inscribed to me.

The liquor store was just around the corner on Hyde Street, and Jack sometimes bought a small bottle, or 'poor-boy,' of Tokay or Muscatel to sip late in the afternoon or after dinner, when he would share it with me. Sometimes I'd go with him to the liquor store to buy beer for Neal. One time when I stopped for beer alone, the proprietor said something about my 'husband's' preference for sweet wine. It wasn't until I was outside that I realized he meant Jack, and I had to laugh. If only he knew how much trouble I had keeping one husband, let alone two.

One afternoon I was feeding John in his highchair when I heard the front door open and slam shut, and Neal came clumping down the stairs dragging his jacket behind him. He threw it down hard on the couch and said, 'Shit.' He hardly ever swore in front of me, so I knew he must be really angry.

'I've got to pack,' he said. 'I've drawn a two-week hold-down in San Luis.' He stood looking out the window, clenching his jaw.

This kind of assignment was the only kind he didn't like. On hold-downs he had to go to a neighboring branch, and it meant staying in either a barren dorm, the 'crummy' (caboose) or a sleazy hotel. He had to work the same local freight early every morning for at least two weeks, sometimes longer.

Neal blew off some steam and then accepted his lot, settling down to his own cheerful self again. He would never expand on his disappointments if it meant bringing someone else down.

He hadn't much time. While he went upstairs to pack, I hurried with the dinner, and he called up to Jack to explain why dinner would be earlier tonight. I was even more sorry than Neal at this sudden development, and I guessed maybe Jack would be, too. When alone together, Jack and I had still not found a firm footing in our relationship, and we needed Neal nearby as a buffer. Consequently, during this dinner we were both nervous, eyeing each other in a new and uncharted way.

Neal stood up from the table and planted his hands on either side of his chest in his Oliver Hardy stance, looking down at Jack and then at me.

'Well, kiddies I must be off. Just everyone pray I get back in fourteen days and no more.'

He retrieved his jacket, kissed me and the children and strode to the stairs. At the landing he turned back as though he'd forgotten something, then said with a grin, 'I don't know about leaving you two—you know what they say, "My best pal and my best gal . . ." Ha, ha—just don't do anything *I* wouldn't do—okay kids?' He bounded up the stairs laughing, knowing, just as we did, that there was nothing he wouldn't do in a similar situation. I wanted to crawl under the table and disappear, I was so embarrassed, and I couldn't look at Jack. Instead, I jumped up and began grabbing dishes off the table and putting them in the sink. Jack bolted for the attic.

Jack had been taught that marriage was a sacrament, whereas my thinking was that if a person agreed to a set of rules and went so far as to choose to take vows, then he should play the game and keep the promises. Otherwise, don't do it—nobody *has* to get married nowadays. Neal, on the other hand, was torn between his beliefs and overpowering desires. Jack's courtesy and gentleness toward me resulted from my being the wife of his best friend, nothing more—at least that was all either of us could admit to, even to ourselves.

The more I thought about Neal's remark, the angrier I got and the more it hurt. Well, maybe I was jumping to conclusions again—maybe he really did mean it only as a joke. But it was no joke to me. During the next two weeks, Jack was out most of the time and rarely sat and talked to me. When he did agree to share a meal, however, it was so pleasant we'd soon forget the circumstances in the joys of conversation. But the silences brought back our discomfort at being alone together, Neal's remark hanging in the air around us.

When he returned we welcomed him with great relief. He seemed a little reserved the first evening at dinner, and I wondered if he supposed we had behaved as he would have done. When Jack hurriedly left us alone, I asked. 'Remember what you said when you left, Neal? How could you say a thing like that? Do you know how that hurt? You made me feel I was no more precious to you than—a towel or something. Can you understand that? Don't you know I'm proud to show you I deserve your trust, that I like chances to prove my loyalty? Tell me, did you sincerely feel we should have made love, Jack and I—or were you just saying that to protect yourself in case we did?'

I was peering at Neal intently, waiting for his answer. He got up from the table looking uncomfortable and started toward the stairs. Then he paused and shrugged.

'A little of both, I suppose . . . yeah, actually . . . why not? I thought it would be fine.' And up the stairs he went.

Goddamn the man! Well, I had asked for this second blow, but how could he be so unfeeling? I should know by now, I thought dejectedly. Hadn't he 'shared' LuAnne—even though they were no longer married—and how many others? Again, I kept supposing I was different, meant more to him. This seemed a greater rejection even than desertion.

Dolefully, I did the dishes, mulling it over, finding no solace. When Neal came down to tell me he and Jack were going out, I got a vision once more of the future as an incessant repetition of the past, and I knew I must do something to change it. None of the old ways had worked, so defiantly, I said half-aloud, 'All right, Neal dear, let's try it your way.' And the anger drained out of me while I felt another conviction torn away as though I'd shed another skin. Suddenly I felt exposed, but with that came a coolness and a spurt of excitement mingled with fear. Never had I known how to play female games of deliberately setting out to trap a man. At least in this case it shouldn't require much aggression, just a few calculated moves. After all, Jack knew better than I how Neal would react. It was worth a try; anything was better than this.

CHAPTER THIRTY

An evening or two later, I made a few plans—nothing elaborate or unusual, but admittedly I manipulated circumstances as best I could. I'd asked Neal about the train he was called for and its schedule. He'd be gone until the following afternoon. When the children were settled for the night, I called softly up the attic stairs. 'Jack?'

He came to the top of the steps. 'Yeah?'

'I wondered if you'd like to join me for dinner. I've made an experimental sort of pizza, and there's way too much for me. It doesn't keep too well, so—how about it?'

'Okay, sure . . .' He looked hesitant. 'Just give me a minute?'

'Oh, no hurry; it'll be another thirty minutes anyway, but there's some wine, too. So whenever you're ready.' Pausing for a minute at my dressing table, I checked my appearance —mustn't be too obvious. I was already feeling like a wanton woman and had butterflies in my stomach. Too bad I could only get away with jeans and a white shirt without arousing his suspicions; but I had been careful with my hair and makeup, and thought just a dab of cologne would be fair.

Downstairs I checked my ammunition there: new candle in the bottle, table set as usual, radio set at KJAZ, the station both Neal and Jack approved of for its ballads and progressive jazz. The oven was ready, so I popped in the pizza. I thought I'd better sample the wine to calm my nerves, and I fancy I appeared quite nonchalant when Jack descended from the attic to join me.

'Pour us some wine. Dinner will be ready in a jiffy.'

I sat down opposite him at the table, raised my glass to my private scheme and smiled.

The wine helped put us both at ease and made us garrulous. Jack praised my cooking long and loud and plunged into stories, all self-consciousness gone. For my part, I forgot my preconceived plot and was lost in genuine enjoyment. He regaled me with the impressions of Bill Burroughs he'd gained in New York, what he knew of that strange individual's childhood, education and brilliant mind. Neither of us could guess why such a man had become so attracted to drugs and firearms. He told me the story of his own first wife, Edie Parker, and the hectic times in New York when he'd met them both. He was planning to visit Bill in Mexico in the summer and eagerly looked forward to another sojourn in that magic country. He loved the music and the slow, easy-going lifestyle. To him it seemed to represent a Utopian existence without hassles, a timeless peace. He and Neal favored Spengler's word *'fallaheen'* to describe the culture, but since to them the term meant a people who weren't going anywhere but had already been and were resting before the next creative cycle occurred, it sounded to me like the impossible dream for these two men who loved dashing about looking for 'kicks.'

When we had finished eating, I knew I had to keep Jack downstairs until I'd finished what I'd started; I'd never be able to repeat it. I poured more wine and walked to the couch we kept opened out to double-bed size. As I sat down on its edge, I held out Jack's glass to him. He followed me, accepted the wine and lay back upon the couch, balancing the glass on his chest. With his eyes closed, he hummed along to 'My Funny Valentine' as it wafted from the radio.

I looked down at him but said nothing until the silence became thick and warm, then I asked, 'Do you remember when we danced together in Denver?'

He turned his head, opened his eyes and looked at me tenderly. Then, smiling, he sat up and said softly, 'Yeah . . . I wanted to take you away from Neal.' He kept looking into my eyes but he had stopped smiling.

Barely audibly, I asked, 'And do you remember the song we danced to?'

He leaned toward me: ' "Too Close for Comfort." '

At that moment I knew plots and plans were foolish; my mind and will floated away and, just as in the movies, we both put down our glasses at the same time, not unlocking our eyes or looking at the table but making perfect contact. When his arms went around me, glints of light sparked in my head as if from a knife sharpening on a wheel, and my veins felt filled with warm, carbonated water.

The first morning light awakened me, and for a second I didn't know where I was. Then it came back, and seeing his form beside me a wave of remorse passed through me. What had I done? I was married to Neal, and now I felt sorry for him as well as afraid of what would happen next. The leather of the old couch was cold under me, and my muscles felt cramped. As quickly and silently as I could, I slid out from under the blanket and ran upstairs to my own bed, hoping for a few more hours of oblivion. It was no use. My mind kept frying the situation on all sides. I felt more shy of Jack than ever, and I didn't see how I could look him in the face. Would he be sorry?

I heard him getting up and come up the stairs, so I pretended to be asleep. All at once I felt his lips on my forehead, lingering, and a flood of soothing warmth poured over me as he climbed the stairs to his attic, and I drifted into sleep.

He accepted our new relationship more enthusiastically than I had expected, but I was pleased my guilt was thus diminished. Jack was a tender and considerate lover, though somewhat inhibited, and I suspected he wished I was more aggressive, but that I could never be. So our temperaments and our guilty feelings about Neal made actual love-making infrequent but more passionate. Although I could be wholly romantically in love with him, my heart still ached for Neal to be enough. Also, my compassion for anyone in Neal's position made me feel even more loving toward him, and I wavered in my resolve to teach him a lesson. I'd have sworn allegiance again in an instant, but I prodded my mind to remember his flippant words of indifference. I hoped sincerely that some lasting good would come from this, but for now there was nothing to do but relax and enjoy it.

Whenever Neal was home, Jack and I were extremely discreet, but there was no concealing the change in us. Neal couldn't help but notice, though the only evidence we had that he cared was his increased attentiveness to me.

The hope that my gamble would change the pattern of our lives was well founded. Like night changing into day, everything was showered with new light. Butterflies bursting from cocoons had nothing on me. Now, I was a part of all they did; I felt like the sun of their solar system, all revolved around me. Besides, I was now a real contributor for once; my housework and childcare had a purpose that was needed and appreciated. I was functioning as a female and my men were supportive. It may have taken two of them to complete the role usually filled by one, but the variety was an extra added attraction. They were such different types. How lucky could a girl get?

I provided for whichever of them was in residence according to his individual preferences. If they were both home during the day, Neal usually slept and Jack wrote, or Jack would go out and leave the husband and wife alone. On occasion, Jack and I would make love in his attic if the children were asleep. He'd produce a poor-boy of wine and play host. I think of him now whenever I smell unfinished wood, and remember how the sun sometimes lay across us like a blanket; or how, huddled under covers, we'd listen to the soft patter of the rain close above our heads.

When both men became accustomed to the idea, they dropped their defenses and joined me downstairs in the kitchen. While I performed my chores, they'd read each other excerpts from their writings-in-progress or bring out Spengler, Proust, Céline or Shakespeare to read aloud, interrupted by energetic discussions and analyses. Frequently they would digress and discuss a musician, or a riff or an interesting arrangement emanating from the radio. I was happy listening to them and filling their cups. Yet, I never felt left out any more. They'd address remarks to me and include me with smiles and pats, or request my view.

They still made forays together in search of tea or to buy necessities, but they were never gone long, and if Neal was at home, Jack and I sometimes took walks in the neighborhoods nearby. In Chinatown we marveled at the weird food displayed in the markets, the gorgeous embroidered clothing and the endless bric-a-brac in the tourist shops. Jack found an old-time Chinese restaurant with a white-tiled entrance on a little street adjacent to St. Francis Park. We'd buy steaming bowls of won-ton soup for 35¢ or fried rice for 25¢. Often we warmed ourselves thus and then sat on a bench in the park beneath the magnificent Benny Bufano steel and marble statue of Sun Yat Sen. Other times we walked down the hill to Aquatic Park and drank Irish coffee in the Buena Vista or down the Union street hill to Washington Square, taking French bread, cheese and wine purchased at the Buon Gusto market to nibble beneath the glittering gold spire of the cathedral. This reminded Jack of his childhood church in Lowell where he'd been baptized, St. Louis en l'Ile, and of his desire to see the original in Paris. On bright days we might hike up Telegraph Hill to Coit Tower and gaze out over the Bay, watching the ships, and that would be his cue to tell me of his seafaring adventures.

The times when Neal and I were alone were happier, too. We had the children's progress, illnesses and antics to discuss, as well as household economics. I felt especially affectionate toward him now, and he accepted and returned these expressions in better grace. I wondered if it was because he tended to appreciate his women more when the relationship was threatened, or whether a rival made him feel less trapped. At the moment I didn't care. Meals together amused me and gratified my ego. Here the two men were like small boys, vying for the most attention, for the best story, and felt slighted if one was allowed to hold the floor too long. Jack was the more sensitive, sometimes taking offense or sulking if Neal talked exclusively to me and behaved as though he weren't there. At times like these, Jack might stalk upstairs, and Neal would have to go and coax him back and make it up to him. Neal still had to prove he was the best man around. By and large, my cup was running over.

Already, in the first couple of months since Jack's arrival, my self-esteem had expanded as I found myself accepted as a desirable companion both mentally and physically. So I decided to go along with Jack's expectation that I would now join him, with or without Neal, on evenings out, although I was apprehensive, still conditioned by past experiences and less comfortable in the Bohemian scene than I had been when younger and unencumbered. Young people now seemed more intense, clutching, and I couldn't help feeling they took themselves too seriously. I wondered if the increasing use of drugs could account for this, but whatever the cause, 'good, clean fun' appeared to be a thing of the past. Or perhaps the aura of suspicion and defensiveness was merely a reflection of my own fears. . . .

Diane DiPrima

Diane DiPrima dedicated her humorous first book of prose sketches, Dinners and Nightmares *(1961), to her "pads & the people who shared them with me." In these wryly affectionate* Dinner *excerpts subtitled* What I Ate Where, *she described a variety of different memorable food experiences in New York, as early as the August 1950 iced coffee she shared with her girlfriends from Hunter High School, and the cheap stews like "menstrual pudding" she and her friends cooked a short time later in the East Village in her earliest years as a writer, as well as the solitary Oreo chocolate cookies and a lover's promise of raw clams that sustained her during some months on her own.*

from DINNERS AND NIGHTMARES

WHAT I ATE WHERE

the first i remember to tell of was the food on east fifth street. all kinds of food on east fifth street but the kind i'm remembering now to tell of we called menstrual pudding. it wasn't so bad really, was merely potatoes in tomato sauce and that's all no spices even and no no meat. but to pretend there was meat and that we were eating stew we put the tomato sauce. the potatoes were just potatoes which are ok if you like potatoes. some people i notice are crazy about potatoes. i'm not and never was, i can't say menstrual pudding turned me against them, i just plain never liked them to start with. not mashed not homefries not even bakedidahowithbutter.

how come we called it that was this cat jack who was staying there at the time, he had that kind of mind, i mean he called things things like menstrual pudding. we ate it for three or four days as i remember, i was going to say for breakfast lunch and supper, but that wouldn't be true because we just gave up on those three, on breakfast lunch and supper i mean, and ate when we couldn't help it, and after a while the potatoes got mushier and mushier and finally the whole thing was almost only mush. we added water too at the end if i remember.

it wouldn't have been so bad, menstrual pudding, if it weren't for the color of the walls, taupe, which just didn't go with tomato sauce, no, and especially not on grey days. how come the walls were taupe was we wanted to paint them beige, that is i did, cause almost everybody else said why not leave them grey in one room and pale yellow in the other and not too dirty why paint them at all. but no i thought beige and black would be very chic and i wanted a very chic apartment especially for this very chic girl i knew who hardly ever came down there anyway but. so but to save money we bought white paint which is the cheapest, a dreadful grade of it that rubbed off like chalk when it dried but it was the cheapest, and we bought four gallons of it and with it a tube of paint tinter whatever you call it. i figured to get beige what you needed was a light offbrownish color, so i figured burnt sienna which i'm fond of anyway, a little of it in white would make beige. it didn't. it made pink. now pink walls (i tried it out) are not chic and they make you want to vomit, and besides i hate pink anything almost there are a couple of things pink which i don't hate but we won't mention them shall we, and they are anyway not walls. so we went out again to the paint store to figure out what to do with these four gallons of something what was it pink light-burnt-sienna which we had rashly mixed all of in a big pot-thing saying if we add a little more it will turn beige until it had become pink indeed and i mean it. and in the paint store we looked at the colors, all of us dancers, writers, folk singers, none of us painters in the least, looked at them and looked and tried to figure what mixed with this pinkstuff would make beige and finally settled on raw umber, which when we added turned the whole thing taupe. and we gave up and painted everything taupe by candlelight so we wouldn't have to see too much the color, and it was within these taupe walls which rubbed off like taupe chalk and were all runny of different shades of taupe that we ate our menstrual pudding on those four grey november days that year and how many of us there were i don't remember.

i remember iced coffee made from powdered skim milk and coffee ice cubes and a sprinkle of cinnamon, and this was very good indeed. it was a very hot night, summer and august, in the same apartment where i later had my first meal in new york, and we were then still in high school or just graduating. it was a veritable gathering of maidens, enough to make your mouth water, enough even to make my mouth water in retrospect, how we were. we were all dressed in this new garment we had just invented, it was a half slip which you hung just above your breast and tied with a sash just under your breasts or around your middle or low like a flapper on your hips if you wanted and if you had a longish one. they stopped high up and they were cool and comfortable in august and they looked good which counted dreadfully with us, though there was only us in the pad and we had all seen each other look good and not look good on a great many occasions. there was a mattress on the floor in the front room, the windows were open, sometimes a breeze, and endless supplies of this drink and it seems to me, i may be wrong, but it seems to me we were happy.

i remember the winter the january i ate nothing but oreos. if you know what oreos are, they're those chocolate cookies two of them at a time stuck with sugar in the middle, and very addictive. i mean i really got hooked on them. there was this low armchair in my pad and i would sit in it and eat oreos and read and sometimes drink a little milk or water cause oreos in large numbers they tend to stick in your teeth.

when i wanted company i would go upstairs and visit these

two girls who were my neighbors. they were a little crazy. they liked oreos too but not as much as i did, i mean not three or four packages a day, but anyway they would sit there and eat them with me to keep me company, and they washed theirs down with ale. ale and oreos i didn't dig too much, together like that. but boy, to hear the wind blow and all that awful january rain and a bunch of windows looking out on old crumbling filthy brick walls, and to sit in the middle of all this eating oreos and reading was—well anyway it was a way to get through january. to get through january in manhattan is hard, to get through january and february the same year almost impossible.

one of the best ways to get through i found was this of eating oreos. except that it makes you fat. really fat. even if you don't eat anything else and you think, shit, how can i get fat i haven't had breakfast or lunch or anything like that, but don't kid yourself. OREOS MAKE YOU FAT.

or maybe it's just me. the girls upstairs ate a lot of them, but i couldn't tell if they were getting fatter or skinnier because they never got out of bed. that was a weird pad. the bed was in the center of the center room and they were in the center of the bed. the edges of the bed were for ashtrays and beer cans and beercan openers and pastels and oreos. and they had these red lights that they turned on all the time with that grey outside it was too much, and dust over everything like you read about in biographies of proust and try to imagine but you hardly ever encounter it. real genuine dust-from-not-moving, from not capering about, not the kind of dust you 'raise' the kind that drifts slowly, settles in through a whole grey winter. we would sit and eat oreos and drink ale if there was any and sometimes one of them would draw in a black book with pastels and everytime it rained we would talk about the fallout.

and one day the girl who never drew said she would draw too, it was snowing, and she got out the other one's water colors, and while the other one drank ale, and i did terrible abstract pastels, she carefully like a child drew an apple and a pear each two inches above a wobbly perspectivy table and carefully like a child she filled them all in with color, the pear yellow the apple orangy-red and the table brown and it was very beautiful. and she said There that's my still life what else is there to paint? and we said Landscapes. and so she drew a tree with a bird in it and a very tall flower stem and the flower on top of the stem was also the sun and it was like blake or redon but much more childlike and lovely, and she said There, that's finished what else is there to paint. and we said People. and she drew and painted all in one color a grey blue a very all wrong lumpy disproportionate person who was not beautiful at all, and then she said There i have finished, i have mastered the art of painting. and we said to her No you haven't because your people aren't right yet. but she said That is how they are, and if they are not right i will be known as a painter of landscapes and still lifes.

and then i went out and brought back from the snow pastrami sandwiches and ale and yes more oreos and we waited for it to get dark.

it happened one night he was leaving, this lover, a lover i was in love with, and he said do you like raw clams? and i said yes i love them, i do i love raw clams i would eat them every day except i can't open them. people have tried and tried to show me how but i can't and so i only eat them at stands and in the cedar. ok he said i'll come by tomorrow in the afternoon and i'll bring clams lots of them i love them too and we'll have lunch. so i said fine and the next afternoon i took a bottle of wine, white wine i had been saving and put it in the icebox, and knowing him how he was always late i went into the study to think up something to do, a thing to do until he got there.

i took out a pair of dice and made some rules and began to write a play by chance, which is a good way to pass time and not very difficult, and at the time i called it six poets in search of a corkscrew, which was a title that had been hanging around. i used the radio and elizabethan plays and pieces of old poems and letters from people and i wrote this play and soon it got dark, i was still writing, i wrote it out by hand, and then it was finished and still he hadn't come. so i cleaned the kitchen and took a shower and started, just about started to study greek, by then it was anyway nine o'clock or so and then somebody knocked on the door and it was him.

it was him he had forgotten all about the clams and i said do you want some wine and he said yes and we went inside, it was dark, we drank wine out of earthenware japanese tea cups and somehow the clams didn't matter one way or the other.

later on we did the play it was called paideuma.

Brenda Frazer

Brenda Frazer published Troia: Mexican Memoirs *in 1969 under her married name of Bonnie Bremser. At the time she wrote the book her husband Ray was serving a five-year prison sentence, and she was living in New Jersey to be near him. She remembers that "we were allowed only infrequent visits and a one page letter per week. So I included two additional pages of prose for him to edit and managed to expand our communication a little that way. Writing discipline consisted of copying my favorite author, Kerouac, and adopting a ritualistic existence centered around the daily hour or so of actual writing. I had only my memories, and recalling them was part of the creative atmosphere I set for myself. . . . I lived on Café Bustelo, beans, and rice. It took about a year at this pace of two pages a day to write the book."*

Frazer considered her book "an attempt at self-analysis and as such the explicit property of me and my husband. The subsequent publication of Troia *was ok only because I was at that time leaving the country again with my husband and never planned to return." She was angry that the publisher sensationalized her book with the title "Troia," meaning adventuress or whore. The dustwrapper for the memoir promised the reader that the book about the Bremsers' adventures in Mexico with their baby daughter Rachel, dodging the American law from Matamoros to Mexico City to Veracruz and beyond, was "a female* On the Road." *The character referred to as "P" was the poet Philip Lamantia.*

from TROIA: MEXICAN MEMOIRS

Once across, we were quickly tired of Matamoros and purchased tickets to Mexico City. Transportes Del Norte, maroon
buses, nothing to complain of in these first class accommodations, we had enough money to get safely to Mexico City
from where we were somehow to get safely to Veracruz, where
we were to find our refuge . . . had I already exchanged one
fear for another? Had the cold damp night of Matamoros put
another chill into my heart? Was my fear at this time all com-
posed of not being able to handle external circumstances,
afraid I would not be able to keep Rachel healthy, or at least
not crying, (and that was a feat I didn't often succeed in,) and
not to be able to satisfy Ray—what was happening in his head,
something similar? And it all was so extremely personal, this
service of responsibility, that the failure of it and maybe the
success I have not had much chance to experience up to this
point was a very lonely thing; we were not really helping each
other too much now. Each of us was just clinging as well as
possible to what shreds of strength were left in the confidential
self. The bus ride to Mexico City, full of this, I am constantly
with the baby on my lap, broken hearted at every spell of
crying, the frustration of not being a very good mother
really—trying to groove, trying to groove under the
circumstances—and in spite of it I have impressions of dark
shrouded nights of passage through the hills, of an oasis of
light in a restaurant stop. 2 A.M. with everyone sitting around
the narrow lighted room—with a sense of it being the only
lighted room for fifty miles around—eating eggs Mexican style
for the first time. Ray got his *huevos rancheros* and me eggs
scrambled with fried beans and this was sort of a prelude to
our Mexican trip. This meal in itself would come to be one of
the great Mexican treats; eggs, how many places have we had
those eggs I came to remember with great pleasure, but then,
at that time, it was fear and anxiety not even to know how to
ask for an egg in Spanish and though I probably exaggerate
now the lostness of not being able to make myself understood,
I can now see that it was not just the language that caused the
fear. Somehow the fear was cumulative, the desire growing as
the inability increased.

The trip—maroon bus awaits us beside the low immigration building, near the broken-down bridge—beer cans clatter in the dusty road afternoon no sunlight but the approaching lowering clouds of a thunderstorm spreading out over the sky into gray vastness of a depressing standstill underneath any tree; lonely your reality here in Matamoros, the streets which carry through the center of town growing in importance to the four central parallels which cut out the square of the plaza, where afternoon *bistek* eaters and shoe-shine boys eye each other from across the unpaved streets; these same streets spread outward into the still mathematically correct city layout but sidewalks disappear and houses rise in midst of a block shacked upwards from a broken down fence entryway by eroded paths; a house may take any shape or position within a block and weeds of menacing aspect care little for the store on the corner so drawn into its cache of paper candies and orange soda signs it has shrunk to the stature of a poverty-struck doll house— the incredible ironies of Mexico—the wild-flung filth of Matamoros. Leaving town on the bus, mud hole crossroads fifty yards wide of rutting and industry—some International Harvester or reaping machine showroom with its economic splendor surveying the city; it will grow on, and the sky disapproves. Pass Sta. Teresa, a cafe faces east on the flat land. Look across to the Gulf, and nothing looks back, save the mesquite bushes, a mangy dog chases a couple of not promising cows across a landscape you would not expect to carry even that much vision of life. Seen from the air, Transportes Del Norte carries on, a vision of good service, sixty people burning up the dust on the first stretch of the roads which do indeed all lead to Mexico City—San Fernando, Tres Palos, Encinal. The sun shines briefly as I change the baby's diaper and we have a cup of coffee and head back to the bus. Santandar Jimeniz, we do not know yet that from here dots one of those "almost" roads perpendicular to the route of travelling civilization. A road which grows out of the solid surety of modern highway dotting in weak secrecy into the plain to Abasolo where another almost not to be seen road, goes nowhere, but goes—we want to see where all the roads go, since then, but this first trip just get us there and quick, get us there where we are going, and we don't know yet that nothing waits but the bottom waiting to be scraped in our own whimsical and full-of-love fashion—got to get there and quick—damn the crying and wet diapers and laps full of Gerbers on the bus, of leg cramps and not much to view—Padilla, Guemez, Ciudad Victoria, chicken salad sandwiches and the unknown feeling of a waterfall. In all of these places we stop, passing through, rushing downward, seeking our level, slowly dying, get it over, let's get there. Ciudad Monte, non-stop Valles, passing in the night the bus driver picks up on lack of sleep, answers on the wheeling whispering pavement. We take our first curves into the hills, the roads start to swing—Tamazunchale, lights seen across a valley, Jacala, pencil marks on maps of future excitement. We turn East in the night approaching Ixmiquilpan, herald Indian feathers, the driver mutters incoherent names over the sleeping passageway, the bus careens as we shoot through Actopan, come another and final turning point at Pachuca. The driver announces the last lap and everyone stirs and gets excited at the news, not realizing it is more than 3 hours of approach to Mexico City. I look out and God drops from his hand the myriad stars and constellations I have never seen before, plumb to the horizon flat landed out beneath the giant horoscopic screen of Mexican heaven.

Why do I hold back and hide, when I am sure at least of one person as understanding as I of my own faults and maybe as proud of our achievements. Oh yes, let's don't get personal about it at this late hour—had we done so earlier, tempestuous natures would have wracked to the lowest hill what now begins to seem almost a peaceful Arcadia we retire to, even in exile, now. . . .

Two o'clock *en la mañana,* we arrive in Mexico City and the bus leaves us off at ADO and not at the Transportes Del Norte bus terminal. In a swelter of homeless appearing people whom we don't recognize there are many who are waiting for the morning bus perhaps, and though they look disreputable something will eventually be brought out of their packs to make them proud—like us, our records, our chevrons at that point I guess, on our way to make the scene at P's and it couldn't be too soon for me. I was cold, tired and ready for the new day to dawn with everything O. K., as usual. Taxi drivers, *caldo* eaters of the night, our soon-to-be-compadres of doubtful reckonings on Mexico City taxi meters. When the meter registers two pesos, the passenger somehow must pay four and even more surprisingly we find out this is not just tourist graft and that the taxi in Mexico is one of the cheapest rides anywhere with privacy like a king; cheapest except for the bus ride, if you are game, but that is more rollercoaster thrills.

P was not at home. We walked looking for a place to have coffee and get warm, for though we travel light we have the burdens of 300 miles in our heads. I remember now the opposite trip for me later when I flew from Mexico City to Washington in five hours and was dizzy for days afterward, unbelieving—and now I make the trip in my head, slowly, in pieces, this morning with the sun I climb the overhanging hills of Acapulco, alone, lonely, alone, full of the meaning of death, and life, either end of it, Mexico, Mexico, your sun crashes me in the head obliterating all bodily care, all shame, shameless Mexico, I am your child, and you have my child as the token.

Like the man who taps you on your waiting-for-hours shoulder, P finally comes to the window, ahh, relief, I give the baby a little jiggle for joy, ooyboy, baby, this is it, we enter. Five flights up, an imposing building, strange this is for us, even in a strange country. In Hoboken we live in houses of the renovated artist type, to put it politely. We live in ramshackle houses where we can and love it—modern apartment buildings for us, whafor? But I am tolerant for once, maybe even glad, I want to flake, a couple of hours of peace, unmoving. But there is no peace for our bodies, more food for the soul on top of all the rest, and maybe it is better, the truth, soul full of food in Mexico. . . . We turn on, do indeed at this point display our chevrons and for once they are appreciated, but we were used to that, Change of the Century, Ray Charles. We all were there at that first meeting, P, L, his blond stage-managing wife, in bed asleep, no doubt working the next day, in spite of our cataclysmic arrival, but P knows and believes, as all groovy poets who dig us, no one otherwise could. We had met P in our marriage year, arriving in San Francisco on foot, having just aired our souls on the Mojave Desert. He took us to his room in the B Hotel and, handing us one enormous reefer, proceeded to read stuff that will knock you out, poetry that cannot fail to hit you in your own personal cause of it all, and therefore we love him, that is P still, I believe. N was there, as I say, the whole Mexico crew, jive N, the first of the absconders, who had I believe invited us to Mexico, in lieu of staying to testify at Ray's trial, whereby we would have had double strength of truth on our side, but what does that matter, all visions of trial and parole past, have we not achieved our escape, have we not disembarked from it all and many mornings together in the waste of a life will prove it's no mistake. Salvage what you can, when there is no hope, run for your life, this is what I felt all along, the closing, around the ears like a bad drug taking hold which has been administered involuntarily.

Melchior Ocampo in the morning light is not half so scary and we all retire to the nearby hip food stand and eat hamburgers and apple pie with ice cream and coffee. It is one of those great pot feasts that are always for all time remembered like some memorial along the road of our beautiful experiences. God praise marijuana, yes, my baby, I will never put you down. A few things stay close to our hearts, definitive, a happy to have habit thing with no pain, no remorse, no sickness—although we did contact some people in Mexico who were profound expostulants of LOCOS who had smoked too much, (this was more a way of bragging that the pot you buy for an arms length thick amount costing less than a dollar is likely to shack you up until you decide to buy again), we have never had more than one or two disagreements with them, and that purely external, say for instance once or twice not having the minimum of survival and therefore having to do without, and only then, and then it was a frenzy to get straight and quick, and nothing wrong with that I guess. Sweet marijuana—lotus blossom I am entitled to call you now, being thoroughly a member of the club.

Ray was perhaps responding to the illusion of everything being beautiful. He always was ahead of me in that respect, and I do respect, although it in fact leaves me behind. He decided to stay in Mexico City for twenty-four hours more while it is decided for me that I will travel to Veracruz by bus with N and the baby. Ah bitter, I was not about to accept with grace my maidenly burdened-by-baby responsibility at this particular time. I should have put my foot down instead of being shuffled because see what it did in rebellion (sure! almost sure! suspecting something really wrong since Matamoros—that Ray had already set his eye on something that didn't include me—what could it be—my perceptions were not sharp) and my survival reflexes were working overtime, I guess. But I go—midway between holding the baby on the eight hour bus trip, the night quickly sets in and I decide to try my seductive powers on N, and the mistaken blue jeans, not to survive this episode, did indeed entice his hand where it should have by any standards stayed away from, the baby on my lap, we arrive in Mexico, me zipping up alone, my lonely pleasure, had I known I could have got in any restroom by my own mechanics—damn N.

If I could only do more than grab at a passing branch over my head, but the trouble with that is everything up until now has taken place fast on the go, the screeching terror of speed of everything falling out from underneath you—the recurring dream of bridges falling and falling away from beneath your very feet into rushing water, the resulting social shock, but more than that, knowing what it is to fall for the last time forever.

I set down in Veracruz, not I alone, me and the little me, Rachel, we arrive there escorted into taxi cab jive and Veracruz barely registers our arrival. The American Consul is not informed, the DA knows not what is about to hit him, the FBI thinks that we are maybe laid up with a cold in Hoboken. And yet we are already doing the dance; the Paso Doble of passionate worth dissembles all other meaning of life and we dance, we all dance, Veracruzano's Negroes, the woman on the corner shakes her wet clothes into a floating heap on some not so precious patch of grass, gelatinas yelled through the streets, the palms again, all dancing dancing, the sun rises, Veracruz rises, some altar on this Easternmost coast, the morning of Mexico, Veracruz rises beyond the sugar fields. Oh Cordoba, the plaza dances, the streetcar certainly dances, this is the dance of the sun I have fallen into and knowing my own heart also at least dance, abide the sacrifice, it is unimportant, but dance. . . .

Brion Gysin

Brion Gysin transcribed his memory of the Beat Hotel in Paris at 9 rue Git-le-Coeur as a bit of "nostalgia" to accompany his friend Harold Chapman's brilliant photographic essay on the hotel in its heyday in the late 1950s, early 1960s, before it was sold in 1963 by its owner Madame Rachou to a Corsican couple who completely renovated it and called it the Hotel Vieux Paris. Burroughs fondly recalled that in the old days a glass of wine cost less than a cup of coffee at the hotel bar. The American Express Guide to Paris *currently lists the hotel in its "Literary Left Bank" tour as the one where "Allen Ginsberg and others of the 'Beat Generation' used to stay." Here Ginsberg wrote his poem "At Apollinaire's Grave" and Peter Orlovsky started to write poetry in 1957. The following year Gregory Corso wrote his poem "Bomb" at the hotel and let Jack Kerouac sleep over-night on the floor of his closetlike room. At the Beat Hotel William Burroughs readied the manuscript of* Naked Lunch *for his publisher Maurice Girodias of Olympia Press in 1959 and collaborated with his friend Gysin on various literary experiments, including the method of composition they called "the cut-up." Gysin also published a grisly humorous pornographic novel about "beatnik" life in the Beat Hotel,* The Last Museum *(1986), in which Burroughs and Corso made brief appearances under the names "William Buroon" and "Gregorio Corsorio."*

from THE BEAT HOTEL, PARIS

Madame Rachou who ran our fleabitten rooming-house with "inflexible authority," as William Burroughs said, was "the perfect landlady" and our guardian angel. She had no use for the police, none at all. If she was "tender" with us, she was "pugnacious" with them, determined not to let them set foot in the place, not even her little bistro on the street with its already old fashioned zinc-topped bar. She may have had to splash out a free drink or two of her sour white wine for a plain clothes cop now and then but if she did, we never knew it. She was so small she had to stand on an overturned wine-case, the better to keep an eye on things. She could peer out into our narrow little street through her aspidistra plants and lace curtains to see who was coming or going. She could also see through a panel in the door onto our filthy entrance hall to see who was trying to slip in or out unnoticed. If some suspicious character zipped in like a flash, she could hop down from behind the bar and get a second look at him or her through her diningroom window which gave on the stairs. It was put there originally no doubt to catch a welshing lodger by the leg.

Madame Rachou was infinitely suspicious of electricity and had good good reason to be, given the primitive 19th century electrical installation in the house whose cellars may well have dated back to Roman times as do many of the buildings in the Latin Quarter. Nevertheless, she had to depend on it to keep track of more or less what was going on in the forty odd rooms on six and a half floors of her territory. This was her "*Espion*," her spy, her "Light Control Panel," as Mr Chapman calls it. Amazing 19th century invention though it was, there were more ways than one to circumvent it. When William Burroughs and Ian Sommerville and I began playing around with tape-recorders all those light years ago, we began by paying Madame Rachou our dollar or so apiece for more wattage. Then Ian wired up our three rooms together with telltale electrical extensions looping over the façade on our alley. This provided enough juice for Cut-Ups and Permutations on tape but we had to listen to them played back by candlelight. "*Dreama-chines*," flashing in the alpha band at eight to thirteen interruptions of the light source per second, came later. Dear old Madame Rachou had no idea of the strange epoch-making inventions which were hatching under the crazy tiled roof of her home for the homeless.

Or did she? William Burroughs used to say sententiously: "Madame Rachou has her orders." Whatever did he mean? I remember once slily "buttering her up" when I could not get off the rent money by praising her for her tenderness toward penniless painters. Airily, she replied: "Oh, ever since I knew Monsieur Monet . . ." I cross questioned her while shuffling through my memory for the dates of the Impressionists. It turned out that she had begun working at the age of twelve in a country inn at Giverny only a short walk from Monet's studio and home in the middle of his waterlily ponds. Monet used to stroll down after a morning's work on his gigantic canvases to have lunch there with his old friend Pissaro. "And whatever became of his son, the young M'sieu Pissaro?" I was happy to tell her that there was a big show of his work hanging at that moment in a national museum in Paris and offered to take her to see it but she had no time to spare from her guardianship of the Beat Hotel.

"This fleabag shrine will be documented by art historians," wrote another alumnus, Harold Norse in his: "*Death of Number Nine Rue Git le Coeur.*" We knew we were working against time. We were well aware of the dangers of too much publicity for our frail little fortress. A well-timed article with photos in a slick rag like LIFE could burn the place down overnight and we would be out on the street or in jail with our memories. We were living on borrowed time as well as borrowed money and very little of it. We looked askance at green young Americans with a fistful of American Express travelers' checks in their hip pockets and that postwar guide to an Americanized Bohemia under their arms: "*Europe on Five Dollars a Day.*" They could damn well go stay somewhere else. Five dollars was a lot of bread and Madame Rachou was particular about who owed her money. She had her orders, wherever they were coming from. If the Beats in the Beat Hotel were going to become a subject for Ph. D. doctoral theses and they have, now being taught in the Sorbonne itself, however are we going to account for all those little Swedish girls with incendiary headresses of lighted candles tottering perilously on their empty blonde heads? That's easy. They are the chorus of Muses whose silvery soprano voices one could hear trilling up the slippery stairs, calling: "Gregory! Gregoooory!" whenever Corso was in residence. And then he would yell back some flippant poetic obscenity from his eyrie under the roof at the top of the last flight of steps to immortality. "Fuck off! I'm too busy becoming immortal but come back later, sweet Poesy."

Joyce Johnson

Joyce Johnson saw her book Minor Characters *(1983) adver-*
tised as being "A memoir of a young woman of the 1950s in
the Beat orbit of Jack Kerouac," but Johnson intended her book
to do more than document her love affair with Jack Kerouac.
She wanted it to celebrate the lives of several anonymous women
friends who wanted to be writers or artists but became instead
the "minor characters" in the background of more famous peo-
ple. One of these women was Allen Ginsberg's girlfriend Elise
Cowen, Joyce's classmate at Barnard College in 1950. It was
Elise who later asked Ginsberg after she'd typed up the man-
uscript of "Kaddish," the long poem about his mother Naomi,
"You haven't done with her, yet?" In 1953, while a junior at
Barnard, Johnson was told by her male creative writing pro-
fessor that she and the other girls in the class should be out
"hopping freight trains, riding through America" if they wanted
to be writers. Ginsberg helped arrange Johnson's blind date
with Kerouac at the Howard Johnson's restaurant in Greenwich
Village in January 1957, during the time that Johnson was work-
ing as a secretary for the publisher Robert Giroux and just before
she sold her first novel to Random House. Minor Characters
won the National Book Critics Circle Award in 1984.

from MINOR CHARACTERS

> *On the Road* is the second novel by Jack Kerouac, and its publication is a historic occasion insofar as the exposure of an authentic work of art is of any great moment in an age in which the attention is fragmented and the sensibilities are blunted by the superlatives of fashion (multiplied a millionfold by the spirit and power of communication).
>
> —Gilbert Millstein, *New York Times,*
> September 5, 1957

There was a newsstand at Sixty-sixth Street and Broadway right at the entrance to the subway. Just before midnight we woke up and threw on our clothes in the dark and walked down there still groggy with the heaviness, the blacked-out sleep, that comes after making love. According to Viking, there was going to be a review. "Maybe it'll be terrific. Who knows?" I said. Jack said he was doubtful. Still, we could stop at Donnelly's on the way back and have a beer.

We saw the papers come off the truck. The old man at the stand cut the brown cord with a knife and we bought the one on the top of the pile and stood under a streetlamp turning pages until we found "Books of the Times." I felt dizzy reading Millstein's first paragraph—like going up on a Ferris wheel too quickly and dangling out over space, laughing and gasping at the same time. Jack was silent. After he'd read the whole thing, he said, "It's good, isn't it?" "Yes," I said. "It's very, very good."

We walked to Donnelly's and spread the paper out on the bar and read the review together, line by line, two or three more times, like students poring over a difficult text for which they sense they're going to be held responsible.

> . . . the most beautifully executed, the clearest and most important utterance yet made by the generation Kerouac himself named years ago as "beat," and whose principal avatar he is.
>
> Just as, more than any other novel of the Twenties, *The Sun Also Rises* came to be regarded as the testament of the Lost

Generation, so it seems certain that *On the Road* will come to
be known as that of the Beat Generation.

It was all very thrilling—but frightening, too. I'd read lots of
reviews in my two years in publishing: None of them made
pronouncements like this about history. What would history
demand of Jack? What would a generation expect of its avatar?
I remember wishing Allen was around to make sense of all
this, instead of being in Paris.

Jack kept shaking his head. He didn't look happy, exactly,
but strangely puzzled, as if he couldn't figure out why he wasn't
happier than he was.

We returned to the apartment to go back to sleep. Jack lay
down obscure for the last time in his life. The ringing phone
woke him the next morning and he was famous.

The call was from Keith Jennison, one of Jack's editors at
Viking, who was rushing up to the apartment with half a case
of champagne. He carried it up the four flights of stairs and
we drank it with orange juice, which seemed more Lost Gen-
erationish than Beat, as the phone kept on ringing with news
of reporters who wanted to interview Jack, and excited old
friends, and invitations to various gatherings, and my mother,
who wanted to know when I was coming to dinner and what
was all that talking going on in the apartment. It was the radio,
I said. But it was Jack, who'd downed a lot of champagne
rather quickly and finally gotten smashed and broken the quiet
that might have seemed gloomy to Keith Jennison, achieving
the boisterous high spirits appropriate to the occasion. Jack
had his own extravagant ideas of courtesy—in some way he
felt honor-bound to meet other people's expectations. Three
bottles of champagne were emptied with a rapidity that astonished Keith Jennison. When he left to go to his office, quite
mellow by then himself, he took me aside for a moment.
Squeezing both my hands in his, he looked urgently into my
eyes. "Take care of this man," he said.

The first of many interviewers of the author of *On the Road*
arrived a few hours later to get the inside story on the Beat
Generation and its avatar. What was it really like to be Beat?

he wanted to know. "Tell me all about it, Jack." When did you first become aware of this generation? And how many people are involved in it, in your estimation? Is America going to go Beat? Are you telling us to now turn our backs on our families and our country and look for kicks? What kind of society will we have in two years?"

"Hey," Jack said. "Have some champagne. My publisher came up with all this champagne this morning."

"Thank you, no. I'll stick to coffee." The interviewer made a note on his pad and explained that he did not want to cloud his impressions. Jack advised him to try writing when he was high. The interviewer said maybe he'd do it sometime, but it didn't go along with journalism when you were dealing with fact. Expansively Jack revealed he'd wanted to be a journalist himself, a great sportswriter, and his father Leo Kerouac had always hung out with newspapermen in the days when he was a printer in Lowell. The interviewer wasn't too interested in that. "Let's get back to the Beat Generation for a minute. Jack, why do you consider yourself and your friends 'beaten'?"

Eavesdropping from the kitchen, where I'm boiling water for coffee, I don't think much of this reporter, who seems to have swallowed Millstein's review without understanding it at all. Millstein had spoken of excesses and kicks and "violent derangements," but had also insisted Jack was expressing the need for affirmation—" 'even though it is upon a background in which belief is impossible,' " he'd written, quoting the Lost Generation critic John Aldridge. Was that so hard to understand?

Beaten? Bewilderedly Jack laughs and shakes his head, then with weirdly courteous patience launches into the derivation of the epithet—first uttered on a Times Square street corner in 1947 by the hipster-angel Herbert Huncke in some evanescent moment of exalted exhaustion, but resonating later in Jack's mind, living on to accrue new meaning, connecting finally with the Catholic, Latin *beatific*. "*Beat* is really saying *beatific*. See?" Jack so earnest in making his point so the interviewer can get it right, respecting the journalistic search for accuracy although he knows accuracy is not the same as truth.

Again and again in the coming months he will go through this derivation with increasing weariness—for other journalists, in labored articles he himself will write. Blinking into the glare of hot white lights he will repeat it before television cameras and deliver it into microphones on the stages of auditoriums, the words slurring progressively, emptying; wine will make them flow disconnectedly from the shamed fool on stage.

No one had much patience for derivations by 1957. People wanted the quick thing, language reduced to slogans, ideas flashed like advertisements, never quite sinking in before the next one came along. "Beat Generation" sold books, sold black turtleneck sweaters and bongos, berets and dark glasses, sold a way of life that seemed like dangerous fun—thus to be either condemned or imitated. Suburban couples could have beatnik parties on Saturday nights and drink too much and fondle each other's wives. I forget when it was that *beatnik* entered the vernacular—could it have been as soon as October? The San Francisco columnist Herb Caen gets the credit for inventing it. How deftly it got the whole thing down to one word. The Russian-sounding suffix (the ascent of Sputnik was in the public consciousness at the time) hinted at free love and a little communism (not enough to be threatening), as well as a general oafishness. "Beat Generation" had implied history, some process of development. But with the right accessories, "beatniks" could be created on the spot.

I went downstairs every morning and found the mailbox jammed with letters forwarded by Viking. "Dear Jack," they invariably began. He'd start reading one thinking an old friend of his had perhaps turned up, and discover the yearnings or fantasies of a stranger.

Dear Jack, I am dying in this little hick town. If I could only meet you, touch you . . .

Dear Jack, I don't know what you're driving at and I've put down your book half a dozen times because it made me dizzy & sick & thrilled & confused, and I said the hell with it. But when I get home at night, fed up with working and all the corny doings of the one-minded people who always know where they are going to sleep at night and where the next meal is going to be, I pick the damn thing up, and wow! Good luck to you. If you ever get sick of New York and don't mind masses of collies and cats, give me a ring and come out for a weekend. I'm so ancient you won't have to be embarrassed . . .

Dear Jack, Jefferson said—Yessir he did—"I have sworn on the altar of GOD ETERNAL hostility to every form of tyranny over the MIND OF MAN," hostility which THE AMERICAN PEOPLE make their own!! Hostility too, of course, to the obscene tyranny of Vaticanism & its evil cabal of celibates . . .

"Fuffnik's fan mail." Jack said sadly.

Hettie Jones

*Hettie Jones was one of the "minor characters" in Joyce John-
son's memoir, a Greenwich Village friend in the late 1950s who
was the wife of the African-American writer LeRoi Jones and
mother of their two daughters. In* How I Became Hettie Jones
*(1990), she described her transformation from Hettie Cohen, a
"small, dark, twenty-two-year-old Jew from Laurelton,
Queens," to Hettie Jones, a radical poet's wife who worked
full-time as a secretary for the conservative* Partisan Review.
*She came home after her secretarial job to help her husband
Roi run* Yugen, *an experimental magazine, and Totem Press,
which fostered the "new consciousness in arts and letters," in
their crowded apartment on West Twentieth Street in the Chelsea
district. Hettie Jones took a quotation from the writer Jane
Bowles as the epigraph of her book: "The idea . . . is to change
first of our own volition and according to our own inner prompt-
ings before they impose completely arbitrary changes on us."*

from HOW I BECAME
HETTIE JONES

Connected to the two front rooms on Twentieth Street was a
narrow kitchen with high, thickly painted cupboards, and over
the sink an oversize window of sooty smoked glass. The vague
shadow of a wall loomed up close, the brightest day came
through dulled. But dead center, onto the window frame, Roi
tacked a poem by Ron Loewinsohn, the opening work in *Wa-*

termelons, the first book issued—in 1959—by our publishing company, Totem Press. The poem brings to the reader the act of the art itself. It begins

> *The thing made real by*
> *a sudden twist of the mind:*

and ends

> *. . . thunders into*
> *the consciousness*
> *in all its pure & beautiful*
> *absurdity,*
> *like a White Rhinoceros.*

I read those words at all hours, in all strained lights, always to see that rhinoceros snorting toward me. The poems *were* our lives. Basil King, the painter who did some *Yugen* and Totem covers, claimed the beast himself. He was walking with Ron in San Francisco, he said, when Ron said, "We need an image that'll knock 'em over." "Well," said Basil, "how about a white rhinoceros?" And then later, pleased and surprised: "Damn if he didn't just go home and *write* about it!"

Whatever its country of origin, the presence of that animal over my sink was due to my husband, the sort of gesture from him that I valued. There's a habit to putting your heart on the wall, to modes of domestic expression. The one we fell into was peaceful and playful.

Another Friday, midwinter 1959, about six on a bitter cold evening. I've just come home from work, in the big black sweater I wear buttoned over an unzipped skirt. Although I always know it's there, I don't *think* about the baby much, most of the time I'm just living my life with it in me. Anyway tonight's a more imminent birth—*Yugen 4.* Something like the baby, its cover will be black with a white abstraction. Over the years every last issue will be sold, it will become, to the book trade, "rare." But now it's only corrugated boxes of reams of paper fresh from the offset printer. I hear the scuffle as they're dragged past the outside doors. Then, with a great show of strength, and moans and exclamations, they're carried inside by three excited young men.

In the lead, fair of face and form, with a midwestern open mien, is the cover artist himself, designer of the Totem logo, Fielding Dawson, known as Fee. He's one of the Black Mountain crowd, a writer and a painter. His blue eyes sparkle, his cheeks are red from the cold. Right behind him, wearing a jaunty peaked cap, is Roi, whose nose is red too, right through the brown, and who drops his heavy box—*bang*—as the cap falls off his head and rolls to the feet of the third man, Max Finstein, who neatly sidesteps, drops the box he's carrying—*crash*—his own hat falls off. The timing's perfect. They're bent over laughing. They think they're the Marx Brothers! I have to applaud. Max is a slight, wise, amber-bearded poet from Boston, the first man I've ever watched iron his own shirts. He's living on our couch at the moment.

In retrospect the three of them seem like a sentiment, a bohemian version of an ad for Brotherhood Week. But there—in that room designed for middle-class life, our formal "front parlor" with its tiled hearth and bay of venetian blinds—they're real, available to me, and revealing. And they're having such fun! Proudly stamping their frozen feet and blowing on their poor bare knuckles. Max produces a pint of brandy. We drink to the birth. Roi slits the boxes with my X-acto knife.

From a quick first look at *Yugen 4* you'd say Beat, as the three Beat gurus—Kerouac, Corso, and Ginsberg—were represented. Except the "new consciousness in arts and letters" was more inclusive. Like Basil King, Joel Oppenheimer, and Fielding Dawson, the poets Robert Creeley, John Wieners, and Charles Olson were out of Black Mountain College, where Olson was the last rector. Frank O'Hara, like the painters he knew, was a poet of the "New York School." Gilbert Sorrentino lived in Brooklyn, Gary Snyder in Japan, Ray Bremser in a Trenton, New Jersey, prison.

Gravely we check all twenty-eight pages. The centerfold is printed sideways, per instructions. But some of the covers are not what they ought to be. Fee looks disappointed.

I glance at Roi, who'd rather be perfect. He's got that tight look at the jaw, but he's still leafing through the box. "Hey, look here, the rest are okay," he says reassuringly, his own relief a little bit hidden. That's just like him. Of them all, he's the smallest, youngest, and skinniest. But he takes charge; he's the editor.

And he spent time at the editor's desk—the *Record Changer*'s huge rolltop, left to us by Dick [Richard Hadlock] and Ruth when they married and moved. (People regularly sat on it, but Joel—one crowded weekend—was the only one who ever slept on it.)

Past the kitchen on Twentieth Street a long hall led to three more rooms. The desk and books filled one, our narrow bed another. As for the third—because I can see in my mind its sunny, dusty window, I can't see why I didn't put a desk of my own there, and at my back a door that shut me into myself so I would write. I didn't even know how much I needed this. The room stayed full of a printing press someone gave us, which never worked, while I worked in the public eye, in the room with the double door that led to the street. Before we could afford to leave printing to the professionals, I put together *Yugen 3–6,* and a couple of small books, on a drafting board propped on the kitchen table.

Meanwhile we'd attracted attention. In late 1958, the critic Gilbert Seldes remarked that even though he wasn't always "with" the poetry in *Yugen* he found in it a lot of *feeling*—his italics. It was this that all my late-night cutting, pasting, aligning, and retyping finally taught me—what comes from reading things over and over, taking apart and putting together, the heart of the matter, the way it feels.

And there goes the doorbell. First Joel, with a scarf up to his nose, squinting from a day at the print shop where he works. After him the Brooklyn contingent: Gilbert Sorrentino and his wife, Elsene, with Cubby Selby, who looks like a sailor in his watch cap and pea jacket; then Joe Early, an editor, his wife, Ann; their friend Larry Hellenberg, a sheet metal worker; poet Sam Abrams and his wife, Barbara; Basil King and his wife, Martha; and Tony Weinberger, later the author of *Max's Kansas City Stories.*

With all these mouths to feed I get lots of instruction. The mysterious kitchen has been more or less revealed. I own a seasoned iron pot and a wooden salad bowl I rub with garlic, and I've mastered the rudiments, mostly of other people's ethnic dishes—though I've yet to shape a matzoh ball, I can make gumbo with okra and also spaghetti for a hundred. That's what we're having tonight. All the Italians are over the sauce. Both sexes—each one a poverty gourmet. No onions is Elsene Sorrentino's theory. She has two children and from my view a world of expertise. "No self-respecting Sicilian . . ." scoffs her husband, a tall, handsome man with expressive gestures and grimaces. "My mother would *never,*" he says, flinging his arms around. Elsene goes on cooking. I see it's all part of the big-life-poem: "With a knife in the kitchen / I cut / a tomato" ("A Fixture," Gilbert Sorrentino, *Yugen 4*).

Spoon in hand I glance at my husband the host, who doesn't cook. But he does clean up these parties: his specialty is mopping the floor. Meanwhile he's standing back to survey the scene. In the parlor Max and Fee are setting out stacks of pages that seem huge to me, at least a night's work. But I'm sure the job will be done, and carefully, and Roi is too. Accomplishment is the virtue of our life together. With a wide, satisfied grin, his chin tucked in and his arms folded tight across his chest, he's leaning against the wall that divides the rooms. It's as if he's trying to contain his pride, to keep it from bursting out of his body the way it has on his face. I know how he feels.

Midnight. We pass around a second wind, a vial of heart-shaped Dexedrines, the kind that look like Valentine candies and should say LOVE ME or I'M YOURS. Bottles line the floor at our feet, an unmistakable smell drifts down the hall. But drugs are expensive, their purchase and use are still risky, and we're for life over death. Even William Burroughs, whose writing is all about using, had warned in *Yugen 3:* "Stay away from Queens Plaza, son . . . Evil spot haunted by dicks screaming for dope fiend lover. . . ."

Three A.M. The last pages have been passed. The dozen of us has doubled, the couch and chairs are crowded, the room is alive with a din that satisfies every emptiness I've ever felt.

I'm adding covers to the final collated folded stacks, then passing the completed copy to Max, who's taking a turn at the stapler. Joel and Roi are having an argument, something about Ezra Pound. I stop what I'm doing to watch. Ray Charles's "What'd I Say?" is on the box. Elsene and Cubby are dancing. Martha King, in a paradoxical reaction to the Dexies, has fallen asleep. Her husband glowers from under his kinky hair; he thinks his wife can't hang. Roi's making a point; he's got his funny finger out while holding a quart of ale and the oversize bottle makes him seem even smaller, more concentrated, a bantamweight fighter going jab, jab, jab jab jab. . . . Suddenly, the strongest it's ever been, the baby inside me turns and turns again—dancing to Ray Charles!—and the copy of *Yugen* in my hand falls open to the sideways printed centerfold, a brief, compelling vision, part of the wide lines of "The Chamber," by Michael McClure:

> *Matchflame of violet and flesh . . .*
> . . . *clear bright light.*
> > . . . *stars outside.*
> . . . *long sounds of cars.*
>
> . . . *the huge reality of touch and love.*
>
> . . . *real as you are real whom I speak to.*

To me the homosexual life seemed the hardest and riskiest, almost certain to drive people crazy at some point. John Wieners stayed with us a while that year. He'd come east from California, and en route had lost his top front teeth. Embarrassed, smiling shyly behind his hand, he perched cautiously on our studio couch, a pale contrast to the bright Indian print spread. I admired not only his poems but the magazine *Measure,* which he'd founded. I told him so, and thought of telling him I liked his (shocking then) ponytail, but he was so bashful I hesitated even to mention it. How did one encourage such a soul?

In a world that denied their existence, I admired gay men who could party. Frank O'Hara and his roommate Joe LeSueur had a loft opposite Grace Church and they often filled it with people, including many women, with whom they were always friendly and careful. I liked gay irreverence, and it was Allen Ginsberg and his lover Peter Orlovsky who starred in my all-time favorite Twentieth Street party. Ambitious, dedicated Allen was in his early thirties by then. His twenties hadn't been easy—from Paterson, New Jersey, to Columbia University, a forced season in Bellevue—but now he seemed used to himself, and like Roi and me he made his own rules. I was drawn to this social ease, to his warmth and his smarts, his matter-of-fact relationship with Peter. The two of them sometimes liked to get nude in the middle of a fully dressed room—Allen dark, balding, bespectacled, Peter with a blond brush of hair and pretty body. Complacent, superior, they would pose—they never even seemed cold!—challenging the rest of us to follow (no one ever did).

Among our few possessions was a hat collection—a collapsible top hat I'd bought in a junk store, a Moroccan fez, a Stetson, a derby, a sombrero with long, grassy streamers. One Saturday night—I don't know how it started—there was a wild competitive rush for hats. After the real ones were claimed we had to invent. When Joel got a pot Gil got the salad bowl, the rest of us followed with paper, shoes, hastily reconstructed clothing. Joe Early looked like a bulky Sikh with his jacket wound on his head, and the woman with Cubby Selby braided her stockings into her hair. When I noticed Allen and Peter, they were stark naked and in a huddle, whispering. Then suddenly they shooed everyone off the couch, and heaving it to their heads began to dance around the room with it, yelling *"Hat! Hat! Hat! Hat!"* A roar of laughter rose and then applause for the winners, and so they took a victory run, around the front parlor, with the bright bedspread flipping and flapping around their bare posteriors!

Jan Kerouac

Jan Kerouac described the two occasions when she met her father Jack Kerouac in her first book, Baby Driver *(1981). Their first meeting was in New York City in 1961, when she was nine years old and living with her twin stepsisters and her mother Joan Haverty, Kerouac's second wife, in a tenement in the Lower East Side. Despite Jan's striking physical resemblance to Jack Kerouac, he denied that she was his child and insisted that his wife had other lovers during their brief marriage. Their second meeting six years later was in Lowell, Massachusetts, Kerouac's birthplace, where he had returned briefly to live with his mother Gabrielle, paralyzed from a stroke, and his third wife Stella Sampas, who was also from Lowell. This was in 1967, two years before his death.*

from BABY DRIVER

Toward late fall [1961] my mother was going to court all the time to try and get child support from our fathers. She must have gotten fed up with waitressing. The day was nearing when I was to meet my father for the first time. I remember a certain gullible part of my young mind thinking that nine and a half must be the age when one was grown-up enough to meet one's father for the first time. It meant I was maturing—a big girl now. Feeling more independent than usual, I went to the pizza parlor all the way up on Fourteenth Street. I had had my hair curled for the occasion, and as I watched the guy twirl the dough, I kept looking in the mirror at my new hair, not at all sure I liked it and worrying what my father would think of me.

In Brooklyn the next day, after a long subway ride, my mother and I met Jack and his lawyer at the appointed place and went strolling down the street together. I couldn't take my eyes off my father, he looked so much like me. I loved the way he shuffled along with his lower lip stuck out.

The lawyer nervously suggested we go somewhere for lunch, and was about to walk into a restaurant when Jack saw a place he liked better, and steered us to a bar across the street, in spite of the lawyer's feeble protests. I thought it was a great idea, wanting, as I did, to be in accord with this naughty bummish fellow. We sat down in a booth, my mother and I facing the two of them, and a hamburger was ordered for me. It was the day the first astronaut went up in space, and the TV up in the corner by the ceiling was showing him up in his capsule all bundled up in glaring black and white.

My mother and father seemed to be getting along just fine, and were talking about old times.

"Yeah," he was saying into his beer, "you always used to burn the bacon," jokingly accusing her. I could see why she had been attracted to him. He was so handsome with his deep blue eyes and dark hair hanging in a few fine wisps on his forehead. I liked hearing them talk about these things they used to do. It made me feel whole, confirmed the suspicions I'd had all along that I was an official bona fide human being with *two* parents.

After that, we had to go get blood tests, Jack and I, to determine if he was really my father. I felt like we were special somehow, as if our blood was some precious substance the laboratory needed, and we were the only two people in the world that had it. Then we went back to my neighborhood, bringing Jack with us.

As soon as we got to the apartment, he wanted to know where the nearest liquor store was, so I took him by the hand to the one on Tenth Street, proudly walking him past kids I knew as if to say, "See—I have one too."

In the liquor store, he bought a bottle of Harvey's Bristol Cream Sherry. That name is indelibly etched in my memory.

As we walked back, he talked to me but seemed shy, like a boy on his first date. I was nervous too, afraid I'd say something stupid.

Upstairs, he sat down at the kitchen table and peeled off the black plastic around the top of the bottle, as my sisters gathered around him curiously. He pointed at each little black peel and, furrowing his brow, said, "Shee im? Shs' Russian—shhhs' no good!" He kept doing this, to their delight, and telling my mother, "This one has laughing eyes and this one has melting eyes."

I was a little jealous that he was paying them so much attention, but I figured he didn't want to be serious, and me being older, maybe he was afraid we'd have to talk about something he didn't want to think about. So I watched his antics and smiled whenever he looked at me.

To my sisters, he was just another funny guy that came over to visit and entertain them, like Ray Gordon or Pete Rivera. But to me he was something special, he was my very *own* funny man out of all the others—like their father, Don Olly, was to them.

When he left, leaving the empty bottle surrounded by its debris on the table, I watched him go through the battered old door into the dark hallway, sitting still and staring at his vanishing point almost as if I knew he was coming right back. A few seconds later, he stuck his head back in and said, "Whoops, I forgot my survival hat."

I looked and found his funny smashed blue hat under the chair and handed it to him. He slapped it on his head and turned around to leave again.

"See ya in Janyary!" he called down the hall.

After the meeting with my father, things went on as always, except that the twins and I were closer, having spent the summer together on the Cape. I did my homework every night to the radio, and hung out in the candy stores by day, and every once in a while I'd take out my one souvenir of his visit—the cork from the bottle of sherry—and stare at it, wishing it would hurry up and be Janyary. . . .

We took the bus from Montpelier to Lowell, Massachusetts, through early autumn roads [1967]. In Lowell, the first place we went was a dark, dreamlike Chinese restaurant for tea while we looked up my father in the phone book. I was astonished to see a whole *list* of Kerouacs. I'd never in my life seen my name in a directory, not even in Manhattan, though I looked occasionally out of curiosity. Now here was a whole passel of them—Kerouack, Kirouack, various odd spellings.

I began by calling the ones spelled like mine, and before I knew it we were at the home of Doris Kerouac, amid a crowd of stocky French-Canadian relatives, all excitedly speaking *patois* and embracing me.

"The daughter! Jean never told us he had a daughter!" Shaking their heads and gesticulating, they bore us over to Jack's house on an ocean wave of strength, morality, and good will. I felt almost mentholated with gladness and security. So these were my *people*, hearty people with souls of gold. I wanted to stay with them and belong.

We arrived at the house where Jack lived. The door of the comfortable suburban house opened, and there was Stella, his wife, and his mother, Gabrielle, in a wheelchair.

My father sat in a rocking chair about one foot from the TV, upending a fifth of whiskey and wearing a blue plaid shirt. He was watching "The Beverly Hillbillies."

The relatives stormed in with boisterous good cheer, berating Jack for not telling them he had a daughter. They all evidently recognized me as a Kerouac from my face, and gave it no further thought. During all this uproar, John chose to wait outside, so as not to confuse matters.

Jack's reaction to me was shrugs and uncertain smiles. He said "Hi" but didn't make much of a fuss. When the doorway back-slapping and bantering was done with, he went back to his rocking again, calling to his brethren across the room, "Hey, why doesn't somebody turn this thing down, I can't hear myself think!" This seemed odd, for he was closer to the TV than anyone else in the room. But someone did turn it down for him, and he continued to guzzle his giant baby bottle, rocking himself as if in a cradle.

The relatives all left, and Jack nodded a casual so-long to them over his shoulder. I watched him curiously, once again with the feeling that I had to be careful of what I said, like I'd felt the first time I met him on Avenue B when I was nine.

He was desperately trying to keep his shield in place, at a loss for what to say.

At some point Jack discovered that John was outside, and, making an unusual effort, he got up and called him in, which made me happy. I thought it was important that they meet.

Upon seeing him, the first thing Jack said was, "Ahh, Genghis Khan, eh?" referring to his Oriental topknot. He managed to start a conversation with John, in order to steer clear of me, where he feared a confrontation. I think he was afraid that I wanted a big emotional father-daughter reunion. Right there in the same room was his mother to whom he had lied long ago, telling her that Joan Haverty's baby wasn't his doing. He knew that wasn't true. I could see the painful recognition in his eyes flash like a tiny blue spark each time our gazes met.

His wife Stella stood by, hospitable and courteous, but not much else. She was like a guard, making sure everything went smoothly, a Greek matron responsible for these two ailing Canucks she'd taken under her wing. Now that his mother could no longer take care of him, Jack had married another mother to take care of them both.

My father had found something he could talk to me about —some paintings on the wall.

"See this? Sa painting of the Pope. I painted it." He nodded proudly and added, "*before* he was the Pope." Then there was a painting of underwear hanging on a line that his friend Stan Twardowiscz had done. Last in line was a portrait of his little brother Gerard, who had died at age nine. When he told me about this one, I thought I heard his voice break, and he quickly went back to his whiskey.

I sat down on the couch next to him and stretched out my palms, asking cautiously. "My mother says we have the same hands . . . can I see your hands? I've always wondered."

He raised his eyebrows and shrugged, giving me a hand to examine. "Oh, she does? Hmmm, dunno."

They were the same, all right, only his were bigger.

John told him that we were on our way to Mexico, and I added that we had wanted to see him before we left, because we might be gone for a while. To which he replied, surprisingly,

"Yeah, you go to Mexico an' write a book. You can use my name."

Just about then, Gabrielle began to stir, calling in a high, disturbed voice, "Is Caroline there?" and "Foreigners! They're all foreigners!"

She might have thought I was Jack's sister, Caroline, whom I had never met. Stella told us we had to leave, since our presence was upsetting Gabrielle and she could have another stroke. So we left, and I felt cheated out of time. I had an idea that my father would have loosened up if I continued to talk to him. But then, I'd come visit when I returned from Mexico someday. . . .

Ken Kesey

Ken Kesey wrote a fictionalized account of the sad day in 1968 on his cattle farm in Oregon when he learned of the death of his close friend Neal Cassady. Cassady had been the driver of the bus on the cross-country trip taken by Kesey's group the Merry Pranksters, which proselytized for LSD five years before. Kesey's story was titled "The Day After Superman Died" and was published in a limited edition by Lord John Press of Northridge, California, in 1980, reprinted in number six of Ken Babbs's magazine Spit in the Ocean *in 1981, and included in Kesey's book* Demon Box *in 1986. Kesey called himself "Deboree" in the story. The "legendary Neal Cassady" was renamed "Houlihan," whose last words in Mexico were reported to be "Sixty-four thousand nine hundred and twenty-eight," the number of railroad ties he'd counted before his death. At the end of the story "Deboree" was reassured to think that "Houlihan wasn't merely making noise; he was* counting. He didn't lose it. We didn't lose it. We were all counting."

from THE DAY AFTER SUPERMAN DIED

He had been up two days, grassing and speeding and ransacking his mental library (or was it three?) for an answer to his agent's call about the fresh material he had promised his editor and to his wife's query about the fresh cash needed by the loan office at the bank. Mainly, since Thursday's mail, for an answer to Larry McMurtry's letter.

Larry was an old literary friend from Texas. They had met at a graduate writing seminar at Stanford and had immediately disagreed about most of the important issues of the day—beatniks, politics, ethics, and, especially, psychedelics—in fact, about everything except for their mutual fondness and respect for writing and each other. It was a friendship that flourished during many midnight debates over bourbon and booklore, with neither the right nor the left side of the issues ever gaining much ground. Over the years since Stanford, they had tried to keep up the argument by correspondence—Larry defending the traditional and Deboree [Ken Kesey] championing the radical—but without the shared bourbon the letters had naturally lessened. The letter from Larry on Thursday was the first in a year. Nevertheless it went straight back at the issue, claiming conservative advances, listing the victories of the righteous right, and pointing out the retreats and mistakes made by certain left-wing luminaries, especially Charles Manson, whom Deboree had known slightly. The letter ended by asking, in the closing paragraph, "So. What has the Good Old Revolution been doing lately?"

Deboree's research had yielded up no satisfactory answer. After hours of trial and chemistry before the typewriter, he had pecked out one meager page of print, but the victories he had listed on his side were largely mundane achievements: "Dobbs and Blanche had another kid. . . . Rampage and I finally got cut loose from our three-year probation. . . ." Certainly no great score for the left wing of the ledger. But that was all he could think of: one puny page to show for forty hours of prowling around in the lonely library of what he used to call "The Movement." Forty hours of thinking, drinking, and peeing in a milk bottle, with no break except that ten-minute trip downstairs to deal with those pilgriming prickheads. And now, back upstairs and still badly shaken, even that feeble page was missing; the typed yellow sheet of paper was as misplaced as his colored glasses.

"Pox on both houses," he moaned aloud, rubbing his irritated eyes with his wrists. "On Oregon field burners poisoning the air for weed-free profit and on California flower children gone to seed and thorn!"

. . . He heard the whine again, returning, growing louder. He opened his eyes and walked back to the window and parted the tie-dye curtains. The pink car had turned around and was coming back. Entranced, he watched it pass the driveway again, but this time it squealed to a stop, backed up, and turned in. It came keening and bouncing down the dirt road toward the barn. Finally he blinked, jerked the curtain closed, and sat heavily in his swivel chair.

The car whirred to a stop in the gravel and mercifully cut its engine. He didn't move. Somebody got out, and a voice from the past shouted up at his office: "Dev?" He'd let the curtain close too late. "Devlinnnn?" it shouted. "Hey, you, Devlin Deboreeeee?" A sound half hysterical and half humorous, like the sound that chick who lost her marbles in Mexico used to make, that Sandy Pawku.

"Dev? I've got news. About Houlihan [Neal Cassady]. Bad news. He's dead. Houlihan's dead."

He tipped back in his chair and closed his eyes. He didn't question the announcement. The loss seemed natural, in keeping with the season and the situation, comfortable even, and then he thought, *That's it! That's what the revolution has been doing lately, to be honest. Losing!*

"Dev, are you up there? It's me, Sandy . . ."

He pushed himself standing and walked to the window and drew back the curtain. He wiped his eyes and stuck his head into the blighted afternoon. Hazy as it was, the sunlight nevertheless seemed to be sharper than usual, harsher. The chrome of the little car gleamed viciously. Like the knife blade.

"Houlihan," he said, blinking. The dust raised by the car was reaching the barn on its own small breeze. He felt it bring an actual chill. "Houlihan dead?" he said to the pink face lifted to him.

"Of exposure," the voice rasped.

"When? Recently?"

"Yesterday. I just heard. I was in the airport in Oakland this morning when I ran into this little hippie chicky who knew me from Mountain View. She came up to the bar and advised

me that the great Houlihan is now the late great. Yesterday,
I guess. Chicky Little had just got off the plane from Puerto
Sancto, where Houlihan had been staying with her and a bunch
of her buddies. At a villa right down the road from where we
lived. Apparently the poor maniac was drinking and taking
downers and walking around at night alone, miles from nowhere. He passed out on a railroad track between Sancto and
Manzanillo, where he got fatally chilled from the desert dew.
Well, *you* know, Dev, how cold it can get down there after
sunset."

It was Sandy Pawku all right, but what a change! Her once
long brown hair had been cropped and chromed, plated with
the rusty glint of the car's grill. She had put heavy eye makeup
and rouge and lipstick on her face and, over the rest of her
had put on, he guessed, at least a hundred pounds.

"Dead, our hero of the sixties is, Devvy, baby. Dead, dead,
dead. Of downers and drunk and the foggy, foggy dew. O,
Hooly, Hooly, Hooly, you maniac. You goon. What did Kerouac call him in that book? The glorious goon?"

"No. The Holy Goof."

"I was flying to my aunt's cottage in Seattle for a little R
and R, rest and writing, you dig? But that news in Oakland
—I thought, Wonder if Dev and the Animal Friends have
heard? Probably not. So when the plane stopped in Eugene,
I remember about this commune I hear you all got and I
decided, Sandy, Old Man Deboree would want to know. So
Sandy, she cashes in the rest of her ticket and rents a car and
here she is, thanks to Mr. Mastercharge, Mr. Hughes, and
Mr. Avis. Say, is one supposed to drive these damn tricks in
D1, D2, or L? Isn't L for driving in the light and D for driving
in the dark?"

"You drove that thing all the way here from the airport in
low gear?"

"Might have." She laughed, slapping the flimsy hood with
a hand full of jeweled fingers. "Right in amongst those log
trucks and eighteen-wheelers, me and my pinkster, roaring
with the loudest of them."

"I'll bet."

"When it started to smoke, I compromised with D1. Goddamn it, I mean them damn manufacturers—but listen to me

rationalizing. I probably wrecked it, didn't I? To tell the truth? Be honest, Sandy. Christ knows you could use a little honesty. . . ." She rubbed the back of her neck and looked away from him, back the way she had come. "Eee God, what is happening? Houlihan kacked. Pigpen killed by a chicken-shit liver; Terry the Tramp snuffed by spades. Ol' Sandy herself nearly down for the count a dozen times." She began walking to and fro in the gravel. "Man, I have been going in circles, in bummer nowhere circles, you know what I mean? Weird shit. I mean, hey listen: I just wasted a *dog* on the road back there!"

He knew he must have responded, said, "Oh?" or "Is that right?" or something, because she had kept talking.

"Old bitch it was, with a yardful of pups. Whammed her good."

Sandy came around the front of the car and opened the right door. She tipped the pink seat forward and began hauling matching luggage out of the back and arranging it on the gravel, all the while relating vividly how she had come around a bend and run over a dog sleeping in the road. *Right* in the *road.* A farmwife had come out of her house at the commotion and had dragged the broken animal out of the culvert where it had crawled howling. The farmwife had felt its spine then sentenced it to be put out of its misery. At her repeated commands, her teenage son had finally fetched the shotgun from the house.

"The kid was carrying on such a weeping and wailing, he missed twice. The third time, he let go with both barrels and blew bitch bits all over the lawn. The only thing they wanted from me was six bits apiece for the bullets. I asked if they took credit cards." She laughed. "When I left, goddamn me if the pups weren't playing with the pieces."

She laughed again. He remembered hearing the shots. He knew the family and the dog, a deaf spaniel, but he didn't say anything. Shading his eyes, he watched this swollen new version of the skinny Sandy of his past bustle around the luggage below him, laughing. Even her breath seemed to have gained weight, husking out of her throat with an effort. Swollen. Her neck where she had rubbed it, her wrists, her back, all swollen. But her weight actually rode lightly, defiantly, like a chip on her shoulder. *In her colored shoes and stretch pants and a silk*

Hawaiian shirt pulled over her paunch, she looks like a Laguna Beach roller derby queen, he thought, *just arriving at the rink. She looks primed,* he thought. Like the hitchhiker; an argument rigged to go off at the slightest touch. The thought of another confrontation left him weak and nauseous.

M'kehla's Great Danes discovered her in the yard and came barking. Sandy sliced at them with her pink plastic handbag. "Get away from me, you big fuckers. You smell that other mutt on my wheels? You want the same treatment? Damn, they are big, aren't they? Get them back, can't you?"

"Their big is worse than their bite," he told her and shouted at the dogs to go home to their bus. They paid no attention.

"What the shit, Deboree?" She sliced and swung. "Can't you get your animals to mind?"

"They aren't mine," he explained over the din. "M'kehla left them here while he went gallivantin' to Woodstock with everybody else."

"Goddamn you fuckers, *back off!*" Sandy roared. The dogs hesitated, and she roared louder. "*Off! Off!* Clear *off!*" They shrunk back. Sandy hooted gleefully and kicked gravel after them until they broke into a terrified dash. Sandy gave chase, hooting their retreat all the way to the bus, out of his view.

The ravens were flying again. The sun was still slicing a way through the impacted smoke. The radio was playing "Good Vibrations" by The Beach Boys. Back in the yard below, at her luggage, Sandy was humming along, her hysteria calmed by her victory over the dogs. She found the bag she had been searching for, the smallest in a six-piece set that looked brand-new. She opened it and took out a bottle of pills. Deboree watched as she shook out at least a dozen. She threw the whole handful into her mouth and began digging again into the case for something to wash them down with.

"Ol' Thandy'th been platheth and theen thingth thinth Mexico," she told him, trying to keep all the pills in her mouth and bring him up to date at the same time. Seen lots of water under the bridges, she let him know, sometimes too much. Bridges washed out. Washed out herself a time or two, she told him. Got pretty mucked up. Even locked up. But with the help of some ritzy doctors and her rich daddy, she'd finally got bailed out and got set up being half owner of a bar in San

Juan Capistrano; then become a drunk, then a junkie, then a blues singer *non*professional; found Jesus, and Love, and Another Husband—"Minithter of the Univerthal Church of Latterday Thonthabitcheth!"—then got p.g., got an abortion, got disowned by her family, and got divorced; then got depressed, as he could well understand, and put on a little weight, as he could see; then—Sunday, *now*—was looking for a place where a gal might lay back for a while.

"A plathe to read and write and take a few barbth to mellow out," she said through the pills.

"A few!" he said, remembering her old barbiturate habit. "That's no 'few.' " The thought of having more than one carcass to dispose of alarmed him finally into protest. "Damn you, Sandy, if you up and O.D. on me now, so help me—"

She held up her hand. "Vitamin theeth. Croth my heart." Pawing through a boil of lingerie, she at last had found the silver flask she had been seeking. She unscrewed the lid and threw back her head. He watched her neck heave as the pills washed down. She wiped her mouth with her forearm and laughed up at him.

"Don't worry, Granny," she said. "Just some innocent little vitamins. Even the dandy little Sandy of old never took *that* many downers at once. She might someday, though. Never can tell. Who the hell knows what anybody's gonna do this year? It's the year of the downer, you know, so who knows? Just let it roll by. . . ." She returned the flask to the suitcase and snapped it shut. Rayon and Orlon scalloped out all around like a piecrust to be trimmed. "Now. Where does Sandy take a wee-wee and wash out her Kotex?"

He pointed, and she went humming off to the corner of the barn. The big dogs came to the door of their bus and growled after her. Deboree watched as she ducked under the clothesline and turned the corner. He heard the door slam behind her.

He stayed at the window, feeling there was more to be revealed. Everything was so tense and restrained. The wash hung tense in the smoky air, like strips of jerky. The peacock, his fan molted to a dingy remnant of its springtime elegance, stepped out of the quince bush where he had been visiting his mate and flew to the top of one of the clothesline poles. Deboree thought the bird would make his cry when he reached the top, but he didn't. He perched atop the pole and bobbed his head this way and that at the end of his long neck, as though gauging the tension. After watching the peacock for a while, he let the curtain close and moved from the window back to his desk; he too found he could be content to let it roll by without resolution.

Over the radio The Doors were demanding that it be brought on through to the other side. Wasn't Morrison dead? He couldn't remember. All he could be sure of was that it was 1968 and the valley was filled to the foothills with smoke as 300,000 acres of stubble were burned so lawn-seed buyers in subdivisions in California wouldn't have to weed a single interloper from their yards.

Tremendous.

The bathroom door slammed again. He heard the plastic heels crunch past below; one of M'kehla's dogs followed, barking tentatively. The dog followed the steps around the other corner, barking in a subdued and civilized voice. The bitch Great Dane, he recognized. Pedigreed. She had barked last night, too. Out in the field. Betsy had got out of bed and shouted up the stairs at him to go check what was the matter out there. He hadn't gone. Was that what offed the lamb? One of M'kehla's Great Danes? He liked to think so. It made him pleasantly angry to think so. Just like a Marin County spade to own two blond Great Danes and go off and leave them marooned. Too many strays. Somebody should go down to that bus and boot some pedigreed ass. But he remained seated, seeking fortification behind his desk, and turned up the music against the noise. Once he heard a yelping as Sandy ran the bitch back to the bus. Sometimes a little breeze would open the curtain and he could see the peacock still sitting on the clothesline pole, silently bobbing his head. Eventually he heard the steps return, enter the barn below, and find the wooden stairs. They mounted briskly and crossed the floor of the loft. Sandy came through his door without knocking.

"Some great place, Dev," she said. "Funky but great. Sandy gave herself the tour. You got places for everything, don't you? For pigs and chickens and everything. Places to wee-wee, places to eat, places to write letters."

Deboree saw the pitch coming but couldn't stop her chatter.

"Look, I blew the last of my airline ticket to Seattle renting that pink panther because I knew you'd want Sandy to bring you the sad news in person. No, that's all right, save the thanksies. No need. She *does* need, though, a little place to write some letters. Seriously, Dev, I saw a cabin down by the pond with paper and envelopes and everything. How about Sandy uses that cabin a day or so? To write a letter to her dear mother and her dear probation officer and her dear ex et cetera. Also maybe catch up on her journal. Hey, I'm writing up our Mexico campaign for a rock'n'roll rag. Are you ready for *that?*"

He tried to explain to her that the pond cabin was a meditation chapel, not some Camp David for old campaigners to compile their memoirs. Besides, he had planned to use it tonight. She laughed, told him not to worry.

"I'll find me a harbor for tonight. Then we'll see."

He stayed at his desk. Chattering away, Sandy prowled his office until she found the shoe box and proceeded to clean and roll the last of his grass. He still didn't want to smoke, not until he was finished with that dead lamb. When he shook his head at the offered joint, she shrugged and smoked it all, explaining in detail how she would refill his box to overflowing with the scams she had cooking in town this afternoon, meeting so-and-so at such and such to barter this and that. He couldn't follow it. He felt flattened before her steamrolling energy. Even when she dropped the still-lit roach from the window to the dry grass below, he was only able to make the feeblest protest.

"Careful of fire around barn?" She whooped, bending over him. "Why, Mistah Deboree, if you ain't getting to be the fussy little farmer." She clomped to the door and opened it. "So. Sandy's making a run. Anything you need from town? A new typewriter? A better radio—how can you listen to good music on that Jap junk? A super Swiss Army? Ho ho. Just tell Sandy Claus. Anything?"

She stood in the opened door, waiting. He swiveled in his chair, but he didn't get up. He looked at her fat grin. He knew what she was waiting for. The question. He also knew better than to ask it. Better to let it slide than encourage any relationship by seeming curious. But he was curious, and she was waiting, grinning at him, and he finally had to ask it:

"Did he, uh, *say* anything, Sandy?" His voice was thick in his throat.

The black eyes glistened at him from the doorway. "You mean, don'cha, were there any, uh, *last words? Any sentences commuted,* any *parting wisdoms?* Why, as a matter of fact, in the hospital, it seems, before he went into a coma, he did rally a moment and now wait, let me see. . . ."

She was gloating. His asking had laid his desperation naked. She grinned. There he sat, Deboree, the Guru Gung Ho with his eyes raw, begging for some banner to carry on with, some comforter of last-minute truth quilted by Old Holy Goof Houlihan, a wrap against the chilly chaos to come.

"Well, yep, our little hippie chick did mention that he said a few words before he died on that Mexican mattress," she said. "And isn't that irony for you? It's that *same ratty Puerto Sancto* clinic where Behema had her kid and Mickey had his broken leg wherein our dear Hooly died, of pneumonia and exposure and downers. Come on! Don'cha think that is pretty stinking ironic?"

"What were they?"

The eyes glistened. The grin wriggled in its nest of fat. "He said—if Sandy's memory serves—said, I think it was, 'Sixty-four thousand nine hundred and twenty-eight.' Quite a legacy, don'cha think? A number, a stinking number!" She hooted, slapping her hips. "Sixty-four thousand nine hundred and twenty-eight! Sixty-four thousand nine hundred and twenty-eight! The complete cooked-down essence of the absolute burned-out speed freak: sixty-four thousand nine hundred and twenty-eight! *Huh-woow woow wow!*"

She left without closing the door, laughing, clacking down the steps and across the gravel. The injured machine whined pitifully as she forced it back out the drive.

So now observe him, after the lengthy preparation just documented (it had been actually three days and was going on four nights), finally confronting his task in the field: Old Man Deboree, desperate and dreary, with his eyes naked to the smoky sun, striding across the unbroken ground behind a red wheelbarrow. Face bent earthward, he watches the field pass beneath his shoes and nothing else, trusting the one-wheeled machine to lead him to his destination.

Like Sandy's neck, he fancies himself swollen with an unspecified anger, a great smoldering of unlaid blame that longed to bloom to a great blaze. Could he but fix it on a suitable culprit. Searching for some target large enough to take his fiery blame, he fixes again on California. *That's* where it comes from, he decides. Like those two weirdo prickhikers, and Sandy Pawku, and the Oakland hippie chick who must have been one of that Oakland bunch of pillheads who lured Houlihan back down to Mexico last month . . . all from California! It all started in California, went haywire in California, and now spreads out from California like a crazy tumor under the hide of the whole continent. Woodstock. Big time. Craziness waxing fat. Craziness surviving and prospering and gaining momentum while the Fastestmanalive downs himself dead without any legacy left behind but a psycho's cipher. Even those Great Danes—from California!

The wheelbarrow reaches the ditch. He raises his head. He still cannot see the carcass. Turning down into the ditch, he pushes on toward the place where the three ravens whirl cursing in and out of the tall weeds. . . .

Michael McClure

Michael McClure was surprised to see his novel The Mad Cub *marketed by Bantam Books in 1970 as an exploitative youth cult paperback, and to find the protagonist described on the jacket of the book as a "Captain Nowhere" who "propelled by drugs, sex and the fantastic pulse of his own existence, explores the possibilities of America." McClure deliberately wrote his autobiography in the style of Kerouac's spontaneous confessional prose, changing the names of the people in his life (his wife Joanna was called "Cathy"), but recalling his memories of his teenage experiences in Kansas and his years of literary apprenticeship in San Francisco before beginning his career as a poet and playwright, including the production of his Obie–award–winning plays* The Beard *and* Josephine: The Mouse Singer.

from THE MAD CUB

"Tell me a story," says Jarman . . . Jarman's wife Norah lies on the floor looking into an imagined rosy sunset that she sees behind her closed eyes . . . Brooder lies looking up and out the window mumbling and humming a song happily to himself . . . Neri sits with her back against the wall and eyes closed. Her lids are heavy and lovely with a stripe of blue make-up on them. Quiet and mysterious Cathy does saintly things in the other room only making a few noises like the moving of dishes . . . The early evening is very still . . .

"Sure," I say . . . "There's a barber shop downtown and I walked by it one day . . . In the big window of the barber shop there was a cat just sitting there . . . hunched down on his hind legs and standing up on his front legs looking out the window at nothing in particular . . . I saw a canary fluttering around in the window like a little yellow streak . . . I stopped to watch. The canary flew down and landed right on top of the cat's head. WHAT I SAW GOING THROUGH THE CAT'S MIND AND SPIRIT WAS TERRIBLE! It was one of those striped alley Toms only big and well-groomed and cared for . . . I saw every detail of the cat's expression when the canary landed on the cat's head . . . An urge to kill started moving up from the cat's insides—from its guts—and the urge rose higher and higher—there wasn't a visible ripple of flesh or movement just the urge to kill rising up through the body of the cat toward that sassy perky little canary sitting on the top of his head . . . The cat's huge yellow eyes rolled upward just a little . . . Then the urge to *kill* reached the cat's head and CLONG! BLOCK! The urge was stopped at the head. CLONG! BLOCK!—It stopped right there and the cat stiffened almost imperceptibly and its face and eyes just blanked out . . . The cat sat there like a ninny . . . The urge to kill met the trained repression of the urge to kill and the mind of the cat was wiped out . . . The cat ceased to exist and became a comical statue of a baffled and stupefied cat . . . It was an agonizing thing to see . . . The people getting their haircuts all sat up to watch but they couldn't see the cat's expression . . . The funny little canary flew off and the cat just sat there. I had to run half a block to get away from the sight . . ."

"I know that men are the size of stars . . . we can't apply standards of measurement—they're false . . . There's no way to measure spirit . . ." I say to Linder.

I have just told Linder that I want to go into biochemistry . . . that I am going to return to college and get a doctor's degree in science . . . I want to do everything and be everything. . . .

"You should keep doing just what you *are* doing," says Linder seriously and smiling from his heavy brows.

Linder is an old high-school acquaintance . . . now he is a resident in psychiatric training at Johns Hopkins . . . He has flown to the city to speak about the new drugs that he has used in his research . . . He has looked me up.

We eat dinner together and he fascinates Cathy and me with his glibness . . .

Why does he look me up when he gets here . . . ? I know it is to bring this message to me . . . *that I should forget about returning to school* . . . it is the only possible reason. Linder is satanic but I do not question the efficacy of my messengers and usually I pay attention to what they say. Linder means me well and he does not realize that he is satanic. He believes that he is merely an impostor and he secretly questions the fault that he sees in himself. Life is totally without meaning to him . . . All of his glibness hides the fact that everything is valueless and meaningless to him . . . Everything is relative to Linder—he is objective and understanding and he poisons himself with his ability to make everything relative to everything else . . . Linder has a name for everything . . . I know I will not see him again for years . . . but I like his message . . . "Goodbye . . ." I wave from the stairs.

The library is ugly. I stand waiting for it to open. The bald old guy grudgingly opens the doors and slides back all of the night locks and the huge thick wooden gate-doors behind the front glass doors . . . Old winos and pensioner-men stumble sadly and happily to read the newspapers and spend hours on the toilet seats.

I run up the long flight of marble stairs three stairs at a time and walk down the corridor to the right . . . past the 1920's murals of sunsets and plowhorses through the halls that smell like sputum and books. I spit on the floor just to show my hatred for a place that will not check out the books I need. But I am happy . . . Working each day in the library for the two hours gives me an early morning purpose and it gives me the information on which I need to dwell when the will-lessness and weakness comes over me.

I open the huge tome . . . Ah! The nervous systems of rare worms, of jellyfish, of crickets . . . I begin to draw . . . Everything is going to be o.k. today. I forget the high ceilings, the bad smells and the resentful faces.

In my head is the picture of all living creatures broken down to their simplest components of muscles and organs and senses and the sub-creatures of which creatures are made . . . When my eyes begin to expand and grow farther and farther apart and my ears spread and my senses numb that picture is still there and loses its beauty and becomes something else . . . I do not like that . . . I know down deep inside that I will someday not believe the knowledge that I assemble now. There is another answer to all that I must know and it is simpler and better but now I must throw myself with all energy into those things that I can learn, do, and feel.

I have totally put down drugs . . . No peyote, no heroin, no cocaine will I touch again . . . But the agony will not go away . . . I know that the peyote has started this but the lights will not stop gleaming out of objects . . . My head wants to divide—to spread farther and farther apart and fly away with my consciousness and my sanity . . . I have an urge that drives me to want to throw myself from windows . . . I think at moments that I will explode to death—and I hope so . . . Anyway it will not have to go on much longer. In a few months it will all be over—I do know that at least . . . I imagine a gun here in my hand. I know how I'd use it . . . I may be dulled and blunted but I would know how to use the gun I have here in my hand . . . I can't think quite right . . . Nothing makes good sense . . . The tables, chairs, dishes . . . wall . . . white . . . red . . . colors

Larry is whispering something to me. Larry only speaks in a whisper . . . I lean way across the table to hear what he's saying . . . I can't understand him . . . He's saying something about yogi . . . I want to hear . . . My mind won't quite focus. Larry makes me feel prosaic. I sit listening to him dressed in my old shirt and pants and shoes—just clothing. Larry opposite me is dressed in the most fantastic costume of a dandy. He is wearing a broad-brimmed black hat that he has doffed and laid on the chair next to him and he is wearing a black turtle-

neck sweater and the jacket of an old suit and jodhpurs . . .
Around all he wears a black Lord Chesterfield overcoat . . .

"So that is the final solution of the Tathagata," says Larry.
Then he politely adds in a final whisper, "as I see it." His dark
boyish eyes peer lively and dreamily from his long hair and
beard.

I want to tell Larry that soon I will be twenty-eight but
before then I will be dead . . . I know it is getting close now.
It is only months or weeks away. I will not kill myself but I
am obsessed with the desire to fling myself to destruction. I
do not want to kill myself . . . I fight to keep the desire abstract
and not let it rest upon definite methods. I am dying anyway.
I do not want to burden Cathy with my death but I am afraid
I am dying of something in my chest and neck. Just now I am
learning to love and adore children and see the life that is
swinging so brightly in people . . . I don't want to die . . . It
is better this way though.

I have enormous revelations and confirmations of my genius
and I know that I am a success and that I have made new
discoveries . . . Then later I cannot reconstruct what they were.
It is better this way that I die soon . . . "What did you say,
Larry?" I say.

Ed Sanders

Ed Sanders set most of his satiric memoir Tales of Beatnik Glory *in New York City in the late 1950s and early 1960s. He said it "focuses on artists, musicians, filmmakers, and writers, and speaks in the language and modes of culture of the time." The book was first published in 1975 but reissued with additional material in 1990, including the chapter "A Book of Verse" that described what happened to a conventional, if bookish, Midwestern teenage boy in 1957 when he unwittingly stumbled on Ginsberg's* Howl and Other Poems. *Himself the "he" in the story, Sanders chose the distanced third person style of narration to contrast humorously with his own explosive emotional reaction to the little black and white City Lights paperback.*

A BOOK OF VERSE

A carload of them drove a hundred and fifty miles to the state university for a fraternity weekend during the spring of 1957. They were all graduating seniors at a high school in a small town near the Missouri-Kansas border. Some of them were thinking about attending State U. so they thought, what the hell, why not let themselves be beered and fed free by obliging fraternities.

They left early in the morning in order to arrive in time for the afternoon beer and barbecue party. He wore his forty-five-dollar R. H. Macy flannel suit with the pink and blue flecks he and his mother had bought for the homecoming dance in 1956.

When they arrived at the state university they were early so they killed time by driving around the campus. He spotted the campus bookstore so he said, "Hey, let's stop and check it out." There was a bit of grumbling, but they whipped into the lot and went inside. It was the usual campus bookstore of the time, with heavy emphasis on thick expensive textbooks written by professors cleaning up on sales to captive students. There was a poetry section and a section dealing with what was called then "the paperback revolution."

They stayed about a half-hour before the urge to guzzle beer tugged them outward. He purchased C. M. Bowra's *Creative Experiment,* plus *Three Ways of Thought in Ancient China* by Arthur Waley, and *Howl* by Allen Ginsberg. That's about all he could afford. Buying *Howl* was a last-minute decision. He had read an article somewhere about a court case and obscenity charges, and he had liked, when glancing at it in the store, the last lines of the William Carlos Williams introduction. And it only cost seventy-five cents so he grabbed it.

The trip visiting the fraternity was otherwise uneventful except that he threw up into the waterfall of a local fancy restaurant when he was drunk. That guaranteed him an invitation to pledge the fraternity. Puking, the symbol of the Fifties.

When he got back home, he read *Howl* and was stunned. Here was a young man whose family had prepared a map of life for him that included two avenues, either a) law school (like his uncle Milton), or b) to work in his father's dry-goods store. *Howl* ripped into his mind like the tornado that had uprooted the cherry tree in his backyard when he was a child. He began to cry. He rolled all over the floor of his bathroom crying. He walked down the stairs in the middle of the night to wake his parents and read it to them. His mother threatened to call the state police. His father went to work an hour early the next morning.

He could not go to school that day, but walked into the field behind his house and strode back and forth all day along a barbed-wire fence shouting and moaning the book in front of a bunch of cows. Over and over he "howled" the poem, till much of it was held in his mind and he'd close his eyes and grab the book, almost tearing it, and shriek passages, stamping the ground. "God! God!" he yelled, "God!" He fell and rolled in the dirt, laughing and shouting, scaring the wet-nosed cows who ran up the hill.

When he returned to school the next day he was a changed person. "Holy holy holy holy holy holy," he must have chanted that word, in long continuous singsong sentences, at least four or five thousand times a day. He felt great. Every care assumed before evaporated. He read the poem to anybody who would listen to him and he got into trouble almost immediately. First it was shop class.

In shop class he had been working for almost the entire school term on a walnut spice cabinet for his mother. It was just about finished after a tortuous slow-motion construction process common to every shop class of the time. In fact, he had finished the project too quickly and was caught having to sand the cabinet for about five straight class days. Then he brought *Howl* to shop class. That day the teacher was called away for a teachers' conference so the students were left on their own, their activities observed by the class snitch.

The bell had barely ended when he began to read the poem to his shopmates, who stood for it for several minutes, staring at him; then right before his eyes they began to go about their business of sawing, soldering, sanding and gluing. He couldn't believe it. Then they started talking loudly as he read, perhaps as a hint. Finally one of them walked over to him and said, "I don't understand what you're howling about"—and poked a bony forearm into his ribs; "Howling, get it? Yar har har!" And a bunch of shopsters joined in to elevate yar har.

He kept on reading the poem, however, and when done, he walked over to his spice cabinet. He pulled a woodburning tool out of the storage shelves and wood-burned a quote upon the door of the spice cabinet:

> *I saw the best minds*
> *of my Generation*
> *destroyed by madness*

which he left on the teacher's desk.

When he arrived in shop class the next day, he found a note

taped to the howl cabinet from Mr. Russell the teach: "Take this with you and please go at once to the principal's office. He is expecting you."

"Johnny," the principal paused—"about this spice cabinet"—picking it up. "Now, we know the source of this quote and we feel it inappropriate for a boy of your background to dabble in such filth."

"What do you mean filth?" he replied. "There's nothing filthy about that sentence."

"Let's not kid ourselves, Johnny. What you allude to in this woodburned"—pausing for words, "woodburned stupidity is immoral and suggestive. It's the despicable ravings of a homo. And we both know the implications of that."

The boy couldn't think of anything to match his indignation. "I think it's great. It's going to change the world. There'll be something new come out of this poem. Things will never be the same."

"Nothing new will ever come to *this* town from this obscene filth, believe you me." The principal tugged at the corner of the flag on his desk.

"You just wait," the boy replied.

"Get out of here!" the principal ordered and gave him a light shove. Tears welled in the boy's eyes. "And I'm going to call up your parents. We can't have you polluting our school with filth. Now get on out of here. Do not—you hear me? Look at me! Do not *ever* recite any part of this poem again on school property, do you understand?"

"I'll recite anything I want any time!"

"Get out. You are expelled from school for three days. I'll just call your mother,"—reaching for an index file.

The boy paused at the door and taunted the principal: "I saw the best minds of my generation destroyed by madness starving hysterical *naked!!*" then ran out to the parking lot and drove home in his pickup truck.

He returned to school three days later wearing what he wanted and saying what he pleased. Gone were the days of shoe polish, clean shirts, and paste-on smiles. He began to spend almost all of his time writing poetry. Things went oddly but smoothly until his senior writing class was assigned to write some poems, which were to be read aloud in class. For days he worked on a howling masterpiece. He typed various versions and gradually the poem evolved into the rageful shape he desired. It was a rather lengthy twenty-seven pages and there was a language problem. He knew he could never get away with the word *fuck* or other similar words. For a while he thought he could get away with *screw* if he, say, mumbled it during the recitation. Finally he chose the word *planked*—good old Missouri locker-room lingo.

Friday arrived and the teacher made each student walk to the head of the class to read their poems. When it was his turn he shuffled forth, stood, eyed the teacher, and began: "This poem is titled *Springtime Shriek*." Right at that moment the nervousness overcame him, and there was a twitch of his hand, and half the poem fluttered to the floor. Gray dabs of floor-dirt covered his fingers, as he reached down frantically to grab up the sheets before the teacher could help him. Then he read:

They dragged their fingers through
their skulls and sang in ambrosia

They lay in the shanks of the night
and screamed for the morn
and dawn was planked atremble on the
couch of the hill

They pulled three aces straight
before they drew the black nine
in the void of cards

They cried for food without profit
They saw in a vision the wheat pour from the
bins enough for the roar of centuries
and drank the champagne of God's eye

They screwed. . . .

"Wait a minute young man!" the teacher roared. "No one's going to read any filth in *my* classroom! I won't and never will stand for it! Now you take that nonsense with you down to the principal's office right now. Scat!"

He didn't even bother to go to the office but instead drove downtown to play pool at Ernie's Tavern. There was fifty cents riding on the game near the end, and he leaned low over the green felt, mumbling, "angelheaded hipsters burning for the ancient heavenly connection to the starry dynamo in the machinery of night . . ." Clack! The ball bounced back and forth and into the pocket. He grabbed the money eagerly and coaxed Sonny Marsh, who was over twenty-one, into buying a couple of beers with it. He and Sonny chugged it down and then he headed home to write.

A month later he graduated from high school. He went on a last and final drunk with his best friend, the one with whom he'd bunked at scout camp, the one he learned how to get drunk with, sneaking over the Kansas state line to purchase 3.2 beer, the one with whom he had driven countless circles around the county courthouse with a six-pack, gossip, and rock-and-roll on the radio. His friend and he got really loaded and then said goodbye. "I'm going to New York to become a poet."

And his friend replied, "Don't do anything I wouldn't do."

PART SIX

"THE UNSPEAKABLE VISIONS OF THE INDIVIDUAL"

Later Work

For many people it seemed as if the Beat movement would end with the deaths of Cassady and Kerouac in the late 1960s, but as essential as they were to defining the mood of the Beat Generation in its earliest years, the spirit of the literary movement has continued into the present in the work of other members of the group. A sample of more recent poetry and prose shows the writers' development of earlier literary themes and techniques over the past twenty-five years, often with increasing artistic maturity.

William Burroughs collaborated with Kells Elvins and Brion Gysin in the production of the section "Gave Proof Through the Night" published in Burroughs's book *Nova Express* (1964). The part of the text based on the *Titanic* shipwreck was first written in 1938 by Burroughs and Elvins while they were undergraduates at Harvard. Then—as Burroughs described the procedure—this early piece "was later cut back in with the first 'cut-ups' of Brion Gysin" produced at the Beat Hotel in Paris. Burroughs also used Gysin's method of the "cut-up" in *The Soft Machine* (1961) and his own method of the "fold-in" in *The Ticket That Exploded* (1962), the trilogy he wrote after *Naked Lunch*. He explained the process of the "fold-in" as folding pages of text down the middle, placing them on a piece of paper and reading across. His friend, the writer Paul Bowles, commented that this method of composition wasn't writing, it was "plumbing." Another version of this text is in Burroughs's *Interzone* (1989), titled "Twilight's Last Gleaming."

Gregory Corso wrote "Columbia U Poesy Reading—1975" as an opportunity to take stock of his friends' accomplishments after a return visit to read at Columbia University in New York with Ginsberg and Orlovsky. In his opening lines he referred to a condescending review of their earlier poetry reading at Columbia in 1959 by Diana Trilling, wife of the English professor and influential critic Lionel Trilling, one of Ginsberg's favorite professors at Columbia. In 1959 only Diana Trilling went to hear Ginsberg's reading, more out of a sense of curiosity than respect for his poetry. In 1975, Corso noted that both Trillings attended the performance. "The Whole Mess . . . Almost" is a poem from Corso's recent collection *Herald of the Autochthonic Spirit* (1981).

Diane DiPrima included "April Fool Birthday Poem for Grandpa" as the introduction to her collection of *Revolutionary Letters* (1971), a group of anti-Vietnam War poems. The five poems from *Loba: Parts I–VIII* (1978) reflect her current interests in occult studies, American Indian mythology, and radical Feminism.

Lawrence Ferlinghetti read "The Canticle of Jack Kerouac" (1987) at the International Jack Kerouac Gathering in Quebec City in 1987, a week-long festival celebrating Kerouac's French-Canadian heritage. "Uses of Poetry" is a recent poem questioning the usefulness of poetry during a time when the flourishing military-industrial complex continues to foster political turmoil in the world. "Short Story on a Painting of Gustav Klimt" is from Ferlinghetti's book *When I Look at Pictures* (1990). It reflects his extensive knowledge of art history and his work for the last forty years as a painter.

Allen Ginsberg wrote "First Party at Ken Kesey's with Hell's Angels" at three A.M. in Kesey's house in the woods at La Honda, California, in early December, 1965. Two months later he embarked on a reading tour in a Volkswagen bus in which he recorded into a tape recorder his spontaneous "poetry no-tations" of what he saw and heard on the road as "Highway Poesy: L.A.-Albuquerque-Texas-Wichita," a section pub-lished as "Wichita Vortex Sutra" in 1972. "Anti-Vietnam War Peace Mobilization" was written during the March on Washington in 1970. "Mugging," first published in *The New York Times,* was a poem about the evening in 1974 he was robbed of his money and wristwatch by a street gang in his Lower East Side neighborhood. "Ode to Failure" described some dark thoughts while at the Naropa Institute in Boulder, Colorado, in 1980. A few years later Ginsberg dreamed what he called "an epilogue in heaven to *Kaddish*" in Boulder. This dream, captured in "White Shroud," was a vision of discovering his mother Naomi surviving as a bag lady in the Bronx. "Fourth Floor, Dawn, Up All Night Writing Letters" was written in 1980 in Ginsberg's East Village apartment.

Michael McClure's short poems "Song (I Work with the Shape)," "It's Nation Time," and "Watching the Stolen Rose" were collected in *Fragments of Perseus* (1983). "The Death of Kin Chuen Louie," also from that volume, was written on the day before McClure celebrated his daughter Jane's twenty-first birthday in San Francisco.

Ed Sanders included "Hymn to Archilochus" in *Thirsting for Peace in a Raging Century: Selected Poems 1961–1985* (1987). "What Would Tom Paine Do?" is a song from his recent opera *Star Peace.*

Gary Snyder distributed "Smokey the Bear Sutra" in San Francisco at the Human Be-In in 1967 as a free broadside to promote ecological consciousness. "I Went into the Maverick Bar" describes an evening in New Mexico after he'd returned to America from his long residence in Japan as a student of Buddhism. "Mother Earth: Her Whales," written for a United Nations conference in Stockholm in 1972, is referred to by Michael McClure in his description of the Six Gallery reading in *Scratching the Beat Surface* as a poem continuing the West Coast writers' early interest in environmental issues. "The Bath" (1974) and "Axe Handles" (1983) are two poems about Snyder's family life at his xendo in northern California, men-tioning his sons Kai and Gen. "Pine Tree Tops" is from the collection *Turtle Island* (1974). Its last line could stand as the basic thought behind the work of all the writers in this literary group: "What do we know."

from William Burroughs
NOVA EXPRESS

GAVE PROOF THROUGH THE NIGHT

(This section, first written in 1938 in collaboration with Kells Elvins who died in 1961, New York, was later cut back in with the "first cut-ups" of Brion Gysin as published in Minutes to Go.*)*

Captain Bairns was arrested today in the murder at sea of Chicago—He was The Last Great American to see things from the front and kept laughing during the dark—Fade out

S.S. America—Sea smooth as green glass—off Jersey Coast—An air-conditioned voice floats from microphones and ventilators—:

"Keep your seats everyone—There is no cause for alarm—There has been a little accident in the boiler room but everything is now/"

BLOOOMMM

Explosion splits the boat—The razor inside, sir—He jerked the handle—

A paretic named Perkins screams from his shattered wheelchair:

"You pithyathed thon of a bidth."

Second Class Passenger Barbara Cannon lay naked in First Class State Room—Stewart Hudson stepped to a porthole:

"Put on your clothes, honey," he said. "There's been an accident."

Doctor Benway, Ship's Doctor, drunkenly added two inches to a four-inch incision with one stroke of his scalpel—

"Perhaps the appendix is already out, doctor," the nurse said peering over his shoulder—"I saw a little scar—"

"The appendix *OUT! I'M* taking the appendix out—What do you think I'm doing here?"

"Perhaps the appendix is on the left side, doctor—That happens sometimes you know—"

"Stop breathing down my neck—I'm coming to that—Don't you think I know where an appendix is?—I studied appendectomy in 1910 at Harvard—" He lifted the abdominal wall and searched along the incision dropping ashes from his cigarette—

"And fetch me a new scalpel—This one has no edge to it"—

BLOOOMM

"Sew her up," he ordered—"I can't be expected to work under such conditions"—He swept instruments cocaine and morphine into his satchel and tilted out of The Operating Room—

Mrs. J. L. Bradshinkel, thrown out of bed by the explosion, sat up screaming: "I'm going right back to The Sheraton Carlton Hotel and call the Milwaukee Braves"—

Two Philippine maids hoisted her up—"Fetch my wig, Zalameda," she ordered. "I'm going straight to the captain—"

Mike B. Dweyer, Politician from Clayton Missouri, charged the First Class Lounge where the orchestra, high on nutmeg, weltered in their instruments—

"Play The Star Spangled Banner," he bellowed.

"You trying to con somebody, Jack?—We got a union—"

Mike crossed to the jukebox, selected The Star Spangled Banner With Fats Terminal at The Electric Organ, and shoved home a handful of quarters—

Oh say can you seeeeeeeeee

The Captain sitting opposite Lucy Bradshinkel—He is shifty redhead with a face like blotched bone—

"I own this ship," The Lady said—

The deck tilted and her wig slipped over one ear—The Captain stood up with a revolver in his left hand—He snatched the wig and put it on—

"Give me that kimona," he ordered—

She ran to the porthole screaming for help like everyone else on the boat—Her head was outlined in the porthole—He fired—

"And now you God damned old fool, *give me that kimona—*"

I mean by the dawn's early light

Doctor Benway pushed through a crowd at the rail and boarded The First Life Boat—

"Are you all right?" he said seating himself among the women—"I'm the doctor."

The Captain stepped lightly down red carpeted stairs—In The Purser's Office a narrow-shouldered man was energetically shoving currency and jewels into a black suitcase—The Captain's revolver swung free of his brassiere and he fired twice—

By the rocket's red glare

Radio Operator Finch mixed a bicarbonate of soda and belched into his hand—"SOS—URP—SOS—God damned captain's a brown artist—SOS—Off Jersey Coast—SOS— Might smell us—SOS—Son of a bitching crew—SOS—URP —*Comrade* Finch—SOS—Comrade in a pig's ass—SOS— SOS—SOS—URP—URP—URP—"

The Captain stepped lightly into The Radio Room—Witnesses from a distance observed a roaring blast and a brilliant flash as The Operator was arrested—The Captain shoved the body aside and smashed the apparatus with a chair—

Our flag was still there

The Captain stiff-armed an old lady and filled The First Life Boat—The boat was lowered jerkily by male passengers— Doctor Benway cast off—The crew pulled on the oars—The Captain patted his bulging suitcase absently and looked back at the ship—

Oh say do that star spangled banner yet wave

Time hiccoughs—Passengers fighting around Life Boat K9— It is the last boat that can be launched—Joe Sargant, Third

Year Divinity student and MRA, slipped through the crowd and established Perkins in a seat at the bow—Perkins sits there chin drawn back eyes shining clutching a heavy butcher knife in his right hand

By the twilight's last gleamings

Hysterical waves from Second Class flood the deck—"Ladies first," screamed a big faced shoe clerk with long teeth—He grabbed a St. Louis matron and shoved her ahead of him— A wedge of shoe clerks formed behind—A shot rang and the matron fell—The wedge scattered—A man with nautical uniform buttoned in the wrong holes carrying a World War I 45 stepped into the last boat and covered the men at the launching ropes—

"Let this thing down," he ordered—The boat hit the water—A cry went up from the reeling deck—Bodies hurtled around the boat—Heads bobbed in the green water—A hand reached out of the water and closed on the boat side—Spring-like Perkins brought down his knife—The hand slipped away—Finger stubs fell into the boat—Perkins worked fever-ishly cutting on all sides:

"Bathdarths—Thons of bidth—Bathdarth—thon bidth— Methodith Epithcopal God damn ith—"

O'er the land of the freeee

Barbara Cannon showed your reporter her souvenirs of the disaster: A life belt autographed by the crew and a severed human finger—

And the home of the brave

"I don't know," she said. "I feel sorta bad about this old finger."

Gave proof through the night that our flag was still there

Gregory Corso
COLUMBIA U POESY
READING—1975

PROLOGUE

What a 16 years it's been
Since last sat I here
with the Trillings again seated
he older . . . sweetly sadder;
she broader . . . unmotherly still

with all my poetfriends
ex-wife & forever daughter
with all my hair
and broken nose
and teeth no longer there
and good ol Kerouacky . . . poofed into fat air
Eterne Spirit of the Age . . . a
Monumental loss . . . another angel
chased from the American door

And what the gains?
Al volleyed amongst Hindu gods
then traded them all for Buddha's no-god
A Guggenheim he got; an NBA award;
an elect of the Academy of Arts & Sciences:
and the New York Times paid him 400 dollars
for a poem he wrote about being mugged for 60 dollars
O blessed fortune! for his life
there is no thief

16 years ago we were put down
for being filthy beatnik sex commie dope fiends
Now—16 years later Allen's the respect of his elders
the love of his peers
and the adulation of millions of youth . . .
Peter has himself a girl so that he and Allen,
Hermes willing, might have a baby
He's also a farm and a tractor
and fields and fields of soybeans

Bill's ever Bill
even though he stopped drugging and smoking cigarettes
Me, I'm still considered an unwashed beatnik sex commie dope
      fiend
True, I don't bathe every day (deodorants kill
the natural redolence of the human form divine)
and sex, yes, I've made three fleshed angels in life;
and I'm as much a Communist as I am a Capitalist
i.e., I'm incapable of being either of 'em;
as for Dopey-poo, it be a poet's porogative

Dear Audience,
we early heads of present style & consciousness
(with Kerouac in spirit)
are the Daddies of the Age
16 years ago, born of ourselves,
ours was a history with a future
And from our Petroniusian view of society
a subterranean poesy of the streets
enhanced by the divine butcher: humor,
did climb the towers of the Big Lie
and boot the ivory apple-cart of tyrannical values
into illusory oblivion
without spilling a drop of blood
. . . blessed be Revolutionaries of the Spirit!

POEM

Summoned by the Muse
I expected the worst
Outside Her Sanctum Sanctorum
I paced up and down a pylon
of alabaster poets
known and unknown by name
and lauded and neglect of fame
I felt weak and afeared
and swore to myself:
"This is it! It's good-bye poetry for me!"
And the eyes of Southey
humbled me

into a nothingness
I braced myself
with self-assurances
muttering: 'Being a poet
limits one's full potential;
I can ride Pegasus anytime I feel;
though my output has been of late
seldom and chance,
it's the being makes the poem
not the poem the being:
and besides, I long ago announced myself poet
long before the poem—"
The great Thothian doors opened
I beheld Her and exclaimed: 'Ah, Miss God!'
She beckoned me sit upon a velvety gold cushion
I sat—and at Her swan-boned feet sat three:
Ganesha, Thoth, Hermes,
and over a pipe of Edgar Poe's skullen ash
they blew a fiery diamond of Balbeckian hash
"O charming poet-stud whom I adore
my Nunzio Corso Gregorio
I twirl churingas, I sing,
you inspire the inspirer
for behold I am the Muse
and music is my sacrament
—I ask you, would you ever deny me?"
"Never!" I swore . . .
From Ganesha's curled trunk to Thoth's ibis beak
to Hermes' Praxitelesean nose She flecked cocaine
from the Dawnman's mirrory brain—
"Would you favor me your ear?"
"Happily so O sweet sister of sestinas"
"It's Emily, Emily D . . .
I implore you regard her chemicry
she who tested a liquor never brewed;
and Percy Bysshe, your beloved Shelley
who of laudanum did partake
. . . but I fear I'll embarrass you
this question I would put to you . . ."
"O soul of Shakespeare, ask me, ask me anything . . ."

I could hear the silent laughter
of Her three messenger-boys
"I have no desire to upset you—"
"Ask; I shall answer"
"What thinkest thou the poppy?"
My silence seemed the lapse of a decade
The eyes of She and the three
were like death chills waved upon me
When I finally spoke I spoke a voice
old so old and far from the child I used to be
"Dear carefree girl of Homer, Madonna of Rimbaud;
morphia is poet-old,
an herbal emetic of oraclry,
an hallucinatory ichor divined by thee
as traditioned unto the bards of the Lake,
theirs and mine to use at liberty
but I am not free to be at such liberty;
the law has put its maw
into the poet's medicine cabinet
. . . I tell you, O sweet melancholy of Chatterton,
the forces of morality
and depresséd gangs of youth,
this God-sick age
and fields farmed by gangster farmers
prevents the poet ferret his mind
halts him his probe of the pain of life
. . . for consider, around that Lake
Coleridge and De Quincey were spared
the Eldorado Caddie connection men
and every other Puerto Rican mother's son
has his stash of laudanum
—for me there is no Xanadu"

"I ask you: Do you favor heroin more than you do me?"
The three each held a bloody needle
each needle a familiarity
"Was I with you when heroin was with you?"
A great reality overcame me
huge as death, indeed death—
The hash, an illusion, was in truth myrrh,

and the cocaine, illusion, was the white dust of Hermes'
      wings
Again Her awful tone:
      "Do you love drugs more than you love me?"
"I'm not ashamed!" I screamed
"You have butchered your spirit!" roared Ganesha
"Your pen is bloodied!" cawed the scribe Thoth
"You have failed to deliver the Message!" admonished Hermes
With tearful eyes I gazed into Her eyes and cried:
"I swear to you there is in me yet time
to run back through life and expiate
all that's been sadly done . . . sadly neglected . . ."

Seated on a cold park bench
I heard Her moan: "O Gregorio, Gregorio
you'll fail me, I know"

Walking away
a little old lady behind me
was singing: "True! True!"
"Not so!" rang the spirit, "Not so!"

THE WHOLE MESS . . .
ALMOST

I ran up six flights of stairs
to my small furnished room
opened the window
and began throwing out
those things most important in life

First to go, Truth, squealing like a fink:
"Don't! I'll tell awful things about you!"
"Oh yeah! Well, I've nothing to hide . . . OUT!"
Then went God, glowering & whimpering in amazement:
"It's not my fault! I'm not the cause of it all!" "OUT!"
Then Love, cooing bribes: "You'll never know impotency!
All the girls on *Vogue* covers, all yours!"
I pushed her fat ass out and screamed:

"You always end up a bummer!"
I picked up Faith Hope Charity
all three clinging together:
"Without us you'll surely die!"
"With you I'm going nuts! Goodbye!"

Then Beauty . . . ah, Beauty—
As I led her to the window
I told her: "You I loved best in life
. . . but you're a killer; Beauty kills!"
Not really meaning to drop her
I immediately ran downstairs
getting there just in time to catch her
"You saved me!" she cried
I put her down and told her: "Move on."

Went back up those six flights
went to the money
there was no money to throw out.
The only thing left in the room was Death
hiding beneath the kitchen sink:
"I'm not real!" It cried
"I'm just a rumor spread by life . . ."
Laughing I threw it out, kitchen sink and all
and suddenly realized Humor
was all that was left—
All I could do with Humor was to say:
"Out the window with the window!"

Diane DiPrima
APRIL FOOL BIRTHDAY POEM
FOR GRANDPA

Today is your
birthday and I have tried
writing these things before,
but now
in the gathering madness, I want to
thank you

for telling me what to expect
for pulling
no punches, back there in that scrubbed Bronx parlor
thank you
for honestly weeping in time to
innumerable heartbreaking
italian operas for
pulling my hair when I
pulled the leaves off the trees so I'd
know how it feels, we are
involved in it now, revolution, up to our
knees and the tide is rising, I embrace
strangers on the street, filled with their love and
mine, the love you told us had to come or we
die, told them all in that Bronx park, me listening in
spring Bronx dusk, breathing stars, so glorious
to me your white hair, your height your fierce
blue eyes, rare among italians, I stood
a ways off, looking up at you, my grandpa
people listened to, I stand
a ways off listening as I pour out soup
young men with light in their faces
at my table, talking love, talking revolution
which is love, spelled backwards, how
you would love us all, would thunder your anarchist wisdom
at us, would thunder Dante, and Giordano Bruno, orderly men
bent to your ends, well I want you to know
we do it for you, and your ilk, for Carlo Tresca,
for Sacco and Vanzetti, without knowing
it, or thinking about it, as we do it for Aubrey Beardsley
Oscar Wilde (all street lights
shall be purple), do it
for Trotsky and Shelley and big/dumb
Kropotkin
Eisenstein's Strike people, Jean Cocteau's ennui, we do it for
the stars over the Bronx
that they may look on earth
and not be ashamed.

from **LOBA: PARTS I–VIII**

THE LOBA DANCES

I.

She raises
           in flames
                        the
city
     it glows about her
                        The Loba
mother wolf &
                mistress
of many
           dances she
treads
      in the severed heads
                           that grow
likc mosses
            on the flood
                          the city
melts it
        flows past her
treading
         white feet they
curl around
            ashes & the ashes
sing, they chant
                 a new
                          creation myth
ghoul lips of
             lovers she
                        left
like pearls
           in the road
                        she
dances, see

her eyes
        glow the
                 city

glows dancing
            in them
                        wolf cry you hear
falls
    from the stars
                the Loba
dances, she
            treads the
salty earth, she
            does not
                        raise
breath cloud heavenward
                        her breath
itself
    is carnage.

II.

HOW DO THE GODS MANIFEST, WHERE DO THEY
HOME AGAIN? SHE SHONE
LIKE A WHITE LIGHT IN THE DARK
NORTHERN FOREST, WOLF-WOMAN AND VALKYRIE RIDING
THE DARK MIST, RIDING
WITH RED SHOUTS OVER THE HILLTOP, HER
LANCE DRIPPING, BLOOD SWELLING
FROM ITS BRASS TIP, OR SHE SWAM
UPSTREAM IN ICY RIVERS, GREEN HER
WHITE PELT UNDER THE FLOWING
WATERS

III.

she strides in blue jeans to the corner
bar; she dances
w / the old women, the men
light up, they order wine,
sawdust is flying under her feet
her sneakers, thudding soft
her wispy hair falls sometimes
into her face

were it not for the ring of fur
            around her ankles
just over her bobby socks
                 there's no one
wd ever guess her name. . . .

IV. SOME LIES ABOUT THE LOBA

that she is eternal, that she sings
that she is star-born, that she gathers crystal
that she can be confused with Isis
that she is the goal
that she knows her name, that she swims
in the purple sky, that her fingers are pale & strong

that she is black, that she is white
that you always know who she is
when she appears
that she strides on battlements, that she sifts
like stones in the sea
that you can hear her approach, that her jewelled feet
tread any particular measure

that there is anything about her
which cannot be said
that she relishes tombstones, falls
down marble stairs
that she is ground only, that she is not ground
that you can remember the first time you met
that she is always with you
that she can be seen without grace

that there is anything to say of her
which is not truth

V. THE LOBA ADDRESSES THE GODDESS / OR THE POET AS PRIESTESS ADDRESSES THE LOBA-GODDESS

Is it not in yr service that I wear myself out
running ragged among these hills, driving children

to forgotten movies? In yr service
broom & pen. The monstrous feasts
we serve the others on the outer porch
(within the house there is only rice & salt)
And we wear exhaustion like a painted robe
I & my sisters
    wresting the goods from the niggardly
     dying fathers
healing each other w / water & bitter herbs

that when we stand naked in the circle of lamps
(beside the small water, in the inner grove)
we show
no blemish, but also no superfluous beauty.
It has burned off in watches of the night.
O Nut, O mantle of stars, we catch at you
  lean   mournful
  ragged triumphant
   shaggy as grass
our skins ache of emergence / dark o' the moon

Lawrence Ferlinghetti
THE CANTICLE OF JACK KEROUAC

I.

Far from the sea far from the sea
      of Breton fishermen
  the white clouds scudding
       over Lowell
  and the white birches the
       bare white birches
   along the blear night roads
      flashing by in darkness
  (where once he rode
      in Pop's old Plymouth)
And the birch-white face
      of a Merrimac madonna

                shadowed in streetlight
                        by Merrimac's shroudy shoes
                —a leaf blown
                            upon sea wind
                    out of Brittany
                                over endless oceans

                            II.

There is a garden in the memory of America
There is a nightbird in its memory
There is an *andante cantabile*
in a garden in the memory
of America
In a secret garden
in a private place
a song a melody
a nightsong echoing
in the memory of America
In the sound of a nightbird
outside a Lowell window
In the cry of kids
in tenement yards at night
In the deep sound
of a woman murmuring
a woman singing broken melody
in a shuttered room
in an old wood house
in Lowell
As the world cracks by
                        thundering
like a lost lumber truck
                    on a steep grade
            in Kerouac America

And the woman sits silent now
                        rocking backward
    to Whistler's Mother in Lowell
            and to all the tough old
                        Canuck mothers

and Jack's *Mémère*
And may still on stormy nights show through
as a phantom after-image
on silent TV screens
a flickered after-image
that will not go away
in Moody Street
in Beaulieu Street
in 'dirtstreet Sarah Avenue'
in Pawtucketville
And in the Church of St. Jean Baptiste

III.

And the Old Worthen Bar
in Lowell Mass. at midnight
in the now of Nineteen Eighty-seven
Kerouackian revellers
crowd the wood booths
ancient with carved initials
of a million drinking bouts
the clouts of the
Shrouded Stranger
upon each wood pew
where the likes of Kerouack lumberjack
feinted their defiance
of dung and death
Ah the broken wood and the punka fans still turning
(pull-cord wavings
of the breath of Buddha)
still lost in Lowell's
'vast tragedies of darkness'
with Jack

IV.

And the Four Sisters Diner
also once known as 'The Owl'
Sunday morning now
March Eighty-seven

or any year of Sunday specials
Scrambled eggs and chopped ham
  the bright booths loaded with families
      Lowell Greek and Gaspé French
           Joual patois and Argos argot
     Spartan slaves escaped
             into the New World
    here incarnate
          in rush of blood of
          American Sunday morning
And *ti-jean* Jack Kerouac
  comes smiling in
         baseball cap cocked up
      hungry for mass
         in this Church of All Hungry Saints
      haunt of all night Owls
            blessing every booth . . .

V.

Ah he the Silent Smiler
  the one
      with the lumberjack shirt
    and cap with flaps askew
      blowing his hands in winter
    as if to light a flame
The Shrouded Stranger knew him
  as *Ti-Jean* the Smiler
    grooking past redbrick mill buildings
down by the riverrun
      (O mighty Merrimac
         'thunderous husher')
  where once upon a midnight then
young *Ti-Jean* danced with *Mémère*
in the moondrowned light
And rolled upon the greensward
  his mother and lover
    all one with Buddha
        in his arms

VI.

And then *Ti Jean* Jack with Joual tongue
disguised as an American fullback in plaid shirt
        crossing and recrossing America
                        in speedy cars
    a Dr. Sax's shadow shadowing him
     like a shroudy cloud over the landscape
      Song of the Open Road sung drunken
          with Whitman and Jack London and Thomas Wolfe
          still echoing through
                        a Nineteen Thirties America
                        a Nineteen Forties America
                        an America now long gone
            except in broken down dusty old
                                Greyhound Bus stations
                    in small lost towns
    Ti-Jean's vision of America
          seen from a moving car window
              the same as Wolfe's lonely
                            sweeping vision
              glimpsed from a coach-train long ago
('And thus did he see first the dark land')

And so Jack
            in an angel midnight bar

    somewhere West of Middle America
          where one drunk madonna
                    (shades of one on a Merrimac corner)
        makes him a gesture with her eyes
                            a blue gesture

            and *Ti-Jean* answers
                        only with his eyes
    And the night goes on with them
          And the light comes up on them
                    making love in a parking lot
              in the mysterious dark
              in the mysterious light
                        of his America

VII.

In the dark of his fellaheen night
  in the light of the illuminated
                Stations of the Cross
      and the illuminated Grotto
           down behind the Funeral Home
              by roar of river
    where now *Ti-Jean* alone
           (returned to Lowell
              in one more doomed Wolfian attempt
              to Go Home Again)
gropes past the Twelve Stations of the Cross
    reciting aloud the French inscriptions
      in his Joual accent
  which makes the plaster French Christ
             laugh and cry
    as He hefts His huge Cross
          up the Eternal Hill
And a very real tear drops
          in the Grotto
      from the face
            of the stoned Virgin

VIII.

  Light upon light
The Mountain
    keeps still

IX.

  Hands over ears
He steals away
    with the Bell. . . .

Writ in Lowell and Conway and Boston, Mass. and San Francisco
March–April 1987

USES OF POETRY

So what is the use of poetry these days
What use is it What good is it
these days and nights in the Age of Autogeddon
in which poetry is what has been paved over
to make a freeway for armies of the night
as in that palm paradiso just north of Nicaragua
where promises made in the plazas
will be betrayed in the back country
or in the so-green fields
of the Concord Naval Weapons Station
where armed trains run over green protesters
where poetry is made important by its absence
the absence of birds in a summer landscape
the lack of love in a bed at midnight
or lack of light at high noon
in the not-so-White House
For even bad poetry has relevance
for what it does not say
for what it leaves out
Yes what of the sun streaming down
in the meshes of morning
what of white nights and mouths of desire
lips saying Lulu Lulu over and over
and all things born with wings that sing
and far far cries upon a beach at nightfall
and light that ever was on land and sea
and caverns measured out by man
where once the sacred rivers ran
near cities by the sea
through which we walk and wander absently
astounded constantly
by the mad spectacle of existence
and all these talking animals on wheels
heroes and heroines with a thousand eyes
with bent hearts and hidden oversouls
with no more myths to call their own
constantly astounded as I am still
by these bare-face bipeds in clothes

these stand-up tragedians
pale idols in the night streets
trance-dancers in the dust of the Last Waltz
in this time of gridlock Autogeddon
where the voice of the poet still sounds distantly
the voice of the Fourth Person Singular
the voice within the voice of the turtle
the face behind the face of the race
a book of light at night
the very voice of life as Whitman heard it
a wild soft laughter
(ah but to free it still
from the word-processor of the mind!)

And I am a reporter for a newspaper
on another planet
come to file a down-to-earth story
of the What When Where How and Why
of this astounding life down here
and of the strange clowns in control of it
the curious clowns in control of it
with hands upon the windowsills
of dread demonic mills
casting their own dark shadows
into the earth's great shadow
in the end of time unseen
in the supreme hashish of our dream

SHORT STORY ON A PAINTING
OF GUSTAV KLIMT

They are kneeling upright on a flowered bed
   He
     has just caught her there
           and holds her still
    Her gown
       has slipped down
          off her shoulder

He has an urgent hunger
                    His dark head
                              bends to hers
                                        hungrily
And the woman the woman
        turns her tangerine lips from his
                    one hand like the head of a dead swan
                    draped down over
                                        his heavy neck
                    the fingers
                        strangely crimped
                                    tightly together
        her other arm doubled up
                        against her tight breast
            her hand a languid claw
                                clutching his hand
            which would turn her mouth
                                        to his
        her long dress made
                        of multicolored blossoms
                            quilted on gold
        her Titian hair
                    with blue stars in it
        And his gold
                    harlequin robe
                            checkered with
                                    dark squares
            Gold garlands
                        stream down over
                                    her bare calves &
                                        tensed feet
Nearby there must be
                a jeweled tree
                        with glass leaves aglitter
                            in the gold air
It must be
        morning
                in a faraway place somewhere
They
    are silent together
                    as in a flowered field

upon the summer couch
which must be hers
And he holds her still
so passionately
holds her head to his
so gently so insistently
to make her turn
her lips to his
Her eyes are closed
like folded petals
She
will not open
He
is not the One

Allen Ginsberg
FIRST PARTY AT KEN KESEY'S
WITH HELL'S ANGELS

Cool black night thru the redwoods
cars parked outside in shade
behind the gate, stars dim above
the ravine, a fire burning by the side
porch and a few tired souls hunched over
in black leather jackets. In the huge
wooden house, a yellow chandelier
at 3 A.M. the blast of loudspeakers
hi-fi Rolling Stones Ray Charles Beatles
Jumping Joe Jackson and twenty youths
dancing to the vibration thru the floor,
a little weed in the bathroom, girls in scarlet
tights, one muscular smooth skinned man
sweating dancing for hours, beer cans
bent littering the yard, a hanged man
sculpture dangling from a high creek branch,
children sleeping softly in their bedroom bunks.
And 4 police cars parked outside the painted
gate, red lights revolving in the leaves.

December 1965

WICHITA VORTEX SUTRA

I

Turn Right Next Corner
  The Biggest Little Town in Kansas
    Macpherson
Red sun setting flat plains west streaked
    with gauzy veils, chimney mist spread
   around christmas-tree-bulbed refineries—aluminum
    white tanks squat beneath
   winking signal towers' bright plane-lights,
     orange gas flares
   beneath pillows of smoke, flames in machinery—
     transparent towers at dusk

In advance of the Cold Wave
  Snow is spreading eastward to
     the Great Lakes
  News Broadcast & old clarinets
  Watertower dome Lighted on the flat plain
    car radio speeding acrost railroad tracks—
Kansas! Kansas! Shuddering at last!
    PERSON appearing in Kansas!
   angry telephone calls to the University
   Police dumbfounded leaning on
     their radiocar hoods
   While Poets chant to Allah in the roadhouse Showboat!
Blue eyed children dance and hold thy Hand O aged Walt
   who came from Lawrence to Topeka to envision
    Iron interlaced upon the city plain—
  Telegraph wires strung from city to city O Melville!
    Television brightening thy *rills of Kansas lone*
I come,
    lone man from the void, riding a bus
    hypnotized by red tail lights on the straight
      space road ahead—
   & the Methodist minister with cracked eyes
     leaning over the table
    quoting Kierkegaard "death of God"
     a million dollars

in the bank   owns all West Wichita
come to Nothing!
Prajnaparamita Sutra over coffee—Vortex
of telephone radio aircraft assembly frame ammunition
petroleum nightclub Newspaper streets illuminated by Bright
EMPTINESS—

Thy sins are forgiven, Wichita!
Thy lonesomeness annulled, O Kansas dear!
as the western Twang prophesied
thru banjo, when lone cowboy walked the railroad track
past an empty station toward the sun
sinking giant-bulbed orange down the box canyon—
Music strung over his back
and empty handed   singing on this planet earth
I'm a lonely Dog, O Mother!
Come, Nebraska, sing & dance with me—
Come lovers of Lincoln and Omaha,
hear my soft voice at last
As Babes need the chemical touch of flesh in pink infancy
lest they die Idiot returning to Inhuman—
Nothing—
So, tender lipt adolescent girl, pale youth,
give me back my soft kiss
Hold me in your innocent arms,
accept my tears as yours to harvest
equal   in nature to the Wheat
that made your bodies' muscular bones
broad shouldered, boy bicept—
from leaning on cows & drinking Milk
in Midwest Solitude—
No more fear of tenderness, much delight in weeping, ectasy
in singing, laughter rises that confounds
staring Idiot mayors
and stony politicians eyeing
Thy breast,
O Man of America, be born!
Truth breaks through!
How big is the prick of the President?
How big is Cardinal Vietnam?

How little the prince of the FBI, unmarried all these years!
How big are all the Public Figures?
What kind of flesh hangs, hidden behind their Images?

Approaching Salina,
Prehistoric excavation, *Apache Uprising*
in the drive-in theater
Shelling Bombing Range   mapped in the distance,
Crime Prevention Show, sponsor Wrigley's Spearmint
Dinosaur Sinclair advertisement, glowing green—
South 9th Street lined with poplar & elm branch
spread over evening's tiny headlights—
Salina Highschool's brick darkens Gothic
over a night-lit door—
What wreaths of naked bodies, thighs and faces,
small hairy bun'd vaginas,
silver cocks, armpits and breasts
moistened by tears
for 20 years, for 40 years?
Peking Radio surveyed by Luden's Coughdrops
Attacks on the Russian & Japanese,
Big Dipper leaning above the Nebraska border,
handle down to the blackened plains,
telephone-pole ghosts crossed
by roadside, dim headlights—
dark night, & giant T-bone steaks,
and in *The Village Voice*
New Frontier Productions present
Camp Comedy: *Fairies I Have Met.*
Blue highway lamps strung along the horizon east at Hebron
Homestead National Monument near Beatrice—

Language, language
black Earth-circle in the rear window,
no cars for miles along highway
beacon lights on oceanic plain
language, language
over Big Blue River
chanting *La illaha el (lill) Allah hu*

revolving my head to my heart like my mother
chin abreast at Allah
Eyes closed, blackness
vaster than midnight prairies,
Nebraska of solitary Allah,
Joy, I am I
the lone One singing to myself
God come true—
Thrills of fear.
nearer than the vein in my neck—?
What if I opened my soul to sing to my absolute self
Singing as the car crash chomped thru blood and muscle
tendon skull?
What if I sang, and loosed the chords of fear brow?
What exquisite noise wd
shiver my car companions?
I am the Universe tonite
riding in all my Power riding
chauffeured thru my self by a long haired saint with eyeglasses
What if I sang till Students knew I was free
of Vietnam, trousers, free of my own meat,
free to die in my thoughtful shivering Throne?
freer than Nebraska, freer than America—
Whatfree to diefreer than NeMay I disappear
in magic Joy-smoke! Pouf! reddish Vapor,
Faustus vanishes weeping & laughing
under stars on Highway 77 between Beatrice & Lincoln—
"Better not to move but to let things be" Reverend Preacher?
We've all already disappeared!

Space highway open, entering Lincoln's ear
ground to a stop Tracks Warning
Pioneer Boulevard—
William Jennings Bryan sang
Thou shalt not crucify mankind upon a cross of Gold!
O Baby Doe! Gold's
Department Store hulks o'er 10th Street now
—an unregenerate old fop who didn't want to be a monkey
now's the Highest Perfect Wisdom dust
and Lindsay's cry

survives compassionate in the Highschool Anthology—
a giant dormitory brilliant on the evening plain
                    drifts with his memories—
There's a nice white door over there
                    for me O dear!   on Zero Street.

February 15, 1966

ANTI–VIETNAM WAR PEACE MOBILIZATION

White sunshine on sweating skulls
Washington's Monument pyramided high granite clouds
over a soul mass, children screaming in their brains on quiet grass
(black man strapped hanging in blue denims from an earth cross)—
Soul brightness under blue sky
Assembled before White House filled with mustached Germans
& police buttons, army telephones, CIA Buzzers, FBI bugs
Secret Service walkie-talkies, Intercom squawkers to Narco
Fuzz & Florida Mafia Real Estate Speculators.
One hundred thousand bodies naked before an Iron Robot
Nixon's brain Presidential cranium case spying thru binoculars
from the Paranoia Smog Factory's East Wing.

May 9, 1970

MUGGING

I

Tonite I walked out of my red apartment door on East tenth street's
        dusk—
Walked out of my home ten years, walked out in my honking neighborhood
Tonite at seven walked out past garbage cans chained to concrete anchors
Walked under black painted fire escapes, giant castiron plate covering a hole
        in ground
—Crossed the street, traffic lite red, thirteen bus roaring by liquor store,
past corner pharmacy iron grated, past Coca-Cola & Mylai posters fading
        scraped on brick

Past Chinese Laundry wood door'd, & broken cement stoop steps For Rent
    hall painted green & purple Puerto Rican style

Along E. 10th's glass splattered pavement, kid blacks & Spanish oiled hair
    adolescents' crowded house fronts—

Ah, tonight, I walked out on my block NY City under humid summer sky
    Halloween,

thinking what happened Timothy Leary joining brain police for a season?

thinking what's all this Weathermen, secrecy & selfrighteousness beyond
    reason—F.B.I. plots?

Walked past a taxicab controlling the bottle strewn curb—

past young fellows with their umbrella handles & canes leaning against a
    ravaged Buick

—and as I looked at the crowd of kids on the stoop—a boy stepped up, put
    his arm around my neck

tenderly I thought for a moment, squeezed harder, his umbrella handle
    against my skull,

and his friends took my arm, a young brown companion tripped his foot
    'gainst my ankle—

as I went down shouting Om Ah Hūm to gangs of lovers on the stoop
    watching

slowly appreciating, why this is a raid, these strangers mean strange
    business

with what—my pockets, bald head, broken-healed-bone leg, my softshoes,
    my heart—

Have they knives? Om Ah Hūm —Have they sharp metal wood to shove
    in eye ear ass? Om Ah Hūm

& slowly reclined on the pavement, struggling to keep my woolen bag
    of poetry address calendar & Leary-lawyer notes hung from my
    shoulder

dragged in my neat orlon shirt over the crossbar of a broken metal door

dragged slowly onto the fire-soiled floor an abandoned store, laundry candy
    counter 1929—

now a mess of papers & pillows & plastic car seat covers cracked cockroach-
    corpsed ground—

my wallet back pocket passed over the iron foot step guard

and fell out, stole by God Muggers' lost fingers, Strange—

Couldn't tell—snakeskin wallet actually plastic, 70 dollars my bank money
    for a week,

old broken wallet—and dreary plastic contents—Amex card & Manf. Han-
    over Trust Credit too—business card from Mr. Spears British Home

Minister Drug Squad—my draft card—membership ACLU & Naropa Institute Instructor's identification

Om Ah Hūm I continued chanting Om Ah Hūm

Putting my palm on the neck of an 18 year old boy fingering my back pocket crying "Where's the money"

"Om Ah Hūm there isn't any"

My card Chief Boo-Hoo Neo American Church New Jersey & Lower East Side

Om Ah Hūm—what not forgotten crowded wallet—Mobil Credit, Shell? old lovers addresses on cardboard pieces, booksellers calling cards—

—"Shut up or we'll murder you"—"Om Ah Hūm take it easy"

Lying on the floor shall I shout more loud?—the metal door closed on blackness

one boy felt my broken healed ankle, looking for hundred dollar bills behind my stocking weren't even there—a third boy untied my Seiko Hong Kong watch rough from right wrist leaving a clasp-prick skin tiny bruise

"Shut up and we'll get out of here"—and so they left,

as I rose from the cardboard mattress thinking Om Ah Hūm didn't stop em enough,

the tone of voice too loud—my shoulder bag with 10,000 dollars full of poetry left on the broken floor—

November 2, 1974

II

Went out the door dim eyed, bent down & picked up my glasses from step edge I placed them while dragged in the store—looked out—

Whole street a bombed-out face, building rows' eyes & teeth missing

burned apartments half the long block, gutted cellars, hallways' charred beams

hanging over trash plaster mounded entrances, couches & bedsprings rusty after sunset

Nobody home, but scattered stoopfuls of scared kids frozen in black hair

chatted giggling at house doors in black shoes, families cooked For Rent some six story houses mid the street's wreckage

Nextdoor Bodega, a phone, the police? "I just got mugged" I said

to the man's face under fluorescent grocery light tin ceiling—

puffy, eyes blank & watery, sickness of beer kidney and language tongue

thick lips stunned as my own eyes, poor drunken Uncle minding the store!

O hopeless city of idiots empty eyed staring afraid, red beam top'd car at
      street curb arrived—
"Hey maybe my wallet's still on the ground got a flashlight?"
Back into the burnt-doored cave, & the policeman's gray flashlight broken
      no eyebeam—
"My partner all he wants is sit in the car never gets out Hey Joe bring your
      flashlight—"
a tiny throwaway beam, dim as a match in the criminal dark
"No I can't see anything here" . . . "Fill out this form"
Neighborhood street crowd behind a car "We didn't see nothing"
Stoop young girls, kids laughing "Listen man last time I messed with them
      see this—"
rolled up his skinny arm shirt, a white knife scar on his brown shoulder
"Besides we help you the cops come don't know anybody we all get arrested
go to jail I never help no more mind my business everytime"
"Agh!" upstreet think "Gee I don't know anybody here ten years lived half
      block crost Avenue C
and who knows who?"—passing empty apartments, old lady with frayed
      paper bags
sitting in the tin-boarded doorframe of a dead house.

                            December 10, 1974

ODE TO FAILURE

Many prophets have failed, their voices silent
ghost-shouts in basements nobody heard dusty laughter in family attics
nor glanced them on park benches weeping with relief under empty sky
Walt Whitman viva'd local losers—courage to Fat Ladies in the Freak Show!
      nervous prisoners whose mustached lips dripped sweat on chow
      lines—
Mayakovsky cried, Then die! my verse, die like the workers' rank & file
      fusilladed in Petersburg!
Prospero burned his Power books & plummeted his magic wand to the
      bottom of dragon seas
Alexander the Great failed to find more worlds to conquer!
O Failure I chant your terrifying name, accept me your 54 year old Prophet
epicking Eternal Flop! I join your Pantheon of mortal bards, & hasten this
      ode with high blood pressure

rushing to the top of my skull as if I wouldn't last another minute, like the
    Dying Gaul! to
You, Lord of blind Monet, deaf Beethoven, armless Venus de Milo, headless
    Winged Victory!
I failed to sleep with every bearded rosy-cheeked boy I jacked off over
My tirades destroyed no Intellectual Unions of KGB & CIA in turtlenecks
    & underpants, their woolen suits & tweeds
I never dissolved Plutonium or dismantled the nuclear Bomb before my skull
    lost hair
I have not yet stopped the Armies of entire Mankind in their march toward
    World War III
I never got to Heaven, Nirvana, X, Whatchamacallit, I never left Earth,
I never learned to die.

Boulder, March 7 / October 10, 1980

WHITE SHROUD

I am summoned from my bed
To the Great City of the Dead
Where I have no house or home
But in dreams may sometime roam
Looking for my ancient room
A feeling in my heart of doom,
Where Grandmother aged lies
In her couch of later days
And my mother saner than I
Laughs and cries She's still alive.

I found myself again in the Great Eastern Metropolis,
wandering under Elevated Transport's iron struts—
many-windowed apartments walled the crowded Bronx road-way
under old theater roofs, masses of poor women shopping
in black shawls past candy store news stands, children skipped beside
grandfathers bent tottering on their canes. I'd descended
to this same street from blackened subways Sundays long ago,
tea and lox with my aunt and dentist cousin when I was ten.
The living pacifist David Dellinger walked at my right side,
he'd driven from Vermont to visit Catholic Worker
Tivoli Farm, we rode up North Manhattan in his car,

relieved the U.S. wars were over in the newspaper,
Television's frenzied dance of dots & shadows calmed—Now
older than our shouts and banners, we explored brick avenues
we lived in to find new residences, rent loft offices
or roomy apartments, retire our eyes & ears & thoughts.
Surprised, I passed the open Chamber where my Russian Jewish
Grandmother lay in her bed and sighed eating a little Chicken
soup or borscht, potato latkes, crumbs on her blankets, talking
Yiddish, complaining solitude abandoned in Old Folks House.
I realized I could find a place to sleep in the neighborhood, what
relief, the family together again, first time in decades!—
Now vigorous Middle aged I climbed hillside streets in West Bronx
looking for my own hot-water furnished flat to settle in,
close to visit my grandmother, read Sunday newspapers
in vast glassy Cafeterias, smoke over pencils & paper,
poetry desk, happy with books father'd left in the attic,
peaceful encyclopedia and a radio in the kitchen.
An old black janitor swept the gutter, street dogs sniffed red hydrants,
nurses pushed baby carriages past silent house fronts.
Anxious I be settled with money in my own place before
nightfall, I wandered tenement embankments overlooking
the pillared subway trestles by the bridge crossing Bronx River.
How like Paris or Budapest suburbs, far from Centrum
Left Bank junky doorstep tragedy intellectual fights
in restaurant bars, where a spry old lady carried her
Century Universal View camera to record Works
Progress Administration newspaper metropolis
double-decker buses in September sun near Broadway El,
skyscraper roofs upreared ten thousand office windows shining
electric-lit above tiny taxis street lamp'd in Mid-town
avenues' late-afternoon darkness the day before Christmas,
Herald Square crowds thronged past traffic lights July noon to lunch
Shop under Macy's department store awnings for dry goods
pause with satchels at Frankfurter counters wearing stylish straw
hats of the decade, mankind thriving in their solitudes in shoes.
But I'd strayed too long amused in the picture cavalcade,
Where was I living? I remembered looking for a house
& eating in apartment kitchens, bookshelf decades ago, Aunt
Rose's illness, an appendix operation, teeth braces,
one afternoon fitting eyeglasses first time, combing wet hair

back on my skull, young awkward looking in the high school mirror
photograph. The Dead look for a home, but here I was still alive.
     I walked past a niche between buildings with tin canopy
shelter from cold rain warmed by hot exhaust from subway gratings,
beneath which engines throbbed with pleasant quiet drone.
A shopping-bag lady lived in the side alley on a mattress,
her wooden bed above the pavement, many blankets and sheets,
Pots, pans, and plates beside her, fan, electric stove by the wall.
She looked desolate, white haired, but strong enough to cook and stare.
Passersby ignored her buildingside hovel many years,
a few businessmen stopped to speak, or give her bread or yogurt.
Sometimes she disappeared into state hospital back wards,
but now'd returned to her homely alleyway, sharp eyed, old
Cranky hair, half paralyzed, complaining angry as I passed.
I was horrified a little, who'd take care of such a woman,
familiar, half-neglected on her street except she'd weathered
many snows stubborn alone in her motheaten rabbit-fur hat.
She had tooth troubles, teeth too old, ground down like horse molars—
she opened her mouth to display her gorge—how can she live
with that, how eat I thought, mushroom-like gray-white horseshoe of
incisors she chomped with, hard flat flowers ranged around her gums.
Then I recognized she was my mother, Naomi, habiting
this old city-edge corner, older than I knew her before
her life disappeared. What are you doing here? I asked, amazed
she recognized me still, astounded to see her sitting up
on her own, chin raised to greet me mocking "I'm living alone,
you all abandoned me, I'm a great woman, I came here
by myself, I wanted to live, now I'm too old to take care
of myself, I don't care, what are you doing here?" I
was looking for a house, I thought, she has one, in poor
Bronx, needs someone to help her shop and cook, needs her children now,
I'm her younger son, walked past her alleyway by accident,
but here she is survived, sleeping at night awake on that
wooden platform. Has she an extra room? I noticed her cave
adjoined an apartment door, unpainted basement storeroom
facing her shelter in the building side. I could live here,
worst comes to worst, best place I'll find, near my mother in
our mortal life. My years of haunting continental city streets,
apartment dreams, old rooms I used to live in, still paid rent for,
key didn't work, locks changed, immigrant families occupied

my familiar hallway lodgings—I'd wandered downhill homeless
avenues, money lost, or'd come back to the flat—But couldn't
recognize my house in London, Paris, Bronx, by Columbia
library, downtown 8th Avenue near Chelsea Subway—
Those years unsettled—were over now, here I could live
forever, here have a home, with Naomi, at long last,
at long last, my search was ended in this pleasant way,
time to care for her before death, long way to go yet,
lots of trouble her cantankerous habits, shameful blankets
near the street, tooth pots, dirty pans, half paralyzed irritable,
she needed my middle aged strength and worldly money knowledge,
housekeeping art. I can cook and write books for a living,
she'll not have to beg her medicine food, a new set of teeth
for company, won't yell at the world, I can afford a telephone,
after twenty-five years we could call up Aunt Edie in California,
I'll have a place to stay. "Best of all," I told Naomi
"Now don't get mad, you realize your old enemy Grandma's
still alive! She lives a couple blocks down hill, I just saw her,
like you!" My breast rejoiced, all my troubles over, she was
content, too old to care or yell her grudge, only complaining
her bad teeth. What long-sought peace!
                            Then glad of life I woke
in Boulder before dawn, my second story bedroom windows
Bluff Street facing East over town rooftops, I returned
from the Land of the Dead to living Poesy, and wrote
this tale of long lost joy, to have seen my mother again!
And when the ink ran out of my pen, and rosy violet
illumined city treetop skies above the Flatiron Front Range,
I went downstairs to the shady living room, where Peter Orlovsky
sat with long hair lit by television glow to watch
the sunrise weather news, I kissed him & filled my pen and wept.

October 5, 1983, 6:35 A.M.

FOURTH FLOOR, DAWN,
UP ALL NIGHT WRITING
LETTERS

Pigeons shake their wings on the copper church roof
out my window across the street, a bird perched on the cross

surveys the city's blue-gray clouds. Larry Rivers
'll come at 10 A.M. and take my picture. I'm taking
your picture, pigeons. I'm writing you down, Dawn.
I'm immortalizing your exhaust, Avenue A bus.
O Thought, now you'll have to think the same thing forever!
New York, June 7, 1980, 6:48 A.M.

Michael McClure
SONG

I WORK WITH THE SHAPE
of spirit
moving the matter
in my hands;
I
mold
it from
the inner matrix.
Even a crow or fox
understands.

"IT'S NATION TIME"

NOW IT IS TIME FOR A NATION,
FOR A SPIRITUAL
NATION,
a spiritual Nation
based
and formed on open freedom,
on flesh and biology—on what we can know
of the shaping
of men and all living creatures
as we grow together
through billions of years! And
IT
MUST
INCORPORATE
(hold the body of the Nation)

our ceaseless need
for liberation, for revolt,
and for CHANGE!

WATCHING THE STOLEN ROSE

THE ROSE IS A PINK-YELLOW
UNIVERSE UNFOLDING

layer upon
luminous layer

petal to petal
spreading

unsteady yet
perfectly balanced

as the curling
of smoke

from a mind
on fire.

THE DEATH OF KIN CHUEN
LOUIE

NOW, ON THE DAY BEFORE MY DAUGHTER'S
TWENTY-FIRST BIRTHDAY,
ON THE AFTERNOON OF HER PARTY,
I REVISIT THE SCENE OF THE DEATH
of Kin Chuen Louie.
He too was between twenty and twenty-one.
The newspapers called him
a smalltime extortionist.
But what are we all but small
time extortionists in the
proportionless

universe?
(I am in awe of the thought
of the coolness and sureness
of his assassin.)
Twelve days ago, on the Festival
of the Lord Buddha, shortly
after two in the afternoon,
Kin Chuen Louie left his flat
on Kearney Street.
Louie's young, long-haired murderer,
in black jacket and army pants,
waited with a .380
Walther automatic pistol holding
fourteen bullets. Kin Chuen Louie,
spotting his assailant, leaped
into his bright red Plymouth Fury.
The murderer stepped
to the driver's side and fired a shot
into Louie. Louie started the ignition
and slammed into reverse.
His foot stuck on the accelerator.
The car, propelled backward with great
force, jammed between
a building and a white car
parked there—knocking loose shards
of red brick painted over with beige.
The murderer stepped quickly
to the passenger side of the trapped
and roaring car and fired seven bullets
through the windshield
into a tight pattern on the head and neck
of Louie. A ninth shot missed,
going finger-deep
into brick. The killer
fled a few yards, turned at the corner,
and disappeared down Sonoma Alley.
A moment later,
we arrived on the empty street
and looked through
shattered glass

at the young Chinese man—
blood pouring out of the holes
in his head—slumped over
on his side. It was like the close-up
in a Sam Peckinpah movie.
He was completely relaxed
—finally and almost pleasantly limp
and serene—wearing an army jacket
and grubby levis . . . a slender, handsome,
clean-cut face with short hair boyishly
hanging in his eyes above
the dime-size bullet holes.
The blood pouring onto the seat covers
was a thick, reddish vermillion.
There was a peaceful, robbe-grilletish,
dim light inside the car.
The shattered window was like
a frosted spider web.
Either death is beautiful to see
—or we learn the esthetic
of death from films. BUT I do know
that our physical, athletic body,
a thing of perfect loops, and secret
and manifest
dimensions and breathings of consciousness
and unconsciousness, emanates
rainbows and actions,
and black flowers
and
it is there
to bear us through this world
and to kiss us goodbye at the doorstep
of any other.
I praise Everything-That-Is
for that blessing.
I drink chrysanthemum
tea in his memory.
Candied ginger, scented with licorice
from Hong Kong,
is on my breath.

I know each death

shall be as fine as his is.

Ed Sanders
HYMN TO ARCHILOCHUS

For Joe Cardarelli

On the rocky isle of Paros[1]
    2700 years ago
      was born a bard
who smote the strings of his lyre
    with a newness
        that made them gasp
          for a thousand years

His name was Archilochus
He was thought by the ancients
      the equal of Homer
The halves of his brain
    shared secrets by the billion
      to make it new.

From Plutarch[2]
we learn that Archilochus
made many inventions:

the ithyphallic trochaic trimeter
the recitative
    (rhythmical recitation
        of poetry to the lyre or flute)
the combination of unlike measures
the epode
    (long line followed by short)
the tetrameter

[1] One of the Cyclades Islands southeast of Athens.
[2] *On Music.*

the cretic
the prosodiac
the combination of epibatic paeon with the iambic
the lengthened "heroic" with prosodiac and cretic
the concept of singing and recitation
        within the same poem
and he was the first to tune his lyre
        an octave higher than his voice

He wrote the
       victory song
         at the Olympics

In later centuries
       they used to
         stitch together
a rhapsody
       of his poems & songs
      & tour the islands
   doing
       A Night of Archilochus.

He was the first great confessional poet
They spoke of his raging iambics
He was engaged to a woman named Neobule
but her father intervened
        and prevented it
and he wrote about him
        with such a bitter pulse
that the verses
    were said to cause a suicide

Critics accused Archilochus of
"slandering himself"
because, through his poesy,
people down the centuries
knew he was the son of a slave woman, Enipo,

that pov drove him from Paros to Thasos[3]
that he was adulterous & lecherous.

He was the first of the poets
          to de-macho his art
Once he let them strip away his shield
          on the field of battle
and laughed of it later in trochees & dactyls

an act that got him thrown
          out of Sparta—
             The South Africa
             of 600 B.C.

What an honor
          when the Spartan secret police
ordered his books removed
for erotolalia.

He was a mercenary
          as well as a bard
He must have looked like a samurai
          standing on the marble chips
             of Paros
          with greaves on the legs
& a horsehair plume on his helmet

his tortoise-shell lyre packed away
             with his poems
          in a sheepskin satchel.

     O bards
        ponder Archilochus
           you who think,
               "Hey, my poems are going to last
               all the way till the Milky Way
               explodes."

[3] Island off the coast of Thrace.

Your archives
bulging in acid-free binders
at U.C.-San Diego
and a staff
of graduate students
sorting them clean!

The fireman felt the wall
above my bed
just where I'd taped
a quote from a poem
by Robert Kelly.
On the blanket were all of the books
of Charles Olson

and my notes for
the Olson Memorial lectures

when I was
wounded by fire in
the frothsome night
"Why are you saving those books?"
the fireman asked
pointing his ax
toward the stereo

hosing down my wall of verse
and chopping the plaster.

As I scooped up the books
I thought of Archilochus

whose work comes down to us
in pitiful tatters

gone
shredded
stomped
abyssed

gone with the fires
      that burned Alexandria
gone with the disrepute
      & disrespect
gone with the book-burning frenzy
      of Christians and Moslems
gone with the mold spores
      alighting atop the
         long chains of molecules
           holding the structure of paper

      for a thousand-year lunch
        of the lines of Archilochus

      The first large magnetic body
      that passes too close to earth
      will erase the tapes
      The one that crashes
        will burn the books

      and the sky shall spit
        your poems out
          like pellets of fire

The home town of Catullus
      was Verona
where they saved a single manuscript
but no one saved Archilochus.

Your wounded verses sing
across the ages
     O Archilochus

I can see you standing
     on a hillside
holding your 4-string lyre
and how you were an inventer!
striking the twisted strings
on the palmwood sounding board
with a limberlimbic meter whose waves

> slosh gently

and faintly
all the way to my burning wall,

and it was you who said
ἐι γὰρ ὥς ἐμοὶ γένοιτο χειρα Νεοβόυλης φιγειν
"if only it could happen
> that I could touch
> the hand of Neobule"

> (*Sung*)

There used to be a poet named Archilochus
one of the greatest of them all
Oh there's nothing of his poetry now
except some scattered lines

I wish we could hear Archilochus
play his four-stringed lyre
Oh to hear some great poetry
to make the world entire

Oh I learned from Archilochus
about the Nightingale
O I long to hold the nightingale
nesting in my hands

and I love to spend the Catskill spring
the Catskill spring with you
but you know that there's a hunger there
to touch the nightingale

Oh they talk so elegantly
about eternity
Oh I sing to you Archilochus
to touch the nightingale &

feel those flashing feathers
> on my fingertips &

feel the fluttering wings
    upon my begging lips

ἀηδονιδεύς

WHAT WOULD TOM PAINE DO?

(Song from Star Peace*)*

What would Tom Paine do
to spread a little *Common Sense*?
What would Tom Paine do—
    the problem's so immense,

that a shout pass mouth to mouth around the world

Protest and Survive
Protest and Survive

Protest and Survive
Protest and Survive

I want to be a pamphleteer
in the name of Tom Paine's *Rights of Man*
But what is the name of the pamphlet
in the age of laser disks
    and satellite time?
What is the name of the pamphlet
that shall soar aloft
and beam from mind to mind
    a million miles?

And the men of war
    need the fresh young minds
        in the labs of doom

We've got to interdict the flow
We've got to interdict

                    the labs of doom
                        labs of doom
                        labs of doom

We vow to go wherever
the malinformed
are dragged aboard
            the ships of death
on a dirty sea

that a shout pass mouth to mouth around the world

Protest and Survive
Protest and Survive

Protest and Survive
Protest and Survive

There'll be times when the struggle shall falter
            in a whirl of ink and stupid strife

There'll be times when we're eaten by chaos
            and everything's a crazy maze
                        of razorblade roads

There'll be times when we'll have to let it go
            and walk away to heal
            pull on the headphones
                        listen to Bach
                        by the garden wall

            You don't want to sew
            a quilt of guilt
            but a lace of grace
                lace of grace
                lace of grace

Oh the archetypal macho man
            with his nuclear spears

pushes his agression   in the high frontier
as if the Milky Way were just a swirl of knives

We have to overcome
        the labs of mega doom
We have to overcome
        the labs of mega doom

Oh it's such an enormous equation
to dance while others moan in pain
But we're never going to find any answers
until we make that simple word

     It's such a simple word
     It comes in simple parts
     I'm talking about p . . . p . . . p . . . peace

     Let it roll
        Let it roll like a rumbling wheel
             for a thousand years
             p . . . p . . . p . . . peace
     Let the feather of justice
            float down and rest
               on the shining scales
            p . . . p . . . p . . . peace

What would Tom Paine do
to spread a little *Common Sense*?
What would Tom Paine do—
        the problem's so immense,

that a shout pass mouth to mouth around the world

Protest and Survive
Protest and Survive

Protest and Survive
Protest and Survive

Gary Snyder
SMOKEY THE BEAR SUTRA

Once in the Jurassic about 150 million years ago,
the Great Sun Buddha in this corner of the Infinite
Void gave a Discourse to all the assembled elements
and energies: to the standing beings, the walking beings,
the flying beings, and the sitting beings—even grasses,
to the number of thirteen billion, each one born from a
seed, assembled there: a Discourse concerning
Enlightenment on the planet Earth.

"In some future time, there will be a continent called
America. It will have great centers of power called
such as Pyramid Lake, Walden Pond, Mt. Rainier, Big Sur,
Everglades, and so forth; and powerful nerves and channels
such as Columbia River, Mississippi River, and Grand Canyon.
The human race in that era will get into troubles all over
its head, and practically wreck everything in spite of
its own strong intelligent Buddha-nature."

"The twisting strata of the great mountains and the pulsings
of volcanoes are my love burning deep in the earth.
My obstinate compassion is schist and basalt and
granite, to be mountains, to bring down the rain. In that
future American Era I shall enter a new form; to cure
the world of loveless knowledge that seeks with blind hunger:
and mindless rage eating food that will not fill it."

And he showed himself in his true form of

SMOKEY THE BEAR.

A handsome smokey-colored brown bear standing on his
hind legs, showing that he is aroused and watchful.

Bearing in his right paw the Shovel that digs to the
truth beneath appearances; cuts the roots of useless attach-
ments, and flings damp sand on the fires of greed and war;

His left paw in the Mudra of Comradely Display—indicating
that all creatures have the full right to live to their limits
and that deer, rabbits, chipmunks, snakes, dandelions,
and lizards all grow in the realm of the Dharma;

Wearing the blue work overalls symbolic of slaves and
laborers, the countless men oppressed by a civilization
that claims to save but often destroys;

Wearing the broad-brimmed hat of the West, symbolic of
the forces that guard the Wilderness, which is the Natural
State of the Dharma and the True Path of man on earth:
all true paths lead through mountains—

With a halo of smoke and flame behind, the forest fires
of the kali-yuga, fires caused by the stupidity of those
who think things can be gained and lost whereas in truth all
is contained vast and free in the Blue Sky and Green Earth
of One Mind;

Round-bellied to show his kind nature and that the great
earth has food enough for everyone who loves her and trusts
her;

Trampling underfoot wasteful freeways and needless
suburbs; smashing the worms of capitalism and totalitarianism;

Indicating the Task: his followers, becoming free of cars,
houses, canned foods, universities, and shoes, master the
Three Mysteries of their own Body, Speech, and Mind; and
fearlessly chop down the rotten trees and prune out the
sick limbs of this country America and then burn the leftover
trash.

Wrathful but Calm. Austere but Comic. Smokey the Bear will
Illuminate those who would help him; but for those who would
hinder or slander him,

HE WILL PUT THEM OUT.

Thus his great Mantra:

> Namah samanta vajranam chanda maharoshana
> Sphataya hum traks ham mam

> "I DEDICATE MYSELF TO THE UNIVERSAL DIAMOND
> BE THIS RAGING FURY DESTROYED"

And he will protect those who love woods and rivers,
Gods and animals, hobos and madmen, prisoners and sick
people, musicians, playful women, and hopeful children:

And if anyone is threatened by advertising, air pollution, television,
or the police, they should chant SMOKEY THE BEAR'S WAR SPELL:

> DROWN THEIR BUTTS
> CRUSH THEIR BUTTS
> DROWN THEIR BUTTS
> CRUSH THEIR BUTTS

And SMOKEY THE BEAR will surely appear to put the enemy out
with his vajra-shovel.

Now those who recite this Sutra and then try to put it in
practice will accumulate merit as countless as the sands
of Arizona and Nevada.
Will help save the planet Earth from total oil slick.
Will enter the age of harmony of man and nature.
Will win the tender love and caresses of men, women, and
beasts
Will always have ripe blackberries to eat and a sunny spot
under a pine tree to sit at.
AND IN THE END WILL WIN HIGHEST PERFECT ENLIGHTENMEN'

thus have we heard.

(may be reproduced free forever)

I WENT INTO THE
MAVERICK BAR

I went into the Maverick Bar
In Farmington, New Mexico
And drank double shots of bourbon
                              backed with beer.
My long hair was tucked up under a cap
I'd left the earring in the car.

Two cowboys did horseplay
                    by the pool tables,
A waitress asked us
                    where are you from?
a country-and-western band began to play
"We don't smoke Marijuana in Muskokie"
And with the next song,
                    a couple began to dance.

They held each other like in High School dances
                    in the fifties;
I recalled when I worked in the woods
                    and the bars of Madras, Oregon.
That short-haired joy and roughness—
                    America—your stupidity.
I could almost love you again.

We left—onto the freeway shoulders—
                    under the tough old stars—
In the shadow of bluffs
                    I came back to myself,
To the real work, to
                    "What is to be done."

MOTHER EARTH: HER WHALES

An owl winks in the shadows
A lizard lifts on tiptoe, breathing hard
Young male sparrow stretches up his neck,
        big head, watching—

The grasses are working in the sun. Turn it green.
Turn it sweet. That we may eat.
Grow our meat.

Brazil says "sovereign use of Natural Resources"
Thirty thousand kinds of unknown plants.
The living actual people of the jungle
        sold and tortured—
And a robot in a suit who peddles a delusion called "Brazil"
        can speak for *them?*

        The whales turn and glisten, plunge
           and sound and rise again,
        Hanging over subtly darkening deeps
        Flowing like breathing planets
          in the sparkling whorls of
            living light—

And Japan quibbles for words on
        what kinds of whales they can kill?
A once-great Buddhist nation
        dribbles methyl mercury
        like gonorrhea
           in the sea.

Père David's Deer, the Elaphure,
Lived in the tule marshes of the Yellow River
Two thousand years ago—and lost its home to rice—
The forests of Lo-yang were logged and all the silt &
Sand flowed down, and gone, by 1200 AD—

Wild Geese hatched out in Siberia
        head south over basins of the Yang, the Huang,
        what we call "China"
On flyways they have used a million years.
Ah China, where are the tigers, the wild boars,
        the monkeys,
           like the snows of yesteryear
Gone in a mist, a flash, and the dry hard ground
Is parking space for fifty thousand trucks.
IS man most precious of all things?
—then let us love him, and his brothers, all those
Fading living beings—

North America, Turtle Island, taken by invaders
        who wage war around the world.
May ants, may abalone, otters, wolves and elk
Rise! and pull away their giving
        from the robot nations.

Solidarity. The People.
Standing Tree People!
Flying Bird People!
Swimming Sea People!
Four-legged, two-legged, people!

How can the head-heavy power-hungry politic scientist
Government   two-world   Capitalist-Imperialist
Third-world   Communist   paper-shuffling male
        non-farmer   jet-set   bureaucrats
Speak for the green of the leaf? Speak for the soil?
(Ah Margaret Mead . . . do you sometimes dream of Samoa?)

The robots argue how to parcel out our Mother Earth
To last a little longer
        like vultures flapping
Belching, gurgling,
        near a dying Doe.

"In yonder field a slain knight lies—
We'll fly to him and eat his eyes
    with a down
    derry derry derry down down."

        An Owl winks in the shadow
        A lizard lifts on tiptoe
            breathing hard
        The whales turn and glisten
            plunge and
        Sound, and rise again
        Flowing like breathing planets

        In the sparkling whorls

        Of living light.

Stockholm: Summer Solstice 40072

THE BATH

Washing Kai in the sauna,
The kerosene lantern set on a box
    outside the ground-level window,
Lights up the edge of the iron stove and the
    washtub down on the slab
Steaming air and crackle of waterdrops
    brushed by on the pile of rocks on top
He stands in warm water
Soap all over the smooth of his thigh and stomach
    "Gary don't soap my hair!"
    —his eye-sting fear—
    the soapy hand feeling
    through and around the globes and curves of his body
    up in the crotch,
And washing-tickling out the scrotum, little anus,
    his penis curving up and getting hard

      as I pull back skin and try to wash it
Laughing and jumping, flinging arms around,
      I squat all naked too,
                      is this our body?

Sweating and panting in the stove-steam hot-stone
      cedar-planking wooden bucket water-splashing
      kerosene lantern-flicker wind-in-the-pines-out
      sierra forest ridges night—
Masa comes in, letting fresh cool air
      sweep down from the door
      a deep sweet breath
And she tips him over gripping neatly, one knee down
      her hair falling hiding one whole side of
      shoulder, breast, and belly,
Washes deftly Kai's head-hair
      as he gets mad and yells—
The body of my lady, the winding valley spine,

      the space between the thighs I reach through,
      cup her curving vulva arch and hold it from behind,
      a soapy tickle   a hand of grail
The gates of Awe
That open back a turning double-mirror world of
      wombs in wombs, in rings,
      that start in music,
                      is this our body?

The hidden place of seed
The veins net flow across the ribs, that gathers
      milk and peaks up in a nipple—fits
      our mouth—
The sucking milk from this our body sends through
      jolts of light; the son, the father,
      sharing mother's joy
That brings a softness to the flower of the awesome
      open curling lotus gate I cup and kiss
As Kai laughs at his mother's breast he now is weaned
      from, we
      wash each other,

this our body

Kai's little scrotum up close to his groin,
    the seed still tucked away, that moved from us to him
In flows that lifted with the same joys forces
    as his nursing Masa later,
    playing with her breast,
Or me within her,
Or him emerging,

this is our body:

Clean, and rinsed, and sweating more, we stretch
    out on the redwood benches hearts all beating
Quiet to the simmer of the stove,
    the scent of cedar
And then turn over,
    murmuring gossip of the grasses,
    talking firewood,
Wondering how Gen's napping, how to bring him in
    soon wash him, too—
These boys who love their mother
    who loves men, who passes on
    her sons to other women;

The cloud across the sky. The windy pines.
    the trickle gurgle in the swampy meadow

this is our body.

Fire inside and boiling water on the stove
We sigh and slide ourselves down from the benches
    wrap the babies, step outside,

black night & all the stars.

Pour cold water on the back and thighs
Go in the house—stand steaming by the center fire
Kai scampers on the sheepskin
Gen standing hanging on and shouting,

"Bao! bao! bao! bao! bao!"

This is our body. Drawn up crosslegged by the flames
    drinking icy water
    hugging babies, kissing bellies,

Laughing on the Great Earth

Come out from the bath.

AXE HANDLES

One afternoon the last week in April
Showing Kai how to throw a hatchet
One-half turn and it sticks in a stump.
He recalls the hatchet-head
Without a handle, in the shop
And go gets it, and wants it for his own.
A broken-off axe handle behind the door
Is long enough for a hatchet
We cut it to length and take it
With the hatchet head
And working hatchet, to the wood block.
There I begin to shape the old handle
With the hatchet, and the phrase
First learned from Ezra Pound
Rings in my ears!
"When making an axe handle
      the pattern is not far off."
And I say this to Kai
"Look: We'll shape the handle
By checking the handle
Of the axe we cut with—"
And he sees. And I hear it again:
It's in Lu Ji's *Wên Fu,* fourth century
A.D. "Essay on Literature"—in the
Preface: "In making the handle
Of an axe
By cutting wood with an axe
The model is indeed near at hand."
My teacher Shih-hsiang Chen

Translated that and taught it years ago
And I see: Pound was an axe,
Chen was an axe, I am an axe
And my son a handle, soon
To be shaping again, model
And tool, craft of culture,
How we go on.

PINE TREE TOPS

in the blue night
frost haze, the sky glows
with the moon
pine tree tops
bend snow-blue, fade
into sky, frost, starlight.
the creak of boots.
rabbit tracks, deer tracks,
what do we know.

THREE COMMENTATORS ON THE BEAT GENERATION

Norman Mailer

Norman Mailer was born on January 31, 1923, in Long Branch, New Jersey. After his graduation from Harvard he served eighteen months in the Pacific in the U.S. Army, an experience that was the inspiration for his first, highly acclaimed novel about World War II, The Naked and the Dead *(1948).*

Reacting to the pressures of the Cold War, Mailer contributed a weekly column to the Village Voice *newspaper, (founded in October 1955) as a way of declaring what he called his own "private war" on the mass media in America. He wrote on May 9, 1956, "There is a universal rebellion in the air, and the power of two colossal super-states may be . . . failing in energy even more rapidly than we are failing in energy, and if that is so, then the destructive, the liberating, the creative nihilism of the Hip, the frantic search for potent Change may break into the open with all its violence. . . ." In the mid-1950s the word "hip" was often used interchangeably with "beat," as when Neal Cassady titled his account of meeting William Burroughs "The History of the Hip Generation."*

In 1957 Mailer published "The White Negro" in Dissent *magazine, expanding his concept of "Hip" to identify American "Negroes" as its source, since they had been "living on the margin between totalitarianism and democracy for two centu-*

*ries." As a middle-class critic, Mailer projected his own fasci-
nation with violence onto his interpretation of the black hipster
as a "philosophical psychopath," assuming that race rather than
social class determined human behavior. To some readers his
view was a degrading stereotype. Ted Morgan's recent sympathetic interpretation is that Mailer's "White Negro" is "the
new man, who feels the danger that a black man feels from a
hostile society, and who says, why not encourage the psychopath
in oneself, as society is doing?"* The White Negro *was published
as a pamphlet by City Lights Books and included in Mailer's*
Advertisements for Myself *(1959).*

THE WHITE NEGRO
Superficial Reflections on the Hipster

Our search for the rebels of the generation led
us to the hipster. The hipster is an *enfant terrible*
turned inside out. In character with his time, he
is trying to get back at the conformists by lying
low . . . . You can't interview a hipster because
his main goal is to keep out of a society which,
he thinks, is trying to make everyone over in its
own image. He takes marijuana because it supplies him with experiences that can't be shared
with "squares." He may affect a broad-brimmed
hat or a zoot suit, but usually he prefers to skulk
unmarked. The hipster may be a jazz musician;
he is rarely an artist, almost never a writer. He
may earn his living as a petty criminal, a hobo,
a carnival roustabout or a free-lance moving man
in Greenwich Village, but some hipsters have
found a safe refuge in the upper income brackets
as television comics or movie actors. (The late
James Dean, for one, was a hipster hero.) . . .
It is tempting to describe the hipster in psychiatric terms as infantile, but the style of his in-
fantilism is a sign of the times. He does not try
to enforce his will on others, Napoleon-fashion,
but contents himself with a magical omnipotence
never disproved because never tested. . . . As
the only extreme nonconformist of his generation, he exercises a powerful if underground
appeal for conformists, through newspaper ac-

counts of his delinquencies, his structureless
jazz, and his emotive grunt words.
—"Born 1930: The Unlost Generation"
by Caroline Bird
Harper's Bazaar, Feb. 1957

Probably, we will never be able to determine the psychic havoc
of the concentration camps and the atom bomb upon the unconscious mind of almost everyone alive in these years. For
the first time in civilized history, perhaps for the first time in
all of history, we have been forced to live with the suppressed
knowledge that the smallest facets of our personality or the
most minor projection of our ideas, or indeed the absence of
ideas and the absence of personality could mean equally well
that we might still be doomed to die as a cipher in some vast
statistical operation in which our teeth would be counted, and
our hair would be saved, but our death itself would be unknown, unhonored, and unremarked, a death which could not
follow with dignity as a possible consequence to serious actions
we had chosen, but rather a death by *deus ex machina* in a
gas chamber or a radioactive city; and so if in the midst of
civilization—that civilization founded upon the Faustian urge
to dominate nature by mastering time, mastering the links of
social cause and effect—in the middle of an economic civilization founded upon the confidence that time could indeed be
subjected to our will, our psyche was subjected itself to the
intolerable anxiety that death being causeless, life was causeless as well, and time deprived of cause and effect had come
to a stop.

The Second World War presented a mirror to the human
condition which blinded anyone who looked into it. For if tens
of millions were killed in concentration camps out of the inex-
orable agonies and contractions of super-states founded upon
the always insoluble contradictions of injustice, one was then
obliged also to see that no matter how crippled and perverted
an image of man was the society he had created, it was nonetheless his creation, his collective creation (at least his collective creation from the past) and if society was so murderous,

then who could ignore the most hideous of questions about his own nature?

Worse. One could hardly maintain the courage to be individual, to speak with one's own voice, for the years in which one could complacently accept oneself as part of an elite by being a radical were forever gone. A man knew that when he dissented, he gave a note upon his life which could be called in any year of overt crisis. No wonder then that these have been the years of conformity and depression. A stench of fear has come out of every pore of American life, and we suffer from a collective failure of nerve. The only courage, with rare exceptions, that we have been witness to, has been the isolated courage of isolated people.

II

It is on this bleak scene that a phenomenon has appeared: the American existentialist—the hipster, the man who knows that if our collective condition is to live with instant death by atomic war, relatively quick death by the State as *l'univers concentrationnaire,* or with a slow death by conformity with every creative and rebellious instinct stifled (at what damage to the mind and the heart and the liver and the nerves no research foundation for cancer will discover in a hurry), if the fate of twentieth century man is to live with death from adolescence to premature senescence, why then the only life-giving answer is to accept the terms of death, to live with death as immediate danger, to divorce oneself from society, to exist without roots, to set out on that uncharted journey into the rebellious imperatives of the self. In short, whether the life is criminal or not, the decision is to encourage the psychopath in oneself, to explore that domain of experience where security is boredom and therefore sickness, and one exists in the present, in that enormous present which is without past or future, memory or planned intention, the life where a man must go until he is beat, where he must gamble with his energies through all those small or large crises of courage and unforeseen situations which beset his day, where he must be with it or doomed not to swing. The unstated essence of Hip, its psychopathic brilliance, quivers with the knowledge that new kinds of victories increase one's power for new kinds of perception; and defeats, the wrong kind of defeats, attack the body and imprison one's energy until one is jailed in the prison air of other people's habits, other people's defeats, boredom, quiet desperation, and muted icy self-destroying rage. One is Hip or one is Square (the alternative which each new generation coming into American life is beginning to feel), one is a rebel or one conforms, one is a frontiersman in the Wild West of American night life, or else a Square cell, trapped in the totalitarian tissues of American society, doomed willy-nilly to conform if one is to succeed.

A totalitarian society makes enormous demands on the courage of men, and a partially totalitarian society makes even greater demands for the general anxiety is greater. Indeed if one is to be a man, almost any kind of unconventional action often takes disproportionate courage. So it is no accident that the source of Hip is the Negro for he has been living on the margin between totalitarianism and democracy for two centuries. But the presence of Hip as a working philosophy in the sub-worlds of American life is probably due to jazz, and its knife-like entrance into culture, its subtle but so penetrating influence on an avant-garde generation—that post-war generation of adventurers who (some consciously, some by osmosis) had absorbed the lessons of disillusionment and disgust of the Twenties, the Depression, and the War. Sharing a collective disbelief in the words of men who had too much money and controlled too many things, they knew almost as powerful a disbelief in the socially monolithic ideas of the single mate, the solid family and the respectable love life. If the intellectual antecedents of this generation can be traced to such separate influences as D. H. Lawrence, Henry Miller, and Wilhelm Reich, the viable philosophy of Hemingway fits most of their facts: in a bad world, as he was to say over and over again (while taking time out from his parvenu snobbery and dedicated gourmandise), in a bad world there is no love nor mercy nor charity nor justice unless a man can keep his courage, and this indeed fitted some of the facts. What fitted the need of the adventurer even more precisely was Hemingway's categorical imperative that what made him feel good became therefore The Good.

So no wonder that in certain cities of America, in New York of course, and New Orleans, in Chicago and San Francisco and Los Angeles, in such American cities as Paris and Mexico, D.F., this particular part of a generation was attracted to what the Negro had to offer. In such places as Greenwich Village, a ménage-a-trois was completed—the bohemian and the juvenile delinquent came face-to-face with the Negro, and the hipster was a fact in American life. If marijuana was the wedding ring, the child was the language of Hip for its argot gave expression to abstract states of feeling which all could share, at least all who were Hip. And in this wedding of the white and the black it was the Negro who brought the cultural dowry. Any Negro who wishes to live must live with danger from his first day, and no experience can ever be casual to him, no Negro can saunter down a street with any real certainty that violence will not visit him on his walk. The cameos of security for the average white: mother and the home, job and the family, are not even a mockery to millions of Negroes; they are impossible. The Negro has the simplest of alternatives: live a life of constant humility or ever-threatening danger. In such a pass where paranoia is as vital to survival as blood, the Negro had stayed alive and begun to grow by following the need of his body where he could. Knowing in the cells of his existence that life was war, nothing but war, the Negro (all exceptions admitted) could rarely afford the sophisticated inhibitions of civilization, and so he kept for his survival the art of the primitive, he lived in the enormous present, he subsisted for his Saturday night kicks, relinquishing the pleasures of the mind for the more obligatory pleasures of the body, and in his music he gave voice to the character and quality of his existence, to his rage and the infinite variations of joy, lust, languor, growl, cramp, pinch, scream and despair of his orgasm. For jazz is orgasm, it is the music of orgasm, good orgasm and bad, and so it spoke across a nation, it had the communication of art even where it was watered, perverted, corrupted, and almost killed, it spoke in no matter what laundered popular way of instantaneous existential states to which some whites could respond, it was indeed a communication by art because it said, "I feel this, and now you do too."

So there was a new breed of adventurers, urban adventurers who drifted out at night looking for action with a black man's code to fit their facts. The hipster had absorbed the existentialist synapses of the Negro, and for practical purposes could be considered a white Negro.

To be an existentialist, one must be able to feel oneself— one must know one's desires, one's rages, one's anguish, one must be aware of the character of one's frustration and know what would satisfy it. The over-civilized man can be an existentialist only if it is chic, and deserts it quickly for the next chic. To be a real existentialist (Sartre admittedly to the contrary) one must be religious, one must have one's sense of the "purpose"—whatever the purpose may be—but a life which is directed by one's faith in the necessity of action is a life committed to the notion that the substratum of existence is the search, the end meaningful but mysterious; it is impossible to live such a life unless one's emotions provide their profound conviction. Only the French, alienated beyond alienation from their unconscious could welcome an existential philosophy without ever feeling it at all; indeed only a Frenchman by declaring that the unconscious did not exist could then proceed to explore the delicate involutions of consciousness, the microscopically sensuous and all but ineffable *frissons* of mental becoming, in order finally to create the theology of atheism and so submit that in a world of absurdities the existential absurdity is most coherent.

In the dialogue between the atheist and the mystic, the atheist is on the side of life, rational life, undialectical life— since he conceives of death as emptiness, he can, no matter how weary or despairing, wish for nothing but more life; his pride is that he does not transpose his weakness and spiritual fatigue into a romantic longing for death, for such appreciation of death is then all too capable of being elaborated by his imagination into a universe of meaningful structure and moral orchestration.

Yet this masculine argument can mean very little for the mystic. The mystic can accept the atheist's description of his weakness, he can agree that his mysticism was a response to despair. And yet . . . and yet his argument is that he, the mystic, is the one finally who has chosen to live with death, and so death is his experience and not the atheist's, and the atheist by eschewing the limitless dimensions of profound despair has rendered himself incapable to judge the experience. The real argument which the mystic must always advance is the very intensity of his private vision—his argument depends from the vision precisely because what was felt in the vision is so extraordinary that no rational argument, no hypotheses of "oceanic feelings" and certainly no skeptical reductions can explain away what has become for him the reality more real than the reality of closely reasoned logic. His inner experience of the possibilities within death is his logic. So, too, for the existentialist. And the psychopath. And the saint and the bullfighter and the lover. The common denominator for all of them is their burning consciousness of the present, exactly that incandescent consciousness which the possibilities within death has opened for them. There is a depth of desperation to the condition which enables one to remain in life only by engaging death, but the reward is their knowledge that what is happening at each instant of the electric present is good or bad for them, good or bad for their cause, their love, their action, their need.

It is this knowledge which provides the curious community of feeling in the world of the hipster, a muted cool religious revival to be sure, but the element which is exciting, disturbing, nightmarish perhaps, is that incompatibles have come to bed, the inner life and the violent life, the orgy and the dream of love, the desire to murder and the desire to create, a dialectical conception of existence with a lust for power, a dark, romantic, and yet undeniably dynamic view of existence for it sees every man and woman as moving individually through each moment of life forward into growth or backward into death.

III

It may be fruitful to consider the hipster a philosophical psychopath, a man interested not only in the dangerous imperatives of his psychopathy but in codifying, at least for himself, the suppositions on which his inner universe is constructed. By this premise the hipster is a psychopath, and yet not a psychopath but the negation of the psychopath for he possesses the narcissistic detachment of the philosopher, that absorption in the recessive nuances of one's own motive which is so alien to the unreasoning drive of the psychopath. In this country where new millions of psychopaths are developed each year, stamped with the mint of our contradictory popular culture (where sex is sin and yet sex is paradise), it is as if there has been room already for the development of the antithetical psychopath who extrapolates from his own condition, from the inner certainty that his rebellion is just, a radical vision of the universe which thus separates him from the general ignorance, reactionary prejudice, and self-doubt of the more conventional psychopath. Having converted his unconscious experience into much conscious knowledge, the hipster has shifted the focus of his desire from immediate gratification toward that wider passion for future power which is the mark of civilized man. Yet with an irreducible difference. For Hip is the sophistication of the wise primitive in a giant jungle, and so its appeal is still beyond the civilized man. If there are ten million Americans who are more or less psychopathic (and the figure is most modest), there are probably not more than one hundred thousand men and women who consciously see themselves as hipsters, but their importance is that they are an elite with the potential ruthlessness of an elite, and a language most adolescents can understand instinctively for the hipster's intense view of existence matches their experience and their desire to rebel.

Before one can say more about the hipster, there is obviously much to be said about the psychic state of the psychopath—or, clinically, the psychopathic personality. Now, for reasons which may be more curious than the similarity of the words, even many people with a psychoanalytical orientation often confuse the psychopath with the psychotic. Yet the terms are polar. The psychotic is legally insane, the psychopath is not; the psychotic is almost always incapable of discharging in physical acts the rage of his frustration, while the psychopath at his extreme is virtually as incapable of restraining his violence. The psychotic lives in so misty a world that what is happening at each moment of his life is not very real to him whereas the psychopath seldom knows any reality greater than the face, the voice, the being of the particular people among whom he may find himself at any moment. Sheldon and Eleanor Glueck describe him as follows:

> The psychopath . . . can be distinguished from the person sliding into or clambering out of a "true psychotic" state by the long tough persistence of his anti-social attitude and behaviour and the absence of hallucinations, delusions, manic flight of ideas, confusion, disorientation, and other dramatic signs of psychosis.

The late Robert Lindner, one of the few experts on the subject, in his book *Rebel Without A Cause—The Hypnoanalysis of a Criminal Psychopath* presented part of his definition in this way:

> . . . the psychopath is a rebel without a cause, an agitator without a slogan, a revolutionary without a program: in other words, his rebelliousness is aimed to achieve goals satisfactory to himself alone; he is incapable of exertions for the sake of others. All his efforts, hidden under no matter what disguise, represent investments designed to satisfy his immediate wishes and desires . . . The psychopath, like the child, cannot delay the pleasures of gratification; and this trait is one of his underlying, universal characteristics. He cannot wait upon erotic gratification which convention demands should be preceded by the chase before the kill: he must rape. He cannot wait upon the development of prestige in society: his egoistic ambitions lead him to leap into headlines by daring performances. Like a red thread the predominance of this mechanism for immediate satisfaction runs through the history of every psychopath. It explains not only his behaviour but also the violent nature of his acts.

Yet even Lindner who was the most imaginative and most sympathetic of the psychoanalysts who have studied the psychopathic personality was not ready to project himself into the essential sympathy—which is that the psychopath may indeed be the perverted and dangerous front-runner of a new kind of personality which could become the central expression of human nature before the twentieth century is over. For the psychopath is better adapted to dominate those mutually contradictory inhibitions upon violence and love which civilization has exacted of us, and if it be remembered that not every psychopath is an extreme case, and that the condition of psychopathy is present in a host of people including many politicians, professional soldiers, newspaper columnists, entertainers, artists, jazz musicians, call-girls, promiscuous homosexuals and half the executives of Hollywood, television, and advertising, it can be seen that there are aspects of psychopathy which already exert considerable cultural influence.

What characterizes almost every psychopath and part-psychopath is that they are trying to create a new nervous system for themselves. Generally we are obliged to act with a nervous system which has been formed from infancy, and which carries in the style of its circuits the very contradictions of our parents and our early milieu. Therefore, we are obliged, most of us, to meet the tempo of the present and the future with reflexes and rhythms which come from the past. It is not only the "dead weight of the institutions of the past" but indeed the inefficient and often antiquated nervous circuits of the past which strangle our potentiality for responding to new possibilities which might be exciting for our individual growth.

Through most of modern history, "sublimation" was possible: at the expense of expressing only a small portion of oneself, that small portion could be expressed intensely. But sublimation depends on a reasonable tempo to history. If the collective life of a generation has moved too quickly, the "past" by which particular men and women of that generation may function is not, let us say, thirty years old, but relatively a hundred or two hundred years old. And so the nervous system is overstressed beyond the possibility of such compromises as sublimation, especially since the stable middle-class values so prerequisite to sublimation have been virtually destroyed in our time, at least as nourishing values free of confusion or doubt. In such a crisis of accelerated historical tempo and deteriorated values, neurosis tends to be replaced by psychopathy, and the success of psychoanalysis (which even ten years ago gave promise of becoming a direct major force) diminishes because of its inbuilt and characteristic incapacity to handle patients more complex, more experienced, or more adventurous than the analyst himself. In practice, psychoanalysis has by now become all too often no more than a psychic blood-letting. The patient is not so much changed as aged, and the infantile fantasies which he is encouraged to express are condemned to exhaust themselves against the analyst's non-responsive reactions. The result for all too many patients is a diminution, a "tranquilizing" of their most interesting qualities and vices. The patient is indeed not so much altered as worn out—less bad, less good, less bright, less willful, less destructive, less creative. He is thus able to conform to that contradictory and unbearable society which first created his neurosis. He can conform to what he loathes because he no longer has the passion to feel loathing so intensely.

The psychopath is notoriously difficult to analyze because the fundamental decision of his nature is to try to live the infantile fantasy, and in this decision (given the dreary alternative of psychoanalysis) there may be a certain instinctive wisdom. For there is a dialectic to changing one's nature, the dialectic which underlies all psychoanalytic method: it is the knowledge that if one is to change one's habits, one must go back to the source of their creation, and so the psychopath exploring backward along the road of the homosexual, the orgiast, the drug-addict, the rapist, the robber and the murderer seeks to find those violent parallels to the violent and often hopeless contradictions he knew as an infant and as a child. For if he has the courage to meet the parallel situation at the moment when he is ready, then he has a chance to act as he has never acted before, and in satisfying the frustration—if he can succeed—he may then pass by symbolic substitute through the locks of incest. In thus giving expression to the buried infant in himself, he can lessen the tension of those infantile desires and so free himself to remake a bit of his nervous system. Like the neurotic he is looking for the opportunity to grow up a second time, but the psychopath knows instinctively that to express a forbidden impulse actively is far more beneficial to him than merely to confess the desire in the safety of a doctor's room. The psychopath is ordinately ambitious, too ambitious ever to trade his warped brilliant conception of his possible victories in life for the grim if peaceful attrition of the analyst's couch. So his associational journey into the past is lived out in the theatre of the present, and he exists for those charged situations where his senses are so alive that he can be aware actively (as the analysand is aware passively) of what his habits are, and how he can change them. The strength of the psychopath is that he knows (where most of us can only guess) what is good for him and what is bad for him at exactly those instants when an old crippling habit has become so attacked by experience that the potentiality exists to change it, to replace a negative and empty fear with an outward action, even if—and here I obey the logic of the extreme psychopath—even if the fear is of himself, and the action is to murder. The psychopath murders—if he has the courage—out of the necessity to purge his violence, for if he cannot empty his hatred then he cannot love, his being is frozen with implacable self-hatred for his cowardice. (It can of course be suggested that it takes little courage for two strong eighteen-year old hoodlums, let us say, to beat in the brains of a candy-store keeper, and indeed the act—even by the logic of the psychopath—is not likely to prove very therapeutic for the victim is not an immediate equal. Still, courage of a sort is necessary, for one murders not only a weak fifty-year old man but an institution as well, one violates private property, one enters into a new relation with the police and introduces a dangerous element into one's life. The hoodlum is therefore daring the unknown, and so no matter how brutal the act, it is not altogether cowardly.)

At bottom, the drama of the psychopath is that he seeks love. Not love as the search for a mate, but love as the search for an orgasm more apocalyptic than the one which preceded it. Orgasm is his therapy—he knows at the seed of his being that good orgasm opens his possibilities and bad orgasm imprisons him. But in this search, the psychopath becomes an embodiment of the extreme contradictions of the society which formed his character, and the apocalyptic orgasm often remains as remote as the Holy Grail, for there are clusters and nests and ambushes of violence in his own necessities and in the imperatives and retaliations of the men and women among whom he lives his life, so that even as he drains his hatred in one act or another, so the conditions of his life create it anew in him until the drama of his movements bears a sardonic resemblance to the frog who climbed a few feet in the well only to drop back again.

Yet there is this to be said for the search after the good orgasm: when one lives in a civilized world, and still can enjoy none of the cultural nectar of such a world because the paradoxes on which civilization is built demands that there remain a cultureless and alienated bottom of exploitable human material, then the logic of becoming a sexual outlaw (if one's psychological roots are bedded in the bottom) is that one has at least a running competitive chance to be physically healthy so long as one stays alive. It is therefore no accident that psychopathy is most prevalent with the Negro. Hated from outside and therefore hating himself, the Negro was forced into the position of exploring all those moral wildernesses of civilized life which the Square automatically condemns as delinquent or evil or immature or morbid or self-destructive or corrupt. (Actually the terms have equal weight. Depending on the telescope of the cultural clique from which the Square surveys the universe, "evil" or "immature" are equally strong terms of condemnation.) But the Negro, not being privileged to gratify his self-esteem with the heady satisfactions of categorical condemnation, chose to move instead in that other direction where all situations are equally valid, and in the worst of perversion, promiscuity, pimpery, drug addiction, rape, razor-slash, bottle-break, what-have-you, the Negro discovered and elaborated a morality of the bottom, an ethical differentiation between the good and the bad in every human activity from the go-getter pimp (as opposed to the lazy one) to the relatively dependable pusher or prostitute. Add to this, the cunning of their language, the abstract ambiguous alternatives in which from the danger of their oppression they learned to speak ("Well, now, man, like I'm looking for a cat to turn me on . . ."), add even more the profound sensitivity of the Negro jazzman who was the cultural mentor of a people, and it is not too difficult to believe that the language of Hip which evolved was an artful language, tested and shaped by an intense experience and therefore different in kind from white slang, as different as the special obscenity of the soldier which in its emphasis upon "ass" as the soul and "shit" as circumstance, was able to express the existential states of the enlisted man. What makes Hip a special language is that it cannot really be taught—if one shares none of the experiences of elation and exhaustion which it is equipped to describe, then it seems merely arch or vulgar or irritating. It is a pictorial language, but pictorial like non-objective art, imbued with the dialectic of small but intense change, a language for the microcosm, in this case, man, for it takes the immediate experiences of any passing man and magnifies the dynamic of his movements, not specifically but abstractly so that he is seen more as a vector in a network of forces than as a static character in a crystallized field. (Which, latter, is the practical view of the snob.) For example, there is real difficulty in trying to find a Hip substitute for "stubborn." The best possibility I can come up with is: "That cat will never come off his groove, dad." But groove implies movement, narrow movement but motion nonetheless. There is really no way to describe someone who does not move at all. Even a creep does move—if at a pace exasperatingly more slow than the pace of the cool cats.

IV

Like children, hipsters are fighting for the sweet, and their language is a set of subtle indications of their success or failure in the competition for pleasure. Unstated but obvious is the social sense that there is not nearly enough sweet for everyone. And so the sweet goes only to the victor, the best, the most, the man who knows the most about how to find his energy and how not to lose it. The emphasis is on energy because the psychopath and the hipster are nothing without it since they do not have the protection of a position or a class to rely on when they have overextended themselves. So the language of Hip is a language of energy, how it is found, how it is lost.

But let us see. I have jotted down perhaps a dozen words, the Hip perhaps most in use and most likely to last with the minimum of variation. The words are man, go, put down, make, beat, cool, swing, with it, crazy, dig, flip, creep, hip, square. They serve a variety of purposes, and the nuance of the voice uses the nuance of the situation to convey the subtle contextual difference. If the hipster moves through his night and through his life on a constant search with glimpses of Mecca in many a turn of his experience (Mecca being the apocalyptic orgasm) and if everyone in the civilized world is at least in some small degree a sexual cripple the hipster lives with the knowledge of how he is sexually crippled and where he is sexually alive, and the faces of experience which life presents to him each day are engaged, dismissed or avoided as his need directs and his lifemanship makes possible. For life is a contest between people in which the victor generally recuperates quickly and the loser takes long to mend, a perpetual competition of colliding explorers in which one must grow or else pay more for remaining the same, (pay in sickness, or depression, or anguish for the lost opportunity) but pay or grow.

Therefore one finds words like go, and make it, and with it, and swing: "Go" with its sense that after hours or days or months or years of monotony, boredom, and depression one has finally had one's chance, one has amased enough energy to meet an exciting opportunity with all one's present talents for the flip (up or down) and so one is ready to go, ready to gamble. Movement is always to be preferred to inaction. In motion a man has a chance, his body is warm, his instincts are quick, and when the crisis comes, whether of love or violence, he can make it, he can win, he can release a little more energy for himself since he hates himself a little less, he can make a little better nervous system, make it a little more possible to go again, to go faster next time and so make more and thus find more people with whom he can swing. For to swing is to communicate, is to convey the rhythms of one's own being to a lover, a friend, or an audience, and—equally necessary— be able to feel the rhythms of their response. To swing with the rhythms of another is to enrich oneself—the conception of the learning process as dug by Hip is that one cannot really learn until one contains within oneself the implicit rhythm of the subject or the person. As an example, I remember once hearing a Negro friend have an intellectual discussion at a party for half an hour with a white girl who was a few years out of college. The Negro literally could not read or write, but he had an extraordinary ear and a fine sense of mimicry. So as the girl spoke, he would detect the particular formal uncertainties in her argument, and in a pleasant (if slightly Southern) English accent, he would respond to one or another facet of her doubts. When she would finish what she felt was a particularly well-articulated idea, he would smile privately and say, "Other-direction . . . do you really believe in that?"

"Well . . . No," the girl would stammer, "now that you get down to it, there is something disgusting about it to me," and she would be off again for five more minutes.

Of course the Negro was not learning anything about the merits and demerits of the argument, but he was learning a great deal about a type of girl he had never met before, and that was what he wanted. Being unable to read or write, he could hardly be interested in ideas nearly as much as in life-manship, and so he eschewed any attempt to obey the precision or lack of precision in the girl's language, and instead sensed her character (and the values of her social type) by swinging with the nuances of her voice.

So to swing is to be able to learn, and by learning take a step toward making it, toward creating. What is to be created is not nearly so important as the hipster's belief that when he really makes it, he will be able to turn his hand to anything, even to self-discipline. What he must do before that is find his courage at the moment of violence, or equally make it in the act of love, find a little more of himself, create a little more between his woman and himself, or indeed between his mate and himself (since many hipsters are bisexual), but paramount, imperative, is the necessity to make it because in making it, one is making the new habit, unearthing the new talent which the old frustration denied.

Whereas if you goof (the ugliest word in Hip), if you lapse back into being a frightened stupid child, or if you flip, if you lose your control, reveal the buried weaker more feminine part of your nature, then it is more difficult to swing the next time, your ear is less alive, your bad and energy-wasting habits are further confirmed, you are farther away from being with it. But to be with it is to have grace, is to be closer to the secrets of that inner unconscious life which will nourish you if you can hear it, for you are then nearer to that God which every hipster believes is located in the senses of his body, that trapped, mutilated and nonetheless megalomaniacal God who is It, who is energy, life, sex, force, the Yoga's *prana,* the Reichian's orgone, Lawrence's "blood," Hemingway's "good," the Shavian life-force; "It"; God; not the God of the churches but the unachievable whisper of mystery within the sex, the paradise of limitless energy and perception just beyond the next wave of the next orgasm.

To which a cool cat might reply, "Crazy, man!"

Because, after all, what I have offered above is an hypothesis, no more, and there is not the hipster alive who is not absorbed in his own tumultuous hypotheses. Mine is interesting, mine is way out (on the avenue of the mystery along the road to "It") but still I am just one cat in a world of cool cats, and everything interesting is crazy, or at least so the Squares who do not know how to swing would say.

(And yet crazy is also the self-protective irony of the hipster. Living with questions and not with answers, he is so different in his isolation and in the far reach of his imagination from almost everyone with whom he deals in the outer world of the Square, and meets generally so much enmity, competition, and hatred in the world of Hip, that his isolation is always in danger of turning upon itself, and leaving him indeed just that, crazy.)

If, however, you agree with my hypothesis, if you as a cat are way out too, and we are in the same groove (the universe now being glimpsed as a series of ever-extending radii from the center) why then you say simply, "I dig," because neither knowledge nor imagination comes easily, it is buried in the pain of one's forgotten experience, and so one must work to find it, one must occasionally exhaust oneself by digging into the self in order to perceive the outside. And indeed it is essential to dig the most, for if you do not dig you lose your superiority over the Square, and so you are less likely to be cool (to be in control of a situation because you have swung where the Square has not, or because you have allowed to come to consciousness a pain, a guilt, a shame or a desire which the other has not had the courage to face). To be cool is to be equipped, and if you are equipped it is more difficult for the next cat who comes along to put you down. And of course one can hardly afford to be put down too often, or one is beat, one has lost one's confidence, one has lost one's will, one is impotent in the world of action and so closer to the demeaning flip of becoming a queer, or indeed closer to dying, and therefore it is even more difficult to recover enough energy to try to make it again, because once a cat is beat he has nothing to give, and no one is interested any longer in making it with him. This is the terror of the hipster—to be beat—because once the sweet of sex has deserted him, he still cannot give up the search. It is not granted to the hipster to grow old gracefully—he has been captured too early by the oldest dream of power, the gold fountain of Ponce de Leon, the fountain of youth where the gold is in the orgasm.

To be beat is therefore a flip, it is a situation beyond one's experience, impossible to anticipate—which indeed in the circular vocabulary of Hip is still another meaning for flip, but then I have given just a few of the connotations of these words. Like most primitive vocabularies each word is a prime symbol and serves a dozen or a hundred functions of communication in the instinctive dialectic through which the hipster perceives his experience, that dialectic of the instantaneous differentials of existence in which one is forever moving forward into more or retreating into less.

V

It is impossible to conceive a new philosophy until one creates a new language, but a new popular language (while it must implicitly contain a new philosophy) does not necessarily present its philosophy overtly. It can be asked then what really is unique in the life-view of Hip which raises its argot above the passing verbal whimsies of the bohemian or the lumpenproletariat.

The answer would be in the psychopathic element of Hip which has almost no interest in viewing human nature, or better, in judging human nature, from a set of standards conceived a priori to the experience, standards inherited from the past. Since Hip sees every answer as posing immediately a new alternative, a new question, its emphasis is on complexity rather than simplicity (such complexity that its language without the illumination of the voice and the articulation of the face and body remains hopelessly incommunicative). Given its emphasis on complexity, Hip abdicates from any conventional moral responsibility because it would argue that the result of our actions are unforeseeable, and so we cannot know if we do good or bad, we cannot even know (in the Joycean sense of the good and the bad) whether unforeseeable, and so we cannot know if we do good or bad, we cannot be certain that we have given them energy, and indeed if we could, there would still be no idea of what ultimately they would do with it.

Therefore, men are not seen as good or bad (that they are good-and-bad is taken for granted) but rather each man is glimpsed as a collection of possibilities, some more possible than others (the view of character implicit in Hip) and some humans are considered more capable than others of reaching more possibilities within themselves in less time, provided, and this is the dynamic, provided the particular character can swing at the right time. And here arises the sense of context which differentiates Hip from a Square view of character. Hip sees the context as generally dominating the man, dominating him because his character is less significant than the context in which he must function. Since it is arbitrarily five times more demanding of one's energy to accomplish even an inconsequential action in an unfavorable context than a favorable one, man is then not only his character but his context, since the success or failure of an action in a given context reacts upon the character and therefore affects what the character will be in the next context. What dominates both character and context is the energy available at the moment of intense context.

Character being thus seen as perpetually ambivalent and dynamic enters then into an absolute relativity where there are no truths other than the isolated truths of what each observer feels at each instant of his existence. To take a perhaps unjustified metaphysical extrapolation, it is as if the universe which has usually existed conceptually as a Fact (even if the Fact were Berkeley's God) but a Fact which it was the aim of all science and philosophy to reveal, becomes instead a changing reality whose laws are remade at each instant by everything living, but most particularly man, man raised to a neo-medieval summit where the truth is not what one has felt yesterday or what one expects to feel tomorrow but rather truth is no more nor less than what one feels at each instant in the perpetual climax of the present.

What is consequent therefore is the divorce of man from his

values, the liberation of the self from the Super-Ego of society. The only Hip morality (but of course it is an ever-present morality) is to do what one feels whenever and wherever it is possible, and—this is how the war of the Hip and the Square begins—to be engaged in one primal battle: to open the limits of the possible for oneself, for oneself alone because that is one's need. Yet in widening the arena of the possible, one widens it reciprocally for others as well, so that the nihilistic fulfillment of each man's desire contains its antithesis of human cooperation.

If the ethic reduces to Know Thyself and Be Thyself, what makes it radically different from Socratic moderation with its stern conservative respect for the experience of the past, is that the Hip ethic is immoderation, child-like in its adoration of the present (and indeed to respect the past means that one must also respect such ugly consequences of the past as the collective murders of the State). It is this adoration of the present which contains the affirmation of Hip, because its ultimate logic surpasses even the unforgettable solution of the Marquis de Sade to sex, private property, and the family, that all men and women have absolute but temporary rights over the bodies of all other men and women—the nihilism of Hip proposes as its final tendency that every social restraint and category be removed, and the affirmation implicit in the proposal is that man would then prove to be more creative than murderous and so would not destroy himself. Which is exactly what separates Hip from the authoritarian philosophies which now appeal to the conservative and liberal temper—what haunts the middle of the Twentieth Century is that faith in man has been lost, and the appeal of authority has been that it would restrain us from ourselves. Hip, which would return us to ourselves, at no matter what price in individual violence, is the affirmation of the barbarian for it requires a primitive passion about human nature to believe that individual acts of violence are always to be preferred to the collective violence of the State; it takes literal faith in the creative possibilities of the human being to envisage acts of violence as the catharsis which prepares growth.

Whether the hipster's desire for absolute sexual freedom contains any genuinely radical conception of a different world is of course another matter, and it is possible, since the hipster lives with his hatred, that many of them are the material for an elite of storm troopers ready to follow the first truly magnetic leader whose view of mass murder is phrased in a language which reaches their emotions. But given the desperation of his condition as a psychic outlaw, the hipster is equally a candidate for the most reactionary and most radical of movements, and so it is just as possible that many hipsters will come—if the crisis deepens—to a radical comprehension of the horror of society, for even as the radical has had his incommunicable dissent confirmed in his experience by precisely the frustration, the denied opportunities, and the bitter years which his ideas have cost him, so the sexual adventurer deflected from his goal by the implacable animosity of a society constructed to deny the sexual radical as well, may yet come to an equally bitter comprehension of the slow relentless inhumanity of the conservative power which controls him from without and from within. And in being so controlled, denied, and starved into the attrition of conformity, indeed the hipster may come to see that his condition is no more than an exaggeration of the human condition, and if he would be free, then everyone must be free. Yes, this is possible too, for the heart of Hip is its emphasis upon courage at the moment of crisis, and it is pleasant to think that courage contains within itself (as the explanation of its existence) some glimpse of the necessity of life to become more than it has been.

It is obviously not very possible to speculate with sharp focus on the future of the hipster. Certain possibilities must be evident, however, and the most central is that the organic growth of Hip depends on whether the Negro emerges as a dominating force in American life. Since the Negro knows more about the ugliness and danger of life than the White, it is probable that if the Negro can win his equality, he will possess a potential superiority, a superiority so feared that the fear itself has become the underground drama of domestic politics. Like all conservative political fear it is the fear of unforeseeable consequences, for the Negro's equality would tear a profound shift into the psychology, the sexuality, and the moral imagination of every White alive.

With this possible emergence of the Negro, Hip may erupt

as a psychically armed rebellion whose sexual impetus may rebound against the anti-sexual foundation of every organized power in America, and bring into the air such animosities, antipathies, and new conflicts of interest that the mean empty hypocrisies of mass conformity will no longer work. A time of violence, new hysteria, confusion and rebellion will then be likely to replace the time of conformity. At that time, if the liberal should prove realistic in his belief that there is peaceful room for every tendency in American life, then Hip would end by being absorbed as a colorful figure in the tapestry. But if this is not the reality, and the economic, the social, the psychological, and finally the moral crises accompanying the rise of the Negro should prove insupportable, then a time is coming when every political guide post will be gone, and millions of liberals will be faced with political dilemmas they have so far succeeded in evading, and with a view of human nature they do not wish to accept. To take the desegregation of the schools in the South as an example, it is quite likely that the reactionary sees the reality more closely than the liberal when he argues that the deeper issue is not desegregation but miscegenation. (As a radical I am of course facing in the opposite direction from the White Citizen's Councils—obviously I believe it is the absolute human right of the Negro to mate with the White, and matings there will undoubtedly be, for there will be Negro high school boys brave enough to chance their lives.) But for the average liberal whose mind has been dulled by the committee-ish cant of the professional liberal, miscegenation is not an issue because he has been told that the Negro does not desire it. So, when it comes, miscegenation will be a terror, comparable perhaps to the derangement of the American Communists when the icons to Stalin came tumbling down. The average American Communist held to the myth of Stalin for reasons which had little to do with the political evidence and everything to do with their psychic necessities. In this sense it is equally a psychic necessity for the liberal to believe that the Negro and even the reactionary Southern White are eventually and fundamentally people like himself, capable of becoming good liberals too if only they can be reached by good liberal reason. What the liberal cannot bear to admit is the hatred beneath the skin of a society so unjust that the amount of collective violence buried in the people is perhaps incapable of being contained, and therefore if one wants a better world one does well to hold one's breath, for a worse world is bound to come first, and the dilemma may well be this: given such hatred, it must either vent itself nihilistically or become turned into the cold murderous liquidations of the totalitarian state.

VI

No matter what its horrors the Twentieth Century is a vastly exciting century for its tendency is to reduce all of life to its ultimate alternatives. One can well wonder if the last war of them all will be between the blacks and the whites, or between the women and the men, or between the beautiful and ugly, the pillagers and managers, or the rebels and the regulators. Which of course is carrying speculation beyond the point where speculation is still serious, and yet despair at the monotony and bleakness of the future have become so engrained in the radical temper that the radical is in danger of abdicating from all imagination. What a man feels is the impulse for his creative effort, and if an alien but nonetheless passionate instinct about the meaning of life has come so unexpectedly from a virtually illiterate people, come out of the most intense conditions of exploitation, cruelty, violence, frustration, and lust, and yet has succeeded as an instinct in keeping this tortured people alive, then it is perhaps possible that the Negro holds more of the tail of the expanding elephant of truth than the radical, and if this is so, the radical humanist could do worse than to brood upon the phenomenon. For if a revolutionary time should come again, there would be a crucial difference if someone had already delineated a neo-Marxian calculus aimed at comprehending every circuit and process of society from ukase to kiss as the communications of human energy—a calculus capable of translating the economic relations of man into his psychological relations and then back again, his productive relations thereby embracing his sexual relations as well, until the crises of capitalism in the Twentieth Century would yet be understood as the unconscious adaptations of a society to solve its economic imbalance at the expense of a new mass psychological imbalance. It is almost beyond the imagination to conceive of a work in which the drama of human energy is engaged, and a theory of its social currents and dissipations, its imprisonments, expressions, and tragic wastes are fitted into some gigantic synthesis of human action where the body of Marxist thought, and particularly the epic grandeur of *Das Kapital* (that first of the major *psychologies* to approach the mystery of social cruelty so simply and practically as to say that we are a collective body of humans whose life-energy is wasted, displaced, and procedurally stolen as it passes from one of us to another)—where particularly the epic grandeur of *Das Kapital* would find its place in an even more Godlike view of human justice and injustice, in some more excruciating vision of those intimate and institutional processes which lead to our creations and disasters, our growth, our attrition, and our rebellion.

Alan Watts

Alan Watts was born on January 6, 1915, in Chislehurst, England and died in Mill Valley, California, on November 16, 1973. As a popularizer of Eastern philosophy for Western readers, Watts published more than twenty books between his debut volume, The Spirit of Zen *(1936) and his posthumously published* Tao: The Watercourse Way *(1975).*

Watts's importance to the Beat literary movement is his article "Beat Zen, Square Zen, and Zen," written for the summer 1958 "Zen" issue of Chicago Review, *which also contained an excerpt from Kerouac's* The Dharma Bums *titled "Meditation in the Woods," and work by Gary Snyder and Philip Whalen. This issue of the* Chicago Review *and its spring 1958 issue featuring the "new San Francisco Poets" were so popular that they tripled the* Review's *circulation. Revised and expanded, Watts's article was published as a pamphlet by City Lights in 1959 and included in his book* This Is It *in 1960.*

In the later expanded version of "Beat Zen, Square Zen, and Zen," Watts discussed Kerouac's portrayal of Snyder as Japhy Ryder in The Dharma Bums. *Watts approved the description of Snyder's shack as being "in the Best Zen tradition of clean and uncluttered simplicity." But as Watts understood, in the novel "we are seeing Snyder through Kerouac's eyes, and some distortions arise because Kerouac's own Buddhism is a true beat Zen which confuses 'anything goes' at the existential level with 'anything goes' on the artistic and social levels. Nevertheless, there is something endearing about Kerouac's personality as a writer, something which comes out in the warmth of his ad-*

miration for Gary, and in the lusty, generous enthusiasm for life which wells up at every point in his colorful and undisciplined prose."

BEAT ZEN, SQUARE ZEN, AND ZEN

It is as difficult for Anglo-Saxons as for the Japanese to absorb anything quite so Chinese as Zen. For though the word "Zen" is Japanese and though Japan is now its home, Zen Buddhism is the creation of T'ang dynasty China. I do not say this as a prelude to harping upon the incommunicable subtleties of alien cultures. The point is simply that people who feel a profound need to justify themselves have difficulty in understanding the viewpoints of those who do not, and the Chinese who created Zen were the same kind of people as Lao-tzu, who, centuries before, had said, "Those who justify themselves do not convince." For the urge to make or prove oneself right has always jiggled the Chinese sense of the ludicrous, since as both Confucians and Taoists—however different these philosophies in other ways—they have invariably appreciated the man who can "come off it." To Confucius it seemed much better to be human-hearted than righteous, and to the great Taoists, Lao-tzu and Chuang-tzu, it was obvious that one could not be right without also being wrong, because the two were as inseparable as back and front. As Chuang-tzu said, "Those who would have good government without its correlative misrule, and right without its correlative wrong, do not understand the principles of the universe."

To Western ears such words may sound cynical, and the Confucian admiration of "reasonableness" and compromise may appear to be a weak-kneed lack of commitment to principle. Actually they reflect a marvelous understanding and respect for what we call the balance of nature, human and otherwise—a universal vision of life as the Tao or way of nature in which the good and the evil, the creative and the destructive, the wise and the foolish are the inseparable polarities of existence. "Tao," said the *Chung-yung*, "is that from which one cannot depart. That from which one can depart is not the Tao." Therefore wisdom did not consist in trying to wrest the good from the evil but in learning to "ride" them as a cork adapts itself to the crests and troughs of the waves. At the roots of Chinese life there is a trust in the good-and-evil of one's own nature which is peculiarly foreign to those brought up with the chronic uneasy conscience of the Hebrew-Christian cultures. Yet it was always obvious to the Chinese that a man who mistrusts himself cannot even trust his mistrust, and must therefore be hopelessly confused.

For rather different reasons, Japanese people tend to be as uneasy in themselves as Westerners, having a sense of social shame quite as acute as our more metaphysical sense of sin. This was especially true of the class most attracted to Zen, the *samurai*. Ruth Benedict, in that very uneven work *Chrysanthemum and Sword,* was, I think, perfectly correct in saying that the attraction of Zen to the *samurai* class was its power to get rid of an extremely awkward self-consciousness induced in the education of the young. Part-and-parcel of this self-consciousness is the Japanese compulsion to compete with oneself—a compulsion which turns every craft and skill into a marathon of self-discipline. Although the attraction of Zen lay in the possibility of liberation from self-consciousness, the Japanese version of Zen fought fire with fire, overcoming the "self observing the self" by bringing it to an intensity in which it exploded. How remote from the regimen of the Japanese Zen monastery are the words of the great T'ang master Lin-chi:

> In Buddhism there is no place for using effort. Just be ordinary and nothing special. Eat your food, move your bowels, pass water, and when you're tired go and lie down. The ignorant will laugh at me, but the wise will understand.

Yet the spirit of these words is just as remote from a kind of Western Zen which would employ this philosophy to justify a very self-defensive Bohemianism.

There is no single reason for the extraordinary growth of Western interest in Zen during the last twenty years. The appeal of Zen arts to the "modern" spirit in the West, the work of Suzuki, the war with Japan, the itchy fascination of

"Zen-stories," and the attraction of a non-conceptual, experiential philosophy in the climate of scientific relativism—all these are involved. One might mention, too, the affinities between Zen and such purely Western trends as the philosophy of Wittgenstein, Existentialism, General Semantics, the metalinguistics of B. L. Whorf, and certain movements in the philosophy of science and in psychotherapy. Always in the background there is our vague disquiet with the artificiality or "anti-naturalness" of both Christianity, with its politically ordered cosmology, and technology, with its imperialistic mechanization of a natural world from which man himself feels strangely alien. For both reflect a psychology in which man is identified with a conscious intelligence and will standing apart from nature to control it, like the architect-God in whose image this version of man is conceived. The disquiet arises from the suspicion that our attempt to master the world from outside is a vicious circle in which we shall be condemned to the perpetual insomnia of controlling controls and supervising supervision *ad infinitum.*

To the Westerner in search of the reintegration of man and nature there is an appeal far beyond the merely sentimental in the naturalism of Zen—in the landscapes of Ma-yuan and Sesshu, in an art which is simultaneously spiritual and secular, which conveys the mystical in terms of the natural, and which, indeed, never even imagined a break between them. Here is a view of the world imparting a profoundly refreshing sense of wholeness to a culture in which the spiritual and the material, the conscious and the unconscious, have been cataclysmically split. For this reason the Chinese humanism and naturalism of Zen intrigue us much more strongly than Indian Buddhism or Vedanta. These, too, have their students in the West, but their followers seem for the most part to be displaced Christians—people in search of a more plausible philosophy than Christian supernaturalism to carry on the essentially Christian search for the miraculous. The ideal man of Indian Buddhism is clearly a superman, a *yogi* with absolute mastery of his own nature, according perfectly with the science-fiction ideal of "men beyond mankind." But the Buddha or awakened man of Chinese Zen is "ordinary and nothing special"; he is humorously human like the Zen tramps portrayed by Mu-chi and Liang-k'ai. We like this because here, for the first time, is a conception of the holy man and sage who is not impossibly remote, not superhuman but fully human, and, above all, not a solemn and sexless ascetic. Furthermore, in Zen the *satori* experience of awakening to our "original inseparability" with the universe seems, however elusive, always just round the corner. One has even met people to whom it has happened, and they are no longer mysterious occultists in the Himalayas nor skinny *yogis* in cloistered *ashrams.* They are just like us, and yet much more at home in the world, floating much more easily upon the ocean of transience and insecurity.

But the Westerner who is attracted by Zen and who would understand it deeply must have one indispensable qualification: he must understand his own culture so thoroughly that he is no longer swayed by its premises unconsciously. He must really have come to terms with the Lord God Jehovah and with his Hebrew-Christian conscience so that he can take it or leave it without fear or rebellion. He must be free of the itch to justify himself. Lacking this, his Zen will be either "beat" or "square," either a revolt from the culture and social order or a new form of stuffiness and respectability. For Zen is above all the liberation of the mind from conventional thought, and this is something utterly different from rebellion against convention, on the one hand, or adopting foreign conventions, on the other.

Conventional thought is, in brief, the confusion of the concrete universe of nature with the conceptual things, events, and values of linguistic and cultural symbolism. For in Taoism and Zen the world is seen as an inseparably interrelated field or continuum, no part of which can actually be separated from the rest or valued above or below the rest. It was in this sense that Hui-neng, the Sixth Patriarch, meant that "fundamentally not one thing exists," for he realized that things are *terms,* not entities. They exist in the abstract world of thought, but not in the concrete world of nature. Thus one who actually perceives or feels this to be so no longer feels that he is an ego, except by definition. He sees that his ego is his *persona* or social role, a somewhat arbitrary selection of experiences with which he has been taught to identify himself. (Why, for example, do we say "I think" but not "I am beating my heart"?)

Having seen this, he continues to play his social role without being taken in by it. He does not precipitately adopt a new role or play the role of having no role at all. He plays it cool.

The "beat" mentality as I am thinking of it is something much more extensive and vague than the hipster life of New York and San Francisco. It is a younger generation's nonparticipation in "the American Way of Life," a revolt which does not seek to change the existing order but simply turns away from it to find the significance of life in subjective experience rather than objective achievement. It contrasts with the "square" and other-directed mentality of beguilement by social convention, unaware of the correlativity of right and wrong, of the mutual necessity of capitalism and communism to each other's existence, of the inner identity of puritanism and lechery, or of, say, the alliance of church lobbies and organized crime to maintain the laws against gambling.

Beat Zen is a complex phenomenon. It ranges from a use of Zen for justifying sheer caprice in art, literature, and life to a very forceful social criticism and "digging of the universe" such as one may find in the poetry of Ginsberg and Snyder, and, rather unevenly, in Kerouac. But, as I know it, it is always a shade too self-conscious, too subjective, and too strident to have the flavor of Zen. It is all very well for the philosopher, but when the poet (Ginsberg) says—

> live
> in the physical world
> moment to moment
>
> I must write down
>   every recurring thought—
> stop every beating second

this is too indirect and didactic for Zen, which would rather hand you *the thing itself* without comment.

> The sea darkens;
>   The voices of the wild ducks
>   Are faintly white.

Furthermore, when Kerouac gives his philosophical final statement, "I don't know. I don't care. And it doesn't make any difference"—the cat is out of the bag, for there is a hostility in these words which clangs with self-defense. But just because Zen truly surpasses convention and its values, it has no need to say "To hell with it," nor to underline with violence the fact that anything goes.

Now the underlying protestant lawlessness of beat Zen disturbs the square Zennists very seriously. For square Zen is the Zen of established tradition in Japan with its clearly defined hierarchy, its rigid discipline, and its specific tests of *satori*. More particularly, it is the kind of Zen adopted by Westerners studying in Japan, who will before long be bringing it back home. But there is an obvious difference between square Zen and the common-or-garden squareness of the Rotary Club or the Presbyterian Church. It is infinitely more imaginative, sensitive and interesting. But it is still square because it is a quest for the *right* spiritual experience, for a *satori* which will receive the stamp (*inka*) of approved and established authority. There will even be certificates to hang on the wall.

I see no real quarrel with either extreme. There was never a spiritual movement without its excesses and distortions. The experience of awakening which truly constitutes Zen is too timeless and universal to be injured. The extremes of beat Zen need alarm no one since, as Blake said, "the fool who persists in his folly will become wise." As for square Zen, "authoritative" spiritual experiences have always had a way of wearing thin, and thus of generating the demand for something genuine and unique which needs no stamp.

I have known followers of both extremes to come up with perfectly clear *satori* experiences, for since there is no real "way" to *satori* the way you are following makes very little difference.

But the quarrel *between* the extremes is of great philosophical interest, being a contemporary form of the ancient dispute between salvation by works and salvation by faith, or between what the Hindus called the ways of the monkey and the cat. The cat—appropriately enough—follows the effortless way, since the mother cat carries her kittens. The monkey follows the hard way, since the baby monkey has to hang on to its mother's hair. Thus for beat Zen there must be no effort, no discipline, no artificial striving to attain *satori* or to be anything but what one is. But for square Zen there can be no true *satori* without years of meditation-practice under the stern supervision of a qualified master. In seventeenth-century Japan these two attitudes were *approximately* typified by the great masters Bankei and Hakuin, and it so happens that the followers of the latter "won out" and determined the present-day character of Rinzai Zen.[1]

Satori can lie along both roads. It is the concomitant of a "nongrasping" attitude of the senses to experience, and grasping can be exhausted by the discipline of directing its utmost intensity to a single, ever-elusive objective. But what makes the way of effort and will-power suspect to many Westerners is not so much an inherent laziness as a thorough familiarity with the wisdom of our own culture. The square Western Zennists are often quite naive when it comes to an understanding of Christian theology or of all that has been discovered in modern psychiatry, for both have long been concerned with the fallibility and unconscious ambivalence of the will. Both have posed problems as to the vicious circle of seeking self-surrender or of "free-associating on purpose" or of accepting one's conflicts to escape from them, and to anyone who knows anything about either Christianity or psychotherapy these are very real problems. The interest of Chinese Zen and of people like Bankei is that they deal with these problems in a most direct and stimulating way, and begin to suggest some answers. But when Herrigel's Japanese archery master was asked, "How can I give up purpose on purpose?" he replied that no one had ever asked him that before. He had no answer except to go on trying blindly, for five years.

Foreign religions can be immensely attractive and highly overrated by those who know little of their own, and especially by those who have not worked through and grown out of their

---

[1] Rinzai Zen is the form most widely known in the West. There is also Soto Zen which differs somewhat in technique, but is still closer to Hakuin than to Bankei. However, Bankei should not exactly be identified with beat Zen as I have described it, for he was certainly no advocate of the life of undisciplined whimsy despite all that he said about the importance of the uncalculated life and the folly of seeking *satori*.

own. This is why the displaced or unconscious Christian can so easily use either beat or square Zen to justify himself. The one wants a philosophy to justify him in doing what he pleases. The other wants a more plausible authoritative salvation than the Church or the psychiatrists seem to be able to provide. Furthermore the atmosphere of Japanese Zen is free from all one's unpleasant childhood associations with God the Father and Jesus Christ—though I know many young Japanese who feel just the same way about their early training in Buddhism. But the true character of Zen remains almost incomprehensible to those who have not surpassed the immaturity of needing to be justified, whether before the Lord God or before a paternalistic society.

The old Chinese Zen masters were steeped in Taoism. They saw nature in its total interrelatedness, and saw that every creature and every experience is in accord with the Tao of nature just as it is. This enabled them to accept themselves as they were, moment by moment, without the least need to justify anything. They didn't do it to defend themselves or to find an excuse for getting away with murder. They didn't brag about it and set themselves apart as rather special. On the contrary, their Zen was *wu-shih,* which means approximately "nothing special" or "no fuss." But Zen is "fuss" when it is mixed up with Bohemian affectations, and "fuss" when it is imagined that the only proper way to find it is to run off to a monastery in Japan or to do special exercises in the lotus posture for five hours a day. And I will admit that the very hullabaloo about Zen, even in such an article as this, is also fuss—but a little less so.

Having said that, I would like to say something for all Zen fussers, beat or square. Fuss is all right, too. If you are hung on Zen, there's no need to try to pretend that you are not. If you really want to spend some years in a Japanese monastery, there is no earthly reason why you shouldn't. Or if you want to spend your time hopping freight cars and digging Charlie Parker, it's a free country.

> In the landscape of Spring there is neither better
>   nor worse;
> The flowering branches grow naturally, some long,
>   some short.

John Clellon Holmes

John Clellon Holmes wrote his essay "The Game of the Name" in 1965, analyzing his response to Mailer's "The White Negro," during the time that the words "beat" and "beatnik" were being replaced in the public's mind by the word "hippie." As his biographer Richard Ardinger understood, Holmes had a "unique ability to describe the questions and psychological dilemmas which plagued his generation and the driving forces behind the ideologies of the movement." "The Game of the Name" was included with the cultural essays collected in Holmes's volume Passionate Opinions, *published shortly after his death from cancer in 1988, by the University of Arkansas where he had taught creative writing.*

from THE GAME OF THE NAME
(1965)

Spiritual quests to the contrary, after the initial furor about the Beat Generation in the late fifties, the public, the Media, and the critics decided that when you spoke of "beatness" you were referring exclusively to the folkways of a group of urban Thoreaus who lived in those limbo-neighborhoods where the nation's Bohemias shelved off into the nation's slums. In other words, the so-called Beatniks.

That sneering diminutive, which is about all that is left of the Beat Generation today ("Among the sit-ins was the usual sprinkling of beatniks," "The moral contagion represented by juvenile delinquents, racial malcontents, and beatniks," "I certainly don't intend to support my son if he wants to be a beatnik"), was originally coined by Herb Caen, a facetious columnist in San Francisco, to describe the bearded, sandaled coffee-house loungers of the North Beach Bohemia, but it was immediately adopted by the mass media as a handy caricature for everyone associated with Beatness, and thereby quickly entered the smear-vocabularies of all those perceptive people who like to call intellectuals "eggheads." And for the same perceptive reason: if you can't understand them, brand them.

The notion (which became universal) that when you talked about the Beat attitude you were speaking of Caen's idea rather than Kerouac's, had the paradoxical effect of at once making the Beat Generation briefly notorious in the popular mind as a species of hip Amish, and more or less permanently obscuring the wider, and deeper, implications of the term. In my not-unprejudiced view, the Beatniks and the Mass Media, between them, succeeded in beclouding most of what was unsettling, and thereby valuable, in the idea of Beatness, and I might as well deal with this aspect of the matter before discussing the more serious critical appraisals of that idea.

The Beatniks were (and, I suppose, still are) essentially Bohemians—that is, *artistes manqués,* colony-establishers, ci-tified Trobriand Islanders. On the run from the ant heaps of the industrial revolution, in flight from its moral cul-de-sacs, they gathered into seedy enclaves on the margins of the arts, where they immediately went about setting up a kind of parody of the society they had fled. The life-style described in *On the Road,* "Howl," and other works gave a direction to their with-drawal, but their dominant preoccupations remained nest-building and Square-baiting. They talked so incessantly about "the rat race" and their own group identity that, with a few changes of reference, they would have gone almost unnoticed in Levittown.

Of course, Bohemians have always, drearily, derived most of their behavior patterns from attentively watching the bourgeoisie and then doing the opposite, but the Beatniks, unlike most Bohemians, could admit that their need to shock the Squares was only the obverse side of the Squares' need to *be* shocked, and this led to such sure-fire merchandising schemes as the Rent-a-Beatnik fad, and the Do-It-Yourself Beatnik Kit. It also led to a rigorous uniformity of language, dress, tastes, attitudes, and values that was almost a mirror image of the very conformity against which they were in revolt. The only difference was that the Beatniks were obsessed with the Squares, while the Squares were not obsessed with them, and a far better gimmick would have been an agency from which one could Rent-a-Square, because every pad needed one if it wanted to really swing. . . .

As should be wearisomely clear by now, a confusion of terminology has plagued the naming of this generation, as it did those of biblical times, and Mailer's vote would probably go to "Hip." I am sure all of us by now would cordially be rid of labels altogether. Certainly I have no fondness for the one with which I am associated, and am only interested in the New Consciousness for which it is a crude and perhaps misleading adjective, but nevertheless Mailer, and Hip, deserve a brief look.

As has been seen, I consider *The White Negro* to be a pioneer exploration of this New Consciousness, a document fully as important to the secret history of this age as *Notes from Underground* was to the Europe of its time. In a footnote to *The White Negro* (written somewhat later), Mailer says, "The Beat Generation is probably best used to include hipsters and beatniks"; he then goes on to detail with fine precision the differences between the two. The Beatniks are more intellectual, less sexy; they are mystic, pacifist, and neurotic, whereas "the hipster is still in life; strong on his will, he takes on the dissipation of the drugs in order to dig more life for himself, he is wrestling with the destiny of his nervous system, he is Faustian." I find little of importance to disagree with in this, as my views of the Beatniks may have made clear. But it is on this matter of "the destiny of the nervous system" where Mailer and I diverge, just as Hipness and Beatness (as I mean it) ultimately reach a crossroads of the consciousness, and must go their different ways.

Mailer's hipster goes back into the jungle of the world, where Power is the prize, and Ego is the weapon, and Hip the sight through which you aim. But the destiny of the nervous system, accumulating Sensation the way Faust's mind accumulated Knowledge, is inexorably violence, just as surely as Faust's destiny was damnation, for neither the mind *nor* the nervous system is a large enough channel for the whole of Consciousness. And it is our consciousness of *more* than either our nerves or our minds can contain by themselves that is the primary fact of this half of the twentieth century.

I have always thought that Mailer stubbed his toe on God. He is a metaphysician snagged in the data of the senses. I do not mean to say that he is immodest when I say that he cannot seem to endure the ego-loss toward which all his finest perceptions are driving him. There is something about the "merging" that all states of heightened Consciousness precipitate that revulses him. And yet he knows, he knows—for in sex, where the dissolving of the ego is most imminent and most intense, his vision comes perilously close to a drunken fusion of the insights of Sade and Swedenborg (if that can be imagined), only to draw back at the final moment when the character armor begins to melt, and insist on once again confusing the Ego with the Self.

His version of Beat (call it what you will) is decidedly "of this world," and, as such, it has proved more comprehensible, and more attractive, than any other version. It has even succeeded in establishing a point of re-entry into the public world (what he has dubbed "existential politics") that a serious man can take seriously, and the consequences of which are as yet incalculable. . . .

It is clear that *my* conception of Beatness was just that—mine; or at best a conception shared to one degree or another by my *crowd*—Kerouac, Ginsberg, Burroughs, Corso, and a few others, like Snyder and Whalen, who turned up on the West Coast. What I was projecting were my own bankruptcies and aspirations, just as Jack projected his in all his novels. But it was the blasting, beering, and bumming in our work, the restless, energetic surface of the life described, and *not* the world-and-mind weariness, the continual moulting of consciousness, and the spirit's arduous venture toward its own reconciliations, that caught whatever fancies—Square *or* Beatnik—that were eventually caught.

Finally, *my* Beat Generation, like the Lost Generation before it, was primarily a literary group, and not a social movement; and probably all that will last out of our Beat years are a rash of vaporous anecdotes, and the few solid works that were produced. We have paid for the audacity of daring to label ourselves a "generation" by being continually ticketed with attitudes of mind and styles of behavior that were not necessarily ours, and having our work dismissed as these attitudes and styles became moribund. But thankfully a book is not as ephemeral as a beard, and, if it is a good book, it will outlast whatever quick-fading labels are attached to it. Time will tell, and not too quickly.

For the rest of it, it seems to me, the Beat Generation (and even the sorriest of the Beatniks) made contributions to the scene which deserve to be assessed—if only because they are in danger of being forgotten now, so radically has that scene changed in the last years.

Culturally, America has gone through something of a "thaw" since 1960. Part of this can be attributed to the fact that we had a president, albeit briefly, for whom culture, if it did not mean Charlie Parker, at least meant more than Lawrence Welk; a man in whose mouth the names of Faulkner and Hemingway did not sound ghost-written; a man who could speak of the inner life without somehow suggesting the digestive process. But whatever the reason, the atmosphere has changed. Among other things, the old puritan structure of censorship has been dismantled, idiocy by idiocy, and the clammy hand of Academia has been returned to the exhumation of dead works, rather than the murder of living ones. It is assumed, once more, that poetry *can* make something happen—other than a plague of exegetics, spreading through the "little magazines" like African sleeping sickness. Novels are published now that couldn't even have been written a few scant years ago. John Cage is no longer spoken of as a demented piano tuner; De Kooning is welcomed in the White House; even Iowa City has its Bergman Festival.

Off-Broadway, LSD, Ornette Coleman; the Frug, Genet, Buñuel—for the first time, the avant-garde is fashionable, experimentation is news, the far-out style is the chic style. Much of this is a mixed blessing at best, for much of it suggests the supermarket gourmand ("More, more! New, new!"), rather than the specialty-shop gourmet ("This, and this, but not that"). Still, it is a more open culture now, a culture at least trying to relate to a real and specific world, a culture in which strongly individual voices can be heard over the mindless din of the entertainment factories.

The poets, playwrights, and novelists, who might be loosely associated with the Beat attitude, were among the first of these voices to be heard, and their insistence on talking in loud, personal terms (whose very negation of certain values was an implicit affirmation of others) provoked those, who were not specifically "beat" themselves, into speaking up as well. The basic *tone* of the culture has changed from the caution, irony, and impersonality of the critical intellectual to the daring, commitment, and diversity of the creative artist, and the Beats certainly deserve a sizable part of the credit for this.

Socially, also, America is a different land. If there has been a new tide running in the nation these past years—a tide of dissent, activism, and involvement (in civil rights, disarmament, poverty, and freedom of speech); a tide that bluntly calls into question the quality of our life here at home, and challenges mere anticommunism as a sane foundation for our policy abroad; a tide that has noisily erupted in the universities, the magazines, the public forums, and the streets themselves —this tide is urged on by a new generation, which grew to awareness in the last half of the fifties, and was exposed to the example of a fragment of my generation, whose fixation with the idea that the emperor had no clothes led it to proclaim the bald and unruly "No!," without which the Free Speechers, and the Ban-the-Bombers, and the white (at least) Sit-ins might not have been able to say the challenging "Yes!" we are hearing at last in the land. For if politics are back "in" among the young, they are a very different sort of politics than those of the thirties or the forties—a much tougher-minded, pragmatic, lifegrounded politics, a politics of personal witness and non-violence, a politics that tries to replace bloodless ideology with the living body interposed between the finger of the Establishment and the various buttons of the Society. All in all, it is a time of possibilities again, for which the Beat revolt is not a little responsible.

Perhaps because of all this, the fever for naming generations may be dying out of our culture at last. Perhaps the future holds no single occurrence that will prove so forming that an entire age group can be characterized by a single term. Sometimes I find myself wondering if this happened, in actual fact, in our case. But deluded though we may have been, it *was* a generation we sought to describe, and not simply a minority group and its exotic mores; it was a unique phenomenon-of-mind in all of us, and not only the eccentric behavior patterns in a few, that we felt impelled to name. And if we were wrong, it was not because we were eclectic. For myself, I believe that we perceived the new sort of consciousness that distinguished us from our elders with a clarity the intervening years have not seriously blurred.

But I cannot leave this matter of the Beat attitude without a word about the generation that has come along since mine. If, as I believe, some of its achievements, and a lot of its style, have flourished on the ground we cleared, nevertheless the differences between us may yet prove to be greater than the similarities. Existentialism, as an example, exerts a powerful influence on both generations, and probably constitutes the only philosophic point of view that is broadly typical of this time. But whereas it was existentialism's conception of the nature of man that spoke so clearly to *us,* it is existentialism's engagement in the community of men that most appeals to *them.* Nonviolence, pacifism, and reverence for life are mostly means of social action to young people today, whereas, to us, they were ends in themselves: you were nonviolent not because it was one way of changing institutions, but because it was the only way of remaining a human being. . . .

Perhaps these are inevitable reactions to a world that twenty years of Cold War have brought closer to insanity than to sense, but if that world is ever to be diverted from its present collision course with the fatality inherent in its own history (an onerous task that will fall on people who are under twenty-five today), my generation's stubborn choice of man over society, the Self over the Ego, and the spirit over psychology may have to be made all over again by those to whom we honestly thought we had bequeathed it already.

But then growing up in America has always been arduous.

Our maturation rites are compounded of equal parts of nihilism and idealism, and we have always smashed our icons with *other* icons. Young Americans have immemorially been as uncritical in their surrender to the present as they are ruthless in their repudiation of the past, and a disorderly, eruptive process of individuation, whose first requirement seems to be a weaning-by-excess, is a tradition so unbroken and so peculiar to us that America's senescence may only be said to have arrived when it no longer produces successive generations-in-revolt.

For my own part, I am weary of labels. Whatever lies ahead for my generation will certainly make them less and less applicable to our experience, for an inevitable part of aging seems to be that one relentlessly becomes less representative of one's times, and more representative of oneself. Something like this, it seems to me, is happening to all of us who shared the Beat years—which, of course, was precisely what the Beat Generation was all about.

BOOKS FOR
FURTHER READING

For bibliographies of individual writers, see listings in *The Beats: Literary Bohemians in Postwar America,* edited by Ann Charters. Vol. 16, Parts 1 and 2, of *Dictionary of Literary Biography.* Detroit: Gale Research Co., 1983.

Allen, Donald M., ed. *The New American Poetry.* New York: Grove Press, 1960. (Editor's introduction defines the different categories of the "new" poetry.)

Allen, Donald M., and George F. Butterick. *The Postmoderns: The New American Poetry Revised.* New York: Grove Press, 1982. (Revised and updated edition.)

Ball, Gordon, ed. *Allen Verbatim: Lectures on Poetry, Politics, Consciousness.* New York: McGraw-Hill, 1974. (Essays on various subjects, including Kerouac and the early poetic community in San Francisco and Berkeley.)

Baro, Gene, ed. *'Beat' Poets.* London: Vista Books, 1961. (Editor of this early anthology of "new" poetry explains why it "has had a desirable and liberating effect.")

Bartlett, Jeffrey. *One Vast Page.* Berkeley, California: Provine Press, 1991. (Essays on Beat writers and their books.)

Bartlett, Lee. *William Everson: The Life of Brother Antoninus.* New York: New Directions, 1988. (Description of Berkeley Renaissance and Everson's career as a small-press printer.)

Bartlett, Lee, ed. *The Beats: Essays in Criticism.* Jefferson, N.C.: McFarland, 1981. (Critical analysis of work by Burroughs, Ferlinghetti, Ginsberg, Kerouac, Snyder, Corso, Whalen, McClure, and others.)

Berlowitz, Leslie, and Rick Beard. *Greenwich Village: Culture and Counterculture*. New Brunswick, N.J.: Rutgers University Press, 1991.

Black, Jack. *You Can't Win*. New York: Amok Press, 1988. (Reprint of 1926 "underworld" classic with an introduction by William Burroughs.)

Breslin, James E. B. *From Modern to Contemporary: American Poetry, 1945–1965*. Chicago: University of Chicago Press, 1984. (Long essay on the composition of "Howl.")

Brossard, Chandler, ed. *The Scene Before You: A New Approach to American Culture*. New York: Rinehart and Co., 1955. (Contains Anatole Broyard's "A Portrait of a Hipster," Milton Klonsky's "Greenwich Village: Decline and Fall," and Marshall McLuhan's "The Psychopathology of *Time* and *Life*.")

Buckley, Lord Richard. *Hiparama of the Classics*. San Francisco: City Lights, 1980. (Hipster versions of the New Testament, Shakespeare, Lincoln, etc.)

Charters, Ann. *Beats and Company*. New York: Doubleday, 1986. (Twenty years of photographic work, with an introduction by John Clellon Holmes.)

Charters, Ann. *Kerouac: A Biography*. San Francisco: Straight Arrow, 1973. (First biography of Jack Kerouac.)

Charters, Ann, ed. *The Beats: Literary Bohemians in Postwar America*. Vol. 16, Parts 1 and 2 of *Dictionary of Literary Biography*. Detroit: Gale Research Co., 1983. (Contains essays on Amiri Baraka by James A. Miller, Bonnie Bremser [Brenda Frazer] by Michael Perkins, Ray Bremser by Arnold Moodnik, William S. Burroughs by Jennie Skerl, William S. Burroughs, Jr., by J. Skerl and J. Grauerholz, Carolyn Cassady by Joy Walsh, Neal Cassady by Gerard Nicosia, Gregory Corso by Marilyn Schwartz, Diane DiPrima by George F. Butterick, Bob Dylan by Joseph Wenke, Lawrence Ferlinghetti by Larry Smith, Allen Ginsberg by Paul Christensen, Brion Gysin by Terry Wilson, John Clellon Holmes by Richard Ardinger, Herbert Huncke by Arthur Knight, Ted Joans by James A. Miller, Bob Kaufman by A. D. Winans, Ken Kesey by Ann Charters, Tuli Kupferberg by Joseph Wenke, Philip Lamantia by Nancy J. Peters, Jay Landesman by John Clellon Holmes, Norman Mailer by Joseph Wenke, Michael McClure by William King, Jack Micheline by Gerard Nicosia,

Peter Orlovsky by Ann Charters, Kenneth Rexroth by Brown Miller and Ann Charters, Ed Sanders by George Butterick, Gary Snyder by Dan McLeod, Carl Solomon by Tom Collins, Anne Waldman by Ann Charters, Alan Watts by Dan McLeod, Lew Welch by Samuel Charters, Philip Whalen by Paul Christensen, John Wieners by Raymond Foye, William Carlos Williams by Paul Christensen. Also included are Holmes's essays on the Beat Generation and George F. Butterick's listing of periodicals of the Beat Generation.)

Cook, Bruce. *The Beat Generation.* New York: Scribners, 1971. (Popular social history and summary of the literary movement.)

Cowley, Malcolm. *And I Worked at the Writer's Trade.* New York: Viking Press, 1978. (Contains "A Note on Literary Generations.")

Davidson, Michael. *The San Francisco Renaissance: Poetics and Community at Mid-Century.* New York: Cambridge University Press, 1989. (Analysis of historical context and poetry of Kerouac, Ginsberg, Snyder, Whalen, DiPrima, Robert Duncan, Jack Spicer, and other San Francisco writers.)

DiPrima, Diane, and LeRoi Jones. eds. *The Floating Bear: A Newsletter 1961–1969.* La Jolla, California.: Laurence McGilvery, 1973. (578 page reprint of the historic newsletter.)

Ehrenreich, Barbara. *The Hearts of Men: American Dreams and the Flight from Commitment.* Garden City, N.Y.: Doubleday, 1983. (Cultural history from a feminist perspective.)

Ehrlich, J. W., ed. *Howl of the Censor.* San Carlos, California: Nourse Publishing Co., 1961. (Full transcript of the trial with Mark Schorer's critical analysis of the poem.)

Faas, Ekbert, ed. *Towards a New American Poetics.* Santa Barbara: Black Sparrow Press, 1978. (Essays and interviews with Olson, Duncan, Snyder, Creeley, Bly, and Ginsberg by Canadian scholar.)

Feldman, Gene, and Max Gartenberg, eds. *Protest: The Beat Generation and the Angry Young Men.* London: Souvenir Press, 1987. (Reissue of 1957 anthology.)

Ferlinghetti, Lawrence, and Nancy J. Peters. *Literary San Francisco.* New York: Harper & Row, 1980. (Authoritative guide to the literary history of the city.)

Fiedler, Leslie A. *Waiting for the End*. New York: Stein and Day, 1964. (Comments on Ginsberg, Mailer, Henry Miller, etc.)

Fields, Rick. *How the Swans Came to the Lake*. Boston: Shambhala Press, 1981. (Narrative history of Buddhism in America, with chapter on "The Fifties: Beat and Square.")

French, Warren. *Jack Kerouac: Novelist of the Beat Generation*. Boston: Twayne, 1986. (Analysis of books in "The Duluoz Legend.")

Fuller, Edmund. *Man in Modern Fiction*. New York: Random House, 1958. (Essay on Kerouac and Mailer titled "The Hipster or the Organization Man?")

Gifford, Barry and Lawrence Lee. *Jack's Book*. New York: Penguin Books, 1979. (Excellent oral history of Kerouac's life and times.)

Ginsberg, Allen. *Howl: Original Draft Facsimile, Transcript and Variant Versions*. Edited by Barry Miles. New York: Harper & Row, 1986. (Background of composition of the poem.)

Goodman, Michael Barry. *Contemporary Literary Censorship: The Case History of Naked Lunch*. Metuchen, New Jersey, and London: Scarecrow Press, 1981. (*Big Table, Chicago Review,* Olympia Press, and Grove Press background and censorship case.)

Goodman, Paul. *Growing Up Absurd*. New York: Random House, 1960. (Early sociological analysis of the Beats.)

Green, Martin. *Mountain of Truth: The Counterculture Begins, Ascona, 1900–1920*. Hanover, New Hampshire: New England University Press, 1986. (History of the development of early radical bohemian communities.)

Green, Martin, ed. *A Kind of Beatness: Photographs of a North Beach Area 1950–1965*. San Francisco: Focus Gallery, 1975. (Photographs of writers in their settings.)

Gruen, John. *The Party's Over Now: Reminiscences of the Fifties*. New York: Viking, 1972. (New York's artists and writers, including Frank O'Hara.)

Halper, Jon, ed. *Gary Snyder: Dimensions of a Life*. San Francisco: Sierra Club Books, 1991. (Biographical reminiscences.)

Harris, Mary Emma. *The Arts at Black Mountain College*. Cambridge: MIT Press, 1987. (Cultural history.)

Harris, William J., ed. *The LeRoi Jones/Amiri Baraka Reader*. New York: Thunder's Mouth Press, 1991. (Development of Baraka's commitment to radical politics.)

Holmes, John Clellon. *Passionate Opinions*. Fayetteville: University of Arkansas, 1988. (Includes the full text of "The Game of the Name" and other essays on the Beat Generation, and Holmes's later commentary on them.)

Honan, Park. *The Beats*. London: J. M. Dent & Sons, Ltd., 1987. (Poetry, prose, and commentary.)

Horemans, Rudi, ed. *Beat Indeed!* Antwerp: EXA, 1985. (Critical essays.)

Hunt, Tim. *Kerouac's Crooked Road*. Hamden, CT: Archon Books, 1981. (Development of Kerouac's prose style.)

Hyde, Lewis, ed. *On the Poetry of Allen Ginsberg*. Ann Arbor: University of Michigan Press, 1984. (Essays by poets and critics.)

Jones, LeRoi, ed. *The Moderns: An Anthology of New Writing in America*. New York: Corinth Books, 1963. (Excellent introduction by Jones on selections by Beat writers and others.)

Kerouac, Jack. "Is There a Beat Generation?" Recorded talk published as "The Origins of the Beat Generation, *Playboy*, June 1959. (Included in *The Jack Kerouac Collection*. Santa Monica, California: Rhino Records, 1990.)

Kesey, Ken. *Kesey's Garage Sale*. New York: Viking, 1973. (Includes playwright Arthur Miller's introduction to this "chaotic volume" comparing the Beat cultural revolution of the 1950s to the social revolt of the 1930s.)

Kherdian, David. *Six San Francisco Poets*. Fresno: Giligia, 1969. (Bibliographies.)

Knight, Arthur Winfield, and Glee Knight, eds. *The Beat Book*. California, Pennsylvania: Unspeakable Visions of the Individual, 1974. (One of several anthologies of Beat writing and interviews published by the Knights.)

———. *The Beat Vision*. New York: Paragon House, 1987. (Collection of largely unpublished writing and interviews.)

Kostelanetz, Richard. *Social Speculations: Visions for Our Times*. New York: William Morrow, 1970. (Contains Ginsberg's 1967 lecture, "Public Solitude.")

Krim, Seymour. *Shake It for the World.* London: Allison & Busby, 1971. (Essays on Kerouac, Mailer, and Frank Harris as the "First Hipster.")

Krim, Seymour, ed. *The Beats.* Greenwich, Connecticut: Fawcett, 1960. (Introduction discusses background of Beat writing.)

Landesman, Jay, ed. *Neurotica: The Authentic Voice of the Beat Generation.* London: Jay Landesman, Ltd., 1981. (Reprinting of the nine issues of the magazine with an introduction by John Clellon Holmes.)

Lipton, Lawrence. *The Holy Barbarians.* New York: Messner, 1959. (Early reportage of Beat life in southern California and discussion of Kerouac, Ginsberg, and other writers.)

McClure, Michael. *Scratching the Beat Surface.* San Francisco: North Point Press, 1982. (Description of the Six Gallery reading in 1955 and discussion of art as "a living bio-alchemical organism.")

McDarrah, Fred. *Kerouac & Friends: A Beat Generation Album.* New York: William Morrow, 1985. (Photographs.)

McNeill, Don. *Moving Through Here.* New York: Citadel Underground, 1990. (*Village Voice* articles from 1967–1968 about Ginsberg, Sanders, Leary, etc.)

Matusow, Allen J. *A History of Liberalism in the 1960s.* New York: Harper & Row, 1984. (Twenty pages on the Beat subculture.)

Maynard, John A. *Venice West.* New Brunswick: Rutgers University Press, 1991. (Insightful history of the Beat generation in Southern California.)

Meltzer, David. *The San Francisco Poets.* New York: Ballantine Books, 1971. (Interviews in depth with Ferlinghetti, Welch, McClure, Rexroth, and Everson.)

Mezzrow, Mezz, and Bernard Wolfe. *Really the Blues.* New York: Random House, 1946. (Well-written saga of a musician's life and times.)

Miles, Barry. *Ginsberg: A Biography.* New York: Simon and Schuster, 1989. (Biography based on Ginsberg's journals and correspondence; excellent bibliography of secondary-source material.)

Miller, Douglas T., and Marion Nowack. *The Fifties: The Way We Really Were.* Garden City, New York: Doubleday, 1977. (Analysis of the role of American intellectuals in their own culture.)

Morgan, Ted. *Literary Outlaw: The Life and Times of William S. Burroughs.* New York: Henry Holt, 1988. (Biography as cultural history.)

Mottram, Eric. *William Burroughs: The Algebra of Need.* London: Marion Boyars, 1977. (Critical appraisal by a noted English scholar.)

Nicosia, Gerard. *Memory Babe: A Critical Biography of Jack Kerouac.* New York: Grove Press, 1985. (Most complete factual account of Kerouac's life.)

Norse, Harold. *Beat Hotel.* San Diego: Atticus, 1983. (Memoirs.)

Parkinson, Thomas, ed. *A Casebook on the Beat.* New York: Thomas Y. Crowell Co., 1961. (First anthology of "a body of material essential to understanding the writing often placed under the rubric 'Beat Generation.' ")

Perloff, Marjorie. *Frank O'Hara, Poet Among Painters.* Austin: University of Texas, 1977. (Critical study.)

Plummer, William. *The Holy Goof: A Biography of Neal Cassady.* Englewood Cliffs, New Jersey: Prentice-Hall, 1981. (Popular biography.)

Polsky, Ned. *Hustlers, Beats and Others.* London: Chivers Penguin, 1967. (Chapter on the Greenwich Village Beat scene.)

Rexroth, Kenneth. *American Poetry in the Twentieth Century.* New York: Herder and Herder, 1971. (Evaluation of changes and innovations in postwar American poetry emphasizing the contribution of the Beat poets.)

Rigney, Francis J., and L. Douglas Smith. *The Real Bohemia.* New York: Basic Books, 1961. (Sociological and psychological study of the San Francisco Beat community.)

Ritchie, Harry. *Success Stories: Literature and the Media in England, 1950–1959.* London: Faber and Faber, Ltd., 1988. (Cultural history, including chapter on "When the Angry Men Grow Older.")

Rodman, Seldon. *Tongues of Fallen Angels.* New York: New Directions, 1974. (Interviews with Ginsberg, Mailer, and others.)

Roszak, Theodore. *The Making of a Counter Culture.* New York: Doubleday, 1969. (Chapters on Ginsberg, Herbert Marcuse, Norman O. Brown, Alan Watts, Timothy Leary, and Paul Goodman.)

Roy, Gregor. *Beat Literature.* New York: Monarch Press, 1966. (Monarch Notes and study guide, including chapters on the tradition of rebellion in American literature and arguments for and against the writing of Beat Generation authors.)

Saroyan, Aram. *Genesis Angels: The Saga of Lew Welch and the Beat Generation.* New York: William Morrow, 1979. (Biography as cultural history.)

Seaver, R., T. Southern, and A. Trocchi, eds. *Writers in Revolt: An Anthology.* New York: Frederick Fell, 1963. (Rebellion in the mainstream tradition, including works by Doestoevsky, Hesse, Céline, Genet, Beckett, Miller, Burroughs, and Ginsberg.)

Skau, Michael. *"Constantly Risking Absurdity": The Writings of Lawrence Ferlinghetti.* Troy, N.Y.: Whitston Pub. Co., 1989. (Critical overview of Ferlinghetti's poetry and plays.)

Silesky, Barry. *Ferlinghetti: The Artist in His Time.* New York: Warner Books, 1990. (Most complete Ferlinghetti biography.)

Skerl, Jennie. *William S. Burroughs.* Boston: Twayne, 1985. (First scholarly biography.)

Skerl, Jennie, and Robin Lydenberg. *William S. Burroughs: At the Front.* Carbondale, Illinois: Southern Illinois University Press, 1991. (Burroughs's critical reception, 1959–1989.)

Stephenson, Gregory. *The Daybreak Boys: Essays on the Literature of the Beat Generation.* Carbondale, Illinois: Southern Illinois University Press, 1990. (Essays on Kerouac, Ginsberg, Burroughs, Corso, Holmes, McClure, Ferlinghetti, and Cassady by a Danish scholar.)

Sukenick, Ronald. *Down and In: Life in the Underground.* New York: Collier Books, 1987. (Greenwich Village in the 1960s and 1970s.)

Sutherland, John. *Offensive Literature: Decensorship in Britain, 1960–1982.* London: Junction Books, 1982. (Response to *Naked Lunch* in the *Times Literary Supplement*.)

Tytell, John. *Naked Angels: The Lives and Literature of the Beat Generation.* New York: McGraw-Hill, 1976. (Pioneering analysis of the work of Kerouac, Ginsberg, and Burroughs.)

Veyscy, Laurence. *The Communal Experience.* New York: Harper & Row, 1973. (Historical survey of countercultures in America.)

Weinreich, Regina. *The Spontaneous Poetics of Jack Kerouac.* Carbondale: Southern Illinois University Press, 1987. (A study of Kerouac's fiction.)

Wilentz, Elias, ed. *The Beat Scene.* New York: Corinth Books, 1960. (Collection of photographs and Beat poetry with an introduction surveying contemporary critical responses.)

Zinsser, William, ed. *Spiritual Quests: The Art and Craft of Religious Writing.* Boston: Houghton Mifflin, 1988. (Chapter by Allen Ginsberg, "Meditation and Poetics.")

INDEX OF AUTHORS
AND TITLES

Grateful acknowledgment is made for permission to reprint the following copyrighted material:

"Keeping the Issues Alive" by Ed Sanders. By permission of the author.

Excerpt from *On the Road* by Jack Kerouac. Copyright © 1955, 1957 by Jack Kerouac, copyright renewed © 1983 by Stella Kerouac, renewed copyright © 1985 by Stella Kerouac and Jan Kerouac. Reprinted by permission of the publisher, Viking Penguin, a division of Penguin Books USA Inc.

Excerpt from *The Subterraneans* by Jack Kerouac. Copyright © 1958 by Jack Kerouac; copyright renewed © 1986 by Jan Kerouac. Used by permission of Grove Press, Inc.

Excerpt from *The Dharma Bums* by Jack Kerouac. Copyright © 1958 by Jack Kerouac, copyright renewed © 1986 by Stella Kerouac and Jan Kerouac. Reprinted by permission of the publisher, Viking Penguin, a division of Penguin Books USA Inc.

Choruses 211, 239, 240, 241, 242 from *Mexico City Blues* by Jack Kerouac. Copyright © 1959 by Jack Kerouac, copyright renewed © 1987 by Jan Kerouac. Reprinted by permission of Grove Weidenfeld, a division of Grove Press, Inc.

"Essentials of Spontaneous Prose" by Jack Kerouac. Reprinted by permission of Sterling Lord Literistic, Inc.

"Belief and Technique for Modern Prose" by Jack Kerouac. Reprinted by permission of Sterling Lord Literistic, Inc.

"Howl," "A Supermarket in California," "Sunflower Sutra," "America," "Kaddish," "Song—The Weight of the World Is Love," "On Burroughs'

Work," "First Party at Ken Kesey's," "Wichita Vortex Sutra," "Anti-Vietnam War Peace Mobilization," "Mugging," "Ode to Failure," "Fourth Floor, Dawn, Up All Night Writing Letters" from *Collected Poems 1947–1980* by Allen Ginsberg. Copyright © 1984 by Allen Ginsberg. Reprinted by permission of HarperCollins Publishers.

Excerpt from *Junky* by William S. Burroughs. Copyright © 1977 by William S. Burroughs. Reprinted by permission of Wylie, Aitken & Stone, Inc.

Selections from *The Yage Letters* by William S. Burroughs and Allen Ginsberg. Copyright © 1963, 1975 by William S. Burroughs and Allen Ginsberg. Reprinted by permission of City Lights Books.

Except from *Naked Lunch* by William S. Burroughs. Copyright © 1959 by William S. Burroughs, copyright renewed © 1987, 1990 by William S. Burroughs. Reprinted by permission of Grove Weidenfeld, a division of Grove Press, Inc.

"Deposition: Testimony Concerning a Sickness" by William S. Burroughs. Copyright © 1990 by William S. Burroughs. Reprinted by permission of Wylie, Aitken & Stone, Inc.

"Elsie John" and "Joey Martinez" by Herbert Huncke. Reprinted by permission of Herbert Huncke.

Excerpt from *Go* by John Clellon Holmes. Copyright © 1952 by John Clellon Holmes. Reprinted by permission of Sterling Lord Literistic, Inc.

Selections from *Mishaps, Perhaps* by Carl Solomon. Copyright © 1966 by Carl Solomon. Reprinted by permission of City Light Books.

"I Am 25," "The Mad Yak," and "Vision of Rotterdam" from *Gasoline & the Vestal Lady on Brattle* by Gregory Corso. Copyright © 1955, 1958, 1976 by Gregory Corso. Reprinted by permission of City Lights Books.

"Bomb" and "Marriage" from *The Happy Birthday of Death* by Gregory Corso. Copyright © 1960 by New Directions Publishing Corporation. Reprinted by permission of New Directions Publishing Corporation.

Letters to Jack Kerouac and excerpt from *The First Third* by Neal Cassady. Copyright © 1971, 1981 by the Estate of Neal Cassady. Reprinted by permission of City Lights Books.

Jack Kerouac's letter to Neal Cassady, 1951. Reprinted by permission of Sterling Lord Literistic, Inc.

Excerpt from *Visions of Cody* by Jack Kerouac. Copyright © 1960, 1972 by Jack Kerouac. Reprinted by permission of McGraw-Hill Publishing Company.

"Thou Shalt Not Kill" from *In Defense of the Earth* by Kenneth Rexroth. "Poems from the Japanese" from *One Hundred Poems from the Japanese.* Copyright © 1956 by Kenneth Rexroth. Reprinted by permission of New Directions Publishing Corporation.

"Rexroth: Shaker and Maker" by William Everson. Copyright © 1980 by William Everson. First appeared in *For Rexroth (The Ark* 14:1980). By permission of the author.

"Dog," "Constantly Risking Absurdity," and "In Goya's Greatest Scenes" from *Endless Life* by Lawrence Ferlinghetti. Copyright © 1958, 1960, 1981 by Lawrence Ferlinghetti. Reprinted by permission of New Directions Publishing Corporation.

"One Thousand Fearful Words for Fidel Castro" from *Starting from San Francisco* by Lawrence Ferlinghetti. Copyright © 1961 by Lawrence Ferlinghetti. First printed in *Evergreen.* Reprinted by permission of New Directions Publishing Corporation.

"Horn on Howl" by Lawrence Ferlinghetti, *Evergreen Review*, I, 4 (1958). By permission of the author.

"Peyote Poem" from *Hymns to St. Geryon & Dark Brown* by Michael McClure. Copyright © 1959, 1961, 1980 by Michael McClure. Reprinted by permission of Grey Fox Press.

Excerpt from *Scratching the Beat Surface* by Michael McClure. Copyright © 1982 by Michael McClure. Published by North Point Press and reprinted by permission. "A Berry Feast" from *The Back Country* by Gary Snyder. Copyright © 1957 by Gary Snyder. Reprinted by permission of New Directions Publishing Corporation. "Plus Ça Change . . ." by Philip Whalen. Reprinted by permission of the author.

"Mid-August at Sourdough Mountain Lookout," "Milton by Firelight," "Riprap," "Praise for Sick Women," "Tōji," and "Higashi Hongwanji" from *Riprap and Cold Mountain Poems* by Gary Snyder. Copyright © 1965 by Gary Snyder. Published by North Point Press and reprinted by permission.

"Night Highway Ninety-nine" from *Six Sections* by Gary Snyder. Copyright © 1965 by Gary Snyder. "Note on the Religious Tendencies" by Gary Snyder. By permission of the author.

"Sourdough Mountain Lookout," "A Dim View of Berkeley in the Spring," and "Prose Take-Out, Portland 13:ix:58" by Philip Whalen. Reprinted by permission of the author.

"High," "The Night is a space of white marble," "I have given fair warning," "There is this distance between me and what I see," and "Fud at Foster's" from *Selected Poems* by Philip Lamantia. Copyright © 1967 by Philip Lamantia. Reprinted by permission of City Lights Books.

"Chicago Poem," "The Basic Con," "Taxi Suite—After Anacreon," "Not Yet 40, My Beard is Already White," "The Image, as in a Hexagram," and "I Saw Myself" from *Ring of Bone* by Lew Welch. Copyright © 1973 the Estate of Lew Welch. Reprinted by permission of Grey Fox Press.

"Round About Midnight," "Jazz Chick," "On," and "O-Jazz-O" from *Golden Sardine* by Bob Kaufman. Copyright © 1966 by Bob Kaufman. Copyright © 1966, 1967 by City Lights Publishing Company. Copyright © 1990 by Eileen Kaufman.

"In Memory of Radio" and "Way Out West" from *Preface to a Twenty-Volume Suicide Note* by LeRoi Jones (Amiri Baraka). Copyright © 1961 by LeRoi Jones (Amiri Baraka). Reprinted by permission of Sterling Lord Literistic, Inc.

"The Screamers" from *Tales* by LeRoi Jones (Amiri Baraka). Copyright © 1967 by LeRoi Jones (Amiri Baraka). Reprinted by permission of Sterling Lord Literistic, Inc.

Letter about Kerouac's Prose by LeRoi Jones (Amiri Bataka). Copyright © 1967 by LeRoi Jones (Amiri Baraka). Appeared originally in the *Evergreen Review*. Reprinted by permission of Sterling Lord Literistic, Inc.

"Funny Lotus Blues" from *Blowing Mouth* by Ray Bremser, Cherry Valley Editions. © 1978 by Ray Bremser. By permission of the publisher.

"Three Laments," "Song for Baby-O, Unborn," "The Practice of Magical Evocation," "Poetics," and "Brass Furnace Going Out" from *Selected Poems 1956–75* by Diane DiPrima, North Atlantic Press. Copyright 1975 by Diane DiPrima. By permission of the author.

"Blowin' in the Wind" by Bob Dylan. Copyright © 1962 Warner Bros. Music; copyright renewed 1990 Bob Dylan. All rights reserved. International copyright secured. Reprinted by permission of Special Rider Music.

"The Times They are A-Changin' " and "A Hard Rain's A-Gonna Fall" by Bob Dylan. © 1963 Warner Bros. Inc. All rights reserved. Used by permission.

Excerpts from *Tarantula* by Bob Dylan. Reprinted with permission of Macmillan Publishing Company. Copyright © 1971 by Bob Dylan.

"Poem to Lee Forest" by Brenda Frazer (Bonnie Bremser). By permission of the author.

"Afrique Accidentale" from *Afrodisia* by Ted Joans. Copyright © 1970 by Ted Joans. Reprinted by permission of Hill and Wang, a division of Farrar, Straus and Giroux, Inc.

"A Few Blue Words to the Wise" from *Black Pow-Wow* by Ted Joans. Copyright © 1969 by Ted Joans. Reprinted by permission of Hill and Wang, a division of Farrar, Straus and Giroux, Inc.

Excerpt from *1001 Ways to Beat the Draft* by Tuli Kupferberg and Robert Bashlow. Copyright © 1966 Tuli Kupferberg and Robert Bashlow. By permission of Tuli Kupferberg.

"Les Luths" from *The Collected Poems of Frank O'Hara*, edited by Donald Allen. Copyright © 1958 by Maureen Granville-Smith, Administratrix of the Estate of Frank O'Hara. By permission of Random House, Inc.

"Post the Lake Poet's Ballad" by Frank O'Hara. Courtesy Tibor de Nagy Editions.

Personal Poem" and "The Day Lady Died" from *Lunch Poems* by Frank O'Hara. Copyright © 1964 by Frank O'Hara. Reprinted by permission of City Lights Books.

"Lepers Cry" from *Clean Asshole Poems* by Peter Orlovsky. Copyright © 1978 by Peter Orlovsky. Reprinted by permission of City Lights Books.

"Poem from Jail" (excerpt), "The Cutting Prow," and "Hymm to Archilocus" from *Thirsting for Peace in a Raging Century* by Ed Sanders, Coffee House Press, 1987. Reprinted by permission of the publisher. Copyright © 1987 by Ed Sanders.

"Our Past" reprinted from *Blue Mosque* by Anne Waldman, United Artists, 1988. Used by permission of author with thanks to publisher Lewis Warsh. © 1988 by Anne Waldman.

"A poem for record players," "A poem for tea heads," "A poem for museum goers," and "A poem for the insane" from *The Hotel Wentley Poems* by John Wieners. © 1958, 1986 John Wieners. Courtesy Black Sparrow Press.

Excerpt from *Notes of a Dirty Old Man* by Charles Bukowski. Copyright © 1969 by Charles Bukowski. Reprinted by permission of City Lights Books.

Excerpt from *Kentucky Ham* by William Burroughs, Jr. © 1973 by William Burroughs, Jr. Published in 1984 by The Overlook Press.

Excerpt from *Off the Road* by Carolyn Cassady. Copyright © 1990 by Carolyn Cassady. Reprinted by permission of William Morrow and Co., Inc.

Selections from "What I Ate Where" from *Dinners and Nightmares* by Diane DiPrima. Copyright © 1961 by Diane DiPrima. By permission of the author.

Excerpt from *Troia: Mexican Memoirs* by Brenda Frazer (Bonnie Bremser). By permission of the author.

Excerpt from *Minor Characters* by Joyce Johnson. Copyright © 1983 by Joyce Johnson. Reprinted by permission of Houghton Mifflin Co.

Excerpt from *How I Became Hettie Jones* by Hettie Jones. Copyright © 1990 by Hettie Jones. Reprinted by permission of the publisher, Dutton, an imprint of New American Library, a division of Penguin Books USA Inc.

Excerpts from *Baby Driver* by Jan Kerouac. Reprinted by permission of the author.

Excerpt from "The Day After Superman Died" from *Demon Box* by Ken Kesey. Copyright © 1979, 1986 by Ken Kesey. Reprinted by permission of the publisher, Viking Penguin, a division of Penguin Books USA Inc.

Excerpt from *The Mad Cub* by Michael McClure. Reprinted by permission of the author.

"A Book of Verse" from *Tales of Beatnik Glory: Volumes I and II* by Ed Sanders. Copyright © 1975, 1990 by Ed Sanders. By arrangement with Carol Publishing Group. A Citadel Underground Book.

Excerpt from *Nova Express* by William S. Burroughs. Copyright © 1964 by William S. Burroughs. Reprinted by permission of Grove Weidenfeld, a division of Grove Press, Inc.

"Columbia U Poesy Reading—1975" and "The Whole Mess . . . Almost" from *Herald of the Autochthonic Spirit* by Gregory Corso. Copyright © 1981 by Gregory Corso. Reprinted by permission of New Directions Publishing Corporation.

"April Fool Birthday Poem for Grandpa" from *Revolutionary Letters* by Diane DiPrima, City Lights Press. Copyright © 1971 by Diane DiPrima. By permission of the author.

Selections from *Loba: Parts I–VII* by Diane DiPrima, Wingbow Press. Copyright © 1978 by Diane DiPrima. By permission of the author.

"The Canticle of Jack Kerouac," "Uses of Poetry," and "Short Story on a Painting of Gustav Klimt" by Lawrence Ferlinghetti. Copyright © 1990 by Lawrence Ferlinghetti. By permission of the author.

White Shroud" from *White Shroud: Poems 1980–1985* by Allen Ginsberg. Copyright © 1986 by Allen Ginsberg. Reprinted by permission of Harper-Collins Publishers.

"Song," "It's Nation Time," "Watching the Stolen Rose," and "The Death of Kin Chuen Louie" from *Fragments of Perseus* by Michael McClure. Copyright © 1983 by Michael McClure. Reprinted by permission of New Directions Publishing Corporation.

"What Would Tom Paine Do?" by Ed Sanders. By permission of the author.

"I Went into the Maverick Bar," "Mother Earth: Her Whales," "The Bath," and "Pine Tree Tops" from *Turtle Island* by Gary Snyder. Copyright © 1972, 1974 by Gary Snyder. Reprinted by permission of New Directions Publishing Corporation.

"Axe Handles" from *Axe Handles* by Gary Snyder. Copyright © 1983 by Gary Snyder. Published by North Point Press and reprinted by permission.

The White Negro by Norman Mailer. Copyright © 1958 by Norman Mailer. Reprinted by permission of the author and the author's agents, Scott Meredith Literary Agents, Inc.

"Beat Zen, Square Zen and Zen" by Alan Watts. Reprinted by permission of *The Chicago Review*.

Excerpt from "The Game of the Name" by John Clellon Holmes. Reprinted by permission of Sterling Lord Literistic, Inc. Copyright © 1988 by John Clellon Holmes.